Special Edition
Using

Adobe®
Photoshop® 6

Richard Lynch

201 W. 103rd Street
Indianapolis, Indiana 46290

CONTENTS AT A GLANCE

SPECIAL EDITION USING ADOBE PHOTOSHOP 6

Copyright © 2001 by Que Corporation

International Standard Book Number: 0-7897-2425-1

Library of Congress Catalog Card Number: 00-101702

Printed in the United States of America

First Printing: December 2000

03   02   01   00   4   3   2   1

TRADEMARKS

WARNING AND DISCLAIMER

Publisher
Robb Linsky

Executive Editor
Beth Millett

Acquisitions Editor
Heather Banner Kane

Development Editor
Laura Norman

Managing Editor
Thomas F. Hayes

Senior Editor
Susan Ross Moore

Copy Editors
Kay Hoskin
Cheri Clark
Margaret Berson

Indexers
Larry Sweazy
Tim Tate

Proofreaders
Maribeth Echard
Benjamin Berg

Technical Editors
Jori Curry
Kate Binder

Team Coordinator
Julie Otto

Interior Designer
Ruth Lewis

Cover Designers
Dan Armstrong
Ruth Lewis

Production
Ayanna Lacey
Heather Miller
Stacey Richwine-DeRome
Mark Walchle

CONTENTS

ABOUT THE AUTHORS

Richard Lynch is currently a Documentation Specialist for a software company and Graphics and Publishing freelancer. He has worked as an Image Editor/Senior Editor for a photography book publisher and has done design, editorial, and consulting work for book and CD covers, Web sites, photographic tradeshow murals, advertising photographers, packaging design, printers, and publishers. He welcomes comments about the book, questions, requests, and interaction through the Web site at `ps6.com`.

Michael Lennox is an Adobe Certified Training Provider for Photoshop and has been providing professional training in Photoshop for the past five years. Michael consulted with Adobe in development of its certification exam for Photoshop. He authored *Short Order Adobe Photoshop 5.5* (Hayden Books) and coauthored the Adobe Press *Adobe Photoshop Certification Guide*. (Michael authored Chapters 1, 2, 6, 8, 12, 13, 38, 39, 42, and Appendix C of this book.)

DEDICATION

For my daughters: Isabel who proved it is possible to walk before crawling; and Julia who likes to prove that anything is possible.

Richard Lynch

ACKNOWLEDGMENTS

Thanks to all who helped with contributions of source images, image ideas, and so on: Lee at Seattle Support Group, Laurie McEachron at PhotoDisc, Steve Lilly at PhotoSphere, Virginia Kinzey, and Mihail Chemiakin. Thanks to Karen Thomas and Olympus for the use of the C2500L digital SLR, and Linotype-Hell for the SAPHIR scanner.

Thanks as well to the great team at Macmillan, especially: Beth Millett, Laura Norman, Heather Kane, and Susan Moore. My appreciation to Michael Lennox and Kate Binder for additional content contributions.

Additional thanks to those who laughed out of turn: Lisa, Frances Hagen, Larry Woiwodc, and Kevin Harvey. Those missing: Dom Leone, Al Weeks, Anthony Tamburrino, Vincent de Paul, and Tony Zenos. Those who provided more opportunity: Mitch Waite, Stephanie Wall, George Hoskins, David Larson, and Dave and Mary Spacone. The guy who showed me my first pixel: Luke Delalio. And anyone who has ever asked a question, or given me anything that has caused me to pause—no matter how briefly.

TELL US WHAT YOU THINK!

As the reader of this book, *you* are our most important critic and commentator. We value your opinion and want to know what we're doing right, what we could do better, what areas you'd like to see us publish in, and any other words of wisdom you're willing to pass our way.

As an Executive Editor for Que, I welcome your comments. You can fax, email, or write me directly to let me know what you did or didn't like about this book—as well as what we can do to make our books stronger.

Please note that I cannot help you with technical problems related to the topic of this book, and that due to the high volume of mail I receive, I might not be able to reply to every message.

When you write, please be sure to include this book's title and author as well as your name and phone or fax number. I will carefully review your comments and share them with the author and editors who worked on the book.

Fax: 317-581-4666

Email: desktop_pub@macmillanusa.com

Mail: Beth Millett
          Executive Editor
          Que Corporation
          201 West 103rd Street
          Indianapolis, IN 46290 USA

INTRODUCTION

In this introduction

ABOUT THIS BOOK

The purpose of this book is to develop the reader's ability to confidently use Photoshop in all applicable situations. The goal is to cover everything from simple, practical application of Photoshop's tools, to development of complex layered images and animations, perfecting color management, and achieving the desired end in print, display, or on the Web. The book can be read from beginning to end as a general tutorial and developmental study, or it can be used as a reference for fast solutions and suggestions on particular topics.

Each chapter begins with an outline of the main topics included, and dives right in to the use of Photoshop and its features. The basic function of tools is described progressing through the chapter toward examples of practical application. References throughout provide links to other portions of the book, which can help the reader to better understand additional concepts being discussed, and tips and notes offer brief insight into techniques and ideas to help the reader understand the application of tools and functions. Troubleshooting sections at the end of each chapter reiterate important concepts and help clarify what to avoid and what can go wrong with tool and function applications.

Because there are hundreds of ways to approach any problem in Photoshop, the solutions given here are meant to be practical and clear, not comprehensive. Other solutions may achieve the same or very similar ends. Although no CD is included, a Web site is available for downloading images from the book, and for interaction with the author and other Photoshop users. Find the site at http://www.ps6.com.

This book assumes that you have a basic understanding of computers and digital images, that you are able to install the Photoshop program, and that you are familiar with your equipment and operating system. Although there are troubleshooting tips throughout, and a section for troubleshooting on both Mac and PC in the appendixes, this book is primarily focused on developing skills with Photoshop and answering questions to achieve real-world digital-imaging solutions.

SECTIONS IN THIS BOOK

The sections of the book are broken into a progression from becoming oriented to the interface and tools, to understanding digital images and how they are used in Photoshop, to applying tools to the images, and to using the images for a final purpose. Each of these concepts is subdivided into a progression from intermediate to advanced concepts. I've grouped these concepts into 12 distinct areas.

- **I. Working with Photoshop**—Understanding the interface and what is new in Photoshop 6.
- **II. Photoshop's Image Building Blocks**—An in-depth overview of tool use that shows more than just tool function, including all the major Photoshop tools: layers, channels, paths, Selection, gradients, freehand tools, Type control, and History use.
- **III. Automating Image Processing and Saving Images**—A look at bulk image-processing capabilities within Photoshop (actions and automated commands) and saving your images.
- **IV. The Image: Format and Resolution**—A complete discussion of the bits and bytes that drive the images that you see. Including advantages of file formats and how to work with resolution and color modes.

- **V. Acquiring the Digital Image**—With the basic tools firmly in hand, it is important to consider how to acquire images—where they come from, how to import them—so you can have elements to work with.

- **VI. Color Handling: Use, Evaluation, and Correction**—After you have the image, you can work with it. Color correction and understanding color functions and changes can help you get what you want to improve images. Covers everything from evaluating through correcting image color, including converting color and the use of spot and duo-tone colors.

- **VII. Cleaning, Repairing, and Altering Images**—Basic image repair for improved quality requires neatening up the obvious problems. Correct dust, nicks, dents, dings, and other flaws using the information in this section. Includes assessing damage and some changes in composition.

- **VIII. Enhancing Images**—When basic alterations and improvements don't take an image where you expect it to go, enhancements might. Combining images and image elements can help make more radical changes in an image, with photorealistic results and improvements. Covers working with highlight and shadows, creating new image elements, compositing, and morphing.

- **IX. Creating Special Effects**—The final stage of image development is the creation of special effects. Effects can range from imitating properties you have seen in other images to creating your own effects. This chapter is dominated by filter use and drastic image alterations.

- **X. Creating and Using Web Graphics**—With the addition of ImageReady, Photoshop became a graphics powerhouse for the Web as well as for photographic purposes. ImageReady covers ground where Photoshop simply did not have functionality, such as processing images as rollovers, creating HTML, and working with image motion. Animation, rollovers, imagemaps, and slicing are all covered here.

- **XI. Image Printing, Output, and Use**—Output to a printing device can be done well or poorly. Knowing the possibilities for output might affect your decisions in creating and working with an image. This chapter gives you not only the knowledge of what is possible, but what to expect if you are sending something out to be printed—and what to demand.

- **XII. Image Protection and Storage**—When you have created and finished an image, there are issues of copyright and digital file storage that should be addressed, both to protect your image during use and to protect it in dormancy.

- **XIII. Appendixes**—Covers several issues and areas that didn't fall neatly into the other categories, which can help the Photoshop user, and provides reference information, also. Find what you need to run Photoshop, information on image concepts, and HTML color guide, Photoshop installation information, and Web resources.

The perspective is that as a user of Photoshop you are serious about images and imaging. The techniques and examples are real-world applications, and should apply whether working in business application, printing, publishing, prepress, image correction, retouching, Web graphic development, or developing images for your own enjoyment.

SHORTCUT KEYSTROKES

Shortcut keystrokes are given throughout the book in Mac and PC form. Mac keystrokes are given in parentheses (Mac) using a hyphen to signify key combinations (Mac-key); PC keystrokes follow Mac keystrokes immediately, wherever they appear, in brackets [PC] using a plus sign to signify combinations [PC+key]. For example, the following might appear in the text: "To create a new file, select New from the File menu, or press the (Cmd-N) [Ctrl+N] keys."

Few shortcuts are actually different on these platforms if the following equivalents are observed:

Mac	PC
[Shift]	(Shift)
[Ctrl]	Right Mouse Click
[Cmd](also known as: Apple; ⌘)	(Ctrl)
[Option](also known as: Opt)	(Alt)
Mouse Click	Left Mouse Click

THE BOOK'S WEB SITE AND PASSWORD

The Web site (PS6.com) is generally open to Photoshop users, but has some additional features just for readers of this book. There will be an email discussion list, a list of frequently asked questions, user support, and new materials, as well as a few surprises.

Your most important visit to the site will be to pick up the PDF workbook. The workbook will require use of a password/key that will change periodically. This password will be encrypted into an image, and you will have to decipher the message. What better, more fitting way to get it to you than to stash it in an image that you can use Photoshop to find? You will have to download both the workbook and the password image, and then follow these steps to get the password. The password is necessary to protect copyrighted materials in the workbook.

1. Open the Password file (password.tif) by pressing (Cmd-O) [Ctrl+O] and locating the file. It will open as an RGB TIFF image, and it will have some blocks of dark color.
2. Save the file as a RAW file by pressing (Shift-Cmd-S) [Shift+Ctrl+S], and selecting RAW from the file type pop-up menu. Change the file Header option when the Raw Options screen appears to 1692 and click OK. The dialog boxes should look like Figure IN.1.
3. Close the file.
4. Open the RAW file you just saved and enter the following in the RAW options dialog box: width 1716, height 329, count 3 and header size 0 (see Figure IN.2). Then, click OK. The image will open in a brownish color.
5. Use Auto Levels to adjust the image (Shift-Cmd-L) [Shift+Ctrl+L], and the password will appear.

Use this password when opening the workbook. This password was hidden in the image as a type of Steganographics, or hiding data in images. Try other settings to open up that password, and you'll see just how protected it is by those simple changes. If you download the workbook at different times, be sure to download the password file as well, as the password will change on occasion. You will find both the workbook and the password when you click the workbook link from the main page of the Web site.

Figure IN.1
Choose RAW as a file type when saving. Change only the Header default for the RAW file.

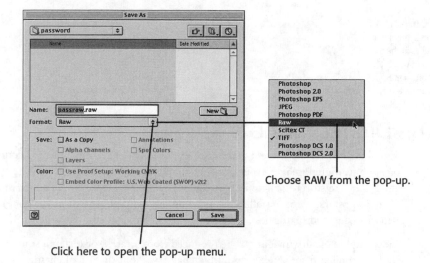

Choose RAW from the pop-up.

Click here to open the pop-up menu.

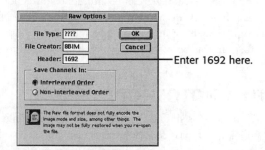

Enter 1692 here.

Figure IN.2
Change the Height, Width, Count and Header. The screen should look as shown here before choosing OK.

Make changes in these fields only.

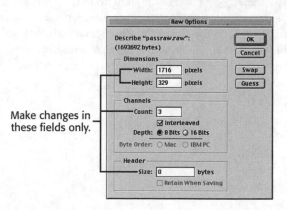

NEW FEATURES IN VERSION 6

Features new to Photoshop 6 are covered in the "New Features" section, but are also noted when they are used in other procedures throughout the book by the appearance of this symbol:

Figure IN.3
This symbol marks places in the text where new Photoshop 6 features are employed.

THE DIGITAL IMAGE

Digital images are the present and future wave of imaging. Unlike printed counterparts and analog storage, digital images experience no degradation (unless there is damage to the data files in which they are stored). These images can be used in a wide variety of applications from digital video, to posters, mural installations, printing (offset, Web, and direct to plate), film creation (negatives and transparencies), Web site development, and computer-generated presentations.

Photographic quality images can be produced from scratch, or (using a scanner or digital camera) can be compiled from single or multiple images without the use of chemicals, developing, and lab processes. Images can be altered, distorted, or implemented in any way a photographic image can. In short, Photoshop puts the power of safe, digital processing and the development and improvement of images in the hands of every user. Learning to use the tools and concepts put forth in this book will give you what you need to use images in any media.

WHY PHOTOSHOP?

Photoshop is simply the best image-editing application available. It can do all the things that this book encompasses. It has extensive features, broad file handling, and raw power. Few applications come close in offering even the versatility of channels and layers, and this says nothing of the function behind the scenes. As a result of the strength of the application, there is very little serious competition, and most of the products that become recognized are more or less plug-ins that provide a very specific functionality to use in conjunction with, rather than instead of, Photoshop. What will this allow you to do with images? About anything you can imagine. And if you can't find the solution in this book, just ask richard@ps6.com.

PART 1

WORKING WITH PHOTOSHOP

CHAPTER 1

What's New in Version 6?

In this chapter

PHOTOSHOP 6—IMPROVEMENTS AND NEW FEATURES

Photoshop 6 contains hundreds of improvements to enhance the efficiency and function of the interface and give greater outlets to your digital artistry. Some of the features increase the similarity of Photoshop's interface to other Adobe products (such as Illustrator and ImageReady). Others improve familiar commands, tools, and processes, providing them with additional functionality. Photoshop 6 also contains some completely new commands that give you additional capabilities for image manipulation.

Table 1.1 lists some of the most exciting improvements, but is by no means a complete list of the changes. There are changes in every nook and cranny and listing them all would simply be daunting. Suffice it to say, you will have plenty to do to explore all the changes as you work through the interface and this book.

TABLE 1.1   NEW FEATURES IN VERSION 6

Feature	Use/Description
Liquify	A brand-new tool used for creating serious freehand image distortions.
Shape Drawing	A library of predefined vector shapes to complement enhanced vector functions and allow quick incorporation of object shapes.
Text Tool Enhancements	Includes onscreen text entry, improved text layout controls, and text warping.
Layer Styles	Allows application of predefined groupings of layer effects for quick enhancements.
Layer Sets	Help with management of image layer groupings, moving groups of layers, managing layer order, and neatening complicated image layer schemes.
Content Libraries	A Preset Manager for choosing available content for Photoshop elements, such as patterns, Layer Styles, shapes, brushes, contours, gradients, and swatches.
Vector Masking	A second and complementary masking type adding to the means of controlling layer content.
Noise-Based Gradients	Improved one-step gradient fills that reduce banding or noticeable steps in color blending.
Gradient Maps	New color correction and color-enhancement tool that affects color based on tone.
Case-Sensitive Toolbar	A centrally localized toolbar that neatens the interface and creates a defined area to look when making tool option changes.
Palette Management Improvements	Palette docking and autoresizing to make the most of the space you have onscreen.

GENERAL INTERFACE ENHANCEMENTS

When you start Photoshop 6 for the first time, the most obvious change is the new placement and look for the Tool Options bar. Instead of being a separate palette, it is a bar that by default is docked to the top of the working area (see Figure 1.1). The Tool Options bar also provides quick access to Boolean operations when you're using a selection or drawing tool, and alignment options when you're using the Move or Path Component Selection tools. The Brushes pop-up palette is also now integrated with the Options bar when a painting tool is being used (see Figure 1.2).

Figure 1.1
The Tool Options bar is dockable to top or bottom, or it can float. The Palette Well, a dark gray area at the right of the bar, lets you store palettes for easy access when not in use.

The Palette Well on the bar displays only if you have screen resolution higher than 800×600 (for example, 1,024×768). If you change resolution to 800×600 or below, the palettes are purged and will float again. To dock the palettes, simply drag the palette tab to the gray window. To access the palettes from the window, click the tab to open the palette; click it again to return it to the well.

Note

The behavior of the well and Tool Options bar is somewhat buggy at the time of this writing, especially when using two monitors and 800×600 screen resolution or lower, and this behavior probably will not be fixed by release time. You can use the feature if the bar is not docked to the top or bottom of the screen, but you may experience some unexpected results. If the left of your Options bar jumps off the screen at any time, you will not be able to get it back by dragging. Use Window, Reset Palette Locations to get the palette back in place. In fact, you can use that anytime you "lose" a palette off the screen.

→ For more information about working with Photoshop's interface, **see** "Using the Interface," **p. 25**.

Figure 1.2
The Brushes pop-up palette is integrated with the Tool Options bar and can be resized. Brushes can be listed by thumbnail, name, or name and thumbnail.

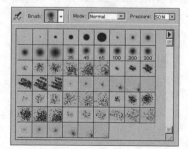

EASIER IMAGE ACCESS

When opening images, Photoshop provides access to a Favorites button so that you can navigate quickly to often-used folders. In addition, recently used files are placed in a separate, configurable submenu. For saving images, the Save As a Copy function has been incorporated into the Save As dialog box (see Figure 1.3). To add items (folders or specific files) to the Favorites menu, simply locate the item in the Open or Save screen and choose Add to Favorites from the Favorites menu. To remove a favorite from the menu, choose Remove from Favorites—there is no need to locate the item you want to remove first. A menu of favorites will appear, and you can remove the item(s) by highlighting and clicking Remove.

Figure 1.3
The Favorites menu is great for quickly locating directories or folders you often save work to. The Save As a Copy command has been integrated into the Save As dialog box.

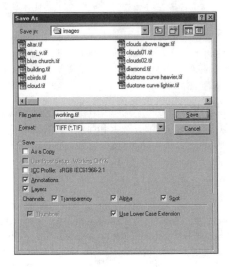

STYLES PALETTE

Similar to ImageReady, Photoshop now has a Styles palette (see Figure 1.4) that enables you to save combinations of layer effects and apply them by single-clicking or by dragging and dropping the style onto a layer or layer set. Photoshop provides a range of style presets, and the styles can be used interchangeably with ImageReady. Styles can be stored for later use—a very handy tool if you have certain tool settings that you use often. Styles can be displayed using thumbnails, names, or thumbnails and names.

Figure 1.4
Photoshop's styles make it easy for you to manage and apply combinations of layer effects that you use regularly. This can help make tasks—like creating button effects—simple and fast.

TEXT ENTRY, PARAGRAPHS, AND WARPING

Instead of the Text palette, Photoshop now supports on-canvas text editing (see Figure 1.5). When creating text, you can create a text box that supports line wrapping, auto-hyphenation, paragraph alignment, justification, and a range of other per-paragraph settings. Text settings are controlled through the Character and Paragraph palettes. To create the box, select the Type tool from the tool palette and click and drag on your image to draw the box. If you resize the box while the Type tool is still selected, the text will reflow according to your settings (for paragraph and character). Changing the box with the movement tool will cause distortion and scaling (as per Transformations). If you don't draw a box, you can handle type and returns/line breaks manually.

Figure 1.5
Text creation in Photoshop is now similar to that in Illustrator, with separate controls for character and paragraph settings.

The new Text Warp options give you unprecedented control over text in Photoshop while maintaining the editing capabilities. With more than a dozen warp presets and the capability to finely tune each, complex effects are easy to create and change without rasterizing and using filters.

The Text Warp can be accessed through the Create Warped Text button on the Options bar. This will open the Warp Text dialog box (see Figure 1.6). Simply choose your settings and click OK. The settings will be applied to the whole text layer (not just selected text) and the layer thumbnail for the text layer will change to the warped-text icon. You can select from 15 presets, select Horizontal or Vertical orientation for the application of the effect, select the amount of the Bend, and choose a level of Horizontal and Vertical perspective distortion. To change the settings, highlight the warped-text layer in the Layers palette and click the Create Warped Text button again.

→ For more information about working with text, **see** "Type Control, Placement, and Settings," **p. 221**.

Figure 1.6
As you warp text, the image shows a preview of the effects caused by the transformation.

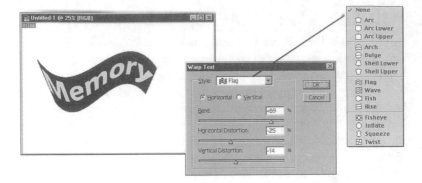

FREEHAND DISTORTIONS USING LIQUIFY

The new Liquify command enables you to smudge, twist, pinch, bulge, and reflect images in real-time using brushes (see Figure 1.7). With the capability to Freeze (or mask) areas of the image, you can precisely control what your transformations will affect. The Reconstruction tool will actually reconstruct image areas that you have distorted, giving you strong control over the results and variations.

Figure 1.7
To open the Liquify dialog box, select Liquify from the Image menu. You have an incredible array of options for altering an image in real-time.

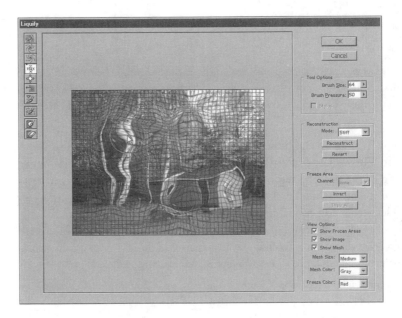

→ For more information about the Liquify command, **see** "Freehand Painting Tools," **p. 203**.

IMAGE EXTRACTION

The Extract tool is used for extracting image elements from an image in order to use them in another or with another background. It works almost as a separate interface with tools that are unique to its function, including the highlighter. Really, this is a substitute for a similar extraction which you can do manually using a somewhat more protracted set of steps (building a complicated selection using channels, changing the channel to a selection, and then using the selection to isolate the image area). This extraction, however, considers the present color of the background and selected areas when extracting to improve blending ability automatically.

Significant improvements have been made to the Extract command to improve performance and utility. Edge touchup and extraction cleanup tools have been added. The Smart Highlighting option performs edge detection while the Highlighter tool is in use. In addition, the Undo command (Cmd-Z) [Ctrl+Z] can be used while you're working in the Extract environment.

To open the Extract dialog box, select Extract from the Image menu. Use the highlighter to define the edge of what you want to select, and then fill the area using the Paint Bucket tool. Photoshop uses the outlining and the settings you choose to automatically build an extraction masking and removes the background when you click OK. This may be best in situations in which you have a complex selection to make, but not a lot of time to do it. It will, however, take some time to master the tool.

GRADIENTS ENHANCEMENTS

Gradients are used to fill areas with color. In Photoshop 6, the use of gradients has been enhanced through interface changes and better application options. The gradient types (Linear, Radial, Angle, Reflected, and Diamond) are now choices in the Options bar when the Gradient tool is selected. Gradients are controlled via presets. You can use the ones provided with Photoshop, alter them, or add all new gradients that you create yourself. To edit a gradient, select the Gradient tool, and then click on the gradient currently selected in the Options bar. This will open the Gradient Editor. To create a new gradient, click the New button, which will create a new gradient swatch, or select a swatch from the existing list and edit it by changing the color and position of the sliders.

The Gradient Editor itself has been updated, enabling you to modify a gradient's color stops and opacity stops in the same view (see Figure 1.8). You can also set the smoothness of the blend between the gradient's color stops. An entirely new type of gradient, the Noise gradient, has been added to generate noise throughout an applied gradient (see Figure 1.9).

Figure 1.8
You may now change the color and opacity settings right on the gradient bar for better control of gradient applications.

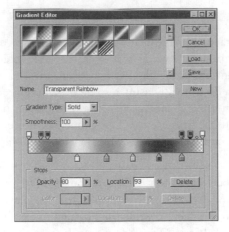

Figure 1.9
The new Noise gradient type uses configurable roughness and color settings to create randomized color blends.

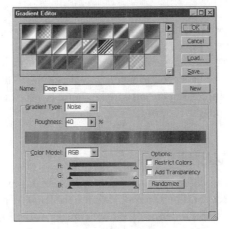

PRESET MANAGER FOR CONTENT LIBRARIES

The Content Libraries define available brushes, swatches, gradients, styles, patterns, contours, and custom shapes (see Figure 1.10). The Preset Manager is used for centralized organization of presets that will be available immediately in the Photoshop Content Libraries. Hundreds of presets and examples of each type of content are available for use within both Photoshop and ImageReady. Proper management of content will help you find what you need easily, instead of having to search through numerous examples to find what you are looking for. Keeping the libraries to a minimum can help lower the memory allocated to those features, and can help you intelligently target groupings of presets for the type of work you are doing. This can, in turn, streamline your workflow and speed results.

Figure 1.10
Photoshop comes with hundreds of preset brushes, gradients, styles, and shapes for you to use in your images. All of your presets can now be controlled in the Preset Manager interface.

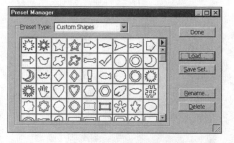

→ For more information about working with gradients and fills, **see** "Color Fills and Gradients," **p. 159**.

LAYER MANAGEMENT AND STYLES

New options have been added for managing layers, including the capability to create Layer Sets, the capability to lock layer content and transparency, and color-coding for layers in the palette (see Figure 1.11). The 99-layer limit of previous versions has been lifted as well, so Photoshop users can be layer-hogs. Improved control over this primary image creation feature gives you more flexibility and stronger control over the development of your images.

Figure 1.11
Layer sets let you group layers together in the Layers palette so that you can focus your attention on only the layers you are working with.

Layer effects are easy to create, change, and manage through the use of the Layer Style dialog box (see Figure 1.12). New layer effects—Contour and Texture, Satin, Overlay, and Stroke—have been added, expanding the layer effects arsenal. The options available for all layer effects have been expanded and the range of values for each tool has been increased.

After you have created an effect using layer styles, you can save the grouping as a style. You can then use the Styles palette (see Figure 1.13) to apply the style to other layers in the current image or other images by dragging and dropping the style to the appropriate layer in the Layers palette. Layer Styles can be reused in other Photoshop images, and can be shared between Photoshop and ImageReady or with other users.

Figure 1.12
Layer styles are easy
to create by combin-
ing layer effects and
layer blending modes
in the Layer Style
dialog box.

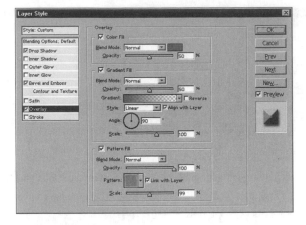

Figure 1.13
Layer Styles are a
powerful new effects
management tool
which can store every-
thing from simple
drop shadows and
opacity changes to
highly complicated
scenarios that apply
many different effects
with one simple
move.

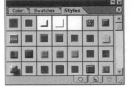

Layer Styles can also contain a layer's blending options. The options for blending
layers have been expanded with improved knockout options and channel controls
(see Figure 1.14).

Figure 1.14
Blending options con-
trol the manner in
which layer informa-
tion mixes in overlays
using settings for
opacity, blending, and
mode.

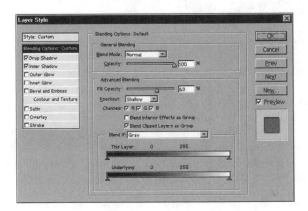

→ For more information about working with layers, **see** "Creating Images in Layers," **p. 53**.

SHAPES AND VECTOR LAYER MASKING

New vector shape creation tools simplify the creation of standard paths such as rectangles, ellipses, polygons, and stars. In addition, a wide range of custom shapes are provided and easily managed in the Shapes Library (see Figure 1.15).

PART

I

CH

1

Figure 1.15
The Shapes library is available directly from the Options bar, and you can select from any of the presets or manage your own custom shape sets.

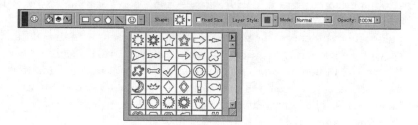

Along with greater control of vector objects and the capability to manage custom shapes, vector objects can be used as layer masks. This gives you greater flexibility and precision when creating masks, and also provides greater compatibility with Adobe Illustrator.

→ For more information about working with shapes and paths, **see** "Paths: Bézier Tools for Creating Vector Effects," **p. 175**.

PRINT PREVIEWING AND 16-BIT PREPRESS SUPPORT

Extensive proofing capabilities for images have been added to Photoshop. These include the capability to preview an RGB image in different CMYK color spaces. Moreover, the Print Options dialog box now displays all printing marks and other printing settings (see Figure 1.16).

Figure 1.16
Print previews allow for accurate onscreen color proofing of a number of different color scenarios, and previews even include printers' markings, as specified.

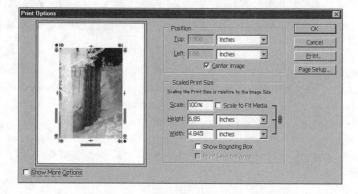

When you're working in 16-bit mode, some commonly used filters are now available that were not available before Photoshop 6. Specifically, you can now use the Unsharp Mask, Gaussian Blur, Add Noise, Median, High Pass, and Dust & Scratches filters. In addition, the new Gradient Map image adjustment is available for tonally mapping gradient color schemes to images. Lab mode is enabled, so now you can convert between Lab and other image modes while working in 16-bit mode.

CROPPING CONTROLS

Cropping can be performed with any selection instead of being restricted to a rectangular selection as you were before Photoshop 6. Even feathered selections can be used for cropping. The result creates the tightest possible rectangle around the selection (to the very edge of the feathering in the case of feathered selections). In addition, you can use the Perspective option to fix perspective anomalies when using the Crop tool, and cropping previews have been improved so that the area outside the crop boundary is dimmed (see Figure 1.17). The improved preview gives you a better visual idea of what will remain when the crop is completed.

Figure 1.17
You can crop using irregular selections, or add perspective to a cropping boundary created with the Crop tool.

The new Trim command can be used to simplify cropping procedures and can offer some advantages for bulk processing images in actions. These controls can conveniently automate cropping actions to help create the smallest rectangular version of an image without losing any image data (as you might if cropping visually). For example, when cropping a button with a drop shadow over a plain background, the automated cropping feature detects gradient changes and crops to the outside of the shadow automatically.

CROSS-PRODUCT COLOR MANAGEMENT

All of Photoshop's color management options now reside in one dialog box (see Figure 1.18). Online help is provided for each option at the bottom of the dialog box to help you make appropriate decisions about managing your color preferences. The interface is identical to the Illustrator 9 interface, and settings can be shared easily between the two applications.

Figure 1.18
When you move the cursor over areas of the Color Management dialog box, embedded help at the bottom of the dialog box describes the setting and the consequences of possible choices.

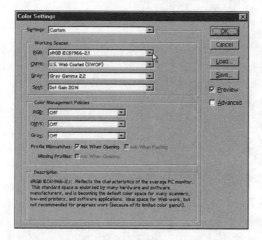

→ For more information about color management, **see** "Evaluating Image Color," **p. 409**.

BATCH PROCESSING AND AUTOMATION TOOLS

 Droplets are actions that are saved outside of Photoshop or ImageReady as separate applications. You can apply a Droplet to an image or a group of images by dropping files onto the Droplet application icon (see Figure 1.19). These images have to be compatible with the function of the droplet. Droplets can be created from actions or by dragging droplet icons to the desktop. Once created, Droplets can be shared with other Photoshop users and are portable between operating systems. Actions can also now be saved in text file format.

Figure 1.19
These icons are created when a droplet is made. Note that they are different for Photoshop and ImageReady and are distinguishable by icon and name.

Extensive filenaming rules are available in the Batch command or when you're creating a droplet so that you can change the case of filenames, add serial numbers, or add date stamps to the names of the files being processed (see Figure 1.20). Expanded options have also been added to the Web Photo Gallery, Picture Package, and Contact Sheet automation tools for processing and saving images with more control.

Figure 1.20
When you batch-process images, you can specify how file-names should be created when saving into a folder. Filenaming can automatically add serial numbers and serial letters, as well as various date and filename formats.

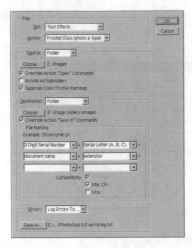

→ For more information about batch processing and automation tools, **see** "Working with Automated Commands," **p. 285**.

PHOTOSHOP AND THE WEB

Photoshop 6 has a Slice tool, for cutting up images intended for use on Web pages. The tool looks and functions exactly like ImageReady's Slice tool, so that you can create and manage slices, including creating image maps directly in Photoshop. When you use Save for Web, individual slice settings and output settings, as well as HTML formatting, can be precisely controlled through the dialog box. This enables tighter integration between ImageReady and Photoshop, but also enables you to use Photoshop with more independence.

→ For more information on slicing and Web images, **see** "Creating Professional Web Effects," **p. 791**.

ANNOTATIONS AND WORKFLOW OPTIONS

You can create annotations and embed sounds into your Photoshop document (see Figure 1.21). These notations can help in the review process for images and documents. For example, the notations can be saved with PDF files and distributed as parts of other documents. They can be task instructions, they can be used as audio captions, they can be notes to yourself about development, and can probably have hundreds of other uses. This is new territory for Photoshop, but something that has been used in other applications and at least one other Adobe product (Acrobat) for years.

Figure 1.21
You can use the Notes tool and Audio Annotation tools to create comments in your Photoshop document.

Photoshop also has new workflow-management tools. Using this control with documents that are stored on a server, many people can access a file, but only one at a time can edit it using the check-in and check-out controls and a WebDAV server. For more information about WebDAV, see www.webdav.org. When the file is saved to the server and opened, the user can check out the file by opening it and then choosing File, Manage Workflow, Check Out. Checking out the file allows editing from that workstation. Other users can open the file, and see the changes that are saved (uploaded to the server), but no other users can edit the same file concurrently. When the file is checked back in (by selecting Check In from the File, Manage Workflow menu), the current user relinquishes control over the document and another user can check it out.

CHAPTER 2

USING THE INTERFACE

In this chapter

CREATING A NEW IMAGE FILE

Before you can really get into Photoshop and explore the functions and interface, you will need to open an image. If you don't, most of the functions will be inaccessible. And, let's face it, how interesting is an imaging program with no images?

Although you could open an existing or scanned image (there are some sample images in the Photoshop program directory in the Sample folder), we'll start here with a blank canvas.

Note

The following information assumes you are using the Photoshop default settings. If you have changed anything as far as placement of palettes and altered preferences is concerned, you should reset the Photoshop preferences to follow along with these results.

Resetting Photoshop Preferences

Although, generally, you will want to retain Photoshop settings (you may even want to back up the settings when you get the interface just how you want it), you may want to revert to the default settings to clean up or just to start anew. You can do this easily when opening Photoshop. Simply launch the program and hold down the following keys (Shift–Cmd–Option) [Shift+Ctrl+Alt]. A dialog box will appear asking whether you would like to delete the current preferences. Click the Yes button to create new preferences and restore all factory defaults.

Note

To create a new image, choose File, New (Cmd-N) [Ctrl+N]. The New dialog box will open (see Figure 2.1). In the New dialog you can enter the name of the file, the dimension, resolution, color mode, and whether the initial canvas should start as white, transparent, or a background color. For this image, enter My Image for the name, 640×480 pixels for the dimension (you may need to change the measure units), 72dpi for the resolution, RGB mode for the color, and White for the contents.

The default image name will be Untitled-1. If you continue to open images without changing the name, Photoshop will name them for you sequentially as Untitled-2, Untitled-3, and so on.

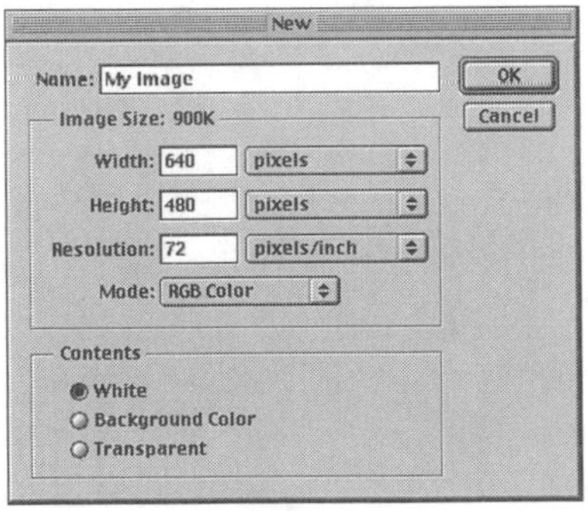

Figure 2.1
When you create a new file, you can set the size, the resolution, the image mode, and the color of the background.

If you are interested in jumping right into setting up your own image with different parameters, see "Setting Up Your Own Image" in the Troubleshooting section at the end of this chapter.

After clicking OK on the New dialog box, the new image will open in a document window. There are several helpful things to note about the image window, including the title bar, sizing, file information, and scrollbars (see Figure 2.2).

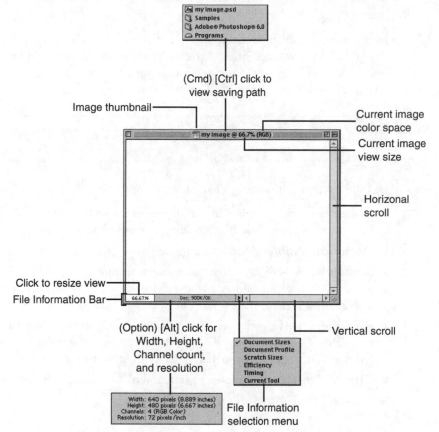

Figure 2.2
The document window shows more than just the image. You can access folders in which the image is stored, find out information about the image size and dimension, and control how the image is viewed.

When the image window is created, various Photoshop functions become available on the menus. Some palettes change as well: A background layer is created in the Layers palette, a composite and three color channels are created in the Channels palette (this varies depending on the color mode selected), the History palette displays an initial snapshot of the image created and records the first step in the history of the image (New), and the Navigator shows a thumbnail of the new image and view. The only items that are not available at this point are items that require other image elements or states to exist before they will be able to be applied. This context sensitivity helps keep you from trying to apply functions that are inappropriate to the current image. As the image changes, the choices fluidly change, activating the deactivating functions that can be used.

IMAGE WINDOW FILE INFORMATION, DISPLAY, AND CONTROLS

The title bar for the image document window contains basic information about the document, including the filename, viewing size (as a percentage), and then layer and channel in parentheses. To the left of the filename is an icon which either shows a thumbnail of the image (if it is saved) or the Photoshop file-type icon. If you (Cmd-click) [Ctrl+click] the icon, the path for saving the image shows in a pop-up menu. These folders can be opened by choosing one from the menu.

 The file information bar is at the bottom of the image window. It offers several options for viewing image information, which can help you manage memory and keep track of—or quickly reference—important image information. To choose between the different options for viewing file information, click the menu arrow.

Note

Menu arrows appear throughout Photoshop, more often in the new interface as a rounded button.

The following list outlines the file information options:

- **Document Size**—Displays image file size in the flattened/fixed dimension size and the full size of the electronic file (including Layers and Channels).

- **Document Profile**—Displays current color profiling.

- **Scratch Sizes**—Displays information about memory use (RAM and Scratch disk). The display shows the amount of memory that is currently being used by the program to display open images, and the amount of RAM available for processing image functions.

- **Efficiency**—Displays the percentage of time in operation versus reading or writing scratch disk information. Lower percentages suggest Photoshop is not working optimally because it is spending too much time writing to the scratch disk.

- **Timing**—Displays the amount of time it took to complete the last operation.

- **Current Tool**—Displays the name of the current tool.

Choices can be made from the list at any time. (Option) [Alt] clicking on the file information bar opens a basic file information pop-up (Width and Height in pixels and the currently selected ruler-unit preference, Channel count, and resolution in dpi). Double-clicking the percentage at the far left enables you to change the viewing percentage between 3.7% and 1600%, by typing in the number and pressing return. This is the view size of the image only and does nothing to change the image information.

Tip

With the cursor in the view size box, press the up arrow to upsize by 1% and the down arrow to downsize by 1%. Hold down the shift key and press the arrows to increase the sizing to 10% up and down.

THE IMAGE MAT

The image mat is the area around the frame of the actual image. To see the mat, you have to size your image smaller than the current window. To do this in the case of the new image you opened, click in the view size box, and change the view to 25% (double-click in the box, type 25, and press Return). The area around the image will be gray. This gray area is the image mat; it is just a background to the image, and will not print. The area will generally act only as a backing, although some operations (cropping and transformations) use this area to display frames (not image contents). This happens only if you distort, skew, or crop the image outside the current visible boundaries.

The image mat color can be changed to your preference. To change the color, double-click the foreground color swatch on the toolbox to open the Adobe Color Picker. When the Color Picker is open, choose a color, and accept the change by clicking the OK button. The foreground swatch on the toolbox should change to the color you selected. Next, choose the Paint Bucket tool (press (Shift-G) [Shift+G]), and then shift-click the paint bucket anywhere in the gray area. The background can be set back to the original gray by resetting the preferences (not recommended), or filling the area with gray again (use the Lab fields in the Color Picker to enter L, a, b values of 80,0,0).

You will probably want to change the mat color to a color other than gray only to see what it would look like as part of a specific color motif. Generally, you will want to use a gray backing, as it will provide a neutral backing for evaluation of the image.

MULTIPLE IMAGE WINDOWS

Photoshop is a multiple-document environment, meaning that you can open more than one image at a time and drag and drop image data between them (see Figure 2.3). You can close, maximize, restore, and minimize documents in the interface, using standard window buttons for your operating system. You can move any of the windows or palettes by clicking and dragging on their title bars.

You can open more than one view of an image by choosing View, New View. This opens a new window with the same contents of the original image. These can be viewed at different percentages, and with different preview/proofing settings. After you have set the views, you can change the contents in one view of the image and see the effects of the changes in the other view (see Figure 2.4). For example, you can make changes zoomed in tight to a small area of the image (for example, 1,000%) and see how these changes alter the overall image by having a second view at a lower zoom (viewed at 100%).

USING A SECOND IMAGE AS A COLOR PALETTE OR LIBRARY

An interesting use of multiple windows is to use another image as a color palette, color mixer, scratch pad, or image element library like a painter uses a paint palette or a layout artist uses a pasteboard. This image might vary in size depending on what you need it for, but, generally, it can stay very small—even if storing large pasteboard items.

Figure 2.3
You can open multiple documents in Photoshop and rearrange the documents so that you can work on them easily. The title bar names and thumbnails provide a quick reference as to which image is which.

Figure 2.4
Working in multiple views lets you see both the overall image and a close-up of the area in which you are working.

Photoshop provides a Swatch palette, but it is better suited for storage of colors and color sets than mixing colors and temporarily storing color. Using the second image enables you to mix colors (on different layers if you prefer), explore brush applications, and create color gradients to use as a swatch for quick selection of color variations. Using the second image for color manipulation will be most useful if doing a lot of freehand painting.

If you want to reuse an image element in multiple images, or store image groupings (such as a logo or logo variations), this extra image can be used as a library to drag and drop image information from or to, and to store reusable elements. Elements stored in the image that are larger than the image itself will not be cropped just because you can't see the image information (see the Image Document Size sidebar). Even very large elements will be retained, and you can access them by name from the Layer palette.

Tip

You may want to keep library image elements separate in some cases, such as with logos. A better means of handling commonly used image elements (rather than an element you are temporarily sharing between several images) may be to save the library and assign a keystroke to open that library image using actions.

Image Document Size

The maximum size of an image is 30,000 pixels by 30,000 pixels. However, an additional 30,000 pixels of potential image area is present around the currently visible document. This area holds image information that goes beyond the edge of the visible canvas. In other words, a maximum document size of 90,000×90,000 pixels is theoretically possible with invisible elements outside the image viewing area. Anything that goes beyond these large dimensional boundaries is removed from the image, but this should generally not be a concern. There is also a 2GB file size limit (which you will reach before the 30,000×30,000 limit in RGB or CMYK modes).

IMAGE VIEW MODES

There are three different view modes for the document window that control how a document takes up space on your monitor. These views are Standard Screen Mode, Full Screen Mode with Menu Bar, and Full Screen Mode (without the menu bar). You can control the views from the toolbox by clicking the button for the appropriate view on the toolbox, or by toggling through the views pressing the F key.

Full Screen mode without the Menu Bar is useful when displaying your work to others without the clutter of the interface. If you turn off the palette views by pressing the Tab key, you get a clear view of the image. Full Screen Mode will use a black background, and is best for displaying images. Full Screen with Menu Bar and Standard Mode will allow you to change the color of the display area around the image.

Tip

Use Full Screen Mode with Menu Bar to do color correction to block out the desktop and thus the desktop colors, icons, and other distractions.

➔ For more information on changing the color of the background around the image, **see** "The Image Mat," **p. 29**.

IMAGE NAVIGATION AND VIEWS

Although the Navigator palette can be used to zoom in and out of your image (see Figure 2.5), the primary method of navigating through the image will be the Zoom and Hand tools on the toolbox. The Zoom In, Zoom Out, and Hand tools can be temporarily accessed using keyboard shortcuts. Hold down the spacebar to temporarily switch to the Hand tool. This enables you to grab the image and move the view of it around in the image window without affecting the contents. Use (Cmd-Spacebar) [Ctrl+Spacebar] to access the Zoom In tool and (Option-Spacebar) [Alt+Spacebar] to access the Zoom Out. You will have to click the mouse on the image for Zoom to act. (Cmd--) [Ctrl+-] and (Cmd-+) [Ctrl++] will also zoom out or in, respectively.

Figure 2.5
Click and drag in the Navigator palette to pan and use the slider or buttons at the bottom to zoom. Hold down (Cmd) [Ctrl] to define a zoom window in the Navigator palette.

Tip

There are a few quick image navigation shortcuts that are handy to know: Press (Shift–Cmd–0) [Shift+Ctrl+0] or double-click the Zoom tool in the toolbox to zoom to 100%; Press (Cmd-0) [Ctrl+0] or double-click the hand tool to fit the image to the available space. Pressing the Page Up key scrolls up by one screen and the Page Down key scrolls down by a screen. Using Shift with either key confines the movement to ten pixels.

NEW TO PHOTOSHOP 6 In the View menu, you can access some common zoom views, preview the image in different modes, and access views of image extras, including Selection, Target Path, Grids, Guides, Slices, Annotation, and Rulers. All of these extra image element views can be toggled on and off: Selection, Target Path, Grids, Guides, Slices, and Annotation can be controlled with (Cmd-H) [Ctrl+H], depending on how you have the Show Extras Options set (View, Show, Show Extras Options). Rulers can be toggled on and off with (Cmd-R) [Ctrl+R].

GUIDES

Guides can be used to help measure, align elements, create slices, and control drawing. In combination with the Snap feature on, freehand tools will cling to guides. To set a guide, turn the rulers on, and then click on the ruler and drag the guide toward the image. You can move guides with the Move tool and remove them by dragging them back to the rulers. You can set guide options in the preferences for color by choosing Edit, Preference, or by double-clicking a guide with the Move tool. Holding down (Option) [Alt] after dragging the guide into the image changes the orientation of the line.

EXPLORING MENUS AND PALETTES

Photoshop's interface uses palettes, menus, and a toolbox to organize functions and help make application of tools more intuitive. Because there is so much functionality (some filter and command dialog boxes have buttons or menu items that open additional dialog boxes that have additional menus and options), the organization may not always seem simplified. Despite this complexity, there are a significant number of similarities throughout the interface and similarity to other applications that you may have used. Because of these similarities, understanding the common principles and use of one set of functions can help you understand and use other functions. Taking some time to learn the function of the interface can help save time in learning to work with the tools.

MENU BAR LAYOUT

Photoshop's menu bar contains categories of items that let you access functions by grouping. For example, the File menu contains all file-related commands such as Open, Save, and Print. By this grouping, menus are meant to help you find what you are looking for. To open a menu, simply click it. Those menu items with arrows contain submenus, and menu items with ellipses (...) after the name open dialog boxes.

In order to access certain functions quickly, Adobe has assigned keystrokes to some items. These keystrokes appear on the menus next to the item—if they exist. Take note of those that you use most frequently. You can also access most items on a PC by using Alt key combinations in a series. For example, pressing Alt-I, I (without releasing the Alt key) will open the Image Size dialog box—which is a useful function that has no keystroke assigned. This can help quickly navigate functions. You can also assign your own keystrokes to frequently used menu items by creating actions that open the function.

→ For more information on customizing function access with actions, **see** "Creating Action Hotkeys," **p. 264**.

Although you will find many Photoshop functions on the menu bars by grouping, you will by no means find all of them there. Toolbars and palettes offer a wealth of other features and a second means of logically grouping functions for intuitive access.

THE TOOLBOX

The Photoshop toolbox is your primary method of accessing freehand tools in Photoshop. Simply click the icon associated with the tool and the cursor will function as your control for application of that tool (see Table 2.1). Click the mouse to apply. The toolbox contains some commonly used functions as well, including background and foreground color control, screen viewing options, masking mode, and quick access to ImageReady and the Adobe Web site (see Figure 2.6).

Figure 2.6
Clicking the
Photoshop 6 splash-
screen image at the
top of the toolbox
opens the Adobe
Online screen. You
can set this up to
receive periodic
updates or to be noti-
fied of updates of
Photoshop.

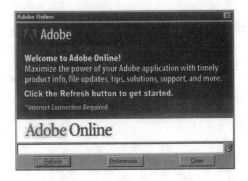

TABLE 2.1   TOOLS: USES AND SHORTCUTS

Tool Icon	Name	Description	Shortcut
	Rectangular Marquee	Selects a rectangular area	M
	Elliptical Marquee	Selects an ellipse or circular area	M
	Single Row Marquee	Selects a single row	
	Single Column Marquee	Selects a single column	
	Lasso	Selects using a freeform shape	L
	Polygonal Lasso	Selects using straight lines	L
	Magic Lasso	Selects along an edge of contrasting colors	L
	Magic Wand	Uses a tolerance to select similar colors	W
	Move	Moves selected pixels	V
	Crop	Reduces the canvas size to the area that you select	C

TABLE 2.1   CONTINUED

Tool Icon	Name	Description	Shortcut
	Slice	Create slices for HTML image maps and rollovers	K
	Slice Select	Selects and edits slices	K
	Airbrush	Paints with a pressure-sensitive soft edge	J
	Paintbrush	Paints with a soft edge	B
	Pencil	Paints with a hard edge	B
	Clone Stamp	Copies pixels from one part of the image to another	S
	Pattern Stamp	Paints with a selected pattern	S
	History Brush	Paints with a previous version of the image	Y
	Art History Brush	Paints with a previous version of the image in an artistic style	Y
	Eraser	Changes areas to either the background color or to transparency	E
	Background Eraser	Replaces background areas with transparency	E
	Magic Eraser	Erases similar colors	E
	Gradient	Fills an area with a smooth blend between one or more colors	G
	Paint Bucket	Based on the tolerance, fills an area with the foreground color	G

TABLE 2.1   CONTINUED

Tool Icon	Name	Description	Shortcut
	Blur	Blurs the area where you drag the pointer	R
	Sharpen	Increases the contrast between colors in the area where you drag the pointer	R
	Smudge	Displaces pixels as you drag	R
	Burn	Darkens the painted area	O
	Dodge	Lightens the painted area	O
	Sponge	Increases or decreases the saturation in the painted area	O
	Type	Places text	T
	Path Component Selection	Selects an individual point or segment in a Bézier path	A
	Direct Selection	Selects an entire Bézier path or subpath	A
	Pen	Creates a Bézier path by placing anchor points and dragging direction lines	P
	Freeform Pen	Creates a Bézier path as you drag	P
	Add Anchor Point	Adds an anchor point to a Bézier path	
	Delete Anchor Point	Deletes an anchor point from a Bézier path	

TABLE 2.1 CONTINUED

Tool Icon	Name	Description	Shortcut
	Convert Anchor Point	On a Bézier path, converts a corner point to an anchor point or an anchor point to a corner point	
	Rectangle	Creates a vector rectangle	U
	Rounded Rectangle	Creates a vector rectangle with rounded corners	U
	Ellipse	Creates a vector ellipse	U
	Polygon	Creates a vector polygon	U
	Line	Creates a vector line	U
	Custom Shape	Creates a custom vector shape	U
	Annotation	Places text comments in an image	N
	Audio Annotation	Places audio comments in an image	N
	Eyedropper	Reports color information and resets the Foreground Color	I
	Color Sampler	Reports color information from up to four sample points	I
	Measure	Measures distances and angles	I
	Hand	Pans in an image	H to select, spacebar to pan
	Zoom	Increases and decreases the magnification in an image	Z

Additional tool functions and tool variations are neatly tucked away behind some of the buttons (see Figure 2.7). These buttons have a tiny arrow in the bottom-right corner. Clicking and holding the mouse button down opens a fly-out menu that shows the additional tools that can be accessed through this button. The menus display the tool icon, tool name, and keystroke (if any). Learning the keyboard shortcuts for frequently accessed tools can help you quickly change functions without moving your mouse. Simply pressing the tool key accesses the last variation on that tool you used. Press Shift plus the tool key to scroll the other tools with the same shortcut.

Figure 2.7

There are two ways to access tool variations directly from the tool palette. You can switch tool variations by holding down (Option) [Alt] and clicking on the tool, or you can click and hold down the mouse button to open the tool fly-out menu, and then select the tool you want from the menu.

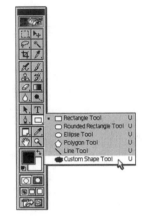

Tip

To remove all the palettes from the screen, except the toolbox, press (Shift-Tab) [Shift+Tab]. This comes in handy if you want to continue to do freehand work and screen real estate is at a premium.

PALETTES

Photoshop's palettes are floating windows that group functions and associated views. The groupings are somewhat like the menu bar, but more dedicated to particular functions. They may share some functional items found on the menu bar. In other words, the palettes offer options for access of some menu bar functions, but they have some unique functionality as well.

Palettes can be moved to any place on the screen—even to a second monitor. This allows you to position the palettes to keep them out of your viewing way or to place them however you find it most convenient to work. Photoshop will remember these placements and open the palettes in the position they were in when you last exited the program.

You can open specific palettes by choosing Show (palette name) from the <u>W</u>indow menu. To close palettes, you can use the palette window button, or the Hide (palette name) option in the <u>W</u>indow menu. Palettes can be docked to one another so that the window grouping can be controlled, and they can be stored in the palette well on the Options bar. Palettes can also be grouped and ungrouped in any combination (with the exception of the toolbox).

- To group a palette with another palette, click and drag the palette tab to the target palette (anywhere below the title bar).

- To ungroup a palette from another palette, click and drag the palette tab away from the current palette. If you drag over to another palette, the palette you are dragging will group with the palette underneath.

- To dock palettes, click and drag the palette tab of the palette that you want to dock to the bottom of the target palette (below the button bar). The very bottom of the palette should highlight when the docking position is correct.

- To temporarily hide all palettes, press the Tab key.

- To temporarily hide all palettes but the Tool palette, press (Shift-Tab) [Shift+Tab].

Tip

By loading the Command action set, you can use function keys to show palettes (see Figure 2.8).

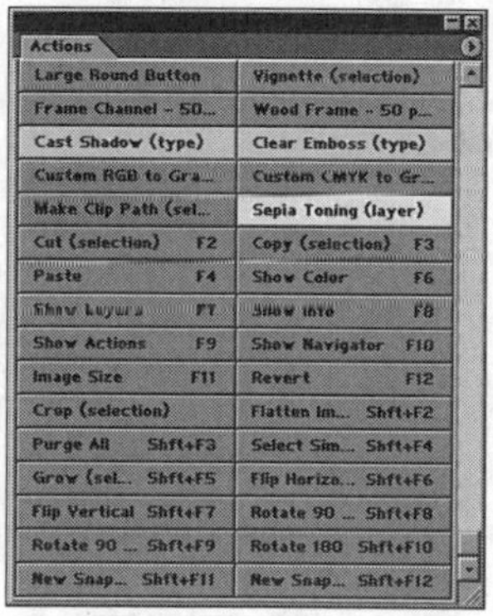

Figure 2.8
The function keys, which are assigned to the Command action set, can be displayed in the Actions palette, by selecting Button mode.

Although the palettes differ in which parts of the image they control, they all have similar elements (see Figure 2.9). Table 2.2 lists the palettes and the functional groupings that they help control.

Figure 2.9
Palette menus are
context sensitive,
based on the palette
and your selection
within the palette.

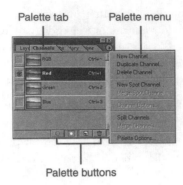

Palette tab   Palette menu

Palette buttons

TABLE 2.2   PALETTE FUNCTIONS

Palette	Palette Name	Palette Function
	Layers	Use the Layers palette to manage image layers (see Chapter 3). Layers are a convenient way to separate image elements within the same image so that you can edit them easily.
	Channels	Use the Channels palette to manage color channels (see Chapter 4). Channels are fundamental color components of an image, (such as the Red, Green, and Blue components in an RGB image), control spot color, or can be used for storage of selections and grayscale masks.
	Paths	Use the Paths palette to manage paths and other stored vector information (see Chapter 7). Paths can be used to define such elements as image clipping, layer clipping, selections, and shapes. They are a resolution-independent means of handling image content.

TABLE 2.2 CONTINUED

Palette	Palette Name	Palette Function
	History	Use the History palette to manage image History states and Snapshots (see Chapter 10). History states are other versions of your image; in a sense, functioning like a multiple undo/redo. Snapshots are image states that you have specifically saved. This palette works in conjunction with the History tool for defining the source of that tool's application.
	Actions	Use the Actions palette to manage action sets, actions, and commands (see Chapter 11). An action is a function, collection of commands, and/or series of filters that is run in succession, similar to a macro.
	Color	Use the Color palette to select or define foreground or background colors.
	Swatches	Use the Swatches palette to manage color sets, or to store frequently used colors or color sets.
	Styles	Use the Styles palette to manage Layer Styles (see Chapter 3). Layer Styles can be used to apply multiple settings to specific layers as a grouping.
	Navigator	Use the Navigator palette to control the screen view of your image interactively.

Palette	Palette Name	Palette Function
	Info	Use the Info palette to view current image information (color, position, direction, and angling) in conjunction with cursor position, free-hand tool application, and/or measurement tools.

TABLE 2.2 CONTINUED

Tip

You should set up Photoshop's palettes so that you can work efficiently—closing the palettes that you do not use. In Photoshop 6, you can clean up the image area and store palettes in the Palette Well.

Tip

In addition to, or in replacement of the Swatches palette, you can open a document that contains color and other image elements that you use often, using it as a layout library or pasteboard.

→ For more information on working with a second image as scratch area, **see** "Using a Second Image As a Color Palette or Library," **p. 29**.

CUSTOMIZING AND OPTIMIZING PHOTOSHOP

The Photoshop interface is highly customizable. You can move the palettes to more convenient locations, group them together by dragging them by their tabs onto other palettes, and resize many of them. The Options bar can be undocked from the top of the window and allowed to float. If you want to return the palettes to their default locations and settings, choose Window, Reset Palette Locations. By setting appropriate preferences, you can further customize the interface.

Preferences are just that: whatever you prefer. There is no real right or wrong to the settings you choose, unless they work against what you are trying to accomplish and are inappropriate to your ends. Photoshop's Preferences enable you to configure how it interacts with the operating system, how it uses RAM and hard drive space, how files are saved, and many other individual preferences. Each of the following areas can be found under Edit, Preferences.

GENERAL PREFERENCES

The General Preferences (see Figure 2.10) lets you set a variety of user preferences. The General Preferences range from color selection options to whether or not Photoshop beeps when it has completed a command.

Figure 2.10
The General Preferences dialog box can be used to control many of Photoshop's settings.

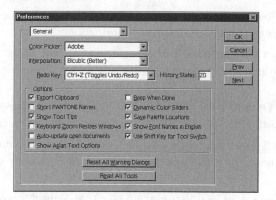

- **Color Picker**—The Color Picker option lets you choose the color picker interface you prefer, offering either Photoshop's color picker or the operating system's color picker. The color pickers for Macintosh and Windows are very different, and are simply options for color selection. Some advantages, such as out-of-gamut color warnings, will not be available with the operating system color palettes.

- **Interpolation**—You can set the default type of interpolation used when resampling an image. Interpolation is the mathematical process of determining intermediate values between pixel colors. In the case of images in Photoshop, intermediate color values are chosen when an image is resized. For example, you might change this to Bicubic when working with photographic images, and to Nearest Neighbor when resampling screen-shots. The type of interpolation can be overridden when performing the actual resampling in the Image Size dialog box.

→ For more information on resizing, **see** "Resizing an Image," **p. 346**.

- **Redo Key**—Lets you choose between three options for the Undo/Redo key: (Shift–Cmd–Z) [Shift+Ctrl+Z], (Cmd-Z) [Ctrl+Z], or (Cmd-Y) [Ctrl+Y].

- **History States**—Allows you to choose any number from 1–100 states to be stored in the History palette as you work. Although a higher number offers more flexibility in working with image states, it also requires more memory.

- **Export Clipboard**—This option determines whether information is left on the Clipboard, for use by other applications, after exiting Photoshop. If you turn on this option, it takes more time to exit because Photoshop needs to convert the information into a format that can be read by other applications before exiting.

- **Short PANTONE Names**—The PANTONE Matching System is a widely used method of designating spot colors. Different programs, such as Adobe Illustrator, Adobe PageMaker, and QuarkXPress, can specify the names for these colors in a variety of ways. To ensure compatibility between the names of spot colors in a Photoshop document and the same names in a page-layout program, this option should be selected.

- **Show ToolTips**—ToolTips are the small description boxes that appear when the cursor moves over a command in the toolbox. This option allows you to turn the descriptions on or off.

- **Keyboard Zoom Resizes Windows**—Automatically resizes the image window when reducing or enlarging the image via keyboard shortcuts.

- **Auto-Update Open Documents**—Automatically updates any images that you have open in both Photoshop and ImageReady when you make a change in the image in either application.

- **Show Asian Text Options**—Allows you to view and set options for Asian (Chinese, Japanese, and Korean) type.

- **Beep When Done**—Tasks that take a long time can be somewhat of a nuisance to wait for. This option turns on a simple tone that chimes when Photoshop completes a calculation or task.

- **Dynamic Color Sliders**—The sliders in the Color palette display color bars that represent the current color model. By default, the Dynamic Color Sliders option is on. It allows the colors of the individual sliders to change so that you can see the effect of changing a particular slider in combination with the other colors by looking at that slider bar. If this option is turned off, the appearance of the sliders remains a fixed representation of the color element (the bar colors vary in accordance with selection of the slider modes).

- **Save Palette Locations**—By default, Photoshop remembers the location of all the palettes when you close and restart it. If you would like the palettes restored to their default locations each time you start Photoshop, turn this option off.

- **Show Font Names in English**—Controls how Asian font names are displayed (English or native language).

- **Shift Key for Tool Switch**—Determines whether you will use the Shift key to scroll tool options. Using the Shift key (default) may keep you from inadvertently switching tools by pressing a hotkey for a tool you already have selected.

- **Reset All Warning Dialogs**—Resets all warnings and dialog boxes to the original state. This removes the flags you may have set for not showing a warning or window again.

- **Reset All Tools**—Restores original settings for all the tools in the Tool palette.

SAVING FILES

The Saving Files preferences give you some control over the ways in which Photoshop saves files (see Figure 2.11).

- **Image Previews**—This option controls whether previews of the images are always saved with the document, never saved, or if you are prompted to decide every time you save an image. The previews are visible after selecting an image in the Open dialog box.

- **File Extension/Append File Extension**—This option determines whether Photoshop should use file extensions (Mac) and whether they should be upper- or lowercase. File extensions are the three-character suffixes that follow the filename. For example, JPEG files have filenames in the form `filename.jpg`. The extension is used by the operating system and by Photoshop to determine the file type. Lowercase extensions are of particular importance to Web developers because Unix servers are case sensitive.

Figure 2.11
Use the Saving Files
Preferences to turn
image previews on
and off and to control
how file extensions
are saved.

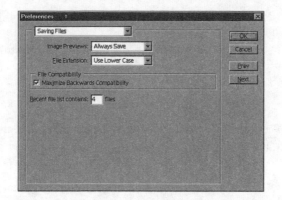

- **File Compatibility**—The Maximize Backward Compatibility options saves a Photoshop file that has the greatest chance of being opened by previous Photoshop versions. Enable Advanced TIFF Save Options opens the TIFF options dialog box when you save a TIFF image (see Figure 2.12).

Figure 2.12
Advanced TIFF
options include the
ability to set compres-
sion methods, byte-
order multiresolution
image pyramids, and
transparency.

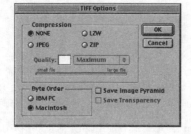

- **Recent File List Contains**—This shows the number of files that will be listed in the Open Recent list. Any number from 0 to 30 can be used.

DISPLAY & CURSORS

Settings in this area of the Preferences control the way the image is displayed on the screen and the type of cursor used by tools during their application.

- **Color Channels in Color**—This option shows channels in the Channel palette as the color they represent rather than as grayscale representations.

- **Use Diffusion Dither**—Specifies whether Photoshop will use Pattern (unchecked) or diffusion dithering in displaying 8-bit images on monitors currently displaying in a more limited color space (for example, a monitor set to 256 colors).

- **Use Pixel Doubling**—Speeds up the previewing of an image by doubling the size of the pixels for the preview.

- **Standard Cursors**—Displays cursors as the tool icons associated with them in the toolbox and in context-sensitive situations.

- **Precise Cursors**—Shows a crosshair during tool application, so you can tell exactly where it is being applied.
- **Brush Size**—Shows an outline of the brush being applied. The outline shows where the brush is more than 50% opaque.

TRANSPARENCY & GAMUT

Settings in this Preference screen allow you to control the appearance of the transparent background in an image and the overlay color used in conjunction with previewing out-of-gamut color.

- **Grid Size**—Allows you to choose the size of the background grid that appears under transparent portions of the image.
- **Grid Colors**—Allows you to adjust the color of the grid with various presets, or you can choose to create custom settings.
- **Gamut Warning**—Allows you to choose a gamut warning color and opacity. This color will display as an overlay on the image when colors are being displayed that will not convert exactly to CMYK, and the Gamut Warning (Shift–Cmd–Y) [Shift+Ctrl+Y] is turned on.

UNITS & RULERS AND GUIDES & GRID

This Preference screen allows you to choose the display units for the type size, rulers, guides, and grid. The units are used for the general sense of measure in the display on the rulers, Options bar, in measurements on the Info palette, and on the Type palettes.

The guides and grid can be set to appear in specific color and as solid or dashed lines. Column Size affects the display size of the image in some layout programs.

MEMORY AND IMAGE CACHE

Photoshop uses cached images to speed up screen refreshes when certain commands are executed. The cached image is a low-resolution copy of the original, which is stored in RAM. The cache levels can be set to values ranging from 1 to 8. A value of 8 uses the maximum caching and provides the fastest redraw times. The default is set to 4. Because the cached image is stored in RAM, if you are running low on memory, you might want to set the cache level to a lower value (see Figure 2.13).

You can also choose to use the cached image when you calculate a Histogram. Photoshop uses the low-resolution copy of the image providing faster results but a less accurate histogram in the Histogram, Levels, and Threshold dialog boxes.

Figure 2.13
Set a lower cache level to use slightly less memory when working with Photoshop.

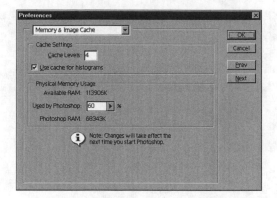

NONIMAGE SETTINGS

Photoshop uses a virtual memory scheme called *scratch disks*. Hard-disk space is used in conjunction with the physical RAM on your computer. In Windows systems, you can specify how much physical memory Photoshop should use in the Memory & Image Cache Preferences. In the Plug-Ins and Scratch Disk Preferences, you can tell Photoshop where to look for plug-ins and where scratch disks should be created. When setting a plug-in search path, you should choose the smallest folder structure that still finds the plug-ins you use because Photoshop looks in all subdirectories at startup. When choosing a scratch disk, you should choose the fastest hard drive(s) available on your computer that contain the most available space.

→ For more information about setting nonimage settings in Photoshop's preferences, **see** "Your System and Photoshop," **p. 907**.

> **Note**
>
> When working with Photoshop, especially when working with large images, you might occasionally need to free up some of the memory that is being used. You can purge Undo, Clipboard, and History information by choosing Edit, Purge, and then selecting the areas that you want to purge.

GETTING HELP

Photoshop's online Help provides a wealth of information about Photoshop features and tools. In Photoshop 6, the help is HTML based and can be accessed from the Help menu by pressing F1 or pressing (Cmd-?) [Ctrl+?] (see Figure 2.14).

Figure 2.14
You can search for specific topics in the Help system or work with specific procedures or concepts. The Help menu also contains links to top technical support issues, downloadable information, Adobe News, and Adobe Online.

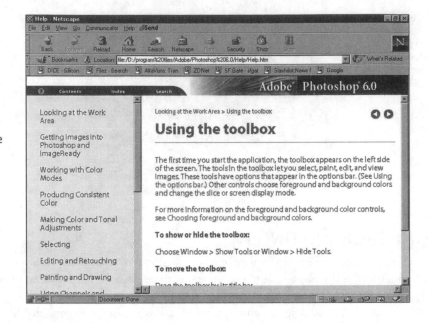

In addition to the online help within Photoshop, there are innumerable resources available on the Web and in Usenet newsgroups. You can find help with specific techniques, tutorials, and technical support information on a number of sites. You might want to start by pointing your browser to www.ps6.com. From there you can access links to a number of helpful Photoshop links, including User Forums, tutorials, and information about how other people are using Photoshop. Two helpful newsgroups are comp.graphics.photoshop and alt.graphics.photoshop. And a helpful free Photoshop community is available to you just for buying this book. Go to www.ps6.com, and you can sign up for the listserver. It was started just for those who have bought this book, and as a discussion group for using Photoshop.

TROUBLESHOOTING

SETTING UP YOUR OWN IMAGE

I'd like to set up my own image rather than use the settings suggested at the beginning of this chapter. What considerations do I need to make?

The first thing you should consider in setting up any image is its intended use. This requires knowledge about the medium, including required resolution and file types. Setting up the files requires knowing what you will do with it so you can determine the

- Size
- Resolution
- Color Mode
- File Type

You should always try to set the correct image size, resolution, and image mode before you begin, because changing these after the image is created alters the image data. It is beneficial to start with the correct image size to avoid resizing damage. The color mode of the image should usually be compatible with the file type—although it is sometimes an advantage to work in other color modes, and then convert the image to the proper color mode before saving. Although the final option when creating a new image is to select the file type, it really has ramifications for the other image choices.

→ For more information on file types, **see** "Selecting a File Format," **p. 319**.

If in doubt, start out at a higher resolution rather than a lower resolution if you think you may need a high-resolution copy of the image. It is better to downsample an image than to sample up.

→ For more information about choosing appropriate resolutions, **see** "Understanding Resolution," **p. 341**.

Different color modes offer specific advantages, both in working with color and compatibility with output and/or use. For example, you will usually choose RGB for onscreen images, CMYK for color printing, and Grayscale for grayscale images. Working properly with files and color modes helps save file size and targets color use to the capability of the final medium.

PHOTOSHOP AT WORK: INTERFACE CHANGES IN PHOTOSHOP 6.0

The most significant changes to the interface in Photoshop 6.0 are small changes to the placement and appearance of common menu items and tools, and the addition of some palettes and tools that might alter some of your Photoshop habits. For users of previous versions of Photoshop, the most significant interface changes you will find are

- Preferences are now located under the Edit menu, instead of the File menu.
- The Save a Copy command has been removed and is now an option in the Save As dialog box.
- The Options palette has been changed into an Options bar that is displayed at the top of the screen all the time.
- The New Character and Paragraph palettes enable you to control text as it is being entered on the screen, replacing the Type dialog box.
- The Styles palette enables you to manage and apply sets of Layer Styles to layers.
- The Preset Manager enables you to manage all your Photoshop presets, including brushes, shapes, gradients, and patterns.
- The Slice tool and Slice Select tool enable you to create and edit slices in a Photoshop image, just as you did in ImageReady.

- New vector-creation tools in the toolbox enable you to create a variety of shapes and edit them as vectors.
- The Color Management dialog box and controls have been completely reworked and are now accessible under Color Settings.

PHOTOSHOP'S IMAGE BUILDING BLOCKS

CHAPTER **3**

CREATING IMAGES IN LAYERS

In this chapter

CREATING IMAGES IN LAYERS

The basic layer is like a transparency, or a clear sheet, which you lay over your image so you can add image elements without affecting other layers (such as the background). Each sheet can be filled completely or partially, and it can be of varying opacity, effectively allowing the user to combine image elements in the stack, where the topmost layers obscure what is below (depending on the content and opacity). Layers allow you abundant flexibility in creating and arranging independent image elements in a single image. This is invaluable for image corrections and combining elements from different images, or essentially for use with any image alteration you might be considering.

Background Layers

Background layers are somewhat different from other layers in that they are completely opaque and cannot be reordered in the image. There is also only one background in any image, and it can only be the layer at the bottom of the stack. In a way, it can be considered the solid canvas behind the transparent layers that lie above. Backgrounds can be converted into layers, images can have no background, and backgrounds can be re-established. To convert the background into a layer, simply double-click it and it will convert to a layer (the default name is layer 0), and the New Layer dialog box will open to allow you to choose options. To restore a background if you have converted the background to a layer, either flatten the image or select New Background from the Layers menu.

Layers have functions that help you work with and blend the elements you are using for an image, and they are integral to creating complex images. These functions include

- Layer Modes
- Opacity
- Blend If
- Clipping Groups (or Layer Groups)
- Layer Masks
- Layer Styles
- Layer Sets

All can be used in different ways and combinations to accomplish specific layer-oriented tasks. Layers can be grouped in Sets, locked in place, and Layer Styles can be stored so that settings you use often for layers can be recalled and applied to layers in other images. The sum of all these parts is an almost limitless control over the means of combining and altering content. Each of these elements will be discussed in context as we progress through this chapter.

Implementation and control of layers are mostly handled via the Layers palette (see Figure 3.1) and the Layer menu. Details for the functions are summarized in Table 3.1.

Figure 3.1
The Layers palette is one of the most used and useful palettes, neatly containing quite a store of functions and information at a glance, yet it is remarkably tidy considering all that is on it. Be sure it is placed in an easily accessible spot in your workspace.

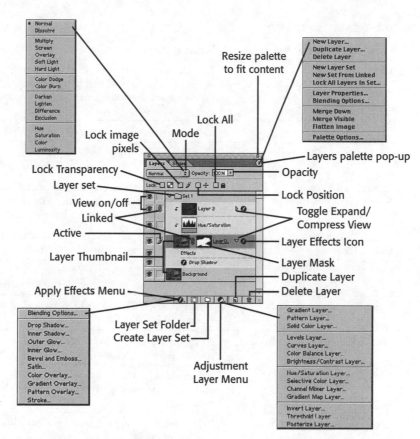

PART

II

CH

3

TABLE 3.1   LAYERS PALETTE FEATURES

Layers Palette Features	What It Does
View On/Off	Turns visibility for the layer on or off. Layers must be visible (On) to work on the content.
Active	Indicates the layer that will be affected by painting applications.
Layer Thumbnail	Shows the content of the individual layer.
Linked	Can show a linking between layers (when it appears in the palette column where the paintbrush icon for the active layer is located), or linking between a layer and its mask or clipping path (when it appears between the thumbnail and Mask or Path).
Mode	Allows the user to make a selection for the layer blending.
Apply Effects Menu	Allows the user to choose specific predefined effects that are applied across the content of the layer. Opens the appropriate Layer Effect dialog box when the Effect is selected.

TABLE 3.1 CONTINUED	
Layers Palette Features	**What It Does**
Layer Set Folder	Provides a means for grouping layers so they can be arranged in the image or transferred between images. Might be in expanded and condensed views so the content of the set is either visible or hidden.
Create Layer Set	Creates a Layer Set folder that can be populated with layers.
Adjustment Layer Menu	Creates an Adjustment layer as per the selection made on the list. Opens the appropriate dialog box when the selection is made.
New Layer	Creates a new layer or duplicates a layer dragged to it with copy appended to the original layer name. The new layer is created above the old.
Delete Layer	Removes the Active layer from the image.
Layer Mask	Acts as a mask, blacking out areas of the layer from view. Affects the image only when linked to the layer content.
Layer Effects	Indicates that Effects have been applied to the layer. If in expanded view, the Effects are listed below the layer.
Toggle Expand/Compress View	An arrow that when clicked will change state from expanded (pointing down) to condensed (pointing right) and vice versa.
Lock All	When checked, this locks the layer, and keeps the user from either moving the content of the layer or changing layer information.
Lock Movement	When checked, keeps the user from moving or repositioning content of the layer.
Lock image pixels	Keeps layer pixel information from changing.
Lock Transparency	Keeps layer transparency intact.
Opacity	Changes the opacity of the layer.
Resize Palette to Fit Content	Resizes the Palette to an optimal size for the current content of the Palette.
Layers Palette Pop-Up	Opens the Layers Palette Pop-Up menu, which contains additional layer functions.

CREATING AND MANAGING LAYERS

Worrying about any of the settings and features having to do with layer information is really wasted effort if you are working with only one layer. If there isn't more than one layer, there is no opportunity for layer interaction, so layer controls will be inoperative. There are innumerable opportunities to take advantage of layers and their controls but you have to create additional layers to take advantage of that opportunity. At times you will have to create layers and sometimes they will be created for you. Understanding the relationship between how to create, control, and activate layers is imperative for proper image editing and development.

CREATING LAYERS

A number of user actions will create a new layer. These include

- Pressing (Shift–Cmd–N) [Shift+Ctrl+N]
- Clicking the New Layer button on the Layers palette
- Pasting a copied image area (either within the same image or in other images)
- Duplicating a layer with the Duplicate function (on the Layers palette or the Layers menu)
- Dragging a layer to the New Layer button
- Dragging a layer from another image
- Entering type by clicking the Type tool on the image
- Creating a New Fill Layer (Layer, New Fill Layer)
- Creating a New Adjustment Layer (Layer, New Adjustment Layer)
- Rendering Layer effects (Layer, Layer Style, Create Layer)

Creating a new blank layer with either of the first two actions in the preceding list will place a new layer above the currently active layer, and will open the New Layer dialog box (see Figure 3.2).

Figure 3.2
In the New Layer dialog box, you get to choose options for the layer you are creating, including the layer name, grouping the new layer with the previous, selecting a Color coding for the layer in the palette, choosing a Mode, and setting Opacity.

Layers can be created from selections or by duplicating layers using the keyboard shortcuts seen in Table 3.2.

TABLE 3.2 SHORTCUTS FOR LAYER CREATION

Action	Macintosh	Windows	Shortcut Requirements
Create a new blank layer	(Shift–Cmd–Option-N)	[Shift+Ctrl+Alt+N]	An open image.
Create a new blank layer and open the New Layer dialog box	(Shift–Cmd–N)	[Shift+Ctrl+N]	An open image.
Create a new layer from a selection (As Copy/Paste)	(Cmd-J)	[Ctrl+J]	Requires an active selection applied to a layer that has pixel content (is not blank).
Create a new layer from a selection (As Cut/Paste)	(Shift–Cmd–J)	[Shift+Ctrl+J]	Requires an active selection applied to a layer that has pixel content (is not blank).
Create a new layer from a selection and open the New Layer dialog box (As Copy/Paste)	(Cmd–Option-J)	[Ctrl+Alt+J]	Requires an active selection applied to a layer that has pixel content (is not blank).
Create a new layer from a selection and open the New Layer dialog box (As Cut/Paste)	(Shift–Cmd–Option-J)	[Shift+Ctrl+Alt+J]	Requires an active selection applied to a layer that has pixel content (is not blank).
Duplicate Layer	(Cmd–Option-Arrow)	[Ctrl+Alt+Arrow]	Requires an active layer with pixel content (is not blank).

You will want to create a new layer every time there is image information you need to isolate from other portions of the image. Isolation is useful for managing image and element blending, as well as aiding in certain types of corrections. Layers provide unique opportunities to indulge complex image arrangement and interaction.

Layering Tool Applications
When doing just about any correction to an image, you will want to use additional layers to allow you several options. If making the correction to a separate layer, you can quickly compare the changes by toggling the view for the changes off and on (before and after), and you will have unprecedented options for blending, merging, smoothing, and otherwise optimizing the incorporation of what you have done in the correction. If you don't think the changes are optimal, you can store the changes and duplicate them to yet another layer to see whether you can improve on them—and you can apply layered changes to the changes! Considering this versatility, the one-shot correct-it-all-in-one-layer approach is not recommended.

If you create a layer and have trouble applying new tools and effects, there can be several things going wrong. See "Getting a Layer to Work" in the Troubleshooting section at the end of this chapter.

MERGING LAYERS

On the other side of layer creation is Layer Merge. Merging is putting together information from two different layers so that the layer information is no longer separate. Merging can be used to combine layers that need not be separate, such as several text applications over an image to which you will want to apply the same effects. In this case you will have to render the type before merging, but merging will help you manage effects and conserve memory.

Note

Layers are tremendously flexible and add a lot of possibility to manipulating images; however, they also require a significant amount of memory to maintain. Keeping layers to a minimum by combining Layers via Merge whenever it will not affect your ability to work on the image can free up memory and maintain a more efficient working environment.

There are a number of options for merging layers and all appear on the contextually sensitive Merge section of the Layer Menu. The menu adjusts options to those that are most probable considering the layer that is currently active. The selection by the program is based on a hierarchy of what Merge variations are possible, approximately in the order that follows (from most likely to be superceded):

- **Merge Down**—Merges the currently active layer into the layer immediately below. Both the active layer and the layer immediately below must be visible.

- **Merge Group**—Merges all the layers in a clipping group. The bottommost layer of the group must be active.

- **Merge Linked**—Merges all linked layers provided the linked layers are all visible and not part of a clipping group (all parts of any group must be part of the link).

- **Merge Visible**—Merges all visible layers. The active layer must be a visible layer.

- **Flatten Image**—Is essentially the ultimate Merge in that it will combine all layers into a single layer. A warning will be issued when the function is invoked if any layers are hidden letting the user know that all hidden layers will be discarded during the flattening.

ACTIVATING LAYERS

 Active layers are really the layers that will be targeted to accept the changes you implement in the course of working with the image. Simply stated, an active layer is the one that is highlighted in the Layers palette. The area of the Layers palette that contains the layer description will be in the highlighted color, and the Paintbrush icon will be to the left of the layer thumbnail. This layer will accept application of any tools or functions invoked.

To activate a layer to work on, simply click it in the Layers palette. Layers can also be activated using keystrokes. This will move up and down through the visible layers or jump to layers at the top and bottom of the stack. Combinations of these keystrokes can help you quickly navigate between layers when working on an image. See Table 3.3 for a listing of the keystrokes.

TABLE 3.3   KEYSTROKE LAYER NAVIGATION

Layer Selected	Mac	PC
Layer above currently active layer (also jumps bottom to top)	Option–[	Alt+[
Layer below currently active layer (also jumps top to bottom)	Option–]	Alt+]
Topmost layer in the palette	Shift–Option–]	Shift+Alt+]
Bottommost layer in the palette	Shift–Option–[	Shift+Alt+[
Topmost visible layer under the cursor (click on image)	Ctrl–Cmd-Option-Click	Alt+Right-click

After a layer is activated, changes can be made to the image content using any of Photoshop's tools that affect pixel information, so long as the tool or function is available. Layer information can be moved within the layer, both by arranging layer order and by horizontal and vertical positioning of the layer information. Positioning can be independent from or in unison with other Linked Layers, Clipping Groups, or Layer Sets.

LINKED LAYERS

Linking is a means of managing layer content by grouping and linking the content of selected layers. *Linked layers* will be affected by layer content movements in the image plane and Transformations applied to any layer in that group, but will not be affected by movement of the layer in the Layers palette. The Layers will move in unison and will not have to be realigned or moved individually to maintain alignment with one another. Linking layers provides noncontiguous control of layers that spans Layer Sets, Clipping Groups, and visibility.

To link a layer to another layer, make one of the layers that will be linked the active layer. This will automatically place the paintbrush icon in the box immediately to the left of the thumbnail. Next, click the link indicator box on the Layers palette immediately to the left of the layer you would like to link it to. A Link icon will appear in the box where you clicked, indicating that the layer is linked to the active layer.

 Items linked together will always appear as linked to one another: Anytime one of the layers in the Linked group is selected as active, the Paintbrush icon will appear next to it showing it is the active layer, and the other links in the group will display the link icon. These links appear in the grouping regardless of which layer is active or the order they were created in. In other words, if you link Layers 2 and 3 to Layer 1, Layer 1 will have the Paintbrush icon at the time of linking, and 2 and 3 will have Link icons. When you select Layer 2 as the active layer, the Paintbrush icon will appear next to it, and the Link icon will appear next to Layers 1 and 3. These links will remain in effect until they are removed.

All movements within the image plane and transformations will affect all linked layers equally. Any number of layers can be linked in whatever order (contiguously or noncontiguously within the stack), and links can be terminated and activated at will. To remove a link, simply click the Link icon when another layer in the linked group is active. This will remove the link only from the layer from which the icon was removed. A quick means of linking a series of contiguous layers is to hold the Shift key down while holding down the mouse button and dragging the pointer over the link boxes. To unlink by clicking and dragging, hold down the (Option) [Alt] key.

Aligning Layer Content

Pixel content in linked layers can be aligned and distributed using the Align and Distribute commands on the Layer menu or the alignment buttons on the Move tool options. Two or more layers have to be linked to use the Align feature and three or more must be linked to use the distribute feature (see Figure 3.3).

Figure 3.3
Layer content can be arranged quickly by linking the items you want to align and clicking the appropriate button on the Movement Options bar for alignment or distribution.

LAYER SETS

Layer Sets are a brand-new feature in Photoshop 6 (see Figure 3.4). They are a means of grouping collections of layers that need to be maintained in a particular order. This provides a means for easy movement of the group (between images or in the layer order). Layer Sets also allow for the contents of the Sets to be collapsed and expanded in the Layers palette view. Viewing and hiding in no way affects the content of the set.

Figure 3.4
The collapsed Layer Set makes it easier to view the remaining layers. This can be moved as a group within the image and without, deleted as a group, or viewed by expanding.

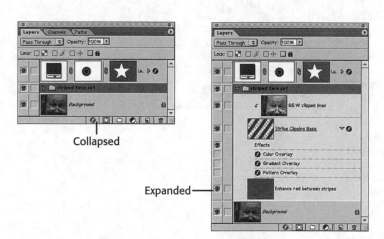

Collapsed

Expanded

Layer Sets can be Masked or clipped as a group by applying a Mask and/or Layer Clipping Path to the Set. The content of the Sets must contain contiguous layers, unlike linked layers, but can contain linked layers and Clipping Groups. Sets are a higher level of order and cannot be used as part of a Clipping Group.

CREATING LAYER SETS

To create a Layer Set, you can either create the folder for the set and then drag layers into it, or link the layers that you want in the set and choose New Set From Linked from the Layers palette pop-up menu. Dragging the layers to a set you create is clumsier than linking the layers and then creating the set if the layers already exist because you have to drag individual layers in one at a time. Layers dragged into a Set folder stack from the top down unless dragged to a specific spot: Each layer you drag in gets added to the bottom of the stack if you just drag it to the folder. This is counter to the way layers generally work, which is from the bottom up. You can rearrange the layers after they are in the folder—or you can drag them one at a time to the spot in which they belong in the order. If you use New Set From Linked, the Linked Layers will retain the layer order they had when the Set was created. To create an empty set, click the New Set icon at the bottom of the Layers palette.

USING LAYER SETS WITH CHANNELS

Another use for Layer Sets, and a rather unique feature for layers, is that the effects of layer Sets can be targeted to specific channels. For example, if working in CMYK, you can create a Layer Set that will affect only the cyan and black channels while not affecting the content of the yellow and magenta channels—even if there are yellow and magenta components in the layers used for the Layer Set. To Target a specific Channel, highlight a Layer Set that you have already created and choose Layer Properties from the Layer Menu or Layers palette pop-up. The Layer Set Properties screen will appear (see Figure 3.5). Simply uncheck the boxes by the primaries that you do not want the changes to apply to.

Figure 3.5
This feature can be handy for some color changes where the color change is content specific, such as redeye. In the case of redeye, limiting the color change to the red Channel in RGB or the yellow and magenta in CMYK might help you make a color change targeted to the red while maintaining other color integrity.

CLIPPING GROUPS

Clipping Groups use the bottommost layer in a group as a mask and apply the content of the layers above (within the group) to the image based on the order of the layers. The base layer of a Clipping Group clips the other layers in the group based on its transparency.

Clipping Groups define a result based on what are essentially substacks of layers. Where an image is the result of all the stacked visible layers on the background, Clipping Groups use the base of the group as the background. The grouped layers use the bottom layer as a clipping path or mask for the grouped layers above it based on its areas of transparency. Unlike the background of the image, however, Clipping Groups can appear anywhere in the layer order.

Using a Clipping Group is like using a Layer Mask or Layer Clipping Path. In fact, Layer Masks, Clipping Groups, and Layer Clipping Paths all essentially do the same thing, although they each do it a little differently.

To create a Clipping Group:

1. Create or open an image with at least two layers in a stack (in addition to the background if you have one).

Note

The bottom layer should probably have some transparent or semitransparent areas.

2. Make the upper layer of the two you are using for the Clipping Group active.

3. Group the layers by pressing (Cmd-G) [Ctrl+G]; the lower layer's transparency clips the information from the upper layer (see Figure 3.6).

Figure 3.6
In this series of images, the top layer is placed on the second layer. When they are grouped, the result is that the base layer of the Clipping Group cookie-cuts the image lying above it. The area of the image above that falls to where the base layer is 100% opaque stays, while the rest falls away.

The upper layer

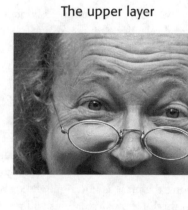

The lower layer

The result of grouping

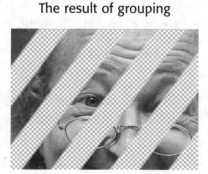

How it appeares in the Layers palette

> **Note**
> If you select the grouping command from the Layers menu, it is called Group With Previous.

The top layer in the pairing will have its content confined by the opacity of the lower layer. Another method for applying a Clipping Group is to link the layers. When one of the Linked layers is selected, Group Linked can be selected from the Layers menu (actually the same command as Group With Previous; its name changes to fit the context).

LAYER MASKS

 A Layer Mask, like a Clipping Group, helps redefine the content of the layer. The masks block out layer information, somewhat like placing a stencil on the layer. One notable difference between a mask in Photoshop and a stencil is that a mask can be semiopaque.

→ For more information on working with masks, **see** "Channels As Selections and Masks," **p. 81** and "Editing Channels," **p. 87**.

To apply a Layer Mask:

1. Create a selection of the area you would like to mask. As an alternative, a selection can be loaded from one you have already created or another Channel can be loaded as a Mask.

2. After the selection is active, choose either Reveal Selection or Hide Selection from Layer, Add a Layer Mask menu. Reveal selection will create a Mask for the layer that masks the unselected portion of the image, revealing the selected area; Hide Selection will mask the selected area of the image.

Masked areas appear black in the layer Mask. Figure 3.7 shows the result of applying a Layer Mask.

 To edit a Layer Mask, highlight the layer that contains the mask you want to edit in the Layers floating palette by clicking once on the layer. The mask will appear in the Channels palette and can be edited just like any other channel at this point; it will not appear in the Channels palette when the layer containing the mask is not highlighted. You can also edit the channel by clicking the thumbnail in the Layers palette. This will not show you the mask you are editing but will allow you to view the effects of the changes as you edit the mask. In either case, when the mask is active, the Layer Mask icon will appear to the left of layer in the Layers palette rather than the Paintbrush icon.

LAYER CLIPPING PATHS

A *Layer Clipping Path* is a resolution-independent means of applying a shaped clipping area to an image layer. The Clipping Path is applied with vectors rather than a pixel-based mask, so the result can be sharper in some instances. The difference between applying a Clipping Path and a Mask is similar to the difference between bitmapped and PostScript fonts. The limitation to a Layer Clipping Path is that the border is absolute; the path denotes a sharp break between inclusion and exclusion of image information. There is no means of blending as there is with a Layer Mask. However, Layer Masks and Layer Clipping Paths are not mutually exclusive: They can be used together and can, in fact, be made from the same selection.

→ For more information on making a path from a selection, **see** "Interchanging Paths and Selection," **p. 187**.

The Mask

The Mask Applied

Figure 3.7
The Layer Mask in this case was loaded from a selection adjusted to fit the subject's eye area. Note the effect of the inner ring in the selection on the result. When the mask is applied to the layer, it blocks out everything outside the selected area, revealing the black background of the image.

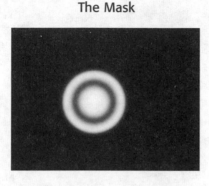

How it appears in the Layers palette

To apply a Layer Clipping Path, you will need to create an active path. After the path is created, it can be applied to the layer in a way very similar to the application of a Layer Mask. Simply select Current Path from the Add Layer Clipping Path submenu on the Layers menu. This will create a Layer Clipping Path from the currently active path. Everything inside the area of the path will be revealed while everything outside the path will be clipped. Figure 3.8 shows the result of applying a Clipping Path to a layer.

Clipping Paths can be used in combination with Clipping Groups and Layer Masks in any configuration. When used in combination Layer Masks show up immediately to the right of the layer thumbnail, and Clipping Paths show up to the right of the Layer Mask. Clipping Paths, Layer Masks, and Clipping Groups can all use Layer Styles as well, which create effects based on the result of the masking(s). Figure 3.9 shows a combination of the previous examples used for Clipping Groups, Layer Masks, and Clipping Paths. You can try your hand at imitating these results in the "Photoshop at Work" section at the end of this chapter.

Figure 3.8
When a Path is active in an image, the outline will show. After the path is applied here, it blocks out the image area outside the path only in the layer it is applied to—unless that layer is the base of a Clipping Group.

How the path looks over the image

The Layer Clipping path applied

How it appears in the Layers palette

Figure 3.9
The original image from these examples was of a somewhat red-faced Ben Franklin imitator. The red face and blue eyes seemed already to be waxing patriotic, and needed only a little further manipulation with the help of clipping and masking to look like a wacky patriot. Various clipping and masking effects are at work here to define the stripes and star.

The result of applying multiple clipping effects

Results in the Layers palette

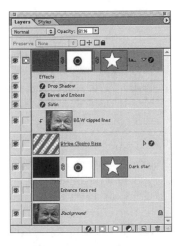

SIMPLE BLENDING MODES

Layers have several basic blending functions including Layer Modes, Layer Opacity, and Preserve settings. These settings can be used to control the intensity and type of interaction between layer information. All are found at the top of the Layers palette just above the stack.

A *Layer Mode* defines how the content of the layer will be applied to the elements in layers below. These Modes are pretty much the same as modes for application of painting tools, but the mode applies to the entire layer as an overlay. Layer Mode is most often used as Normal, but can be used in other modes both for special purposes and special effects.

Table 3.4 gives some details on the Layer Mode types. Rankings in the Frequency of Use column of Very Often, Often, Sometimes, Rarely, and Almost Never are based on photographic reproduction and application. For all applications, Layer opacity can be controlled by pressing a number key where 10 times the number is the opacity the layer will assume. Typing the exact opacity desired quickly will change the opacity to that number.

TABLE 3.4   LAYER MODE TYPES, EFFECTS, USES, AND SHORTCUTS

Blend Mode	Effect	Use	Frequency of Use	Quick Key
Normal	Takes on the color/tone of the pixels in the upper layer.	Normal use; unblended result.	Very Often	(Shift–Option–N) [Shift+Alt+N]
Dissolve	Takes on the color/tone of the pixels in the upper layer, but dithers selection between upper and lower layer based on the strength of the opacity. The greater the opacity, the more selection is weighted to the upper layer.	Special effects; method for adding noise; rough, gritty blending.	Almost Never	(Shift–Option–I) [Shift+Alt+I]
Multiply	Darkens the result by increasing the darkness of the lower layer based on the darkness of the upper layer. No portion of the image can get lighter.	Used for shadow effects.	Often	(Shift–Option–M) [Shift+Alt+M]
Screen	Brightens the values of the lower layer based on the lightness of the upper layer. No portion of the image can get darker.	Used for highlight effects.	Often	(Shift–Option–S) [Shift+Alt+S]
Overlay	Multiplies (darkens) the dark colors and screens (lightens) the light.	Work with contrast and image blends.	Sometimes	(Shift–Option–O) [Shift+Alt+O]

PART

II

CH

3

TABLE 3.4 CONTINUED

Blend Mode	Effect	Use	Frequency of Use	Quick Key
Soft Light	Multiplies (darkens) the dark colors and screens (lightens) the light. Soft application of the upper layer.	Work with contrast and ghosted image overlays.	Rarely	(Shift–Option–F) [Shift+Alt+F]
Hard Light	Multiplies (darkens) the dark colors and screens (lightens) the light.	Work with contrast and image overlays.	Rarely	(Shift–Option–H) [Shift+Alt+H]
Color Dodge	Dodges (lightens) color of underlying layer with upper layer, brightening the result. No portion of the image gets darker.	Washing out, overexposing, highlighting.	Rarely	(Shift–Option–D) [Shift+Alt+D]
Color Burn	Burns in (darkens) color of underlying layer with the upper layer, darkening the result. No portion of the image gets lighter.	Underexposing, darkening.	Rarely	(Shift–Option–B) [Shift+Alt+B]
Darken	Chooses the darker color values for each pixel in comparing the two layers. No portion of the image gets lighter.	Some dust correction applications, shadowing, darkening.	Sometimes	(Shift–Option–K) [Shift+Alt+K]
Lighten	Chooses the lighter color values for each pixel in comparing the two layers. No portion of the image gets darker.	Some dust correction applications, lightening, highlighting.	Sometimes	(Shift–Option–G) [Shift+Alt+G]
Difference	Reacts to difference between later pixel values: Large difference yields a bright result; small difference yields a dark result (no difference yields black).	Special effects.	Almost Never	(Shift–Option–E) [Shift+Alt+E]

TABLE 3.4   CONTINUED

Blend Mode	Effect	Use	Frequency of Use	Quick Key
Exclusion	Uses darkness of lower layer to exclude the Difference effect (described previously). If the bottom layer pixel is dark, there is little change in the upper layer; if the bottom layer is black, there is no change; the lighter the lower layer, the more intense the Difference effect.	Special effects.	Almost Never	(Shift–Option–X) [Shift+Alt+X]
Hue	Changes hue of the lower layer to the upper while leaving Saturation and Luminosity.	Color changes and correction.	Rarely	(Shift–Option–U) [Shift+Alt+U]
Saturation	Changes Saturation of the lower layer to the upper while leaving Hue and Luminosity.	Color changes and correction.	Almost Never	(Shift–Option–T) [Shift+Alt+T]
Color	Changes the Hue and Saturation of the lower layer to the upper while leaving the Luminosity.	Color changes and correction.	Sometimes	(Shift–Option–C) [Shift+Alt+C]
Luminosity	Changes Luminosity of the lower layer to the upper while leaving Saturation and Luminosity.	Color changes and correction.	Almost Never	(Shift–Option–Y) [Shift+Alt+Y]

PART II

CH 3

Note

Also see images 5.51 to 5.66 in Chapter 5 for a simple black-and-white demonstration of how blending modes work.

Layer Opacity determines the amount the current layer will obscure or affect the image information in layers below. An opacity of 100% means that the image information in the layer will interact completely with information below. A lower percentage means the effect and/or coverage will be less intense.

Settings for locking transparency and pixel content affect application of tools to the current layer depending on the opacity and content of each pixel in the layer. If neither is checked, images can be freely edited. If the transparency is locked, the layer will preserve current opacity for each pixel no matter what tool or effect is applied, but the content (color and tone) can change. If the pixel content is preserved (color, tone, and opacity), the layer will retain the information in the image essentially locking pixel values and disallowing any application of filters or tools that change content.

It is important to note that pixel information within the layer can be partially transparent, as it might have been applied to the layer with a tool that used partial opacity. In other words, if black was applied to a 50% opaque layer with 50% opacity, the result would be 25% opacity. Although you will probably most often use an opacity of 100%, you might find a number of reasons to reduce opacity in blending images and elements. This will affect the application of other tools if the layer transparency is locked.

Note

Although there is no difference in the result in the image if applying a 50% opaque tool to a 50% opaque layer, applying a 100% opaque tool to a 25% opaque layer, or applying a 25% opaque tool to a 100% opaque layer, the result in the layer itself is different. The choice as to how to set opacities can be important and can be noticeable if duplicating the channels, applying additional changes via clipping groups.

LAYER BLENDING OPTIONS AND LAYER STYLES

Layer Blending Options and Layer Styles are grouped effects for the layer controlled through the Layer Styles palette and dialog box. Layer Styles are really saved sets of Layer Blending Options. Selecting Blending Options from either the Layers palette pop-up or the Layer menu (under the Layer Styles submenu) will open the Layer Styles dialog box. The Layer Style dialog box is a one-stop management area for what were Layer Effects and blending modes (see Figure 3.10).

The Layer Styles dialog box actually allows you access to all the following and then some: Layer Styles, General Blending, Drop Shadow, Inner Shadow, Outer Glow, Inner Glow, Bevel & Emboss, Contour & Texture, Satin, Overlay and Stroke. I say "and then some" as there are numerous subeffects that can be applied using patterns, fills, gradients, curves, and so on. See Table 3.5 for a listing of the effects and the features each supports. These effects will be examined further in later chapters as the effects are applied.

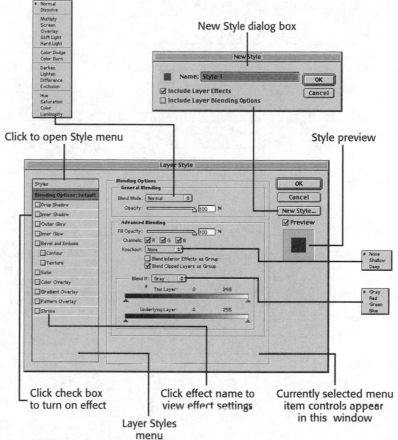

New Style dialog box

Click to open Style menu

Style preview

Figure 3.10
To view the palettes/dialog boxes for each of the Effects, click the name of the effect. To apply the effect, click the check box. To shut the effect off, click the check box again so that the check is removed.

Click check box to turn on effect

Click effect name to view effect settings

Currently selected menu item controls appear in this window

Layer Styles menu

TABLE 3.5   LAYER STYLE EFFECTS

Effect	What It Does	Features
General Blending	Defines how the current layer will blend with layers below.	General Settings: Mode setting, Opacity Advanced Settings: Fill Opacity, Channels, Knockout, Blend Group, and Blend If settings
Drop Shadow	Defines drop-shadow effects behind layer content based on transparency of the layer.	Structure: Blend Mode, Opacity, Angle, Distance, Spread, Size Quality: Contour, Noise, Knockout Dropshadow
Inner Shadow	Defines shadow effects on the inside edge and above layer content as if the layer were the base of a Clipping Group.	Structure: Blend Mode, Opacity, Angle, Distance, Choke, Size Quality: Contour, Noise

TABLE 3.5   CONTINUED

Effect	What It Does	Features
Outer Glow	Defines glow around and below layer content based on opacity.	Structure: Blend Mode, Opacity, Noise, Solid Color/Blend Elements: Technique, Spread, Size Quality: Contour, Range, Jitter
Inner Glow	Defines Glow effects on the inside edge and above layer content as if the layer were the base of a Clipping Group.	Structure: Blend Mode, Opacity, Noise, Solid Color/Blend Elements: Technique, Source, Choke, Size. Quality: Contour, Range, Jitter
Bevel & Emboss	Creates beveled effect inside or outside the edge of the opaque area of the layer (depending on settings).	Structure: Style, Technique, Depth, Direction, Size, Soften Shading: Angle Altitude, Gloss Contour, Highlight Mode, Opacity, Shadow Mode, Opacity
Contour & Texture	Allows control of Bevel Contour and application of textures over the beveled area.	Contour: Contour, Range Texture: Pattern, Scale, Depth, Invert, Link with Layer
Satin		Structure: Blend Mode, Opacity, Angle, Distance, Size, Contour
Overlay	Applies an Overlay to the image using a color, gradient, or pattern.	Color Fill: Blend Mode, Opacity Gradient Fill: Blend Mode, Opacity, Gradient, Style, Angle, Scale Pattern Fill: Blend Mode, Opacity, Pattern, Scale
Stroke	Strokes the edge of the image area where it turns from opaque to transparent either outside, on center, or inside the edge.	Structure: Size, Position, Blend Mode, Opacity Fill: Color, Gradient, Pattern

The preview box to the right on the Layer Styles palette allows you to view how the effects would look on a small square. The current effects can be saved for later use as Layer Styles by clicking the New button. This will allow you to choose a descriptive name for the new style and select options for what to save from the current style set. To recall the style you saved, all you have to do is open the Blending Options and select the style from the style menu. To view the saved Styles, click Layer Styles on the menu to the left. This will reveal all the Styles that are currently loaded. From this view, you can load more Styles and manage sets. You can also change the style views by selecting the desired view from the Layer Styles pop-up menu. See Figure 3.11.

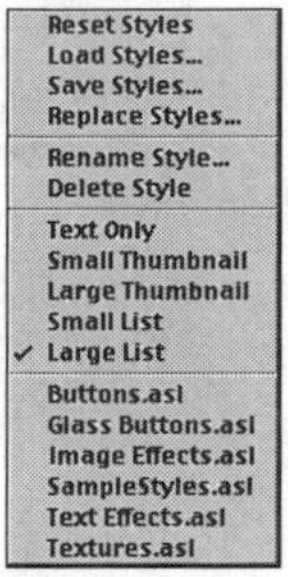

Figure 3.11
Layer Styles can be viewed either with or without previews, with or without descriptions, and in varying thumbnail sizes. I find viewing the thumbnail and descriptions together helpful.

Reset Styles
Load Styles...
Save Styles...
Replace Styles...

Rename Style...
Delete Style

Text Only
Small Thumbnail
Large Thumbnail
Small List
✓ Large List

Buttons.asl
Glass Buttons.asl
Image Effects.asl
SampleStyles.asl
Text Effects.asl
Textures.asl

ADJUSTMENT AND FILL LAYERS

Adjustment and Fill layers allow the user to apply Photoshop functions as layers. This provides an advantage in that the application of the function does not actually change the image information. The layer can be applied to the images later or discarded without stepping back in the History.

Fill and Adjustment layers are actually applied and managed through four separate menu items. Selecting New Fill Layer or New Adjustment Layer from the Layers menu adds a new layer to the image above the currently active layer. Upon selection, the New Layer dialog box will open to allow selection of the layer name, grouping (with previous), color code, mode, and opacity. When the New Layer dialog box is closed, the dialog box for the adjustment or fill function opens and the layer will be created. The layers are automatically assigned a mask and appear with an icon that is unique to the function selected. The mask can be turned into a layer clipping path by simply drawing a path or layer mask by using pixel-editing tools to change the channel information. A complete list of the icons appears in Figure 3.12.

Figure 3.12
The icons here represent the thumbnails that are created to identify the layer types.

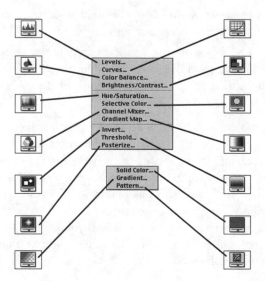

Levels...
Curves...
Color Balance...
Brightness/Contrast...

Hue/Saturation...
Selective Color...
Channel Mixer...
Gradient Map...

Invert...
Threshold...
Posterize...

Solid Color...
Gradient...
Pattern...

After the layers are created, the layer content can be edited or changed. Change Layer Content enables you to change the function currently assigned to the layer. For example, if Levels are assigned to the layer and you would like to change it to Curves, select Curves from the Change Layer Content menu. To adjust the settings for the function currently assigned to the layer, choose Layer Content Options from the Layers menu, or double-click the function icon in the Layers palette. Either of those actions will open the dialog box for the function with the current settings.

THE BLEND IF LAYER FUNCTION

The *Blend If* function allows the user to create conditions in which image information will blend between layers. The sliders allow the user to target specific areas to blend from and to in consideration of color and tone. With measurements, application of color changes, repairs, and so on can be based on tonality.

This is useful for colorizing images, targeting tool application, blending back details lost in corrections, and a number of other applications. This might be infrequently used, but it is a powerful and exacting tool. Used in combination with new Layer options and in tune with the new interface for control of Layer Styles, this can more easily be targeted to your needs than in previous versions of Photoshop.

→ For more information on using the Blend If function, **see** "The Blend If Layer Function," **p. 76** and "Colorizing a Grayscale Image," **p. 520**.

TROUBLESHOOTING

GETTING A LAYER TO WORK

Occasionally, I will run into a problem where the layer I am working with will not accept the changes I am making. Is this a bug in the program or is something else going wrong?

With all the versatility that Photoshop offers, sometimes there are some unexpected results—although the true surprises and bugs are few and far between. In this case there are several ways Photoshop might be keeping you from applying what you'd like, and all are valid reasons (not bugs).

Hopefully, most of these problems can be taken care of by Photoshop error messages. These are not crash messages, but contextually sensitive, helpful notes that let you know what might be going wrong. For example, if you try applying a History brush to an image's eighth layer and the Snapshot you are painting from had seven layers, you will not be able to apply the History Brush. The Can't Apply icon will appear instead. If you attempt to apply anyway, you will get the message "Could not use the History Brush because the History State does not contain a corresponding layer." In other words, if you see the pointer icon turn into the Can't Apply icon, try applying it anyway. The result might be a helpful message that tells you why you can't apply the tool.

Reasons why difficulty in applying tools might be occurring might stem from opacity or mode selections for the tools you are using to Layer Opacities, pixel and transparency locks, inappropriate application of color modes, sampling mistakes (the Stamping tool), and such. Really, you probably need to check only a few things: Layer Opacity, Tool Opacity, Layer Mode, Tool Mode, Image Mode, Layer Masking, Layer Clipping Paths, Clipping Groups, Selection, Pixel Lock, and Transparency Lock. You will note this can be summarized as Opacities, Modes, Masking, Selection, and Locks.

■ **Opacity**—Any setting for opacity that is too low might keep you from seeing the result. This is especially true if there are multiple opacity settings at work. For example, it is possible to apply a 10% opaque tool to a 10% opaque Layer and end up with a 1% application of the original color. If that color is less than 50% gray in intensity, it might not show up at all.

■ **Modes**—There are two types of Mode to be concerned with, Image Mode and application Mode. Image Modes are the color spaces you are working in, and application Modes apply to the Mode of tool and Layer application. Image Modes will need to be compatible—and in most cases this means the same. If you are attempting to stamp CMYK information into an RGB image, you probably will have a mismatch and experience some problems. On the application Mode side, if you are using a Lighten mode and are attempting to apply a black to an image, nothing will happen. Selecting an appropriate Mode (such as Darken) will help get the results you need.

→ For more information on Color Modes, **see** "Choosing an Image Mode," **p. 309**.

■ **Masking**—If you use Masking in the form of Layer Masks, Layer Clipping Paths, or Clipping Groups, you might actually make valid application of tools that you simply can't see because it is being masked. Be sure you are not painting to a layer that has either a Clipping Path or Mask applied, and be sure it is not in a Clipping Group.

■ **Selection**—Selections can sometimes hide in an image: you might be too close to see the selection which is loaded over another part of the image, selections might not encompass any pixels at more than 50%, or you might have hidden the selection and forgotten. In any case, you can shut off the selection by pressing (Cmd–D) [Ctrl+D]. After the Selection is disabled, you will be able to apply the tool as desired.

■ **Locks**—This is probably the lowest possibility, as you have to set the Locks fairly consciously (whereas tool settings can carry over from session to session and are easier to forget). However, if you turn on the Pixel Lock, you will not be able to change existing Pixels in a layer. Be sure the layer you are working on has the Pixel Lock off (unchecked).

With all this checked, there are still other valid things that can go wrong, such as having a Channel active and painting to that instead of the layer you think you are working on. If you are really in a quandary and have checked everything, open a brand-new image and try doing what you want to do there. If it works, rebuild the image a layer at a time to find the problem. If it doesn't work, you might want to re-evaluate what you are trying to do.

PHOTOSHOP AT WORK: CREATING LAYER EFFECTS

If you have read the whole chapter, you probably saw it coming: The exercise for this chapter is to re-create the wacky patriot. Page 3 of the PDF workbook (download the workbook at the Web site http://www.ps6.com) has the original cropped version of the fellow that was used for the image. This exercise will require creating new layers, a Layer Mask, a Clipping Group, a Layer Clipping Path, and applying at least one layer effect. With all that done, you will have a pretty good idea of how layers work and you'll know how to handle them. This series of events could be handled differently to create the same effects, but this series exercises as many options as possible.

1. Open the image Page 3 in the PDF workbook as an RGB image.

2. Be sure you can see the Channels, Layers, and Path palettes. This image will have a single layer, two alpha channels, and a Path.

3. Duplicate the original layer (Layer, Duplicate Layer).

4. Desaturate the duplicate layer (Shift–Cmd–U) [Shift+Ctrl+U].

5. Create a new layer (Layer, New Layer).

6. Move the layer created in Step 5 below the Duplicate created in Steps 3 and 4. Use (Option–Cmd–[) [Ctrl+Alt+[] to move the layer down one level.

7. Load Alpha 1 as a Selection (Shift–Cmd–Click Alpha 1) [Shift+Ctrl+Click Alpha 1].

8. Fill the selection with the foreground color (Edit, Fill). The Foreground color really doesn't matter, but it should be 100% Opaque.

9. Click the Link box next to the Desaturated layer created in Steps 3 and 4.

10. Choose Group Linked from the Layer menu (Layer, Group Linked). The result should be that the duplicate created in Step 3 is clipped by the layer filled with the foreground in Step 5. The face will show with alternating stripes of white and red.

11. Create a new layer (Layer, New Layer).

12. Move the layer created in Step 12 to the top of the layer stack. Use (Shift-Option–Cmd–]) [Shift+Ctrl+Alt+]] to move the layer.

13. Fill the new layer with blue. To do this, double-click the foreground color, select a blue; then choose the Paint Bucket tool (K) and click it over the image. The new layer should be filled with blue and obscure the rest of the image.

14. Load Alpha 2 as a Selection (Shift–Cmd–Click Alpha 2) [Shift+Ctrl+Click Alpha 2].

15. Change the selection to a Mask by choosing Layer, Add Layer Mask, Reveal Selection. This should mask out the blue over the eye and reveal the image below.

16. Click the Path in the Paths palette to activate it.

17. Add the Layer Clipping Path by choosing Layer, Add Layer Clipping Path. This should clip the outside of the blue into a star shape, revealing the rest of the face outside the star area.

18. Apply a Bevel to the star by choosing Blending Options (which opens the Layer Styles), and click the Bevel and Emboss effect on the menu at the left of the dialog box. Increase the depth of the effect as desired.

At this point you will have something very close to the result shown earlier, but in full color red-white-and-blue. Try variations by altering the effects for Step 18, and changing the shape of the Mask, fill layer content, and clipping path.

CHAPTER 4

WORKING WITH CHANNELS

In this chapter

WHAT CHANNELS DO

Channels serve two purposes: to store color image information and to store selections and masks. Each channel is a grayscale representation of intensity: For color, greater intensity generally means stronger application of the individual color represented (a and b channels in Lab color are an exception to this); for masks, greater intensity means a stronger application of masking—or what essentially amounts to protection from change. Intensity ranges from 0% (by default, represented as white in the channel) to 100% (by default, represented by black in the channel). Most often this percentage is recorded and displayed in 256 levels of gray, from 0 to 255 levels (bitmap images are an exception to this). Channel information can be manipulated directly in grayscale, and will be affected by changes to the color information as it is currently viewed in the layers.

→ For more information on selections, alpha channels and masking, **see** "Selection and Masking," **p. 93**.

→ For more information on layers, **see** "Creating Images in Layers," **p. 53**.

CHANNELS AS COLORS

Color images have channels that use the interplay of the color set (or color space) to define the color of individual pixels. This information is stored in the image bits for each channel. Channels by default have 8 bits per channel, each with the potential to be on or off. This leads to the 256 potential grayscale combinations. The bit depth can vary depending on color mode selection.

→ For more information on bit depth, **see** "Pixels and Bit Depth," **p. 894**.

Like color, each channel represents one of the primary colors of the color mode for the image. For example, an image in RGB has three color channels, one representing each of the three colors in the Red, Green, and Blue primary colors that make up the RGB color set. Although only three colors make up the primary set, the colors can be combined in any intensity (from 0%–100% of each color individually). In the case of RGB, this leads to more than 16 million different color possibilities: Each channel has 256 possibilities, so 256×256×256= the total potential colors.

→ For more information on color modes, **see** "Choosing an Image Mode," **p. 309** and "Color Conversions," **p. 485**.

While representing color, channels themselves will be grayscale, again representing intensity of an individual color. It is possible to view channels in the palette as colors by switching the Preference for Color Channels in Color to checked in the Display & Cursors Preferences (Edit, Preferences, Display & Cursors). Checking the box displays the channel in its defined color (a red channel displays red instead of as grayscale). This is strictly a preference in that it offers no advantage to the user and doesn't change anything about the image data.

Additional colors can be represented and used if necessary by adding spot colors as additional channels. Spot colors can be used to augment the current color possibilities (known as the color space) and achieve colors that would otherwise be out of gamut, or for other special purposes, such as achieving better ink coverage or varnishing in printing.

→ For more information on spot colors, **see** "Selecting and Using Spot Color," **p. 543**.

CHANNELS AS SELECTIONS AND MASKS

A second function of channels is as storage for selection and mask information. Selections and Masks are essentially the same thing: They allow the user to target an area of an image. As Masks, channels can obscure image information that is still present in the image, limiting what can be viewed to a selected area; as Selections, channels can section off parts of an image to confine applications of tools, filters, and so on. You can save selections by choosing Select, Save Selection, or reload a saved selection by choosing Select, Load Selection.

→ For more information on selection and masks, **see** "Selection and Masking," **p. 93**.

Neither masks nor selections directly become part of the visible image information, yet they can certainly help influence the final look of an image by providing tools for shaping an image and limiting the areas of change. Either can be stored as an alpha channel and are, in fact, interchangeable, and can be converted to spot colors or can replace other channel information.

CHANNELS VERSUS LAYERS

The distinction between layers and channels sometimes confuses newer Photoshop users or those who have not had an opportunity to explore channels at length. Much of the look and function is the same, and they both display image information. Information can be swapped between the two (although the result might differ as per the mode), and both can perform masking functions (although in quite different ways). Put simply, and for the sake of the visual image, the difference lies in the purpose as described previously and in the previous chapter: Layers show composite color information of the separations stored in the channels. In other words, the layers and channels are a different means of displaying the same image information. *Channels* are a breakdown of the source into its color components, whereas layers are a representation of the actual display and mixture of colors separated in the channels (a visual summation of the result of the channel components).

Of course, this gets more complicated, and can sometimes blur completely. For example, in working with a single-layer grayscale image, editing the channel or the layer produces the same results. However, the fact remains that the utility of layers and channels is fairly distinct: If you need to edit an image based on the visual content, you use layers; if you need to edit color components of the image, you use the color breakdown in the channels. Using layers is probably the more intuitive means of correction. Knowing when to use channels is more a reflection of your understanding and comfort level with color theory and breakdowns.

Neither layers nor channels are superior, although working with either has advantages and disadvantages. Understanding both is imperative to using Photoshop to its fullest extent.

PART

II

CH

4

WORKING WITH THE CHANNELS PALETTE

Channels are viewed and activated using the Channels palette (see Figure 4.1). The palette is very similar to the layers palette, and by default is actually located on the same palette under a different tab. To access channels, simply click the Channels tab on the palette. Channels appear listed on the palette in the order of their color mode description, following the composite view (if the image is in a color mode). For example, an RGB image will show the composite RGB channel at the top of the palette list, followed by the Red, Green, and Blue channels, respectively.

 If you are trying to change the order of the RGB channels in an RGB image, see "Changing Primary Color Order" in the Troubleshooting section at the end of this chapter.

Figure 4.1
Channels will be ordered with the composite at the top of the list, followed by the primary colors, spot colors, and alphas. The spot colors and alphas can be rearranged by moving them on the palette (simply click and drag as with layers), but the composite and primaries cannot be moved.

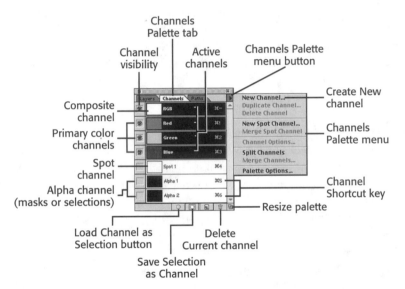

→ For more information on each channel palette feature and function description, **see** "The Channel Palette Functions," **p. 83**.

 Clicking the view icon (Adobe eye) on the composite channel displays all the primary colors for the image. Clicking the view for individual colors displays those colors only; if you select more than one of the individual channels to be viewed, they will display in combination, and in color. When viewing a channel by itself, the default settings will display the channel information in black-and-white. These display options can be changed in the General Preferences which you can open by selecting Edit, Preferences, General (see Figure 4.2).

Figure 4.2
The Preferences for viewing channels in their primary color or grayscale is controlled on the Display & Cursors Preferences.

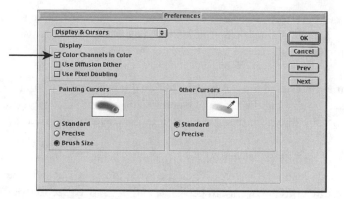

Alpha and spot channels can be renamed by double-clicking the channel to open the Channels dialog box for either Spot Channel Options or Channel Options (see Figure 4.3). Renaming will not work with primaries or the composite, and although Spot channels will assume the name of colors selected from the Custom color palette, these colors can be renamed if desired (it is recommended that you keep the custom color names).

Figure 4.3
The Spot Channel options and Channel Options are used for Spot color channel and alpha channel preferences, respectively.

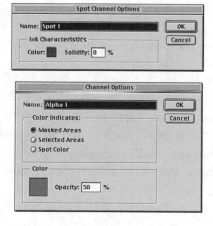

PART

II

CH

4

THE CHANNEL PALETTE FUNCTIONS

The following Channel palette menu descriptions are listed in accordance with the descriptions shown earlier in Figure 4.1.

→ For more information on and description of the functions on the Channels palette menu not covered in this section, **see** "Additional Channel Menu Functions," **p. 85**.

■ **Active Channels**—Highlighted channels in the Channels palette are considered active. When the channel is activated, changes made to the image will affect only that channel (no matter what the current Layer view).

■ **Channel palette menu button**—Opens the channel pop-up menu, which contains additional functions for channels. See Channel palette menu, later in this list.

- **Channel palette tab**—Allows selection of the Channels palette within a palette grouping (by default channels are grouped with layers and paths). It also allows the user to grab the Channels palette from the grouping to move to another group, or to stand alone.

- **Channel palette menu**—A list of additional functions for Channel operations, and is accessed by clicking the Channel palette menu button. The list is context sensitive in that only the functions that can be used in the current conditions are highlighted (black type).

- **Channel visibility**—The Adobe eye for each Channel indicates whether or not the associated Channel is visible: When the eye is in the box, it indicates that the Channel is currently visible. Layers can be visible and not active. See Active Channels previously in this list.

- **Composite channel**—The composite channel serves as a control for the primaries more than as an editable single channel. It displays the current composite, as if the image were currently a single layer—no matter how many layers are currently visible. Changing the view or active status of the composite will affect all the primaries. You can shut off the active status of the composite channel only by selecting another channel.

- **Primary Color channels**—The channels that make up the color breakdown of the color mode. For example, in CMYK, this would be Cyan, Magenta, Yellow, and Black. In Lab, this would be Lightness, a (or Red-Green) and b (or Blue-Yellow). In RGB it would be Red, Green, and Blue. The primary color channels will be created each time you create an image in or switch to a color mode.

- **Spot Channel**—A spot color is an additional color added to the primaries to either expand on the potential colors, control specific color (for example, Pantone use), or for special purposes. These are most often used in printing, either for special effects (varnish) or solidifying color areas. Spots are often used with Duotone mode images.

- **Alpha Channel** (masks or selections)—Alpha channels hold grayscale mappings of selections and masks. As a means of storage, they can record information identical to active selections (unlike storing selections as paths).

- **Channel Shortcut key**—When the Channels palette is open, pressing these keys activates the associated channel. The keys are assigned in order from the top channel down, starting with the composite that is represented by a tilde (Cmd-~) [Ctrl+~]. The rest of the channels are assigned numbers from one to nine. After nine, no more assignments are made. If channels are reordered, the numbers are reassigned in descending order as per the new arrangement.

- **Resize palette**—Allows the user to resize the palette grouping vertically and horizontally.

- **Delete Current Channel**—When clicked, this deletes a highlighted channel. By holding down the (Option) [Alt] key when clicking, the channel deletes without invoking the Warning dialog box.

- **Create New Channel**—When clicked, this button creates a new channel. Holding down the (Option) [Alt] key when clicking the button creates a new channel and opens the new Channel dialog box. To create a new Spot color channel, hold down the (Cmd) [Ctrl] key when clicking the New Channel button (this opens the Spot Channel dialog box). When a channel is dragged to this button, a duplicate is created.

- **Save Selection as Channel**—When clicked, this saves an active selection as an alpha channel while leaving the current selection active. Pressing the (Option) [Alt] key while clicking the button saves the selection and opens the new Channel dialog box.

- **Load Channel as Selection button**—Clicking the button with any channel highlighted loads that channel as a selection. Key shortcuts cover the Operations in the Load Selection dialog box. Pressing Shift while clicking the button uses the highlighted channel to add to the current selection. Pressing (Option) [Alt] while clicking the button uses the highlighted selection to subtract from the current selection. Pressing (Option-Shift)[Alt+Shift] while clicking the button uses the highlighted channel to Intersect with the current selection.

 Other Channel Keyboard Shortcuts

Several additional shortcuts exist for using channels. One is strictly a keyboard combination. Pressing (Cmd-Option-#) [Ctrl+Alt+#], where # equals the number of the channel 1–9 or the tilde, will load the associated channel as a selection. These other operations use key combinations and a single click directly on the channel desired to complete the operation. Press (Cmd-Shift) [Ctrl+Shift] and click the channel whose contents you would like to add to the current selection. Press (Cmd-Option) [Ctrl+Alt] and click the channel whose contents you would like to subtract from the current selection. Press (Cmd-Option-Shift) [Ctrl+Alt+Shift] and click the channel whose contents you would like to intersect with the current selection.

PART

II

CH

4

ADDITIONAL CHANNEL MENU FUNCTIONS

Many of the Channel Menu functions can be accessed through palette controls, shortcut keys, or combinations of those as described in the previous section. New Channel, Duplicate Channel, Delete Channel, New Spot Channel, and Channel Options can all be reached by those other methods; however, Merge Spot Channel, Split Channels, Merge Channels, and Palette Options are not found anywhere else, and must be accessed via the Channels menu. Duplicate Channel has a slightly different function on the menu than the palette button, but generally those functions with the same name have the same functionality as the palette commands.

- **Duplicate Channel**—Duplicate Channel is available on the Channels pop-up menu when an individual channel is selected. When the function is chosen from the menu, the Duplicate Channel dialog box appears (see Figure 4.4). The channel can be named and targeted either as a duplication to the same image, or to a new image.

Figure 4.4
When duplicating a channel by selecting from the menu, the Duplicate Channel dialog box opens. To open the dialog box when dragging to the New Channel button to duplicate, hold down the (Option) [Alt] key.

- **Merge Spot Channel**—Allows the user to merge a selected spot color channel into the existing color space, and appropriately distributes the information to the primary colors for the color mode you are in. This can be very useful if, for example, you are using a spot channel to situate a particular color, yet want to save the charges of an additional ink on press (using CMYK printing). The merged channel is deleted. Color differences because of the conversion might become apparent after the deletion (this depends on the type of conversion).

→ For more information on color conversions, **see** "Color Conversions," **p. 485**.

→ For more information on using spot color, **see** "Using Duotones and Spot Colors," **p. 521**.

- **Split Channels**—Allows the user to split all the current channels into individual documents, one for each of the channel colors. The original is not retained (if desired, make a copy of the original or save it before splitting). This can be useful for a number of purposes, but is probably most often used in conjunction with the Merge Channels function. For example, if you would like to change channel order, simplify channel components in an image, replace channels, and the like, you would split the channels into separate documents using the Split Channels command and then reassemble using Merge Channels (see Merge Channels, as follows). Split channels retain channel names as appendages for easier identification after they are split. For example, the Red channel of a document named `mydoc` would be renamed to `mydoc.red` and would be a single-layered, flattened grayscale document in the result file. This command can be used only on Flattened images.

- **Merge Channels**—Allows the user to Merge open, single-layered, flattened grayscale documents into a single RGB, CMYK, Lab, or Multichannel image. The process allows the user to select the number of channels to merge, the mode of the image, and the order of compiling. RGB and Lab images require three channels, and CMYK requires four channels—no more, no less. Any other option will need to be created in a Multichannel image. The dialog boxes essentially lead you through the process of reassembly intuitively. After the image is compiled into a Multichannel image, it can then be converted to other color modes.

→ For more information on converting a Multichannel image to a standard color mode, **see** the example in "Photoshop at Work: Replacing Object Color with a Spot Color," **p. 550**.

■ **Palette Options**—The Palette Options are strictly options for viewing the channel thumbnails. These options are the same as those for layers; however, the options show only grayscale renderings as the channels appear only in grayscale (see Figure 4.5). Selecting None will save some memory (only the names of the channels will appear on the Channels palette), and might help save some space on the monitor if that is precious. Choosing any of the other Thumbnail sizes will display the channel contents with approximately the thumbnail size shown. The size of the thumbnail will vary depending on the actual size of the canvas; the palette options show maximum potential viewing size.

Figure 4.5
To select a Thumbnail view, simply click the option button associated with the size you would like to view the channels. Larger Thumbnails will require more memory for rendering, so using the smallest size (or none) is recommended for quicker processing.

Click the radio button by the view you want to choose.

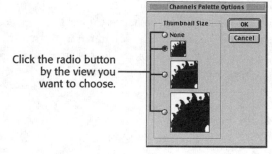

EDITING CHANNELS

Channels can be edited independently from one another or as a composite of current color so that all primary colors are edited at one time for the currently active layer. Changes to the channel will be reflected only in the active layer. Channels can be activated by clicking the desired channel in the Channels palette; layers are activated independently of channels in the Layers palette.

→ For more information on working with layers, **see** "Creating Layers," **p. 57**.

Channels can be edited using freehand tools and filters that do not only affect color (tools in the Hue mode, for example). Painting can be accomplished using colors or colored patterns; however, only the tonality (gray levels) will affect the result.

→ For more information on working with masks to create selections, **see** "Selection and Masking," **p. 93**.

→ For more information on manipulating image information, **see** "Cleaning, Repairing, and Altering Images," **p. 569** and "Enhancing Images," **p. 637**.

Although any channel can be edited individually as part of the image, and although individual editing might often be desirable for Alpha channels, the true power of primary color channels is in making color changes in the image. Generally, these color changes are larger sweeping changes in the whole image, and are best taken care of in the composite (after layers have been flattened). However, if color correction has not been completed before compositing an image or if composite pieces need to be more closely matched before finalizing, layered corrections might certainly be in order.

→ For more information on color correction, **see** "Color Corrections," **p. 465**.

Beside channel duplication via the channel functions, channels can be copied between images by drag and drop. To duplicate in this fashion, simply click the source channel (the channel to be duplicated), hold the mouse button down, and drag the channel to another open document. If the channel is either a primary color or masking channel, it will be created as a new Alpha, called Alpha [#], where the number is the next in the sequence of alpha channels (if there are no other Alphas, it will be named Alpha 1; if you already have Alphas 1, 2, and 4, it will be Alpha 5). The channel will be centered in the new document. The background will be white if dragged from a color channel or black if dragged from a masking/selection channel. Spot colors retain their names and color associations.

TROUBLESHOOTING

CHANGING PRIMARY COLOR ORDER

I am trying to change the order of the primary colors in my Photoshop document, but the channels won't move. How do I move the channels?

You can mean one of two things here: Either you are trying to reorder the color order in that you'd like to see BRG rather than RGB, or you want to rearrange the information in the color plates so that, for example, Red is Blue, Blue is Green, and Green is Red.

The answer to the first is that it can't be done. In an RGB image, for example, the primary colors will always appear in the order Red, Green, Blue. They will always be in the same name order, even if you are successful in switching the information around.

To switch the information around in the channels is probably only going to be done for a special effect. However, if you want to change the information around, it can be accomplished in a variety of ways. For example, you can copy and paste information from one color channel to the next, and in that way simply replace what is there. This can get a little awkward. Probably the easiest method is to split the image and reassemble it in the desired order. Simply choose Split Channels from the Channels palette menu; then reassemble the image by changing the order in the Merge RGB Channels dialog box (the dialog box in this case is for an RGB image—the name will be different depending on the target color set you choose for the merged image). Figure 4.6 shows the screens you will see and use during splitting and reassembling an image using Split Channel and Merge Channel functions.

Figure 4.6
The colorful butterfly is easily split into its component channels. Reassembling will change the color of the butterfly (see the color section), but maintain the tonality.

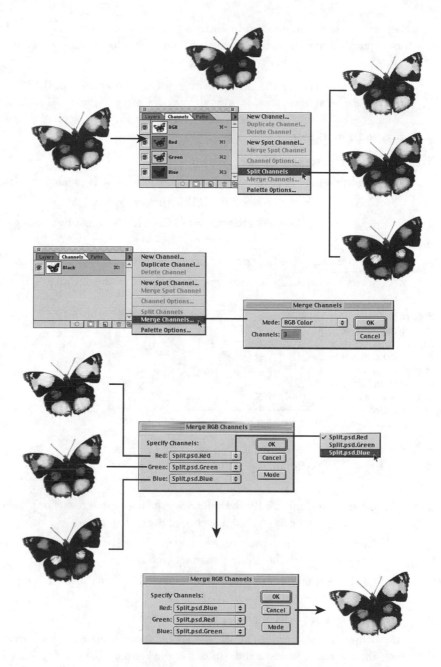

PHOTOSHOP AT WORK: CREATING TWO ALPHA TYPES

No matter what level you are, you will need to be able to control channel information in a variety of ways to have the most versatility in working with images and controlling your results. A distinction needs to be clear in your mind as to the function and result of assigning a purpose to a channel—and how that channel information can serve more than one purpose.

For this example, open the butterfly image included on page 4 of the PDF workbook (get the workbook at http://www.ps6.com). What we are going to do is make a selection of the black area of the image using channel information and then apply the result both as a selection and a spot color.

1. Open the workbook image on page 4 in RGB.

2. Duplicate the image (on the History palette, choose New Document).

3. Convert the new document to CMYK (Image, Mode, CMYK).

4. Activate only the Black channel of the CMYK document by clicking it in the Channels palette.

5. Choose Duplicate Channel from the Channels palette pop-up menu.

6. Select the original document opened in Step 1 as the destination (see Figure 4.7).

Figure 4.7
The pop-up menu will have the name of the current document, the original that was duplicated, and New, which will target a new document. The name of your target document might be different from what you see here.

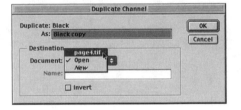

7. Choose OK, and the Black channel will be duplicated to the original document as Alpha 1 (as long as you did not change the default name).

8. Close the CMYK version of the image without saving. This will leave the original image open with the Alpha 1 channel highlighted.

9. Click the thumbnail for the RGB channel. This will show the image in color and switch the channel views to RGB.

10. Choose Load Selection from the Select menu.

11. When the Select menu appears, it should have the name of the current document as the Source Document and Alpha 1 as the Source Channel. Click the Invert button and choose OK. This will load the dark part of the channel as a selection.

12. Feather the selection by 2 pixels; from the Select menu choose feather (Cmd–Option-D) [Ctrl+Alt+D] and put 2 in the Feather Radius before clicking OK. This will smooth out the selection and change the appearance of the dotted selection line onscreen.

13. Press D to switch to the default foreground and background colors. This will have no effect if the defaults are already in place.

14. Delete the information in the selection by pressing the Delete key on the keyboard. This will turn the black area of the butterfly white and leave the selection.

At this point you have applied the alpha channel to the image and used it to effectively clear the black and darkest portions of the image to accept a new color. We will use the same alpha channel to apply a spot color.

1. Duplicate the selected area to a new channel (Cmd-J) [Ctrl+J]. This will copy the white area of the butterfly that you have just cleared to a new layer.

2. Double-click the Alpha 1 channel. This will open the Channel Options and allow you to change the channel to a Spot color (by clicking the Spot Color option button).

3. (Option) Change the color for the replacement spot color.

Note

I suggest something dark in keeping with the color scheme. This can be adjusted later.

4. Change the opacity of the spot color channel to 0%. This will allow the spot to blend with the background.

Note

At this point you have created a layer (in Step 1) that is mostly white and will allow the spot color to be implemented without interference—but will also allow you to shade and adjust the effects of the spot color. Step 4 will not have much effect at this point, but it will be important to later changes.

5. Choose OK. This will apply the spot color settings to the channel. The result will essentially be a flat spot color fill of the black area in the image.

Note

You might prefer to slightly blur the spot color application by applying a slight Gaussian Blur to the spot channel.

Although this result is not a finalized image (there is still a lot more that you can do to improve the result), it shows the basic application of a single alpha channel as both a selection and a spot color. If you understand the applications, you understand much of what you need to about channel function—although there is more to how channels help get results.

Using this result, you could extend this exercise by applying other filters and effects to the image. A simple effect to try is to apply a Satin Effect to the layer created in Step 1 of the second set of steps. This will create a pattern based on the information already in the layer. Use the following settings for Satin: Multiply, Opacity 64%, Angle 19°, Distance 28, Size 5, Contour Gaussian, Anti-aliased, and Inverted. With some additional effects you can re-create detail in the black portion of the image that might have been missing or excluded, or to enhance the image (see Figure 4.8).

Figure 4.8
Continuing from the result from the steps in the example, you can add effects to the area of the Spot color application by changing the layer created in Step 1. Tonalities and colors applied to the layer will change and enhance the application of the spot color.

→ For more information on working with and applying spot colors, **see** "Selecting and Using Spot Color," **p. 540**.

CHAPTER 5

SELECTION AND MASKING

In this chapter

HOW SELECTIONS WORK

Selection is one of the most important concepts to master in developing images with Photoshop. In simple application, it allows you to section off active areas of an image. After a selection has been made, applied effects are confined to only the selected area. This is also known as *masking*, which is a photographic term meaning, essentially, blocking out. The idea is that you want to block changes from being made to other portions of your image, restricting changes to the selected area only. Commonly, selection is used for clipping out parts of images to use in other images.

As you become more familiar with the techniques and features in Photoshop, mastering selection becomes important in making image alterations and improvements. It can be used not only for simple applications (fills) but also for complex or automated alterations, such as loading a predefined texture in an action to apply to a portion of an image automatically. There are a number of specialized tools that help make basic selections. These basic selections can then be modified by using other selection tools—other tools that directly affect pixels—or by combining a selection and application of other tools. These selections can then be deactivated after use, or saved for use again later in the same image, with other images, or for other purposes (for example, they can be used as textures with the Lighting Effects filter).

→ For more information on Actions, **see** "Creating Effective Actions," **p. 263**.

→ For more information on the Lighting Effects filter, **see** "Creating and Using Bump Maps," **p. 762**.

Several modes are available for working with selections, including direct selection, Quick Mask, and alpha channels. *Direct selection* involves making and modifying a selection onscreen by simply adding and subtracting selection areas using selection tools. *Quick Mask* is a little more versatile, allowing selections to be manipulated with pixel tools and other selections. *Alpha channels* are Photoshop channels created to store selections. Storing selections allows creation of complex selections that would not be possible otherwise, and also allows duplication and reuse of completed selections.

→ For more information on alpha channels, **see** "Channels As Selections and Masks," **p. 81**.

The boundaries of a selection are defined by a *marquee*, which is a dashed line that contrasts with the underlying image. The marquee appears to shimmer or move about in a circular path. These boundaries of the marquee are sometimes referred to as "marching ants." The line defines where the selection is 50% or more—that is, it shows where the selection will affect the image with at least 50% strength of the applied tools.

Note

It is possible that no marquee line will appear when a selection is active if the selection has no areas where selection is greater than 50%. This does not mean that pixels will remain unaffected by tool use or that the selection is not active. Photoshop will issue a warning when such a selection is made.

USING BASIC SELECTION TOOLS

It isn't as important how you make the selections as it is that you make them as effectively as possible. This means understanding the tools and the strengths and weaknesses of each selection tool, and what effect the selection will have on an image and tool applications.

The basic tools for selection appear on the toolbox. These include the Marquee tool, Lasso tool, and Magic Wand. Other selection tools appear on the Selection menu on the menu bar, most of which are used for modifying existing selections. The real power of selection tools, however, goes far beyond the basic, obvious tools, which are really just building blocks for creating useful selections.

→ For more information on the selection tools described in the following sections, **see** "Working with Channels," **p. 79**, "Paths," **p. 175**, and "Freehand Painting Tools," **p. 203**.

The simplest selection functions can be accomplished by keystrokes (see Table 5.1), or by choosing from the Select menu. The keystrokes will function no matter what tool you use to make a selection.

TABLE 5.1   SELECTION KEYSTROKES

Selection Function	Mac	PC	Description/Explanation
All	(Cmd-A)	[Ctrl+A]	Selects entire canvas area
Deselect	(Cmd-D)	[Ctrl+D]	Deactivates any active selection
Reselect	(Cmd-Shift-D)	[Ctrl+Shift+D]	Reactivates the last selection used in the Photoshop session whether saved or not
Invert	(Cmd-Shift-I)	[Ctrl+Shift+I]	Inverts the current selection
Hide/Show	(Cmd-H)	[Ctrl+H]	Shows or Hides selection area without deselecting

Note

The Reselect command will pick up the last selection made even if many other moves have been made and the memory has been purged. Although this is handy in a lot of situations, it may not be best to depend on this when a selection was difficult to accomplish. Better to save difficult selections to be safe.

PART

II

CH

5

THE MARQUEE TOOL

The Marquee tool draws a standard shape for selection based on the shape selected in the toolbox (see Figure 5.1). This might include squares, rectangles, circles, elliptical shapes, and the selection of a single line of pixels, either horizontally or vertically.

Figure 5.1
To select a Marquee tool type, click the Marquee icon and hold the mouse button down. When the pop-up menu appears, drag the mouse to the desired tool.

To make a selection with the rectangular or elliptical Marquee tool, choose the tool shape you want from the Marquee fly-out menu, and then click and drag the shape diagonally across an open image area that you want to select. Release the mouse button when the selection is the desired size.

You can constrain selections to perfect square or circle shapes by holding down the Shift key as you drag your selection. Normal selections are made by dragging diagonally over the area to be selected. It is as if an imaginary box were being drawn between the initial click and the release of the mouse to put the selection in. Selections can also be made from the center of the area being selected. To select from center, hold down the (Option) [Alt] key; in this case, the initial click point is the center of the selection. Holding down (Option-Shift) [Alt+Shift] while dragging your selection selects a constrained shape (perfect circle or perfect square) from center.

Tip

Most often you will create rectangular selections dragging corner to corner, which is the default (see Figure 5.2). Elliptical shapes are often easier to place by dragging from the center of what you would like to select. Selection from center requires holding down the (Option) [Alt] key.

Tip

To reposition the selection while you are making it, press the spacebar while continuing to hold the mouse button. When the spacebar is depressed, the current selection area drags in the direction of mouse movement.

MARQUEE TOOL OPTIONS

Options for the rectangular and elliptical Marquee tools include Constrained Aspect Ratio and Fixed Size, as well as an option for Feathering. These options can be accessed on the Options bar when the Marquee tool is selected (see Figure 5.3).

Figure 5.2
The initial click of the mouse sets a pivot point for the selection. The pivot is either on the corner of the selection (left) or from center (right). This type of selection is the most basic selection you can make. Generally, these selections need to be modified to be effective for more complicated tasks. However, they can be very useful for cropping, limiting effective work area, and creating simple shapes.

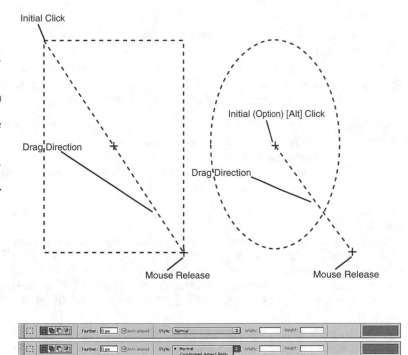

Figure 5.3
To view the Marquee Options bar, click the Marquee tool in the toolbox or choose Window, Show Options.

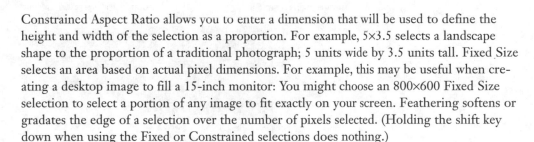

PART
II
CH
5

Constrained Aspect Ratio allows you to enter a dimension that will be used to define the height and width of the selection as a proportion. For example, 5×3.5 selects a landscape shape to the proportion of a traditional photograph; 5 units wide by 3.5 units tall. Fixed Size selects an area based on actual pixel dimensions. For example, this may be useful when creating a desktop image to fill a 15-inch monitor: You might choose an 800×600 Fixed Size selection to select a portion of any image to fit exactly on your screen. Feathering softens or gradates the edge of a selection over the number of pixels selected. (Holding the shift key down when using the Fixed or Constrained selections does nothing.)

→ For more information on feathering, **see** "Feathering Selections," **p. 116**.

SELECTING SINGLE-PIXEL ROWS

Selecting a single row of pixels can simplify a task that has come to have a rather specific use in Web design. This eliminates the tedious process of magnifying and selecting a single row of pixels. Cropping or copying the single-row selection to a new document can help create fill elements quickly, such as wallpapers or backgrounds. You also can use this technique to fine-tune scanned image crops by removing a slight edge or borderline of pixels. To do this, select the edge or borderline of pixels with the single-pixel, row-selection tool, invert the selection, and then choose Crop from the Image menu.

To make a selection, select the Single Row Marquee tool or Single Column Marquee tool and click the image. The tool automatically selects a single row of pixels across the entire document, edge to edge. The selection is made to the right of the cursor (for vertical selection) or below the cursor (for horizontal selection). For tight selections, it's still a good idea to magnify significantly to be sure that the proper row is being selected. The only tool option available for selecting a single-pixel row is Feather.

Caution

Be careful when using single-pixel row selection with feathering, because feathering quickly diminishes the visibility of the marquee. The selection you do make can lurk in the image. It can stop you from applying tools and may cause unintentional damage to your image.

Cropping

 Although not strictly one of the selection tools, the Crop tool (Image, Crop) can perform a kind of selection by changing canvas size. The Crop tool is usually used to reduce the size of an image by cutting off portions that might detract from the image, or to help reposition elements to improve the composition. The Crop tool can, however, be used to increase canvas size by cropping outside the image. The Background color is used to fill the area of the crop where new canvas is created. See Figure 5.4 for an example of cropping outside the canvas.

Cropping can also be done with the rectangular and single-pixel row Marquee tools. After creating the selection, simply select Crop from the Image menu. Selections for cropping cannot extend beyond the canvas, and selections must be rectangular, without deviation—feathered selections will not crop.

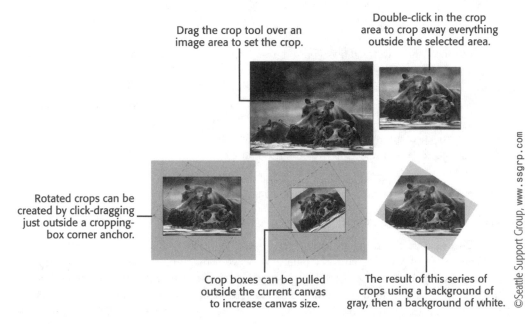

Drag the crop tool over an image area to set the crop.

Double-click in the crop area to crop away everything outside the selected area.

Rotated crops can be created by click-dragging just outside a cropping-box corner anchor.

Crop boxes can be pulled outside the current canvas to increase canvas size.

The result of this series of crops using a background of gray, then a background of white.

©Seattle Support Group, www.ssgrp.com

Figure 5.4
The Crop tool can be used to increase and decrease the size of the canvas, as well as change image composition.

THE LASSO TOOL

The Lasso tool is for drawing freehand selections. The tool has several variations, including the default freehand Lasso tool, the Polygonal Lasso tool and the Magnetic Lasso tool. These options appear in the fly-out menu shown in Figure 5.5. Each of the Lasso tools offers feathering and anti-aliasing during selection.

Figure 5.5
Each tool works differently to accomplish selection and the strengths of a tool should be used to your advantage.

Anti-aliasing

Anti-aliasing slightly softens the edges of a pixel selection when it is applied, creating a slight blend, rather than adhering to a hard edge of pixels. This helps selected elements appear less pixelated when copied and pasted to other images, by softening jaggies and allowing a better area of blending. Using anti-aliasing is similar to applying a slight blur to a mask or feathering to a selection edge. Although there are instances in which it is desirable to use an aliased final selection, anti-aliasing is probably the way to go with 99% of selections and image applications. See Figure 5.6 for a magnified comparison.

Figure 5.6
The white areas in the images shown here show the effect of anti-aliased (left) and aliased (right) selection on the same selection area, magnified 1,600%.

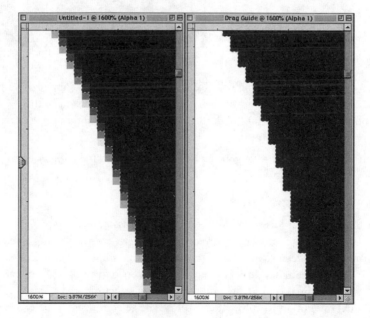

PART

II

CH

5

To make a selection with the Lasso tool, choose an area to start the selection, and then click and hold down the mouse button as you drag the cursor. When the mouse button is released, the selection is completed automatically; the program draws a straight line from the point of release to the beginning point of the selection. This can sometimes produce unexpected results. Often it is best to complete the selection by drawing back to the point of origin, unless releasing the mouse will have predictable results (see Figure 5.7).

Figure 5.7
If the mouse button is released prematurely, selections may not provide expected results.

Release Point   Initial Mouse Click

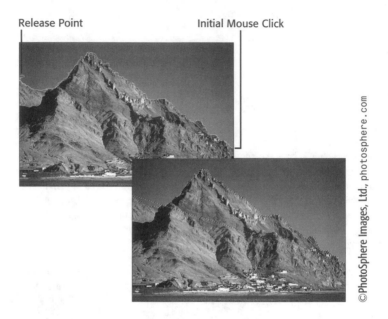

©PhotoSphere Images, Ltd., photosphere.com

The Lasso tool will take some practice and a steady hand to control. Using a better controller device such as a good trackball or tablet device might make this easier. Toggling the function of the Freehand tool with the Polygon and Magnetic options can help you make the best of this selection tool.

→ For more information on the Polygon and Magnetic lasso, **see** "The Polygonal Lasso" and "The Magnetic Lasso," **pp. 100-101**.

THE POLYGONAL LASSO

Using the Polygonal Lasso, unlike the Freehand Lasso, does not require holding down the mouse button. This tool works more or less point-to-point, creating a straight edge of a selection area between each click of the mouse. To complete a selection with the Polygonal Lasso tool, you again have to complete the geometric form. The form can be completed by either making a final click at the point where the selection area started, or (Cmd-click) [Ctrl+click] on a point to automatically close the selection. Essentially, (Cmd-click) [Ctrl+click] is the same action as taking your finger off the mouse button when selecting with the freehand Lasso tool.

The Polygonal Lasso tool can also be toggled to the freehand Lasso by pressing the (Option) [Alt] key. When the (Option) [Alt] key is depressed, the freehand tool engages. Toggling the tool by releasing the button automatically creates a pivot point for the polygon. Holding the Shift key while using the Polygonal Lasso tool confines the selection's sides to increments of 45°. This is useful for selecting reasonably even, geometric shapes without having to do a lot of complicated measuring.

Although the Polygonal Lasso tool is a straight-edged tool, it can be useful for making selections around a curved element, (although there may be even better options, such as using the Pen tool to create a curved path). Clicking at short intervals along the curve in a selection may provide a close enough selection for many applications. Techniques for modifying selections can help quickly improve these results.

➔ For more information on making selections on curved paths, **see** "Creating Vector Paths with the Pen Tool," **p. 178**.

➔ For more information on modifying selections, **see** "Feathering Selections," **p. 116**.

THE MAGNETIC LASSO

The Magnetic Lasso offers an option to aid in selecting image elements semiautomatically. The tool uses differences in contrast to choose likely edges for the selection, based both on preferences chosen in the Options bar and the standard function of the tool. The selection is drawn by Photoshop based on where you move the cursor, how anchors are placed for the selection, and the contrast among pixels in the immediate area of the cursor.

To guide the selection, the program looks at the pixels around the cursor and chooses which pixels to have the selection cling to, based on the contrast. A line is drawn showing the chosen path, with anchor points that indicate confirmed segments (see Figure 5.8). Anchors placed by Photoshop can be accepted or rejected as they are placed (using the Delete key to remove unwanted points). Also, you have the option of interactively adding anchor points to the line as it is drawn to help the selection progress as you want it to. (Option) [Alt] keys switch to the freehand Lasso or Polygonal Lasso tools, depending on mouse clicks: a mouse click with (Option) [Alt] key pressed initiates a Polygonal Lasso point; holding the mouse button down with (Option) [Alt] key pressed activates the freehand Lasso. Releasing the (Option) [Alt] key returns the Magnetic Lasso.

Selection areas can be closed the same way they are controlled with the Polygonal Lasso: (Cmd-click) [Ctrl+click] closes the selection, as does pressing the Enter key, and selection can be completed by clicking the initial point to complete the circuit manually. Closing the selection with the (Cmd-click) [Ctrl+click] option may follow an obvious path to completing the circuit based on the current settings. This may result in a curve completion rather than a straight line as occurs with the Polygonal and Freehand Lasso tools.

As the tool's controls are based on contrast values, the tool works best in making selections of high-contrast image areas. For example, selecting products from images taken using high-contrast backgrounds is probably one of the best uses for this tool. There is an advantage to using this over the Magic Wand (see the next section) in cases where the background is textured or contains multiple colors, yet still provides enough contrast between it and the subject of the image for the selection to be made.

Figure 5.8
The Magnetic Lasso attaches a selection to elements in the image based on contrast values among surrounding pixels.

The Options bar for the Magnetic Lasso is a little different from the dialog box for other Lasso tools as it allows control over the sensitivity of the tool as well as the final selection (see Figure 5.9). Feather and Anti-aliased still have the same effect on the final selection. Three other preferences—Width, Frequency, and Edge Contrast—help Photoshop decide where to place the selection. Width refers to the area, or pixel radius, which the tool will consider in choosing the best place to place the selection line. This number is a pixel value and must be between 1 and 40. Frequency gives the tool a relative frequency for placing anchors automatically. A higher number places anchors more frequently; the number must be between 0 and 100. Edge Contrast allows control over the sensitivity to contrast. The higher the number, the greater the contrast must be for the consideration of selection. Values for Edge Contrast are in percentage and must be between 1 and 100.

Figure 5.9
Settings chosen for the Magnetic Lasso tool will affect the speed of the tool operation. Keep the Width as low as possible and Frequency and Edge Contrast high without compromising the goal of the selection.

Tip

While making a selection, the Width can be adjusted with the bracket keys. The left bracket ([) will decrease width by 1, and Shift-[will switch the width to 1; the right bracket (]) will increase width by 1, and Shift-] will switch the width to 40.

THE MAGIC WAND

Despite the name, the Magic Wand does not perform magic in making a selection. It has calculated responses to an image, based on the Options bar settings and applies those settings based on the exact pixel clicked to make the selection. It is not, as is implied by the name, a tool that will magically select what you want it to. The Magic Wand is not the best tool for every selection, but used wisely it can drastically reduce the time you need to make complex selections.

The color of the initial pixel, clicked with the Magic Wand, is used by Photoshop as a standard by which other pixels are judged. Judgment, according to Photoshop, is made considering the options selected for the Magic Wand in the Options bar. Double-clicking the tool will display the Magic Wand Options bar. Your selections for Tolerance, Anti-Aliased, Contiguous, and Use All Layers will affect the final selection (see Figure 5.10).

Figure 5.10
Selections made in the Magic Wand Options bar greatly affect the impact and application of the tool.

TOLERANCE SETTINGS

The Tolerance setting is used to allow selection of additional pixels based on deviation from the initial pixel. The Tolerance number reflects the number of levels above and below the tone of the exact pixel selected that the Magic Wand will capture. The higher the Tolerance number, the more levels of color and the greater the number of pixels the Magic Wand will select. The Tolerance can be set between 0 and 255 (representing 256 shades) in whole numbers only. So, for example, with the tool set to a tolerance of 32 (the Photoshop default), Photoshop would select 32 levels of gray above and below the value for the selected point in a grayscale image (or channel). The range for the selection could not extend above 255 levels, or below zero levels.

Tip

Although it might be more natural to think in terms of percentage when using grayscale, using levels of gray (0–255) will help you think more like Photoshop.

If you were to set the tool's tolerance to 32, and click a point that was 50% gray (128 levels of gray), Photoshop would select all grays from level 96 to level 160 (or about 37.5% to 62.5% black, which display at 38% to 63% black).

Note

Selection based on calculated values in percentage might appear to be approximate. This is because calculations are based strictly on levels. Decimal values are not allowed in selecting the Tolerance, and gray percentages displayed for the eyedropper are in whole-number percentages only—so they do not reflect actual percentages. Selecting 10% (25.5 levels) would not be possible to do exactly as you have to round off the tolerance to the nearest whole number (25 or 26) in order to enter it. This compromises exact results based on percentage.

Tolerance in color images is used in a similar way. The tolerance setting creates a range of color values based on the color of the original selection. So, if selecting a color in RGB, Photoshop will calculate a limit for each color channel (Red, Green, and Blue) and any colors selected must fall within that range. The calculation actually goes a little further than that, taking into account both the information on individual channels as well as the composite information, and involving the Gaussian equation in the selection. It is sufficient to know that the area selected in a color image will be smaller than simply creating a range for each channel based on the tolerance.

As an example, if you were to select with a Tolerance of 32 from an orange pixel with an RGB value of 255,128,0, Photoshop would create a range of values that would be considered for each channel based on that selection. Pixels would be selected in a range, as noted, above and below the selected value of the initial pixel (without going above 255, or below zero). In this case, the range for red would be 255 to 223, the range for green would be 160 to 96, and the range for blue would be 16 to zero. Pixels selected with the wand would be those that simultaneously fall within the specified range for each channel. This is strictly a mathematical calculation. Being mathematical, it will not always render exactly the results expected in the visual sense. For example, although 238,130,17 may appear to be a closely related orange—or more closely related than 255,96,0 red—it would not be selected.

Tip

Selecting Tolerance values is easier to do with experience but it is often just trial and error using your best guess. If the area of the image you want to select has little image noise and little gradient, use a lower tolerance; if the image area has more image noise and greater gradient, use higher tolerance. A higher tolerance is also desirable when the area you are selecting has a high contrast with the elements in the image you are selecting from.

USE ALL LAYERS AND CONTIGUOUS SELECTIONS

The Use All Layers option allows you to choose whether you are going to select from a particular layer (regardless of what you see onscreen) or from what you see onscreen (regardless of what is on a current channel). When checked, the selection will take into account everything you see onscreen; if this is not selected, the Magic Wand will consider only the pixel values on the layer that is currently active. Choose this option if you want to select only from the currently active area.

Making a selection with the Contiguous option checked will select only pixels attached to the initially selected pixel that meets the criteria for selection (including those connected by the corners on diagonal). Unchecking the box will allow selection of pixels anywhere in the image, based on the original selection. Choices made for Use All Layers or Contiguous options will affect one another and additionally be affected by the choice for Anti-aliased selection.

Note

It might be harder to control the Magic Wand in some circumstances with the anti-aliasing option on; selections can bleed into areas you had not intended to select, and you might get surprising results. For example, a Magic Wand selection in an area filled with noise, using low tolerance and anti-aliasing without the Contiguous option checked, might not yield the expected result. Keep wand selections aliased for greater control in images that do not show a good deal of contrast in the areas you will be selecting. You can always adjust the edges of the selection later.

THE COLOR RANGE FOR SPECIFIC COLOR SELECTIONS

Several tools can help you select specific colors, in addition to the Magic Wand (discussed in the previous section). Probably the most useful is Color Range (Select, Color Range), which is very much kin to the Replace Color command. Although the Color Range and Replace Color commands are similar—and, in fact, selections created with one can be passed to the other through Save and Load—Replace Color does not create an active selection as a result of use. As that is the case, the focus here is on Color Range, which creates an active selection as the result of its use rather than changing the colors included in the selection (see Figure 5.11).

Figure 5.11
The Color Range function is a very powerful tool for selecting a specific range of color from an image.

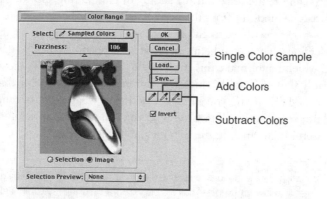

Single Color Sample

Add Colors

Subtract Colors

The Color Range dialog box is accessed through the Select menu (Select, Color Range). The dialog box offers the following options:

- Automatic selection of predefined ranges (Red, Yellow, Green, Cyan, Blue, Magenta, Highlights, Midtones, Shadows, Out of Gamut)
- Fuzziness slider for scaling the range of color selection

- Viewing in the Preview area (preview the selection or the image in the palette)
- Options for viewing the preview (preview in the image as None, Grayscale, Black Matte, White Matte, Quick Mask)
- Loading and saving of Color Range settings
- Selection of tools (eyedroppers for single color, adding to the colors selected or subtracting from those selected)
- Enabling the user to invert the selection created

The Color Range command works as a standalone selection tool, or in conjunction with any current selection. When used in conjunction with selections, the command allows you to select color range in the image freely, and then confines the areas of selection to those which intersect the active selection, as if it were an isolated area.

When you are finished making the selection, Color Range converts that to a standard marquee selection, no matter which modes were used for preview of the selection. You can save, use, or alter the selection any way you want after it is created. Generally, the selection will not be perfect for immediate use and you will have to make some alterations, but this method will go a long way in quickly selecting out colors in the most efficient manner.

Note

Despite the name, Color Range will work with selections of black-and-white or grayscale images.

Generally, this function is most useful when in the Sampled Colors mode, which is found on the Color Range dialog box's Select pop-up menu. This allows you to sample colors with the eyedropper(s) and refine selections by adding or eliminating specific sampled colors within the selection. Choosing from the predefined list is rather special purpose, and somewhat stagnant as you can choose to either work with the eyedroppers or the predefined color range selections. These can help you isolate image color quickly—although no range can be defined which might make this considerably more useful. The most useful of the ranges is probably Out of Gamut, which will automatically select color that will not print as an equivalent in CMYK, giving you a quick selection of what is out of range. This identifies color that will not reproduce well in CMYK so you can work on it as an isolated problem. It is really most useful if the final destination for the image is print.

Tip

It might be a good idea to confine the application of Color Range by roughly selecting a target area in your image—if there is one—before choosing the command from the Select menu. Doing this will keep touchup to a minimum.

The dialog box preview has limited function considering it is small, and that anything you can do on the dialog box preview you can do on the image. It really functions only as a second view. Most often, the views can be set to Image (for the dialog box) and Quick Mask (for the image window preview). This will show you a thumbnail of the image in the dialog box while you work on the document to make your selection. It will also show you a preview of the selection as if the selection was a Quick Mask or already saved to a channel. The preview in the document combines the active selection (if any) with the selection made by use of the Color Range command so you'll know what the final selection will look like. The preview on the dialog box ignores any current selection.

Use the following steps to make a selection with the Color Range command:

1. Open an image for use in the selection (see Figure 5.12).

Figure 5.12
This image shows blue bushel baskets in a field of greenery. Color range can be used to quickly isolate the color so it can be altered to match a color theme or to preference.

© PhotoSphere Images, Ltd., photosphere.com

2. (Option) Make an initial rough selection to confine the area of application for the Color Range selection as seen in Figure 5.13.

PART

II

CH

5

Figure 5.13
It can save some work later to section off an area of the image you want to work on by roughly preselecting and confining the activity of the Color Range selection. In this case the freehand Lasso was used to roughly grab the area.

3. Choose Select, Color Range to open the Color Range dialog box.

4. Select options for viewing on the dialog box and previewing the selection in the image document.

Note

You can temporarily toggle between the Image and Selection views in the dialog box by holding down the (Cmd) [Ctrl] key.

5. Make a selection on the Select pop-up menu on the Color Range dialog box. Most often, and for this example, this will be Sampled Colors (which is the default).

Note

If you select anything but Sampled Colors, the range will be automatically selected. You can load that selection and use it to create a more refined selection if desired. If a selection is made of a portion of the image before opening the Color Range, the preview area on the dialog box will crop the view to the affected area.

6. Make color selections with the eyedroppers if Sampled Colors has been selected. To do this, click an eyedropper and sample colors either from the image document or the preview on the palette. (It doesn't matter which you use, although the document will probably offer the best view.) Select the plain eyedropper for single-color selection (this will create a new selection with each click); select the eyedropper with the plus (+) sign to add to the current Color Range selection; select the eyedropper with the minus (−) sign to subtract colors from the current selection. These tools are not available if a predefined color range has been selected from the Select pop-up.

7. Next, use the Fuzziness and Preview (see Figure 5.14) to help define the selection. This is not available if a predefined color range has been selected from the Select pop-up.

Figure 5.14
After making the samples and adjusting fuzziness, the selection will most probably leave some areas that will need to be touched up. Worry about these later.

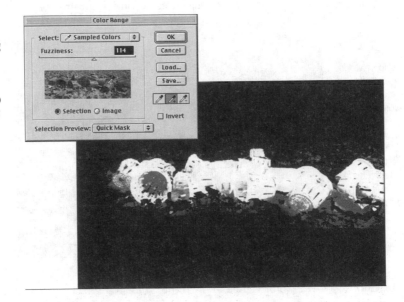

8. When you are satisfied that you have the best selection, convert the Color Range selection to a selection by clicking OK. Save the selection, if desired (Select, Save Selection).

Clarifying Fuzziness

Choosing a level of fuzziness is somewhat like choosing a feathering value, but not exactly. The idea is more like the Magic Wand option for tolerance. The selections you make with the Eyedropper will select a certain number of additional pixels outside that exact color range of the pixel selected as defined by the fuzziness. The great advantage to the Fuzziness slider is that you can make selections and then use the slider to tune your selection so that the selection is confined best to the area of color you were looking to isolate. If a selection looks a bit broad, don't go for the deselecting Eyedropper without checking by reducing the fuzziness first; you might have selected exactly what you need.

After the selection is converted, you can touch it up, if necessary, as you would any other selection (or saved mask). After the selection was saved in the previous example, a Lasso tool with slight feathering was used to grab most of the extra portions of the area outside the baskets, and those areas were filled with black to mask them off. Finer areas were filled in with the Airbrush, and a small, slightly soft brush (using white to open the selection and black to mask).

→ For more information on touching up selections, **see** "Editing Selections," **p. 112**.

Do not worry that some of the area inside your selection may not be perfectly hard. This accounts for shift in the color (such as might happen in shadowed areas, specular highlights, and possibly by color reflection), and will keep a better color balance when you apply color changes later. You might want to duplicate the channel and apply a slight Gaussian blur to soften the edges of the selection (see Figure 5.15).

Figure 5.15
The final mask confines the selection nicely to the area where color change or alteration is desired.

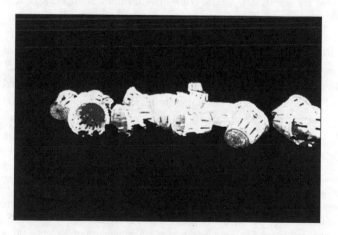

The final step is really applying the resulting mask and selection to the image. You might be interested in changing the color of a portion of an image for a variety of purposes, even though the color is fine as it is. For example, you might be doing a brochure with a color theme and changing a particular color in the image might emphasize that.

To quickly apply a color alteration, use the following steps:

1. If the selection is not currently active, load the selection created with Color Range by choosing Select, Load Selection, and then choose the channel where you saved the selection.

2. Switch the image to Lab Color mode by choosing Image, Mode, Lab Color.

> **Tip**
>
> The Lab Color mode works best with this type of color change because it retains the tonality and works with the hue only. Other color modes tend to be less obedient and color changes will not be nearly as pure or well defined.

3. Create a new layer and move it above the other layers.

4. Change the layer's blending mode to Color in the Layers palette.

5. Fill the selection with the color. The Paint Bucket tool will work just fine. Be sure to click inside the active area of the selection to complete the fill.

6. Create an adjustment layer by selecting Layer, New, Adjustment Layer, Hue/Saturation.

7. Check the Group with Previous check box.

8. Adjust the Hue/Saturation slider to fine-tune the color you have selected for the fill.

> **Tip**
>
> Some colors look wrong when you select them with the slider. The colors won't blend well or tones might look unnatural. Playing with the lightness and saturation might improve the results somewhat, but stick to the colors that look best without such adjustments if possible.

9. When you are satisfied with the color alteration, click the OK button to accept the changes.

This is only one of many variations that are possible in making color changes. Try using various layer-blending modes as well as Blend If sliders in the Layer Style dialog box to achieve the color effects you are looking for when making changes of this sort. Making one change and taking a Snapshot and then making another change from the original state allows you to quickly compare the two possibilities.

→ For more information on making color changes, **see** "Color Corrections," **p. 465**.

→ For more information on Snapshots, **see** "Creating with Image Histories," **p. 251**.

Replace Color

You can use Replace Color (Image, Adjust, Replace Color) to perform essentially the same function in creating the selection as Color Range, but there is an added step as the Replace Color command does not automatically make the selection (see Figure 5.16). You need to save the settings out of Replace Color and then reload them into the Color Range anyway to work with the selections. It is possible to work only using Replace Color, but you need to be sure that the selection does not need revision or you might find that some areas of color change unexpectedly when you use the sliders. You might also want to work on a duplicate of the layer or image (although you can always undo the changes with Histories or Undo).

Figure 5.16
The Replace Color dialog box allows simultaneous access to Color Range selections and the Hue and Saturation functions.

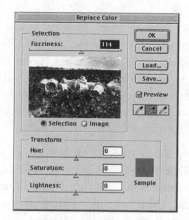

In addition to color changes, Color Range selection might be valuable in creating masks for large area dust correction and correcting image stains or miscoloration. For example, a red dress that is dusty and linty or that was scanned from a dirty negative will have a variety of problems due to unwanted noise. Making a selection of the red area and then inverting it will give you control over the noise only. With the noise selected, the dress will be masked from changes. In other words, you can worry only about making good choices in fixing the selected areas.

→ For more information on dust correction, **see** "Removing Dust from an Image," **p. 580**.

Some color changes are better done with selection of a larger area and are better not confined to a single color. For example, say you have a photograph of a swimsuit model and she is in a stunning multicolored suit that has a blue you know is unobtainable in CMYK—yet the image is meant for four-color printing in a brochure. You might be tempted to work with the blue only, but it might be far better to select the entire suit and change the colors in unison using Hue/Saturation or other color tools. To do this, make a broad Quick Mask selection with paint tools that ends at the boundaries of the suit, rather than the end of the area of blue. The color change will affect appearance, but the or contrast in the colors of the suit will be more or less maintained. Hue/Saturation is probably still the easiest tool to use to make these changes. In a case such as this, be cautious of reflected color from the suit; it might change the hue of neighboring skin tones and other articles in the image as well (for example, reflections).

Tip

Be sure your color changes don't create problems. You might do a good job of changing the color, as in the swimsuit example, but keep reflectivity in mind, as a reflection of the original colors in the water might ruin your best efforts.

 If you have trouble getting tools to apply after you have been using selections, see "I Can't Apply the Tool I Am Trying to Work With" in the Troubleshooting section at the end of this chapter.

EDITING SELECTIONS

It is possible to add to and edit selections with any of the tools specifically designated as selection tools (those on the toolbox and on the Select menu). A variety of other tools in Photoshop not meant for selection can be used to alter or manipulate selections that already exist. Manipulating and saving selections will help you make the most of selections by providing flexibility in the way you can work with creating the selections you need. Selections can be duplicated so that you can alter them, and they can be moved to other documents.

Manipulation of selections runs from the simple (Invert), to the quite complex (Calculations). You can work using straightforward application of additional tools to alter unsaved selections, work on fledgling selections in Quick Mask to get them in shape before committing them to a channel or applying them to images without saving, or you can save selections in alpha channels to allow the greatest flexibility and application. Although there is a limit of 24 channels (including color and alpha channels), and certainly there will be a limit for the capability of your computer system as channels do use memory, you can create and combine as many channels, selections, and colors as you need to create an image. This might require multiple documents, which you can use to store selections as alpha channels. However, even complex images don't often require too many masks and saved selections, and, generally, there will be plenty of room to accomplish what you have to in one document. Sometimes the simplest tools can quickly accomplish what you need.

Note Understanding manipulation of saved selections requires a working knowledge of channels.

→ For more information on alpha channels, **see** "Working with Channels," **p. 79**.

Tip Channels take up memory, and if they are not pivotal to the development of an image they should probably be removed. Try to keep channel use to a working minimum wherever possible. To help you along those lines, use Quick Masks and remove duplicate or unnecessary alphas, or store channels in another image.

It might be necessary to alter selections in order to get them to fit your purposes. Any tool in Photoshop that directly affects pixels can alter your selection. Some tools will prove more useful and selection friendly, however. These altered selections can be used simply to section off portions of an image that need a little extra work, or selections can be used to apply effects or can be used with other, complex tools (Calculations and filter applications) to create effects.

Several tools on the Selection menu allow you to modify active selections. These are special general function tools that are applied evenly across the selection. These include Feather, Modify, Grow, Similar, and Transform.

MODIFYING SELECTIONS WITH SELECTION TOOLS

With any selection tool from the toolbox, holding down the Shift or (Option) [Alt] key with the tool selected will add or subtract from the selection, respectively. Simply hold down the appropriate key while using the tool as you normally would (described in the previous section). This will freeze the current selection onscreen while you drag a new selection. The new selection will be drawn just like an initial selection, but the result will either be subtracted from or added to the frozen selection—depending on the function you have selected. When the Shift key is pressed, the selection tool will display a small plus sign (+) below the selection icon when the icon is over an active image; when the (Option) [Alt] key is pressed, the selection icon will display a minus sign (−) below the selection icon when the icon is over an active image. These keys will have no effect if there is no active selection.

The current selection can be cropped by a selection as well. That is, a new selection can be used to redefine an existing selection by encircling the area of the selection you desire to keep (see Figures 5.17 through 5.19). Everything outside the area you select while holding these keys will be deselected when you release the mouse. To crop a selection, hold down the (Option-Shift) [Alt+Shift] keys together while using any selection tool. This will again freeze the selection onscreen while the new selection is created. When the (Option-Shift) [Alt+Shift] keys are pressed, an x will appear below the selection icon when the icon is over an active image. Again, these keys will have no effect if there is no active selection.

Figure 5.17
This selection picks out the center fish, but if you want to refine that selection you don't have to redo it.

Figure 5.18
To crop the selection hold down the (Option-Shift) [Alt+Shift] keys and freeze the current selection, and then draw a selection around what you want to retain. This will intersect the current selection.

Figure 5.19
The final selection retains only the portion of the original selection that falls within the cropping selection. Note that the cropping selection does not add to the original selection area.

Tip

The (Option-Shift) [Alt+Shift] keys are fine tools for working with an active selection, but you might want to retain the original selection you are cropping for other purposes—or in case you may need to come back to that selection for any reason. Although the History palette and Undo offer means of returning to the selection, saving to a channel is your best bet in retaining selection information.

RETAINING MODIFIED SELECTIONS

It is easy to retain several versions or alterations on a selection without losing the original selection. To be sure selections don't get away from you, complete the following steps:

1. Save a selection in an image you are working on. The easiest way to do this is to choose Select, Save Selection. You can also use Quick Mask, located at the bottom of the toolbox; however, with Quick Mask the channel needs to be duplicated (see Figure 5.20).

Figure 5.20
To duplicate a Quick Mask, make a selection, activate the mask by clicking the Quick Mask button on the toolbox, and drag the channel titled "Quick Mask" to the duplicate channel button on the Channels palette.

2. With step one completed, either continue to work on the active selection (if you saved the selection) or the Quick Mask (if you duplicated the Quick Mask to save the channel).

> **Tip**
>
> You can turn an active selection into a Quick Mask at any time by clicking the Quick Mask button on the Tool palette, or by toggling with the Q key.

→ For more information on Quick Masks, **see** "Using Quick Mask to Work with Selections," **p. 135**.

3. When finished with alterations on the selection, save the new selection (see Step 1). This will give you two alpha channels: one with the original selection and the second with the changes you created. Either of these selections can be reloaded at any time using the menu option Selection, Load Selection. To create additional variations, repeat Steps 2 and 3.

4. Save the document. This will permanently save the channels in the image.

> **Tip**
>
> Information in the channels will not be saved to the hard drive without saving the document. Save the document frequently to avoid losing your selection work because of crashes.

Saving enables you to come back to selections as you need them. Saving selections can be handy for a variety of reasons, including reverting to an earlier selection, using the selection in other images, making complicated masking effects with calculations, and so on. Adding to and subtracting from selections in various ways help in creating intricate selections.

Intricate and accurate selections help accomplish the most difficult and involved image-creation tasks.

Note	If you have selections saved in alpha channels, you will find that you may not be able to include them in the document when using some file format options—most notably, EPS. Save a second version without the channels for portability or to change the image to other formats that cannot retain channel information.

FEATHERING SELECTIONS

Essentially, feathering a selection results in the selection having a blurred or softened edge. This makes the selection affect the application of tools with a blended effect. The greater the feathering, the more pronounced the blending effect. A slight feathering (less than one pixel) is akin to anti-aliasing.

There are quite a few ways to blur, so there are as many ways to create a feathered selection. The basic techniques range from simply using the Feather command to using masks and blurring (either with filters or the Blur tool). It is possible to create special-effect featherings with filters and custom brushes. Your technique should depend on what you are trying to accomplish.

Combining selections made with different tools into a single, evenly feathered selection is not always easy. For example, you might want to combine two selections made at different times—or even within the same channel of an image—one with feathering and one without. If you just globally blur a selection or set a feather at this point, as it may end up being broader in some areas of the image. If this is not an effect you want, it could be time-consuming to repair. A Threshold technique can help get it in line without much fuss at all.

→ For more information on merging and blending selection edges, **see** "Threshold and Blur Techniques," **p. 118**.

Photoshop provides a Feather command, which can be used for the simple application of feathering existing selections. However, you can be in complete control of the hardness of feathering and feathering edges by working with masks, using Threshold (Image, Adjust, Threshold) and Curves. Steps later in this section show how to soften a hard edge and how to harden a soft edge. This will give you ultimate control over soft feathering using Curves and the Threshold slider. You will be able to re-create blurred edges for feathers and define the falloff, or feathering effects, any way you want. You can use these same tools to restore an even feathering to your images without rebuilding the selections.

→ For more information on controlling feathered edges with Threshold and Curves, **see** "Controlling Feathered Selections," **p. 118**.

THE FEATHERING FUNCTION

Feathering can be applied to an active selection to blur it, rather than leaving an edge of hard pixels. The benefit of feathering a selection is in blending images. If you plan to cut and paste a selected area of an image into another image, a hard edge will leave a jagged selection of pixels, which might not blend very well with what you paste in above it. Feathered selections can help you blend image elements more seamlessly, as what you use them to copy from and/or paste into will have a softer edge, and therefore a less abrupt transition into the surrounding image.

The Feather command can be found on the Select menu, and it is available only when there is an active selection in your current document. When the function is selected from the menu, the Feather Selection dialog box appears (see Figure 5.21).

Figure 5.21
Feathering is effective on a specific range of pixels that you enter in the dialog box. A higher number causes a broader softening.

After entering a number for the radius of the feathered edge, simply click OK and the selection will be feathered according to the radius you have chosen. The feather may or may not show any visible changes in the selection onscreen depending on the radius you have chosen and the % you are zoomed into the image.

Feathering Radius
Feathering does not affect only the number of pixels within the radius assigned—the blurring is actually controlled by a Gaussian equation. In a black-on-white application, blurring of about 70% of tonal levels occurs between the radius specified, but the effect actually extends quite a bit beyond the radius (2.55×the radius). The application is very similar to the effect of Gaussian blur. (It is not an evenly stepped gradient effect.) The purpose is to soften blending more effectively. If you need to control the width of the feathering in a black-on-white blend more exactly, select a radius that is 38.25% of the area you want to affect (Distance of Effect×.3825 = Feather Radius). Or you can use feathering and adjust Curves to change the affected area. To do this, save the selection and apply a Curve; move the Curve points to 38,0 and 217,255 (as shown in Figure 5.22). The feathering will remain, but will drop off more steeply.

Figure 5.22
This Curve adjustment will alter the existing feathering to the origi-nal setting of the radius.

(217,255)

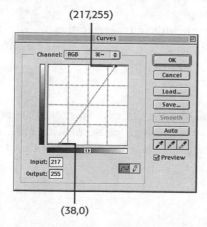

(38,0)

CONTROLLING FEATHERED SELECTIONS

It is possible to control feathered or blurred edges of selections that have been saved to alpha channels to achieve a variety of effects. Although numerous effects can be achieved with application of filters and additional selections, this discussion will concentrate on manipulating falloff of the selection edge. This can mean softening a hard-edged selection, hardening a soft-edged selection, or manipulating an existing feather, which already exists in a selection. Two tools prove especially useful in making adjustments to selection edges: the Threshold command (Image, Adjust, Threshold) and Curves (Image, Adjust, Curves or (Cmd-M) [Ctrl+M]).

Threshold changes an image to hard black and white, removing shades of gray between pure black (100% black) and pure white (0% black). It changes gray values according to a Threshold setting made on the Threshold slider (see Figure 5.23). This slider position defines the level where grayscale will become either black or white. As the Threshold command eliminates grayscale, it is very useful in redefining a hard selection line. This can help in joining a mixed bag of selections that have varying degrees of feathering applied. When the selections are combined and Threshold applied, they can then be feathered (or blurred) when applied as selections (see the steps for hardening a soft edge later in this section). This gives you greater control of the uniformity of the feathering.

Figure 5.23
Every gray level to the left of the slider becomes black, and every level to the right becomes white when Threshold is applied. To apply changes, click the OK button.

Curves can be used to adjust falloff for the feathered or blurred edges of a saved selection. This gives you the ability to change the way edges of a selection will be used in blending, or can help in creating special effects with image masks. For example, you might want a selection to drop off sharply, or perhaps you want to apply a rippled effect to the feathering. These effects can be achieved easily with Curve applications.

→ For more information on controlling feathered edges with Curves, **see** "Using Blurring and Curves to Define Selection Falloff," **p. 123**.

THRESHOLD AND BLUR TECHNIQUES

Threshold and blurring (more specifically, the Gaussian blur filter) can be used to combine feathered and unfeathered masks, and redistribute feathering with uniformity. Threshold is useful for hardening a soft edge, whereas the blur filters come in handy for putting a feather back into the selection.

To soften a hard edge on a selection, follow these steps:

1. Open a new file or an existing image to use for making a selection.
2. Create a hard selection with the tool of your choice. For example, a brush with 100% hardness can create this effect in a Quick Mask using the Airbrush tool and a black foreground swatch (see Figure 5.24).

Figure 5.24
A close-up of this image segment will be used to focus on the softening effect being described. The selection appears in grayscale against the image, which is a black-and-white scan.

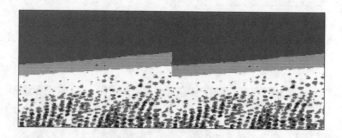

3. Save the selection to a channel. (This step is not necessary if you are using Quick Mask.)
4. Choose the channel where the mask was saved from the Channels palette. This will be called Quick Mask in italic if you did not save the channel.
5. Deselect any active selections (Cmd-D) [Ctrl+D].
6. Choose Gaussian Blur from the Filter menu (Filter, Blur, Gaussian Blur) (see Figure 5.25).

Figure 5.25
Select the Gaussian Blur filter from the Filter menu. Gaussian Blur is a useful and versatile filter, important, in this case, for creating or restoring feathering.

PART

II

CH

5

7. Select the width you want to make the blur. Be aware that you are choosing a radius, not a diameter, and that the actual affected area for the blur is greater than the radius selected (see Figure 5.26).

Note

The Gaussian Blur filter does not create a linear blurring (evenly stepped gradient). Although a radius is input, the actual effect of the blur can extend far beyond the radius. The actual effect is based on an equation named for Carl Friedrich Gauss, a mathematician.

Figure 5.26
The Gaussian Blur dialog box has a preview that will show you the effect of the blur before it is applied to the image.

8. Select OK, and the channel will blur (see Figure 5.27) according to the radius you have selected in the Gaussian Blur dialog box.

Figure 5.27
This image was sectioned to show how different radius blurs would affect the outcome of the blur. The sections from left to right were blurred with a radius of 15, 7, 3, and 0 pixels.

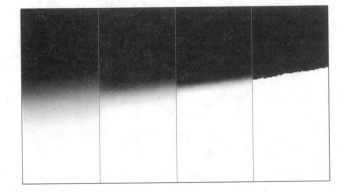

To harden a soft edge on a selection, follow these steps:

1. Open a new image and make a feathered selection, or use the result of the preceding steps for softening a hard-edged selection.

Tip

It can be most helpful to create a new selection using tools with different feathering settings to see the full benefit possible with this technique.

Note

The sample illustrations use the selection created in the previous exercise, although it has been slightly altered for purposes of demonstration. Without alteration, the result of Step 3 would be a straight selection that matched the original.

2. Choose Select, Save Selection to Save the selection to a channel.

3. Highlight the alpha channel in the Channels palette by clicking it.

Open up the Threshold dialog box by selecting Image, Adjust, Threshold (see Figures 5.28 and 5.29).

Figure 5.28
When the Threshold dialog box is opened, the slider will be in the middle of the levels graph. Moving the slider to the right will lower the threshold, making more levels of gray turn black; moving the slider left will raise the threshold, making more levels of gray turn white.

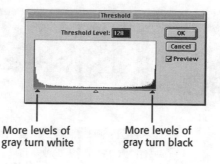

More levels of
gray turn white

More levels of
gray turn black

Figure 5.29
The initial selection in Figure 5.28 is reformed by the Threshold function to this stepped shape. Further adjustment will bring the segments of the selection back into line.

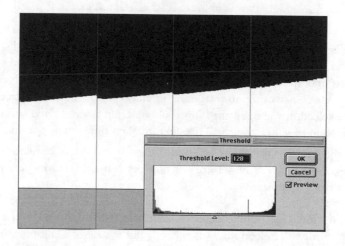

5. Use the slider on the Threshold dialog box to even up the edges of the selections into a continuous line (see Figure 5.30). As you move the Threshold slider to the right, it chooses a greater percentage of gray pixels.

> **Tip**
>
> If the gray tones of two selection areas overlap with the same tonality at any point, the selections will meet and form a continuous edge. If not, you might have to create a slightly larger blur area, repeat a procedure of blur and Threshold several times, or concentrate on keeping the more difficult parts of the selection intact while planning to redo portions of the selection to compensate.

6. When the selection is aligned to your satisfaction, select OK to commit the change and close the Threshold dialog box.

7. To preview how well the selection matches the image, view the color channels and mask together by switching on views for all channels in the Channels palette.

→ For more information on viewing channels and channel views, **see** "Working with Channels," **p. 79**.

Figure 5.30
The Threshold slider is moved to the right to align the selection edge, forming a continuous line, and restoring the original selection.

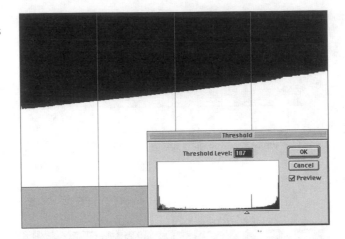

8. The selection might align perfectly with the image, or it might need some adjustment. If several selections are being combined (as in the sample image) make necessary alterations to smooth out the transition areas in the mask with a hard-edged brush or other tool of your choice using no feathering or aliasing. To adjust the selection to the image, blur the selection and open the Threshold function again. While still viewing the image and selection together, use the Threshold to align the selection to the image.

9. When the selection is to your satisfaction, save it and the document before making changes to the image. The selection is now permanently saved where it can be reloaded without being re-created.

Using blurring and Threshold as described can help redefine the edge of a selection without having to go through reselection. This is handy in the case of a complex selection that you do not want to create again. Using this technique on a selected portion of the mask localizes results and helps you fine-tune selections where areas don't seem to fit quite right.

In some cases, it's easier to remake portions of a selection by re-creating them than by fussing too much with blurring and Threshold. To re-create an area of a selection, simply choose the channel and paint over the area you want to rework. Use a hard-edged brush if working with a hard-edged selection. If working on a feathered selection, use a soft-edged brush, or convert the selection you are working on to hard-edged using the Threshold function before making changes with a hard-edged brush. Working with hard edges will help you keep the feathering even, if that is a concern.

Blurring and Threshold methods can help you expand and contract selections with more flexibility than is currently offered by Photoshop's Expand and Contract functions for selections. These tools allow only an increase/decrease of 16 pixels per application. With blurring and Threshold, you can increase that dramatically (limited by the size of the image more than the radius of the blur). For example, if you wanted to expand or contract a selection past the 16 pixels available in the Modify functions, you could use the Gaussian Blur tool to create a blur for the selection you want to change (say, 100 pixels). When the blur is complete, open the Threshold function and use it to define how much you want to expand and contract the selection. This is easy to do, and you can have precise control over the effects you want to achieve. Using blurring/Threshold will allow you to preview the changes if you keep the visibility on both the mask and the composite channels. The effective possibility for expansion or contraction of your selection is changed to hundreds of pixels in this case, with the ease of slider control.

USING BLURRING AND CURVES TO DEFINE SELECTION FALLOFF

Blurring and Curves can be used to define the falloff of a selection. By blurring a selection, you can apply Curves to the tones created to shape the edge of the selection. For example, if you want a selection to fall off hard (shifting quickly from dark to light), you can redefine the edge of the selection with a Curve. Essentially, the Curve can be seen as a graphic depiction of the shape of the falloff. The following Figures (5.31 through 5.36) demonstrate some of the possibilities for using Curves to redefine feathered or soft grayscale edges.

Figure 5.31
A selection with a soft edge created by feathering with Gaussian Blur.

Figure 5.32
The Curve redefines the edge of the mask, making the edge fall off rapidly. This can be useful where little blending is necessary or desired, such as when using a selection to snip out part of an image to use as foreground to a drop shadow.

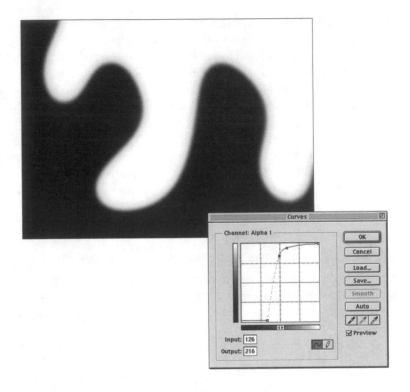

Figure 5.33
Bowing the curve downward creates a lingering feather that will spread broadly after a quick falloff. This can be useful for attempting to blend an image with a new background while keeping the edge clearly defined.

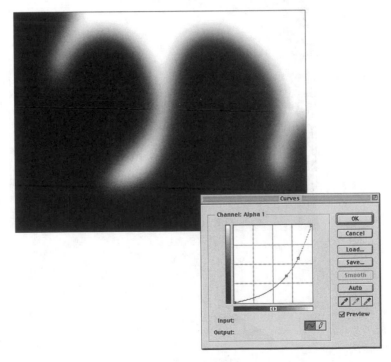

Figure 5.34
Curves can help create a variety of special effects. This Curve creates a rippling or wavelike feathering.

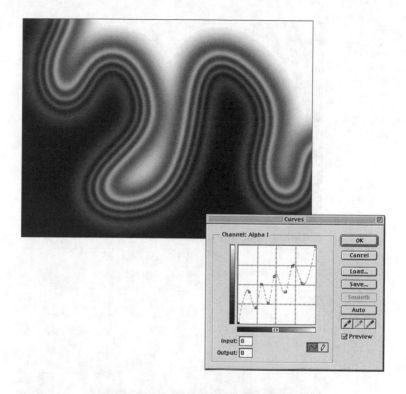

Figure 5.35
This Curve could be used to create a selection for painting in glossy, specular highlights.

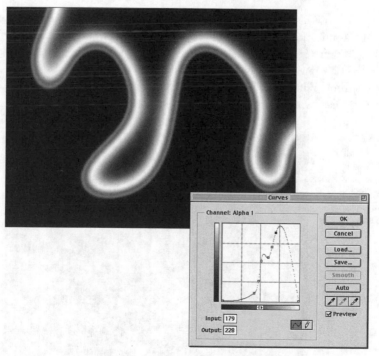

PART

II

CH

5

Figure 5.36
Using the Pencil tool
to sketch in random
curves can yield some
interesting results.
The effect can be
smoothed out if
desired by clicking the
joined-line button.

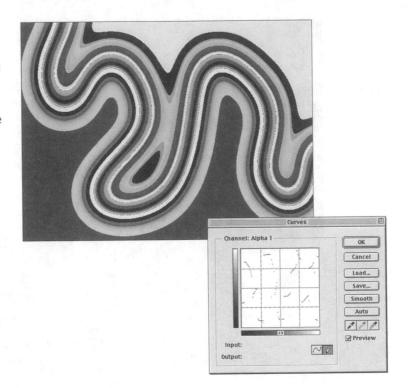

Creative work with masking is great for developing frames, special effects, and custom blends. Application of multiple filters to a feathered edge can yield interesting results as well. In Figure 5.37, a sine wave (Filter, Distort, Wave) was applied to the original selection, then the Chrome filter (Filter, Sketch, Chrome) with the selection loaded, then the Lighting Effects filter (Filter, Render, Lighting Effects), and finally a Glass Block filter (Filter, Distort, Glass with the texture set to Blocks).

Figure 5.37
It is possible to build
some wild masking
effects with applica-
tion of filters on top
of controlling edge
blends in a mask.

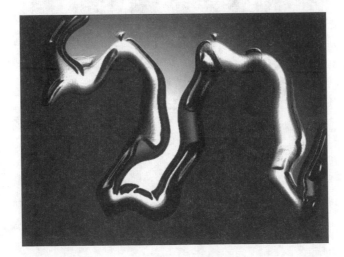

Selection edges can be controlled with a variety of methods to help you achieve the effects you need for a specific instance or image. Don't just depend on the dedicated selection tools to get it done: Use creative selection techniques to create selections that do what you need them to.

USING THE TRANSFORM SELECTION FUNCTION

The Transform Selection function allows you to modify an active selection by changing its position, shape, and orientation. This feature supports scaling, rotation, distortion (movement of a single-corner anchor), stretching (movement of a pair of corner anchors), skewing (horizontal or vertical movement of corner pairs—like side or opposite), perspective changes, numeric distortions, flipping, inverting, and the like. There is also a Transform Again command (Cmd-Shift-T) [Ctrl+Shift+T], which will change the current selection based on the last transformation you accepted. Really, these are the same transform operations you can perform with Layers and Paths, only these movements will affect the selection only—not the path or image.

Simply invoking the function (Select, Transform Selection) accesses the simplest of these transformations. The current selection will be placed in a transform box, which has a center point and handles (they look like Pen tool anchors) on each corner of the box and at the midpoint of each side (see Figure 5.38). The Center point defaults to the center of the transformation outline, but can be moved to achieve some rotational effects, as well as control the application of some transformations.

Tip

Rotation can be confined to 15° increments by holding the Shift key.

The mode will default to Free Transform, which allows simple *scaling* (move a single side with the center point, move two sides with a corner point) and *rotation* (about the center point). After the function is invoked, menu commands for altering the selection can be accessed by selecting Edit, Transform or by pressing (Control) [Right Mouse] to invoke the menu. Certain key combinations will help you toggle between functions, as seen in Table 5.1.

TABLE 5.1   TRANSFORM FUNCTION KEYSTROKES AND DESCRIPTIONS

Type of Transformation	Keystroke	Description
Free Transform	(Cmd-T) [Ctrl+T]	Allows simple vertical/horizontal scaling (click midpoint) and Rotation (click just outside corners or midpoints).
Scale	([Shift])	Scales with confined ratio (click corner).

TABLE 5.1   TRANSFORM FUNCTION KEYSTROKES AND DESCRIPTIONS

Type of Transformation	Keystroke	Description
Scale on Center	(Option-Shift) [Alt+Shift]	Scales with confined ratio according to the center point.
Distort	(Cmd) [Ctrl]	Free movement of corner points (click corner) and sides (click midpoint).
Skew	(Cmd-Shift) [Ctrl+Shift]	Skews whole side along side axis (click midpoint) or corner point along one axis or the other (click corner).
Skew on Center	(Cmd-Option-Shift) [Ctrl+Alt+Shift]	Moves opposite sides along opposite side axis (click midpoint) based on positioning of the center point.
Perspective	(Cmd-Option-Shift) [Ctrl+Alt+ Shift]	Moves corner points in opposite directions along the line axis (click corner) based on positioning of the midpoint. Can be used to fix perspective, such as to vanishing points.
Perspective	(Cmd-Option) [Alt+Ctrl]	Moves opposite sides on Center in opposite directions (click midpoint) based on position of the center point.
Call Transform Menu	(Control-Click) [Right Mouse+Click]	Opens the Transform menu, which will offer the preceding options as well as Numeric (a Transform dialog box), set rotations of 180° and 90° (clockwise and counterclockwise, and flip (horizontal and vertical)

Figure 5.38
The Transform box handles are used to alter the shape of the box, and the selection inside is reshaped accordingly.

Midpoint Handle

Center Point

Corner Handle

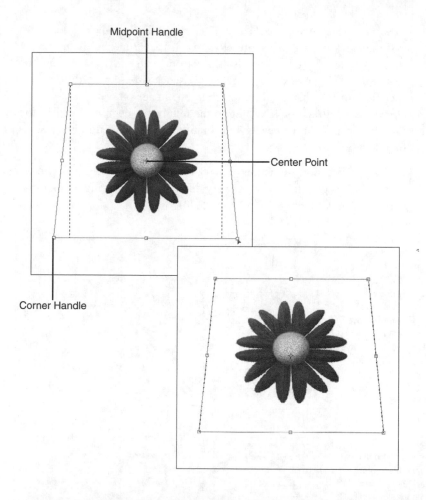

Tip

To undo a move during a transformation, choose Undo from the Edit menu, or (Control-Z) [Right Mouse+Z]. This will remove the last step only, and will toggle between Undo and Redo—it is not a multiple Undo.

The numeric entry fields on the Options bar appear when you invoke the Transform Selection. They will allow you to control position (in terms of x and y coordinates), scaling (in terms of Width and Height values), skewing (horizontal and vertical independently) and rotation of your selection. Each function can be selected independently or all can be applied at the same time. These options are a great advantage when trying to accomplish a precise movement or an application of several alterations in one move.

Position can be a controlled movement of up to 2,000 pixels in any direction; x controls left (–) and right (+) position, y controls up (–) and down (+). Scaling can be controlled up to 2,000% horizontally or vertically (based on the size of the selection and size of the image; negative and positive number entries have the same effect). Skewing can work with between

–180° and 180°. Areas are skewed on center with the right and left sides of the selection shifting clockwise (+) or counterclockwise (–) according to the number of degrees specified for the change. Vertical skew also shifts from center with the top and bottom sides of the selection shifting clockwise (+) or counterclockwise (–) according to the number of degrees specified for the change. Rotation shifts the image on center in a clockwise (+) or counter-clockwise (–) direction according to the number of degrees specified for the change. Degrees specified for skewing and rotation can be applied in increments as small as a tenth of a degree.

Using the Transform functions, you can change the shape of selections, and make basic geometric shapes that are otherwise very difficult such as triangles, egg shapes, figure 8s, and parallelograms (see Figures 5.39 and 5.40).

Figure 5.39
Triangles and egg shapes can be made by taking a simple rectangle or oval (respectively) and using the Perspective Transformation. Pulling the perspective across the midpoint when working with the oval will make a figure 8.

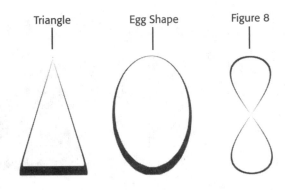

Triangle   Egg Shape   Figure 8

Figure 5.40
This water droplet was formed by creating a figure 8, transforming again two times, and then using half the shape and distorting it with a rotated square selection (for the process, see Figure 5.41).

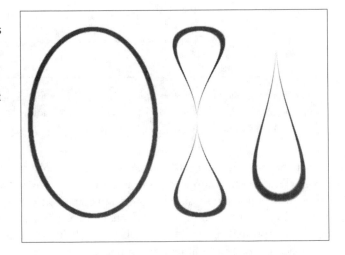

Figure 5.41
After the basic form of the droplet is created, it can be turned back into a selection using the Magic Wand tool and clicking outside the drop area, and then inverting and saving the selection.

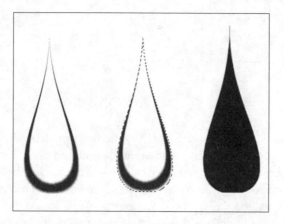

Tip

When doing distortions of this type, it is good to work in a high resolution, or far larger size than you will need in the end. Although it takes up memory to create the effect, the result can be scaled down to lessen pixelation and other effects that might be caused by the alterations.

MODIFY, GROW, AND SIMILAR SELECTION FUNCTIONS

Modify, Grow, and Similar commands, such as Feather, also affect active selections. These functions can be very useful in performing specific tasks, even though they are somewhat limited. All appear on the Select menu, and must be initiated from there unless you customize an action for invoking them.

→ For more information on using actions to create keystrokes, **see** "Creating and Editing Actions," **p. 269.**

MODIFY SELECTION SUBMENU

Modify has four options on its submenu: Border, Smooth, Expand, and Contract. These selection changes are controlled by the selection itself, independently of the image area it is selecting.

The Border function creates a new selection based on the edge of a current selection (the selection line as it appears onscreen). It turns the edge of the current selection into a border with an evenly stepped gradient from the border line to the background, which is controlled by the distance entered as a radius in the border dialog box. The width can be from between 1 and 64 pixels, and it is an actual, evenly stepped gradient result that is not controlled by Gaussian equations. The Border function chooses pixels along the selection edge to be the center of the border, assigning them a value of 0% black. The function then uses each of these border pixels as the center of a diamond gradient, which is applied in the Width designated on the Border dialog box (see Figure 5.42). The lightest value for any pixel is assigned considering the calculated possibilities.

PART

II

CH

5

Figure 5.42
The Width is used to apply an evenly stepped gradient between the chosen border edge and the background.

The choice of the pixel edge is made differently by the function depending on whether the number entered for the radius is an odd or even number. For an even number, pixels whose side (not corner) touches the selection line are chosen—these can lie inside or outside the selection. For odd numbers, only those pixels on which the side touches the selection line inside the selection (inside the active area of the selection) are chosen. This makes the appearance of the center of borders with an odd number radius thinner than those made with an even number radius. See Figure 5.43 for an example of each of these.

Figure 5.43
A comparison shows (left) the resulting mask of a single pixel selection that has had a 10-pixel border applied; (center) a single row of selected pixels with a border applied at a radius of 2; (right) a single row of selected pixels with a border applied at a radius of 3.

Odd number Width value makes white border pixels inside the selection line only

Even number Width value makes white border pixels inside and outside the selection line

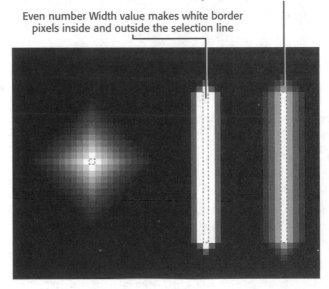

This function can be used to select borders, of course, but combined with other tools (such as Curves to control feathering) can produce unique opportunities to embellish selections, and poses opportunities as a creative tool. For example, confining sharpening to the edge of a selection that outlines a specific object in an image will effectively sharpen only that area, which might be a help in making the image element stand out.

→ To control the gradation of the border created using the Border command, you can use feathering controls; **see** "Feathering Selections," **p. 116**.

Smooth looks at each pixel in the current selection (as the selection would appear in grayscale, not according to what the selection would affect in the image) and assigns a new value to it in grayscale based on the surrounding pixels. The newly assigned value is based on an average of the grayscale values of pixels in a square surrounding the pixel being examined. The size of the square is determined by the radius entered in the Smooth dialog box. The average is determined, and then used as a measure to select the closest existing value currently in the selection. The value closest to the average is assigned to the pixel being evaluated. The size of the sampling square is based on the radius; the radius becomes the length of the square sides—or the sampling area that is used to determine the average.

The effect is really meant to soften harsh differences and noise in selections, and can remove fringes or ragged edges while maintaining the general shape of the selection. It can be very effective in working with simple noise; however, it will also soften selection corners (see Figure 5.44).

Figure 5.44
If the mask on the left is loaded as a selection, and smooth is applied with a radius of 2, the result (after saving the selection) would be the mask at right. Note that the noise is gone, but the corners of the mask are slightly softened as well.

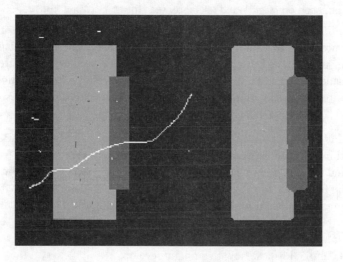

Expand will evaluate each pixel in a selection just like Smooth, and assign a new value. In this case, the function will adopt the black percentage value of the lightest pixel that falls within the radius of the square and assign that to the pixel being evaluated. This effectively expands a selection while maintaining the general shape, removing dark noise, increasing light noise, and increasing intensity (the selection will affect more pixels in a broader area). Contract works in just the opposite manner of Expand, looking at all the pixels within the square and selecting the darkest one for reassignment of the value for the original pixel. This effectively shrinks the selection while maintaining the general shape, removing light noise, increasing dark noise, and lowering intensity. These functions effectively shrink and expand selections.

GROW AND SIMILAR

Grow and Similar use currently selected areas of an image (layer or channel) to expand a selection. To do this, the functions look at pixels that are in the existing selection to collect a list of values of everything that is in the selection. Each uses this list to select additional pixels that are outside the selection that are like those in the list. The difference between Similar and Grow is that Grow looks only at pixels that are adjacent (contiguous) to the current selection and Similar looks at pixels over the entire image—whether they are adjacent or not.

The pixel values in the list can be affected by the Tolerance setting on the Magic Wand tool. If the value for the tolerance is zero, the Grow and Similar functions will use only the list of pixel values found within the current selection to derive the new selection. If the Tolerance contains a value (1–255), the list is re-evaluated and expanded based on the tolerance as set in the Magic Wand preferences.

→ For more information on Magic Wand tolerance, **see** "The Magic Wand," **p. 103**.

Grow and Similar are very effective tools in expanding rough selections or picking foreground elements out of a solid-colored background. Their link to the Magic Wand seems not to be an accident, as I often find I use Grow and/or Similar immediately following a selection made with the Magic Wand to fine-tune the results. Fine-tuning usually means extending into nooks and crannies or selecting secondary areas that are isolated from the first.

Figure 5.45 is a good example of this type of use. Here I would select the sky and replace it with something a bit more dramatic. A Wand selection in the two areas (the sky area above the rocks and the area in between) would accomplish the selection—if the tolerance were set perfectly the first time. However, it would take a lot of trial and error to get the selection perfect the first time (so, it wouldn't really be the first time). A better course of action is to select from the larger area of the sky with low-tolerance levels and then select Similar after the upper area is selected. Selecting Similar will grab the spot of sky between the rocks. Figures 5.45 and 5.46 show how this might develop.

Figure 5.45
Selection of the sky can be done in a number of ways, but here the Magic Wand is used to select the blues in preparation for application of several Grow commands.

Figure 5.46
The Grow function is applied several times, and then clouds are added using the Lasso to complete the selection.

USING QUICK MASK TO WORK WITH SELECTIONS

If you use a lot of selections and often just want to do a simple alteration to the mask before applying it to some purpose, it can be to your advantage to use Quick Mask. With Quick Mask, you can alter the mask or selection and then quickly return it to an active selection by clicking the Standard Mode button on the toolbox immediately to the left of the Quick Mask button (see Figure 5.47).

Figure 5.47
The Selection mode buttons appear at the bottom of the toolbox. Selection modes can be toggled by pressing Q on the keyboard as well.

Standard Selection Mode

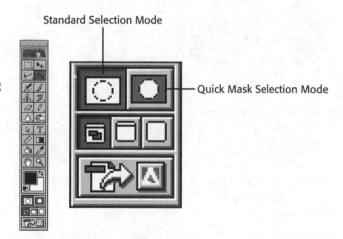

Quick Mask Selection Mode

The power of Quick Mask is in automating the process of creating an editable alpha channel. Using Quick Mask saves several steps in switching between working on channels and activating channels as selections before they are altered and viewed. Quick Mask also makes it easy to toggle back and forth between selection and alpha channel without repeated saving. It is ideal for making spot alterations and quick changes using the painting tools, because of the control offered by alpha channels. The only disadvantage is that it does not save to the document and is more or less a temporary channel. However, selections created with Quick Mask can still be saved as alpha channels at any point in the process of change—only one Quick Mask channel is available at a time.

Note

Make a conscious effort to save masks that you make in the Quick Mask mode that you believe you will have use for in the future.

You might use Quick Mask in a situation where you may need to make several attempts at a selection before getting the right results. The following steps show an example of how this might be used:

1. Open an image and make a selection using the selection tool of your choice (see Figure 5.48).

Figure 5.48
For this example, a selection is loaded that captured the head and mask from another image. The selection was previously made for another purpose and had been saved for future use.

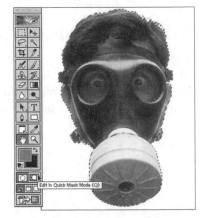

2. Switch to the Quick Mask mode by clicking the button on the Tool palette. This will display the current selection as a channel mask along with the image, and the marquee line will disappear.

3. Edit the Quick Mask to fit to the desired area. I used the Airbrush to fill in or remove parts of the mask. To mask, paint with black; to select, paint with white. The eyes in the mask were selected using the Ellipse Marquee and the Transform tool—the latter to distort the shape to make it fit.

4. When you have completed the changes to the mask channel, switch the selection back to Standard Editing mode (see Figure 5.49).

5. With the mask converted to a selection in the Standard mode, make the changes to your document that you created the selection to facilitate (see Figure 5.50).

Figure 5.49
In switching to Standard Editing mode, the Quick Mask is removed from the channels and is converted to a selection. If for any reason you want to save the selection, duplicate the Quick Mask channel before converting, or save the selection after converting.

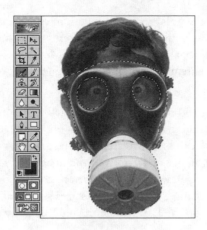

Figure 5.50
Cutting from the background and pasting back to the original document yields the results in a new layer.

It is probably best to become comfortable with selections and mask use before diving right into Quick Masks. However, there is no compromise in using Quick Masks. The only thing you need to remember to do is save important selections made in Quick Mask mode. Don't let seeing the Quick Mask in the Channels palette fool you into believing it is permanent or saved. Converting to the Standard mode deletes the Quick Mask channel. Be careful to save, and you will quickly become accustomed to using Quick Mask as a tool of choice for working with active selections.

⚠ *If you have trouble seeing your Quick Masks, see "I Can't See the Quick Mask" in the Troubleshooting section at the end of this chapter.*

ISOLATING AN IMAGE AREA: CREATING LAYERS FROM SELECTIONS

Selections isolate image areas, but they don't physically remove them from the surrounding image, and sometimes more complete separation might be necessary to accomplish your goals with an image. Working a little with layers in conjunction with selection offers further options for image manipulation, changes, and revision that are not possible in one layer—or, if possible, require quite a bit of additional effort to complete. Moving selected areas of an image to another layer offers better potential for control, layer blending, and comparison between before-and-after images.

Making a selection and then copying and pasting the results back to the image lets you make image edits without worrying about the surrounding portions of the image. Using this along with Snapshots in the History palette can help you attempt changes in a variety of different ways without opening and saving a number of versions of the image. The technique is simple: Duplicate the isolated image area you want to work with to another layer before making changes. This way you can see how changes blend with the area surrounding the selected one by showing and hiding the layer on the Layers palette, and can easily revert by deleting the layer.

Tip

You can also compare multiple versions of the changes using Snapshots or layer views.

The following steps outline how to move an image area to its own layer using selection:

1. Open an image with an area that you want to alter (see Figure 5.51).

Figure 5.51
Selecting out one of these bottles to alter can add some action to this image and allow the bottle colors to be changed.

2. Make a mask or selection of the area you want to isolate. It doesn't matter how complex the selection is. The selection can be loaded from a saved selection if one is available.

Note

It is often a good idea to use slight feathering or anti-aliasing on a selection that you will be incorporating into other elements so that the image blends at the edges.

→ For more information on feathering, **see** "Feathering Selections," **p. 116**.

3. Copy the image area to a new layer (Cmd-J) [Ctrl+J].

Note

Do not cut the selection as this will remove the original image information from the layer and replace it with the background color.

    4. Alter the image layer or apply effects as desired (see Figure 5.52).

Figure 5.52
Without altering the shape of the bottle at this point, the color can be changed using adjustment layers, and additional selections can be loaded to further control tool applications without having to create complex selections first.

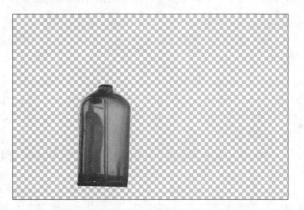

    5. Compare the altered image to the original by simply toggling the visibility option for the layer on the Layers palette.

    6. To retain the layer, save the document as a Photoshop document (psd). To accept the effects, Merge Down (Cmd-E) [Ctrl+E] or Flatten the image. If you saved the mask and did not make shape changes to the information on the layer, you can still load the selection to reselect the area and make further changes even after the image is flattened.

Tip

The only way you can revert to the original state after saving an image with the same name is by using the initial Snapshot from the History palette. After you have closed the image, that initial state will be gone. Saving the second document by a different name (for example, image02.psd) will help you keep track of the versions of any image in sequence as you develop them.

Although color changes described previously could be accomplished without separating the image element, distortion is not often terribly effective in a single layer. Using the Pinch filter (Filter, Distort, Pinch) and two applications of the Wave filter (Filter, Distort, Wave), it was possible to achieve an effect with the bottle that made it appear agitated. The background was duplicated and altered to accommodate the bottle's new shape. Areas behind the new, agitated bottle layer were filled in by cloning from the sky with the Clone Stamp tool. Part of the bottle in the background (just left of the agitated bottle) was re-created from the bottle that was altered, which still remained unaltered in the background layer. Again, the Clone Stamp tool was used to clone that portion of the image.

PART

II

CH

5

→ For more information on repairing images, **see** "Correcting Image Damage," **p. 579**.

Work done to the background image, in the case of this example, was actually done by cloning to a duplicate of the background image. Cloning could have been done to a blank layer as well, and probably would have provided more flexibility (if more memory intensive). In a way, working on duplicate layers or cloning to blanks is similar to putting a portion of the image on its own layer, as it allows you to test an improvement before committing to it.

To make clones between layers, first activate the layer you want to clone from in the Layers palette. Next, click the point you want to clone from. Activate the channel you want to clone to, and, finally, apply the clone.

The bottle top was selected and put in its own layer as well, so it could be positioned easily, regardless of the background. Finally, a slight spritz effect was added to the image in yet another layer. Using layers for image-element separation made creation and placement of these image elements much easier.

→ For more information on using the Clone Stamp tool for cloning, **see** "Working with the Stamp Tools," **p. 206**.

Creating selections around areas to isolate them from their surroundings is one step shy of isolating elements on their own layer as described here. Isolating part of the image to its own layer lets you work on it separately to create effects that would be impossible otherwise, and allows you to alter the background if necessary to match the changes in the foreground elements. Isolate elements to their own layers for better control.

 If you have trouble with isolated elements or composites fitting in well with their surroundings, see "My Composite Images Look Rough" in the Troubleshooting section at the end of this chapter.

COMBINING SELECTIONS

Often making a single selection will get you only part of what you need. You may need to make multiple selections to make the best selection result, and sometimes it will be helpful to subtract one selection from another or intersect to simplify what you are trying to accomplish. The Load Selection command will perform several additional functions that are often helpful in redefining selection areas. When you need a really complicated or creative solution, Calculations may be the way to go.

LOADING SELECTIONS IN COMBINATION

To combine selections, you might need to use different techniques, depending on how you want the selected areas to combine. The simplest method is to load one selection, and then choose Load Selection a second time (see Figure 5.53). Load Selection offers several options for the new selection:

- **New Selection**—Removes current selection.
- **Add to Selection**—Adds to the existing selection.

- **Subtract from Selection**—Subtracts the loaded selection from the current selection.
- **Intersect with Selection**—Keeps only areas of the selection that are common between the selection being loaded and the existing selection.

Figure 5.53
The Load Selection dialog box can be used to choose a selection to load for the current document from any open document. Simply choose the document name (on the Document pop-up) and the available choices will appear in the Channel pop-up for selection.

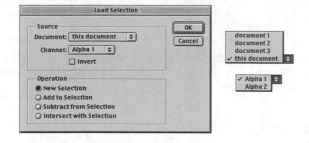

CALCULATIONS FOR COMBINING SELECTIONS

A second possibility is combining selections or channels and masks with Calculations (Image, Calculations) to make another masking channel. Calculations combine channels by predetermined criteria. Controlled use of calculations can accomplish a wide variety of effects and embellishments and will save the step of having to save the result to a new channel. Calculations can create the effects offered in the Load Selection dialog box (Add is Add; Subtract is Subtract; Intersect is Multiply), plus 11 additional effects. The dialog box (see Figure 5.54) offers options for creating the new element (not necessarily a mask) as a New Document, New Channel, or New Selection. Additional control is offered by the capability to select information pertaining to individual layers as well as channels to use in the merge. Each type of calculation produces different results by using different means to combine the channels. Channels can be chosen for calculations from any open image and combined in any fashion—even onto themselves. If the Mask option is checked, yet another channel can be selected from open images to use as a mask for the changes.

PART

II

CH

5

Figure 5.54
The Calculations dialog box offers a lot of choices and can prove to be a challenging tool to master.

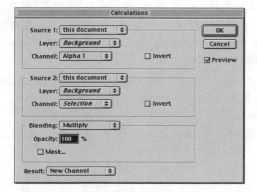

To create a new image element from existing channels with Calculations, follow these steps:

1. Open the image(s) that contain the channels you want to combine.

2. Open the Calculations dialog box (Image, Calculations).

3. Choose a document for the first source (Source 1). The selection list will be limited to open documents.

> **Note**
>
> The documents selected for these steps must be open, but none of the selections has to be from the currently active image. The order in which you make selections for documents can impact the calculations.

4. Choose the layer from the document that reflects the image information you would like considered for the calculation. This list will be limited to those layers in the chosen document. Choosing Merged will use visible information in the document. This selection will default to Merged in a document with more than one layer, or Background (Layer 0) for images that do not have multiple layers.

5. Choose the channel from available list in the Channels pop-up for the first document.

6. (Optional Step) Check the Invert box. This will apply the mask in the calculation as inverted from its current state.

7. Choose the second document (Source 2). This should contain the channel information you hope to use for the second part of the calculation. This can be the same as the first document.

8. Choose the layer from the Layer pop-up menu, which reflects the image information you would like considered for the calculation.

9. Choose the channel from available list in the Channel pop-up menu for the second document.

10. (Optional Step) Check the Invert box.

11. Choose the Blending mode you want to use for combining the selected channels.

→ For more information on blending modes, **see** "Simple Blending Modes," **p. 66**.

12. Select the opacity with which the blending mode should be applied.

13. (Optional Step) Check the Mask box if there is a mask/selection you would like to apply to the calculation. If this box is checked, you will have to make additional selections for Source, Layer, and Channel to define the mask. The mask may also be applied as inverted by checking the Invert box.

14. Choose the destination for the result. This can be a New Channel (in the active image), a New selection (in the active image), or a new document (which will be created as a multichannel document).

15. Select OK. The result will be placed, activated, or created in a new document according to your choice for the result.

Tip

The Preview check box can come in handy when trying to figure out the results of a calculation. Calculations are often too complex to figure out, and the visual aid is a huge help.

Combining channels is simply a way of combining and altering selections. Calculations can be used in refining selections (such as adding together two color selections), creating special effects, or experimenting with images and combinations.

The results of calculations are much more difficult to figure out than to simply try out. The preview button will help with this. I have also created an action (available on the Web site ps6.com, called Calculations Generator) that takes any two channels and creates all 14 effects, so that you can take a look at the options. The result will be basic combinations and reflect only applying channel one to channel two—and in that order. Reversing the order changes the effect in some of the calculations. You can use this to quickly generate a series of calculation possibilities, and then simply browse through them to find the result you need.

To use the Calculations Generator Action:

1. Download the Calculations Generator action from the Web site (ps6.com).
2. Load the action into your Actions palette.

→ For more information on loading an action, **see** "Loading Prerecorded Actions," **p. 267**.

3. Create a new document called Untitled-1 and place the channels you want to experiment with there as channels titled Alpha 1 and Alpha 2.

Note

If you copy one of the channels you want to apply before creating the document, Photoshop makes the new document the size of the image you have in the buffer when you make a new file (File, New). This can simplify the process of making the new document, and will also help ensure the two selections are overlapping properly (Preview might show you some results you do not expect if working with two images that are the same size but different dpi). Getting the images to fit might require resizing the second alpha channel.

4. Select Calculations Generator from the list of actions.
5. Start the action by highlighting the action and clicking Play, or by double-clicking the action's name in the Actions palette.

Depending on the size of the file, the action may take a few moments to complete. When the action is done, browse the results by clicking through the resulting channels.

A sample of the results using the Calculations Generator follows. The two test images (see Figures 5.55 and 5.56) were designed to show a variety of imposition possibilities, and hopefully this helps clarify what each blending mode accomplishes. Looking at the original figures and results in Figures 5.57 through 5.68 gives you a better idea of how each type of calculation might react. You can use the Calculations Generator on any two alpha channels as long as you set them up in a document as previously described.

Tip

I used to try to figure out the calculations, but the number of potential variations just doesn't make it worthwhile. Run the generator and browse—it is a lot easier and quicker. When you find the mask you want, copy it and paste to the document you are working on and just delete the Untitled file. Using the generator will save create multiple Calculation combinations for you. It enables you to compare between several calculation types quickly. When you are done comparing, you can select what you need and just throw away the generated document—which saves you from scrapping all those alphas one at a time.

Figure 5.55
These are the initial alpha channels. Alpha 1 will be used as Source 1 and Alpha 2 as Source 2 for each of the calculations to follow.

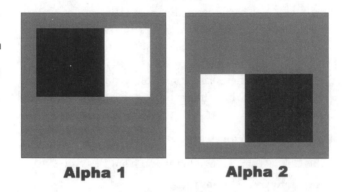

Figure 5.56
Multiply darkens all tonal results by increasing the darkness of the Source 1 based on the darkness of Source 2. No portion of the image can get lighter.

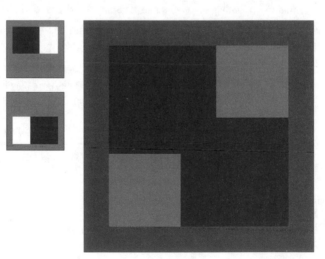

Figure 5.57
Screen brightens the tonal result of Source 1 based on the lightness of Source 2. No portion of the image can get darker.

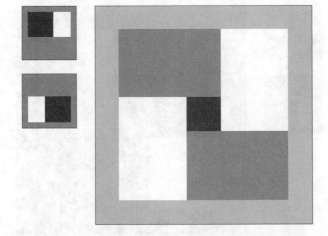

Figure 5.58
Overlay multiplies (darkens) the dark tones and screens (lightens) the light with Source 2 dominant. 50% tones in Source 2 will not affect information on Source 1.

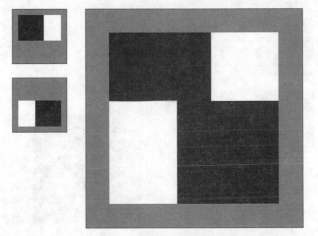

Figure 5.59
Soft Light multiplies (darkens) the dark tones and screens (lightens) the light with Source 2 dominant. 50% tones in Source 2 will average with information in Source 1.

PART

II

CH

5

Figure 5.60
Hard Light multiplies (darkens) the dark tones and screens (lightens) the light with Source 1 dominant. 50% tones in Source 1 will not affect information in Source 2.

Figure 5.61
Color Dodge dodges (lightens) the tone of Source 2 with Source 1, brightening the result. No portion of Source 2 gets darker.

Figure 5.62
Color Burn burns in (darkens) the tone of Source 2 with Source 1, darkening the result. No portion of Source 2 gets lighter.

Figure 5.63
Darken chooses the darker tonal values for each pixel in comparing the two sources. No portion of the result gets lighter than either of the original sources.

Figure 5.64
Lighten chooses the lighter tonal values for each pixel in comparing the sources. No portion of the result gets darker than either of the original sources.

PART

II

CH

5

Figure 5.65
Add takes the tonal value (in levels) of Source 2 and adds it to Source 1. Gray levels equal to or greater than 255 present as white.

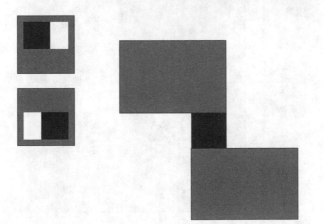

Figure 5.66
Subtract takes the tonal value (in levels) of Source 1 and subtracts it from Source 2. Gray levels equal to or greater than 0 present as black.

Figure 5.67
Difference reacts to difference between source pixel values: large difference yields a bright result, small difference yields a dark result (no difference yields black).

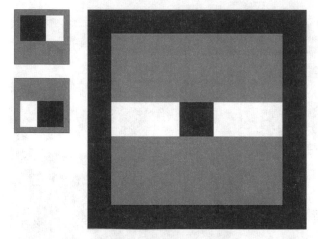

Figure 5.68
Exclusion uses darkness of Source 2 to exclude the Difference effect (described in Figure 5.67). If the Source 2 pixel is dark, there is little change in the Difference result; if Source 2 is black, there is no change in the Difference result; the lighter the tone of Source 2, the more intense the Difference effect.

TROUBLESHOOTING

I Can't Apply the Tool I Am Trying to Work With

I am trying to apply a selection tool to my image, but every time I click, nothing happens.

Although there may be other problems, chances are that if you have selected a tool and can't apply it there is a hidden selection lurking out there somewhere. This selection might be outside the viewing area of the screen, it might be hidden ((Cmd-H) [Ctrl+H] hides the marquee line) or it might be a selection of a low threshold of the image, so that the marquee does not display. To remove the selection, press (Cmd-D) [Ctrl+D]. This will remove the selection.

It may be another problem entirely. If you get an ⊘ when the cursor is over the image, that tells you Photoshop has a reason for not allowing you to apply the tool. Click on the image anyway, and you may get a helpful message that tells you what the problem is.

I Can't See the Quick Mask

When using Quick Mask on a red image, I can't see where the image ends and the mask begins.

Change the mask color so it will show up better against the red image. A bright green would probably work very well. To change the color, double-click the Quick Mask channel. This will open the Quick Mask Options dialog box. Click the color swatch and the Color Picker will open, allowing you to select whatever color you want for the mask. If that isn't enough, you can raise the opacity of the mask color so it stands out more strongly from the image.

My Composite Images Look Rough

When I make a selection and use that to copy and paste portions of one image into another, the pasted portion of the image doesn't blend well into the new background.

Assuming that this refers to the edges of the pasted image and not the composition, there is probably too little or no feathering on your selection. Click the channel for the selection if it is saved and apply a blur to the mask, and then load the blurred mask as the selection; if the selection is active and you don't want to change the mask, apply a feather (Select, Feather). When this selection is used to cut the image area out of the source, it will have softer edges and will probably blend better with what you are pasting it into.

PHOTOSHOP AT WORK: A COMPLICATED SELECTION SCENARIO

There are many methods and tools for selection but they all accomplish the same thing: separation of a portion of the image. Selections can be complex, as in the following example, or simple, requiring a single application of the Marquee or Magic Wand tools—it all depends on what you need to accomplish. If you can understand the principles behind making the selection in this example, you can select just about anything.

For complex selections, you have to take some time and may need to use a variety of tools. The example in this section shows how to make a specific selection, but the tools and techniques can be carried over and used in making many different types of selections.

It is best to follow a sort of order to make sure you make the best selections. First, make a rough general selection; you might find the basic tools are best for this purpose. Next, fine-tune the selection by getting in a little closer and touching up the rough selection. Add and subtract carefully from the selection to bring it in tight on your subject. You might see some areas that need to be altered to achieve an effect in blending or edging. Finally, you may want to soften the selection so the edges are not too harsh—although critical selections may require another level of fine-tuning before moving on to that last step.

Figure 5.69 is an image used in the example that follows. The image is interesting for a variety of reasons. A number of elements might be used in other images; there is room to add to the image and portions can be confined and used for different purposes. The goal for this example will be to cut out the head and gas mask. Get a working copy of the image from the workbook which you can download from `ps6.com`.

Figure 5.69
This selection becomes difficult in some areas because there is not a tremendous amount of separation in color or contrast—especially around the lower portion of the gas mask.

© PhotoDisc, photodisc.com

This is a difficult selection and covers much of the techniques used in real-world design work. Many tools will be utilized for their specific advantages to make the process of selection easier.

Follow these steps to complete this sample selection:

1. Open an image.
2. Crop the image down to the portion you want to work on. This saves file size and confines the amount of the image considered by your tools in making selections.

Tip

Immediately after cropping, save the cropped image separately so you don't accidentally save over the original. It may be smart to save your file as something else as soon as you open it if you know you will be making changes. This will help you avoid accidentally saving over your original.

3. Take a look at the individual color channels to see whether they offer any opportunity to simplify making selections (see Figures 5.70 through 5.72). It might be advantageous to switch back and forth between color channels during the selection process to make portions of the selection.

Figure 5.70
This shows the Yellow channel from the image in Figure 5.69. The channel provides little advantage for selections as the contrast is low and the tone is uneven.

Figure 5.71
The Cyan channel from the image in Figure 5.69 offers better contrast and more even tonality than the yellow channel, but it is a little soft around the edges.

Figure 5.72
The Magenta channel from the image in Figure 5.69 has the best contrast of the three and a nice, hard edge to select. Choices won't always be this easy, and sometimes different channels offer advantages in different areas.

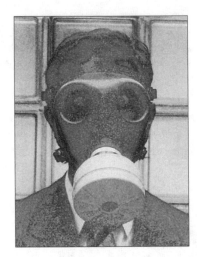

Tip

In versions of Photoshop before the History palette was added, it may have been advised to warn against switching color modes frequently to achieve a selection. However, the image's History palette and Snapshots can return an image to the original state without much fuss, so this type of manipulation is more tolerable.

➔ For more information on working with channels and color separations, **see** "Color Conversions," **p. 485**.

4. Choose a selection tool, set the options, and begin to tighten the selection around the desired area of the image. Continue until you make a satisfactory rough selection (see Figure 5.73).

Figure 5.73
A rough selection of the head area is made with the Magic Wand using the Magenta channel.

Note

For this example, I chose to work with the Magic Wand. I shut off the anti-aliasing and set the tolerance at 40 for selection of the area of the head. After attempting to select both inside the head and the area outside, selecting the area outside the head and inverting seemed slightly more difficult. The selection from inside requires less cleanup.

Tip

Other tools might have worked out just as well—or better. For example, the Magnetic Lasso might have been good for selecting the high-contrast edge while offering the manual control to select the joints for the glass blocks at the same time.

5. Zoom in closer and do some tighter cleanup. For the example, I continued to work with the Magic Wand with lower-tolerance settings.

Note

The channel you are working on is used as the basis for the selection, no matter which channels you are viewing. Be sure to change active channels to the one you are viewing to get the selection you expect (see Figure 5.74).

Figure 5.74
The active channel in the Channels palette will appear highlighted. To highlight a different channel, simply click it with the mouse, or use the keyboard shortcut (which can be seen in each channel of the Channels palette).

6. After you create the rough selection, save it. You should save selections in progress several times throughout the process. Then, save the image as well. To save the selection, convert it to a channel using Save Selection (Select, Save Selection). After you save the selection to a document, you need to save the document; it's a two-step process.

7. After you've roughed in the selection, view the document in color and the mask and alpha channel at the same time to determine what is left to be done. To do this, select the channel visibility in the leftmost column of the Channels palette for the alpha channel as well as the color mode (for example, the RGB or CMYK composite). The eye icon should be on in each channel. The black area of the mask will display as an overlay in the color selected in the Channel Options dialog box. By default this is red and 50% opaque. The areas that still need fine-tuning are evident by red that overlaps the edges of the area you are attempting to select.

Note

To change the color or opacity of the alpha channel, double-click the channel in the Channels palette to open the Channel Options dialog box. Set the color by clicking the swatch and choosing a color from the Color Picker dialog box. To change the opacity, type a new number in the Opacity box. Higher numbers make the mask more opaque. The Opacity affects viewing of the channel only, not application as a selection.

8. Choose the alpha channel for the selection on the Channels palette and begin fine-tuning by painting with your favorite painting tool and a hard-edged brush. If necessary, use selection and masking as appropriate, and change brush sizes as needed. Paint with black to fill in mask areas; paint with white to remove mask where it isn't necessary.

Tip

To toggle the foreground and background color swatches, press X on the keyboard. Go for the obvious discrepancies between the masking channel and head first. Fill in the refinements as you go at greater magnification for better viewing and accuracy.

It may be advantageous to use different tools as you go about your selection; don't just stick with the Magic Wand because it was the first thing you chose. For example, after making the initial selection with the Magic Wand and fine-tuning the upper area, there is a difficult area still to select where the torso meets the gas mask. It's difficult to use the Magic Wand for this. A better choice for making the selection would be the freehand Lasso or the Pen tool.

In Figure 5.75, the Pen tool is used to outline the bottom of the gas mask. You can convert the area to a selection quickly by choosing Make Selection from the Paths palette (see Figure 5.76 and Figure 5.77).

Figure 5.75
The Pen tool controls work well to refine a selection around evenly curved shapes.

Figure 5.76
Choose Make Selection from the Paths palette to convert an active path to a selection.

Figure 5.77
There are options for making a New Selection, Add to Selection, Subtract from Selection, and Intersect with Selection, as well as choices for anti-aliasing and feather radius.

With the path converted to a selection, fill the mask channel with black. This makes the area over the gas mask solid (see Figure 5.78). You could also invert the selection to use in clearing the area below the gas mask using any Paint tool with the foreground set to white. Another method for filling the area would be to use the Lasso to crop the inverted selection to just the torso. Hold down the (Option-Shift) [Alt+Shift] keys and use the Lasso to circle the area of the selection you want to clear. Pressing (Option-Shift) [Alt+Shift] retains only the portion of the current selection that you select with the Lasso.

> **Tip**
>
> Clicking the Default Foreground and Background Colors button on the Tool palette (or pressing the D key) will restore the foreground to absolute white and the background to absolute black.

Touching up noise outside the immediate area of your selection is relatively easy. Instead of going after it dot by dot, select the portion of the mask you are creating that you want to save, invert that, and click Delete. For example, you might use the Magic Wand with a high tolerance and simply click inside the head area. This selects the masked area over the head and gas mask—along with a few stray pixels of noise along the edges. Invert the selection (so you can work in the area outside the head) and erase the rest of the problem area without worrying about the head selection; you can't paint inside the head at this point, so the selection is safe. The result should be your final selection (see Figure 5.79). All that is left to do is feather the selection slightly with a Gaussian blur.

Figure 5.78
After the area of the torso is selected, it can be deleted from the channel (with white as the background color), or it can be painted in with a tool if you need more selective control.

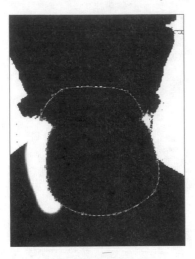

Figure 5.79
The final selection neatly covers the head and mask. This can be loaded as a selection to extract the element from the image, isolate it for changes, or change the background without altering it.

There are numerous variations to selection, and as many methods for selecting. For example, instead of roughing in a selection with the Magic Wand, you can rough in the whole outline with the Magnetic Lasso, use the Pen tool to create the entire path, which you can change to a selection later, or even duplicate the channel that best represents the area you want to select, and then alter that. A highly controlled manual method of selection is to zoom in tight and hold the Shift key down while moving and clicking often along the outline of the area you want to select using a slightly soft Airbrush. The decisions you make should be based on how you like to work with the available tools, what information is in the image, and how easily you can get that image information to work for you.

When you have mastered selection, it is easy to cut out and use selected portions of images in other images or work more selectively on portions of your images. For example, Figure 5.80 was created using the head and gas mask from the previous example. The eyes and hair (and other human features) were removed from the image using selection and erasure. When the gas mask was isolated, it was shaped and altered to fit the meerkat's head. Fine-tuning required burning in inappropriate highlights on the shadow side of the gas mask, and removal of the weasel hair where the straps would wrap around. After that, the gas mask took on a pretty decent fit.

Figure 5.80
Borrowing image elements from one image and placing them in another is a source of creative image development.

© PhotoDisc, photodisc.com

This type of compositing can be easy, as it was in this case (the gas mask fit remarkably well over the meerkat without much resizing), or it can take hours and might be very complex. Either way, selection is the function that makes it possible.

→ For more information on composite images, **see** "Combining Images: Collage and Composites," **p. 703**.

CHAPTER 6

COLOR FILLS AND GRADIENTS

In this chapter

QUICK FILLING WITH PAINT BUCKET

The Paint Bucket tool and Gradient tool are used to create fill areas in your image. The Paint Bucket creates these fills using a single color or pattern. The application is controlled depending on which exact pixel you click in the image—using a process similar to that of the Magic Wand. The areas in which the fill will be applied are determined by a tolerance setting that ranges from 0 to 255. At 0, only the pixels that exactly match the selected pixel are filled with the foreground color or pattern. At 255, almost the entire image is filled. The Tolerance and other Paint Bucket settings, such as Blending mode and Opacity, are controlled in the Paint Bucket Options bar (see Figure 6.1). Turn off the Contiguous setting in the Paint Bucket Options bar to fill every matching pixel in the layer or selection with the fill color, regardless of whether it touches the originally selected pixel. Turn on All Layers to fill every pixel in the image that falls within the tolerance. You can also choose to use either the foreground color for the fill or any available pattern.

Figure 6.1
Here you can set the fill to be anti-aliased so that the edges blend with the surrounding area.

 Having trouble choosing Pattern as an option in the Paint Bucket Options bar? See "Defining and Loading Patterns" in the Troubleshooting section at the end of this chapter.

To use the Paint Bucket tool, select it and click in the image. An area based on the tolerance is filled with either the foreground color or a pattern (see Figures 6.2 and 6.3).

Figure 6.2
A low tolerance fills only areas in which the colors closely match those of the pixel where you click. For this fill, the tolerance was set to 32.

Figure 6.3
A higher tolerance fills large areas of the image. For this fill, the tolerance was set to 64.

⚠ *Do your fills have jagged edges even with the Anti-Aliased option turned on? See "Creating Smooth Fills" in the Troubleshooting section at the end of this chapter.*

PHOTOSHOP GRADIENTS

Gradients are like multicolor swatches that you can use to fill areas of image with color. The appearance of the gradient is controlled by a linear color relationship and the means by which it is applied. These relationships can be created from scratch, loaded from Photoshop defaults, or can be created by editing existing gradients. They can be applied through use of the Gradient Tool, Gradient Map, or through several Layer Styles (Outer Glow, Inner Glow, Gradient Overlay, and Stroke). Gradients can be used to create a variety of common image effects—from backgrounds and shadows to fills, to overlays and color and tonal enhancements (the latter via the Layer Styles and new Gradient Map adjustment tool). They can also be used to affect masks when used in channels and to help create layer blending effects. Careful use of gradients can produce subtle, photorealistic results.

Photoshop's gradient tool enables you to create fills that transition between two or more colors and that also transition between different levels of opacity. Photoshop provides several different gradient libraries that can be loaded and used when creating gradients. In addition, gradients can be customized to add or remove both color and transparency.

USING THE GRADIENT TOOL TO CREATE FILLS

 The Gradient Tool will be the way you will most frequently apply gradients in regular use. The tool has five variations as seen in Table 6.1.

TABLE 6.1 GRADIENT TOOL VARIATIONS

Gradient Tool Variation	Tool Icon
Linear	▣
Radial	▣
Angle	▣
Reflected	▣
Diamond	▣

PART

II

CH

6

All the gradients behave and are applied essentially the same way. With the specific gradient tool selected, and the options set in the Options bar, click and drag in the image. The first point you click determines the starting point of the gradient. The line you drag determines the direction of the gradient, and the length of the line determines the area of transition between the first and the last color (see Figure 6.4). The gradient is completed (or filled in) when you release the mouse button. Tool options on the Options bar allow you to select a blending mode and the opacity of the application as well as allowing control over the direction (reverse), dithering, and transparency of the application.

Figure 6.4
Gradients fill an area based on the start and endpoints you choose and the variation of the tool which you have selected.

As with other Photoshop tools, the options for controlling the creation of gradients and the selection of gradient presets are in the tool's Options bar (see Figure 6.5). Changing options for one gradient type affects all the other gradient types, if you switch to another gradient tool variation. You also can select from an assortment of gradient presets and even create your own.

Opens the
Gradient Picker
Gradient Picker   Menu

Figure 6.5
The Gradient Picker has a pop-up menu as well that allows you to manage the gradients that are available. With it you can load presets or initiate creation of new gradients.

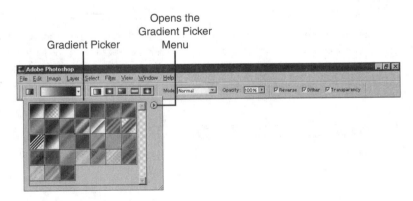

Besides the standard Mode and Opacity options, the three check box options on the Options bar give you greater control over how the gradient is applied. Reverse will run the gradient you have selected in the opposite direction, applying the blend from last color to first from the starting point rather than first to last. Dithering will dither the color to create a smoother blend and reduce banding, which can give a gradient application an undesired stepped appearance, as color changes from one to the next. Transparency turns on or off the transparency built into the blend. If turned off (unchecked), any transparent portions of the blend will be filled in as if you had edited the transparency markers out of the gradient.

 Do your gradients appear to be banding even with the Dither option turned on? See "Adding Noise to Gradients" in the Troubleshooting section at the end of this chapter.

→ For more information about blending modes, **see** "Simple Blending Modes," **p. 66**.

→ For more information about customizing gradients, **see** "Creating Custom Gradients," **p. 166**.

LINEAR GRADIENTS

 The Linear Gradient tool creates a blend between two or more colors that run along a line. Hold down Shift while dragging to constrain the linear gradient to horizontal, vertical, or a 45-degree angle. Horizontal gradients can be used to create a skylike background (see Figure 6.6). Linear gradients at various angles can be used to create dissipating shadows (see Figure 6.7). Linear gradients are also commonly used when creating layer masks (see Figure 6.8).

Figure 6.6
The Clouds filter can be used with a gradient to create a sky effect. In this image, the clouds were added to another layer and set to Screen mode.

Figure 6.7
Shadows created using gradient blends can more effectively fade as they get longer or broader. Creative use of selection combined with gradients can create very effective shadows.

Figure 6.8
When you're creating a layer mask, the length of the gradient determines the amount of mixing between the two layers.

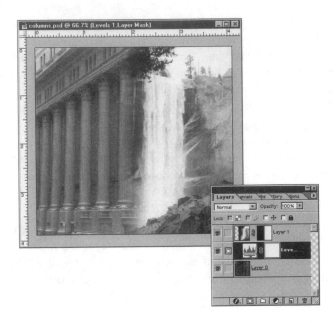

RADIAL GRADIENTS

 The Radial Gradient tool creates a blend between two or more colors in a circular pattern radiating from a center—the initial point you pick for the gradient application. Radial gradients are useful to highlight specific areas of an image (see Figure 6.9) or to create a variety of effects (see Figure 6.10).

Figure 6.9
Working with gradients as backgrounds to selected or isolated image elements can enhance separation of elements and define what is important in an image either subtly or with strength.

Figure 6.10
This image was created by using multiple gradients, applications, and modes.

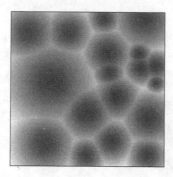

ANGLE GRADIENTS

Angular gradients create a blend between two or more colors in a counterclockwise sweep around the starting point (see Figure 6.11). Used primarily for special effects, angle gradients can be combined with transparency levels and other gradient types with interesting results (see Figure 6.12).

Figure 6.11
When you're using only two colors, angular gradients create a sharp distinction between the colors where they meet. To create a smooth transition in a radial gradient application, use a custom gradient with three colors, with the start and finish colors being the same.

Figure 6.12
By varying the transparency of the gradient at intervals, you can create radial stripes or bursts.

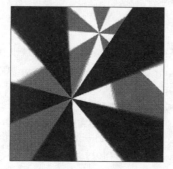

PART

II

CH

6

REFLECTED GRADIENTS

 The Reflected Gradient tool creates symmetrical linear gradients on each side of a starting point. Reflected gradients are most commonly used to create highlights and shadows as they appear on cylindrical objects (see Figure 6.13).

Figure 6.13
Reflected gradients can be used to simulate corrugated materials or cylindrical objects, such as pipes.

DIAMOND GRADIENTS

 The Diamond Gradient tool creates a blend from a starting point outward in a diamond pattern (see Figure 6.14).

Figure 6.14
This is really a simple variation on the Radial gradient that gives a more angled appearance or shape to the gradient as it radiates from center.

CREATING CUSTOM GRADIENTS

You can edit Photoshop's preset gradients or create some of your own. Gradients come in two types: solid gradients, which allow you to control color blends and transparency, and noise gradients, which generate gradient patterns for color and transparency based on randomized generation. When editing solid gradients, you can control both the range of colors that are used and the transparency throughout the gradient. When editing noise gradients, you can control the range from which the random colors are chosen, the roughness, and whether or not the gradient contains randomly generated areas of transparency. Creating either of these gradient types starts in the Gradient Editor, which can be accessed through any gradient view bar—which shows the currently selected gradient. To open the Gradient Editor, simply click the gradient view.

CREATING A GRADIENT WITH THE GRADIENT EDITOR

In the Gradient Editor, the points along the gradient at which a color reaches a maximum and then begins to fade are Color Stops. Similarly, points along the gradient that control the transparency are Opacity Stops. The Gradient Editor shows linear previews of the color and opacity as you edit the gradient by changing color and opacity applications.

Use the following steps to create a solid gradient:

1. Select the Gradient Tool from the Toolbox.

2. In the Options bar, click the currently selected gradient as it appears in the preview box. This will open the Gradient Editor.

3. In the Gradient Editor dialog box, select a gradient to edit from the list by clicking it (the gradient will then appear in the editing preview bar); choose New or click in the Presets box in the field outside the thumbnails (between the thumbnails and the scrollbar, for example) to create a new gradient (see Figure 6.15).

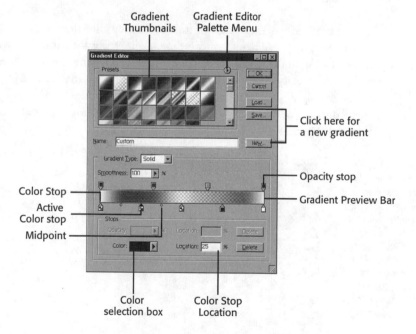

Figure 6.15
You can save your gradients and share gradients with others by choosing Save or Load in the Gradient Editor.

PART
II
CH
6

4. Change the color of the gradient by adjusting, adding, or deleting Color Stops.

   - To add a Color Stop, click below the gradient editor preview bar in the position where you want to enter the Color Stop.

   - To delete a color stop, select the color stop and drag it away from the gradient bar, or click it to highlight and then click the Color/Delete button.

- To change a Color Stop's color, double-click an existing Color Stop to access the Color Picker. You can also choose a color in your image with the Eyedropper tool. If you want to use the foreground or background color as the gradient's start color, choose Foreground or Background from the Colors pop-up menu.

- To change the location of a Color Stop, click and drag the stop or enter a location in the Color/Location field. The field uses a percentage that runs 0%–100% from left to right.

- To change the blend between Color Stops, change the position of the blending midpoint. Photoshop will automatically insert a midpoint for each pair of Color Stops created. Simply click and drag the midpoint, or click the midpoint to highlight it (the midpoint will fill black when highlighted) and enter a number in the Location field. The percentage in this case represents the distance between the two Color Stops left to right as a percentage.

- To duplicate a Color stop, hold down (Option)[Alt] and click-drag on a Color stop.

5. Change the Transparency mask of the gradient by adjusting, adding, or deleting Opacity Stops. You add and remove the Opacity stops the same way you add and remove Color stops, except they are controlled above the Gradient Editor preview bar, not below. Opacity and position are entered using the Opacity and Opacity/Location Stops controls. If you change the opacity, the color of the Opacity Stop changes: Black represents opaque and white represents transparent. Gray values are used for Opacity Stops that are partially transparent (see Figure 6.16).

Figure 6.16
Although gradients will become completely transparent at the point in the gradient where the Opacity Stop is 0%, by placing two Opacity or Color Stops at the same location, you can create distinct edges in your gradient.

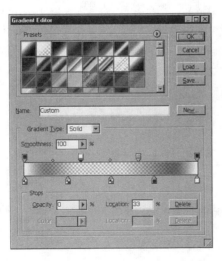

6. To save the gradient you created, click OK, or enter a name for the gradient and click the New button.

Clicking OK will close the Gradient Editor and make the gradient you created available for application using the tool you select. The gradient will also be saved in the Presets so it can be used from other areas where gradients can be applied.

Tip

It is a good idea to save gradients you create by using the Save button in the Gradient Editor. This will save your gradient to a file. If at any time you lose your Photoshop preferences and you have not saved the gradient, it will be lost. Saving it to a file will help you retain the gradient permanently.

NOISE GRADIENTS

 Photoshop 6.0 lets you create gradients based on randomly generated noise. Noise gradients use color range and roughness settings to determine the noise content (see Figure 6.17). These are really just another variation on solid gradients, and they can be used with any gradient shape. You can use noise gradients to create visual effects such as linear static or complex masks.

Figure 6.17
Noise gradients enable you to create organic gradient effects, such as Jacob's ladders, or ripples.

To create a noise gradient, open the Gradient Editor and choose Noise as the Gradient Type. Photoshop will automatically generate the noise pattern and result based on the current settings for Roughness, Color Model, and Options. Increased Roughness adds to the strength of the noise effect; the color model allows you some control over color bands, which will be allowed values. The Restrict Colors option keeps color CMYK compatible, and turning on the Transparency option generates opacity noise as well as color noise. Use the Randomize button to regenerate/resample the noise effect using the same settings.

CREATING GRADIENT BACKGROUNDS

Gradients are often useful in providing an uncluttered, but contrasting, background with a foreground object. More interesting than flat backgrounds, a gradient background can be

PART

II

CH

6

used to focus the viewer's attention on a particular part of the image (see Figure 6.18). It also can be used as a replacement for missing or damaged backgrounds.

Figure 6.18
Use a radial or diamond gradient to focus on a specific area of an image.

To create a gradient background, carefully select and isolate the foreground object. You can use traditional selection techniques or the Extract command. After the foreground object is selected, copy and paste it onto its own layer. Use the gradient tool to fill the Background layer behind the object. You can experiment with different fills until you achieve the effect you want (see Figure 6.19).

→ For more information on creating a selection to isolate image areas, **see** "Isolating an Image Area," **p. 137**.

Figure 6.19
When creating a gradient background, be sure to select colors and a gradient direction that provide sufficient contrast with the foreground object.

TROUBLESHOOTING

DEFINING AND LOADING PATTERNS

I would like to apply a pattern fill but when I choose the Paint Bucket tool there are no patterns available (the box is gray, and there is nothing in the preset manager for Patterns). How do I make patterns available so I can use part of an image I already have in mind as a pattern?

In order to fill with a pattern using the Paint Bucket or the Fill command, you need to have at least one pattern in the Patterns Presets. Photoshop has several pattern sets that you can load by choosing the pattern set from the pattern menu (off the pattern selection menu) or by using the Preset Manager. To load in one of Photoshop's presets using the Preset Manager, choose Edit, Preset Manager, and then choose Patterns. Use the Load button and then browse to find the default patterns in Photoshop's Presets folder, or choose a preset from the bottom of the menu. These new sets can also be appended to your existing patterns, if you have any, in the same way.

To define a new pattern, use the Rectangular Marquee tool to select an area of any image and choose Edit, Define Pattern. This will automatically create the pattern and store the thumbnail. Remember to Save the pattern set so that your new pattern will be saved if you want to keep it.

CREATING SMOOTH FILLS

I used anti-aliasing when I did a Paint Bucket fill and now I want to get more of a blend. Is there any way I can do that?

Instead of just using the Paint Bucket tool to apply the fill directly, use the Magic Wand to select the area that you want to fill, and then feather the selection. After the selection is made, just choose Select, Feather, and enter a radius for the feathering to create a broader blend. After the selection is feathered, create a new layer and apply the fill to the layer with the selection active. Putting the fill on a second layer will let you adjust the blending and will give you better control over how the fill will affect the image.

ADDING NOISE TO GRADIENTS

After creating a blend, it still seems stepped or banded and I can tell where the colors change. Is there any other way to improve these results?

If your gradients appear banded (there isn't a smooth transition between colors), you can select the area that appears banded or the entire area of the fill and choose Filter, Noise, Add Noise. Small amounts with a Uniform distribution usually work best. If a gradient application proves particularly difficult, you may want to fill the gradient in its own layer and use multiple applications of noise and blur to smooth out the results. If you are still not satisfied, you may want to take a look at what you are trying to accomplish in the blend and alter it so that you will achieve better results.

PHOTOSHOP AT WORK: CREATING A CHROME EFFECT ON TEXT

Metallic effects are often difficult to produce quickly in Photoshop. There are, however, gradient presets you can use to create simple metallic fills. This exercise will lead you through creation of a metallic effect that is relatively easy to apply.

1. Begin by creating an image with a black background. You can use this effect with other backgrounds, but it works best against black or dark backgrounds.

2. Create text in your image (see Figure 6.20).

Figure 6.20
You may also want to use some layer effects on the text you create. In this image, a small inner bevel was applied.

3. Choose Layer, New, Layer, and check the Group with Previous box in the Layers dialog box before choosing OK to close it. This creates a clipping group so that the gradient you create is seen only on the text.

4. Select the Linear Gradient tool in the Tool palette.

5. Be sure the default gradient set is loaded. Specifically, you will need the Chrome Gradient or Copper Gradient. You can either do this through the Preset Manager or by selecting the preset group from the Gradient Picker menu.

Tip

To check the preset list by name, you can change the display to Text Only, Small List, or Large List by selecting the desired display option from the Gradient Picker menu. Any of these will display the names of the gradients.

6. Select the Linear Gradient tool in the Tool palette. In the Options bar, choose Chrome as the gradient type. You can also choose the Copper gradient preset if you prefer.

7. Click near the top of the text and drag down while holding down the Shift key (the Shift key will keep the drag line vertical). When you release the mouse button, the layer you created in Step 3 will fill with the Chrome gradient, which will appear clipped by the text layer below it. The result is a metallic-type fill over the letters (see Figure 6.21).

Figure 6.21
You can experiment with the top, bottom, and midpoints of the metallic fill until you achieve the effect you want. You can also edit the chrome and copper presets and use different colors in the fill. Application of filters for distortion (such as Wave) may improve the effect.

Paths: Bézier Tools for Creating Vector Effects

In this chapter

VECTOR EFFECTS IN PIXEL IMAGES

Vectors are perhaps the primary imaging mechanism in popular drawing programs such as Illustrator. Photoshop is a pixel-based, photographic image editor, so there might seem little use for vectors. However, vectors can be used to help manage the distribution of pixels in a different way from—and in conjunction with—other Photoshop tools (notably masks and selections). Just as there is a difference between using various color correction tools, using vectors has distinct advantages and disadvantages over using pixel-based techniques in performing tasks—and sometimes they simply offer an alternative, which might be preferable to some users.

Note

A number of terms are used almost interchangeably and in conjunction when discussing vectors and vector tools, including Bézier (tools, curves, and paths), curves, paths, vectors, pen tools, line and anchor, and more. These are all the same thing. It can get confusing in that several of these terms (curves, paths) can have another meaning within and without the context of vector use. Attempts have been made to simplify this as much as possible in this discussion.

A *vector* is simply a mathematically described line or curve. Although these elements are mathematically described, little or no math is involved in using them—or no more than using other Photoshop tools. The shape, or path, of the vector is defined by anchor points and control handles that you use to shape and position the curves (see Figure 7.1).

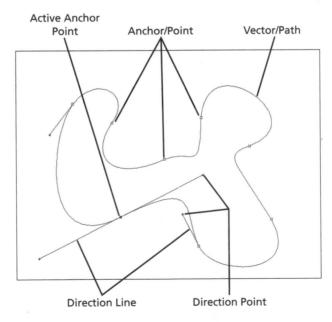

Figure 7.1
This shape was drawn with the Pen tool by placing anchor points and dragging direction lines. Anchor points are placed with the Pen tool by simply moving the cursor and clicking the mouse. To create a direction line, click the mouse, hold down the button, and drag.

Active Anchor Point

Anchor/Point

Vector/Path

Direction Line

Direction Point

One distinct thing to note about vector paths is that they exist independent of the image resolution. You can draw a curve in an image and resize the image up or down dramatically without affecting the curve's quality and shape—although resizing an image might have a dramatically different effect on the pixels in the image. You can also resize and reshape vectors easily, without having to disturb or supplant other parts of the image. Figure 7.2 shows the vector shape from Figure 7.1 at the original size and ten times larger, but with the screen view scaled down so the shapes appear to be the same size. Filling either of these with black produces very different results in pixels although the shape remains the same.

Figure 7.2
The series on the left shows the original vector and the right the vector at ten times the size. Any visible difference in the path is due to the positioning of the element in the video projection grid. Each series shows the vector, the vector and fill together, and finally the fill result alone. The fill result is actually the mask equivalent of the path.

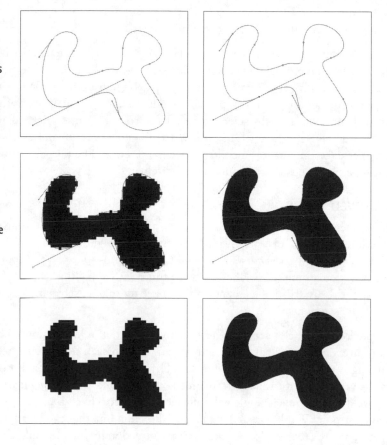

Vectors perform a number of tasks within images. They can act as clipping layers and clipping paths, they can be used to define masks and selections, and they can be stroked and filled with painting tools. By nature they are great for reproducing complex curve selections and making smooth selection lines where your freehand selection with the Lasso or other tools never seems to be controlled or adjustable enough. Generally, it is another way of managing selection and the shape of image elements, and, in fact, the shape of the image itself.

CREATING VECTOR PATHS WITH THE PEN TOOL

 The Pen tool is used to create vector paths, and is one of two ways to create paths. Working with the Pen tool, if you haven't done it before in an illustration program, is something you might need to get used to. Really, it is as simple as doing dot to dots, but with a little twist in creating curves. To create a path with the Pen tool, select the Pen tool from the Tool palette, click to place an anchor point, move the Pen, and click again. A line will be drawn between the two anchor points defining the vector you have created. The vector and anchor points are not part of the visible image, and they won't print out. What will happen is that the elements will be added to the current Work Path, found in the Paths palette. This path is created automatically when you begin using the tool.

To hide the path you have drawn, either click another path in the paths palette (this will make the path you clicked on visible), click below the list of paths in the palette to deactivate all paths, or select Turn Off Path in the Paths palette pop-up menu. When the path is removed from view, it is not lost, but stays hidden as the current Work Path, much like an inactive channel. If saved (by selecting Save Path from the Paths palette pop-up menu when the path is active), the path will be given a default name (Path #) and will be stored in the Paths palette for the image, much like a channel or layer. The purpose of saving is to allow multiple paths to be activated and used separately in one image.

MAKING CURVED PATHS

Paths, as mentioned, can be created as curves, also. This saves a lot of time rather than attempting to draw a curve by creating a number of straight segments. Because the vector represents a mathematical curve, they tend to be smooth—or at least smoother than they would be if you attempted to draw the same thing with straight segments. Curves will help you shape paths to existing elements in the image more precisely with less work than using straight line segments.

To create a curve, click to create a new anchor point, but hold the mouse button down and drag. A direction line will appear—actually two, one to each side of the anchor point, in equal length and proportion. The direction line can be lengthened or shortened and angled from the anchor point to change the direction of the vector. The longer the direction line, the more its direction and angle will influence the vector. Each time you click and drag, a new anchor point will be created with a new direction line that can be adjusted to influence the path you are creating. When you drag the direction line, you should drag it in the direction you want the curve to continue in. Each time you click to create a new anchor point, the previous anchor point will become inactive, but the direction line you dragged from the anchor point will remain visible until you set another anchor point. This allows you to see the influence all direction lines have on the active portion of the path while you continue to draw.

TIPS FOR DRAWING VECTOR PATHS

While drawing paths, a few shortcuts might come in handy. First, holding down the Shift key will place the next point horizontally, vertically, or at 45° angles to the previous point depending on where the cursor is located. Second, holding down the (Option)[Alt] key while creating an anchor point allows you to create an angled juncture at the anchor point. The direction lines will be able to be controlled independently (see Figure 7.3).

Figure 7.3
Holding down the (Option)[Alt] key when creating a new anchor point creates only the forward direction line. Placement of anchor points and direction lines of the same intensity and angle have very different effects. Hold (Option)[Alt] when you want an angle at the anchor point, and simply continue to place anchor points by click-dragging when you want to draw smooth curves.

Click and drag   Click and drag holding (Option) [Alt]

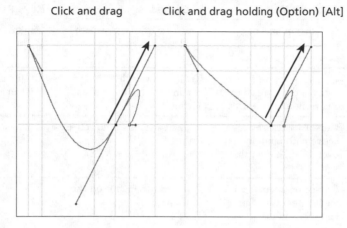

Paths can be edited while you draw them. In other words, you can go back two anchor points or more, activate the anchor point you want to move or adjust, make changes to the position and/or direction lines, then return to the anchor point you were working on, and continue drawing. To make these changes, you will want to change temporarily to the Direct Selection tool to select the anchor to change. You can use this to select the anchor points, move them, and adjust the direction lines. Toggle to the Direct Selection tool temporarily and hold down the (Cmd)[Ctrl] key. To switch to the Direct Selection tool, press A on the keyboard. You might have to press (Shift-A)[Shift+A] to toggle between the Direction Selection tool and the Path Component Selection tool. The latter will require changing back to the Pen tool by pressing P to continue drawing, but it might be a better choice if there are a lot of anchors to arrange.

Adobe has helped the user out quite a bit by making the Pen tool act and react in a context-sensitive manner. This cuts down on the number of times you have to change the tool. If you keep in mind the two keyboard toggles, you probably won't have to change Pen tools at all. (Cmd)[Ctrl] changes the Pen to the Direct Selection tool and (Option)[Alt] changes the pen to the Convert Point tool. The way the context sensitivity works depends on where the cursor is on the screen—for example, close to or on an active or inactive path—the cursor will change the tool function. This can be overridden with the shortcuts mentioned. A list of the cursors, the state that causes them to appear, and each of their actions appear in Table 7.1.

TABLE 7.1   CONTEXT-SENSITIVE PEN TOOL CURSORS AND ACTIONS

Cursor	Appears When	Action If Mouse Is Clicked	Keys Required
	No current anchor exists and cursor is not over a path or anchor.	Creates start of a new path by placing an anchor.	Can be chosen by pressing P when no path is active.
	Cursor is not near paths and anchors, but a current anchor exists.	Creates new anchor to continue path from current anchor.	Can be chosen by pressing P when a path is active.
	Cursor passes over an active path but not over an anchor on that path.	Adds an anchor to the active path.	
	Cursor passes over an anchor that is not an endpoint on the active path.	Removes the anchor on the active path.	
	Cursor passes over the end of a path which is not the current anchor.	If the current anchor exists (has not been deleted or deactivated), the current and the selected point will join. If the current anchor does not exist, the anchor selected will become the current anchor.	
	Cursor passes over the current anchor.	Selects the current anchor and allows Adjustment (length and direction) of the leading direction line of a smooth anchor. The trailing arm changes direction accordingly.	
	Cursor passes over the current anchor or an active path while holding down the (Option) [Alt] key.	Selects the current anchor and allows adjustment (length and direction) of the leading direction line of a corner anchor point. The trailing direction line remains unaffected.	

TABLE 7.1 CONTINUED

Cursor	Appears When	Action If Mouse Is Clicked	Keys Required
	Cursor passes over the anchor on the opposite end of the path that contains the current anchor.	Closes the path by joining the current anchor back to the beginning of the path.	
	Moving a direction point or anchor.	Adjusts the direction line according to the movement of the mouse. Also indicates movement of selected paths and Anchor points.	
	Cursor passes over an anchor that is not the beginning or end point of an active path, while holding down the (Option) [Alt] key.	Removes (Option)[Alt] influence of anchor direction lines or end point forming an angled anchor with no direction lines. Continuing to hold the mouse click and dragging will create smooth anchor controls.	
	Holding down (Cmd)[Ctrl].	Allows selection of anchors and direction points. This is the same as the Direct Selection tool.	(Cmd)[Ctrl] To choose the Direct Selection tool: Press [A] (A) and (Shift-A) [Shift+A] as necessary.
	Holding down (Cmd-Option) [Ctrl+Alt] when a path or anchor is below the cursor.	Allows selection of a path to duplicate.	(Cmd–Option) [Ctrl +Alt].
	Holding down (Cmd-Option) [Ctrl+Alt] when no path or anchor is below the cursor.	Indicates there is no path to select for duplication. This looks but does not act the same as the Path Component Selection Tool.	(Cmd–Option) [Ctrl +Alt] To choose the Path Component Selection tool: (Shift-A) [Shift+A] as necessary.
	Moving duplicated paths.	Indicates duplicated path has moved.	
	Path being moved snaps to. Will appear only after path duplication or selection and movement of a path with the Path Component Selection tool.	Indicates moving path has snapped to successfully.	

The current anchor point is the anchor point from which any new path segment will be drawn. Usually, it is the last anchor point created, although it can be an anchor point that has been changed to the current anchor by selection if that anchor point is an end point. Selected anchors are shaded. Active paths have visible anchor points (shaded or not).

By controlling placement of anchor points and whether the anchor points are corner or smooth point, you can create vectors that fit any shape. Although we've seen a number of tools here already for the construction of paths, there are more. Two other Pen tools offered on the Tool palette are the Freeform Pen and Magnetic Pen. These have been combined in Photoshop 6 and they work a little differently from the basic Pen tools, although the result is still a work path.

The Rubber Band Option

The Rubber Band option on the Tool Options bar for the Pen tool draws a preview path onscreen between the last anchor placed and the tip of the pen (see Figure 7.4). This can help two things while you are using the tool. First, it continuously shows you what the vector result will be based on the placement of the cursor created. Second, it serves as a reminder to let you know that you still have to place a point to complete the path and that the tool is still in an active anchor-placing mode. This really doesn't affect the function of the tool; however, it is really just a selection of personal preference. Use it if you like to see the Pen connected to its active path.

Figure 7.4
The Rubber Band option for the Pen tool keeps the path continuous from the initial anchor placement to the Pen tip until the path is terminated. Paths can be terminated either by closing the path (returning to the origin) or making it inactive (clicking the Direct Selection or Path Component Selection tool off the path).

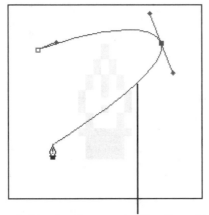

Rubber band connecting Pen tip and last Anchor

OTHER PEN TOOLS AND OPTIONS

 The Freeform Pen tool is the tool to select from the Tool palette for using either the Freeform or Magnetic Pen. These can be selected with the P or (Shift-P) [Shift+P] shortcut as well. After the tool is selected, the Magnetic option can then be turned on in the Options bar (see Figure 7.5).

Figure 7.5
The Options bar presents in three different states for the Freeform and Magnetic Pens. The first and second bars show options for paths before you start creating them: Create New Work Path and Create New Layer Shape. Before you create a path, you can toggle these buttons. The third bar shows the change in the options after you start creating the path by placing anchors.

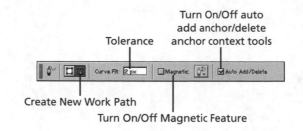

Tolerance

Turn On/Off auto add anchor/delete anchor context tools

Create New Work Path

Turn On/Off Magnetic Feature

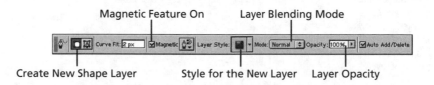

Magnetic Feature On

Layer Blending Mode

Create New Shape Layer

Style for the New Layer

Layer Opacity

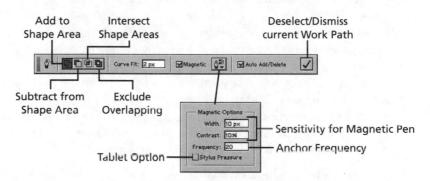

Add to Shape Area

Intersect Shape Areas

Deselect/Dismiss current Work Path

Subtract from Shape Area

Exclude Overlapping

Sensitivity for Magnetic Pen

Anchor Frequency

Tablet Option

The Freeform Pen allows the user to draw a vector, and upon completion (letting go of the mouse) Photoshop creates the path and anchor points based on the vector (see Figure 7.6). This gives the user flexibility and speed in creating some potentially difficult paths. Simply select the tool, choose your options, click the mouse, and draw the line of any shape—while attempting to follow an outline or not. Photoshop fills in the anchor points and direction lines. The idea here is you get to draw completely freeform, without the hassles of following an outline (if you don't want to) or placing anchor points and direction lines.

The Magnetic Pen option for the freeform tool works much like the Magnetic Lasso. As you draw a freehand path, Photoshop detects edges in the image based on Options bar settings for the tool and draws a line that attempts to cling to the edge that it sees. It is really a semiautomatic means of placing anchor points and curves along an obvious edge. The advantage over the Freeform Pen is that as long as the settings are right and the edge is defined, you can get a resulting path that is reasonably close to tracing existing image edges.

PART
II

CH
7

Figure 7.6
After the movement of the Freeform tool from left to right, Photoshop places anchor points based on the tolerance setting to define the curve as closely as possible. Even if these freehand paths are rough, they can be adjusted. Depending on the path application, this can be a great timesaver.

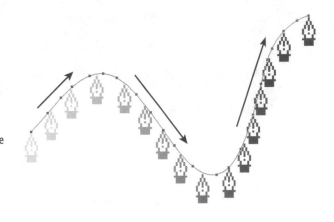

The reason I say it is semiautomatic is that you can switch the Magnetic option on and off as you go, and you have control over the placement of additional anchors. To turn on the Magnetic option, click the Magnetic check box in the Options bar after selecting the Freeform tool (see the Options bars shown earlier in Figure 7.5). Simply press the mouse button and run the cursor over the edge you want the Magnetic Pen to cling to as it draws. You can place additional anchor points by pressing the (Option) [Alt] key at any time. Holding down (Option) [Alt] toggles temporarily to the Freeform Pen tool (in other words, it turns off the Magnetic option). Pressing (Cmd-click) [Ctrl+click] will finish the path by closing it from wherever the cursor is currently. It will follow the Options bar settings in creating that path but will do so in as direct a line as possible.

The tool's controls are based on contrast and are adjusted using the Magnetic Options. The controls can be opened by clicking the Magnetic Pen tool icon on the Options bar after checking the Magnetic check box (see Figure 7.5). The preferences include Width, Contrast, and Frequency (outlined in the list that follows), and there is a check box for Stylus Pressure. The *Stylus Pressure* option will be available only if you are using a graphics tablet. When checked it enables you to use stylus pressure to control edge tolerance.

- **Width**—Refers to the area, or pixel radius, which the tool considers in choosing the best place to place the vector. This number is a pixel value and must be between 1 and 40.

- **Contrast**—Allows control over the sensitivity to contrast in the image. The higher the number, the greater the contrast must be for the consideration of vector placement. Values for Contrast are in percentage and must be between 1 and 100.

- **Frequency**—Gives the tool a relative frequency for placing anchors automatically. A higher number places anchors more frequently; the number must be between 5 and 100.

Tip

When drawing with the Magnetic Pen tool, attempt to stay as close as you can to the edge you want to outline. Although the tool can seemingly automatically trace an outline, it can't read minds.

The advantage of the Magnetic Pen is that it can help you quickly place a rough outline for a shape around even difficult objects quickly. You can always go back and adjust these later, and you will save some time in creating anchor points and direction lines, as most of that work will be done for you.

PATH MANAGEMENT

Paths are stored in the Paths palette, which performs a number of useful functions in helping you manage and apply the paths that you create. Photoshop 6 also has new features for combining and aligning path segments. These new tools can help you limit the need for performing some tasks in other illustration programs.

THE PATHS PALETTE

The Paths palette, like the Layers palette and Channels palette, is a powerful control center for the management of paths, although it is perhaps much simpler than either the Layers or the Channels palettes (see Figure 7.7). The palette's pop-up menu provides access to path functions (see Table 7.2).

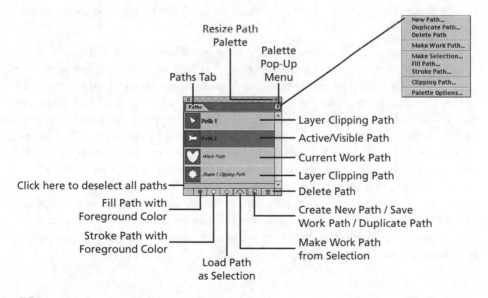

Figure 7.7
The Paths palette shows all the paths created and stored in the current image. These paths include saved paths, the current Work Path, and any active layer clipping paths, where the layer is the active layer.

TABLE 7.2   THE PATHS PALETTE POP-UP MENU FUNCTIONS

Pop-Up Menu Item	Function	Available When
New Path	Creates new saved path	Always
Duplicate Path	Creates duplicate saved path from currently active (highlighted) path	A path is active
Delete Path	Deletes path from image and palette	A path is active
Make Work Path	Creates a Work Path from a selection	A selection is active
Make Selection	Creates a selection from the active path	A path is active
Fill Path	Fills a path area with the Foreground color	A path is active
Stroke Path	Strokes a path with the last brush selected	A path is active
Clipping Path	Assigns a clipping path for the image	A path exists (active or inactive)
Palette Options	Allows user to pick thumbnail viewing options for the Paths palette (None, Small, Medium, and Large)	Always

Palette menu items will become active and inactive as conditions within the image change.

As new paths are added to the palette, they are added in number order by default. New paths appear at the bottom of the list of saved paths. The Work Path and layer clipping path will appear below the saved paths if they exist. The saved paths can be reordered in the palette as per your preference, although ordering really has no effect on their use as it does with layers or the color channels.

The Work Path is really a somewhat different animal when it comes to Photoshop—coming somewhere between a channel and a selection as far as its existence and temporary status are concerned. The Work Path is where you build paths before saving them as paths in the image. Elements in the Work Path are sometimes dropped without warning if you create a new Work Path—much like an active selection will be dropped if you create a new selection without holding down a modifier key. The Work Path can be deceiving as it gives the appearance of permanence: It is saved with the image, and can be re-employed after closing and opening the image again, unlike selections (that are not saved to channels). However, if you are using the Direct Selection or Path Component Selection tool, click in the palette's empty area to deselect the current path, and add a new anchor point; the subpaths that were in the Work Path will be gone. You can recall them with Undo or the History palette. There is only one Work Path, but there can be many saved paths and layer clipping paths (although only one layer clipping path will appear in the Paths palette at a time).

If you are having some trouble with paths mysteriously disappearing, see "Hey, Where'd That Path Go!?" in the Troubleshooting section at the end of this chapter.

The Work Path is for the most part just a semipermanent selection; unless you save it as a path, it can be lost if you inadvertently replace it. Unlike selections, you can make it inactive without saving it and it just goes into hiding (although the new Reselect function for selections is almost the same as it recalls the last selection). Be careful to save the paths you want to keep, just like you save important selections as channels.

To simplify the perception of working with paths, you should probably think of them simply as an alternative to hard-edged selections. The advantage is that you can adjust the shape of the borders using the anchor point placement and direction lines. The fact is that paths and selections can be readily interchanged using the Paths palette functions.

INTERCHANGING PATHS AND SELECTION

 Paths can be turned into selections and selections can be turned into paths by using the Paths palette. To turn a selection into a path, simply make the selection and either choose Make Work Path from the Paths palette pop-up menu, or click the Make Work Path from Selection button at the bottom of the Paths palette. Choosing from the menu will open the Make Work Path dialog box. The only choice you have here is to adjust Tolerance, which controls the amount of leeway Photoshop has in creating the path. With higher resolution images this value can be somewhat lower. Lower tolerance places fewer points with smoother curves and takes less time (sometimes a lot less, depending on the size of the image). When you choose OK, elements currently in the Work Path (if any) will be discarded and replaced by the new path. The path will approximate the 50% line for the selection over gradient areas; that is, the selection as it appears in outline on the screen will be what Photoshop will try to approximate. Before the Path is created, it can be edited using the Pen tools and selection tools.

> **Tip**
>
> It is recommended that you not view the selection as a saved channel or a Quick Mask version of the selection to understand how it will look when converted to paths. The dotted selection line (marching ants) will give you the best preview of the path that will be generated.

To make a path into a selection, choose one of the paths you have created and want to convert (this can be either a saved path, the Work Path, or a layer clipping path), then choose either Make Selection from the Paths palette pop-up menu, or click the Load Path As Selection button at the bottom of the palette. Choosing from the menu will open the Make Selection dialog box. You can enter a Feather Radius (between 0 and 250 pixels), make the selection anti-aliased or not, and choose make a New Selection, Add to Selection, Subtract from Selection, or Intersect with Selection. The last three options exist only if a selection is currently active in the image. When the selection is made, both the path that created it and the selection will appear onscreen in the image. You can hide the path by clicking the Dismiss Target Path button on the Options bar if the Direct Selection, Path Component Selection, or Pen tool is selected, or by clicking in the Paths palette below existing paths. After the selection is made, it can be saved and edited like other selections.

→ For more information on manipulating selections, **see** "Selection and Masking," **p. 93**.

CLIPPING PATHS AND LAYER CLIPPING PATHS

Clipping paths and layer clipping paths are very similar things, except in scale. Clipping paths serve to shape an entire image. If an image is sent in the proper format (TIFF, EPS, or DCS) to a PostScript device for printing, the clipping path will act as a cookie cutter to slice away the image area outside the path. The result will be that the image will imprint with the shape of the clipping path over anything below it in a layout page. Effectively, this changes the output shape of the image from the usual rectangle to the shape of the clipping path.

Note

Some layout programs such as QuarkXPress or Adobe InDesign have the capability to shape image boxes so they can act like clipping paths. This can be a viable alternative to using clipping paths.

A layer clipping path does essentially the same thing as a clipping path, but the Layer clipping path acts only on a layer or clipping group. Also, you can see the results of a layer clipping path in the Photoshop image, but not the result of the clipping path as there is no preview.

To assign a path as a clipping path, create the path, then select clipping path from the Paths palette menu, and choose the path from the Path pop-up menu (see Figure 7.8).

Figure 7.8
In addition to picking the path, you have the option of entering a Flatness value.

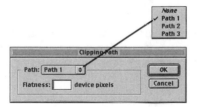

Note

Flatness acts somewhat like Tolerance when creating a path from a selection, but it does this on output of the image. Higher numbers can cause more variance while increasing the speed of printing. Smaller numbers keep more closely to the original path. The value must be between .2 and 100, but you can leave the field blank and the value will be selected for you. If choosing a value, it should probably be about 8 or less.

A layer clipping path can be inserted in several ways. I'll mention two here. The first method is as follows:

1. Choose the Pen tool and click the Create New Shape Layer button on the Tool Options bar.
2. As you draw a shape with the Pen, a new layer will be created with the path you are working on as the layer clipping path, and it will be filled with the foreground color.

This method works in a similar way with the shape tools (see the section on the Shape tools later in this chapter). The only real difference is that you choose one of the shape tools to create the path rather than the Pen tool.

The second method is to assign a path you create to an existing layer:

1. Create the layer you want to use.
2. Create the path you want to clip the layer with. Be sure the layer is active.
3. Activate the path (these might already both be active if they were the last items you were working on in the Layers and Paths palettes, respectively).
4. Choose Layer, Add Layer Clipping Path, Current Path. This will assign the path as a layer clipping path for the layer.

You can continue to adjust and edit clipping paths and layer clipping paths as you wish.

Note The layer clipping path might not be visible if the layer which contains it is not active. Simply choose the layer that contains the layer clipping path and it will appear in the Paths palette.

ALIGNING PATH SEGMENTS

The capability to align path segments is new to Photoshop 6. Paths can be aligned relative to one another, but all subpaths must all be in the same path (Work Path, layer clipping paths, or saved paths). Two or more segments can be aligned and three or more can be distributed vertically according to top edges, centers, or bottom edges, and horizontally according to left edges, centers, or right edges. Figure 7.9 shows the Options bar for the Direct Selection and Path Component Selection tools.

Alignment can come in very handy for some tasks. For example, say you wanted to align a bunch of paths so they were evenly spaced over a few inches. Doing this is easy with the path alignment tools. Just create the paths, move one to the leftmost position, one to the rightmost position, and then click the appropriate buttons to indicate how you want the items to distribute. In this way, you save a lot of painstaking measuring and tedious alignment.

Figure 7.10 shows this example with 14 spindle-shaped path segments. The paths were created from a single segment by duplication (using the Path Component Selection tool and the (Option) [Alt] key along with click and drag). Without bothering to vertically align the paths, one segment was selected as the start and one as the end and they were placed to control the alignment of the other segments. After placing those two, the segments were all selected, and then distributed horizontally on center and then vertically to create a cascade.

Figure 7.9
The Direct Selection and Path Component Selection tool options have a number of useful features not previously available in Photoshop for management of paths, including alignment and combining. Combining is discussed in the next section of this chapter.

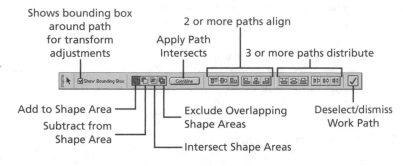

Shows bounding box around path for transform adjustments

2 or more paths align

Apply Path Intersects

3 or more paths distribute

Add to Shape Area

Subtract from Shape Area

Exclude Overlapping Shape Areas

Intersect Shape Areas

Deselect/dismiss Work Path

Figure 7.10
A single spindle from a proposed banister is duplicated and then aligned using the Distribute function for the paths. When the resulting cascade is finished, the addition of a wood grain and a few extra pieces completes the effect.

The wood grain was incorporated using a grouped layer that was filled with one of the provided Photoshop patterns and angled for the direction of the wood. Bevel and Emboss styles were applied separately to the spindles and the other wood.

 If you try this type of cascade effect and don't get the results you expect, there could be a problem with the ordering you created with the paths. See "Getting the Right Alignment" in the troubleshooting section.

COMBINING AND INTERSECTING PATH SEGMENTS

 The spindle in the previous example was created using shapes, the Align buttons, and the Combine function. Combine is also new for Photoshop 6. This feature is available with the Path Component Selection tool on the Options bar and allows you to draw multiple objects in a path and then use them interactively to reshape the result. There are four functions: Add to Shape Area, Subtract from Shape Area, Intersect Shape Area, and Exclude Overlapping. Generally, these work like combining selections, almost identically to the Load Selection options that appear when you load a selection and one already exists. You will see a slight difference in that multiple objects can interact at one time as paths and only two selections can interact (as selections).

Path objects interact in stacking order—that is, they interact according to the order in which they were created. Their combining properties are selected before you start creating them, but these can be changed. To assign the combining properties, Select the Pen tool and click the button on the Options bar for the property you want your path to have. The properties can be changed at any time by selecting the object with the Direct Selection tool (toggle from the Pen by pressing (Cmd) [Ctrl]) to highlight it and then click the property you want to change to.

The stacking order can be rearranged by cutting and pasting the path objects; every time you paste an object back in, it becomes the topmost object.

- **Add to Shape Area**—Will combine the selected path into a single outline with the path below.
- **Subtract from Shape Area**—Will subtract the current path shape from the path below.
- **Intersect Shape Area**—Will retain only the common area between the current path and the path below.
- **Exclude Overlapping Shape Area**—Will retain everything except where the two paths overlap. As objects are added to the path, each new object interacts with the final result of the others already drawn.

Tip

Drawing the paths using the Create New Layer Shape option will allow you to preview how the paths you are drawing interact.

PART

II

CH

7

In the previous example with the spindle, the Add to Shape Area property was used to combine several hastily drawn objects. After everything was aligned, all the objects were selected by click-dragging over them using the Path Component Selection tool, and then the property for combining was changed to Add to Shape Area. When the Combine button was clicked, the elements were joined (see Figure 7.11).

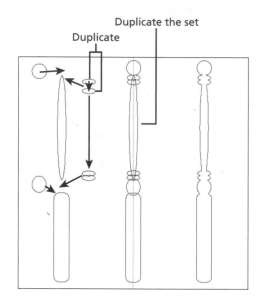

Duplicate the set

Duplicate

Figure 7.11
The paths at left show the separate parts of the spindle, mostly drawn with the Ellipse shape. These parts were assembled by roughly placing them together and then clicking the Align Horizontal Centers button. After they were together, clicking the Combine button joined the paths into one, and that result was used for the spindle.

The capability to combine shapes in this way offers a creative versatility that Photoshop lacked before—a lack that sent users looking to other programs to fill the void. Although there are still improvements to be made, and reasons to go to illustration programs for some tasks, this functionality goes a long way toward bridging the gap in providing the user with flexibility and power in handling vectors.

OTHER PATH SOURCES

You can get help both from inside and outside Photoshop for drawing and manipulating paths. For example, you can make paths from predefined shapes using a custom shape tool and import paths as vectors from other programs. These can, in turn, be combined with elements you have created in Photoshop.

THE SHAPE TOOL

To create a path using a shape tool, select the shape tool from the Tool palette. There are several different tools in this group, including the Rectangle tool, the Rounded Rectangle tool, the Ellipse tool, the Polygon tool, the Line tool, and the Custom Shape tool whose icon varies depending on what shape set you have loaded and which shape you used last. Selecting any of these will enable you to access all of those in the Options bar (see Figure 7.12 and Table 7.3).

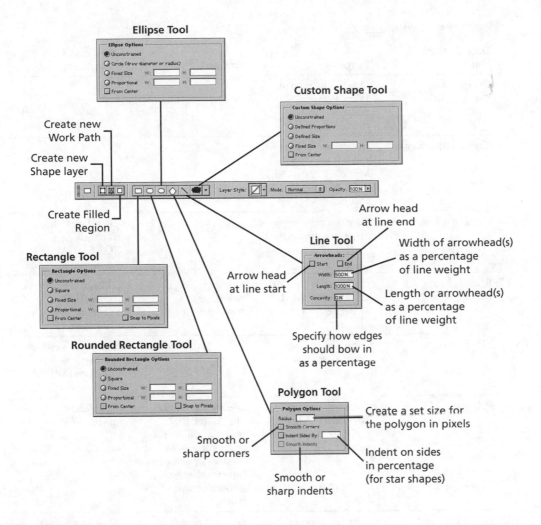

Figure 7.12
The options for shape tools include combine options, tool selection, context-sensitive constraint selection, layer style selection, blending mode selection, and opacity selection.

TABLE 7.3	SHAPE TOOL OPTIONS DETAILS			
Tool Options Name	**Purpose**	**Options**	**Keyboard Shortcuts**	
Create New Shape Layer	Creates a layer clipping path for a new layer that is filled with the foreground color.			

TABLE 7.3   CONTINUED

Tool Options Name	Purpose	Options	Keyboard Shortcuts
Create new Work Path	Deletes the current Work Path and replaces it with created shape.		
Create Filled Region	Creates a new layer and fills the shape with the foreground color. No path is created.		
Rectangle tool	Confines drawing shape to a rectangle.		Shift key: constrain proportions (Option) [Alt]: Draw from center.
Rounded Rectangle tool	Confines drawing shape to a rounded rectangle.	Specify the corner radius for the rounding.	Shift key: constrain proportions (Option) [Alt]: Draw from center.
Ellipse tool	Confines drawing shape to an ellipse.		Shift key: constrain proportions (Option) [Alt]: Draw from center.
Polygon tool	Confines drawing shape to a polygon.	Specify the number of sides for the polygon, smooth or sharp corners, indent on sides in percentage (for star shapes), and smooth or sharp indents.	Shift key: constrains angle to 45°.
Line tool	Confines drawing shape to a line at specified width.	Specify line weight, arrowhead inclusion, and size/geometry as percentage of line weight.	Shift key: constrains angle to 45°.
Custom Shape tool	Confines drawing shape to the selected custom shape.	Select custom shape. See Figure 7.13.	Shift key: constrain proportions (Option) [Alt]: Draw from center.

After the tool and options are selected, applying the tool is simple and automated. Click the mouse and drag to create the path. Assign the combination and intersection properties to the paths you are creating to affect how the paths combine.

Figure 7.13
When the Custom Shapes tool is selected, the Options bar shows a Shape drop-down menu. Click the menu to select a shape from the custom shapes loaded, or manage the shapes with the pop-up menu. Shapes can be deleted by holding down (Option) [Alt] and clicking.

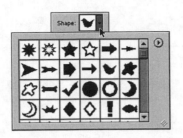

→ For more information on combining paths, **see** "Combining and Intersecting Path Segments," **p. 191**.

 If you are having some trouble with paths mysteriously disappearing, see "Hey, Where'd That Path Go!?" in the Troubleshooting section at the end of this chapter.

COPYING PATHS FROM OTHER PROGRAMS

Paths can be copied from other programs that can create them. Often these programs are more vector oriented than Photoshop so the strength of the controls is broad and at times some of the features can prove to be real timesavers. For example, I often use Illustrator to fine-tune alignment of individual points, or create vector outlines from type, which I then bring back into Photoshop. Although other Adobe products are probably most user friendly and seamless when it comes to this sort of import/export of vector information, other programs can do a fine job of integrating, also. Any program that can export paths to Illustrator format (.ai) can create paths that Photoshop can use.

To move Paths into Photoshop from other programs (CorelDRAW, FreeHand, AutoCAD, or Illustrator and so on), one of the following methods should work:

- Drag and drop the paths from an open document into Photoshop (Illustrator only).
- Copy the paths from the origin program and paste the paths into Photoshop (the Work path should be active).
- Save the paths to an Illustrator format from the origin program and then open in Photoshop.
- Save the paths in the native format, open in Illustrator, save as an Illustrator file, and move to Photoshop (drag and drop, save and open).

There are other possibilities, but chances are it is easier to re-create the paths if these methods don't provide a solution. Another choice is to work with programs that are generally more compatible with Photoshop and Adobe products.

To export paths from Photoshop, choose File, Export, Export Paths to Illustrator.

PART

II

CH

7

STROKING AND FILLING PATHS

Paths can be stroked or filled with color, gradients, and images, as well as being used to define clipping areas and selections. Filling is fairly simple, and works much like filling a selection—in fact, it can work exactly like filling a selection if you convert the path to a selection before filling.

Tip

You might want to assign a keystroke to the Make Selection menu item on the Paths palette if you use paths a lot.

→ For more information on creating keyboard shortcuts as actions, **see** "Creating and Editing Actions," **p. 269**.

If converting the path to a selection, simply choose Make Selection from the Paths palette pop-up menu and fill the selection as desired. The menu option will allow you to select Feathering, Anti-aliasing, and Operations for combining the selection you are creating with existing selections. Choosing to create the selection using the Load Paths As Selection button will use the settings previously used with the Make Selection function.

There are a lot of possibilities after the area is a selection. You can use freehand tools, although the more mundane Edit, Fill will allow you to fill the area with foreground and background color, any stored pattern, the active painting history state (as selected in the History palette), black, 50% gray, or white. These choices are exactly the same as if using the Fill command from the Paths menu (see the dialog box in Figure 7.14), except the Path menu command will allow you to choose feathering and antialiasing for the application of the path. If you are using the Edit menu Fill command, you don't have to worry about that conversion as you have already set those parameters when you converted the path to a selection. If you forget to convert the path to a selection before using the Edit menu Fill command and nothing else is selected, you will fill the entire image with your choice in the Fill dialog box.

→ For more information on feathering selections, **see** "Feathering Selections," **p. 116**.

Figure 7.14
The Fill dialog box from the Paths palette menu is exactly the same as the Fill dialog box from the Edit menu, except for the Feather and Anti-aliasing options. To complete the fill, choose the Content and Blending options, and then click OK.

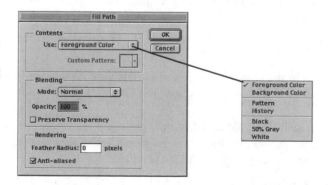

Stroking, on the other hand, can be unique with Paths. You can convert to a selection and stroke (using Edit, Stroke), and you can make a layer clipping path and stroke (with layer styles), but there is no other stroke command like the one on the Paths palette menu (see Figure 7.15).

Figure 7.15
This dialog box looks deceptively simple in that you choose a tool only for the stroke. However, the result is that your choice for the tool will allow application of all the current settings you have for that tool, including selected brushes and the options for those as well.

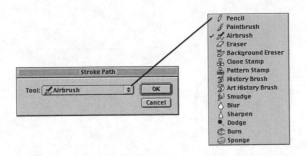

All you have to do is choose a tool and click OK and the active path will be stroked from end to end. However, you need to pay attention to the brush selection for the tool you will be stroking the path with, the tool options you have set, and perhaps some other things such as foreground color, History state, Pattern Stamp pattern, and so on before selecting Stroke Path. This opens a plethora of opportunity for creating with path strokes.

An example of a useful effect created with creative stroking techniques is making a dashed line on a curve—which you cannot do directly in Photoshop. The following steps show how to make a complex dashed line using stroke functions.

1. Create a new layer (Layer 1).
2. Draw a path you want to define as a dashed line.
3. Stroke the path with a painting tool and a hard, round brush whose width is the width you want the dashed line to be. The foreground color should be the color of the final dashed line (see Figure 7.16).
4. Create a new layer (Layer 2) and stroke the path again using a hard, round brush whose radius is the size you want the space between the dashes to be. Set the spacing for the brush to 200% or 300%.
5. Make a selection from the unstroked area using the Magic Wand set to 0 tolerance.
6. Invert the selection (see Figure 7.17).
7. Activate the layer in which you first stroked the path (Layer 1) and press Delete. Hide the other layer (Layer 2) to see the results (see Figure 7.18). The line should appear to be dashed.

PART

II

CH

7

Figure 7.16
This path (top) is stroked with the brush you have selected for the tool you choose in the Stroke Path dialog box, giving you the result (bottom).

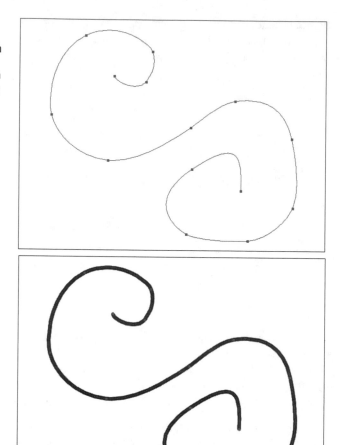

Figure 7.17
You use the second stroke to define the size and spacing of the dash. The size of the brush and spacing can be refined to change the width and length of the dash as well as the spacing.

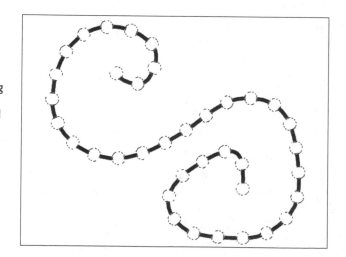

Figure 7.18
The result can be altered using different brush sizes and spacing. You can also vary these steps. For example, the foreground color was switched to white before stroking, so the result could have been flattened at that point without making the selection and deleting. As described, this will work with any foreground color.

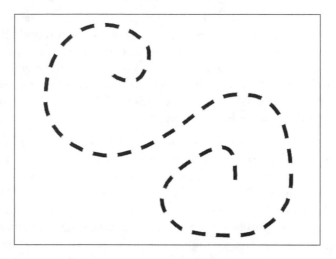

This is but a hint of what you can do with stroking in Photoshop, and creative stroking begins with mastery of creating paths.

TROUBLESHOOTING

HEY, WHERE'D THAT PATH GO!?

I was working on a path and it seems to have disappeared. Where did it go?

Again, this is one of those cases where this problem could be caused by a number of different things. Although a path can disappear from the visible image, it is not necessarily gone from the file. Actually, this is very simple: If the path becomes inactive, the outline for it will not be visible on the screen. There are several ways to shut off the visibility, such as clicking in the open area of the Paths palette, clicking the Dismiss Target Path button on the Options bar, or selecting Turn Off Path on the Paths palette menu. Most of the time you will have to be concentrating to shut off paths this way, but it can happen with an inadvertent click.

Layer clipping paths hide when you are not working on that layer. That is, if you create a layer clipping path from an active path, it will still be visible in the Paths palette and onscreen. If you switch to another layer, however, it will vanish. The only place you will see it is in the Layer palette's thumbnails as a layer clipping path, unless you activate the layer again.

Applying the wrong properties to a path can also result in the path effectively disappearing. There are a lot of combinations that can perhaps create the wrong result. Most combinations will at least leave some remnant of the paths you combined. It is possible, for example, to create a duplicate of the current path object so it is exactly on top of itself, then change the property to subtract, and then combine the results ending up with nothing. It is, however, improbable.

In any case, if you lose a path, the first place you should look is the Paths palette. Paths you have saved will almost all appear there. I say almost, as one or two could be hiding as layer clipping paths. As this is the case, the next place to look is the Layers palette. Your path might be hiding in a layer clipping path there. If you find it in the thumbnails, click it. It will become available in the Paths palette, and you will be able to duplicate it as a regular path. Again, paths become hidden when you click the Dismiss Paths button on the Path Component Selection options bar.

If checking in the Paths and Layers palettes fails to turn up the path you are looking for, it is time to head toward the History palette and examine the History states. You will be looking there to see whether you can locate something that says either Delete Layer, Clear Path, Cut Path, Make Path, New Work Path, or Combine Path Components. Delete Layer and Cut Path might obviously be where you deleted the path by removing the layer containing the path. Make Path is a little trickier way for you to have lost your Path: If you turned another selection into a path while the work path was unsaved, you can lose the path. In a similar way you can lose the path if you Dismiss it (or turn off the view) and begin drawing another path. The next anchor that you draw will create a state called New Work Path which signifies you have replaced the current Work Path. If the path is absolutely gone then this is probably the way you lost it. Combine Path Components would have required that you click the Combine button on the Path Component Selection tool's Options bar. In other words, if you did this, you probably would have known it, so this is not a likely (although possible) culprit.

To save yourself from the heartache of searching for your lost path, save the paths you want to keep by choosing Save Path from the Paths menu when you create something you don't want to lose.

GETTING THE RIGHT ALIGNMENT

In working with the Alignment buttons, the results seem unpredictable. Is something wrong with the program?

A very clever thing goes on with the Alignment buttons, and really paths in general. Photoshop remembers which path you drew and in which order. This is good for most things and bad for Photoshop reading your mind. The following should explain.

For example, create an outline for the spindle as in the example earlier in this chapter. Place it in the upper left, just as in the example. Next, duplicate that spindle a number of times— say four. Put the first duplicate where you want the cascade to end, put the next three consecutively to the left of the previous duplication, but keep between the original and the first duplication. Besides the first and the last, it doesn't matter where you place the spindles vertically so long as they don't go above the original or below the first duplication.

Next, highlight all with the Path Component Selection tool, and then click the Distribute Horizontal Centers button. The spindles will spread out nicely across the area—perfectly even. After that, click the Distribute Top Edges button. A perfect cascade will form for the three center spindles, but it will fall right to left rather than left to right. The original and its duplicate will stay right where you put them. The cascade from right to left happened because Photoshop puts the first created element highest and places them essentially in descending order of age, oldest to youngest.

To solve this problem, you would roughly move the spindles into the proper cascade order and click the Align and Distribute buttons again. If Photoshop has the opportunity to consider the spindles in the right order, it will order them effectively. This might seem like a pain but actually it is great for producing more complicated effects without additional adjustments.

To avoid the problem, always consider the Align and Distribute functions as *fine-tuning*. Place all the objects you will be aligning or distributing in order in the approximate positions you want them to end in, and this will get you the results you want and expect.

PHOTOSHOP AT WORK: CREATING THE STAIRCASE

A good example that will combine many, if not all, the tools discussed in this chapter is to build the staircase segment. This will require using shape tools, the pen tools for editing the shapes, Alignment to get the spindle straight, Combine to add the paths, the Path Component Selection tool to duplicate the spindles, Align and Distribute to straighten the spindles, and you might even use layer clipping paths to apply a wood-grain effect or a layer style. If not all, this exercise covers quite a lot of the tools and their uses.

Use the following steps and check back to the figures to re-create the staircase.

1. Open a new document at 72dpi and 480×480 pixels.

2. Create the shapes for your own spindle. You can duplicate the one I made in Figure 7.10, but it will be more fun to create your own—or even more difficult, duplicate one you've seen in real life. Those seeking a little more of a challenge will create a spindle with holes in it!

3. Align the elements of the spindle with the Align Horizontal Centers button.

4. Combine the spindle elements into a single path with the Combine function.

5. Duplicate the spindles into an array that roughly approximates the desired cascade.

6. Distribute the spindles on center to space them evenly left to right.

7. Distribute the spindles vertically (either by tops, centers, or bottoms). This will finish the cascade.

8. Make the path into a layer clipping path (create a new layer and then choose Layer, Layer Clipping Path, Current Path).

9. Create a grouped layer above the layer created in Step 8 and fill with a wood-grain pattern.

At this point, you have created the spindles. Adding the banister and the wood base is up to you. If you have been able to complete this successfully, you are capable of using the most difficult of the path tools and some practice with the Pen tool (if you are not already proficient) will make you a Paths Master.

CHAPTER

8

FREEHAND PAINTING TOOLS

In this chapter

FREEHAND TOOLS

Freehand tools are the artisan's delight in Photoshop only because some work like the actual tools used for drawing or painting in other media. Many of these tools really must be learned and used whether you consider yourself an artist, photoretoucher, or novice. Freehand tools help you do a number of things that are essential to getting good results in Photoshop, such as creating selections, repairing image damage, and creating effects. Although most tools will be used alone, some can be used in combinations—most often with selection (which limits where a tool can be applied) and paths (which can be stroked with freehand tools, limiting the need for a very steady hand).

USING THE AIRBRUSH AND PAINTBRUSH TOOLS

The Airbrush tool and Paintbrush tool both enable you to apply the foreground color to the canvas, and they have similar options. The Paintbrush tool generally applies color more densely and evenly through the stroke. The Airbrush can apply color with softer edges (see Figure 8.1). The density of color applied by the Airbrush tool increases as you hold your cursor over a set location, while the density of color from the Paintbrush tool remains constant.

Figure 8.1
Although many of the freehand tools have similar options and are controlled by the same brush sets, there are subtle differences in the effects they create. The Pencil tool, shown here with the Airbrush and Paintbrush, works with hard-edged brushes, exclusively.

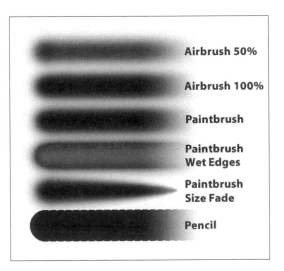

Airbrush 50%

Airbrush 100%

Paintbrush

Paintbrush Wet Edges

Paintbrush Size Fade

Pencil

Tip

All tool-painting cursors can be set in the preferences (Edit, Preferences, Display & Cursors). The view can be toggled between a brush shape preview (which shows the size of the brush application) or the standard icon and the precise (crosshairs) mode, by using the Caps Lock keyboard shortcut.

SETTING THE AIRBRUSH AND PAINTBRUSH TOOL OPTIONS

When using the Airbrush tool, you can set the brush shape and size, blending mode, and pressure of the tool in the Options bar (see Figure 8.2). The pressure setting determines the rate, or density, at which the foreground color is applied to the canvas. In addition, the Airbrush, like other freehand tools, has controllable Brush Dynamics, accessed by choosing the Brush Dynamics button in the Options bar. Under Brush Dynamics, you can choose various fade options, and the number of steps it takes to fade as the tool is applied. The fade is controlled over the distance of the application, considering the brush spacing; the greater the brush spacing, the greater the distance of the fade (when the fade is held constant). You can fade the size of the brush (radius), the pressure (opacity), or color (from foreground to background).

PART

II

CH

8

Figure 8.2
You can reset a tool's options by clicking the tool icon at the left side of the Options bar and choosing Reset Tool from the menu that appears.

Click for Reset menu

Brush Dynamics menu

When using the Paintbrush tool, you can choose to use Wet Edges to create a spray-can effect when painting. To turn the Wet Edges on, choose the Paintbrush tool and click the Wet Edges box on the Options bar. In addition, like the Airbrush tool, you can set the Brush Dynamics to fade the size of the brush, the opacity, or the color from foreground to background (see Figure 8.3).

Figure 8.3
You can use fade effects with many of the painting tools including the Paintbrush. Furthermore, you can combine Brush Dynamics with other brush effects, such as Wet Edges.

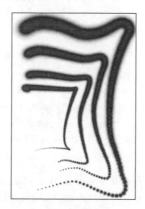

Tip

You can reset a tool to its default options by choosing Reset Tool from the Options palette menu. Open the palette menu by clicking the tool icon on the left of the menu. Choosing Reset All Tools returns all tools to their default settings.

WORKING WITH THE STAMP TOOLS

The Stamp tools—Clone Stamp tool and Pattern Stamp—enable you to paint with parts of an image. In the case of the Pattern Stamp, you must define a pattern by selecting an area and then choosing Edit, Define Pattern. After a pattern is defined, you can paint with that pattern, using the same options and dynamic brush controls (see Figure 8.4) to fade size and opacity as the Paintbrush tool. In Photoshop 6, instead of being limited to using the pattern in the pattern buffer, you can use any of the patterns that you have previously saved in the Patterns palette or Preset Manager.

Figure 8.4
When using Brush Dynamics to change opacity with the Clone Stamp tool, it is often best to use a soft brush so that cloning is not obvious.

The Clone Stamp tool paints with areas of your image that you define. You can use the Clone Stamp tool to fix blemishes or scratches in the image, or use the tool to remove unwanted objects or people from a photograph. The Clone Stamp tool is one of the most valuable tools when retouching an image because you can copy from adjacent areas of the image and create seamless blends.

To use the Clone Stamp tool, click the tool in the toolbox and then select an origin area to duplicate in the image by holding down (Option) [Alt] and clicking in the image. This will be the area of the image you will clone from. Release the (Option) [Alt] key and move the cursor to the area you want to clone to. Click and drag with the tool to clone the original area over the target.

The options for the Clone Stamp tool are similar to those for the Paintbrush tool. In addition, you can use the Clone Stamp tool in aligned or unaligned modes. In aligned mode, the distance between the paintbrush and source is fixed for each stroke of the brush. In unaligned mode, the source remains the same for each brush stroke. You can also choose Use All Layers to sample from all the visible layers when generating the image origin instead of selecting only from the current layer. Using all layers is a helpful way to create new, cloned areas on a separate layer so that you can compare it with the original image.

When using the Clone Stamp tool, you might find it useful to use a brush with a soft edge. By choosing a soft-edged brush, you can more easily blend adjacent applications so that they are not obviously repeated.

UNDERSTANDING THE HISTORY TOOL

The History Brush applies image information from a previous version of your file. Essentially, the tool functions as a selective undo, allowing you to paint back specific information with control of a brush. You can use either a Snapshot or a History State as the source for the History Brush. A History State is a frozen moment in the history of an image. The older history states are automatically eliminated as new states fill the available spaces. A Snapshot history states which you save temporarily so that it is not overwritten with newer states. Neither Snapshots nor History States are permanently saved with an image.

Using the History Brush, you can paint with the effects of a filter over an image. This gives you significant control of the area of a filter's effect.

The History Brush can be applied only to an image that contains a History or Snapshot. As Histories and Snapshots are not saved with images, you have to have been working with an image after it was opened to be able to apply the History. If there are no History states or Snapshots, there will be nothing to apply with the History Brush.

Follow these steps to apply the History Brush to an image that you have been working on:

1. Choose the History Brush from the toolbox.
2. Set the History Brush options on the Options bar, including Brush selection, Mode, Opacity, and Brush Dynamics.
3. In the History palette, select the source for the History Brush by clicking in the box next to the Snapshot or History State.
4. Paint the image. Wherever you paint, the selected History State or Snapshot is applied, reverting the image information under the brush to how the image was in that state.

Tip

In addition to using the painting tools, you can select an area of the image and fill it with the selected History State or Snapshot by choosing Edit, Fill and selecting History as the source.

The Art History Brush lets you paint with a previous version of the file using a History State or Snapshot, but with more impressionistic options (see Figure 8.5). You can use the Art History Brush to add artistic effects based on filters, mode changes, or image adjustments.

→ For more information on working with the History Brush, Art History Brush, and Histories in general, **see** "Creating with Image Histories," **p. 251**.

Figure 8.5
The Options bar has various settings that can be used creatively in applying the Art History Brush. Application combines the current state of the image with the source state or Snapshot, based on sampling from the history source.

GETTING THE MOST OUT OF THE ERASER TOOL

The Eraser tool works much like other painting tools, but removes image information rather than adding to it. If you use the Eraser on layers, with Preserve Transparency turned off, you replace image pixels with transparent ones—essentially erasing the image area as the name implies. In a layer where Preserve Transparency is turned on or is on a background layer, using the Eraser paints with the background color instead of adding transparent pixels. The eraser has the ability to behave like the Paintbrush, Airbrush, or Pencil tool, or in a Block mode (see Figure 8.6). In Block mode, the eraser uses a square brush and the size is fixed, so it looks the same no matter what percentage you are zoomed into the image.

Figure 8.6
You can use the Eraser tool to erase to a previous History State or Snapshot by enabling the Erase to History option.

Note

You can achieve results similar to Block mode by using the Eraser tool in Pencil tool mode with a square brush.

THE BACKGROUND ERASER TOOL

 In addition to the standard Eraser tool, the Background Eraser tool erases background pixels to transparency. By setting the options for this tool, you can use it to detect edges in your image so that you can erase areas on a layer to transparency. Although similar to the Extract command, the Background Eraser tool gives you greater control over the areas of the image that get removed and also how they are removed. This tool is best used to isolate objects with clearly defined edges (see Figure 8.7). For less-defined objects such as hair or fur, you can use the Background Eraser tool to clean up after you perform an initial extraction.

Figure 8.7
When using the Background Eraser tool to remove a flatly colored area, use Sample Once for the sampling option. This will keep erasure to the first color you sample. With Continuous Sampling turned on, you will need to be more careful where the brush is placed so that you don't sample colors you want to keep.

When the Background Eraser tool is selected, you can set options for Erasing mode, Tolerance, and Sampling method on the Options bar. In Discontiguous mode, the Background Eraser erases the sampled color (based on the tolerance) anytime it falls under the brush. In Contiguous mode, only pixels adjacent to the sampling point (center of the brush) that fall within the tolerance of the sampled color are erased. Choose Find Edges to maintain existing image edges, while removing the sampled color.

Lower values for Tolerance erase only colors very similar to the sampled color. Higher Tolerance values erase a wider range of colors. For Sampling Method, choose Continuous to erase colors based on the color under the cursor as you drag. Choose Once to erase colors based on the first color that you sample and Background to erase based on the background color.

THE MAGIC ERASER TOOL

The Magic Eraser tool erases similar colors on a layer to transparency based on a sampled color and a Tolerance setting. Options do not include a brush setting, because its area of effect is based on the initial sampled color. The Magic Eraser tool can work in Contiguous mode so that only adjacent pixels are removed, or you can turn off this option to erase all the pixels within the tolerance throughout the current layer. You can also turn on the Use All Layers option to remove all the pixels within the tolerance throughout the entire image. The advantage to using the Magic Eraser over other methods of accomplishing the same thing (by selection and deletion) is that the Magic Eraser does it all in one step.

USING THE SHAPE TOOLS

Like illustration applications, you can draw basic shapes in Photoshop. You can create lines, circles, rectangles, or select from dozens of custom shape presets. When creating these shapes, you can create them as raster objects directly on the current layer, as a shape layer or vector mask (see Figure 8.8), or as a work path. If you create the objects as rasters, you cannot edit them with the path tools. If you create the shapes as a vector mask or a work path, you can continue to manipulate the vector information in the Bézier paths.

Figure 8.8
When you create a shape with the Create Shape Layer option turned on on the Options bar, Photoshop creates a Fill layer with a vector Layer Mask.

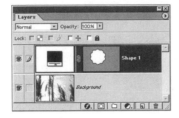

Note

In Photoshop 6, the default when creating lines and shapes is to create a shape layer. When using the Line or Shape tools on a nonshape layer, a new fill layer is created based on the current foreground color. You can change the color of the fill layer, or alter its properties, making it a gradient fill or pattern fill layer. You can also choose a layer style in the Shape Options bar.

→ For more information about creating paths, **see** "Paths: Bézier Tools for Creating Vector Effects," **p. 175**.
→ For more information on using Layer masks, **see** "Layer Masks," **p. 64**.

When using any of the shape tools, you need to select the shape that should be created by using button options on the Options bar (see Figure 8.9). Choose Create New Shape Layer, Create New Work Path, or Create Filled Region. You can also select the shape that you want to create. Note that when a shape layer is current, if you select and use one of the shape tools, the result is a vector mask. If you create shapes on a Shape layer, you can control how the shapes combine by using the Options bar (see Figure 8.10).

Figure 8.9
Choose how you want to handle layers for the shapes that you create on the Options bar. You can also choose other shapes.

Figure 8.10
After you have created the first shape in a layer, the Options bar changes and you can control how all the shapes combine or interact.

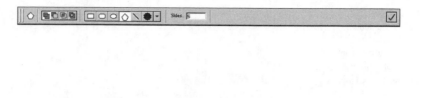

You can also restrict the area of shape creation or control the shape's components by setting the Geometry Options (see Figure 8.11). Furthermore, to use filters or other image effects with a shape layer, the contents must be rasterized. You can rasterize a fill layer, vector mask, or both. Select the layer in the Layers palette and choose <u>L</u>ayer, Rasteri<u>z</u>e to convert a layer to pixels.

Figure 8.11
Context-sensitive Geometry Options for the shape tools can be accessed from the drop menu to the right of the shape buttons. This menu lets you to set shape constraints, and control how the shapes are created.

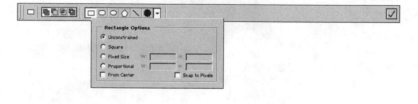

THE LINE TOOL

The Line tool creates lines of a specified thickness. When using the Line tool, you can also apply arrowheads by selecting Start or End from the Line Tool Options bar (see Figure 8.12). If you place arrowheads on the start or end of the line segment, you can control the width and height of the arrowhead as a percentage of the width of the line. In addition, you can control the concavity, or amount that the arrowhead doubles back into itself.

CREATING RECTANGLES, ELLIPSES, AND POLYGONS

By using the Rectangle, Rectangle with Rounded Corners, Ellipse, or Polygon tool, you can create regular geometric shapes that are editable either as rasters or vectors (see Figure 8.13). If you create a rectangle, you can determine the width and height as you draw, or you can constrain the size of the rectangle. When creating a rectangle with rounded corners, you can also set the radius of the corners.

Figure 8.12
You can create leaders and dimensions in your Photoshop image by adding arrowheads to the ends of the Line tool. You can also control the size of the arrowheads by setting their relationship to the width of the line.

Figure 8.13
If you create your shapes as work paths or as a shape layer, you can use the path editing tools, such as Direct Select or Convert Point, to change the shapes you create.

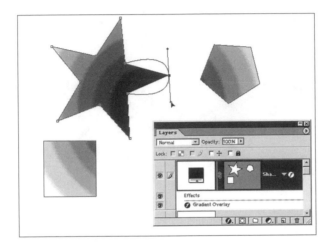

When drawing a polygon, you can set the number of sides in the Options bar. In the Polygon Options menu, you can also set a specific radius for the polygon (the circle in which the polygon is inscribed) and control the smoothing of corners and indentation of the sides (see Figure 8.14).

Figure 8.14
If you indent the sides of a polygon by clicking the Indent Sides By option in the Geometry Options menu, a star is created. The star has the same number of points as the setting for the number of sides.

CREATING CUSTOM SHAPES

 Beyond simple rectangles and circles, Photoshop 6 lets you create a variety of custom shapes. You can create and save your own shapes, or choose among the many preset shapes provided. After you choose the Custom Shape tool, you can choose from any of the shapes available in the Shape palette (see Figure 8.15). These shapes are also available when using the pen tools and in the Preset Manager. You can control the size of the shape as you draw it by dragging, or by setting a size constraint in the Custom Shape Options bar. You can use the Custom Shape tool to create a shape layer (a fill layer/vector mask combination), or use the shape to create a mask with a standard layer (see Figure 8.16).

Figure 8.15
Photoshop 6 has libraries of predefined shapes that you can use with the Shape tool. You can delete, load, and save shapes using the Shapes palette or by using the Content Manager.

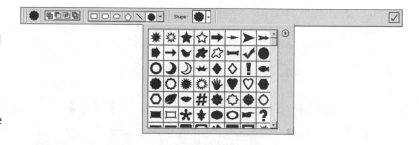

Figure 8.16
Create a Vector mask for an existing layer by creating or copying a path and then choosing Layer, Add Layer Clipping Path, Use Current Path.

THE PENCIL TOOL

Like the other painting tools, the Pencil tool uses the Brush palette to determine how and where the foreground color should be applied to the canvas. The Pencil tool, however, does not have any soft edges. It is like painting with the Paintbrush set to maximum hardness, with the additional step of eliminating any gray areas in the brush. The Pencil tool does not create any areas that are partially opaque or transparent within the brush shape itself, and any existing brushes are converted to 1-bit (see Figure 8.17).

Figure 8.17
The Pencil tool uses only hard-edged brushes. Any brushes that you have loaded are converted to 1-bit, black-and-white.

When using the Pencil tool, you can choose the brush in the Options bar. You can also set the Blending mode and the Opacity of the pencil stroke. The Pencil tool also has an Auto Erase option that determines whether to use the foreground or background color depending on where you begin your stroke. With this option turned on, if you begin to drag with the Pencil tool in an area that contains the foreground color, the background color is used. If you begin to drag from an area that does not contain the foreground color, the foreground color is used.

WORKING WITH THE BLUR AND SHARPEN TOOLS

Like the filters of the same name, the Blur tool and the Sharpen tool selectively obscure areas of an image or attempt to add detail by increasing contrast between pixels. Both tools give you control over specific areas of your image, and both tools have similar options in the Options bar (see Figure 8.18). You can set brush size and shape, blending mode, and pressure. You can also choose Use All Layers to blur or sharpen across all layers.

Figure 8.18
The blending modes available when using these tools are limited to Normal, Darken and Lighten, and Hue, Saturation, Color, and Luminosity.

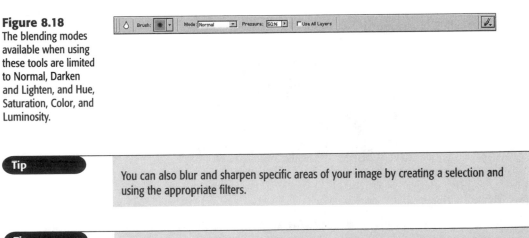

> **Tip**
>
> You can also blur and sharpen specific areas of your image by creating a selection and using the appropriate filters.

> **Tip**
>
> It is best to use a light pressure with both the Blur and Sharpen tools so that you do not create unwanted effects. With a high pressure on the Sharpen tool, for example, it is relatively easy to create unwanted artifacts. You might find it easier to use a slightly lower pressure setting and stroke over a specific area more than once until the desired effect is achieved.

CONTROLLING EXPOSURE WITH THE DODGE AND BURN TOOLS

The Dodge and Burn tools are named after traditional photographic techniques for controlling exposure in the darkroom. The Dodge tool selectively lightens areas of your image. The Burn tool selectively darkens areas of your image. These tools give you control over the exposure in areas of your image. You can use the Dodge tool to create highlights, or to punch up existing ones. Similarly, you can use the Burn tool to create or deepen shadows.

Both the Dodge and Burn tools enable you to select a brush size and shape, an exposure, or intensity of the effect, and a range of effect. You can choose whether you want to lighten and darken highlights, midtones, or shadows. Again, the setting for the pressure on these tools should be kept low in most cases as application of the effects can quickly overwhelm your intention.

BLENDING WITH THE SMUDGE TOOL

The Smudge tool blends areas of your image by dragging image information through your brush strokes—much like dragging your finger through wet paint. Use the Smudge tool to spot blend new image element edges seamlessly into the background, or correct some smaller image defects such as scratches. Control how the Smudge tool interacts with the image in the Options bar. Overapplication will blur and remove finer texture (such as image grain), so this should probably be used sparingly. The options include brush size, blending mode, and pressure. You can also choose to smudge in Finger Painting mode so that each stroke starts with the foreground color.

CREATING NEW BRUSHES

Brushes are used with many of the freehand tools, and it is important to understand the basics of creating them. The preset brushes might not give you exactly what you need for a certain project. You can create your own circular or elliptical brush by choosing New Brush from the Brush Palette menu (see Figure 8.19).

Figure 8.19
You can manage your brushes in the Brush palette from the Options bar of any of the Freehand tools that use brushes.

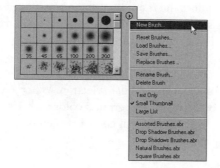

Use the following steps to create your own custom circular or elliptical brush:

1. To create a new brush, choose New Brush from the Brushes palette menu. The New Brush dialog box displays (see Figure 8.20).

Figure 8.20
You can adjust the roundness and angle of the brush dynamically by dragging the handles on the ellipse and by dragging the angle arrow in the New Brush preview.

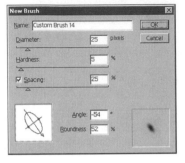

2. Enter a name for the new brush.

3. Set the Diameter, or size of the brush, measured in pixels. Brush sizes range from 1 to 999 pixels.

4. Choose a Hardness (the sharpness) of the edge. A hardness of 100% creates a very crisp edge, whereas a hardness of 0% creates a very fuzzy one.

5. Set a value for the Spacing. Spacing is the distance between brush marks as you paint, measured as a percentage of the brush diameter. Larger values create skips as you paint. You can turn the spacing off to have your brush create a continuous application.

Tip

Broad spacing (greater than 100%) produces a dotted line effect. The greater the spacing, the greater the distance between the dots.

6. Next you'll want to set the Roundness of the brush. Changing Roundness creates an oval-shaped brush, which is more pronounced as the roundness setting gets smaller, based a percentage. For example, if you set Roundness to 50%, the minor axis of the ellipse is 50% of the major axis. Choose Angle if Roundness is set to something other than 100%. Angle determines the rotation of the major axis of the ellipse. You can set Angle if Roundness is set to 100%, but painting with a circular brush is the same at any angle. Changing Roundness and Angle enables you to paint with calligraphic effects.

You can also create a new brush from any rectangular selection. When creating a brush, regions of black within the selection apply the foreground color with 100% opacity. Regions of white apply transparency, and regions of color between black and white apply the foreground color at various opacity levels.

Use the following steps to create an image-based brush:

1. Create a rectangular selection using the Rectangular Marquee tool. The selection must be smaller than 1,000×1,000 pixels. The opacity throughout the brush is based on the color in all visible layers (see Figure 8.21).

Figure 8.21
If the area under a selection is 100% black, the created brush is completely opaque. Where the area under the brush contains white (0% black), the brush is transparent.

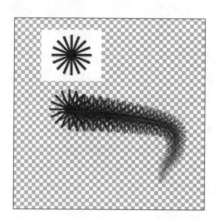

2. Choose Edit, Define Brush.
3. In the Brush Name dialog box, enter the name for the new brush (see Figure 8.22).

After you have created a new brush, you can select it in the Brushes palette (see Figure 8.23), and then use it with any of the painting tools.

Figure 8.22
Enter the name of the brush when prompted. The preview in the dialog box and in the Brushes palette might clip the brush if it is too big to preview.

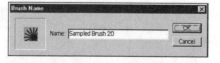

Figure 8.23
You can display the brushes in the Brushes palette as small thumbnails, a list with the brush name, or as text only.

> **Tip**
>
> You can save custom brushes by choosing Save Brushes from the Brushes pop-up menu, which is on the upper right of the Brush selection menu on the Options bar. You can also load brush presets or other custom brush sets. Brushes and brush sets can also be managed from the Preset Manager.

IMAGE WARPING USING LIQUIFY

In Photoshop 6, you can smudge, stretch, and pinch your image in real-time using the Liquify command. Choose Image, Liquify to start the command and open the Liquify interface (see Figure 8.24). The tools along the left side of the window enable you to control how the image is transformed. You can twirl, pinch, bloat, shift pixels or reflect pixels (see Figure 8.25). You also have the ability to selectively reconstruct parts of the image and to freeze, or protect, areas from change.

You can control the size and pressure of the brush as you alter the image, how the image should be reconstructed, and how frozen areas should be generated and controlled. Note that you can determine an area to freeze before using the Liquify command by saving a selection as an alpha channel, and using that to select the area to freeze in the Liquify interface. You can also control how the image is viewed in the interface. Turning on the grid makes it easier to see how the pixels are transformed as you use the Liquify tools (see Figure 8.26).

Figure 8.24
The Liquify interface provides you with all of the Liquify tools as well as access to each of their options in one convenient location.

Figure 8.25
This example shows the result of applying the Liquify tools to an image.

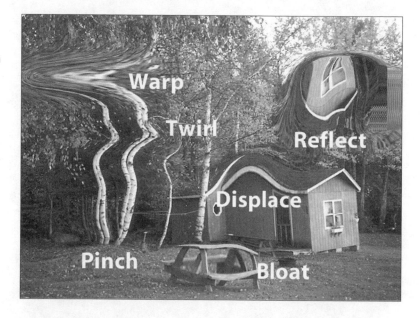

Figure 8.26
The grid can give you a better idea of how the image is being bent and shaped.

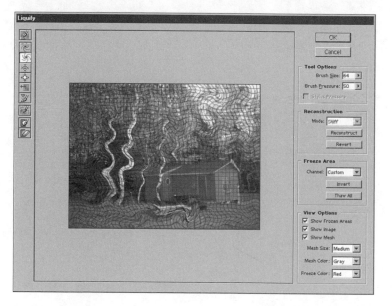

CHAPTER 9

TYPE CONTROL, PLACEMENT, AND SETTINGS

In this chapter

WORKING WITH TYPE

Using type goes far beyond just spelling the words right and selecting a typeface name from a pop-up menu. Designing with fonts can be challenging and can add style to images rather than just a message. Fonts can be used as a graphic element to complement and enhance images. Finding the right font to complement your image and setting the words properly is integral to making effective design. Treating text as part of the image, rather than as a tack-on will make using type more than just placing words on a page. Although it is not necessary to have a comprehensive understanding of type before using it, some background can give you more insight into character design and can affect your choices in use of fonts.

UNDERSTANDING FONTS

Typefaces are compiled as *fonts*, which are complete character sets of an available typeface at a particular size—at least in printing. Fonts on the computer are often thought of as sets in varying size which are contained in a single file or even as a font family. A *font family* is a set of characters that is created in various styles—for example, bold or italic along with the standard set. A standard or complete set of a font does not mean that every character in a font will be available among the 255 keyed English-character possibilities. In fact, most fonts are not complete in that sense. For example, some designer sets are rather limited, perhaps using only the standard letters (A–Z) and numbers (0–9). The font characters are mapped to the keyboard and stored in font files, which are stored in specific areas for reference on your computer system. This mapping selects the letter of the current font based on the key (or key combination) you press on the keyboard. Certain programs (such as Fontographer by Macromedia) allow you to design your own font sets.

The basic imprint of a typeface is defined by the weight of the stroke, the size of the character, the length of ascenders and descenders, and the presence or absence of serifs. The imprint provides a basic rule of thumb for a font's use. The *stroke* is any of the curved or straight lines drawn to make up the appearance of a letter. The *size* of a character is the selected point size of the font. *Ascenders* and *descenders* are the upward and downward strokes of the letter set which make up the total height or point size of the font (see Figure 9.1). These extend above and below the x-height of letters (see Figures 9.2 and 9.3 for information on x-height). Strokes are most readily recognized as the upper portion of the lowercase letters such as *d* and *b* or the lower stroke on the lowercase letters such as *y* and *q*. *Serifs* are extensions from the strokes (see Figure 9.4). A *sans-serif* font is a font that does not have these extensions.

Figure 9.1
Ascenders and descenders add to the total height of the font and define how the font is measured in size. Point size is actually a measure from baseline to baseline, defined by the designer. The total height of the font is a very rough approximation of the point size.

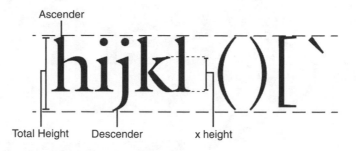

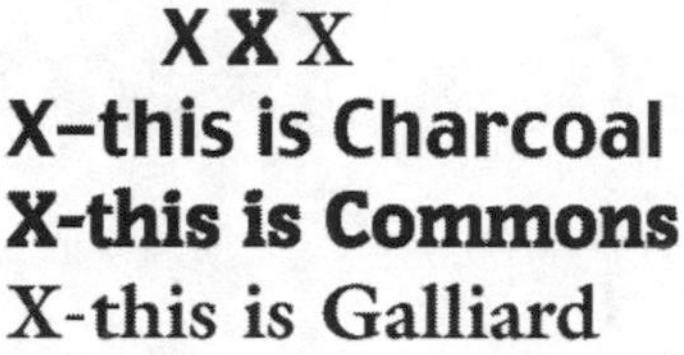

Ascender

Total Height   Descender   x height

Figure 9.2
The three fonts pictured in this window are all the same point size, although they might appear to be different sizes because of the way they imprint on the page.

X X x
X–this is Charcoal
X-this is Commons
X-this is Galliard

Figure 9.3
A close-up and comparison of the x height of each font in Figure 9.2 shows almost a 10% difference in size. The font with the shorter x height will have longer ascenders and descenders to make up the rest of its size.

SERIF VERSUS SANS-SERIF

Serifs essentially help letters in words appear more cohesive and linked by connecting the letters of individual words. This can help the reader pick words out, and leads to greater readability. Most body text is set in serif type, probably for this very reason: It can help the reader pick out the words as they read (see Figure 9.5). Sans-serif type is usually found in headings and titles (see Figure 9.6).

Figure 9.4
A close-up of the left-most stroke on a *W* in Palatino, a popular serif typeface. See Figure 9.5 for more of what Palatino looks like.

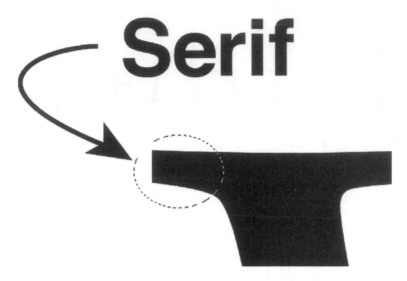

Figure 9.5
A sample of Palatino, a serif typeface.

Word

Figure 9.6
A sample of Helvetica, a well-known sans-serif typeface.

Word

It is not mandatory to use serif type for body text, just as it isn't mandatory that sans-serif type be used only for headlines. It is merely a general guideline for purpose. Serif typefaces can come in a number of shapes, sizes, and intensities—from extremely bold to wispy to almost nonexistent. With some faces, there might be a question as to which category the face falls into. It is not so important to categorize as it is to understand the purpose of the design, and what the importance is in the influence of the type's shape. Other fonts are available that might not fall into either of these categories, such as pictorial fonts (dingbats), decorative or designer fonts, and scripts. These font types are rarely used for body text, and are almost exclusively used as headline type or design elements. Figures 9.7 to 9.10 show a variety of typeface looks.

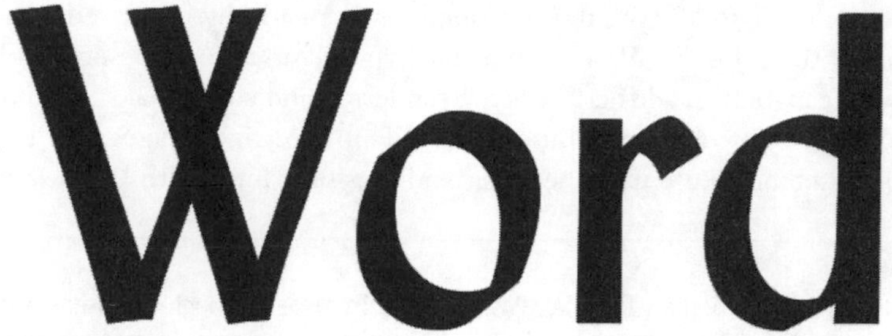

Figure 9.7
Lydian MT, shown here, is an example of a designer font. Broadening at the end of some letter strokes (note the *r*) may make it seem like a serif font, although it is really sans-serif.

Figure 9.8
Taxidermist is a funky font, with a mixture of serif and sans-serif letters.

Figure 9.9
Courier is a classic typeface branded as a typewriter face. It has prominent, heavy serifs.

Figure 9.10
Script types such as French Script, shown here, might have connectors built into the face to imitate the connection of cursive writing.

Word

word

Word

Word

Although the use of type in Photoshop has dramatically improved over the last several versions of the program, Photoshop is not typically used for typesetting. The addition of the newest capabilities adds crisper type rendering and additional style and type controls. However, Photoshop is still used primarily for creating images. For this reason, you will probably tend to use more designer and sans serif fonts with Photoshop than serif fonts.

Font Files

Fonts come in two primary file types: PostScript and TrueType. Although Photoshop was friendly to both types, more recently TrueType support has dwindled. There are several reasons (and rumors) surrounding this, but perhaps the most valid is that TrueType fonts are not completely reliable—especially when considering high-resolution output. Granted, the reliability of TrueType doesn't matter if the font is rendered into pixels, as the output of the font itself no longer has to be handled by the output device. The choice of consistent use of PostScript rather than TrueType fonts extends beyond Photoshop and into getting consistent results from your digital output. Maintaining PostScript type only, if more expensive, can actually save headaches in the long run. If you absolutely must use a TrueType, consider purchasing a utility that can convert fonts from TrueType to PostScript.

To properly use font files, there must be a means of rendering the type onscreen and in print. These files are saved separately for PostScript fonts, and you must have both to view and output files. Again, this is not as important as if the type had been rendered into pixels, but sharing files between computers or users who have different font sets—or even different versions of the same font—can cause viewing and/or output problems. Considering the ability to save type in layers without rendering, this becomes more of an issue in Photoshop. For example, if you create a file with a type layer and send it from your home computer to your work computer and open it there, and the version of the font you are using is probably different, the alignment you worked on so painstakingly might change. Amazingly, when you send it back home and view it there, it will be correct again. This would be due to the difference in the font versions.

 So, how do you solve potential font problems where a font is rendering differently on different computers? See "Keeping Fonts Looking the Same on Different Computers" in the Troubleshooting section at the end of this chapter.

CONTROLLING TYPE

The look and feel of a font is not just controlled by the appearance of the typeface, its imprint, or its size. Settings in Photoshop allow you to control how type works by controlling the spacing between letters overall (*tracking*), between the individual letter pairs (*kerning*), between the baseline and the character (*baseline shift*), and between the baseline of different character rows (*leading*).

Photoshop's type tools have options that enable you to create horizontal and vertical type. Additional functions appear on the Layers menu, which can change the orientation of the type from horizontal to vertical or vice versa, and let you render the type. Type can also be rendered by flattening an image, merging down, or merging visible (these options are not always available depending on the image circumstances). After you render type, it becomes uneditable.

Note   *Rendering* is the redefinition of image or font form as pixels.

Use the following steps to place type in an image:

1. Choose an image to which you want to add type, or open a new file.
2. Choose the Type tool from the toolbox.
3. Choose attributes to use for the type. You can choose to leave the selections at the default settings and proceed to Step 4. These selections, shown in Figure 9.11, can be changed later as well.

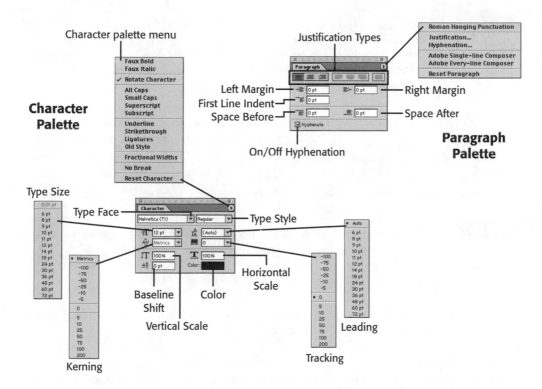

Figure 9.11
The Type Options bar and the two type palettes (Paragraph and Character) give the user a broad range of control over the appearance of type, including the selection of typeface and size, spacing, color, alignment, smoothing, and orientation.

4. Click the mouse where you want to place the type. Type can be placed as flush left, centered, or flush right to the position where you click the mouse. These options are selected on the Options bar.

Note

The color of the type will default to the current foreground color on the Toolbox. You can change the color on the Toolbox before clicking in the image window, or change it in the Options bar. To change the color in either swatch, click the swatch to open the Color Picker dialog box.

→ For more information on selecting font attributes, **see** "Choose a Point Size," "Tracking," "Kerning," and "Leading," following this section.

5. Type the words you want to use and they will appear in the image window.

6. When the type has been entered, click the Commit Any Current Edits button (check mark) on the Options bar. The type will appear in the foreground color (or color you have chosen for the type) on a separate layer, in the typeface and size you have chosen.

Tip

While you are typing with a live cursor, you can change tools by using the keyboard letters, but only if there is no active cursor. Otherwise, you will get the letter you type. To get out of the live typing mode, click the Commit Any Current Edits button to exit live typing mode with the changes, or press the Escape (Esc) key on the keyboard to exit the live typing mode and remove the changes.

After the type is placed, it can be moved with the Move tool [(V)], or edited. The text is fully editable and will remain that way until the layer is rendered (Layers, Type, Render). That is, you can fix misspellings or change the font, font size, kerning, tracking, and so on—per letter, or across the entire layer. Type that flows off the edge of the image is not lost. It remains editable until you have rendered the layer, even if it flows out of the image.

Tip

Settings for fonts can be changed per letter by highlighting the letters you want to change and altering the settings on the Options bar or Character and Paragraph palettes. Change everything on the layer by choosing the layer with nothing highlighted (click the Commit Any Current Edits button on the toolbox), and changing the settings.

If you have lost text off the edge of the image and can't get it back, see "When Type Disappears" in the Troubleshooting section at the end of this chapter.

CHOOSING A POINT SIZE

Point size determines how large a letter appears. The greater the point size, the larger the letters. A point is 1/72 of an inch. Type is measured from the top of the ascender to the bottom of the descender. Although typefaces may be the same size they can appear to fill the page differently because of their bulk, known as *x height* and *stroke weight*.

If you are used to measuring in inches, points can prove a little confounding. To convert a measure from points to inches, simply take the point size and multiply it by .0139. Using a similar conversion, you can take the decimal of the inch measure and multiply by 72 to get the point size. Selecting a type size after that is as simple as placing the point size in the Options bar or the Character palette. A conversion equivalent chart appears in Table 9.1.

TABLE 9.1   MEASUREMENT CONVERSIONS

Inches	Decimal Equivalent	Point Size	Picas
1"	1"	72 pts	6 picas
7/8"	.875"	63 pts	
3/4"	.75"	54 pts	4.5 picas
5/8"	.625"	45 pts	
1/2"	.5"	36 pts	3 picas
3/8"	.375"	27 pts	
1/4"	.25"	18 pts	1.5 picas
1/6"	.167"	12 pts	1 pica
1/8"	.125"	9 pts	
1/16"	.0625"	4.5 pts	
1/32"	.0313"	2.25 pts	
1/64"	.016"	1.16 pts	
1/72"	.0139"	1 pt	

Currently, you can control the point size of text in Photoshop to hundredths of a point, which is a little more than 1/10,000 of an inch (see Table 9.2). Such precise control is not generally needed, because full point sizes will do for most purposes. When making a scaling change to a layer with active type, however, the dialog box displays the corresponding shift in point size when reopened (by clicking the type layer you want to edit). This precise measurement helps you keep type consistent if you work with it on several layers or in different documents.

TABLE 9.2   TYPE SIZE KEYSTROKE SHORTCUTS

Function	Mac	PC
Increase type size by two points	(Cmd-Shift->)	[Ctrl+Shift+>]
Decreases type size by two points	(Cmd-Shift-<)	[Ctrl+Shift+<]
Increases type size by 10 points	(Cmd-Shift-Option->)	[Ctrl+Shift+Alt+>]
Decreases type size by 10 points	(Cmd-Shift-Option-<)	[Ctrl+Shift+Alt+<]

The *pixel* measurement is interesting, as type is not often considered in pixels. However, this makes sense in Photoshop, as the program is a pixel-based image editor. The feature offers some interesting options for fitting type without making a lot of calculations as to size. For example, measuring in pixels can come in handy when designing Web graphics, which can be better defined by absolute pixel sizes. However, if you are working in 72dpi for Web graphic development, pixels and points will have the same measurements.

Note

Type sizes can be entered between .1 and 1,296 points. Generally, these limits are far beyond what you will need in normal use. Point sizes between 7 and 36 are commonly used for print in books and for Web sites—although, Web controls for application are not necessarily handled in points.

TRACKING

Tracking is the control of spacing between letters over an expanse or a block of text. Tracking controls only the space between the letters and does not distort the typeface, as stretching the type would. You can use it to spread type widely across (or down) the page or push the letters together. Proper use of tracking can help with the readability of text, or it can just be used to create effects.

Use the following steps to place type in an image:

1. Open an image in which you want to place type, or open a new image.
2. Select the Type tool from the toolbox.
3. Click the image in which you want to place the type.
4. Type in the text you want to use. (If you have nothing to use, type in word; it works in all situations.)
5. Select the text by double-clicking it. You can select only a portion of the text by click-dragging over a set of letters (see Figure 9.12).

Figure 9.12
You can double-click a word to select it. To select a string of letters or words, click and drag the cursor over what you want to select.

Selecting only a portion of the text

6. Press (Cmd-T) [Ctrl+T] to display the Character palette.

7. Click in the tracking field and select a tracking number between –1,000 and 1,000 (see Figure 9.13). Selecting a negative number moves all the letters and words together; selecting a positive number spreads them apart (see Figures 9.14 and 9.15).

Figure 9.13
This text has no tracking applied.

Figure 9.14
This text is tracked at −150, which decreases the space between letters. In this case, it causes the letters to touch or slightly overlap.

Figure 9.15
Here the word from Figure 9.13 is tracked at 150, which provides more space between letters. Extreme spacing like this might be used when creating a headline or other design effect.

Be sure that you are accomplishing something with tracking and are not just using it because it's available. Tracking type too much in either direction can affect the readability in a negative way, although this is sometimes desirable in design. Whatever the result, be sure it is what you want. Effective tracking adds emphasis; tracking at random leads to random results. For example, tracking is often used to tighten letters in a headline (by setting tracking at less than zero) and can be used to spread lines of text across pages to fit into a given space.

Tracking can be controlled with keystrokes, when specific text is highlighted. See Table 9.3 for a list of valid key combinations for Photoshop 6.

TABLE 9.3   TRACKING KEYSTROKE SHORTCUTS

Function	Mac	PC
Decrease tracking by 20	(Option-la)	[Alt+la]
Increase tracking by 20	(Option-ra)	[Alt+ra]
Decrease tracking by 200	(Cmd-Option-la)	[Alt+Ctrl+la]
Increase tracking by 200	(Cmd-Option-ra)	[Alt+Ctrl+ra]

> **Note**
> The codes "ra" and "la" in the preceding table represent right arrow and left arrow, respectively.

> **Tip**
> When using the type controls in the Character palette, you can tab from one entry field to the next, and increase or decrease the values using the up-arrow or down-arrow keys on the keyboard. Pressing the arrows changes the point size, leading, baseline shift, and scaling by one, and kerning and tracking by 20. Pressing the arrow in combination with the Shift key changes the point size, leading, baseline shift, and scaling by 10, and the kerning and tracking change by 200. Arrows will also scroll the font list; pressing the Shift key in combination with the arrow jumps to the top or bottom of the list in accord with the direction of the arrow.

KERNING

One of the more subtle differences between type that looks good and reads well on the page and type that doesn't is precise control of spacing between the letters. Kerning is like a fine-tuning knob for the tracking. Some letters are notorious for not fitting well in the general scheme of the defined spacing between letters. Kerning is like tracking in that it affects spacing between letters, but kerning is available only to affect letter sets, working independently of tracking. In other words, you can apply kerning between letters and track them as well—the effects are retained separately. Tracking controls the feel of the lettering overall, and kerning controls the distance between the distinct letter pairs.

Photoshop's automatic kerning takes care of most problems for the casual type user, but when seeking more control, it is time to turn off automatic kerning by entering a kerning value rather than leaving the setting at Metrics. The Kerning field can be entered only when the cursor has been placed between a pair of letters. To change the kerning, insert the cursor between two letters and enter a kerning value. To change back to automatic kerning, place the cursor between the letters where you want to reinstate the automatic kerning, and select Metrics from the pop-up menu.

Kerning is most effective in controlling distinct letter sets that don't seem to sit right when next to each other. It can help, for example, by tucking a lowercase *o* a little closer to a capital *W*, or inserting some space between two letters that seem to situate too close together.

Use the following steps to kern type in an image:

1. Open an image in which you want to place type, or open a new file.
2. Select the Type tool from the toolbox.
3. Click the image where you want to place the type.
4. Type in the text you want to use. (Use word if nothing springs to mind.)

5. Hold the pointer between any two letters and click once. This will place a flashing cursor between the letters.

6. Select a kerning number between –1,000 and 1,000 to move the letters closer together or farther apart (see Figure 9.16).

Figure 9.16
Kerning is applied to the original letter pairs in this type to even out the apparent spacing between letters. Kerning is applied as follows: W-O, –75; O-R, –50; R-D, –10. Each kerning value here tightens the space between letters.

Kerning is really necessary only in headlines or creating special effects. In typesetting larger sets of letters, you cannot set absolutes for pairs of letters in Photoshop, although this is a feature available on some high-end layout programs (QuarkXPress). If you could set kerning for specific pairs of letters in a kerning table, for example, and then save that table for use with that particular font, you could make the kerning adjustment one time and save it permanently. This way, it doesn't have to be adjusted each time you use the font or letter pairing. As this is the case, you may want to set type that needs extensive kerning, using another program.

Applying kerning to a set of letters is more of an art and individual preference than a science. However, keeping the letters of words evenly spaced makes them more cohesive and, again, they are easier to read.

Kerning can be controlled with key commands if the type you want to control has a flashing cursor between the pair. The shortcuts for adjustment are the same as for adjusting the tracking, and are listed in Table 9.4.

TABLE 9.4   KERNING KEYSTROKE SHORTCUTS

Function	Mac	PC
Decrease kerning by 20	(Option-la)	[Alt+la]
Increase kerning by 20	(Option-ra)	[Alt+ra]
Decrease kerning by 200	(Cmd-Option-la)	[Alt+Ctrl+la]
Increase kerning by 200	(Cmd-Option-ra)	[Alt+Ctrl+ra]

LEADING

Leading is a vertical control of the spacing between the lines of text. It is measured in point size (currently with an upper limit of 1,296 pts to –1,296 pts), and defaults are controlled by the chosen point size for the type. As a standard automatic setting, Photoshop adds 20% to the point size to determine leading (that is, when no measurement is in the leading box, Photoshop automatically defaults to the point size of the type plus 20%). A 10-point type has 12-point leading, and a 100-point type has 120-point leading. This leading measure works for a wide variety of cases. You can, however, control and change the default leading by entering a number in the leading field after selecting a portion of the text that you want to affect.

The idea behind leading (for readability) is to provide vertical graphic space between lines of text. This is meant to facilitate moving the reader's eye from one line to the next. Creating too much or too little distance makes it awkward for the reader's eye to make a smooth transition from one line to the next. Various typefaces require different leading for the best readability due to their imprint. Generally, a heavier type will require more space and a lighter type less. Leading in Photoshop works in spacing between both line breaks and hard returns.

Note

Leading is measured baseline to baseline from the line below to the line above.

Use the following steps to apply leading to the type in an image:

1. Open an image in which you want to place type, or open a new file.
2. Select the Type tool from the toolbox.
3. Click the image in which you want to place the type.
4. Type in the text you want to use. (You will have to use more than one word, as leading works on a series of text lines.) There needs to be at least one return typed in what you enter to make more than one line of text.
5. Select a portion of the line you want to lead.

Note

It is necessary to select only the bottom line in a pair of lines to apply leading to a pair of lines, but you can select all the type in a text block by pressing (Cmd-A) [Ctrl+A]. Leading can be applied differently to successive lines of text and is controlled by the bottom line in any pairing.

6. Enter the number of points of leading you would like between the lines (see Figure 9.17).

Figure 9.17
The Photoshop default or Auto setting for leading is determined by Photoshop by adding 20% to the point size and using that value. The example to the right of the original shows the type leaded at 20% less than the point size, and the bottom example is shown using leading that is two times the point size.

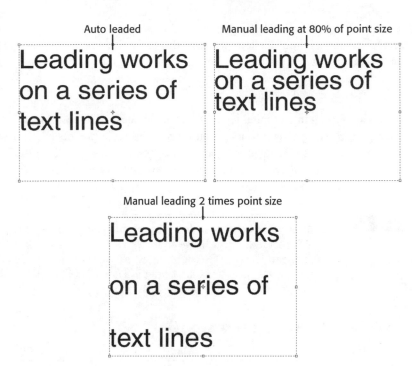

Auto leaded

Leading works on a series of text lines

Manual leading at 80% of point size

Leading works on a series of text lines

Manual leading 2 times point size

Leading works

on a series of

text lines

PART

II

CH

9

Tip

Generally, point size and leading should be at least equal. Most layout programs insert a greater value for the leading than the type size to make type seem less cramped.

The default is generally acceptable, but you should consider several things before choosing a different leading:

- The length of the line of type
- The style of type
- The appearance or absence of ascenders and descenders

Generally, the longer the line of type is, the more leading you will want to use between lines. This helps the eye pick out the next line when shifting from one line to the next.

Note

The length of the line is somewhat dependent on the size of the text. A six-inch line of text is not so long when written with 72-point type. In four-point type, that same six-inch line of text might seem very long, and will probably require that the leading be increased from the default to help the reader pick out successive lines of text.

When considering leading for a particular type because of its style, choosing a leading becomes more subjective. There is no absolute way to measure the correspondence between what a letter looks like and how it should be leaded. The density or imprint of a letter, however, might be considered the standard to go by—that is, the amount of space the letters fill. The base height of the letters affects this presence. The x-height defines the relative bulk of a character. A character with a greater x-height generally requires more leading because it takes up more space on the page—or has a larger imprint. A very slight type might use a reduced leading.

If you are typing in all capital letters or have a typeface that has only caps (Copperplate, for example), you might want to lead a bit more tightly than the default. These letters will not have descenders, so the effective point size is less. In other words, nothing will go below the letter's baseline, so there is significantly more room between lines of text. Consider tightening the leading in such instances.

Tip

Leading does not work on the top line of text as there is no line above. If you need space above a first line of text, move the text with the Move tool [(V)]. If you need precise spacing, place a return on the first line of the text you are inputting. This allows you to lead from the first line, even though nothing appears in it (see Table 9.5).

TABLE 9.5   LEADING KEYSTROKE SHORTCUTS

Function	Mac	PC
Decrease leading by 2	(Option-da)	[Alt+da]
Increase leading by 2	(Option-ua)	[Alt+ua]
Decrease leading by 10	(Cmd-Option-da)	[Alt+Ctrl+da]
Increase leading by 10	(Cmd-Option-ua)	[Alt+Ctrl+ua]

Note

In the preceding table "ua" and "da" represent up arrow and down arrow, respectively.

CONTROLLING BASELINE SHIFT

Baseline shift is to leading what kerning is to tracking. Using this baseline shift control, you can move an individual character above and below the baseline in the line of text where it appears. The *baseline* is the invisible line which characters seem to rest on (see Figure 9.18). Adjusting baseline shift can help achieve a finer typeset look in controlling special characters, such as exponents, or it can be used to create jagged and designed effects. The baseline can be shifted between –1,296 and 1,296 points.

Figure 9.18
Baseline shift is measured in points as the distance between where the letter rests initially and where it ends up due to the shift.

Use the following steps to apply baseline shift to type in an image:

1. Open an image in which you want to place type, or open a new file.
2. Select the Type tool from the toolbox.
3. Click the image where you want to place the type.
4. Type in the text you want to use. (Use word if nothing springs to mind.)
5. Select a letter or letters to which you would like to apply baseline shift.
6. Enter the number of points of baseline shift you would like to set the letter off by (see Figure 9.19).

PART

II

CH

9

Figure 9.19
This effect was accomplished by choosing baseline shifts for individual letters to bring them both above and below the baseline.

Creating a custom exponent or fraction is relatively easy using the baseline shift, and far more uniform than trying to place numbers manually using different layers. Your preferences for the look of the type might vary.

> **Note**
>
> Exponents (or Superscripts) and footnote numbering (or Subscripts) can be created using the new Photoshop Superscript and Subscript attributes. However, you may find you will want additional control in designing some type elements. See the next section for more information on Superscript, Subscript, and a host of other type-attribute controls.

Use the following steps to create an exponent:

1. Open an image in which you want to place type, or open a new file.
2. Select the Type tool from the toolbox.
3. Click the image in which you want to place the type.
4. Type in the text you want to use. (For this example, I used `15x3 + 1/2x2`.)
5. Select the number you want to alter and apply the settings to create exponents, numerators, and denominators, by selecting individual numbers and applying font sizing, kerning, baseline shift, and tracking (see Figures 9.20 and 9.21). See Table 9.6 for baseline shift keyboard shortcuts.

Figure 9.20
The exponent here was sized to 40% and fraction numbers are 50% of the size of the rest of the type line. Baseline shift for the exponents was 45% and baseline shift for numerators was 35%. These numbers work for a variety of type-faces but may need to be altered for different type imprints.

$$15x^3 + \tfrac{1}{2}x^2$$

Figure 9.21
Combinations of type attributes can be used to design type effects using multiple layers, faces, colors, and controls. The ability to control each letter individually allows for some complex arrangements even on a single layer.

TABLE 9.6 BASELINE SHIFT KEYSTROKE SHORTCUTS

Function	Mac	PC
Decrease baseline shift by 2	(Shift-Option-da)	[Shift+Alt+da]
Increase baseline shift by 2	(Shift-Option-ua)	[Shift+Alt+ua]
Decrease baseline shift by 10	(Shift-Cmd-Option-da)	[Shift+Alt+Ctrl+da]
Increase baseline shift by 10	(Shift-Cmd-Option-ua)	[Shift+Alt+Ctrl+ua]

OTHER TYPE CONTROLS

 There is a broad range of other type controls that can affect the appearance of type, and many are new to Photoshop 6 with the broad Type Tool enhancements. Character features include Faux Bold, Faux Italic, Rotate Character, All Caps, Small Caps, Superscript, Subscript, Underline (Right and Left for vertical type), Strike Through, Ligatures, Old Style Numbers, Fractional widths allowance, No Break, and Reset. All of these are accessed on the Character palette menu. Additional paragraph features include Roman Hanging Punctuation, Justification, Hyphenation, Every-Line Composer, Single-Line Composer, and Reset Paragraph. Anti-aliasing methods can be controlled on the Options bar using the anti-alias selection drop menu. Some of these settings affect individual characters while others affect the entire layer. Table 9.7 lists and describes these features.

TABLE 9.7   ADDITIONAL TYPE ATTRIBUTES

Type Control	Function/Description	Effects (Character, Word, Line, Paragraph, Layer, and/or Image)	Location
Faux Bold	Simulates a bold weight style for a typeface, even if one does not exist in the character set or family.	Character or layer	Character palette menu
Faux Italic	Simulates an italic style for a typeface, even if one does not exist in the character set or family.	Character or layer	Character palette menu
Rotate Character	Rotates character orientation 90° counterclockwise, so that type appears to be vertical. This is selected by default and works only with vertical type orientation.	Layer	Character palette menu
All Caps	Changes type case to all capital letters no matter how the type was entered. Capitalization can be reverted to how it was typed by unchecking this option.	Character or layer	Character palette menu
Small Caps	Changes type case to all small capital letters no matter how the type was entered. Capitalization can be reverted to how it was typed by unchecking this option. Uses Small Capitals in the letter sets, or creates faux small caps if the letter set does not contain them.	Character or layer	Character palette menu

Table 9.7   Continued

Type Control	Function/Description	Effects (Character, Word, Line, Paragraph, Layer, and/or Image)	Location
Superscript	Automatically reduces point size and elevates the text off the baseline to create type elements such as exponents (X^2) or footnote numbering.	Character or layer	Character palette menu
Subscript	Automatically reduces point size and lowers the text off the baseline to create type elements such as variable reference, scientific notation (chemistry H_2O) or permutation index ($X_1, X_2, \ldots X_n$).	Character or layer	Character palette menu
Right and Left for vertical type)	Creates underlining for text. Vertical text offers the option of placing the line to the right or left of the text rather than under.	Character or layer	Character palette menu
Strike Through	Creates a slash through letters as if they were meant to be struck or eliminated.	Character or layer	Character palette menu
Ligatures	Connects letters of certain character sets, such as æ for ae, or fi for fi. Works only with Open Type fonts (extended letter set fonts).	Character or layer	Character palette menu
Old Style Numbers	Allows use of old style numbering if these characters are included in font sets. Works only with Open Type fonts.	Character or layer	Character palette menu

TABLE 9.7   CONTINUED

Type Control	Function/Description	Effects (Character, Word, Line, Paragraph, Layer, and/or Image)	Location
Fractional Widths	Allows spacing between characters to be defined as partial pixels. When turned off, considers whole pixel value spacing only.	Layer	Character palette menu
No Break	Removes hyphenation in a single word. General settings for hyphenation controlled with the Hyphenation attribute (see the following).	Selected word only	Character palette menu
Reset	Resets all character attributes (spacing, sizing, and so forth) to defaults.	Character or layer	Character palette menu
Roman Hanging Punctuation	Allows punctuation (hyphens, commas, and so on) to extend into the margins.	Line or layer	Paragraph palette menu
Justification	Allows user definition of rules for determining character width and spacing that can be used in justifying type.	Paragraph, layer, or image	Paragraph palette menu
Hyphenation	Allows user to define how hyphenation will be handled.	Paragraph, layer, or image	Paragraph palette menu
Every Line Composer	A set of composition rules used to determine the hyphenation and scaling within a paragraph, using an approach that considers multiple lines.	Paragraph or layer	Paragraph palette menu

TABLE 9.7   CONTINUED

Type Control	Function/Description	Effects (Character, Word, Line, Paragraph, Layer, and/or Image)	Location
Single Line Composer	A set of composition rules used to determine the hyphenation and scaling within a paragraph, using an approach that considers the single line only.	Paragraph or layer	Paragraph palette menu
Reset Paragraph	Returns paragraph settings to defaults.	Paragraph or layer	Paragraph palette menu
Anti-aliasing	Affects the amount of anti-aliasing used in presenting fonts. Includes four levels of blending.	Layer	Options bar

JUSTIFICATION

 Justification defines how multiple lines of type will fall within the margins defined by a type box. There are really four options for justification, although there are additional variables such as justify left, justify center, justify right, and full justify. Justify left will consider the left of the text bounding box or insertion point (if using no bounding box) as a left margin, align successive lines of text to that point. This creates a straight left margin. Justify left is also known as *rag right*, as the text will end up with a jagged margin on the right side. Justify center aligns the text in the center of the text box or uses the insertion point to locate the center of each successive line. This balances the text lines so that they are weighted evenly and creates a ragged margin on both right and left sides of the text. Justify right considers the right of the text bounding box or insertion point (if using no bounding box) as a right margin, aligning successive lines of text to that. This creates a straight right margin and a jagged left.

Full justify can be used only with text contained in a bounding box. This type of justification will align full lines of type to both the right and left margins of the bounding box using the scaling options and rules entered in the Justification dialog box (see Figure 9.22).

When using full justify, there are four options within that option, and all affect the final line of the paragraphs. The final line is the only difference in the control. It can be justified left, center, right, or full (All), using the same general parameters described for justification. When using Justify All, you might get some final paragraph lines that are greatly distorted.

Figure 9.22
To open the Justification dialog box, choose Justification from the Paragraph palette menu. This dialog box gives you control of the maximum, minimum, and constants that Photoshop will use when scaling type for the purpose of justification.

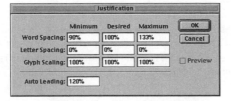

HYPHENATION

 When the Hyphenation check box is enabled on the paragraphs palette, hyphenation settings as defined in the Hyphenation dialog box (see Figure 9.23) affect the appearance of type—specifically affecting word and line breaks.

Figure 9.23
The Hyphenation dialog box can be opened by selecting Hyphenation from the Paragraph palette menu. These settings are used to determine hyphenation in word breaks.

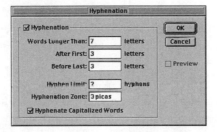

You can affect the way hyphenation is applied by specifying the minimum length of a word that can be hyphenated and the number of letters that must be used before and after the break. If Photoshop cannot meet the criteria you set and, depending on the composer settings (Every Line or Single Line), no hyphenation will occur on the line, and scaling may be employed as per the justification settings, if you are in full-justify mode.

Every Line or Single Line composer considerations affect the result of the hyphenation, in that each has different criteria in measuring how to allow automatic text effects to be employed. Whereas using Every Line should generally give you the best overall results because it considers multiple lines at one time, you may want to use Single Line to gain more manual control.

No Break

No Break on the Character palette menu works in tandem with hyphenation by selectively letting you eliminate hyphenation. To remove an unwanted hyphen, highlight the word involved (all of it) and choose No Break from the Character palette menu. The hyphen will be removed and Photoshop will decide where the word belongs based on other justification and paragraph-control settings.

THE ANTI-ALIASING TYPE OPTION

 The anti-aliasing option for type works like anti-aliasing a selection. It is a little more versatile as it allows four different levels of blending: None, Crisp, Strong, and Smooth. None applies no anti-aliasing, while Crisp, Strong, and Smooth apply anti-aliasing to varying degrees. Crisp is somewhat like sharpening, Strong like a slight emboldening, and Smooth maximizes the smoothness of the edge. All three of the aliasing effects affect the same number of edge pixels in the letters. To use anti-aliasing, simply choose a text layer and then select an option from the Anti-Aliasing drop menu on the Options bar. This option can be applied per layer only.

For the most part, your choices here will affect the appearance of smaller type to a greater degree than larger type, and your choices will impact lower-resolution images more than high-resolution ones. Your choice is subjective, based on the content of the image, and how well you want the type to stand off from the background. However, generally, as the dpi of the image and/or size of the image go up, so can the amount of anti-aliasing.

THE FRACTIONAL WIDTHS CHARACTER SETTING

Fractional Widths (or Fractal Character Widths) is concerned with maintaining spacing with smaller fonts. Spacing varies between fonts slightly because fractions of pixels are rendered at the edge of characters. Depending on how the edges of the type fall, the letters might be too close together and actually will join in some cases. Turning off Fractional Widths keeps the smaller fonts in better alignment and stops them from blending together (see Figure 9.24).

Figure 9.24
Here the same word is shown with Fractional Widths on and with them off. Note that the version where they are off does not have a problem with the fonts running together.

Fractional Widths On

Fractional Widths Off

Although use is again somewhat subjective, this will generally be most useful when using small type in low-resolution images, and will probably be used often when working with images destined for the Web.

OTHER TYPESETTING SHORTCUTS

There are quite a few additional shortcuts built in with Photoshop that revolve around increased functionality in the Type tools. These are presented in Table 9.8 as useful additions to your shortcut arsenal.

TABLE 9.8   MISCELLANEOUS TYPESETTING KEYSTROKES

Function	Mac Keystroke	PC Keystroke
Toggle to move tool	(Cmd)	[Ctrl]
Align left (h) or top (v)	(Shift–Cmd–L)	[Shift+Ctrl+L]
Align center	(Shift–Cmd–C)	[Shift+Ctrl+C]
Align right (h) or bottom (v)	(Shift–Cmd–R)	[Shift+Ctrl+R]
Select 1 character left (h), or up (v)	(Shift-la)	[Shift+la]
Select 1 character right (h), or down (v)	(Shift-ra)	[Shift+la]
Select from insertion to next line down (h), or left (v) at insertion point	(Shift- la)	[Shift+la]
Select from insertion to next line up (h), or right (v) at insertion point	(Shift-la)	[Shift+la]
Select all characters from insertion point to mouse-click point	(Shift-click)	[Shift+click]
Toggle type selection view on/off	(Cmd-H)	[Ctrl+H]
Toggle Underlining on/off	(Shift–Cmd–U)	[Shift+Ctrl+U]
Toggle Strikethrough on/off	(Shift–Cmd–/)	[Shift+Ctrl+/]
Toggle All Caps on/off	(Shift–Cmd–K)	[Shift+Ctrl+K]
Toggle Small Caps on/off	(Shift–Cmd–H)	[Shift+Ctrl+H]
Change to 100% horizontal scale	(Shift–Cmd–X)	[Shift+Ctrl+X]
Change to 100% vertical scale	(Shift–Cmd–Option-X)	[Shift+Ctrl+Alt+X]
Change to Auto leading	(Shift–Cmd–Option-A)	[Shift+Ctrl+Alt+A]
Change to 0 for tracking	(Shift–Cmd–Q)	[Shift+Ctrl+Q]
Justifies paragraph—left-align last line	(Shift–Cmd–J)	[Shift+Ctrl+J]

TABLE 9.8   CONTINUED

Function	Mac Keystroke	PC Keystroke
Justifies paragraph—force last-line justify	(Shift–Cmd–F)	[Shift+Ctrl+F]
Toggle paragraph hyphenation on/off	(Shift–Cmd–Option-H)	[Shift+Ctrl+Alt+H]
Toggle single/every-line composer	(Shift–Cmd–Option-T)	[Shift+Ctrl+Alt+T]

Note

The codes "la" and "ra" in the preceding table represent left arrow and right arrow, respectively.

TROUBLESHOOTING

KEEPING FONTS LOOKING THE SAME ON DIFFERENT COMPUTERS

I have sent Photoshop files with unrendered type layers to friends, and although the words are correct, the fonts end up looking wacky. How do I stop that from happening?

There are several solutions to this problem. The easiest is to render the type and/or flatten the image before sending it. Unless the type needs to be editable for some reason, it doesn't have to remain unrendered. If this would leave the quality unacceptable, it is also possible to turn the type into paths using either the Create Work Path or Convert to Shape command on the Layer, Type menu. Create Work Path will make a path that you can save with the image (perhaps to compare rendering), and Convert to Shape will create a layer-clipping path in the shape of the type. The path can later be loaded as a selection and filled independently of the image resolution. There are creative ways to influence the result in this fashion. For example, if the image is just text, but too large at the resolution you are trying to use to send effectively through email, you can convert to paths and then reduce the resolution. When the receiving party gets the file, they can increase the resolution and render the high-resolution results.

If the type must be editable (unrendered), there are several options for transferring the file. The easiest of these is probably to send a PDF, by saving the file in that format from Photoshop and using the Embed Fonts option. The file will be editable in Photoshop 6 and Adobe Acrobat. You might also consider sending the fonts (screen and printer if applicable and legal—see your agreement with the font company) along with the image. If there are anticipated problems and the destination machine (for example, you expect that it will attempt to replace the font), it might be best to use a common typeface, or simply suggest a type-style replacement. Short of suggesting a specific replacement, simply describe the typeface (serif/sans-serif, bold/medium/light, x height, and so on). You cannot expect perfect results with the last method, but at least whatever you send won't be substituted for by Courier (which is the default in many cases).

It is further possible, if using Photoshop functions alone to generate the file, that you could create an action to simply re-create the image. In this case, you wouldn't send an image file at all—just the action that would be used to create it. This can reduce the file size of something potentially enormous to a very small, highly portable size. Best of all, the results will be fully editable at the destination.

WHEN TYPE DISAPPEARS

Usually, I can edit my type and move it around as I please—even pulling it back when it runs off the edge of a page. However, there was one image I was working on in which the type became uneditable and got cut off where it left the edge of the document. I am sure I didn't render the type. How did that happen?

There is a difference between rendered and unrendered text, and that difference is edibility. When your type becomes rendered, you will no longer be able to access it with the type tool and change it. That type in your image became both rendered and cut off suggests one thing: You used Merge Visible to combine the type layer and another layer (the same thing can happen with Merge Down, but only if you merge to the background layer). This and other methods of physically combining layers will cause type to render before the layers are merged. Of merging options, only Merge Down will allow you to keep the full content of layer information intact when combining layers (except when merging to the background). In any case, there is no warning that will tell you that text is being rendered, although it is.

For now, the solution to the problem would be to back up using the image history to get back the portion of the image that you lost due to the merge. Then, you can use Merge Down instead to combine the layers and keep the text you had. It might be a good idea to take a snapshot of where you were with the image as some of what you had accomplished might be able to be painted back in.

In the future, it might also be a good idea to duplicate type layers before combining them and then hide the duplicate by shutting off the view. This will leave you with a fresh start and editable type if you want to change your procedure and result.

PHOTOSHOP AT WORK: SETTING TYPE IN AN IMAGE

Situating a great line of text in an image where it will get lost makes the line less effective. To have the text work well with an image, you need to evaluate the best place to put it. Without good placement, it can become a nuisance or hindrance to the message the image is trying to convey.

Before placing type, you need to consider the landscape the type will fall into in the image when it is finally placed. What looks good in black on white might be awful over a background image and might not be defined well in color if the colors are too similar. For example, you probably would not want to run an ocean blue type over an area of water unless you are looking for some special effect. Better to use a color with more color contrast.

If the goal of incorporating type is most often to have it remain legible and help make a point linguistically, the reader will have to be able to pick it out with relative ease. Making it more obscure will keep it from having strong impact, unless there is a method to your design. A simple check of the background and selecting the best place for the type first will not only help your message stand out but will help you design the type to fit the image in the space allotted.

This example (you can get the sample image on page 9 of the workbook, which you can download from ps6.com) lets you work with placement of type in creating a fictitious ad for a product.

Use the following steps to place type in the image:

1. Open an image into which you can incorporate some type.

2. Look for areas in which you can easily place type without too much image interference, so the type stands out clearly from the background. The best areas to place type are relatively flat areas without much background noise. Watch out for areas that can run over the subject, or places that force you to downplay the type size too much (see Figure 9.25).

Figure 9.25
This image has lots of space for type and a darker, blurred background, so lighter type will show up pretty well, no matter what the color. This leaves a lot of potential options.

3. After you've found a good spot, click the Type tool where you'd like to start the type, and enter it.

4. Adjust the type to fit that area by controlling fonts, type size, kerning, leading, tracking, and color (baseline shift might also come in handy for some specialized work, as can drop shadows and other type effects).

For the example, I used the slogan "Don't forget important stuff, Use Time Trax" as my text in advertising the fictitious product (see Figure 9.26). I wanted the name of the product to stand out, and let the viewer know they didn't want to be in the same situation as the guy in the image who looks like he's forgotten something. You can use another slogan and product, or even another image, to vary the exercise (see Figures 9.27 and 9.28).

Figure 9.26
Clumping the words together might not be the best choice for this image, as no matter where they land, they fall on the subject and look a little like a mistake.

Figure 9.27
Breaking up the type might work a little better. Here, because of cropping, the image looks a little crowded.

Figure 9.28
This time the type fits a little better. The words at left hug the contour of the subject's arm a little, and it seems like a better fit. There are still other options.

Tip

If an image is noisy and does not have much free space for type, consider running it over the image with some sort of device to help separate it from the background (for example, dropping a shadow behind the type). You might add to the image, either by creating a false border or extending the image with some of the information already in the background. Any of these ideas could be your solution for this example.

→ For more information on adding to an image and extending backgrounds, **see** "Composition Changes and Improvements," **p. 603**.

Type placed in the proper area of an image or background increases its legibility. The correct decision in placement or separation can help type do its job. To make your job easier, look for and choose images that are compatible with text when you know you are going to be incorporating it, and create type to make your words stand out to achieve the best results (see Figure 9.29). Look to make your words stand out.

Figure 9.29
Properly executed type can even stand out of a distracting and seemingly conflicting background clutter.

CHAPTER 10

CREATING WITH IMAGE HISTORIES

In this chapter

WHAT AN IMAGE HISTORY DOES

When the History feature was added to Photoshop, many seemed to think it was just some glorified undo that ate up memory. The fact is, this glorified undo is a very powerful tool for working with and creating images. It would be just a glorified undo if it simply stepped back in the process but there are other features, including Snapshots and the History Brush tool. *Snapshots* allows you to freeze image states while you are working with the image. The *History Brush* allows you to paint with any previous version of the image. These are incredibly powerful creative and correction tools.

USING HISTORY STATES TO UNDO/REDO CHANGES

The basic function of a History is its capability to undo. Like Edit, Undo, or pressing (Cmd-Z) [Ctrl+Z], you can step back after you do something you don't think worked and want to take back. However, with a History you can undo up to 100 changes to an image, depending on the setting in your preferences. Each time you do something to an image, what you did is listed as an image state in the History palette (see Figure 10.1). The steps are listed in chronological order from the oldest step at the top to the newest at the bottom. You take a new step and it is added to the bottom of the list. When you reach the number of History states you have set in the preferences, the top item on the list is removed when the bottom one is appended.

Note

Examining a History is like reviewing recorded actions, but a History cannot be saved and reproduced after the image is closed.

You can step back in single steps from the current position on the History palette by pressing (Cmd–Option-Z) [Ctrl+Alt+Z], and you can go forward again by pressing (Shift–Cmd–Z) [Shift+Ctrl+Z]. You can also select a state, as long as it still exists, by clicking it in the palette. In this way you can look at a step-by-step development of the image, compare states in a nonchronological order, or simply undo and redo quite a few events with a single click. It gives you some room to experiment without worrying about starting all over again in working on corrections or changes.

Note

To have the History palette record image states, you don't have to do a thing—the feature is always enabled.

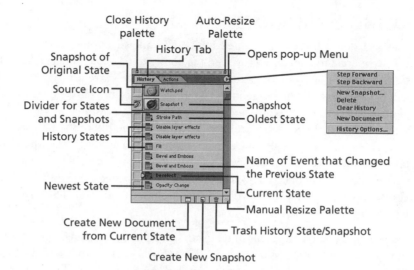

Figure 10.1
The History palette,
like the Layers,
Channels, and Paths
palettes, is really a
command center for
History states.

Close History palette
Auto-Resize Palette
History Tab
Opens pop-up Menu
Snapshot of Original State
Source Icon
Divider for States and Snapshots
History States
Newest State
Snapshot
Oldest State
Name of Event that Changed the Previous State
Current State
Manual Resize Palette
Trash History State/Snapshot
Create New Document from Current State
Create New Snapshot

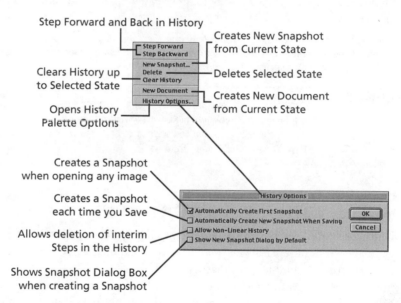

Step Forward and Back in History
Creates New Snapshot from Current State
Clears History up to Selected State
Deletes Selected State
Opens History Palette Options
Creates New Document from Current State
Creates a Snapshot when opening any image
Creates a Snapshot each time you Save
Allows deletion of interim Steps in the History
Shows Snapshot Dialog Box when creating a Snapshot

SETTING HISTORY STATES

By default the History palette holds 20 History states, but you can alter that between 1 and 100 states by changing the setting in the General Preferences. The advantage to more states is obviously more flexibility with being able to return to earlier image states; the disadvantage is that a History takes up memory: the more states you have, the less available memory you will have for other functions. If you don't have a lot of memory in the first place, you might want to keep only a few History states at a time—especially if your computer's performance seems slow. However, after you start playing with what they can do, you might want to purchase more RAM instead, so you can retain the History.

CREATING SNAPSHOTS

Using Histories presents a unique advantage by allowing you to backpedal through what you have done to an image. However, the ability to take Snapshots adds to this advantage significantly. When you take a Snapshot, it freezes the current image state—layers and all—and places a copy of the image in the upper portion of the History palette. This might seem like a glorified History state—and it is. But this poses a distinct advantage over the History state list in that the Snapshot will not disappear off the top of the History list and be lost forever—at least not until you close the image. In other words, Snapshots allow you to hold on to History states in a semipermanent fashion; Snapshots will be retained in the session with the image whether you go through 10 or 10,000 steps. As you are working along, and you see a state you know you will probably want to retain, take a Snapshot and you won't have to worry about losing it.

Snapshots are semipermanent in that they are discarded when you close the image. In other words, they are session specific. If you crash, shut down, or even close an image on Photoshop to get working on something else, the Snapshots will not be retained. Be sure to plan accordingly.

 You created several snapshots in an image, and then you closed it. When you opened it again, the snapshots weren't there any more. If you want to save the snapshots, too, see "Saving the Snapshots" in the Troubleshooting section at the end of this chapter.

Note

When in doubt, take a Snapshot. Although Snapshots eat up memory, it is better to save a state that you think you might want to return to by taking a Snapshot of it than it is to decide after it is gone that you want to go back to it. You decide that too late and you will have to re-create the effect from scratch.

WORKING WITH THE HISTORY BRUSH

 The third and probably most potent use of History is in using Snapshots and prior states of an image to aid in repairing or creating images and image elements. This is done using the History Brush and fill features that support History as a selection. The History Brush and fills allow you to paint between image states. For example, if you step back in the History palette and see an area of the image that looked better than it does now, but you like the rest of the current image, you can use the History Brush or a fill to paint that portion of the older image state back into the new one. Doing this allows you to make the best use of multiple states in an image to attain the best result. Unless you have changed alignment (either in layering, position, document size, or so on), these changes can be accomplished very easily. Simply place the History palette source icon next to the state you want to paint with. With the painting source indicated, select the History Brush from the Toolbar and start painting, or choose History from the Use menu in the Fill dialog box.

What does this do for you? It opens the door to painting with filter applications and painting with variations of the image for corrections (such as adding back lost detail or making spot corrections).

For example, say you want to add a special effect to a portion of an image. You can create the effect on the whole image, take a Snapshot, revert to the earlier state and use the History Brush to paint in the areas you want with the effect (this is taken care of another way in the next section—harder to envision, but easier to use). In the case of corrections, you can run the Dust & Scratches filter to remove the dust and scratches, revert to an earlier state after saving the snapshot, and then use the History brush to paint in the damaged areas you want to cover, while leaving the rest of the image unaffected by the Dust & Scratches filter (which can be damaging). Using the History brush in this way is similar to what you can do with the Sharpen or Blur tool, where a filter is applied only to a small portion of the image based on the brush you are using.

To apply a filter or state, it is best to do so in a second layer, or one above what is currently visible. This can be tricky if you've never done it before, but it really ends up being pretty simple when you know how. Use the following steps to apply the History Brush to a topical layer:

1. Open the image you want to work on.

2. Get the image to the state where you want to apply the History Brush.

3. Duplicate the flattened image to a new layer by pressing (Shift–Cmd–C)[Shift+Ctrl+C] (this copies a merged version of the image), and then Paste. This copies everything you can see into a new layer.

4. Run the filter or apply the effects/changes on the layer you have just created. This keeps the image as you have created it safe on the other layer.

5. When you have finished applying effects, take a Snapshot of the image. You will use the Snapshot for the application of the History brush in a later step.

6. Select all and clear the layer.

7. Click to the left of the snapshot taken in Step 5 to place the Source icon for the History Brush beside the Snapshot you took of the image after creating the effect.

 8. Select the History Brush and choose the brush and options from the Tool Options bar.

9. Apply the History Brush to the layer you cleared. The effects you deleted will fill in where you paint. After you have painted in the effects you want, you can adjust the opacity, blending mode, layer style, and so on to get the most from the History Brush application.

The extra secret step in there (that you didn't even notice—which is why I have to point it out) is the step in which you simply delete the contents of the layer and continue working. The History Brush will paint only to layers that exist in the state you are painting from. Creating the effect on its own layer and then deleting it does several things: It creates a unique layer for the application of the History Brush so you will have more control over how it is finally incorporated, and it creates a valid layer for application of the History Brush without having to do any checking or receiving annoying errors.

 If you are having trouble trying to apply the History Brush to an image, see "I Can't Paint with the History Brush" in the Troubleshooting section at the end of this chapter.

Figure 10.2 shows a before-and-after depiction of one of the sample images included in the Photoshop Samples folder with an application of a filter with the help of the History Brush and the technique described. It is combined with other features and abilities in using Photoshop, such as using selection, path stroking, brush shapes, layering, and the like. The variations on application of image states are really infinite in both a creative and reparative sense.

Figure 10.2
Following the steps for application of the History Brush, the image layer was duplicated, altered, deleted, and reapplied. Here the image was altered by applying Solarize and then Auto Levels. After the result was deleted, it was reapplied with a shaped brush over the numbers (using the Fade Size option for the brush), and then filled over the arms and edge after a selection was made. Bevel & Emboss and Shadows were applied separately to the fill and painting by duplicating the target layer after the painting was done and deleting it to prepare for the fill.

INTRODUCING THE ART HISTORY BRUSH

The Art History Brush is an interesting new addition to the toolbar. It seems to be intended as a purely creative tool which offers options for painting and stroking images with redefined stroke shapes, which you can manipulate using the tool settings. See the Options bar in Figure 10.3.

Figure 10.3
The History Brush's different controls, including Style, Fidelity, Area, and Spacing are the key to creating different effects with the tool. These controls enable you to change the brushstroke shape, method of sampling, and result.

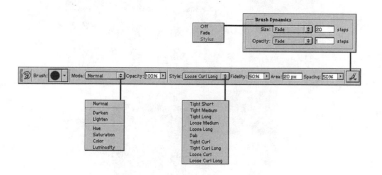

PART

II

CH

10

The tool samples a pixel area based on the History source and uses that sample to determine a color and shape for strokes. These strokes are sent out from the brush you are using in random directions from the point of application.

- The Style has to do with the shape of the preset strokes.
- The Fidelity has to do with the amount the tool will adhere to the color set in the sample—the lower the number, the more the color will be allowed to vary by random generation.
- The Area has to do with the width of the sampling, and the spacing affects the spacing between samples.

Although there is some predictability using a 1-pixel brush with pure (100%) Fidelity, a 1-pixel area and 0% spacing, this predictability quickly disappears and is lost in the wild bursting shapes that get created (see Figure 10.4).

The tool works best on higher resolutions, but also seems more geared toward generating effects than other solid results. The result in Figure 10.5 was achieved using just the History brush with varied layer settings for layers created both above and below the Type Layer. Opacity and layer style options were changed to meld the effects.

Figure 10.4
These strokes are the result of using a pure white History source and painting over a 50% gray background with each of the tool's stroke shapes (as marked). The settings used are as follows: Fidelity 50%, Area 20px, Spacing 50%, Size Fade 20%.

Figure 10.5
In all, the Art History Brush is generally geared to experimentation and play than structured how-to. However it is a new tool in its infant stages which will likely be developed more in upcoming versions of Photoshop.

TROUBLESHOOTING

SAVING THE SNAPSHOTS

Every time I save an image with Snapshots they aren't there when I open the image up. Isn't there a way to save the Snapshots with the images?

It might seem discouraging that Snapshots are lost when the image is saved, but there is an option. Instead of just closing the image, save it, choose the image state you want to keep by highlighting, and then click the Create New Document from Current State button on the History palette. When the new document is created (complete with layers, channels, and so on), save that as well, or flatten and save if you want only the result as that can save space. Do this for every state you want to retain. If there are a number of states you want to retain when working on a particular image, you will want to create a folder to save them all into so you can keep them grouped. If you want to regather the Snapshots into your original image, open the saved images created from the Snapshots and the original image and then drag the opening Snapshot in the History palette from each of the saved Snapshot images to the image window of the original document. This will restore the image to the working state before you closed, including all the Snapshots that were present in the History palette. If the option for Automatically Create First Snapshot isn't turned on in the History Palette Options dialog box, you'll need to create a new Snapshot in each saved Snapshot image first.

I Can't Paint with the History Brush!

I am trying to apply the History Brush and I am getting the icon telling me that I can't apply the brush. What do I do?

The History Brush needs to have a layer in the image that corresponds to the layer in the snapshot or state you are painting from. That is, if you are painting to Layer 1 in the image you are working on, the snapshot or state you are painting from has to have that same layer (not a substitute). A workaround is to do the following:

1. Take a Snapshot of the current image.
2. Open the image state or Snapshot you want to paint with and press (Shift–Cmd–C) [Shift+Ctrl+C] to copy merged layers.
3. Switch back to the image state you were working on by clicking on the Snapshot you took in the History palette.
4. Paste the copy you made of the merged Snapshot above the layer where you want it to apply. Do this by highlighting the image immediately below and pressing (Cmd-V) [Ctrl+V].
5. Take another Snapshot of the image.
6. Select all and press Delete to clear the layer.
7. Click to place the History source icon next to the newest Snapshot.
8. Paint with the History Brush.

What these steps do is re-create the merged Snapshot or History state in the current state. You can then use that layer to apply as much of the History as you want using selection, Fill, and various History Brush shapes, as well as layer styles, to get the results you want.

Photoshop at Work: Styling an Image with Histories

I don't need to send you to the Web site (www.ps6.com) for this one, but the image is included on page 10 in the PDF workbook found there just in case. You should also find it in the Photoshop Samples folder (Adobe Photoshop 6\Samples\watch.psd). Here you will reproduce the results I got in the example for Figure 10.2.

1. Open the image.
2. Switch to RGB (depending on where you get the image from, it might already be RGB).
3. Duplicate the background.
4. Solarize the result (Filter, Stylize, Solarize).
5. Apply Auto Levels.

> **Note**
> Here is one of the cases in which Auto Levels does what you need it to: You are simply looking to extract some useful information from the previous step. Feel free to apply the Levels command manually instead.

6. Take a Snapshot.
7. Select All.
8. Cut.
9. Select the History Brush.
10. Place the Source icon to the left of the snapshot taken in Step 6 by clicking the Set the Source for the History Brush box in the History palette.
11. Choose a brush and settings. The brush I used is from the Assorted Brushes set in the Photoshop Presets folder, called Star 42 pixels. If you open the Brush palette and hold the cursor over the brushes, the names will appear. I used a Fade Size of 200 steps, and a layer style with Bevel & Emboss as well as a texture.
12. Paint.

Of course, the last step is a little vague. You will want to try some variations to see the kind of thing that you can do, even with this simple application. The more daring will use multiple layers and additional filter effects and will not worry about making a mess. You can always go back to the beginning by clicking the initial Snapshot in the History palette.

PART III

AUTOMATING IMAGE PROCESSING AND SAVING IMAGES

CHAPTER **11**

CREATING EFFECTIVE ACTIONS

In this chapter

EXPLORING ACTIONS AND THEIR USES

Actions are a method of recording and playing a series of steps in the order used to accomplish a specific task. This can serve the purpose of repeating common behaviors or reusable effects, but it can also be used as a means to record what you do with an image or as a teaching and learning tool. If created properly, actions re-create a set of events in order so that the set of events can be modified to fit another image. Prompts can be added at crucial junctures to let the user know what to do next, what to enter, or what the action is going to do over the next steps as the user waits.

For example, a set of steps could be created to implement the flaming text effect presented in Chapter 33, "Type Effects." After the set of steps is recorded as an action, prompts can be added to tell the user what to do, and a keystroke can be assigned to the action so that the series of events can be initiated by the Photoshop user at the touch of a button. When you want a flaming text effect, just open the image you want to apply it to, click the action, and follow the prompts. This can save a lot of trouble in re-creating the steps necessary to produce a particular result, and it can ensure that successful results are repeated. It can also speed up processing and can be useful in doing batch processing of images, in which multiple images in a folder need the same action applied.

→ For more information on how actions can be used in batch processing files, **see** "Automating for Efficiency," **p. 286**.

CREATING ACTION HOTKEYS

Actions can be complex sets of events, or they can record very simple steps. In fact, sometimes the simplest actions are the most useful, and these can be assigned hotkeys via actions so that you can implement them by pressing a single key. For example, it may be desirable for the Photoshop user to make often-used menu items that have no keystroke, such as the Flatten function, into actions. In doing this, you can assign your own keystroke while simplifying and personalizing your use of the program.

Assigning hotkeys to complex actions can be useful if the action is a set that is used often, but more often than not, complex actions are effects that are used only once in a while and that the user can tolerate activating from the Actions palette. Hotkey or not, using long actions still saves time over trying to re-create a series of events.

PROMPTING USERS DURING ACTIONS

Actions can't do everything for you. In some instances it will be difficult or impossible to make an action scalable to any image. Actions also won't record absolutely everything you do. For example, they will record freehand movement, but they won't scale that to an image according to the size. However, prompts (Stops) can be inserted to remind the user to select a tool, and can also explain what to do with it, or Insert Paths can be used to add a path that can be stroked to repeat the freehand action.

Editing and modifying actions can make them more generally useful in taking care of a broader set of situations, in correcting them for repeated use on a broader range of images (various sizes and DPI, for example), or in sharing them with other users. For example, it might be helpful to include some information when you insert a Stop that will help you when you're using the action later, or if you're sharing the action with other users. In this way, pertinent notations for the use of actions can be stored and transferred with the actions themselves; this will prompt the user without extensive explanation or documentation that might otherwise be necessary to use the action properly (depending on how complex it actually is). Adding steps to modify a procedure after it is recorded can help you refine the process and perfect application of effects.

ACTIONS AS LEARNING TOOLS

Actions are also a wonderful learning tool. Freely recording the steps you take in experimentation or attempts to create a specific effect might help you learn more about combining events and give you a better idea of how to effect changes in your images. It is far easier and more productive to let Photoshop do the recording than to take notes as you go along. By simply recording your actions and reviewing the resulting steps, you can learn what worked and what didn't in a series, or review and save portions of events that created an interesting effect—even if it wasn't the one you were seeking to accomplish. With that knowledge, you can re-create the series of events, modify the events to your satisfaction, and create reusable effects from your experimentation and mistakes.

Playing back actions you find on the Internet, share with other users, get off the Photoshop installation CD, and the like can help you learn how to use both actions and Photoshop itself. Playing back interesting effects one step at a time enables you to follow along with the development of the effect and review how it was achieved. To this end I have included several listings in Appendix E, "Web Resources Library," showing where actions are available online. Several from this book are available online at www.ps6.com.

→ For more information on where to get and exchange actions, **see** "Web Resources Library," **p. 929**.

USING ACTIONS

To use an action, click it in the Actions palette to highlight it and then click the Play button on the palette. Playback can be relegated to a single click if you're using the Button mode (see Figure 11.1) or to a keystroke if one has been assigned (see Figure 11.2). Initiating the action will begin playback and apply effects to the currently active image (unless other images are requested during the process).

The default list of actions supplied with Photoshop during the installation is pictured in Figure 11.1. These range from the relatively simple (two or three steps) to the relatively complicated (an action that uses another action in the process of implementing an effect). Any of these actions can be used as is or modified for your purposes. You can add actions to this Action Set or other Action Sets by creating actions (see the section "Creating and Editing Actions," later in this chapter) or loading existing actions.

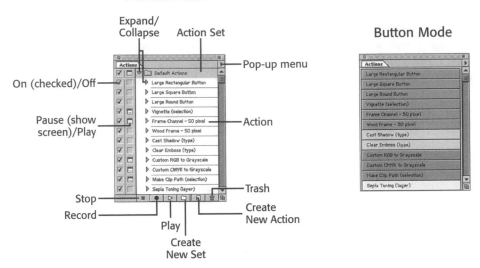

Figure 11.1
The Photoshop Default list of actions provided during the installation in Standard and Button mode. The default list is a good source to begin to quarry for ideas about how to use actions and what they can accomplish.

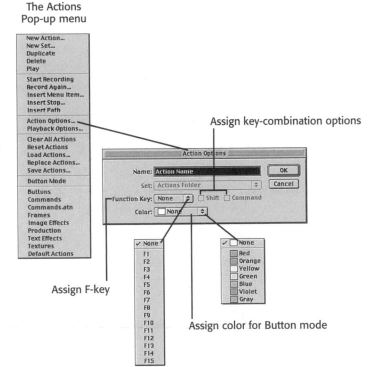

Figure 11.2
Another option for action playback is assigning a keystroke to the action in the Action Options dialog box, which can be accessed from the Actions palette pop-up menu.

The Actions palette helps you manage your actions, enabling you to keep the palette view effective and useful. To delete an action or action set, drag it to the Trash. To duplicate an action, drag it to the Duplicate button. To move an action in the palette list, drag it to the folder and position where you want it to reside. Keep on top of the organization of your Actions in the palette by using appropriate grouping, and getting rid of what you don't need; this will help you work efficiently.

ACTION PLAYBACK OPTIONS

When playing back actions, you have three options to choose from in the Playback Options on the palette menu: Accelerated, Step by Step, and Pause (see Figure 11.3). The Accelerated option is the default setting for playback. It means the action will play back at maximum processing speed, not waiting to redraw the screen between steps or pausing between steps. Step by Step is somewhat slower than Accelerated; the action will play back without pause between steps but will redraw onscreen between each step. *Pause* allows the user to enter a period of seconds between steps from the moment the redraw is completed to the initiation of the next step in the process for the action. Pause may also be useful if it seems your action is memory intensive and hangs up your machine, or if you want to see exactly in which step problems occur.

Figure 11.3
Here the Pause option is selected with a 5-second duration.

Step by Step and Pause modes are helpful in watching the playback of existing actions. You can watch what happens and follow along as each step occurs. Watching the actions can teach not only how to set up actions but also how to proceed in Photoshop.

Really, there is a fourth mode for playback: manual. All you do is expand the action you want to play. You have to be in Standard rather than Button mode if you do a manual play-back so that you can see the details. This allows you to play the details one at a time by double-clicking each step in order. This mode can be useful in playing back very slowly, playing back while allowing user interaction with the image, or playing back while trying to troubleshoot an action.

LOADING PRERECORDED ACTIONS

To use Prerecorded Actions, you must load them into Photoshop. After they are loaded, they can be used immediately. To load the actions, choose Load Actions from the Actions palette pop-up menu. You can then locate the action set and select it. When you choose the set and click Open, the set will appear in the Actions palette menu.

> **Note**
>
> You can find prerecorded actions on the Internet (see Appendix E) or on your hard drive (in the Photoshop Actions folder, inside the Presets folder). They are part of the default installation, so unless you have done a custom install, they should be on your hard drive.

→ For more information on Internet sites where you can find actions, **see** "Photoshop: Finding Plug-Ins, Filters, Brushes, and Actions," **p. 930**.

→ For more information on installation options, **see** "Photoshop Installation Options," **p. 913**.

Actions can be traded between Mac and PC machines, so you can send them back and forth through email to anyone. However, the best actions you will find will be those you create yourself, because they will meet your specific needs.

NEW TO PHOTOSHOP 6 Several new features on the Actions pop-up menu (Clear All Actions, Reset Actions, and the Photoshop Actions listing) can help you manage the actions you have available. This can help keep the Actions palette uncluttered, and can help quickly manage sets of actions you may have adjusted to particular tasks or varied keystroke sets. Clear All Actions removes all the action folders currently on the palette. It also permanently removes any unsaved actions; be sure that those you want to keep have been properly saved using Save Actions. Reset Actions removes all action folders from the palette except the Default actions. The user does have the option of appending the current list with the default set, or removing the list and replacing it with the default set (see Figure 11.4). Selecting Clear All Actions opens an alert (left) that gives the user the opportunity to cancel deletion of all loaded actions. Selecting Reset Actions opens an alert (right) that allows the user to continue with replacement of the current set with the default set, cancel the reset, or append the default set to the current list.

Figure 11.4
Although the message sounds threatening, it is okay to delete the actions as long as they have been previously saved, because you will be able to load them as needed.

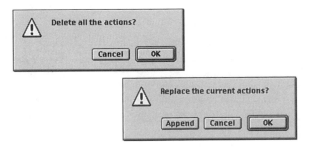

The bottom of the palette menu now lists all the available sets of actions that are stored in the Photoshop Actions folder (in the Photoshop directory under Presets). Simply selecting any of these from the palette pop-up menu will load the Actions folder into the palette.

CREATING AND EDITING ACTIONS

 A few actions have been included on the companion Web site for this book (www.ps6.com) to help the reader understand the process in various examples included in this chapter. Actions can range from the simple to the complex. For example, a function button can be assigned to any menu item (such as Flatten, Unsharp Mask, Bevel, or Emboss) so that you can call up that feature using the function key you assign; this will save you from pulling down menus and searching through lists of filters, especially for frequently used items. This can be a big timesaver. If you often use the function in conjunction with another feature, both items can be assigned to a single keystroke as a single action. Actions can also be used to assign keystrokes to features that already have keystrokes assigned to them that you find inconvenient, or to reassign function keys that are preset (such as the Brush dialog box, which can be summoned using the F5 key by default). Depending on how you work, this can be very impor- ⸢ tant in saving steps, frustration, and time. Actions can play other actions, so a series of actions can be grouped in a set. In fact, actions can be used to create actions!

RECORDING AN ACTION

Recording can be accomplished in two ways: by recording the action using the Actions palette buttons or by adding a menu item to an action using the Actions palette pop-up and the Insert Menu Item, Insert Stop, and Insert Path commands. Recording and using Insert Menu Item are only slightly different in the result. Recording actions and events as they occur assigns settings to the dialog box, so you need to turn on the toggle in the Actions palette to get the dialog box if the settings need to be different from when recorded. Inserting the menu item calls up the dialog box with current settings or defaults—no toggle option for the dialog box appears in the Actions palette.

The best way to get acquainted with actions is to jump right in and create one. Use the following steps to assign a keystroke to a favorite menu item:

1. Decide which menu item you want to assign a keystroke to. This item should be one you use frequently and should be one that does not already have a keystroke assigned.

2. Choose or create a folder in the Actions palette where you want to store the action you are about to create. To choose an existing folder, highlight it by clicking it once in the palette. To create a new folder, select New Set from the Actions palette pop-up menu. The Folder button at the bottom of the palette also creates a new set. If you're creating a new set, select a title for the folder that will indicate which actions are inside when it is collapsed. See Figure 11.5 for more on expanding and collapsing Action menu items.

Figure 11.5
Folders, actions, and action elements can all be expanded to view the details of what they include. Click the arrow to change the state.

Click to Expand

Click to Collapse

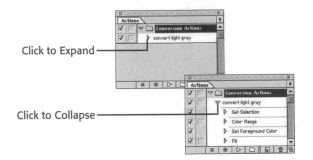

 Tip

A folder titled Menu Keystrokes is an obvious choice for storing simple, single menu items. When they're grouped, it is easy to find them, turn them on or off, or view the names together in the Actions palette. See the action naming tip in Step 4.

3. After you have selected the set in which to save the action, create a new action. Do this by selecting New Action from the Actions palette pop-up or by clicking the Duplicate button at the bottom of the palette.

4. When the dialog box appears, name the action, assign the keystroke, and choose the color for the Action button (available only in the Button mode).

 Tip

It is best to use the exact menu-item name when naming the action. It might be good to show the path, if that helps you identify the function (Menu>Item). Include the keystroke in parentheses as part of the name. For example, if you're defining the Find Edges filter with Shift and F1, the name might be "Find Edges (Shift+F1)" or "Find Edges (^+F1)." Try to abbreviate names if possible so that the whole naming scheme will be visible in the Actions palette. Putting information in the name will keep you from having to examine the action to find out what it is or how to use it.

5. Click OK to accept the changes, and the action will begin recording. See Figure 11.2 for the Action Options dialog box.

6. Apply a menu item function to your image. For this example, if you chose Find Edges, choose Filter, Stylize, Find Edges.

→ For more options on inserting menu items, **see** "Inserting Menu Items in Actions Manually," **p. 272**.

→ For more information on recording a series of steps, **see** "Creating a Complex Action," **p. 273**.

7. Stop recording. To do this, choose Stop Recording from the Actions palette pop-up, or click the Stop button at the bottom of the Actions palette (see Figure 11.6).

Figure 11.6
Locate the Stop button on the Actions palette and click it to stop the recording in Step 7. Then, consider changing options for the action by double-clicking the action to open the Action Options dialog box (Step 8).

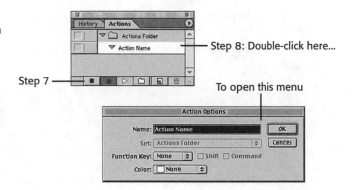

Step 7

Step 8: Double-click here...

To open this menu

8. If you want to change or add any options to the action, recall the Action Options dialog box by double-clicking the action name in the Actions palette or by choosing Action Options from the Actions palette pop-up. You can rename the action, assign or reassign keystrokes, and change the button color.

9. Save the action set. If you don't save at this point, a crash or other problem with Photoshop in which you have to reload can cause you to lose the actions you have created.

Tip

It is probably best to save actions in the Actions folder in the Photoshop program folder so that you know where the actions can be found if you need them later or want to share them with someone else.

Using actions to assign keystrokes to menu items that do not have them might be, far and away, the best use of the actions. This capability helps the user customize the program to fit his own needs and can simplify and speed up working with Photoshop. Creating more involved effects with actions can be challenging because not everything you do in Photoshop will record. Also, changes in image size might cause different effects depending on the way the action was originally set up. You can add prompts and compensate by other means, such as using Stops to add commentary on what to do in the next dialog box that appears, or to archive notes about using the action.

If a series of events is one that is often used, or one you want to repeat, the effort to record the events as an action will be worth the time. For example, if you use any manual version of a standard effect (like creating a perspective drop shadow, which can borrow from Photoshop Effects but requires several steps to apply), you might create an action that completes the steps for you. In the case of the drop shadow, you could make the action perform the following steps after you make a selection: Copy and Paste the selected area to a new layer; apply Effects from the Layer menu (Layer, Effects, Drop Shadow); Create the Layers from the applied Effect (Layer, Effects, Create Layer); Select the drop-shadow Layer; and open the Transform tool in whatever mode you prefer. This will leave you with only having to position the shadow.

Tip

It might be helpful to assign Shift and Command keys to entire action sets. This helps group them for your use and helps cut down on the length of the action names (if you use the conventions mentioned previously). In other words, if you have a folder titled Text Effects, it might be best to assign the same option keys (Command and/or Shift)[Ctrl and/or Shift] with every function key in the grouping. If you change the folder name to Text Effects (Shift), you will know that all the function keys in the names of that set are assigned using the Shift key. This can simplify the names in the set. For example, "Ice Letters w/Icicles (Shift+F7)" can be shortened to "Ice Letters w/Icicles (F7)." This might keep the name from truncating in the palette.

USING THE INSERT PATH COMMAND

 Insert Path gives the user an option for playing back freehand movements with various freehand tools, creating selections with a specific shape, and so on. After a path is created, it can be stroked by recording a Stroke Path command (selected from the Paths palette pop-up menu), turned to a selection, used as a clipping path, or it can function in any other way you might use a path. This feature might require some editing, depending on how you go about creating the action and determining the necessary paths.

To create a path to use in the insertion, simply select the desired pen tool and draw the path. After the path is drawn, the Insert Path command becomes available on the Actions pop-up menu. When selected, it records the coordinates of the path as part of the action. This appears in the action palette as a detail called Set Work Path.

Note

To manipulate several paths in the same action, it may be necessary to record Save Path commands to save the paths separately. If you only record the Set Work Path command, additional paths will replace the paths you create because Work Paths are temporary.

INSERTING MENU ITEMS IN ACTIONS MANUALLY

Another option for inserting menu items is to insert the menu items into the recording using the Insert Menu Item option from the Actions palette pop-up menu (Figure 11.7 shows the Insert Menu Item dialog box). The Insert Menu Item function can accomplish some things recording cannot. For example, the Options palette can be summoned while recording, but the event will not be recorded. Using Insert Menu Item, the event can be added to the recording. Simply type the name of the menu item and click OK.

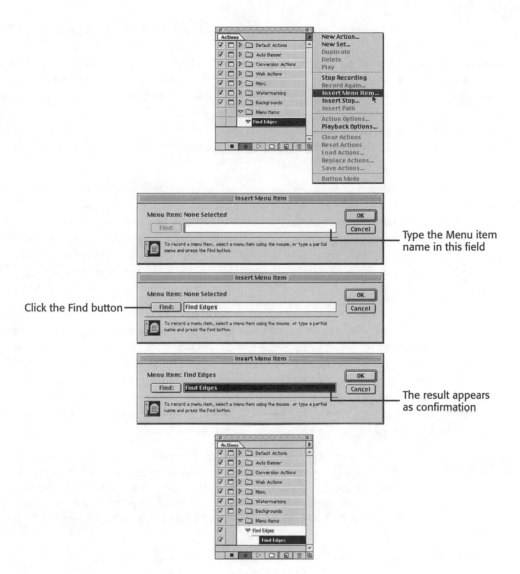

Type the Menu item name in this field

Click the Find button

The result appears as confirmation

Figure 11.7
To insert a menu item, Select Insert Menu Item from the Actions pop-up menu. Then, type the name of the menu item in the Find field. When you click the Find button (or press Return/Enter), Photoshop finds the menu item and inserts it in the Find field. Clicking OK inserts it into the action.

CREATING A COMPLEX ACTION

I would define a complex action as one that requires editing and contains multiple steps. In other words, unlike with the drop-shadow action discussed previously (which is actually a simple action), you cannot simply record a complex action by clicking the Record button and completing a set of steps. The progression of events might require editing and supplementation. Recording actions is similar to basic computer programming. All the steps and events need to work together to produce the desired result. Because recording a series of events as an action can record undesirable events—as well as fail to record some desirable events—you will have to edit the recordings to make them do what you intend. For example, you may need to add unrecordable events and Stops to prompt the user as to what to do during the course of playback, or you may include subactions (other actions created to use in the action you are recording).

Actions can be combined or piggybacked via the creation of an action that incorporates several actions in it. For example, the Cut It Up action for cutting up images intended for the Web (you can locate the action on the companion Web site, www.ps6.com) combines several actions that were recorded separately. This helped in developing the action and creating further utility by making the action easier to modify. The Cut It Up action itself is antiquated by new Slice features in Photoshop and ImageReady, but it is a good example of what can be accomplished.

Actions can also be used in some instances to work on low-resolution versions of images in preparation for working on larger versions. For example, if you're working with a very high-resolution image and you want to test some effects, attempt the effects on a lower-resolution version of the image while recording your actions. When you are finished, you can use the recording you made to help you apply the same series of events to the larger version of the image. This can help speed up the work and experimentation. When you play back the action created when you recorded the steps on the low-resolution image, you will probably have to make adjustments to filter settings to create the same effects.

Caution

Although it might speed things up to work on a lower-resolution image, it is not always completely advisable, depending on the tools you plan to use. Some tools and effects will apply very differently at varying resolutions—for example, using any filter based on pixel radius—and simply scaling the results may not be possible because of tool limitations.

Although you may have a particular end in mind in creating an action, it will sometimes be best to record a rough series of steps by simply recording whatever you do and then refine these steps later by editing. This keeps you from dwelling too much on the effort of creating an action and lets you keep in the flow of the effect you are creating.

Use the following set of steps to prepare and record a complex action:

1. Open a document to the size you want to use in creating the effect.

2. Save the image by another name. This keeps you from losing the original if you want to return to it for other purposes.

3. If you do not have the option on in Histories to automatically take the initial snapshot, take a snapshot of the image (select New Snapshot from the History pop-up menu, or click the New Snapshot button at the bottom of the palette).

Tip

> Increase the number of states retained by the History. This will help you retrace your steps when attempting to verify the action in later steps. Be aware that using an extended History may eat up a lot of memory, so this may not be a practical step, depending on your equipment and configuration.

4. Choose or create a folder set for the recording in the Actions palette. If you're creating a new set, choose New Set from the Actions palette pop-up menu.

 5. Click the Duplicate/New Action button from the bottom of the Actions palette, or choose New Action from the Actions palette pop-up menu. This starts the recording.

Tip

> Plan to save the action at several stages throughout the recording. A crash or system hang loses the action and all your work. Considering that multiple documents and several lengthy histories might be involved, both of which might sap your available memory, frequent saving is highly advisable.

6. Take the steps necessary to produce your effect. Although it is best to get the steps perfect the first time, this might not be a realistic expectation—especially if you are experimenting with a technique or new effect. Don't be afraid to try variations; failed steps can be weeded out either as you go along or at the termination of the recording when you edit/troubleshoot/supplement the steps in the action.

→ For more information on editing actions, **see** "Editing Actions," **p. 276**.

Tip

> Be sure to record all the steps necessary to the effect. For example, although it may be obvious that the first step in the effect will require making a manual selection, include that in the recording. Choose the selection tool desired while recording and insert a prompt (Stop) rather than leaving that step out of the recording.

7. When you have completed the effect you were trying to achieve, stop the recording by clicking the Stop button at the bottom of the Actions palette.

8. Duplicate the action by dragging it to the Duplicate/New Action button on the Actions palette. This will let you keep the original recording in case you have to refer to it.

9. Read through the action to see whether you want to eliminate or add any steps. This step is important if you did not carefully edit the action as you proceeded.

10. Add Stops anywhere they might be helpful.

11. Set the action's Playback Options to Step by Step so that you can watch each step as it occurs.

12. Create a new image from the original snapshot of the image you were working on. To do this, click the initial snapshot in the History and then click the Create new document from current state button at the bottom of the History palette. This will leave what you have of the History intact in the original document.

PART

III

CH

11

13. Play back the action you recorded on the new document. If the series of events does not produce the expected result, or you want to add a prompt, go to Step 14. If the series of events produces the expected set of events without any problems, skip to Step 17.

14. If you note errors, the playback does not follow the expected set of events, or you want to add prompts, stop the playback. Note where the errors occurred and fix the series of events so that the proper effect is produced. Fixing the series might require adding steps, recording steps that were inadvertently deleted, and consulting the image histories (which you have conveniently retained in the original document).

15. Close the document created in Step 13.

16. Repeat to Step 13 and Step 14.

17. Unless you are going to use the action for development of other effects, delete the original action in the Actions palette and rename the copy by removing "copy" from the name. To summon the dialog box to rename the action, double-click the action.

18. Save the action to the Actions folder in the Photoshop application folder.

Using the advantages of Histories and multiple documents makes it easier to re-create effects exactly. Using Histories enables you to step back in an image state and look more closely at the series of events, and creating a new document allows you to test the action without losing the original History. Take snapshots at points where it seems you have achieved strong advancement toward the final goal of the effect or image. An action will step you through the corrections, but if something fails to record, you might lose a step that can become obvious if you backtrack with the Histories.

Tip

Although it might be nice to set the History steps very high and keep a record of everything you do, it may not be practical because of memory considerations. If you run out of room on the History, consider taking a screenshot of your progress. This won't help you revert directly, but it will, at least, make a visual record of the steps you took. A screenshot utility is probably best for this purpose.

Taking appropriate snapshots helps mark the progress of the image; this is especially desirable if you need to use short histories due to memory limitations. Actions record the steps you take, and snapshots can act like mile markers, depicting image states that you want to return to or use as visual markers to the image progress. When you are done creating the effect, you can use the snapshots to check against a re-enactment of the series of events while editing the action.

EDITING ACTIONS

As mentioned in Step 6, there are essentially two options for editing actions: editing as you go and editing after you have completed the "rough draft." Most likely you will use a combination of these techniques, editing as you go along to be sure you have a solid basis for the final action and then editing afterward to fine-tune the result.

To edit as you go, keep the Actions palette visible (if your screen is too small, this might not be at all practical). When you find yourself wanting to backtrack, simply stop the recording by clicking the Stop button at the bottom of the Actions palette. The action must be stopped before it can be edited.

To edit the action, simply remove the steps you have recorded that are unnecessary. To remove the steps, drag them from the list in the Actions palette to the Trash at the bottom of the palette. Steps you might consider removing are those that have no effect on the outcome. For example, if you have used the Histories to compare states or retrace steps, these steps will be added to the action and will have no effect on the end result except for making the action bulky and longer than it has to be. The editing does not have to be perfect at this point, but keeping the action trim by editing as you go can help you fine-tune it later because you won't have as much junk to weed through.

Another good consideration to make while recording is to add Stops along the way just to prompt what you did at certain points of the action. You can add Stops without stopping the recording. These can be used to prompt the step, discuss what you were trying to accomplish, or make other notes to yourself. For example, a prompt might be useful when you're recording the use of a painting tool to give a brief synopsis of what needs to be done with the tool. A Stop at this point can be useful in breaking the action so that you can use the selected tool. To break the playback of the action, leave the Allow Continue box deselected in the Record Stop dialog box. Figure 11.8 shows the dialog box and a sample message.

PART

III

CH

11

Figure 11.8
This Stop is used as a prompt for what to do when the stamping tool is selected. Because the Allow Continue box is unchecked, the action will stop playing at this point so that the user can interact manually with the image. The action can be restarted with a click of Play.

When any editing is complete, you are ready to return to work on the image and continue developing the action. Be sure the last step of the action is highlighted, and begin recording again by clicking the Record button. If steps other than the last one in the actions list are highlighted, the steps you record will be inserted at that point.

If you have trouble with an action even after editing it, see "Troubleshooting Actions" in the Troubleshooting section at the end of this chapter.

RECORDING WORKFLOW WITH ACTIONS

 It is possible to use action recording to document workflow anytime you are experimenting with an image or a procedure. This not only lets you create actions for useful effects but also helps backtrack and replay an edited series of events on the same image. Although reverting with Histories will roll back the time on the image clock, it will not progress from that point with any other series of events. Combining the power of Histories to move back through states of the image and the capability of actions to record steps and events, it is possible to not only revert but also modify a string of events (as long as they are all recorded in the action). This can be quite a timesaver, because instead of an entire series of events having to be reconstructed, the reconstruction can occur from essentially any point in the chain.

It is possible to use a string of events recorded as an action to make several different actions or variations. At times, accidents occur in using different combinations of tools and filters that are quite unexpected. Usually, this happens when you are experimenting with filters rather than trying to effect a specific change such as when doing dust correction. These accidents can be used as a creative well—and if saved as recorded actions, they can be re-created with ease. It also can be helpful to save some actions to look at later, either to see what went wrong in a series of events or to learn from mistakes. For example, if a series of events brought you to a quite unexpected end, it might be useful to review the steps so that you can gain a better understanding of the application of Photoshop tools and effects. This is possible using Histories, but you have to do it right away; recording and saving as an action, however, will let you revisit the events anytime, and allows the opportunity to apply those events to other images as well.

TROUBLESHOOTING

TROUBLESHOOTING ACTIONS

I have edited a complex action, and it is not doing what I thought I had designed it to do. How do I go about fixing the action?

The easiest way to fix an action is to see what it is doing step by step. Although it can be helpful to do this by adjusting playback options to either Step by Step or Pause, it is probably best to play back the action manually. To play back manually, open your test image and then show the action details by clicking the arrow next to the action (it should be pointing down to open the detail list). Next, click the steps one at a time. As you click the steps, note what you expect to happen, and what actually does, and then make appropriate adjustments. It can be helpful to add Stops as you go if you run into a potential problem area: You can use the Stops to make notes to yourself right in the action—this way you can't lose them as you might if you make notations on scraps of paper.

What will often be missing from actions are events that failed to be recorded. Some of these can be inserted using the Insert Menu Item command from the Actions palette pop-up menu. Others may have to be noted in Stops or via the Insert Paths command. Be sure to use stops to note not only what steps do, but the size, DPI, and content of the original image that the action was developed for. This information can help in troubleshooting the action for other images that differ in size.

Many of these situations can be taken care of with the proper use of Stops as described in the section on "Prompting Users During Actions." You can use prompts to fill in actions that just can't be recorded like "Use the Airbrush to dust correct the image." There may be other prompts for the sizing and scaling of paths and brushes, and so on. Really, it isn't a bad idea to use a prompt every time you use a tool or function that isn't completely automatic. That way you can always shut off the prompts (by unchecking the Item Toggle), but they are there if you need them.

If you are just having trouble getting things to work and you know the actions are recordable actions, you probably need to edit the action as discussed in "Creating and Editing Actions," also in this chapter. When creating and editing actions, two of the handiest items are "Insert Menu Item" and the Stop button. The Stop button enables you to simply stop the recording. Do this whenever you need to edit as you go along, or if you need to make image-specific adjustments that should not be included in the recording. For example, if several steps down in the development process you think that the image would have been a lot better had you sharpened a layer or selection before continuing on, stop the recording, go back to the step where you want to sharpen using the History and apply the sharpen. You can add that to the action at the same time if it belongs there by clicking the Record button before sharpening, or leave it out by not recording it. To get back to where you were in the image, stop the recording if you inserted the step, click the step after your insertion, and press Play. This should take you right back to where you were. Next, press Record and keep going from where you left off.

Insertion of menu items plays another important role because you will not always want the action to record certain things. Some things are recorded in too much detail to be useful in a particular action. For example, if you record a save using Save As, and then you enter a filename, every file you create with that action will be named the same thing. Neat, huh? Not really. You might save over something you thought was pretty neat. When recording, the save name can come in handy for certain tasks. You might want a choice or you might want the image to save with only the original name. Inserting the Menu Item introduces it to the action without the settings you used. Recording for different purposes will require direct menu selection and selection using the Insert Menu Item function.

There are still other instances where the program can't do everything for you. Many of these instances require some thinking or judgment, and other instances arise from the lack of ability to scale actions to different image sizes on-the-fly. Most of the solutions require lowering your expectations a little. Although you should expect reliable recording, you need to know when the recording reaches the limits of its utility. You need to know what actions can do, accept what they can't, edit as necessary, and make good notes in the stops to tell you what to do. This process will help you use actions to your benefit. When the actions fail, play them back slowly and look carefully at the point in which the problems appear.

PHOTOSHOP AT WORK: EMBEDDING A WATERMARK WITH ACTIONS

A good example of a repetitive process that might be useful as an action is embedding a watermark. This example shows how to create this specific action using any watermark you have created and saved as a black-and-white PSD of any size.

Note

The PSD I will be using for the watermark has unrendered text. The reason for this is that when the image is resized during the action to fit to the image it will be embedded into, the text will resize as type size in points, rather than being rendered through interpolation. This will give a better result.

Use the following steps to create a watermarking action:

1. Create and save your watermark as a PSD. This should be a square watermark so that it is applicable to the broadest range of images. You might consider making different watermarks for portrait (vertical) or landscape (horizontal) images. See Figure 11.9 for an example of what a watermark might look like.

Figure 11.9
Although you are creating the watermark in a layer, the watermark should be treated like an alpha channel: Keep it black and white. The white represents the area that will be affected by any changes. This will simplify application of the watermark.

➔ For more information on creating and using watermarks, **see** "Watermarking for Protection," **p. 883**.

2. Open an image you want to watermark.

Note

Although you will be including an Open statement in the action itself, you will insert this later. Inserting it now will insert the name of the file to be opened, and the same file will be opened every time.

It is not necessary to retain the watermark on the image for the action to be recorded, so you can choose any image.

3. Choose an Action Set for the action you will create by clicking it once, or create a new one by selecting New Set from the Actions palette menu.

4. Start the action recording by clicking the Create New Action button at the bottom of the Actions menu. Name the action "Watermark."

5. Flatten the image (Layer, Flatten Image). If this menu item is not available, insert it using the Insert Menu Item function on the Actions palette menu.

6. Check the image dimensions with Image, Size, and write down the dimensions. You will need them in a later step. Don't change anything and click Cancel on the Image Size screen.

7. Insert the Image Size menu item using Insert Menu Item from the Actions palette menu. This will not be recorded in the previous step.

8. Select All (Cmd-A) [Ctrl+A].

9. Copy (Cmd-C) [Ctrl+C].

10. Close the document (Cmd-W) [Ctrl+W]. Do not save.

11. Open a New document (Cmd-N) [Ctrl+N].

12. Stop the recording.

13. Remove the Make detail by dragging it to the trash and insert a new Make detail using Insert Menu Item. Choose Insert Menu Item, and then select New from the File menu.

> **Note**
>
> This Step may seem odd, but it will take out the preference for the size that would have been set otherwise. If you ran the action with the recorded Open, it would open the image at the same size every time. If you toggle the dialog box on, it will still put in those parameters. By inserting the menu item, there are no preferences, and the item will open at the size of the image you just copied—which is far more convenient and automatic.

14. Be sure the Make detail is highlighted and restart the recording.

15. Paste (Cmd-V) [Ctrl+V].

16. Open the `watermark.psd` file that you created in Step 1.

17. Choose Fit Image (File, Automate, Fit Image).

18. Put the dimensions of the image to be watermarked in the Fit Image fields (from Step 6).

19. Close the dialog box by choosing OK.

20. Click the Toggle dialog box on/off in the Actions palette for the Fit Image detail.

21. Flatten the image (Layer, Flatten Image).

22. Select All.

23. Copy.

24. Close the watermark (Cmd-W) [Ctrl+W]. Do not save. This will leave only the copy of the image you are watermarking open (from Steps 11 and 15).

25. Create a new alpha channel in the image you are watermarking and name it "Watermark." To create the channel, select New Channel from the Channels palette menu.

26. Paste (Cmd-V) [Ctrl+V] the copy of the watermark into the channel.

27. Click on the composite layer that you pasted in Step 15.

28. Load the watermark as a new selection (Select, Load Selection)

29. Copy and paste. This will move the selected area of the watermark to its own layer.

> **Note**
>
> At this point, the area of the watermark is on its own layer, and you can use that layer to create the watermarking. I used Steps 22–25 to make a simple, yet effective marking that will work on a broad variety of images. Your effects may vary depending on what you are trying to achieve with the watermark.

30. Invert (Cmd-I) [Ctrl+I].

31. Fade Invert to 10% (Cmd-Shift-F) [Ctrl+Shift+F]. This setting can vary depending on the image and the impact you want the watermark to have.

 32. Click the Toggle Dialog on/off selector for the Fade detail. This will call up the dialog box when the action is run, but with the 10% setting.

33. Add Drop Shadow and Bevel and Emboss Layer Styles (Layer, Layer Styles, Drop Shadow). The settings used for the example were the defaults with the following changes: Drop Shadow opacity was changed to 10%, Bevel and Emboss highlight and shadow Opacity was changed to 15%. Other effects (such as opacity changes) can be used as well.

34. Click the Toggle Dialog on/off selector for the Set Layer Styles detail. This will call up the dialog box when the action is run with the settings you chose in Step 33, and you can alter them as desired.

35. Flatten the image (Layer, Flatten Image). See Figure 11.10 for an example of what the watermark might look like at this point.

36. Stop the recording (click the Stop button on the Actions palette).

37. Go back and insert a Stop prior to the Image Size detail generated by Step 5. To do this, click once on the detail before (which should be Flatten Image) and choose Insert Stop from the Actions palette pop-up. Type the following prompt: "Write down the pixel dimension for this image (Height and Width)." Then, click the Allow to Continue check box.

38. Insert the Open menu command in the action as the first detail using Insert Menu Item. In this case you would click once on the first detail (Flatten Image), insert the menu item, and then drag it into place. To move it, click and drag the detail to just below the action name.

39. Insert a Stop before the Open command created in the previous Step, and add the following prompt: "Open the Image you wish to watermark." And click the Allow to Continue check box. Start with the Open detail highlighted, and then insert the Stop by choosing Insert Stop from the Actions palette menu. When the Stop detail is created, drag it up before the Open detail.

Figure 11.10
This is how the watermark appears when applied to a plain white and plain black canvas. Because the area was inverted (Step 22), the results will have some effect on any element that falls within the area of the watermark.

40. Insert a Stop before the Fit Image detail, and add the following prompt: "Put the document dimensions you wrote down in the Fit Image window." To insert the stop, click on the detail before (which should be Open) and select Insert Stop from the Actions palette menu.

41. Save the action by clicking the Action Set the action is included in and select Save Actions from the Action palette menu.

42. Close the image without saving.

Although you may still want to tinker with a few things, these steps will save you hours in application time—especially if you use watermarking a lot. If you do use watermarking, be sure to check the section "Batch Processing" in Chapter 12, "Working with Automated Commands." To test the action, double-click the action in the Actions palette and follow the instructions as they appear.

→ For more information on batch processing, **see** "Batch Process Images," **p. 286**.

Now that the basic process is complete, you can duplicate this action to use different water-marking processes, different watermarks, and so on. All you have to do is duplicate the action by dragging it to the Duplicate button on the bottom of the Actions palette, and edit the details created by Steps 30–33.

See the watermark action on the companion Web site (www.ps6.com) for what the result should look like, as well as a variation with some additional Stops and a slightly different feel.

CHAPTER 12

WORKING WITH AUTOMATED COMMANDS

In this chapter

AUTOMATING FOR EFFICIENCY

Many of the chapters in this book focus on individual commands and processes that can be used to transform single images. Photoshop, however, also gives you the ability to apply a command or process to a collection of images. These automation tools enable you to significantly increase the efficiency of image processing, and they make Photoshop ideally suited to working with images in a production environment. For example, you can convert an entire collection of images to JPEGs for use on the Web or modify the curves for a series of photographs with similar tonal densities.

BATCH PROCESS IMAGES

You can use actions to perform a series of commands on an image. By using the Batch command, you can apply an action or other automation command to a series of images. You can start a batch process and leave it while Photoshop completes the process. Use batch processing for repetitive tasks, such as changing size or mode for hundreds of images, to make your work more efficient.

1. Choose File, Automate, Batch.

2. In the Batch dialog box (see Figure 12.1), choose the action set and action that you want to apply.

Figure 12.1
In the Batch dialog box, choose the source of the images to be processed and where you would like them to be placed after they are processed. Choose Override Action "Open" Commands to open the images in the specified folder if the action starts with an Open command.

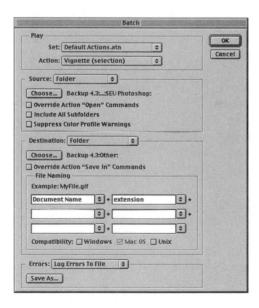

→ For more information on creating and managing actions, **see** "Creating Effective Actions," **p. 263**.

3. Choose a source for the images to be processed. You can process images from a specified folder. All you do is select the folder that contains the images that you want to process and choose OK (see Figure 12.2). Choose Suppress Color Profile Warnings if you do not want the batch process to halt because of profile mismatches.

Figure 12.2
You can choose any folder, local or remote, that you have access to. If you choose a network folder for the destination, make sure that you have permissions to write to the folder.

4. Click the Choose button to select a <u>D</u>estination for the processed images.

   • Choose None to keep the files open after running the action.

   • Choose Save and Close to save the files and overwrite the originals.

   • Choose Folder to save the files to a different folder using the same names as the originals.

Caution

> If the action contains a Save command, choose Override Action "Save In" Command—otherwise, every processed image is saved to the same file, so you would modify and see only the last image you process. Photoshop does not warn you if original files are being overwritten.

5. Choose a filenaming pattern. Using the drop-down lists, you can concatenate up to six filenaming components, including the name of the file in lowercase or uppercase, serial number, date, and extension. You can also choose the operating system compatibility for the output files.

6. Choose OK to begin the batch process.

 If Photoshop is continually notifying you that you are out of scratch-disk space, see "Maximizing Scratch-Disk Space" in the Troubleshooting section at the end of this chapter for some helpful tips.

Tip

> It is often helpful to copy all the images that you want to process into a particular folder, and also get in the habit of using a particular folder for batch process output. You could create folders called In and Out, for example. Establishing procedures can be especially valuable when working in a group. A consistent workflow can help reduce the chance of error, such as overwriting or losing files.

USING CONDITIONAL MODE CHANGE WITH ACTIONS

The Conditional Mode Change command converts the image mode so that the image can be used with an action or batch process. Some filters, tools, and commands work only with images in a specific mode. For example, Indexed Color images do not support the use of any

PART
III

CH

12

filters. Therefore, an Indexed Color image must be converted to RGB before a filter is applied. If one of these filters or commands is included in an action without the mode change, errors will result (see Figure 12.3). This can be especially frustrating if a series of images is being batch processed and the process stops because one or more of the images is in the wrong image mode. To prevent these errors, the conditional mode change can be inserted at the start of any action that contains mode-specific filters or commands.

The reason to use a conditional mode change, rather than a straight conversion across the boards, is that you will want to keep mode changes to a minimum to reduce conversion damage. For example, if a filter works with CMYK, Lab, and RGB, yet you use the action with images in other modes, you can set the Conditional Mode Change to convert everything but the CMYK, Lab, and RGB images. The target mode would be one of the modes that the filter works in (in this case, Lab or RGB would be the best choices, unless the eventual target mode is CMYK). Inserting the Conditional Mode Change allows you to control the conversions so that they are applied only as necessary, rather than converting every image whether they need it or not. Some of the most common conditional mode changes are from Indexed Color or CMYK to RGB.

Figure 12.3
Certain filters and commands can be used with images only in a specific mode. Inserting a Conditional Mode Change will automatically convert images that need to be converted—as long as you set up the command correctly.

Choose File, Automate, Conditional Mode Change as the first step when recording an action, and set the options as appropriate (see Figure 12.4). If you need to insert a conditional mode change into an existing action, choose Insert Menu Item from the Actions palette menu (see Figure 12.5). You can double-click the command in the action to alter the defined modes.

Figure 12.4
Click the source mode(s) in the Conditional Mode Change dialog box. Be sure to select all the possible image modes that you may be using with an action.

Figure 12.5
To add a menu command to an action, choose the command from the menus with the mouse.

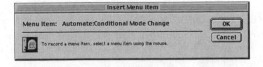

 Are you getting an error that certain tools, filters or commands are not available when executing an action? See "Missing in Action" in the Troubleshooting section at the end of this chapter for some additional information.

SIZING AND SORTING IMAGES

Photoshop has several automation tools that rely on the principle behind the Fit Image command. The Fit Image command resizes an image to fit within a set of horizontal and vertical constraints while maintaining the image's aspect ratio. You can use this to create thumbnails of images, or let Photoshop create thumbnails on contact sheets or in a Web gallery. This same process is used when you create a picture package, or collection of the same image on one page at various common sizes.

USING FIT IMAGE TO CREATE THUMBNAILS

You can create thumbnails for any image that can be opened in Photoshop. The thumbnails can then be used on a Web page, printed, or used with a document or image management system. You can create actions to automatically create thumbnails with predetermined sizes. The action contains only the Fit Image command. This can be particularly effective when combined with batch image processing.

1. Choose File, Automate, Fit Image.
2. In the Fit Image dialog box (see Figure 12.6), enter the maximum horizontal and vertical dimensions for the thumbnail.

Figure 12.6
The aspect ratio of the image is preserved as the image size is changed to match the width or height that you enter.

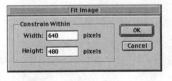

3. Choose OK to accept the resizing change.

Tip

To produce thumbnails of a series of images, record the previous procedure and choose File, Automate, Batch. Select the action in the Batch dialog box. Because you probably want to maintain your original images, choose folders for Source and Destination (you may want to create a new folder for the destination).

WORKING WITH CONTACT SHEET II

The Contact Sheet II automation command uses the Fit Image command to create thumbnails and place them in rows and columns on a page specifically designed for printing.

Note

To create a series of thumbnails for use as a Web page, use the Web Photo Gallery command.

→ For more information about the Web Photo Gallery command, **see** "Web Photo Gallery," **p. 292**.

Contact Sheet II is a revised version of the Contact Sheet that originally appeared in Photoshop 5.0. The new version's primary advantage over the original is the ability to include filenames under the thumbnails.

1. Choose File, Automate, Contact Sheet II.

2. In the Contact Sheet II dialog box (see Figure 12.7), click the Choose button to select a folder that contains the images to make the contact sheet from.

Figure 12.7
If you select a folder or drive on your computer that contains subdirectories and click Include All Subdirectories, contact sheets are created for all the images in the folders.

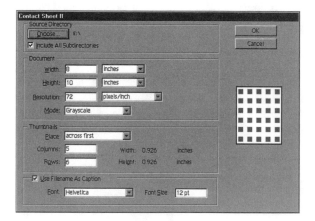

3. In the Document area, enter a Width, Height, Resolution, and Mode for the new Contact Sheet file (or files if there are more thumbnails than fit on a single page).

→ For more information about choosing an appropriate resolution, **see** "Image Resolution for Varied Application," **p. 342**.

4. In the Thumbnails area, choose a number of columns and rows, and how the images should be placed. Photoshop calculates the appropriate size of the thumbnails.

5. Click Use Filename as Caption to place the filename under each thumbnail. You can also choose a font and font size for the caption text.

6. Choose OK to begin the process.

Photoshop processes all the files in the folder you chose, resizing and placing them on the page (see Figure 12.8). This process can be time-consuming based on the number of images and size of the files being processed.

Figure 12.8
Photoshop's contact sheets can be printed so that you have a catalog of all the images in a folder or on your computer.

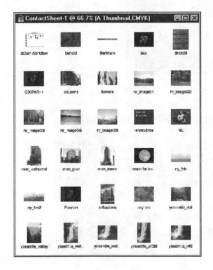

CREATING A PICTURE PACKAGE

Photoshop enables you to create picture packages. A *picture package* is a single page that contains several sizes of the same image, similar to the sets of pictures provided to elementary school students after picture day (see Figure 12.9). Use this tool to create sets of standard photograph sizes, such as 5×7 or 4×5, complete with trim areas.

1. Choose File, Automate, Picture Package.

2. In the Picture Package dialog box (see Figure 12.10), click Choose to select an image to process, or if a file is already open, click Use Frontmost Document.

3. Select a Layout from the list.

4. Choose an image mode and resolution for the resulting page.

Figure 12.9
This page contains one 5"×7", two 2.5"×3.5" and four 2"×2.5" (wallet-size) images.

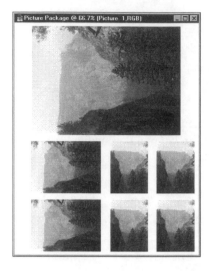

Figure 12.10
The Picture Package command resizes and orients an image several times on a page.

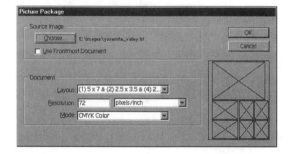

> **Note**
>
> If you intend to print the page, choose Grayscale or CMYK mode, and choose a resolution appropriate for your output device.

→ For more information about choosing an appropriate resolution, **see** "Image Resolution for Varied Application," **p. 342**.

5. Choose OK to begin processing the picture package layout.

WEB PHOTO GALLERY

A Web photo gallery is an HTML page containing thumbnails of a group of images. Each thumbnail is linked to a page that contains a larger version of the image and buttons to move to the next and previous image or back to the home page containing the thumbnails.

Using the Web Photo Gallery command, you can create an electronic catalog of your images, ideally suited for use on the Internet or an intranet.

1. Choose File, Automate, Web Photo Gallery.

2. In the Web Photo Gallery dialog box (see Figure 12.11), choose a Source and Destination folder.

Figure 12.11
The Web Photo Gallery dialog box enables you to select the images for the gallery as well as choose the settings for the output images and HTML.

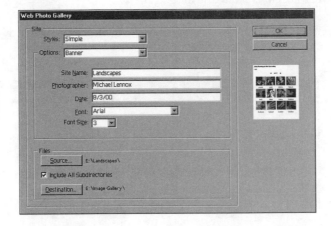

3. Under Styles, choose the format for your Web gallery. The Style determines the HTML structure for the gallery. You can choose between simple thumbnail styles, horizontal or vertical frames, or table formats.

4. Under Options, choose Banner and enter a Site Name, Photographer, and Date.

5. Under Options, choose Gallery Images, and select the settings for the large images that are linked to the thumbnails in your gallery. You can choose a border size, a size for the image, and set the JPEG compression.

6. Under Options, choose Gallery Thumbnails (see Figure 12.12). Choose a size and layout for the thumbnails, and the font and size for the caption text. If you want the filename to be placed under the thumbnail, click Use Filename.

Figure 12.12
You can use the caption information from the File Info command as the caption under your thumbnails by choosing the Use File Info Caption option.

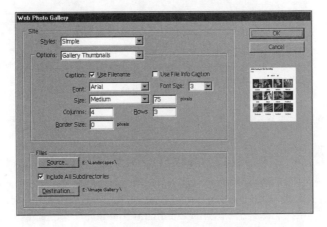

7. Under Options, choose Custom Colors and set the colors that you want for the elements in your gallery. You can set the colors for the background, the text, and all the links.

8. Choose OK to begin creating the image gallery.

The process produces an HTML page, which you can view in a Web browser (see Figure 12.13).

Figure 12.13
The Web Gallery that Photoshop creates can be uploaded directly as part of a Web site on the Internet, or incorporated into an intranet site.

 Are you seeing the error message "Some of the files could not be opened by Photoshop" and wondering why you're getting it? See "Files with Color Profile Mismatches" in the Troubleshooting section at the end of this chapter for details.

Tip

You can change the arrows used in the photo gallery by creating new arrows in Photoshop or ImageReady and editing the HTML.

You can also combine the Web photo gallery with other ImageReady effects such as rollovers and animation.

→ For more information on working with rollovers, **see** "Constructing Rollover Buttons," **p. 796**.

CONVERTING PDFS TO PHOTOSHOP IMAGES

When opening a PDF file in Photoshop, only the first page of a multipage PDF file is used. If you want to open a PDF file that contains more than one page, you should use the Multi-Page PDF to Photoshop native format command to convert the pages to Photoshop files.

> **Note**
>
> Note that Photoshop does not have the capability to save multipage PDF files. You must save each page individually as a PDF file and then collect them together using Adobe Acrobat.

1. Choose File, Automate, Multi-Page PDF to Photoshop native format.
2. In the Source PDF area of the Convert Multi-Page PDF to Photoshop's native format dialog box (see Figure 12.14), click Choose to select a PDF to convert to an image.

Figure 12.14
You can convert each page of a PDF file into an image in Photoshop's native format.

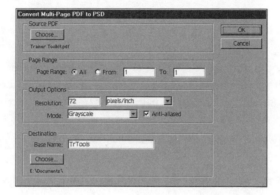

3. Choose the range of pages from the PDF file to convert.
4. Set a resolution and image mode for the conversion.

> **Note**
>
> Many PDF files are created with images at a resolution of 72 pixels per inch (ppi). Increasing the resolution does not improve the quality of the images if this is the case, but any text will be rasterized at the increased resolution.

5. Choose a destination folder for the files and a base filename. A number will be added to the base filename to create the filename for each image as it is created from the PDF file.
6. Click OK to begin the conversion of PDF files to Photoshop native format.

TROUBLESHOOTING

MAXIMIZING SCRATCH-DISK SPACE

Why does Photoshop warn me that I have run out of scratch-disk space?

Photoshop requires hard disk space to use as virtual memory. Really, it is a little bit of a space hog. You should have between 4 and 10 times the size of the file(s) you are working on available in free disk space.

To counteract any warning messages, you might want to rearrange your Scratch disk setup. To do this, choose Edit, Preferences, Plug-ins & Scratch Disks. In the Plug-Ins & Scratch Disks dialog box, choose disks that have the most available space, if you have more than one. You may also need to create more space on your scratch disks by removing files, and you might consider adding more hard drives if this is a frequent problem. If you are in the midst of working with an image and can't save, try closing all other open images and purging the memory (Edit, Purge, All).

→ For more information on memory management and options, **see** "Hard-Disk Space," **p. 900**.

MISSING IN ACTION

Why does Photoshop warn me that a filter, command, or tool is unavailable when executing an action?

Some filters, commands, and tools are available only in specific image modes. To apply an action to an image that is in a color mode which won't allow the application, you should insert a conditional mode change to switch image modes to one supported by the command in the action.

→ For more information on working with conditional mode changes, **see** "Using Conditional Mode Change with Actions," **p. 287**.

FILES WITH COLOR PROFILE MISMATCHES

Why does the error message "Some of the files could not be opened by Photoshop" display?

Photoshop does not automatically open images that require user input regarding color profile mismatches. To ensure that all the images are processed, change profile handling for images to Ignore or to a Convert option.

→ For more information on color management, **see** "ICC Profiles and Color Management," **p. 420**.

CHAPTER **13**

SAVING AN IMAGE

In this chapter

HOW OFTEN TO SAVE?

The best way to protect the hard work that you put into an image is to save regularly and often. Few things are as frustrating as attempting to re-create a complex effect that was perfect the first time. You should save after you do anything significant to your image, particularly anything that you would not want to repeat. It is a good work practice in Photoshop (or any application) to use the save shortcut combination (Cmd-S) [Ctrl+S] almost habitually—particularly if you are leaving the workstation.

SAVE COMMANDS AND OPTIONS

Photoshop provides several different options for use while saving and also has an important addition to the typical Save and Save As commands. You can access some of Photoshop's save options by choosing Edit, Preferences, Saving Files (see Figure 13.1). When saving a file, you can choose to save a preview or thumbnail of the image with the file that is shown in the Open dialog box. On a Macintosh, you can also choose whether or not to save with file extensions, and on both Windows and Macintosh, whether file extensions should be uppercase or lowercase by default. If you are sharing your files with users with other versions of Photoshop, you should choose the Maximize Backwards Compatibility option.

Figure 13.1
You can also access the Saving Files Preferences using the shortcut (Cmd-K) [Ctrl+K] and then (Cmd-2) [Ctrl+2].

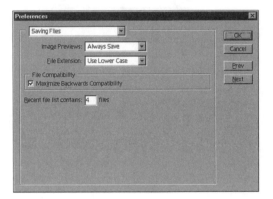

Tip

It is good practice to save files with lowercase extensions when saving for use on the Web. Operating systems such as Windows are case preserving, but not case sensitive, so image.gif and image.GIF both preview correctly in a WYSIWYG HTML editor. When these images are stored on a UNIX system, however, they won't be seen as having the same filename because UNIX is case sensitive.

You can use the Save command to replace the file on disk with the current version of the open image. The Save As command enables you to save the current image to a new file with a new filename. When you are using the Save As command, Photoshop lets you select file formats that are appropriate only for the current image mode, number of channels, or layer usage. When using the Save As command, you can choose to use a lowercase extension, and if it is available based on your preference settings, to save a thumbnail of the image (see Figure 13.2).

Figure 13.2
The Thumbnail check box is available only if the Image Previews option in Saving Files Preferences has been set to Ask When Saving.

Having trouble saving a file as a GIF or a JPEG? See "Why Can't I Save My File As a GIF?" or "Why Can't I Save My File As a JPEG?" in the Troubleshooting section at the end of this chapter.

The As a Copy option in the Save As command saves a copy of the current file with a new filename, while leaving the current file open for editing with its original name. The As a Copy option also enables you to set a number of save options, depending on the type of file that you want to create (see Figure 13.3). The As a Copy option enables you to save in any format that supports the image mode of the current image, flattening layers or discarding alpha channels as necessary for the format.

Figure 13.3
The available file formats in the Save As dialog box are determined by the image mode. Many of the Save Options check boxes select automatically after you select the format that you want.

PART

III

CH

13

Tip

You can use the Save a Copy command to save your work at stages of development while continuing to work in the original file.

Tip

Use the Discard Non-Image Data check box to make the file as small as possible. Do not click this option if you want to save paths with the image.

Tip

It is often valuable to save an image in more than one format by using the Save a Copy command. For example, by saving in the native Photoshop format in addition to the format needed for display on a Web page or for insertion into a page layout application, you can retain text and image layers so that you can continue to modify the image later.

EXPORTING FILES

Photoshop's export commands enable you to extract components of a Photoshop file for use with other applications or in other settings. Two options are available for export: GIF89a and Paths to Illustrator.

EXPORTING GIF FILES FOR THE WEB

In Photoshop 6.0, the GIF89a export filter is not automatically installed. If you want to use the GIF89a export filter, you should install it by copying the appropriate file from the Goodies folder on the Photoshop CD into your plug-ins folder.

Tip

Instead of using the GIF89a export filter, you may want to consider using the Save for Web command because it provides greater flexibility and control over the saved file.

Unlike the Save As command, the GIF89a export command creates a GIF file that supports transparency and interlacing. Furthermore, the GIF89a export command can be used with images in both Indexed Color and RGB mode.

To use the GIF89a export command, your file must first be in either Indexed Color or RGB mode. Choose File, Export, GIF89a Export. If the image is in RGB mode, Photoshop determines the areas of transparency based on transparent areas in the image. The Transparency Index Color is used to indicate areas of transparency when you view a preview of the conversion (see Figure 13.4). Photoshop enables you to select from a shortened list of palettes and to determine the number of colors in the palette. After you have selected the appropriate options, you can preview the image and then save it.

Figure 13.4
By clicking the Load button, you can use a previously saved palette or color table to convert an RGB image to Indexed Color during the GIF89a export process.

Tip

If you want greater control over the conversion of the RGB image to Indexed Color, convert the image mode first.

If the image is in Indexed Color mode, the current indexed color table is used when exporting the GIF file (see Figure 13.5). You can select whether the GIF file should be interlaced, and whether the image caption (if it has been created in File, File Info) should be included with the file. You can also select the transparency preview color, as well as which colors in the image should be transparent in the exported GIF. You can select these colors using the eyedropper, either from the image itself or from the palette displayed under the image. If you have saved an alpha channel in the image to determine transparency information, choose the name of the alpha channel from the Transparency From list. When you have selected your options, choose OK.

Figure 13.5
You can choose as many colors as necessary for the transparency in the GIF file.

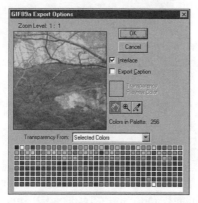

Tip

To create an alpha channel to control transparency in an exported GIF, create a selection of the areas that you want to remain opaque, and choose Select, Save Selection.

Note

Note that GIF images support only one level of transparency, so you cannot have transparent areas fading smoothly into areas of opacity. To create smooth transitions of transparency to opacity in GIF files, use the Dissolve Layer mode.

EXPORTING PATHS TO ILLUSTRATOR

The Export Paths to Illustrator command enables you to save any paths that you have created in Adobe Illustrator's native format. You can open these files in Illustrator to use as placeholders for Photoshop images, or to control the exact placement of information between the two applications. For example, if you want to import text that is placed along a path into a Photoshop image, you can create the path in Photoshop, export it to Illustrator, create the text, and then import the text into Photoshop. The imported text's placement is already determined because the path used to create it originated in Photoshop.

1. To export paths in Illustrator format, choose File, Export, Paths to Illustrator.

2. In the Export Paths dialog box (see Figure 13.6), enter a name for the file that you want to create, and choose which paths you want to export from the Paths list. You can export a single path, all the paths in the Photoshop file, or a path representing the document bounds.

Figure 13.6
To export paths from Photoshop to Illustrator, you must have named paths in the Photoshop image.

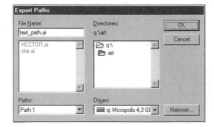

→ For more information about working with paths, **see** "Paths: Bézier Tools for Creating Vector Effects," **p. 175**.

EXPORT TRANSPARENT IMAGE WIZARD

Photoshop has a collection of wizards that walk you through some common tasks. These include Color Management, Resize Image, and Export Transparent Image. The Color Management and Resize Image wizards are covered in detail in other chapters of this book. The Export Transparent Image Wizard is covered here.

The Export Transparent Image Wizard enables you to easily create an image that contains transparency for use on the Web or in print. To use the wizard, choose Help, Export Transparent Image. In the Export Transparent Image Wizard (see Figure 13.7), follow the prompts and select your desired options. Photoshop performs the necessary operations (creating masks or paths) and selects the appropriate file format based on your choices.

Figure 13.7
The Export Transparent Image Wizard is easiest to use if you have already selected the area that you want to be transparent in the final image.

TROUBLESHOOTING

WHY CAN'T I SAVE MY FILE AS A GIF?

Photoshop enables you to save images as a GIF only when they are in Indexed Color mode. You can convert the image to Indexed Color mode (Image, Mode, Indexed Color), although you are better off using the Save for Web command or Export, Gif89a Export command instead.

WHY CAN'T I SAVE MY FILE AS A JPEG?

Photoshop does not support saving as a JPEG if the image contains more than one layer or extra alpha channels. Use the Save a Copy command, or for even greater control, use the Save for Web command.

PHOTOSHOP AT WORK: CREATING A QUICKSAVE ACTION

 Photoshop does not have an automatic save feature, but you can create something that works similarly. The following action saves your current image in a temporary file whenever you press the action's associated function key. Use this action whenever you want to save your file temporarily, and use the Save command whenever you want to commit to changes in the file. If you get in the habit of pressing the action's function key constantly when using Photoshop, at least some version of the file will always be available.

→ For more information on creating and managing actions, **see** "Creating Effective Actions," **p. 263**.

1. Open the Actions palette by choosing <u>W</u>indow, Show <u>A</u>ctions (see Figure 13.8).

Figure 13.8
In the Actions palette, either select an appropriate action set, or create a new action set by choosing New Set from the Actions palette menu.

2. From the Actions palette menu, choose New Action. In the New Action dialog box (see Figure 13.9), enter QuickSave for the name of the action, choose the appropriate action set, and choose a function key to use with this action.

Figure 13.9
If you prefer to use actions in button mode, choose a color for the button.

3. Choose <u>F</u>ile, Save <u>A</u>s. In the Save As dialog box (see Figure 13.10), choose a location and enter a filename. This location and filename are used every time the action is run. Be sure to select Photoshop native as the file format to use, and select the As a Copy, Layers, and Alpha Channels options in the Save area of the dialog box.

Figure 13.10
If you choose a filename of "temp" and place the file in a temporary folder, you will always be able to locate the QuickSave file to either open it or delete it.

4. Click the Stop Recording button in the Actions palette.

The action is now available for use in Photoshop (see Figure 13.11).

Figure 13.11
When finished, your action should look something like this.

Now, whenever you want to quickly save your work without replacing the actual file, press the function key that you assigned to the action.

THE IMAGE: FORMAT AND RESOLUTION

CHAPTER 14

Choosing an Image Mode

In this chapter

CHOOSING THE RIGHT IMAGE MODE

Before working on an image, it is important to know exactly how you are going to use it and how you plan to display it. Even if you are just beginning to play with images and possibilities, considering your needs from that vantage can save you time and trouble by keeping the file sizes small and allowing you to work faster. Having the end in sight helps you make the proper choices in meeting the goals for the image and your purposes.

Some projects require high dpi, some low; some are determined by pixel size and others by dpi; some are determined by the colors or file type which need to be used. Having to resize, change color modes unnecessarily, or redo an image completely because of a bad choice early in the process will prove frustrating, waste time, and not produce the best possible results. Conversions of any sort result in interpolation, and therefore, loss or distortion of image data. Although this loss or distortion may not always be serious or have detrimental effects on the image, it can compromise image data and may cause unwanted changes in an image. The severity of the changes depends on numerous factors, including which modes the information is moving from and to and whatever discrepancies might be in available colors. Knowing what the risks or advantages are can help in making intelligent decisions about color management.

Choosing the proper color mode can save you work or create more. Although Photoshop's tools can correct almost any mistake you start with, working most closely to the final need will most often and most consistently yield the best results in the least amount of time. For example, working on a Web image in CMYK does not serve your purposes or make for the best image potential; colors will be drab, file sizes will be larger than necessary, and you will have to convert to a proper color mode (RGB or indexed color) before saving the file in a Web-compatible format. A better choice is to simplify your workflow by starting in the right place.

Each of the image modes has drawbacks and advantages. Choosing the right mode at the right time and limiting the number of mode switches helps maintain the color integrity of the images you work on (see Figure 14.1).

Use the following steps to make the best decision in choosing a color mode for a new image:

1. Determine what the image will be used for.
2. Create a new file (Cmd-N) [Ctrl+N]. This step may vary in actual workflow. For example, you may be importing a file that has already been created or you may be scanning a new image. In these cases it is good to be familiar with color conversions and how to approach them.

→ For more information on making color conversions, **see** "Color Conversions," **p. 485**.

3. Select a color mode in the New dialog box based on the use determined in step 1 and an understanding of the choices available.

Although new files can be created with five color modes, there are actually three additional color modes available to the user: duotone, indexed color, and multichannel. These file types require additional setup or have additional initial criteria and can be converted to after opening the image and creating the criteria. These will be discussed following the choices available for new files.

Figure 14.1
The Mode choices for a new file include any of the five choices on the pop-up screen: Bitmap, Grayscale, RGB Color, CMYK Color, and Lab Color.

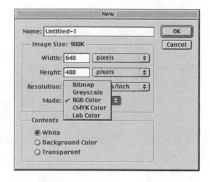

To understand which mode is best suited for a particular purpose, the following sections help describe the advantages and disadvantages of each color mode.

RGB COLOR

RGB stands for Red, Green, and Blue. This can be thought of as display color, where red, green, and blue lights are combined with different intensities to arrive at the result. RGB display is used with color monitors and some big-screen projection displays. This is an additive color model where the more intense the light and combination, the brighter and closer to white; the less intense the addition of color, the closer the result is to black. Although the addition of more of any one color causes the resulting color to brighten or get lighter, the interaction of colors provides a shift in hues. Each of the three colors is assigned a unique channel in Photoshop, and each pixel of color has the potential for 16,777,216 variations. In actuality, all color modes in Photoshop are eventually interpolated through RGB when viewed on your monitor, so it is potentially the most accurate color when it comes to viewing—in the sense that the data from the image file can be used to create the display. Other complex color models need to temporarily be converted to RGB for presentation on your monitor.

RGB is the color mode of choice for most instances when creating color images, and is the default selection in Photoshop. It gives a broad range of possibilities and good color depth, while facilitating color correction and being reasonably compatible with many other color modes and file formats—it can be saved to all the available formats but DCS and Filmstrip. RGB is best for graphics intended to be displayed via video (TV, Web sites, monitors, and so on) and output to some film recorders and RGB friendly output devices which use the RGB color model to interpolate the best color choices based on the system (they do not actually print in RGB). It also provides a means of doing relatively easy and intuitive color correction. Filter applications are most readily available in this mode, while curtailed in some of the other modes.

→ For more information on RGB color correction techniques, **see** "Basic Color Correction Using Tonal Correction Techniques," **p. 465**.

Although generally the most functional, RGB is not always the best choice for color mode. In printing, inks do not come in red, green, and blue, and the process of printing ink accumulation is subtractive, not additive (see the information on CMYK in the next section).

PART

IV

CH

14

In order for printing to work in RGB, one would have to print in luminous inks, which, unfortunately, are not currently available. Because of this and the inherent limitations in printing colors, RGB will show the user more color than is really available for output. Although this may sound like a good thing, when the RGB image is converted to a less friendly color space, the results can be disheartening. Notably, bright blues, greens, and reds lose some vivacity, and colors flatten out or shift—sometimes dramatically. The result of printing RGB images to CMYK process output is often a surprise to newer users.

RGB is also not optimal for working on grayscale images, as the file must carry three sets of identical image information. This simply bulks up the file to three times the size that it needs to be and may slow processing of the image.

→ For more information on grayscale possibilities and limitations, **see** "Grayscale," **p. 314**.

The color model for RGB is also not the broadest one available as it is limited to projection or display modeling. That is, the color model was made for compatibility and operation on computer systems and displays. Other available color models such as HSB and Lab are based on human perception of color and may be broader.

→ For more information on Lab color, **see** "Lab Mode," **p. 313**.

CMYK COLOR

CMYK stands for Cyan, Magenta, Yellow, and Black, or the initials for the colors used in process printing. Printing with colored inks is a subtractive color process: The more ink that is put on the printing surface, both in percentage (0%–100% coverage, not saturation) and number of inks, the darker the result. The less ink, or the less color added, the brighter the result. This is essentially the opposite of the RGB process. Cyan, yellow, and magenta work together to control the hue, much like RGB. However, due to certain limitations, the culmination of 100% of each of the three inks (cyan, magenta, and yellow) reaches a deep brown rather than pure black. The fourth ink, black, is introduced to the mix to overcome this limitation, and allow for pure black print.

Files for CMYK images are created with four channels—one for each color ink. It would seem that the potential for color is greater than with RGB as an additional color should lead to more combinations, but this is not the case. Black ink allows for duplications of color (a single color may have multiple CMYK equivalents), and in effect the number of available colors is actually less than in RGB. The most obvious of these is the result for black, which could be 100% black ink plus any combination of the other three (although this is theory more than practice).

→ For more information on the practice of printing color, **see** "Printing Considerations," **p. 558**.

As the CMYK color mode is based on color process printing, it is the most useful in creating files intended for printing color images. Although it is not necessary to work only in CMYK when producing images for print, it is certainly a desirable endpoint. In other words, you can scan and work on images in other color models and then print to CMYK process, but the best final control over the printed output will come from working with the image in the final process colors. This can also be the color mode of choice for developing logos or other corporate identity materials so that color will be consistent in print and on Web pages. CMYK files can be saved to print compatible formats, including DCS (Desktop Color Separation) 1 and 2.

→ For more information on converting color to CMYK, **see** "Converting an Image from RGB to CMYK," **p. 506**.

The drawback to CMYK images are manifold, including color limitation, larger files size (33% larger than RGB or Lab), and less intuitive color correction (than RGB). However, the reality of print color is that CMYK is the predominant imaging process despite the limitations. Filter application is limited with loss of Artistic, Brush, Sketch, Texture, and Video filters, along with some portion of Rendering and Distortion filters.

Note

Although it is possible, do not save images intended for use on Web pages as JPEG files in CMYK. Although it may be smart to work in CMYK to have consistent color in corporate identity, images saved in CMYK will not show up in a browser. Switch them to RGB from CMYK and resave for use as Web graphics.

⚡ *If you're having trouble trying to save your image in a specific file format, see "I Can't Save My File to the File Format I Need," in the Troubleshooting section at the end of this chapter.*

LAB MODE

Lab (or CIE L*a*b) is an international color standard based on the range of human color perception. The components are broken down into three parts: two scales of hue (the a component which measures between red and green and the b component which measures between blue and yellow) and the lightness (L). The hue scales interact to form colors, and the lightness controls the brightness of those colors (from white to black). This is similar to the HSB (Hue, Saturation, Brightness) model of color mixing that may be familiar to those who have taken color theory or art classes. The file is created in three channels, one for each of the color components and the third for the lightness. Color in channel a is represented as green (100% black) to neutral (50% black) to red (0% black); color in channel b is represented as blue (100% black) to neutral (50% black) to yellow (0% black); lightness will scale the mixture of color in channels a and b from their darkest to lightest tones. These lightest and darkest tones may not be white and black. Shades of gray are achieved by balancing the color channels (a@50%, b@50%) and adding the appropriate percentage of black to the result (0%–100% black in the l channel).

Although the spectrum may appear to have limitations—only two colors are combined in ratio at any one time—the additional color and flexibility of the lightness control extend the possible range of colors beyond what is available in RGB. The advantage to Lab color is clearly the broader color possibilities. Although rarely used by most Photoshop artisans, and not often suggested for use in manuals or other support materials, Lab is integral to Photoshop's color management. It is also a sort of mirror by which color conversions take

PART

IV

CH

14

place. As far as user function is concerned, it can be useful for some color corrections—for example, those that take place across areas of light and darkly shaded areas of flat tone. In an RGB correction, this would require shuffling color mixtures and may not end with the expected result. Lab is also superior for color storage in source images (scans). There are also some advantages to working on images in Lab, such as adjusting contrast, changing selected colors, and converting images to Grayscale.

 If you are having trouble using Lab for color corrections, see "Lab Color Is Confusing!" in the Troubleshooting section at the end of this chapter.

→ For more information on Lab mode use for conversions, **see** "Color Conversions," **p. 485**.

The reason Lab is not more widely used is mainly because it is not an endpoint as a color mode but rather a transitional state; images for print or projection are saved in RGB (for color display) or CMYK (for printing). It is also a little less intuitive to handle in making general color corrections and adjustments. The files can be saved only in Photoshop (native, EPS, PDF), Raw, and TIFF formats. Loss of filter use is much like that of CMYK.

Finally, as with conversion from RGB to CMYK, the actual information in the file cannot be displayed, but for rendering in RGB—which is a more limited model. It is very difficult to work with that which you can't see.

GRAYSCALE

Grayscale files are used for black-and-white images. The term black-and-white is a little deceiving in that there are 256 levels of gray (0-255) to work with. The grayscale file is created with a single channel, which controls the black content.

The advantage of working in grayscale is the capability to correct and manipulate single-tone images (generally black-and-white) without excess file bulk or potential complications from additional color channels. Tonal correction is rather straightforward. Considering the simplicity, the value of Grayscale mode as a learning tool should not be overlooked. Grayscale images can be saved in a number of different file formats—in fact, one more than RGB. It can also be saved to any other mode, including bitmap, duotone, and indexed color, which are often sticking points for conversion of other modes. This is the only mode that will allow conversion to duotone.

It would be hard to note lack of color as a flaw or drawback in a mode that is not intended to be used with color, but I am sure some would feel that it is. The ability to use spot color application would seem to offset this, as really a grayscale image with spot colors could be turned into an RGB or CMYK image—although with significant increase in size and lacking some of the more useful controls.

BITMAP

Bitmap mode files are the simplest of all. Pixels in bitmap mode are either turned on or off meaning that they appear as black or white—with no grayscale or levels. These files are created with one channel. They are different from Bitmap file types, which contain color information.

Note

Bitmap mode should not be confused with the creation of Bitmap (.bmp) files, which do retain color and can be used in a number of color compatible modes.

A bitmap file is the smallest file you can create at a given size (pixel dimension). These are advantageous for storing line art or scans which should be printed as black-and-white line art—pen and ink, and so on, for use at 600+dpi. They can also be used in some applications for special purposes, such as creating a floating drop shadow for printing from a layout program or posterizing.

→ For more information on creating a floating drop shadow with bitmap files, **see** "Creating a Drop Shadow," **p. 645**.

The drawback in bitmaps would be the lack of color and inability to build grayscale—except in likeness at high resolution. The compatibility is surprisingly limited considering the simplicity of the file type, and that filter application and correction controls are absent.

ADDITIONAL COLOR MODES

Several color modes are available after you have created an image that is not available as an initial mode selection. These include indexed color, duotone, and multichannel. These modes require additional image information, which is not currently part of the New dialog box, in order to be created.

INDEXED COLOR

Indexed color images (see Figure 14.2) are essential for creating GIF files, once pretty much the lone staple of Internet graphics. The files are composed using a color palette that is limited to a maximum of 256 colors. A color from the palette is assigned to each one of the pixels. This mode requires that you set up the color palette before it can be created. There are presets available (such as a Web-safe 216-color palette). It is also possible to make and save your own presets (see Figure 14.3).

Figure 14.2
When selecting indexed color as a mode, the Indexed Color dialog box will open. Here a number of selections can be made to control the colors in the palette.

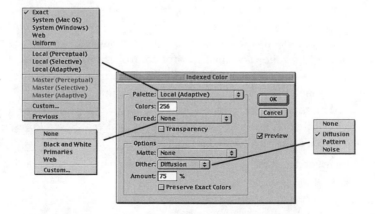

Figure 14.3
Selecting custom color
is also possible if you
know specific color
use you want to
include. Colors can be
subtracted, added, or
changed as necessary.

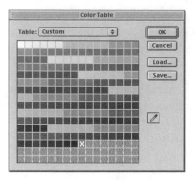

Indexed color files are a compact way to create limited color files. Because of the limited colors, the files are small, they transmit quickly, and are easily viewed in a variety of image-editing and viewing packages. This mode offers control over bit depth and color parameters unavailable in other modes.

However, indexed color as a special use mode comes with a number of limitations. It is severely limiting in working to develop an image. Images developed in indexed color tend to be blocky and work with few Photoshop effects or filters. They can be saved only as native Photoshop, GIF, or PNG files.

Tip

It's generally better to start Web images in RGB and modify them than it is to try and build them in indexed color. The image in RGB can be converted to a Web-safe palette. To modify indexed color images, do one of two things: Switch the image to RGB before making changes, or use the original RGB image to make the changes and then convert to indexed color again.

→ For more information on working with and converting to indexed color, **see** "Converting an Image from RGB to Indexed Color," **p. 499**.

DUOTONES

Duotone images are actually grayscale images whose single channel of information is used as a source to control two colors using duotone curves. The curves offset the tonality for the application of colors (really inks, but we are discussing the file here, not the result). Duotone files in Photoshop actually allow for control of one to four colors without really increasing the size of the file itself. As files in Duotone mode are essentially grayscale files, they behave in much the same way for the sake of manipulations and they allow most filter applications. Duotone images require a grayscale image and setup of the duotone curves (see Figure 14.4) before the mode change can be completed. Several presets are available and you can make and save your own.

→ For more information on adjusting and working with Duotone images, **see** "Creating a Duotone," **p. 528**.

Figure 14.4
Technically, duotones are two colors but Photoshop allows the user to assign from one to four colors. Curves and color palettes are opened for manipulation by double-clicking the swatch and curve, respectively.

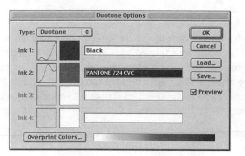

The true advantage to duotone images is seen in print. Smart use of colors and application can reduce the appearance of printer dots in two ways: first, by application of multiple inks which will apply ink on two passes and in smaller dots, rather than one pass and fat dots; and, second, by allowing you to combine inks that will get better coverage. For example, a 50% gray ink can be used at 100% coverage to replace a 50% black. This reduces the feel and appearance of the image dots and also, used correctly, can greatly improve tonal quality and look of the image. Duotone also has some advantages for controlling tonal changes in black-and-white corrections.

→ For more information on the effect of duotone printing on results, **see** "Understanding Duotones and Spot Color," **p. 522**.

The disadvantages of duotones is that they are not so easy to break up into separate channels. You can switch to other modes but the result you get might not be the expected one (which would be retention of the image as you planned it in duotone). If using duotones in print (the primary purpose for this mode), there is an increased expense in printing because you will use more inks and perhaps a better press, or a press that requires more passes. Duotones can be saved only in native Photoshop, EPS, PDF, or Raw file formats.

MULTICHANNEL

Multichannel mode allows you to assemble an image in any configuration of channels as colors and alphas up to the full extent of channels available in Photoshop. It used to be more frequently used to separate color channels in earlier versions of Photoshop.

Multichannel mode is sort of a seldom-used catchall; however, it can be adapted to a number of utility purposes. For example, multichannel can be used to reassemble channels that have been separated, as a storage vehicle for saved selections which you may want to close to free up memory, or as a nonstandard color configuration.

Multichannel images are limited to native Photoshop and DCS 2.0 file formats on save. With the addition of multiple spot colors to most image file types, the purpose of multichannel has somewhat waned.

PART

IV

CH

14

Color Onscreen

Color onscreen for the various modes you are working in may be reasonably accurate or not really accurate at all. For example, Lab colors cannot be accurately displayed and CMYK color is interpreted via RGB mapping. The goal, no matter what your output, is to strive to have the color onscreen match, as closely as possible, your output. In a lesser way, your choice of image Mode influences the success of this quest. Make good choices, and be sure to keep your system calibrated—always check results against your display with frequency.

➔ For more information on calibrations and color management, **see** "Evaluating Color Images Onscreen," **p. 411**.

TROUBLESHOOTING

I CAN'T SAVE MY FILE TO THE FILE FORMAT I NEED

When I try to save my file, the type of file I want to save to does not appear. How do I get my file to save in the format I need?

Color Mode can affect what file types you can save a file to. For example, if you are trying to save a CMYK image as a Targa file, the Targa type will not be available, as it is strictly associated with RGB images. The acceptable color modes for file types are covered under the chapter on "Choosing a File Format."

➔ For more information on saving in specific file formats, **see** "Selecting a File Format," **p. 319**.

 Another option for saving images as the file type you want to use might be to choose Save a Copy from the Save As dialog box. When you choose to Save a Copy, Photoshop will let you select from an increased range of file types and will adjust the image accordingly during the save. The changes are limited to management of extraneous image information, layers, channels, and paths. The good part about this is that it simplifies your tasks somewhat; the bad part is that you may not be able to depend on the choices that are made automatically to retain all you have built into an image.

LAB COLOR IS CONFUSING

I am trying not to lose the extra information in my files by doing corrections directly on Lab scans that I have saved. However, I am finding the controls are confusing to use to make the corrections I need. Is there anything I can do to simplify these corrections?

The first thing you should do is save the image by another name and switch to RGB or CMYK color to make your corrections. It is fine to store the extended information of your scans in a *Lab* file, but corrections are not at all intuitive, and, in fact, you can't even see what you are doing on the screen with any measure of precision. The Lab scans will have more information than can be displayed in RGB, and even if the corrections were not unwieldy, you can't currently use the information anyway. Until a better process comes along, you will have to be satisfied with the results you can get from the current processes. Storing the original scan as Lab will keep safely until that time; for now, use the mode that will get you as far as you need to go. Your corrections will go more smoothly.

➔ For more information on color correction in RGB, **see** "Color Corrections," **p. 465**.

CHAPTER 15

SELECTING A FILE FORMAT

In this chapter

EFFECTIVE USE OF FILE TYPES

Selecting the proper file types ensures compatibility with your intended use of the image you are creating. Choosing the right file type to save in is crucial to any project. To select the right one, it is very important to know which image color modes are compatible with which file types. It is also possible that a mode will be compatible with a file type with the exception of certain qualities (for example, addition of layers or alpha channels). In other words, you might choose the right image mode, but the image information you create will make it so you can't save the file in the format you desire. Being aware of the potential problems can help you either avoid or correct this.

TIFF FILE FORMAT

Tagged-Image File Format (TIFF) files are often used for a variety of print-oriented imaging purposes, including layout and output. TIFF files save with additional channels (in CMYK, RGB, and Grayscale Modes), support clipping paths, and, as of Photoshop 6, allow saves with layers. This format can also be used with Lab, Indexed color, and bitmap images although options for saving with layers and channels vary. This format is a workhorse that is popular for use with layout programs and is widely supported by graphics programs in general for editing and incorporation into high-resolution output. The images provided for this book, for example, were provided to the publisher as TIFF files. Although popular, the TIFF format can vary and there occasionally can be compatibility problems.

Tip

When saving TIFF files, there is an option for Macintosh or PC compatibility. I have never noted this to be a problem in moving TIFF images from my Mac to my PC or vice versa no matter what choice I make, so long as compression is not used. I choose PC most often as it seems any compatibility problem will be more likely to occur there—and this reasoning is based only on the broader potential number of variables in the PC format for program use and configuration. If I know I am going to be sending the images to a second platform (Mac to PC or PC to Mac), zipping the uncompressed files with a Zip utility will usually compress as well as LZW (see Figure 15.1). If the images are staying put, using LZW can save disk space, and it is lossless compression.

Figure 15.1
When saving a TIFF file, the TIFF Options dialog box will appear. Choose between Macintosh and PC compatibility, as well as from a variety of compression types.

Some printers and service bureaus prefer TIFF files rather than EPS files for color image production, although EPS (DCS) saves output time since it's already color separated. Several compression methods are available for TIFFs. LZW, the most common and safest, is lossless encoding. Zip compression, the same algorithm used in Zip utilities such as PKZIP, is also *lossless*, whereas JPEG compression is lossy, meaning that it causes varying degrees of image degradation. If you choose JPEG compression, you can choose the amount of compression applied. The higher the compression level, the more the image's pixels are manipulated to make it smaller, and the greater the likelihood that this image degradation will be noticeable to the viewer.

Lossy Versus Lossless Compression

Some file compression encoding is known as *lossy* in that it loses information from the original image information due to translation. In some instances, it is desirable to sacrifice some image quality for file size. For example, this is done with JPEG Web images to speed transfer. You might want to stick to lossless translations unless loss of information in images is okay or even desirable for your purposes. Image type compression (JPEG, LZW, GIF, and so on) should be considered differently than file compression. File compression (ZIP, SIT, SEA, MIME, and so on) is always lossless as it acts on the file information independent of it being an image. Image-type compressions act to compress based on image information.

Images should probably be provided to your service bureau or printer in uncompressed form to save imaging time and potential compatibility problems. If your images are LZW compressed, the imaging unit must decompress the file before outputting it, which takes additional memory and time. If there are a lot of compressed images and this adds significantly to the imaging time, the service or printer might want to charge you for the added time.

→ For more information on concerns to consider when using a service for printing, **see** "Prepping for Printing: Prepress," **p. 869**.

You might not always want to save TIFF images with channels and layers because it increases the file size. If you do not need the alpha channels or layers for your purposes, simply uncheck those options in the Save As dialog box when saving. Photoshop will automatically flatten the image and remove channels which are incompatible with the format you save to. You might consider saving the file in more than one way. That way, you can keep it both flattened and portable, and with the channels and layers available.

EPS FILE FORMAT

Encapsulated PostScript (EPS) files are most often used for PostScript printing of color images—although they can be used for black-and-white (grayscale) as well. EPS files can be saved in grayscale, RGB, and CMYK so long as the layers for the image are flattened and additional channels are eliminated. Desktop Color Separation (DCS 2.0) is a related format that supports additional spot color channels and alpha channels, but neither EPS nor DCS 1.0 supports alpha channels.

The EPS format also supports a number of functions not supported in any of the other formats, including transfer functions, color management profile embedding, and halftone screen settings. Like TIFF files, EPS files support clipping paths, so you can import an image into other programs and effectively crop out unwanted portions of an image in shapes other than rectangular form (see Figures 15.2 and 15.3). Because EPS files use PostScript encoding, printing errors can be reduced and printing speed improved over other format types when printing to PostScript devices (see Figure 15.4). This file type is, more or less, the choice of professional artists in layout and design as it offers several higher-level controls over the content of the image file than TIFF formatting.

Figure 15.2
Clipping paths are assigned from completed paths (paths that are closed). These paths can be drawn with the Pen tool or a path can be created from a selection in the desired shape.

Figure 15.3
When saved with an active clipping path, the image will appear in Photoshop as it does in Figure 15.2, but when it prints to PostScript, the clipping path will clip off the portions of the image that fall outside the path.

Tip

Although EPS files do not support alpha channels, paths can be converted to and from selections (if they are hard-edged or evenly feathered), so simple selections can be stored in EPS files.

EPS COLOR SEPARATION OPTIONS

Options for saving color-separated PostScript files in Photoshop 6.0 include DCS 1.0 and DCS 2.0. DCS 1.0 supports separation into multiple files; one each for the channels of the image colors and one for the FPO (for CMYK, that would be five files: C, M, Y, K, and the low-resolution placement file). DCS 2.0 can save preseparated files as multiple files or as one composite file. Each format has options for encoding (ASCII, Binary, and JPEG compression) and the type of preview image to build for the placement file (None, TIFF, and Macintosh). The dialog boxes that appear when saving are slightly different for each type, but in practice the choices are handled in a very similar fashion. Check boxes at the bottom of the EPS Options dialog boxes are Include Halftone Screen, Include Transfer Function, PostScript Color Management, Include Vector Data, and Image Interpolation. The two DCS formats include four of those five check boxes, leaving out PostScript Color Management (see Figures 15.4 and 15.5).

Figure 15.4
The EPS dialog box contains options for controlling, which will affect the image reproduction.

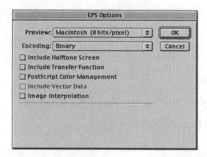

Figure 15.5
Pop-up menus for the Preview image (left) and Encoding (right) allow more control over how the content gets written to the file than any other file type.

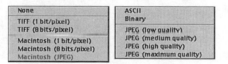

FOR PLACEMENT ONLY (FPO) IMAGES

The preview image for an EPS is a low-resolution image (sometimes called FPO, or For Placement Only). It can be 1-bit (black-and-white) or 8-bit (color). This image is used when putting an EPS image into a layout program to set placement. These FPO images can often look pretty horrible onscreen (depending on the settings you choose, of course), but the idea is to save space in the layout file (QuarkXPress, PageMaker, InDesign, and so on) and, to a lesser extent, in the saved file. Choosing None for Preview in the EPS Options dialog box will still create the placement file—however, there will be no preview or placement image. When the placement image is called up into a layout program and it has no preview or FPO, the program will put in a default PostScript *test pattern* (see Figure 15.6). These test pattern images do not print or affect printing, and are present only to let you know there is something placed where you thought you put it. They might just be text, a simple image, or a pattern.

Figure 15.6
This is a test pattern from QuarkXPress. This merely lets you know that you have successfully placed an EPS image, but might not give any hints as to cropping or placement in the image box.

There are several advantages to using the FPO. Most tangible is that they might help speed layout and keep memory needs lower for open documents in the layout program. When the file is printed to a PostScript printer, the layout program references the full resolution version of the file, so the image will print fine (to PostScript printers). Part of the downside, especially with five-part files (DCS 2.0, Multiple Files), is keeping track of all the parts. When using image files in a layout, it is usually required that the images be sent with the layout file for imaging. In other words, the files are usually placed with the preview image rather than being embedded in the layout file. EPS files saved in multiples of five increase the chance that a file will be inadvertently left out when packing up the job.

Caution

When attempting to send an EPS image to a non-PostScript printer, the image will be sent as the low-resolution file. This can cause some frustration or confusion if you aren't aware of the fact. Unless your non-PostScript printer is equipped to mimic PostScript, the result will be blocky and probably awful. This doesn't mean that the files are bad—although the same thing will happen if components are missing. It might be best to stick to TIFF files if you have a non-PostScript printer that you use for printing proofs.

EPS ENCODING

Different encoding options can affect the file size and, the time it takes to process, and it also can affect some compatibility issues. As a rule of thumb, you'll want to use binary encoding rather than ASCII or JPEG—unless your service specifically requests ASCII.

ASCII and Binary, unlike JPEG, are lossless encodings. JPEG compression does some interpolation of image data and throws some of it out. If you use the highest settings, and save the image for use only—that is, you don't plan to open, work on, and resave the image from Photoshop—it might be okay to use JPEG for encoding. However, because of the interpretation of data, images can change somewhat in appearance or color, especially in lighter colors where a small change can make a great difference. Images tend to get a blocky JPEG quality about them, which is easy to recognize when working at high magnification (see Figure 15.7). To me, any unnecessary image damage is cause for dismissing use of JPEG compression. The only time you should really use JPEG encoding is if space is at a premium and there is no other way to transport the file.

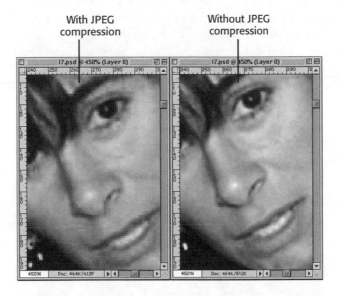

With JPEG
compression

Without JPEG
compression

Figure 15.7
EPS images saved with JPEG compression will alter the information in the image; you won't be able to tell ahead of time exactly how the image will be altered by the JPEG compression when it is saved. Here, the same image is shown with JPEG compression and without at 450% magnification.

Note

Usually, the differences in JPEG/non-JPEG images are harder to discern in print as paper and ink absorption tend to smooth some of the anomalies. You might have to look very closely to see the differences in the images shown in Figure 15.7. If you experiment with JPEG compression, the differences will become very apparent onscreen.

→ For more information on JPEG encoding, **see** "JPEG," **p. 329**.

Binary encoding is merely a more compressed form of ASCII. Both are methods of encoding the raw data, but binary encoding will encode more efficiently. As this is the case, binary files will be smaller, and can be processed more quickly than ASCII. ASCII encoding might have a slight advantage in compatibility, but generally processes and programs that are up to date can handle binary data.

EPS DIALOG BOX OPTIONS

Include Halftone Screen, Include Transfer Function, PostScript Color Management, Include Vector Data, and Image Interpolation options are all options for EPS files that work in interpreting file information for output. *Halftone* screening is related to the angle at which the lines of dots from the printer are put down for different color inks. The screen angle refers to the actual angle in which the lines are skewed. This is used to help offset the appearance of the dots as rows, and to cut down or eliminate *moiré patterns*—repetitive dot patterns formed in areas of consistent color.

TRANSFER FUNCTION

A transfer function is a method of controlling ink intensities with curves, and without affecting the appearance of the image on the screen. The idea would be to adjust and/or fine-tune the output of your images to the output of specific devices. For example, if you usually print to an offset printing device and know that your proofs always run a little hot in the more saturated areas of the magenta (whether due to the paper or the printer itself), loading a transfer function for the image will enable you to adjust print to your proofing device to match the offset printer without further alterations to the image.

To work with and create transfer functions for your images, choose (File, Print Options) [File, Page Setup] and click the Transfer button. This opens the Transfer Functions dialog box. You can then adjust the output overall (leaving the All Same check box checked), or work with inks separately (see Figure 15.8).

Figure 15.8
This transfer function will reduce the intensity of the black ink in the shadow areas. Usually, transfer functions are created for output to a specific device.

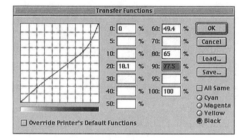

After you note a tendency in a specific output device, you can add a transfer function and save it to recall with any image that goes to the device (using the Load button). If you find you need to create a transfer function for every device you print to, you probably need to recalibrate, and not spend more time with transfer functions.

→ For more information on calibration, **see** "Evaluating Color Images Onscreen," **p. 411**

POSTSCRIPT COLOR MANAGEMENT

PostScript Color Management will embed ICC profiles, which will be used in PostScript Level 2 and 3 devices to attempt to match output as it appears on the original device and configuration. Print devices that do not use this information will generally just ignore the settings. However, this doesn't mean you should always use the embedding. This is a preference and should be managed according to how you feel you best achieve the output results you are looking for.

→ For more information on halftone screens, transfer functions and other printing options, **see** "Image Output Options," **p. 859**.

→ For more information on PostScript Color Management and ICC profiles, **see** "Evaluating Image Color," **p. 409**.

INCLUDE VECTOR DATA

 Including vector data in an EPS is a new feature for Photoshop 6 and it enables you to save vector-defined image elements as vectors (rather than rastering or dropping them). This allows you to get better results with printing type that has been converted to paths and shapes used to define layer data. Saving with this option makes the information ready for other applications, but opening the image again in Photoshop forces the vector information to rasterize to the dpi of the image. When you use this option, you should save in more than one format (such as Photoshop native) in case you need to change the information in the file and want to keep the vector data intact.

→ For more information on working with paths and converting selections to paths, **see** "Interchanging Paths and Selection," **p. 187**.

→ For more information on working with paths for defining image information, **see** "Layer Masks," **p. 64**.

IMAGE INTERPOLATION

Checking this box will help reduce the jagged appearance of images that are resampled during printing. Generally, you will want to have the image information correct in the first place (meaning the resolution will be adjusted to the size of the use), so this will hopefully be unnecessary in most cases. Although this option may improve results of images being printed that do not have the proper resolution, it will not fix images for you, and may cause some loss or blurring of details. It is probably best in every case to resize the image properly instead of using this option.

→ For more information on working with proper resolution, **see** "Understanding Resolution," **p. 341**.

PHOTOSHOP NATIVE FILE FORMATS

Photoshop offers two native file formats: the Photoshop format and the Photoshop 2.0 format. The Photoshop format saves your document with full features according to the current version of Photoshop that you are using. Photoshop 2.0 is not an improvement, as the name might imply, but a means of backward saving so that files can be read by earlier versions of the program (as far back as version 2.0) or can be more widely shared with other graphics programs.

PHOTOSHOP

PSD stands for *Photoshop Document* and is the filename extension for the native and default Photoshop image file format. Photoshop native format is the only file format which supports all Photoshop's image modes and features, including layers, channels, paths, effects, adjustment layers, guides, grids, eyedroppers, and so on. The only things that are not saved in a PSD are image Histories and Snapshots—and no format retains those. By default, Photoshop-format files use lossless compression on saving. This is the best format to use when saving an image in the midst of production or for storage with all the production parts intact. In other words, save working versions of an image in this format. Photoshop format is not a good format for final images that you expect to use in layout programs, as there is only limited support for it, and it cannot be viewed in Web browsers or most simple image viewers.

Although the file format is native for Photoshop, many other graphics applications support the file type (due obviously to the popularity and broad use of Photoshop). This makes the files somewhat more portable than would normally be expected of a native format. However, new features are not backward compatible and will be dropped if opened in earlier versions of Photoshop, and might not function with other graphics programs. For maximum portability, it might be necessary to remove some image features, save backward (see the following section), or choose another file format.

PHOTOSHOP 2.0

This file format backward saves Photoshop files so that they are compatible with Photoshop version 2.0 and later. These files are not compressed, and will be flattened as a result of the save. The format does not support 16-bit channels, Lab color, or ICC profile embedding; however, channel information is retained. This is a method of saving native Photoshop files for transfer to other applications or other users that have not upgraded. The Photoshop 2.0 format saves as a Macintosh file format only, and drops the file extension even if you have your preference set to Always Append File Extension because the Mac OS does not require them. This format is somewhat limited in utility as it can strip out a lot of what is useful in maintaining native Photoshop formatting in the first place.

➔ For more information on options for saving images such as always appending file extensions, **see** "Saving an Image," **p. 297**.

GIF FILE FORMAT

GIF files (or CompuServe GIF/Graphic Interchange Format, named after the organization that developed the format for image transfer) are one of two mainstays in transferring image information over the Internet (as attachments, on Web pages, and in email). There are several GIF versions, including GIF87a and GIF89a. Photoshop uses GIF89a, but can open both. These formats are both indexed color only, supporting 8 bits of color or grayscale and a single alpha channel. Special features of this format include the capability to save animations and allow loading of the image in progressive steps. GIF89a supports transparency as well. The GIF file type is great for supporting images with a limited number of colors and simple two-color gradations. It is lossless compression (LZW), but the losslessness is relative. After you convert an image from RGB to Indexed Color mode to save to GIF format, the reduction from 16.7 million colors to a maximum of 256 (the most a GIF file will support) has probably already done some damage to the image. However, planning images with the color limitation in mind can yield fine results for Web images while taking advantage of the compact size for quick downloads.

Note

GIF images are best used with limited color images (like developed graphics—such as buttons). It is not intended for use with photographic images. For color photos, use JPEG images on your Web pages. PNG images are another format that hopefully will soon be more widely supported.

→ For more information on PNG images, **see** "Other Formats for Save," **p. 332**.

Tip

Upon saving to GIF, you will be prompted to make Indexed Color selections for the file if the image has not already been converted. This dialog box is identical to the Indexed Color dialog box that appears when you choose Image, Mode, Indexed Color. Saving as a GIF will be possible only if the image is RGB or Indexed color. It is, however, possible to use the export Wizard/Assistant for transparent images (Help, Export Transparent Image) or the Save for Web command (File, Save for Web) with any color mode, and this will lead you through semiautomatic export of the current image.

→ For more information on the Indexed Color dialog box, **see** "Indexed Color" in "Additional Color Modes," **p. 315**.

→ For more information on saving and exporting using different Save commands and export options, **see** "Saving an Image," **p. 297**.

→ For more information on GIF images and using them on the Web, **see** "Creating Professional Web Effects," **p. 791**.

JPEG

JPEG (Joint Photographic Experts Group) is a file format and compression type used for conserving file size. It is lossy compression, and generally irreparably damages images. This damage and compression is reapplied every time the image is saved with the JPEG format. That is: The images get progressively worse each time you save, reopen, and save the image again. The compression averages and alters a tremendous amount of image information during a downsampling process (part of which is aptly referred to as decimation). Even areas of flat color are altered.

The premise for compression is based on visual standards. For that reason, the compression considers human color perception, and even though the damage is ample, the overall result of JPEG encoding is more acceptable for the look of photographic images used on the Web than GIF images. This is because JPEG can support RGB color and can retain more colors than the GIF format (which is limited to 256 colors). The format is best suited for transmission of graphic information in compressed format as a suitable alternative to GIF images on the Web in the proper situations (saving images for the Web that have more colors than a GIF can handle well). Although JPEG files can be used with print images in an increasing number of programs, it is not recommended unless compression of image files is crucial.

The JPEG file format supports RGB, CMYK, and grayscale color modes; however, CMYK images will not display on Web pages. It does not have parameters for animation, allows no alpha channels or spot colors, but supports paths. The compression can be controlled on a sliding scale from zero to 12—zero being the highest level of compression and lowest quality, and 12 being the best quality and lowest compression (see Figure 15.9). As compression increases (as the number goes down), the quality of the resulting image goes down.

Tip

It is suggested that you use only High or Maximum Quality when saving JPEGs to reduce the possibility of noticeable image damage.

Figure 15.9
The JPEG Options dialog box has options for selecting Matte, image quality (using slider, pop-up menu, or number entry), Format, and Preview of the saved image. The selector at bottom shows resulting file size and an approximation of download time.

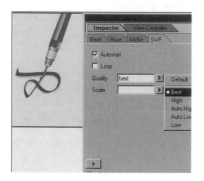

JPEG SAVE OPTIONS

Format for the JPEG can be Baseline Standard, Baseline Optimized, or Progressive. *Baseline standard* is standard JPEG encoding supported by the widest range of browsers. *Baseline optimized* is a slightly more efficient encoding that might not be compatible with some older browsers. *Progressive* allows you to make the image appear in several passes as it opens in the browser (see Figure 15.10).

Figure 15.10
The number chosen denotes the number of loading passes that will occur to fully load the image. Progressive loading of a JPEG image will show the image in steps, increasing the visibility with each pass.

Start of download

End of download

Tip

Using the progressive format for JPEG files helps Web site visitors have the sense that something is going on during download which can keep them from leaving your site when a page with a lot of large images is loading. The image will appear progressively throughout the download and may help keep the visitor interested in the contents of the page.

The JPEG Matte Option

The Matte option for JPEGs is really a substitute for transparency. Although transparency is not directly supported, it can be mimicked by selecting the Matte color. This color fills in to match the background color used for the Web page. To add a matte, follow these steps:

1. Prepare the image by making it a single layer. To do this, flatten the image if necessary, and then double-click the layer in the Layers palette. This will open the New Layer dialog box and rename the layer to Layer 0.

Note

A layer will support transparency, a background (layers with the name Background in italic) will not.

2. Remove any portion of the image which you would like to have transparent (for example, by selecting with the Magic Wand and pressing the delete key). This will show the checkerboard background grid in the areas where the image information was removed.
3. Choose Save for <u>W</u>eb from the <u>F</u>ile menu.
4. Select JPEG for the file type in the Settings window of the Save for Web dialog box.
5. Choose from the options on the Matte list in the JPEG Options dialog box for the Matte color you want to use. You can select the color using an eyedropper.
6. Save the image by clicking the OK button.

When you save the image, the Matte color will be filled into the open areas of the image. Partially transparent areas will fill with a percentage of the matte color. Although it appears to work in the same manner as transparency, this image will appear to be transparent only on pages that have the Matte color as a background. Although this is a handy feature, it might be best to control color for blending/matte when creating the image by substituting the color before saving.

JPEG Preview

The Preview box in the Save for Web window shows a preview of the effects of the compression you have selected when checked. The File Size will display according to the selected options at the bottom of the Options dialog box, and the download time will be approximated based on your selection of speed (14.4K, 28.8K [default], or 56K downloads). These features should help you make intelligent decisions about saving JPEG images and will show you exactly what your tradeoff will be between smaller image size and the damage compression will create.

→ For more information on using images on the Web, **see** "Using Photoshop Images on Your Web Site," **p. 827**.

→ For more information on alternative formats for Web images, **see** the section on PNG image files in the following section.

OTHER FORMATS FOR SAVE

Quite a few additional formats can be used for saving images in Photoshop. These are often somewhat specialized or used only in specific instances. Chances are you will rarely use most of them (except in opening or transferring images to another source) and might never need to use some (IFF, or Filmstrip, which meets needs of a specific group of users). However, you might find a format or two here that you will find useful and use frequently depending on your needs—BMP, for example, might be highly useful on Windows systems.

Note Some formats that appear in this section will not be save options for Photoshop (such as Photo CD). Photoshop will open these images although it cannot save in the original format.

AMIGA IFF

The IFF (Interchange File Format) is an Amiga file format developed for use with Amiga computer systems (Commodore), one of the first computer systems to include color monitors. IFF is the standard bitmap image file format on the Amiga. It supports indexed color, RGB, and grayscale with no channels and uses lossless *Run-Length Encoding (RLE)* compression. Use IFF for exchanging images with Amiga systems. Unless there is a specific reason to save to this format, images tend to be more highly portable and smaller when saved in more efficient and portable formats.

BMP

Bitmap (BMP) is a Windows-based file format for retaining color file information (as opposed to Bitmap mode, which is black-and-white only). Really, this is a standard or default image file format under DOS and Windows. You can save to BMP from Indexed Color, Grayscale, and RGB modes; however, it does not support alpha and spot color channels or layers, so these check boxes will not be available if you choose BMP for the file format. These files are highly portable in the Windows environment (for example, can be pasted into email or used in word processing), and is the default format for screenshots on PCs. Compression is supported with RLE (Run-Length Encoding) compression, which will create shorthand for rows of pixels with the same value—a lossless compression. File sizes can tend to be large, depending on the content. For example, a picture of a leafy tree would be large using this compression because the image information and color changes often; a screenshot of a dialog box, on the other hand, might compress fairly well in bitmap format because the solid gray is more easily defined with the shorthand.

Filmstrip

The Filmstrip format is used for RGB animation or movie files created by Adobe Premiere. Premiere does not allow extended editing of individual frames, so export to Photoshop can be beneficial. After the file is in Photoshop, resizing, resampling, or removing alpha channels, or changing the color mode or file format will keep you from saving back to the Filmstrip format. The Adobe Premiere User Guide can help you more with this. Use this format for saving back to Premiere.

PICT File

The Macintosh PICT image file format is the Mac equivalent of the Windows BMP format. PICT files can be Indexed color, RGB, and grayscale, with one alpha or spot color channel for RGB mode only. PICT files use lossless RLE (Run-Length Encoding) compression. This is used in creating screenshots on the Mac (Shift-Option-3), and is used with desktop patterns. PCT is highly portable in the Mac environment, but there is usually a better, more efficient, choice for most image purposes.

PICT Resource

PICT Resource is another Macintosh PICT image file type which is used to store images in file Mac resource forks. You can save to PICT Resource format from RGB, Indexed Color, Grayscale, and Bitmap mode images. All but RGB must be saved without an additional channel.

You can use import or open commands to open a PICT Resource file. When saving a file as a PICT Resource, you can specify the resource ID and resource name. As with other PICT files, you also specify bit depth and compression options.

PCX

The PC Exchange image file format (PCX) is another PC bitmap format, not unlike PCT, IFF, and BMP in type. It supports indexed color, RGB, and grayscale, with no alpha or spot color channels. The PCX format uses lossless RLE (Run-Length Encoding) compression as well. Again, this is a targeted file format, and images might be better saved in more highly portable and efficient formats.

PDF

The *Portable Document Format (PDF)* image file format was designed by Adobe Systems essentially to allow viewing of PostScript documents (with Acrobat Reader or other PDF viewing utilities). The PDF format has grown in use, popularity, and flexibility, and can now be saved to directly from a number of programs (word processing, layout, and graphic). Where documents cannot be saved directly to PDF from a program, they can be converted using Acrobat Distiller. Any program with a Print command (provided Distiller is available to the user) can turn a file into a PDF. Depending on the compression use and settings chosen, the resulting files are typically small and are used with everything from display on Web pages (via browser plug-ins) to independent viewing with a viewer, to sending single, complete files to a printer or service bureau for high-resolution color printing. It can offer advantages for reducing proofing costs for some output, and is nearly essential to print-on-demand services (short-run, cost-effective, digital book, or content printing).

PDF documents are highly portable in the sense that they can be viewed by nearly anyone with a computer. Free viewers are available for Unix, PC, and Macintosh computers. PDF files are to viewing content what plain text (Text Only, ASCII) files are to word-processing programs—only with the formatting included.

Although PDF is not generally thought of as editable other than with Adobe's Acrobat software, Photoshop changes the perspective on editability to some extent by offering the capability to open PDF files. Individual pages of multiple-page documents can be opened and altered, and then resaved and reincorporated into the original document with Acrobat, or the files can be saved as standalone PDFs. The possibility allows for some exciting potential integration between programs.

OPENING A PDF

To open a page from a PDF document, simply choose File, Open, select the PDF, and a dialog box will open that allows you to select the page you want to edit (see this step-by-step procedure as follows). Opening the PDF file may rasterize the vector elements—depending on how the file was saved—so, working with and editing these documents can be a little tricky, especially if working with type.

In opening a PDF file, there are several dialog boxes that the user must navigate. Use the following steps to open a PDF as an image:

1. Select File, Open.
2. Browse to select the PDF you want to open. If this is a multiple-page document, the Generic PDF Parser dialog box appears. This shows a preview of the first page (if available) and allows selection of the page you want using the navigation arrows.
3. Select a page and click the OK button. This opens the Rasterize Generic PDF Format dialog box (see Figure 15.11).

Figure 15.11
The Generic PDF Parser dialog box allows selection of the single PDF page that you want to open as a document in Photoshop. Navigation arrows move views by single pages, or to the beginning or end of the document. Clicking the Current Page button opens the Go to page dialog box (see Figure 15.12).

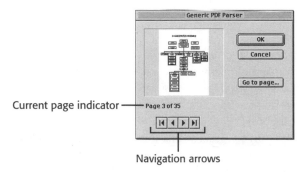

Current page indicator

Navigation arrows

Figure 15.12
In the Go to page dialog box, simply enter the number for the page you want to navigate to and click the OK button. This page will be selected in the Generic PDF Parser dialog box.

Note

For opening multiple pages from a PDF, it might be better to use the Multi-Page PDF to PSD command on the Automate submenu (File, Automate, Multipage PDF to PSD). This will convert multiple PDF pages to PSD documents at one time, whereas you can open pages via Photoshop's Open command only one at a time.

4. In the Rasterize Generic PDF Format dialog box, choose the size, resolution, and color mode for the document when it opens. You can change the proportions of the document by unchecking the Constrain Proportions box, or turn off antialiasing for the text. Clicking OK will begin opening the image. A progress bar will appear if rastering a complex image or working with high dpi.

Tip

You might want to change the defaults for the purposes of editing the page as an image. For example, you might want to edit a text page that suggests a resolution of 72dpi at something quite a bit higher (300–800, depending on how you plan to use the image) if you have to raster the text. PDFs with embedded text allow text elements to be resolution independent, so you are limited only by the resolution of images included in a document.

PDF supports all Photoshop's image modes except duotone and multichannel, but has no direct support for alpha or spot color channels. Photoshop's PDF output offers a choice between lossless Zip and JPEG compression. Use PDF for versatile documents that can be converted into pages of longer documents (using Acrobat Exchange) and that you would like to have both viewed and printed on multiple platforms.

Tip

Printing can be suppressed if you generate the PDF and then save again using the security options in Acrobat Exchange. Creating a PDF of your artwork might be an interesting way of providing a portfolio that is easily transported and viewed. Securing a document from being printed will not, however, stave off screenshots. Watermarking images and artwork might be smart in any case.

→ For more information on watermarking images, **see** "Protecting Images," **p. 881**.

SAVING A PDF

When saving a PDF, simply choose File, Save As and select Photoshop PDF from the Format drop list. When you click the Save button, the PDF Options dialog box will open. This screen offers a variety of controls for saving the PDF, including Encoding, Save Transparency, Image Interpolation, Include Vector Data, Embed Fonts, and Use Outlines for Text.

- **Encoding**—Allows you to select between lossless Zip encoding or JPEG. If JPEG is selected, you will also be able to define the amount of compression.

- **Save Transparency**—Saves any transparency in the PDF for use in other applications (transparency is retained for use in Photoshop whether or not the box is checked if layers are saved).

- **Image Interpolation**—Allows image elements to be viewed and printed from other applications with aliasing. This can soften or blur pixel information. Although it is not desirable for certain image types (screenshots, for example), it may be desirable for affecting the appearance of higher-resolution images.

- **Include Vector Data**—Includes path information, including clipping layers and clipping paths. Choosing this also enables options for embedding fonts and using text outlines.

- **Embed Fonts** and **Use Outlines for Text**—Options for including text information in the PDF after the Include Vector Data box is checked. Embed Fonts includes the fonts used in the PDF with the saved file so that they will be available in the document to enhance editability, viewing, and searching. Using Outlines for Text saves the text as vector outlines. Saving as outlines retains the resolution advantages of vector text, but removes editability and search possibilities.

PDFs saved with Photoshop are generally more Photoshop friendly to Photoshop than PDF files saved with other applications. You will be able to retain more of the editable features in the image while using the advantages offered by the PDF format.

PNG

Portable Network Graphics image file format (PNG) was developed by a dedicated group of volunteers as a royalty-free replacement for GIF and TIFF-LZW. PNG supports indexed color, RGB, and grayscale, with one alpha channel for RGB and grayscale mode. The channel is used for transparency, and allows grayscale application for feathered transparency effects. PNG uses lossless compression, has capability for 16-bit color, and can be used with animation. It has been thought for a while to be a potential replacement for GIF and JPEG images on the Web, but is not currently supported by browsers (except through plug-ins). It is the native file format for at least one Web image tool (Macromedia Fireworks). This is more a file format with future potential than one with immediate need. There is almost no reason to save in this format currently. However, if you choose to save in this format, you will see the PNG Options dialog box (see Figure 15.13). This dialog box allows you to choose additional compression, or to load the image in passes (such as JPEG progression).

Keep in mind that the choice for filter is *additional* compression; the file gets sufficiently (if slowly) compressed by normal process. All the additional filters alter the image information during encoding (see Table 15.1).

Figure 15.13
Options on the PNG Options dialog box allow progressive/interlaced display using image downloads and additional lossy compression controls.

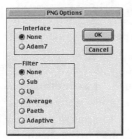

TABLE 15.1   PNG DIALOG BOX OPTIONS

Option	Compression/Action	Example Use/Explanation
None	No interlacing	
Adam 7	Interlacing	Incrementally increases image resolution for appearance of loading activity
Sub	Optimization with consideration for horizontal element retention	Used with horizontal background patterns
Up	Optimization with consideration for vertical element retention	Used with vertical background patterns
Average	Averages adjacent pixel color values to reduce color noise.	Reduces number of colors by changing values
Path	Reassigns/replaces adjacent pixel color values to reduce color noise.	Reduces number of colors by retaining dominant values
Adaptive	Auto select for compression type.	Choose if you are unsure of the compression to use. This will not select None.

Note

Interlacing (None, Adam 7) is selected independently of compression in the PNG.

PIXAR

Pixar image file format is designed for the Pixar Image Computer. This is of severely limited utility unless opening Pixar images created on Pixar workstations to convert to another format or other purpose. Supports only RGB and grayscale, with no channels. You might also use Pixar to edit rendered images to return to the Pixar format.

RAW

Raw is pretty much as described by the name: undefined image data compiled in a file. It is meant to be a flexible image file format. Photoshop's Raw output supports all image modes, with any number of alpha channels, but no layers. Duotones cannot contain alpha channels). It has no compression, and will not open compressed files—at least it will not reproduce the original image, although it might show you something. The intent for using Raw is if you want to exchange your images with a platform that doesn't use any of Photoshop's other formats, however unlikely that might be.

During attempts to import some unknown file types, Raw will be offered as the import file type. To use Raw successfully, you have to know parameters for the file, such as height and width, the number of channels, if the channel data is interleaved, and any header value. *Interleaved* data means that channel data is described for each pixel one at a time; noninterleaved data will store the data in channel segments, completing the description of each channel, one at a time, before moving on to the next. If you do not have the file specifications, you can have Photoshop guess at the file parameters by clicking the Guess button (see Figure 15.14). Photoshop will make a best guess in choosing the parameters for you.

Figure 15.14
The Raw Options screen allows you to create parameters for mapping the import of any file.

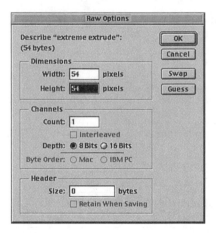

Generally, this format is rarely used, although there are some creative uses for the format such as hiding or scrambling images and image information (steganography). This can also be used to open proprietary formats.

→ For an example of scrambling information in a Raw image, **see** the Password section in the Introduction section of this book, **p. 4**.

However impractical, one thing the Raw format might allow for is some fun with turning text (or really any) files into patterns. Simply pick a file and open it as a Raw file. Fill in the dimensions to take up the bulk of the file size (each pixel on each layer is one byte), and then balance the total with the number of bytes in the header. Generally, this just produces noise, but at times you can create some interesting patterns.

SCT

The Scitex Continuous Tone (Scitex CT) image file format was developed by Scitex for their image-processing systems. This used to be a format in which high-end scans were provided from some service bureaus which used Scitex equipment, but seems to be becoming more scarce. Photoshop's Scitex CT files support RGB, CMYK, and grayscale, with no channels. Scitex CT images are uncompressed. Use Scitex CT if you are submitting your images for processing on Scitex systems.

TARGA (TGA)

Targa is another proprietary bitmap format for the PC. Targa supports indexed color, RGB, and grayscale, with one alpha or spot color channel for RGB and grayscale mode. Photoshop's Targa images are uncompressed although the Targa format itself supports RLE and other compression methods. Most common in the video industry, this file format is also used by high-end paint and ray-tracing programs because of expanded bit depth. Use Targa only for specific application in video output.

OPEN-ONLY FORMATS

Photoshop reads some file types in addition to those it can save in, but requires that you save in another format. If you happen to run into a file type that Photoshop does not open directly, you will be offered the option of opening the file as Raw. There is also some possibility that there will be a plug-in available from vendors of newer products (or those currently unlicensed by Photoshop), which will allow import or opening of these images. Failing in this, there are some image applications that specialize in translating and opening image files in any number of arcane and esoteric formats. DeBabelizer might currently be the most powerful of these applications. Unless you will be using the application a lot, or have a number of files to go through, it is probably best to request the files from the source in another format rather than invest in additional software.

 If you know what an image type should be and are still being offered only Raw as a possibility, or Photoshop is claiming it does not recognize the file format, see "A Known File Type Won't Open" in the Troubleshooting section at the end of this chapter.

PHOTO CD

There are common file formats that Photoshop does not save to, yet can open. For example, Kodak Photo CD is a format developed to store Kodak Photo CD scans. The files support five different resolutions contained in one file. When Photoshop is directed to open one of these files, the user is offered options for the conversion. After the selection is complete, the file is converted according to the selections and opens at the desired resolution. Photo CD is a CIE (Lab-type) color space that does not support additional channels, layers, paths, or placement on Web pages or in layout programs. The only benefit to the format is the availability of multiple resolutions.

It is a fabulous technology from the vending and archival standpoint. These are images that are scanned to CD and are an inexpensive means to get high-resolution image scans. The cost per scan at standard resolution (18MB files) is under $2. A higher resolution is available for larger transparency and negative scans that is under $12. The images are always encoded to CD for archive. This system allows users to open only what they need of an image as far as size is concerned. These images are clearly intended as source images.

➔ For even better support of Kodak Photo CD images, get the Kodak Photo CD plug-in; **see** http://kodak.com/global/en/service/software/pcdAcquireModule.shtml (on the Web).

However, Photoshop does not allow saves to this format. Because of limitations, the file format is not really desirable for many purposes. As the consumer will have purchased the original scans (few people will afford the necessary equipment for Kodak Scanning for home use), and the images are on CD, the user can access the raw scans whenever he/she needs to. There is no real reason to resave the image to a multiple resolution format, as the image can be saved at the desired size and scaled down as necessary.

Although a multitude of options is probably desirable, it seems that the efforts here by Adobe are to offer a blend of the popular and the effective so as not to leave potential transfers, platforms, and programs out of the loop. The only thing that is essential about Kodak Photo CD is opening them; there is no proprietary system that can't read other formats, and no program considers Photo CD as native; there is no reason why the images can't be changed into something more friendly and versatile—nothing is lost.

TROUBLESHOOTING

A KNOWN FILE TYPE WON'T OPEN

I often have trouble opening files from a specific friend. He sends Photoshop native format files but I am unable to open them although we both have updated versions of Photoshop. How can I get Photoshop to consistently recognize and open my friend's files?

This can be damage to the files, or might be compression and formatting details, but often it has to do with simply leaving off extensions. My guess is that the friend is on a Mac. Macintosh computers do not always use the filename extension to recognize file type and are a little more forgiving with file naming. Mac users can fall into some very PC-unfriendly habits with ease. There are two things you can do: 1) Rename the files when they arrive to include the PC three-letter extension (in this case, .psd), or 2) have your friend switch the way she/he saves files. Photoshop can automate the process by adding the extension automatically during the save. Simply have your friend change the current preference for Append File Extension in the Saving Files preferences to Always. Photoshop will automatically append the extension and change it when file types are changed. This actually might help your friend keep from accidentally saving over an image she/he desires to keep.

CHAPTER 16

UNDERSTANDING RESOLUTION

In this chapter

IMAGE RESOLUTION FOR VARIED APPLICATION

Before working on an image, it is best to know exactly how you are going to use it and how you plan to display it. Obviously, that is not always possible; and sometimes it isn't even desirable. You don't always know what you are going to do with an image before you create it. But, even if you are just setting out to play with images and possibilities, considering your needs from that vantage can save you time and trouble by allowing you to keep the file sizes small, work faster, and target the end result. Having the end in sight helps you make the proper choices in meeting the goals for the image or your purposes—play has its purpose.

In short, it is best, if possible, to streamline your work by targeting it to exactly what you need. Some projects require high dpi, some low; some jobs or results are determined by pixel size and others by dpi. Some will require multiple resolution uses for the same image. Just like choosing the proper color mode can save you work, or create more, choosing the proper resolution can help you get the results you need.

Although Photoshop's tools can correct almost any mistake, one thing it can't really correct is getting more information into an image. Having just the right amount of image information by choosing the right file type, dpi, and color mode will consistently yield the best results in the least amount of time. Having to resize, change color modes unnecessarily, or redo an image completely because of a bad early choice (image size, resolution, or color mode) will prove frustrating, will waste time, and will not produce the best possible results. You need to know about resolution in your images and how to handle it to get the best results. So, even when playing, you might want to play with an image that will result in something you can use. If you always work at 300dpi and you are using a test image at 72dpi to save time in running filters, you might really be learning nothing about the filters or settings because some will react very differently at higher resolutions.

DEFINING IMAGE SIZE

The size of an image should not be measured only by size as a linear dimension. By measuring an image in inches, it really doesn't describe the digital information, because digital images are not physical. Certainly, linear measurement gives a physical idea of size, but this idea doesn't translate directly to digital information and the amount of information in the image. What matters most is how much information is in that dimension. The usable size of an image can vary widely depending on the dpi. The element that makes up the dots part of the dpi (dots per inch) is the *pixel*. In the digital world, images are referenced more often by the size in pixels rather than dimension in inches, as pixel size is the final unit of measure for the elements that comprise the image. The number of pixels in an image doesn't change, unless the image is resampled or the crop of the image is changed.

DEFINING IMAGE RESOLUTION BY PIXEL DIMENSIONS

You are probably familiar with the use of pixel dimensions as they relate to capture in a digital camera (for example, 1,712×1,368) or display on a monitor (for example, 800×600).

These are absolute pixel dimensions. A linear dimension can have any number of pixels in it depending on the dpi without the digital information in the image (or file size) changing, but the number of pixels in an image cannot change without altering the information (and file size). For example, a 2×2-inch image at 300dpi should be printed at about 2×2 inches in output to an offset press (150lpi); on a Web page the same image would be more than eight inches square because display requires less resolution (only 72dpi, rather than 300dpi). The same image information will cover different expanses depending on the resolution. All the example means is that monitors project at a lower resolution than the resolution you get in print. Because print images at 150lpi are higher quality and resolution (or clarity), they demand more image information, which in turn gets used up over a smaller area. In other words, the higher the quality of the output, the smaller an image will be when used in that medium (if used properly). Table 16.1 shows the proper dimensions for an image using different output. The required dpi can vary somewhat depending on processes, equipment, and so on.

→ For more information on lpi (lines per inch), **see** "Working with lpi (Lines per Inch)," **p. 347**.

Note

The information in the table is for a 2,000×2,000-pixel image. The information does not change, but the applicable size does. The required dpi are examples, they are not meant to dictate the dpi you should always use with these output types.

TABLE 16.1   SAMPLE dpi RESULTS BASED ON OUTPUT

Output Type	Required dpi	Final Size of Square 4,000,000-Pixel Image
Web	72	27.8×27.8 inches
Poster Printing	100	20×20 inches
Print (175lpi)	271	7.4×7.4 inches
Film Recorder	650	3.1×3.1 inches

→ For more information on resolution, **see** "Resolution," **p. 371** and "Image Size or Scaling," **p. 373**.

DEFINING IMAGE RESOLUTION BY FILE SIZE

File size is sometimes used to define image resolution, although this method is not at all as reliable as defining by pixel size. File size is a measure of the information in a file in bytes, kilobytes, megabytes, and so on. Although it can be useful in working in situations where output or use is limited by file size (to fit on a transferable media, for example) and where the shape of the file and color mode are predefined, it might not be as useful for determining whether something will fit physically to an output method or not. For example, if I didn't note that the four-million-pixel image was square, it could have been any dimension—even 1×4,000,000 pixels, which is about two-tenths of a mile at 650dpi. No service with a film recorder could output a file that long, and you wouldn't even be able to create it in Photoshop in that shape. However, the file would be the same file size with four million pixels whether it was 2,000×2,000 pixels, 1×4,000,000 pixels or 400×10,000 pixels. This tells you the digital weight, but not how it is configured. Working with pixel dimension rather than file size (especially considering other factors such as different color modes and the potential for storing additional information as channels, and so on) is simply more reliable.

RESOLUTION AS PIXEL CONTENT AND LINEAR DIMENSION

You won't usually be asked for a pixel dimension, and having a pixel dimension for an image alone does not tell you how the information will be used. It will be up to you to supply the right information for an image depending on your output. If you know the output medium, you know a target range for the dpi, and you can scale your work accordingly by working with both the linear dimension and pixel size. If you don't know the target range, find out. The listing in Table 16.2 is a general guideline.

TABLE 16.2 APPROXIMATE DPI RANGE BASED ON IMAGE USE

Image Use	Approximate dpi Range (Final Size)
Web pages	72 [72–96]
Poster Printing	100–150
Newsprint	120–240
Uncoated Paper	180–266
Coated Paper	233–350
Art Books	271–400
Line Art/Bitmaps	600–800
Film Recorders	400–1000

Note

These are approximate ranges (minimum–maximum) of the output listed. Check with your service before following these guidelines.

WORKING WITH IMAGE MEASURES

The working range provides a target for the output dpi. That is, if you have a space on a page for a 5×7-inch image, you will want to work as closely as possible to that size and range from scanning to output. If the image is going to print on coated paper—that is, between 1,165×1,631 pixels and 1,750×2,450 pixels (multiply the size in inches by the dpi to get the dots)—scan and work within that scale. You can work either with the dpi and dimension, or the pixel size after you've determined that, whichever you are more comfortable with.

Tip

Photoshop can do a lot of conversions for you. For example, if you know the dpi and size in inches, open the Image Size dialog box (Image, Image Size). Plug in the numbers and you will see the result as pixels at the top of the dialog box. This dialog box is a handy calculator for figuring those conversions. You will have to do your calculations while an image is open, so don't click OK unless you are sure you want to commit the change.

Keep in mind that the scale of an image is not dependent on the linear dimension. You have to understand the relationship between the various image measurements and apply them according to what you have to work with. For example, if you have an image at 300dpi and you are going to implement it for the Web you have to convert the dpi to see the current size. Divide the current dpi by the target, and you will get the multiplier for the dimension (300÷72=4.17). The same image will be a little more than 4 times the print size when it is used on the Web. (Again, the Image Size dialog box can do this conversion for you.)

Tip

Working with a target of 288dpi rather than 300dpi can sometimes be very convenient and actually provide better results if you are targeting images for use both on the Web and in print. When you resize the image for the Web you can convert to exactly 1/4 the dpi (check the resample box when using image size), and you will get better conversions sizing up from Web dpi. Working with whole number multipliers is easier and 288dpi works well with anything from 144lpi to 192lpi.

→ For additional information, **see** the sidebar "Screenshot Resizing and Resampling," **p. 347**

If you don't get the dpi or pixel dimensions right, you will not get the expected result. Images will lose detail or resize accordingly, per the medium that is used for display or output. Work with the resolution of images in coordination with the output, not against it.

USING AN IMAGE FOR MULTIPLE PURPOSES

If you are going to use an image for multiple purposes, there are really two ways to approach this: Use the maximum target range for the resolution and size the image down for other purposes, or use several versions of the image, each scanned for its specific purpose. The latter might be more work but can produce better-targeted results. The former might produce better color consistency across media.

If you are going to play or experiment with images, use a normal image for your workload (dpi and size). If your RAM allows, increase the number of saved History states in the Preferences, and consider recording your playtime as an action: You never know what you will come up with.

→ For more information on using actions to record your moves, **see** "Creating and Editing Actions," **p. 269**.

RESIZING AN IMAGE

Resizing an image either requires a change in dpi with a corresponding change in linear dimension, or resampling of image information to either create more information or remove it. *Resampling* is a means of changing the dpi or effective pixel dimension of an image. If you don't have to, it is not something you want to do—or do to an extreme. Resampling takes image data and digitally computes a result for either upsizing or downsizing an image via interpolation. *Interpolation* makes assumptions about image data based on averaging, and adds or subtracts assumed data to and from the image. That is, a calculation will decide what your final result will look like. This can change the appearance of an image, blur edges that were sharp, cause pixelation—in other words, it can insert problems where there were none.

However, you might not always have the opportunity to work with images that are exactly the right size, and you might have to scale the whole thing or elements within it. When you have to resize, there are several things to keep in mind:

- Scaling up generally delivers worse results than scaling down.
- Scaling with the proper resampling type can improve perceived results.

Resizing is usually done using the Image Size dialog box, accessed by selecting Image, Image Size(see Figure 16.1). All you have to do to resize the image is check the Resample Image box and choose the resampling type, and then click OK. The image will be resized for you.

Figure 16.1
If resizing an image, you will generally want to keep the Constrain Proportions box checked. This will keep the width of the image in proportion to the height according to the original size. Unchecking the box can cause distortion of the image.

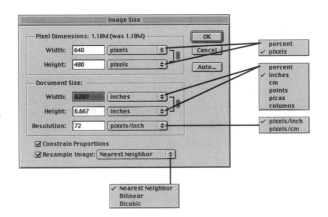

The real key to achieving the best results is choosing the right resampling type. Your choice can vary due to image types and your perception of the results. Generally, bicubic resampling produces the best results for purposes of resampling photographs and images up or down. However, sometimes bilinear may produce a better perceptual result in downsizing, and results of scaling screenshots are best accomplished with nearest neighbor (and downsizing or upsizing in whole number multiples). My general guideline is to use bicubic for upsizing, bilinear for downsizing, and nearest neighbor for screenshots or hard-color images in which there is no color blending. Bicubic resampling tends to blur edges slightly while resampling; bilinear holds an edge better, and nearest neighbor works with existing color and shape (rather than blurring or interpreting). Although the last might sound attractive, it generally leads to a blocky result: It works well for screen shots, but not for photographic images. It is often best to apply an unsharp mask after resizing with bicubic or bilinear resampling, but not with nearest neighbor.

Screenshot Resizing and Resampling

If you ever have to work with screenshots, you can usually just save a screenshot in the proper format to put on a Web page, or copy and paste into Word documents or email. You can usually do this without changing the dpi and get the right results. However, if you ever want to go to print with one or scale it in any way, there are a few guidelines to follow. Generally, you will want to scale screenshots only to be larger, and when you scale, be sure you scale in squares of the size (2^2=4×, 3^2=9×, and the like, … not 2.7^2=7.29×) using Nearest Neighbor resampling. Scaling this way prevents distortion as single pixels simply form larger squares of pixels. If sizing up 4 times, each pixel turns neatly to a 4-pixel square. If you size up 9 times, each pixel turns neatly to a 9-pixel square. The result of scaling this way is that everything looks exactly as it did before, only larger. If you work in multiples that are not whole numbers, Nearest Neighbor will not scale neatly because it will have to be remapped to fractions of a pixel. Pixels have to be a single color, so fractions create distortion. Because of the higher resolution, these larger versions of the image can be used and resized in a layout program without getting those annoying fuzzy edges.

Getting good results with screenshots gets only slightly trickier in some applications. For example, if pasting screenshots into some Microsoft products, the expected resolution is 96dpi and the program uses the dimension for display. If the screenshot is 72dpi, and most are, they appear 33% larger and blurry. To fix that, open the screenshot in Photoshop, change the dpi to 96, and then copy and paste the screen back into the other application. Although you have not changed the image, it is interpreted differently by the receiving software, and will look quite a bit better.

Don't resize an image a lot and expect great results. For example, you most likely will not be able to take a sharp 2×2-inch snapshot and size it up to 18×18 inches and get good results using any scanner, interpolation, or other magic—depending on what you expect. You won't be able to make that little image large and sharp. With the best quality scan, all you will get is that image in all its minute and gory detail, enlarging details of the qualities of the paper along with the image.

Resizing, like changing color mode, requires reinterpretation of *all* the image information. Photoshop does an admirable job (so much so that it is easy to get sloppy with resizing), but eventually the image information will stretch too far and break down. Resample only when you have to, keep it to a minimum, and resample carefully using the resampling type and scaling that is to your advantage. Keep in mind that transform functions will also force interpolation of image information. In short, if you resize and don't get the results you think you should, consider reacquiring the image, or using another one more suited, or more appropriately sized.

Working with lpi (Lines per Inch)

Many factors can play into the selection of a resolution for images you want to print. Often, resolution is referred to as line screen, or lines per inch. This refers to the number of rows of dots per inch, which in turn suggests the size of the dot in the line. The higher the line screen, the smaller the dot and the higher the resolution of the image that can be used and printed with accuracy. The translation that occurs here changes images from a continuous tone in the digital state to a noncontinuous tone as a series of dots. The shape of the dot— or phosphors in the case of display—and other factors play into the final result.

→ For more information on translating digital images to print, **see** "Understanding Duotones and Spot Color," **p. 522**.

If someone needs an ad for a magazine, for example, the parameters for the line screen are predetermined by the practices of the magazine. In doing your own printing, you can run the line screen of your choice, but only in comparison to the capability of paper to absorb the ink. In other words, there are limitations, considerations, and accepted (or at least often used) practices.

OPTIONS TO CONSIDER WHEN SELECTING AN LPI

Knowing the options helps you make an informed decision on what line screen to set up for and use. The solution to this problem is less a series of steps than making an observation and an informed choice. Most of the options to consider are covered in the following list.

Note

Choosing a line screen based on knowing the advantages and disadvantages will yield fewer surprises on the press and will help you manage production better.

- **Advantages and disadvantages of High-Line Screens**—The advantage of a higher line screen is the capability to get more dots per inch on the paper, a finer image feel (smoothness), and better general tonality (with proper resolution in the images). The disadvantages are that High-Line Screens are more susceptible to gain-related shifts in tonality. Improperly compensated images might darken or lose detail depending on the paper and absorption.

- **Paper quality**—The absorption of the paper is critical in line screen choices. Good paper (coated, heavy stock) will absorb ink without spreading (known as holding the dot). If you use better paper, you will be able to take advantage of higher-line screens. The disadvantage to better quality paper is the cost. Newsprint and thinner papers are cheaper, but have strong dot gain.

- **Image color**—Color should run at a high-line screen to avoid patterning (moiré patterns) and to get good color blending. With decent paper, you will want to run color at 175 lines or above. Black-and-white (grayscale) images can run at 133–150 if you are running a fairly decent stock, but not much more. Blending the dots is not desired, as with color and there is no real risk of patterning, so high screen frequency is a little less important than with color images. Duotones are considered color for printing purposes.

- **Image resolution**—If images are already scanned and have a low dpi, consider running a low-line screen to run images bigger. Just because you have a lot of resolution, don't be tempted to run images at a high screen frequency if the paper can't take the dot gain. All elements should achieve a balance.

- **Cost**—It can cost more to image at a higher-line screen because service bureaus and printers have to take more time to output film or image digitally, and higher-line screen will require better print stock, probably better printing devices, and printers who are able to handle those demands.

New Printing Technologies

Digital imaging methods and technologies seem to change almost daily. Although many of these methods are fantastic technologies, the requirements of a different output require different approaches to designing and implementing images. If in doubt, or when doing a new type of output, consult with printers and service bureaus for their recommendations before committing time to creating new work.

Running a higher-line screen on newsprint or paper with high absorption results in images darkening considerably. Even with good, coated stocks, dot gain (or the amount that ink spreads when it hits the paper) at 200 lines can cause a noticeable shift in image tonality if not corrected properly. Check with your press before making any hasty decisions. If possible and not cost prohibitive, do a print test under the actual conditions (usually called a press proof). Even with good image management and careful correction, variables on the press and with paper can change the look of an image between proof and final product. Make decisions on line screen before scanning and correction begin. The decision can affect correction, scanning, and the amount of time it takes to work on the images.

→ For more information on printing and printing concerns, **see** "Image Output Options," **p. 859**.

GETTING GOOD RESULTS IN PRINT: KEYS TO SELECTING A DPI

Getting the right dpi for the final result of the image resolution in print can be somewhat confusing. For example, you might print an image at 233dpi or 300dpi in 150lpi, and the results might look almost exactly the same. The best way to understand how the image information is applied is to look at the digital relationship of the image to the resulting dots. The continuous tone digital image is filtered, really strained, through an array of dots to get the end result. Where the size and amount of information in the image itself might differ considerably, because the dots stay the same size, the results can be almost the same. They should actually be the same until the point at which the information no longer fits correctly with the holes in the filter/strainer. There can be too much information in the strainer, forcing too much information through any one hole: The information will resample from too broad a range of information to define meaningful result. On the other hand, there can be too little information so that the continuous tone of the image is distorted and the information intended for one hole falls through more than one. The goal is to get the right amount of information distributed to each hole.

This distribution is governed by a simple calculation. The dpi can fall in a range 1.55 to 2 times the line screen. Many say 2 and leave it at that to simplify. However, thinking of this in a range can sometimes give you slightly more flexibility without affecting the results, and it is handy to know. So, if you are going to print at 150lpi, you need to have a dpi between 233 and 300. The images in Figure 16.2 attempt to show the relationship and why you can get away with anything between that range. The same image, created in Photoshop by rendering type in three separate resolutions, is printed using 233dpi, 300dpi, and 450dpi for the image. The enlargement shows a portion of the digital image to show what the dpi looks like in the digital file (these are screenshots increased to 400% so that the printed dots on this page don't affect viewing of the result considerably). The result shows that although the digital file is noticeably different when enlarged and in the amount of information stored, the printed result is really the same.

Figure 16.2
As you increase the size of a digital image, the resulting quality in print does not necessarily increase. To increase print quality you have to increase lpi, as well as the paper quality, cost of the job, and time it takes to image.

Never assume you have the right resolution. Check the resolution first when you get an image that you are supposed to work with, and be sure that the pixel dimension or size and dpi match the intended application before you commit to working on it. Work only within what you need and don't try to overpower the medium by supplying too much information—whether it is print, Web, or creation of digital film. If you do work with the dpi too high, the processor must strain away additional information by combining it, and files will take longer than needed to process and print—without improving results.

ACQUIRING THE DIGITAL IMAGE

CHAPTER **17**

OBTAINING SOURCE IMAGES

In this chapter

BORROWING IMAGES

There are a number of ways to obtain images, some of which are legal, some of which are in a gray area between legal and not, and some of which are flat-out illegal. For example, although most pictures you take with your digital camera will be yours to do with as you please, not all will. You can take a picture of a national monument and use that image royalty free to create postcards for sale, but even taking pictures of or scanning some items can be illegal, such as The Lone Cypress Tree at Pebble Beach or U.S. currency. Luckily, most of this type of concern is a matter of common sense and special cases are more the exception than the rule.

On first impression, it might seem harmless to borrow images from a Web site, magazine, book or other source. Really, it is if you are just going to use the images for your own purpose in fiddling with Photoshop and have no intention of distributing the images in any form. In the long run, however, it could prove very harmful if, for some reason, you are found liable for copyright violation either through willful violation of known copyright or by accidentally including copyrighted information in something you distribute as your own. Generally, you will want to get permission or at least ask whenever you have any doubt. As a rule, don't take a picture or make a replica of someone else's logo, design, recognizable character, and so on without expectation of clearing rights and perhaps paying a use charge, depending on what it is you are using and what you are using it for.

While borrowing might make your life easier in certain circumstances, and might prove cheaper than securing proper rights, it is a bad practice. The following sections list image sources and ways to get what you need for images and images elements, either free, for a price, or with some effort in creating it yourself.

STOCK PHOTOGRAPHY

Stock photography images are photographs that are already taken, usually by professional photographers, which are made available for use for a variety of purposes. The images are sold individually or in groups or packages—often on CDs—as royalty or royalty-free images. Images in stock collections can cover a broad range of subjects or they might be targeted to specific subjects and objects—for example, wild animals. Images can also be taken in both studio and natural settings.

Prices will vary depending on the rights purchased for use and whether or not images are purchased as part of a package deal. Images will also vary widely in quality from vendor to vendor and often between images. Be sure to check around for pricing, but certainly be aware of image quality. This includes sharpness and color correction of scans, not just quality of the photography and content. The images might also come in various resolutions and sizes. You'll need to be sure the images are large enough for your purpose. When you buy them, you can have them delivered to you on CD, or you can download them from the Internet—in some cases immediately.

→ For more information on evaluating image quality, **see** "Evaluating Image Color," **p. 409**.

Royalty Versus Royalty Free

Royalty-based images are leased based on use. Generally, these images are used in a limited number of areas and by fewer people than royalty-free images, which might be licensed to many people for many purposes. The difference between the two essentially is that royalty or fee-based images will be more unique and that fee-based images will prove more expensive. Although royalty-free images might be best for working with and creating composites, they should be used sparingly for development of product or corporate identity as they might be frequently used images that can become tired or cliché, or might be used by competitors. Put simply, when using images you are paying for and the shot is critical as unique, use royalty-based images; when it is not critical that the image be unique or a focal point, use royalty-free images and save a little money.

Note

For more information on royalty-based images and a broader discussion of the pros and cons of either, see `http://www.comstock.com/web/instructionshelpfaq/college/compareguide/PrintGuide(hs).html`

Stock photography is certainly the way to go if you can find what you need and can't accomplish it yourself, or if you want to gather a small library of images quickly to have on hand as you need them. Royalty-free images supply a lot of materials that you can freely excerpt as you need them. Generally, this will be much cheaper and quicker than the alternative (having a professional photographer take contracted images for you) and can often save you time and trouble—especially if you don't feel reasonably accomplished as a photographer.

CLIP ART AND FREEHAND ELEMENTS

Clip art is very much like stock photography in use and availability, but the content is freehand illustration, drawn by an artist rather than captured on film or as a scan. Clip art is creative, nonphotographic digital artwork (often, but not necessarily, vector graphics) created by artisans and made available through services or vendors.

More often, and in greater quantity than stock photography, clip art can be found for free—either on the Web or in various program installations that are often found in word-processing and Web programs. As clip art is often given away, it is often best to limit use of free images, unless the images are performing a specific function in which familiarity might be desirable.

Clip art is desirable for a number of functions, and can speed you along if you are looking for something that looks generic or official and you aren't yet too proficient with the drawing tools so that you can make your own.

Tip

Although there might be a perfect piece of clip art to fit your need, this might be a perfect opportunity to exercise your abilities with the freehand and drawing tools to create your own unique piece.

Probably the safest legal means of creating image elements for any purpose is to generate them yourself. Again, this requires the use of some sense; for example, you can't use images of Mickey Mouse without getting permission from Disney even if you draw them yourself. You can make everything from photorealistic images and enhancements to line art using Photoshop's freehand and Bézier tools. Developing these skills can be invaluable to image correction, development and creating the look you need.

→ For more information on freehand and Bézier tools, **see** "Freehand Painting Tools," **p. 203** and "Paths: Bézier Tools for Creating Vector Effects," **p. 175**.

IMAGES AND ELEMENTS FROM OTHER APPLICATIONS

A variety of other applications can help provide you with image source materials, and can provide you with an interface that you find simpler to use for specific tasks. Other programs might also provide a library of images or clip art, which can be exported or used directly in Photoshop royalty free.

For example, if you need more sophisticated path tools (such as in Illustrator), want to create a complicated 3D environment (Bryce), need sophisticated type layout features (Quark, InDesign, PageMaker), tools other than Photoshop might be best for generating these elements. Use the tools that you know and those that will get you the results you desire.

Although Photoshop has generally supported a wide range of file types, improved PDF support gives Photoshop nearly infinite versatility in translating files from a variety of programs. In essence, Photoshop can import image information from any program you can print from successfully using a PDF printer driver or PDF utility. This greatly simplifies transferring image information and removes compatibility issues. One thing you need to pay attention to is resolution in the output—during printing—to be sure you have enough resolution when you bring the elements into Photoshop. With improved support for PDF files, import and export of image information in Photoshop is much better.

Tip

Whereas I used to export some materials from Quark through the Quark EPS feature, I feel I get better results with less fuss using PDFs.

→ For more information on opening PDFs in Photoshop, **see** "Converting PDFs to Photoshop Images," **p. 294**.

Some image information can simply be copied and pasted or, in the case of Illustrator, even dragged from other applications in either bitmap or vector form, so long as it can be retained in the Clipboard (buffer). Some issues that might affect the transfer of information via copy and paste are color type, image type, and sizing. In instances where you cannot copy and paste directly to the intended document in Photoshop, try copying, creating a new document, and pasting to that instead. This might give you the opportunity to make the needed adjustments to the image element in Photoshop before moving it again to the target image. Copy and paste can offer an advantage over PDF files in transferring vector information. Opening an image as a PDF in Photoshop will render the vectors rather than transfer the path.

SCREENSHOTS

Screenshots are images taken from your computer screen that show exactly what is on the screen (in whole or in part, depending on how it is accomplished). Screens can often be a great source of image information for a variety of purposes, but are probably most useful in instructional materials and freezing screen information. However, in a pinch, and when there is nothing else to work with, or seemingly no other way to convert image information, this can be a faithful, although perhaps last-resort, technique.

Screenshots can be taken on a PC using the Print Screen key, usually located above the Insert key on the keyboard, or a screenshot utility. Print Screen will enter the screen information into the Clipboard or buffer, replacing what is there. This can then be pasted to a new document in Photoshop. Screenshot utilities might offer additional capabilities for sectioning or automatically selecting screen areas such as palettes, menus, or buttons. One fine, easy-to-use, and free utility is offered with Microsoft's HTML Help package, and it is definitely worth the download (`http://msdn.microsoft.com/library/default.asp?URl=/library/tools/htmlhelp/chm/hh1start.htm`). A number of other utilities are available for the PC as well.

Screenshots on a Mac can be taken using the (Cmd-Shift–3) key combination. This saves a PICT file of the current screen(s) on the System hard drive; however, if you have more than one monitor, the entire screen area is saved as a single image. A number of screenshot utilities are available for the Mac as well. Snapz Pro by Ambrosia is an excellent example of the available utilities, with capabilities of recording movies of screen activity as well as saving in a number of formats. You can customize the control buttons, include or exclude the cursor, and choose options for automatically or manually naming resulting files. It is shareware well worth the price of the license if screens are important to what you do.

Note

For more information on Snapz Pro, see `http://www.AmbrosiaSW.com`.

Caution

When creating screens, be sure, as with any image or capture, that you are not capturing otherwise copyrighted images or information to use in distribution as your own. Be sure to get permissions as necessary.

SCANNING AND DIGITAL PHOTOGRAPHY

There are clear advantages to creating your own photographic images similar to using the freehand tools to create your own clip art or artwork. Collecting your own image elements photographically is generally cost-effective—unless, for example, you decide to fly to Africa to get a picture of a white rhino—and you'll be able to use them in numerous projects without paying additional royalty fees or asking anyone's permission. A scanner, digital camera, or both will allow you to create your own photographic image elements.

Images can be captured using a video recorder as well. Several devices are available that will grab a frame from your video footage and export it as a still image. This can give you an inexpensive avenue to digital capture if you already own a video camera.

Not all these have the same potential for quality. Standard negatives in 35mm are currently rivaled by some of the better digital cameras, but medium and large format cameras remain essentially in a league of their own when it comes to image quality. The quality of both the print and the scanner, as well as the skill of the operator, play into the results you get from scanning your own photographic images. And although digital cameras provide a direct link from the physical to the digital, there are limitations on quality and potential size of an image depending on many factors from storage to camera ability. Although video cameras might offer an easy link to digital images, the quality of the results might not be suitable to many purposes.

However, it is not really even necessary to own a scanner, digital camera, or video camera to create your own images, so long as you have a camera. Newer scanning options at services such as Photo CD can prove cost-effective in providing high-quality, high-resolution images from standard negatives. These options might be more attractive and cost-effective for those who cannot invest in additional expensive equipment, or those who do not want to learn additional skills with other software and hardware for scanning negatives.

Good technique in using any equipment selected for incorporating images is essential to getting the desired results in any still images produced. This means there will be a learning curve, a need to develop technique, and probably some frustrating downtime. However, any skill you choose to learn will eventually make you better at Photoshop and implementing images.

Techniques and ideas for creative use of scanners and cameras in collecting image elements are covered in the following chapters.

→ For more information on scanning, **see** "Scanning to Create Images," **p. 361**.

→ For more information on taking images with a digital camera, **see** "Creating Images with Digital Cameras," **p. 397**.

CHAPTER 18

SCANNING TO CREATE IMAGES

In this chapter

SCANNING AND PHOTOSHOP

Scanning is one of the most convenient ways to incorporate images of many sorts into the computer. Although scanning is not directly a part of Photoshop, the capability to scan materials, and understand how to do it, is. Getting good, consistent results, enables you to use a much broader scope of existing materials to create image elements. Notice I did not say pictures. There is far more that you can do with a scanner than just scan images you have already taken.

A scanner can work like a limited digital camera for 3D objects, a color photocopier, a means of translating sheets of text into editable documents, and a generator for patterns, textures, borders, and image replacement parts. It can be good for creating product shots or capturing the likeness of any number of items that you want to incorporate into your Photoshop images. From paper clips to camera gears, statuettes, and fabrics, a scanner can help provide raw and finished materials that you can use in developing images. You can also use advanced scanning techniques such as multiple scans to get more information out of an image and improve your results. The ability to do these things immediately can greatly enhance your work in Photoshop and increase the ease with which you complete it.

SCANNING PURPOSE AND GETTING RESULTS

The purpose of good scanning is not to get the most amazing scan in the world, but to get the best scans possible with your available equipment (hardware and software). This usually means getting a scan closest to your purposes. To do this you'll have to make the best possible choices when preparing for the scanning and in setting the scanning options.

Too often people either rely on the presets of a scanning program or just press the auto setting and hope for the best. Certainly, you can use the tools in Photoshop to fix whatever goes wrong. Someone who knows how to scan, however, will take somewhat more care in scanning and start with a better scanning result in the first place. They will save time, frustration—and perhaps money—by getting the better scan. Usually, getting a good scan requires more than pressing the Auto button.

Tip

When operating a scanner, remove jewelry (especially anything with diamonds). You can easily and inadvertently scratch the glass on either the bed or the lid when handling the objects you are scanning. After the glass is scratched, you are doomed to see the scratch in every scan you make until you replace the glass.

IF YOU DON'T OWN A SCANNER

Don't despair if you don't own a scanner. There might be a scanner accessible at a local self-service copy place and perhaps in a local library if you are lucky. If you must use someone else's scanner, collect some interesting things to scan before you go and be sure you bring enough compatible removable storage to save the images. For the most flexibility with scan size, use larger format removable drives. Zip disks are common and a convenient size to hold even large scans. Most desktop scanners have a maximum scan size of 8×14, and a Zip can hold a file that large at a bit more than 450dpi in CMYK without compression.

However, using someone else's equipment does not give you the flexibility that you have when you own a scanner. You probably won't have the guide for the software or scanner and will have to rely on someone else's ability to calibrate, clean, and upkeep the equipment. If they are not involved in getting results with the device, they might just neglect it a little. Being able to do your own calibration and becoming intimate with the software can help target your scans and scanning to your needs. If cost is a concern, inexpensive scanners can be had for the price of a scan or two from a service (under $100) and some of these models rival good consumer scanners of just a few years ago. Although this is not the best long-term solution, these scanners can be worth the investment so you can practice scanning, learn about scanners, and save some money on scans before making a more critical purchase. This is certainly a recommended accessory for Photoshop work.

If you aren't convinced, keep in mind that there are scanning effects and advanced scanning techniques you will never get to try and use if you do not own a scanner. The cost of getting someone to do any of those techniques for you would easily outweigh the cost of the scanner.

GETTING THE BEST IMAGE IN A SCAN

A scanner can get different image information from the same object depending on how it is used. Getting a better scan is the difference between fighting with an image that doesn't have the right information and simply using the images you need after you scan them. Scanning requires some skill and practice to get the best image information and to scan images correctly to fit your needs.

To get the best results from any scanner, you need to take full advantage of the tools at your disposal. Being ordered and methodical in the preparations for scanning will help you develop good scanning technique and will reap the best results.

Use the following steps to make sure that you get the best image. These are the basic steps—more information follows in this chapter on the specifics of each step.

1. Read the manual about the scanner's software, tools, and functions to become familiar with the scanner, its operation, options, and abilities.

→ For more information on learning about your scanner, **see** "Getting Familiar with the Scanner," **p. 364**.

2. Keep the scanner and objects you will be scanning clean and free of dirt and dust.

→ For more information on keeping scans clear of dust and so on, **see** "Keeping Things Clean for the Scan," **p. 365**.

3. Place the item on the scanner in an orientation best suited to your needs and the capability of the scanner.

→ For more information on orientation and placing images or objects on the scanner, **see** "The Scanner Sweet Spot," **p. 367** and "Scanning an Oversized Image," **p. 390**.

4. Choose appropriate software settings for the scan you are creating. These might include some or all of the following: Reflectivity, Color Mode, Resolution, Image Size/Scaling, Descreening, and Sharpness (among other things).

→ For more information on which settings to choose when making a scan, **see** "Choosing Scanner Settings," **p. 368**.

5. If an option for Preview is available, Preview the scan and use any available tools to optimize the image information when scanning. This will create a low-resolution preview of the scan, which will allow you to crop to the image area you intend to use (see Figure 18.1).

Figure 18.1
Cropping the image at this point can speed scanning time, prescan time, and keep the size of the resulting image low.

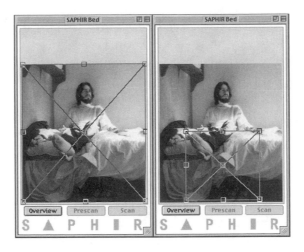

6. (Option) Prescan the image. Depending on the software package, this can produce a result that is high or low resolution that is used for evaluations and adjusting settings before the final scan.

7. (Option) Make adjustments for the prescan. For example, this opportunity can be used to set White and Black Points or to make other fine adjustments, such as with Curves (if available).

→ For more information on curves and their use in corrections, **see** "Corrections with Curves," **p. 456**.

8. Make the scan.

9. Open the scan in Photoshop and make evaluations of the result. If the results are not completely satisfactory. Make adjustments to the scanner setting (see Step 4) and rescan if necessary.

→ For more information on evaluating your scans, **see** "Evaluating Image Color," **p. 409**.

Getting Familiar with the Scanner

Reading a manual can teach you things about a scanner's unique abilities and functions—many of which might be found in the software. In fact, it can often be argued that the scanner software, not the hardware, makes the most difference in the final result of the scan. When reviewing a scanner's operation and software, pay special attention to the section on calibration, and calibrate your scanner according to the manufacturer's instructions. A calibrated scanner will yield the best results. While reading the materials, run tests to see how the scanner's tools work and to see what the software is capable of.

All scanner software is not the same. A few packages, such as LinoColor (see the interface in Figure 18.2), offer superior color-management capabilities and a full range of controls. The scanner's software can make quite a difference in the potential of the scans and performance of the hardware. Good scanning software will build ICC profiles for color management. It will also have tools for previewing and correcting the approach to the scan before the final scan is made.

Figure 18.2
The LinoColor scanning interface offers a broad range of tools and means of controlling how you make your scans. Control can lead to better results and less work in color correction and changes.

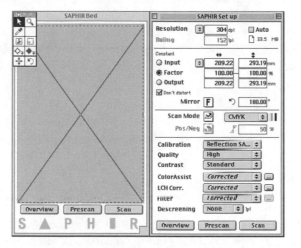

Some scanning packages offer Sharpening, Descreening, Cropping, Histograms analysis, Curves for color correction, or a variety of other tools. Try the tools and see how they work, but don't blindly depend on them. Photoshop happens to be the most powerful image editor around, so if the scanner's tools are less powerful or don't offer a clear advantage to Photoshop's, don't employ those tools during or after the scanning.

KEEPING THINGS CLEAN FOR THE SCAN

Cleaning dust from a scanned image is frustrating and time-consuming. Dust always crops up whenever you scan. At times, it is accentuated by the scanner and becomes more prominent even when software adjustments are made for dust (generally not recommended). There is no real solution to keeping it completely out of a scan, even building a dust-free environment, wearing plastic suits, and handling items to be scanned with sterile tongs reduces only the accumulation. Regretfully, a dust-free environment does not eliminate dust on whatever it is you are scanning. Some care helps keep the dust, fingerprints, and scratches to a minimum. Cleaning the scanner and the item being scanned means less for you to correct after the scan is done and saves a lot of unnecessary Photoshop work. Keeping dust and grime out of an image that is being scanned goes a long way toward lessening the demands of dust removal.

Before placing an image or object to be scanned, be sure that both the scanner glass and the object or image are clean and free of debris, dust, and fingerprints. Dust on the objects being scanned might require far more time and effort to correct in a scan than it would take to quickly wipe objects clean. Use manufacturer-suggested directions for cleaning and maintaining the scanner, and get dust-free soft scanner cloths for wiping objects and scanner glass. Compressed air can help blow away dust on the scanner glass and objects as well.

Use the following steps to maintain a clean scanner environment:

- Schedule scanner cleaning and maintenance. This means cleaning the scanner, scanner area (underneath the unit), glass inside and out, and perhaps cleaning the lamp and internal parts as well. Check with your scanner manual to decide on a maintenance schedule and stick to it. Follow the scanner instructions for disassembly (if necessary) and for any suggestions on using cleaners, solutions, and wipes. This keeps natural accumulations of dust to a minimum.

- Wash your hands before scanning or handling objects to be scanned. This reduces, not eliminates, the possibility of fingerprint smudges. You might consider wearing dust-free white mesh gloves while working with a lot of scans as this keeps items free of fingerprints as well.

- Clean the object you are scanning. Use pressurized air, soft dust-free wipes, and the sticky edge of a sticky note (or other light adhesive tape that won't leave deposits). Depending on the object, you might just run it under water. (I know someone who used to do this with record albums and he got phenomenal results with seemingly unplayable vinyl.) Use cleaning solvents on objects to be scanned only as applicable and practical, and only if you are sure they will not damage the item, or cause a film or residue that will be picked up by the scanner. Be extra careful applying any liquid or solvent to any type of film, print, or original artwork.

- Clean the scanner glass frequently while using it between scheduled cleanings. Use soft, dust-free wipes. When things get really bad, you might have to resort to a glass cleaner. Just a bit on a dust-free cloth takes care of your problems. It is suggested that you don't spray the glass. Put the cleaner on the cloth, use it sparingly, and never douse your scanner with it.

Caution   Do not use cleaning fluids of any kind unless suggested by the scanner manufacturer.

Rely on your tools in Photoshop to help you accomplish the rest of the cleanup.

Sometimes, a simple wipe at the right time saves hours of correction. Suppose, for example, that in scanning a pile of 100 or so 8×10 photos, you place the first one on the scanner with the wrong orientation. In getting it off the scanner, you barely touch the glass, but your finger leaves a mark. You choose not to notice it because a wipe isn't handy. When you are done with the pile, you spend an average of an extra minute on every photo cleaning off the same smudge. That is an hour and a half of wasted time when you could have spent 30 seconds with a wipe (even if it took five minutes to find one).

However, there is a point of diminishing returns, where time spent cleaning the object and scanner will exceed the time it takes to correct the problem in Photoshop. Obviously, that is the time to stop cleaning and start scanning. Work to get rid of the obvious dirt and dust before scanning and leave the rest for corrections.

→ For more information on correcting dust, fingerprints, scratches, and other damage, **see** "Correcting Image Damage," **p. 579**.

THE SCANNER SWEET SPOT

Scanners are not all made alike. In fact, even those of the same brand and model will function somewhat differently, and react to its shape and varying reflectivity in unique ways. Because of the variation, each scanner has its own *sweet spot*, which will render the best scans. It is an area where the scanner reacts most consistently and gives the flattest response. This is something you will have to test for.

PART

V

CH

18

There are a number of tests you can try, but the simplest is placing a large white sheet of paper over the scanner glass, closing the lid and scanning that. The results will have slight variations, which you can emphasize in Photoshop. Simply open the scan of the white paper in Photoshop and correct the levels or hit the auto button. This will radically exaggerate the variation in tonal response to the paper and show you where the most even response areas are (see Figure 18.3). The results will probably show an area away from the sides of the scanner glass. When the area has been determined, you might want to create a template of some sort to help you place the images on the spot. The template should be removable, and probably made of some type of dustless material—in other words, use plastic instead of cardboard to create the template.

Figure 18.3
When the variation of the scan is exaggerated, the better places to scan on the bed become apparent. You can cut a template to help you place images and objects in the best places for scanning.

Scan of white paper
after RGB adjustment

Outline of the
sweet spot

Template created
from the sweet spot

Testing and the results reveal the sweet spot on the scanner, which is the area that you should use if you have the choice. This does not mean that you can't use the rest of the scanning area or that you should necessarily avoid other areas for every scan. This is the area you will want to use for critical scans and optimal results.

→ For more information on orientation and scanning oversized objects, **see** "Scanning an Oversized Image," **p. 390**.

CHOOSING SCANNER SETTINGS

Generally, there will be several settings you will have to choose from when making a scan. The defaults might not be the best choice in all situations, but a radical departure is not often the way to go, either. Options you might encounter include the following: Reflectivity, Color Mode, Resolution, Image Size or Scaling, Descreening, Sharpness, and adjusting Black-and-White Points.

REFLECTIVITY

Reflectivity might go by a different name, but the purpose is to select the method you would like to use in scanning the original. Scans can be reflective, where the scanner looks at the object, or transparent, where the scanner looks through it. You choose one or the other, primarily based on the object and what you want to accomplish. Generally, solid and opaque objects will be scanned using the reflective setting, meaning that the scanned image will be a result of light reflecting off the surface. For scanning transparent objects, such as a chrome or color transparency, use settings for transparent or negative scanning. Using a transparent setting will scan color as it appears (for use with slides and chromes), while scanning using a negative setting will convert a negative to a positive result (for use with negative films).

Note

Transparency options usually exist only if the scanner has the capability to scan negatives and transparent objects as well as opaque objects. If there is no adapter, there may be no transparency setting to select.

Transparency Adapters

Transparency adapters allow your scanner to scan transparent objects such as negatives. Adding the adapter is often a significant increase in the cost of the scanner, as it requires a second set of moving parts. Getting a scanner with a transparency adapter and paying a lot for it is probably a mistake unless you plan to be scanning medium-format transparencies, larger chromes, or medium-format slide film (6cm×6cm and higher), or plan to use the adapter for other creative purposes—or just for fun. Regardless of the maker or resolution, I have yet to see one perform to the level that would produce a good sharp scan from any 35mm film image with the hope of good reproductive quality. For 35mm negatives and transparencies, slide scanners are far better than an adapter. Again, Photo CD or other similar scans might be a less expensive option. Don't depend on a better consumer model to produce effective results with smaller scans that you hope to enlarge.

Unless you are going for a special effect, the choice of scan type should be relatively simple, based on observation of what you are scanning. However, some objects will prove very difficult to scan as either reflective or transparent—usually a problem with clear objects.

→ For more information on scanning clear or translucent objects, **see** "Scanning a Translucent Object," **p. 384**.

Choosing the proper object reflectivity tells the scanner how to scan the object. Choosing the proper setting is important for getting the right effect, but those settings also might change the settings for other options. For example, changing the reflective setting to transparent will probably disable the descreening, as descreening is useful only in capturing screened prints (which are reflective). Note the differences in the scanning choices and make the best use of them.

COLOR MODE

Choosing a color mode for a scan depends on the end use of the image as well as the image itself. Don't just select RGB because you use it most of the time. The technique here is as simple as selecting a button, but choosing the right one is a matter of looking objectively at the thing you want to scan and knowing the purpose you will use it for. Sometimes, the RGB 36-bit color option is not the right way to go, just because it will get more information than you really need. If the image is a black-and-white line drawing, RGB or CMYK are overkill: You'll get a file that is three or four times the size and with no better quality. Making an intelligent choice for color mode will save excess file size and get you the information you need. If you are looking for portable images and a quick scan, your choice in color mode might need to be based on utility and not optimal quality.

The following options might be available in your software as scanning modes: Line Art (or Bitmap), Grayscale, RGB, CMYK, or Lab. Scanning softwares can also offer an option for scanning with different bit depths. These bit-depth options might be offered with the scanning modes (for example, 16-bit CMYK), or as a separate selection. Table 18.1 outlines most of the modes you will encounter and the reason for choosing each, and also expands on these choices with suggestions for use.

TABLE 18.1 SUGGESTIONS FOR CHOOSING A SCANNING MODE

Mode	Choose If	Use Notes
Line Art or Bitmap	The item you are scanning is hard black-and-white with no grayscale.	This works best for most pen-and-ink drawings (not mixed media), text-only, single-color logos, and so on. The advantage of using bitmap over grayscale is you can use higher resolution and retain a smaller file as there is less bit depth—there is approximately 1/8 of the information to deal with in a similar-size grayscale scan. You can use two or three times the resolution (as dpi), have a smaller file size, and cut a nice sharp edge or line.

PART

V

CH

18

TABLE 18.1   SUGGESTIONS FOR CHOOSING A SCANNING MODE

Mode	Choose If	Use Notes
Grayscale	Scanning an image to use in black-and-white grayscale or if the image itself is black-and-white.	This works for black-and-white images, converting most color images to grayscale and might have some creative use in developing textures (for example, scanning fabrics). The advantage over RGB is saving disk size. Some color images which will be converted to black-and-white are better scanned in RGB. This is the case only when the tonality of the colors is too similar to provide proper separation.
RGB	Scanning an image for multiple and general purpose images, as well as for images to be used on the Web.	A second choice for most scanning only if Lab mode is available. This will be your scanning choice 90% of the time. Scanning to RGB, even if the image is going to be grayscale, might offer opportunities to fix the image before converting to grayscale. See the sidebar on "Colors Scanned to Grayscale" that follows.
RGB 16-bit	Using the scan for archiving color or to work in applications that support extra bit depth.	Without the capability to use the extra information, this will waste file size by creating a larger file, and may leave the file unreadable in some applications. It will, however, retrieve more image information, and might be preferable to 8-bit images if the scan will be used for multiple purposes.
CMYK	Scanning images strictly for print reproduction.	This generally gives you a good color conversion from RGB to CMYK. Although you might want to convert to RGB in Photoshop to color correct after the scan, converting back to CMYK again can usually be accomplished with less effort than will be required if the scan is originally RGB. Results will vary depending on the scanning package, calibration of the scanner, and generation of correct ICC files.
CMYK 16-bit	Scanning images strictly for print reproduction using output devices that accept 16-bit CMYK color.	Can capture more accurate CMYK color. Useful when outputting to devices that can handle higher bit depth.
Lab	Scanning multiple-purpose images.	Better than RGB for archiving color with the advantage of the broader color range offered by Lab.Presents good opportunity for conversion to other color modes.
Lab 16-bit	Scanning multiple-purpose images.	Greater bit depth offers the potential to get the maximum information from a scan. Great for archiving image information and color with the broadest range and potential accuracy.

If the image has multiple purposes, scan in a mode with broader gamut. In most instances, the scanner default will be RGB, but some better manufacturers (again, Linotype-Hell, for example) rely on Lab color for color management and conversions. This broader color space will allow for better conversions and color mappings.

→ For more information on color spaces and the use of each, **see** "Choosing an Image Mode," **p. 309**.

→ For more information on scanning a color image to grayscale, **see** "Change an Image from Color to Grayscale," **p. 487**.

If you can target your scanning, you can scan more efficiently and can make the proper adjustments to get the best results. For example, choosing CMYK to make a scan that will be used in grayscale is wrong for just about any purpose; you get too much information and a larger than necessary file size. Correction for tonality and color would be easier in RGB anyway. Stick to your purpose and it will yield the best results. For general scanning, use RGB.

Note

Scanning in CMYK is really converting to CMYK from another color space using the scanner software's conversion routine. In most instances, scanners' manufacturers that claim to be able to scan in CMYK have made the effort to optimize the process and the results are often desirable. If you prefer the results you get in Photoshop, scan to RGB or Lab and convert in Photoshop.

Tip

Calibration of the scanner is essential for getting good scans and good CMYK conversions. Some might insist that RGB scanning is the only way to go—and to use maximum bit depth—but files that are not produced as close as possible to their final intent still need to be converted to the destination color mode. It might be best to always scan to the destination color mode first.

RESOLUTION

As with choosing an image dpi, you want only as much information as you will use for the scan. Knowing an end size is the optimal way to scan, but if an item is going to be used for several purposes, scan with maximum potential for the resolution in mind. Don't just select the maximum dpi for the scan, because it will get more information to use in the image. Proper selection of dpi keeps file sizes in line with use and keeps you from having to resize images.

Tip

When scanning, remain within the limits of the scanner's optical range and don't stretch into the interpolated range if it isn't absolutely necessary. *Interpolation* is simply electronic resizing, which Photoshop can do for you if you choose that route. If you need a larger scan than can be provided by your scanner, consider having the scan done for you. This might require using a service bureau or other imaging professional.

For example, assume you are scanning an image for a Web site that requires only 72dpi. However, consider a situation where you know you are also going to use the image in a color magazine advertisement at a similar size later on. The magazine (printed at 175 line screen) might require between 271dpi and 350dpi, which is approximately four to five times as much image information. You can scan and store the image separately for each, but it might be easier (and provide more consistent color) to scan for the two purposes at one time, work with the image to make corrections and then save two versions of the result. You would want to scan at the greater of the two resolutions you need, and then resize the image for the purpose requiring less dpi.

Another, and perhaps the better, choice is to make two targeted scans: one for the Web site and one for the magazine. In choosing between the two courses of action, you need to determine which set of options and trade-offs best serves your purpose. In creating one original scan, you will have to resize the image, which can render some problems during the resizing; however, the color consistency between the two images should be fairly good. In creating two images, you can better target the end result for each and will probably end up with two better scans overall; however, the color will be less likely to match.

Use the following steps to determine a dpi for scanning:

1. Determine what you want to use the image for.
2. Determine the dpi needs for the output and use of the image as outlined in Step 1. The scanning resolution (ppi/dpi) should equal the dpi necessary for the end use.

TABLE 8.2   APPROXIMATE DPI RANGE BASED ON IMAGE USE

Image Use	Approximate dpi Range (Final Size)
Web pages	72–96
Poster Printing	100–150
Newsprint	120–240
Uncoated Paper	180–266
Coated Paper	233–350
Art Books	271–400
Line Art/Bitmaps	600–800
Film Recorders	400–1000

Note

These are approximate ranges (minimum–maximum) of the output listed. Check with your service before following these guidelines.

Optimally, the scanning resolution equals the output resolution without resizing. A scan can be larger and resized down, but working on a larger image than necessary takes more time in processing, wastes effort, and can cause unnecessary damage to the image. It is easiest and most efficient to keep images at the resolution needed.

If the scan is going to be a utility image—that is, one you will use for various purposes over a period of time—you might consider scanning and storing the image at several sizes to have it ready whenever needed. Kodak Photo CD scans, which offer multiple scan resolutions, are well suited to this purpose. If you plan to keep a library of source images that you will reuse, a more permanent type of removable storage might be in order so you are not left with huge libraries of images clogging up your hard drives. A CD-R drive offers reliable long-term storage and compatibility, both with different operating systems and hardware, large disk capacity, and compact size, and they are inexpensive for both media and drives.

Tip

Although technologies are changing all the time and DVD recordable drives are attractive storage devices because of sheer size, CD-R and CD-RW drives currently offer the best combination of capacity, compatibility, and cost. The disks, if formatted correctly, work well even across platform in standard CD-ROM drives. The media is very inexpensive compared to any other storage source in cost per megabyte.

DVD Drives

DVD (Digital Video Disc, sometimes referred to as Digital Versatile Disc) drives are much like the current standard CD-ROM drives but with two layers of digital information on a disc side. This leads to a big difference in storage capacity: DVD has 7 to 13 times the storage space on a single-sided disc than a standard CD-ROM has. These are not readable in standard CD-ROM drives and will generally be less compatible than standard CDs.

→ For more information on storage and storage systems, **see** "Image Storage," **p. 885**.

IMAGE SIZE OR SCALING

The size or scaling of the scan is usually a simple scaling of the result. For example, if you are scanning a 5×7 image at 300dpi/ppi and scale to 200%, the result would be a 150dpi image at 10×14. In other words, the software scales the image dimension, but uses the information per the dpi/ppi you chose for the sampling. As you increase the scaling over 100%, you effectively decrease the dpi from how you have set it; if you decrease the scaling to less than 100%, you effectively increase the dpi.

Generally, you will be working in the reverse order: You will know the size that you want the image, the current size of the image, and the resulting dpi. You will need to determine the % Sizing, and the sampling dpi/ppi from that. You can determine the factor for the scaling, and determine the resulting dpi using that scaling factor.

To determine scaling, divide the result size by the actual size. Use either the width or the height as a dimension to do your calculations. If you had a 5×7 that you wanted to increase to 10×14, you would divide 10 by 5 (or 14 by 7). Because 10/5=2, you would need double the dpi.

The dpi/ppi you choose for scanning would be the desired result dpi multiplied by the scaling—(2 in the case of the example). If the desired result is 300dpi, the scanning dpi/ppi is 300×2, or 600dpi/ppi. To check your calculations just remember that the dpi/ppi moves in the same direction as the percentage. If you are scaling up (getting larger than the original), the dpi/ppi will have to get higher than what you actually want as the result. If you are scaling down (getting smaller than the original), the dpi/ppi will have to get lower than what you want as the actual result.

SHARPNESS

The intensity of the sharpening filter on your scanner software might not function the same way as Photoshop's or the same as the sharpening filters in other scanning programs. Often the application (even with better scanners and software) is rather vague, offering something comparable to Low, Medium, and High for sharpening settings. If this is the case, it is probably best to leave the sharpening for later and do it in Photoshop, rather than use filters that are not as good as those in Photoshop.

> **Tip**
>
> Even if the scanner's sharpening filter offers percentages, it is hard to say what scale it is using to measure those percentages. The scanner's advantage is in providing raw data. Let it do what it does best.

However, if you do choose to use the scanner software's sharpening filters, keep the intensity of the sharpening low so that sharpening enhances rather than damages your images. You can always go back to the image later and sharpen it more with Photoshop if you want to increase the effects.

Become familiar with the way sharpness works with your scanner and software by running several tests on the same image. Test how the scanner applies sharpening at different dpi/ppi and in combination with scaling.

Sharpness accentuates the edges of tonal change by affecting local contrast. In other words, when sharpening, a dark tone that aligns with a light tone gets darker, and the light tone gets brighter. Oversharpening causes halation (a noticeable glow in areas of high contrast) and can accentuate film grain and make flaws stand out more prominently.

→ For more information on using the Unsharp filter, **see** "Sharpening with Unsharp Mask," **p. 618**.

Waiting to use Photoshop for sharpening has the additional advantage of leaving sharpening until after an image has been relieved of damage and dust. Sharpening first accentuates the damage and dust in an image.

DESCREENING

Descreening is used to blend the dots of pictures printed by press using line screens; it attempts to digitally remove the screening from these printed images during the scanning process. The results vary depending on selection of the descreening level and matching that to the actual screens used in printing. Knowing the screening will help you select the proper level of descreening to select to get the best results.

Note

Descreening is not an absolute solution to smoothing out the effects of printing an image and making it into a continuous tone. It is merely an aid to bettering the potential of the result of scanning such images and won't perform miracles.

Considering the paper an image was printed on and knowing the source of the image will give you a good idea of what line-screen was used in printing. Because paper has different absorption qualities, some types hold printed dots better than others. When using different paper stocks, printers use a certain range of line-screen to get the best results based on known absorption and dot gain. Understanding the choices a printer makes can help you know the line-screen he printed at and infer a descreening level. Simply selecting a descreening level based on the paper type can generally deliver the results you need.

Descreening diffuses halftone dots and smoothes the tonality of an image using a combination of Blur and Sharpen effects. The results are not often completely desirable, but the alternative (no descreening) is often worse. You can accomplish similar effects with Photoshop tools but probably not without significant trial and error. Using descreening will save some time and heartache in these cases. If the lack of quality is not acceptable for your purposes and the screened image is the only source, use another image (see Figure 18.4).

PART

V

CH

18

Figure 18.4
The image at the upper left is a close-up of a scan done without descreening. The image at the lower right is the same image scanned using descreening.

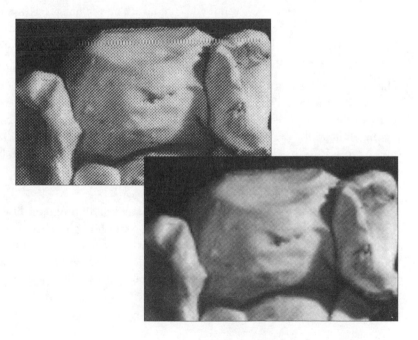

Caution

Do not use descreening on images that were not printed with line-screens unless you want to experiment with effects. The resulting image will be blurry, soft, and generally unpleasant.

Unless the original image is unavailable or you are seeking to create an effect, scanning a printed image should be a last resort—even if using descreening to improve the results. As with any type of image integrity, each step farther from the original loses measurable quality. Scanning from a printed image will prove somewhat extreme as far as steps removed from an original goes, as the image that you have seen in print has already been scanned, prepped for printing, and printed. If at all possible, getting closer to the source will yield better results. Also, be aware of copyright on images and be sure you are not in violation.

→ For more information on copyright and copyright violation, **see** "Copyrighting Your Work," **p. 882**.

SCANNING BIT DEPTH

Bit depth can vary depending on the claims of the scanner maker or software manufacturer. Eight bits per channel actually translates to 24-bit color in RGB, or 8 bits for each channel of the three colors (8×3=24). Twelve bits per channel scanning in CMYK is 48-bit color (12×4=48). Impressive depth, but many Photoshop features are disabled using images with more than 8 bits per channel. (Photoshop 6 has added more support for images with up to 16 bits per channel.) You will generally end up translating images into 8 bits per channel to use full Photoshop features. Even if you could work on the images with more bit depth, the increased size of the files (approximately 50% larger for 12-bit/channel images over 8-bit/channel images and approximately double for 16-bit/channel images) might prove prohibitive to your equipment if the image is large.

The number of bits per pixel is the total number of bits for all the channels that make up the pixel information. For example, RGB has three color channels (red, green, and blue), each of which has a specified bit depth (usually 8 bits). To get the total bits per pixel, multiply the bit depth by the number of color channels (16×3=48 bits per pixel). Grayscale has one channel, RGB has three, CMYK has four. Spot colors are additional, but will not be separated in a scan. To check the bit depth of the channels in an image, look at the Mode menu (Image, Mode). The current bit depth will be noted with a check.

High bit depth is not supported by all types of output or all programs in which you might be using the images. Scanning with the highest bit depth might mean you have to convert the image anyway. Although it is technically a better scan, it might not be best suited for your end use. Also, any additional conversions lead to a generated loss or alteration of information in the scan. Some alterations are potentially positive, but most are not. Let the software work for you and do your best to help it do its job by properly targeting your output.

→ For more information on bit depth, **see** "Pixels and Bit Depth," **p. 894**.

SETTING BLACK-AND-WHITE POINTS

Put simply, black-and-white points are the darkest and lightest areas in the image. Setting the black-and-white points is the act of making a choice for the scanner as to what you want to be considered as white or black. Setting these points allows the scanner to concentrate on the desired tones. The result is much like making a Levels adjustment, but before making the scan. A good scan will get as much information from an image as possible without going to the point of compromising tonality. Setting black-and-white points can help you achieve the best scan from the information available.

Although steps for your software can vary, generally you will want to follow these procedures in setting black-and-white points for the scan.

1. Place the image on the scanner.
2. Preview the image if possible and crop to the size you want.
3. Prescan the image and use the scanner's tools to select black-and-white points. To select a white point, select from the darkest part of the image that you want to be considered as absolute white. To select a black point, select the lightest portion of the shadow areas that you want to be considered as absolute black. Your selections should, optimally, not remove important detail.
4. Be sure other scanning parameters are correct, and then complete the final scan.

Choosing the black-and-white points for the scan limits the range in which the scanner searches for information. Initially this might sound like a bad thing—why limit the scanner? However, the limitation on the range enables the scanner to concentrate on the detail and bit depth over the rest of the image. Tailoring the scanning range to the tonality of the image specifically allows the scanner to make the absolute best scan considering the range of information in the image being scanned.

 If you have adjusted your settings and made scans but are having trouble opening the results in Photoshop, see "I Can't Open My Scans in Photoshop!" in the Troubleshooting section at the end of this chapter.

ADVANCED SCANNING

There are many techniques you can use with a scanner that go above and beyond what a standard scan will accomplish. Generally, these are not techniques you will use all the time, but certainly they serve to show the versatility of what you can do with a scanner and can offer interesting possibilities for image development.

Multiple scans of a single image can help you extract image detail over shorter tonal ranges, which you can then use to adjust lacking areas of a normal, full-range scan. A variation on this is using two or more scans to knit together larger images or objects that just won't fit on the scanner glass. A third variation can be found in methods for scanning translucent objects that may require more than one scan to really help bring out details of both reflectivity and

PART

V

CH

18

translucence. Scans can be made of 3D objects as the scanner will have some depth of field. An interesting twist to this is adding additional external lighting to create different lighting effects.

MULTIPLE SCANS

Instead of making just one scan of an image, it can be better to make two and superimpose the results. This will allow you to take the best information you can from what is available in the two scans. This is very much akin to compositing photos, or taking several pictures of a group and using the best faces and expressions to build a good portrait.

The technique of multiple scanning can be illustrated well by using a high-contrast photo where the subject is backlit. In this case, you would make one scan with the intent of getting good general image information (scanning what the image was exposed for) and another trying to bring detail out of the shadows for the subject. In the first scan, set the White-and-Black Point as you would normally. In the second, set the White-and-Black Point to the area of the image that has fallen into shadow due to the exposure for the backlighting. This gives you the general tonality from the image in the first scan and some better detail from the shadows to blend in and improve what would be available by incorporating the second scan.

The composite of the two scans can be accomplished fairly easily using Layer Modes, Blending, Masks, and other advanced Layering techniques. A key to success is making the second scan without touching the image in between scans—that is, make the second scan just by changing the scanner parameters for the white-and-black point without changing the cropping or placement of the image on the scanner. In doing this, the images will be exactly the same size and will be perfectly aligned when brought together as separate layers in a document. Depending on the image, you might find yourself doing several scans of a single image to fully extract the potential information available there.

→ For more information on using Layers and Layering techniques, **see** "Creating Images in Layers," **p. 53**.

Figure 18.5 shows an image with three distinct tonal ranges. Highlights are overexposed from the sunlight coming in and striking the white sheets. The results of the image itself are a bit distracting because of the limitation of film and equipment used to capture the image. This would be very difficult to repair in the darkroom.

In that same situation, the human eye would see the scene with more detail and a bit less drastic contrast, which perhaps leads us to expect a little more from the result. To get the same details as you would by looking at the scene, the photographer would have to take the image by using separate exposures for the highlights, midtones, and shadows. The next best course, if three images are not taken, is to use the single image and extract all you can from it. Scanning separately for the highlights, overall tonality, and shadows will help produce the best results. Figures 18.6 through 18.8 show how more than one scan can lead to better image information over an isolated tonal range.

Figure 18.5
The bright light on the white areas lead to some loss of detail. The image is exposed for the midtones, which seem to suffer the least. The shoes are in shadow, and seem to have lost some detail as well, yet there are some details that can be brought out so that they stand out more from their surroundings.

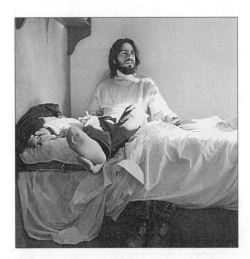

Note

For sake of brevity in the example, the discussion is limited to the midtones and shadows.

Figure 18.6
This portion of the scan from Figure 18.5 shows a decided lack of detail in the shadow area of this image.

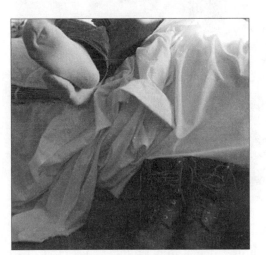

To finish up this image, you could try to pull more information from the highlights to bring back into the image in a similar way. Force the scanner to look at the highlights, paste them back into the scan done for the midtones, and blend the result to bring back the highlight detail. Using your scanner and scanning in this way helps you get more out of the original and helps you bring more to Photoshop to get the image results you want.

Figure 18.7
This scan was made with the black-and-white point set in the shadow area of the image so that the scanner would concentrate on the tonality in that area only.

Figure 18.8
The scan from Figure 18.7 is superimposed on the scan from Figure 18.6 and the two are blended using Blend If, Layer Mode (Lighten), and selective erasure (to remove unnecessary or unwanted detail). The result is a better representation of the portion of the image in the shadow area.

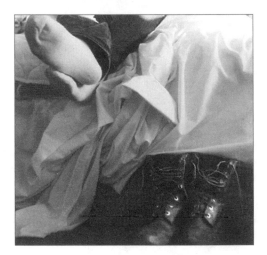

SCAN A 3D OBJECT

Scanning a 3D object is a little different from scanning a flat piece of art. Realistically, there are a number of limitations as to what can and can't be accomplished because of equipment limitations. You need to be careful of the scanner glass—more so than with flat items as the weight of the scanner lid might drive the object through the glass (on either or both the bed and glass—and perhaps the bulbs as well). One of the most difficult aspects of 3D scanning is getting the best lighting for the scanned object. This sometimes requires some creative additional lighting.

→ For more information on additional lighting with scanners, **see** "Scanning with Additional Lighting," **p. 383**.

Caution

Although regular scanner lids may cause a problem as well, be sure to hold on to lids that have transparency adapters in them when scanning 3D objects. These adapters are weighty and are almost guaranteed to do damage to the equipment as well as the item being scanned if they drop on any object left on the bed's glass.

When you scan an object, you really follow the same basic procedures as when doing a normal scan. Pull up the top of a flatbed scanner and place the 3D object where you want it and then scan. However, during object scans more things can go wrong. The lid becomes a greater concern and the possibility of scratching the glass increases.

To keep the glass from being damaged or scratched and to keep it clean, it is a good idea to separate the object from the glass. This actually provides a twofold benefit, depending on the depth of the object. First, you need to protect your glass and second, placing your object so that it is not too close to the scanner light will provide better, more even lighting. A little distance lets the light disperse more evenly, rather than harshly lighting the areas of the object that are closest to the glass.

Transparency plastic (used with overhead projectors) can be used to protect the glass, but something that creates a bit more distance between the object and the light might actually work better—such as clear Plexiglas. Obviously, you need to use something that is completely transparent and large enough to fit the item you intend to scan. The one drawback to placing something between the object and the glass is that any additional surfaces create a greater opportunity for dust and dirt to accumulate.

PART

V

CH

18

Tip

A personal favorite for glass protection is using a CD jewel case cover (obviously with the insert removed). This raises the object about 1/4 inch off the glass, is transparent enough to give reasonable results, and is usually readily available around computers. The drawback is that it works only with small objects.

Use the following steps when scanning an object.

1. Prepare for scanning by cleaning and wiping the scanner glass, additional surfaces of the protective barrier, and the object itself.

2. Place the protective barrier on the scanner glass.

3. Place the object on the protective barrier. Orient it to get the view you want from the scanner's perspective.

Note

Keep in mind that the scanner looks up at everything from the base when you are scanning reflective items, and down (from a transparency adapter lid if you have one) when scanning transparent.

4. Set the scanner options.

5. Complete the scan.

In Figure 18.9, a small gargoyle statuette was placed on a new CD-ROM case over the scanner glass and balanced on its ear. After scanning, a little extra clean-up was necessary because two additional surfaces were placed between the object and scanner eye. The more surfaces, the more dust and scratches. However, the results are satisfactory, if not perfect, and there is enough detail to leave room for reconstruction and alterations if desired. Another attempt to complete this scan without anything between the object and scanner glass just didn't work—light was too intense on the parts of the object closest to the glass (the ear and nose) and the image detail washed out irreparably at those points.

Figure 18.9
This statuette was scanned over a CD-ROM jewel case. Lighting from external sources would help the image, which right now looks similar to a result of a picture taken with on-camera flash.

You might keep a few fat computer books (such as the one you are reading) on hand to help prop up the scanner cover when scanning objects. Especially when employing the transparency adapter for the scan, propping up the cover will keep pressure off the scanner glass. Using a black or white background (depending on the color of your objects) can help separate your scanned objects from the rest of the image area and can help you make selections, masks, and clippings more easily. Use a black background with light objects and a white background with dark objects. Lay the backgrounds over the object after it is in place. A background can be anything from paper (plain old typing paper) to fabrics (black velvet can provide good separation, although it is a dust magnet) and can actually help to hold objects steadily in place. Aluminum foil might be useful in helping to provide more even lighting around an object.

Make a Mask of Things
Using a transparency adapter can prove to be an interesting way to create masks for other images. To do this, you would scan a solid object using the adapter. As the light will not pass through the solid object, the object will effectively create a mask. You can do this with anything that fits under the transparency adapter (see Figure 18.10).

Figure 18.10
The pile of cotton swabs is an example of the type of masking you can create. These masks are easily applied to images to create interesting effects.

violin © PhotoDisc, photodisc.com

It is easy to make a mask, frame, or silhouette out of almost anything that will fit on the scanner glass. Crystal and other translucent objects can produce interesting results when scanned as transparencies as well.

→ For more information on scanning crystal, **see** "Scanning a Translucent Object," **p. 384**.

SCANNING WITH ADDITIONAL LIGHTING

Some objects call for creative techniques in scanning, such as additional lighting. The purpose of additional lights would be to lighten dark 3D objects and add some depth to the object (usually the scanner bulb has a very short effective range). Figure 18.11 shows a scanner set up with a spotlight and aluminum foil reflector. A camera lens was scanned by placing it inside the aluminum cave. The cave helps surround the object with light to pick up more detail and depth. In this case, it helped create special effects as well: the light created reddish highlight color casts as the bulb used was not balanced to the temperature of the scanner bulb. This is because the scanner is calibrated to the scanner bulb that is rated at a bluer color temperature (about 5500°K compared to about 2700°K for incandescent). Unless you make changes in the calibration—which is not suggested—the scanner will be expecting the object to be lit with the scanner light it was calibrated for. Any difference can cause a fairly pronounced shift in the color result.

If this type of effect is undesirable, you will have to get appropriate lighting. Match the rated color temperature for the scanner bulb with added lighting to achieve spotlighting without color casts. Check the scanner manual to be sure of the color rating for the bulb. Any lighting you get needs to be continuous, rather than strobe, as lighting that is not continuous will cause other effects.

Note

Color correction becomes difficult or impossible when using two different color temperature light sources.

Figure 18.11
The aluminum acts as a reflector and background in this case to wrap light around the object being scanned. Using different reflector shapes can guide the light differently and create different effects.

SCANNING A TRANSLUCENT OBJECT

Scanning a translucent object such as a glass might produce sketchy results whether you choose to scan it either as a reflective or transparent object. Varying scanning technique to make multiple scans of the same item can help bring out the details of both. Although the technique described here might not work for all transparent objects, it adds depth to almost anything that you might have difficulty scanning conventionally because of its transparent nature. Transparent objects might be glass, items made of clear plastic, and so on—anything that you can see through.

The idea is to take advantage of an object's translucence, or its capability to deflect light. Superimposing a transparent scan with the reflective information can yield results that would be impossible with other straightforward reflective or transparent scans. The reflective scan will normally show some reflective highlights that the transparent scan would not, and the transparent scan will show some interesting light deflection that would not occur in a reflective scan. The information from the two scans put together can reveal a better visual representation of the object.

Figures 18.12 through 18.20 in the following example show how a rather difficult scan of a plain wineglass is completed. The technique involves making both a reflective and transparent scan of the object and then putting the scans together in Photoshop to complete the result.

Note

Do not move the object or change the cropping when using this technique to composite a scan. If you do, the parts will not match.

Although a scanner might allow some limited play in detaching the transparency adapter (Linotype-Hell scanners offer some 3–4 inches of play in the detached state with the supplied cord), some adapters function only when secure. Be very careful if operating the transparency adapter when it is detached from the base and be sure it is secure where it is situated. Not only might movement ruin the scan, the detached adapter might move or settle during operation and the results can be disastrous for the scanner. Any scanner vibration, which happens during the movement of internal parts, might cause the seeming balance you created to change.

Use the following steps to scan a translucent object.

1. Be sure the item you are scanning is clean. Especially in the case of this type of scanning, it might be good to handle the object with gloves to keep fingerprints off.

2. Scan the item with normal reflective settings. Depending on the object and your scanner, you might want to provide a background. In Figure 18.12, the scan was made using a flat white background. Scanning with different backgrounds produces very different results, because clear objects will show the background through the object.

Figure 18.12
The reflective scan leaves little to see in the glass except a few highlights. Although you could probably trace the result of the glass and pick it out of the image using the background to give it some substance, there is more you can get from this object.

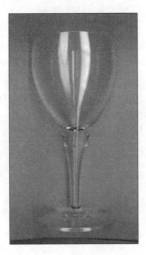

3. Save the reflective scan.
4. Scan the item again, this time using transparent scanning (see Figure 18.13).
5. Save the scan.
6. Open both scans in Photoshop.
7. Copy the second scan (transparent) into the first scan (reflective). This will create a new Layer. The technique you use to move the image may vary depending on your preferences. Copy and Paste works just fine.
8. Reduce the opacity of the upper layer in the composite image to 50%. You should be able to see both objects, the reflective scan through the transparent.

Figure 18.13
This scan was done using a transparency adapter. As the light passes through the glass, it is deflected, blocking the results from reaching the optics. This results in shadows where the scanner light has to pass through more of the glass.

Tip

You can adjust opacity in several ways. To use the Layers palette, highlight the Layer for the transparent scan and either enter the number in the box for opacity or click the arrow at the right of the box and use the pop-up slider. If you choose the Move tool (which you will be using in the next step anyway), you can change the opacity of the Layer by quickly typing the numbers you want to use as the percentage of opacity.

9. Move the upper Layer to fit the images of the scanned objects as best you can (see Figure 18.14). They might be slightly different in size and orientation, depending on how they were situated on the glass, the orientation or angle of the transparency adapter, and so on. You can move the Layer by highlighting it, selecting the Move tool (V), and either by clicking the pointer on the image to drag the Layer into place or by using the keyboard arrows.

Figure 18.14
When the opacity of the upper layer is reduced, elements of both images merge together. Here it becomes apparent that the shape of the glass is well defined by the transparent scan, but the highlights from the reflective scan add interesting dimension.

10. Use Transform (<u>E</u>dit, <u>T</u>ransform) functions to fit the objects together better. It may be necessary in some cases to selectively distort the image (for example, using Selection and Distort).

Note

Object information from either the transparent scan or the reflective scan will need to be considered dominant/subordinate, depending on what you want to accomplish. In the next step, we will be creating a selection for the Layer that will be trimmed in Step 13. The object in the layer you choose to trim should optimally be as big or ever so slightly larger than the layer that will not be trimmed, and this needs to be accounted for in the resizing/shaping you do in Step 10. Sizing appropriately will help make sure the information meets or overlaps the outside bounds of the other scan and does not appear to be cropped just short of where it should be—which will appear in the image as an obvious mistake.

In the case of this example, I have chosen the reflective scan as the subordinate for several reasons. Most important of these is that the black border of the transparent scan is both easy to select and will clearly be the dominant element in the result. I chose it for the example because of this, but either scan could potentially be used.

11. Make a selection of the space around the dominant object (see Figure 18.15).

→ For more information on making selections, **see** "Selection and Masking," **p. 93**.

Figure 18.15
Selection of the glass is made quickly using the transparent scan and the Magic Wand. A single click in the white area outside the glass selects the whole thing. Antialiasing was on, Contiguous off, and the Tolerance was set to 2 in case there was any variance in the white area.

12. (Option) After making the basic selection, apply a soft feather or blur to the selection (1–3-pixel radius, more or less, depending on the dpi). This keeps the selection from being too hard-edged, and may help blend the result of later steps. If you have made the selection using a soft edge of some sort, this additional feathering will be unnecessary (see Figure 18.16).

→ For more information on feathering selections, **see** "Feathering Selections," **p. 116**.

Figure 18.16
When the selection is complete, the mask should fit the shape of the object tightly.

13. Save the selection.

14. With the selection active, activate the subordinate Layer and then select Clear from the Edit menu. This will clear all the information outside the area of the reflective scan in the case of the example (see Figure 18.17).

Figure 18.17
When the image area outside the reflective scan is cleared, the glass takes on better shape, although it is still too dark. Mixing in the high contrast of the transparent scan and lowering the impact of darker tones in the reflective scan through blending will help this situation.

15. Open the Blending Options dialog box by double-clicking on the reflective Layer. While viewing as much of the image as possible onscreen (the Layer Styles palette is large), work with the sliders to produce the most pleasing blend of information on the Layers. See Figure 18.18 for the settings I chose to complete the blend. See Figures 18.19 and 18.20 for the result.

The Blend If Sliders

Blend If sliders are powerful image-editing tools—seldom discussed, yet quite useful. Extreme reactions and pixelation can occur if you fail to set up the blends by splitting the sliders. To split the sliders in the Blend If dialog box, hold down the (Option) [Alt] key and click the right or left portion of the slider and move it. Splitting the sliders makes the area between the split points blend as a gradient.

Figure 18.18
An Opacity of 50% was used in combination with Blend If settings. The Opacity was set first to blend the images overall. Then, the Blend If was used to fine-tune the blending in the highlight and shadow areas.

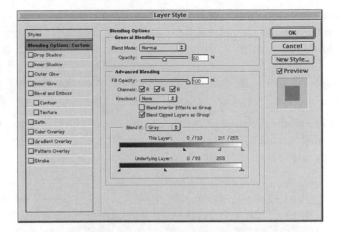

→ For more information on using Blend If functions, **see** "Colorizing a Grayscale Image," **p. 514**.

Figure 18.19
The composited result leaves hints of the highlights from the reflective scan which both soften the contrast of the transparent scan and fill in some missing information. Figure 18.20 shows a side-by-side comparison of the scans and the final result.

PART
V

CH
18

Figure 18.20
In comparing the results side by side, the transparent and reflective scans both look a bit harsh. The final result mellows the flavor of each.

Using the best information from the transparent and reflective scans resolves the problem of getting both reflective and transparent information into the single-result image. You might like more or less detail from the reflective scan, but you can control that any way you like using the Blend If option and Layer opacities (perhaps Modes as well). This technique might need to be adapted to work in scanning other clear objects, but will follow a similar procedure.

The theory is essentially the same as in making other scans: Get what you can out of the information available. Creative scanning techniques offer many image possibilities you might have otherwise dismissed as impossible.

Note

Scanning an image in the fashion described in this example will distort it, somewhat like a wide-angle lens. It is best to keep the object centered on the glass if you are looking for the most faithful reproduction. Orienting it to the side of the scanning area may tend to increase distortion.

SCANNING AN OVERSIZED IMAGE

It is possible to scan an image that is larger than your flatbed's maximum size. This is another two-scan technique where you scan the image or object in two parts and then put it together in Photoshop side by side rather than Layer over Layer. You will need to consciously divide the scan into two parts (or more if the image or object is larger) and scan the parts separately. When the scans are complete, the parts can be added into a composite image where the parts are fit together.

The transparent scan for the wineglass in the previous example was actually constructed in two parts, as the transparency adapter on the scanner could not be detached from the bed and would not allow a single scan result. There was no way to get the object into the scanner to scan it all at once. To solve the problem, two scans were made and knitted together (see Figure 18.21).

Figure 18.21
Scans made with overlaps can be fitted and blended well enough so that the result will appear to be a single scan.

The part of the process for this technique that is most critical is the alignment during scanning, with the knitting in Photoshop running a fairly close second. It is far more difficult to complete the technique at all if the alignment for the image is bad. The better the job you do of aligning the scans and attention you pay to those scanning details, the easier the knitting will be. Although much of the result will be based on your effort to maintain the alignment during the scanning, this will never return a perfect result as there is some distortion during the scanning process that you will have to adjust for (see Figure 18.22).

Figure 18.22
The object you are scanning should remain aligned with one of the sides of the scanner glass. In situations where the transparency adapter is not detachable (shown here) the object will have to be placed as far from the hinge as possible while still remaining in an area that the optics can see. Much of the alignment for objects will have to be done by eye.

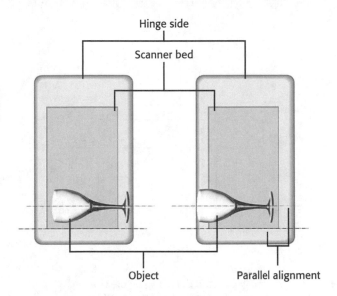

Hinge side

Scanner bed

Object   Parallel alignment

Use the following steps to scan an oversized image or object:

1. Determine how many scans you want to make of an object to get the images you need into your computer. You will have to leave some room for error and overlap to be sure you can blend the image parts. Plan to leave about a 1-inch overlap so that putting the image pieces together will be easier. For example, if your scanning area is 8×14 and your image is 14×16, you might try to get it done in two passes, but it is more realistic to do it in three.

2. Determine which edge you will align to in order to keep the image straight. Scans from a large sheet of paper (on which you can be reasonably sure the edge of the paper is straight) will be easier to keep in line than something without a hard edge (fabric, statue, and so on). The latter will usually require more work after the scanning is complete.

3. Disable automatic color and tonal matching or corrective functions for scanning. (Consult your manual for the features and how to shut them off.) You will want the scanner to scan exactly the same way to get information that is the best match. If your scanner has an option to choose the settings from the previous scan, use it in making successive scans for the parts of the image you are trying to rebuild after you have made the first portion of the scan.

4. (Option) If the object is flat, place targets with tags or sticky notes to help with the alignment. See Figure 18.23 for a diagram of how this might work with a simple two-part scan.

Tip

When placing targets, I like to use a double crosshair: one long line that runs parallel to the image and two short perpendicular strokes (see Figure 18.23). The double crosshairs give you better opportunity to see just how any misalignment might be occurring while you are knitting the images together.

Figure 18.23
Use the ridges at the edge of the scanner glass or a template you have created to help keep multiple scans parallel. On flat items, secure sticky notes or tags on the back at a point where the scans will overlap and make crosshair targets to help line up the scans later. These junctures should also be scanned on the same portion of the scanner to help keep distortion to a mini-mum. To do this prop-erly, it might be necessary to flip the image.

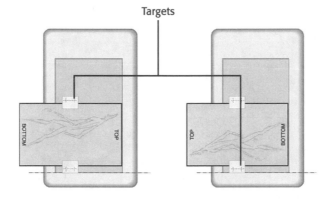

Targets

Images should face down on the scanner.
For demonstration of orientation only.

5. Make the scans in sections, being sure to leave an overlap of about an inch for each joint. Number them and save as appropriate. Be sure to get the targets in the scan.

Tip

If there are several pieces to your scan and if there are multiple rows, you might want to sketch a map showing how the pieces should go together.

6. Open the first scan in the series and enlarge the canvas size to the appropriate dimen-sions for the size of the final image plus an extra two inches in each direction.

7. Cut and paste all the pieces roughly into the large canvas (see Figure 18.24). If the image was rotated to scan, rotate the canvas back (Image, Rotate Canvas, 180°) before cutting and pasting.

8. Save this file with another name so you will not save the image over your first scan.

Figure 18.24
As the glass was 6 inches tall, the canvas was enlarged to 8 inches to allow for resizing and movement. If you need more room, this is now less of a problem than in earlier versions of Photoshop. Simply move your Layer object and if it goes off the canvas, choose Reveal All from the Image menu.

9. Fit the pieces one at a time to the original using Rotation and the Move tool (see Figure 18.25). To do this as accurately as possible, magnify the areas you are connecting to several hundred times their size and change the opacity of the upper layer (the one you are working to maneuver into place) to 50% to see through it to the layer below. Change the opacity back to 100% when you feel the image part is in the proper place.

Figure 18.25
The halves of the scan are fitted together as best as possible. There is a distinct line where the edges of the scans meet. The next step will be to blend by selectively removing overlapping information.

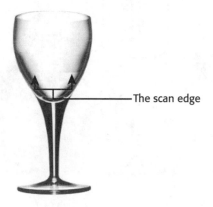

The scan edge

Note

Alignment is where the targets can come in handy in alignment. Make alignments in an orderly fashion (for example, work right to left and top to bottom if there are multiple pieces) and be sure you are completely done placing one element before moving on to the next. This will save problems later with readjusting, which might cause a domino effect of changes: Changing image part 3 after placing part 10 might cause you to have to rearrange the whole image. If necessary, use transformation tools to alter the image parts for a better fit. Transformation tools should be a last resort.

10. When everything is straight, save the image again. If you are fitting several pieces, you might consider saving after you fit each piece. Although you can undo multiple times using the Histories, you do not want to lose your work to a crash, power outage, and so on.

11. Change all the Layer opacities back to 100% if you have not done so already.

12. Blend the edges of the upper Layers with the Layers below starting with the top layer and working your way down. If the images are placed well, and the scans match, you will be able to blend the images by erasing the hard edges of the upper Layer. You can do this quickly by selecting the area of the Layer outside the image with the Magic Wand (W) using zero tolerance, and then applying a feather to the selection and pressing the Delete key. This can be handled manually in a number of ways. For example, you might use a soft brush (0% hardness) and the Eraser tool (E). Manual removal will give you the most control over the end result. The diameter of the brush and width of the feathering will vary depending on the dpi of the images you are knitting together. Sometimes the blending will be simple, but often it will be a little challenging (see Figure 18.26).

Figure 18.26
Having the advantage of a wide overlap left more choices as to where to blend this image. The thinner part of the glass stem was chosen as there was simply less that could go wrong— anything that did would be easier to fix as there was less image to worry about. To get the stems to blend well, a combination of erasing and cloning with the stamping tool was necessary.

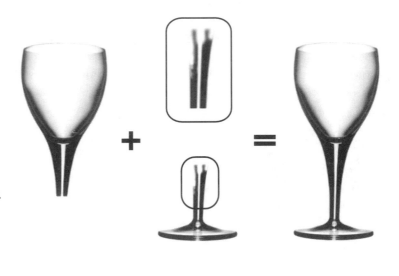

Tip

If you try the quick method and the blends don't look quite right, or they appear too linear and you can make them out, you might have to redo them manually. Look for natural break in the image along the overlaps and erase along the edges of image element contours wherever possible.

13. When all edges have been smoothed to your satisfaction, flatten and save the image.

Putting together larger images this way can be involved, but care in your approach will get reasonably good results. Paying strict attention to placing targets, keeping images parallel to the scanner edges, and aligning the overlap areas on the scanner helps to reduce scanner distortion.

I once used this technique with 12 parts of a topographical map on a computer that was running 16MB of RAM and a 66MHz processor. The image was put together using a prelayer version of Photoshop (v. 2.5). The resulting image was 250MB, which stretched the limits of the capacity of the hard drive (which was only 420MB) and its capability to use scratch disk space. That is to say, almost anything is possible considering the advantages offered by newer computers and the power of Photoshop's Layers. Patience and care help get all the lines straight. Good scanning techniques and attention to detail get the raw material in scans so you can knit the parts of any image together.

TROUBLESHOOTING

I CAN'T OPEN MY SCANS IN PHOTOSHOP!

I got a scanner and scanned some images but I can't open them in Photoshop. What's wrong?

Although it will probably not be a problem often, you might run into proprietary formats that Photoshop won't handle directly. You also might scan something that is not supported by Photoshop, such as an HSB color space. This is best handled either by checking in your scanner manual to see what options you have, or looking for an option for export preferences. At the very least, you will probably have some type of proprietary software, which you got with the scanner, that will allow you to open and view the images, as well as export and save them to other formats. This is inconvenient and adds a step in the process.

Another avenue that you should not overlook is that there might be a plug-in or TWAIN driver that will allow you to scan images directly into Photoshop. Chances are that this software is included with your software for the scanner, but you can also look on the Web to see whether there are compatible drivers or utilities available. The best place to start is on the manufacturer's Web site.

→ For more information on working with and installing plug-ins, **see** "Using Filters and Plug-Ins," **p. 755**.

The fact that Photoshop does not read a particular file type should not be in the least disconcerting. If you look for a solution and just can't find one either in the user manual for the scanner or on the Web, a last resort would be to print the image to a PDF. This may not be your optimal route, but with proper settings (Zip compression rather than lossy JPEG, shutting off color options, and using dpi to match the resolution of the scan), this could be a means of porting the image to Photoshop without a lot of to-do.

CHAPTER 19

CREATING IMAGES WITH DIGITAL CAMERAS

In this chapter

DIGITAL CAMERAS: THE PORTABLE SCANNER

A digital camera can really be an advantage for the Photoshop user. To a limited extent, it can perform the services of a scanner, and it can be used to gather image materials in a way that you would probably never use with an analog (film) camera or a scanner. It is great for taking stock images to use for source and/or additive image elements, such as backgrounds, textures and patterns, or for help in creating those. And it is immediate: You take a picture and it is in a digital format, often ready to be used directly in Photoshop. All you have to do is download the images from your camera to the computer, and you'll be able to work with them in Photoshop (either after opening and resaving from the camera's image software, or by opening the files directly in Photoshop).

 If you have trouble working with your camera's files in Photoshop, see "My Camera Takes Pictures That Photoshop Can't See!" in the Troubleshooting section at the end of this chapter.

To me, the greatest benefit of a digital camera over an analog is that you don't have to worry about expense and time consumption in developing film. The freedom to shoot without wasting film is somewhat liberating, and the ability to toss out what you don't want right away keeps you from dwelling on or accumulating bad shots. You preview and if it isn't what you want, you just delete it and try again or move on to another shot. In this way it is somewhat similar to the evolved use of Polaroid cameras in studio photography: A photographer might shoot a Polaroid to check the results of a shot before exposing larger format film. The digital camera is both the check and the result.

Of course, cameras for serious digital work are expensive, but even the less expensive cameras can be useful in generating image materials. There are some drawbacks to having a somewhat limited maximum result: There is no negative to scan at a higher resolution. To generate negatives, you have to output to a film recorder, which can prove expensive. But even considering everything, the digital camera is just a great source for material—and a different way to shoot.

Video Capture

An alternative to using a digital camera might be to use a video camera and a capture device, or "frame grabber." These can range from video cards and proprietary software to serial devices. These enable you to search through video that you shot previously and clip out portions or stills. In the case of Photoshop, stills are probably what you are looking for. But these devices can turn your video camera into what is essentially a digital camera. Depending on your choices and current equipment, it can do so for relatively little cost. Resolution and quality vary from device to device, and results can vary depending on the quality of the camera.

IMAGE COMPOSITION AND LIGHTING

One thing to be very aware of when taking images with your digital camera is the composition of the image. As the pixel dimensions are limited from the outset, try to make the most of what you have. Sometimes with an analog camera you might just take a shot and expect that you will be able to crop it later if you want. Of course, this is true of digital images as well, but to make the most of the available pixel dimensions, it is probably best to compose shots through the viewfinder. What this means is that you try to see the snapshot before you take it in the viewfinder—cropped tightly and composed. Not only is this good practice for shooting with your digital camera, but it is a good way to practice, and can actually help you get better results over the long term using your analog camera as well.

Several composition concepts can help you improve the images you create. There are certain things you will want to observe about lighting, as well as placement of physical objects in a scene. While this might seem slightly outside the scope of a Photoshop book, these concepts are very important both to creating the images for use with Photoshop and perhaps for creating images in Photoshop as well. Keep in mind that none of the rules are hard or fast rules that you must adhere to in order to achieve excellent results, but they are suggestions that should help you make the proper considerations for shots that you might take and to help you create images.

LIGHTING CONCEPTS

Lighting in your images should generally appear to come from realistic directions. For example, if the sun is the source in your image and there are apparent shadows cast in a scene, you probably won't get away with taking an image of your intended subject using studio lighting in a studio scene, and then clipping the result and pasting it over the background. Being able to drop a convincing shadow from the subject will help, but the lighting on the subject will probably be the greatest problem. In other words, if the light source and direction of the light striking the subject are completely out of sync with the scene, you are going to have trouble placing and combining elements convincingly.

→ For more information on dropping a convincing shadow, **see** "Creating a Drop Shadow," **p. 645**.

The alternative is to use the same lighting in the different settings where you gather your image information. For example, if you take an image of a scene that you intend to use as a background with the camera facing east at 4 p.m. in the afternoon in full sunlight, take the subject in similar light. Similar light would be at or about the same time of day, facing the camera in the same direction, in full sunlight (as long as you stay in the same part of the country). What this really means is, be aware of the quality and direction of the light you are using when creating an image that you plan to use as part of a composite. The *quality of light* is the source, and the *direction* is the angle at which the light strikes the subject. Direction can simply relate the angle between the subject and the source (or sources) of the light.

PART
V

CH
19

> **Tip**
>
> Direction can be determined fairly easily in a situation of direct sunlight by using a compass.

Light quality is defined by a number of things, including the color, size, and focus of the light source. The color is measured in degrees K (Kelvin). When a lighting source is a different color, this will taint the color of the subject, and cast the color accordingly. Size and focus play into the appearance of shadow and the harshness of contour on the subject. A large light source tends to make softer light and fill in shadows, whereas a smaller light will be somewhat harsh. Focused lights will cast defined shadows, whereas diffuse lighting will soften shadows. Again, the point is to attempt to match the original qualities.

→ For more information on the effects of lighting color, **see** "Scanning with Additional Lighting," **p. 383**.

→ For more information on directional light, **see** "Creating a Drop Shadow," **p. 645**. Specifically, note Figure 30.12.

Some of these qualities can be changed by filtering—and actually by adjustments in Photoshop as well. However, using the same conditions is really most simple and most accurate.

Note

A color temperature meter can be used to rate the color of a light source, and adjustments can be made with precision using color filters and jells.

COMPOSITION CONCEPTS

Composition plays a big part in having an image look interesting. If you take a subject, place it in a noisy, distracting background, the result does not focus on the subject well. If you always place your subject dead center in a scene, your images might lack variation and dynamics. There are several considerations to make in composing an image, and these same concepts affect the results whether creating a snapshot, a composite image, or a drawing—in other words, any Photoshop image. Several of the most useful and important considerations are center of interest, image density and noise (clutter), inclusion and elimination, sharpness and depth of field, symmetry, asymmetry, and balance. Keep these in mind when considering images to help you add variation and perhaps improve results.

CENTER OF INTEREST

The center of interest in an image is usually the main subject. There should be something in an image that the viewer's eye is drawn to. An image that has too much in it can be hard to look at and might lose the viewer's interest, as there is nothing to focus on clearly. Making the center of interest stand out somewhat from the image is usually important to the image's success in that the viewer will know what to look at and what the point of the image is. Controlling a number of elements in the image is important to achieve this goal, including being conscious of foreground and background elements that interfere with viewing, as well as image noise, the area included in the framing, depth of field, and so on. Put simply, be sure that the result that you want to stand out from the image has the chance of doing so.

IMAGE DENSITY AND NOISE (CLUTTER)

Image density, image noise, and clutter refer to how busy an image is. If there are a lot of things in an image, it can be harder to pick out a subject easily, or the subject might get lost by blending in too much with other elements. Often simplifying the number of elements in a composition will help the subjects stand out and will help the viewer know what is supposed to be important. Generally, it is a good idea to keep images uncluttered and simple to point the viewer toward what you want them to see. Not all image clutter is bad, and sometimes it is necessary, but be sure you know what is distracting and attempt to eliminate it.

→ For an example of clutter and distraction, **see** "Removing Distractions from an Image," **p. 604**.

INCLUSION AND ELIMINATION

Cropping can help you include or eliminate image elements from the frame area. Often, the result of the image can be dramatically different, depending on the cropping. For example, if taking an image of a vista from the shade of a tree, leaving the tree out completely produces one effect, whereas using the trunk and branch to frame the side and top of the image produces yet another, and if it is an interesting tree, placing it completely in the image will change the feel dramatically—and perhaps the subject as well. Deciding what to include or eliminate in a scene using the viewfinder frame is important to the end result of the image.

SHARPNESS AND DEPTH OF FIELD

The sharpness of elements within an image can help create and lose focus on the intended subject. For example, in a noisy image where you can't reduce the noise of the background, throwing the background out of focus by using depth of field can help reduce its impact as a distraction. Having a blurry subject, on the other hand, will rarely produce a desired result. Be conscious that you can affect the appearance of the scene by using depth of field and focus to your advantage, in turn forcing the viewer's eye to what you want them to see.

→ For an example of working with depth of field, **see** "Shortening Your Depth of Field," **p. 615**.

SYMMETRY, ASYMMETRY, AND BALANCE

Placing the subject dead-center in every image will lead to a rather drab portfolio of images. Sometimes playing with the balance of objects in a scene or purposely skewing the balance can create interest where there might otherwise have been little. The *rule of thirds* is often used to help work with balance and symmetry in working with images. Put simply, the rule of thirds suggests you compose images based on dividing the viewing area of an image into thirds rather than halves to give you more opportunity to create an interesting composition (see Figure 19.1).

Essentially, the viewing field is divided into equal thirds horizontally and vertically, and where the crosshairs meet, that is a potential target for placing your subject. This can be achieved through composition in the viewfinder of the camera, or later by cropping the result (see Figure 19.2).

PART

V

CH

19

Figure 19.1
The rule of halves (left) provides a singular image target where the subject is always placed dead center. The rule of thirds (right) provides more compositional options and as an option can give you an option for placing image subjects.

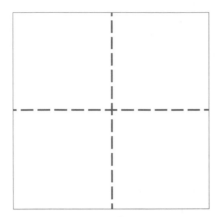
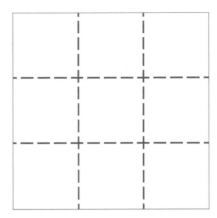

Figure 19.2
This example of cropping from the type placement example (from Chapter 9) shows the subject position changed by cropping to conform to the rule of thirds. The result is quite different from earlier images in the same set of examples.

→ For the other examples in this series, **see** "Photoshop at Work: Setting Type in an Image," **p. 247**.

INCIDENT ANGLE

The angle between the camera and the subject might also come into play. For example, say you are taking pictures at a zoo where the habitat was below the level plane of view. As you are looking down into the setting, the camera will have a perspective on the subject that is not level. If you plan to put a composite element down in the habitat, you need to be aware of the angle at which the element would appear to the camera. Whereas you might get away to some extent with a beach ball (although the shadows would fall the wrong way), you will not get away with elements that will have a definite up and down, like people, tables and so on—anything whose shape in two dimensions will be altered by the perspective in three. Attempt to take image elements from the proper perspective to yield the best result.

PLANNING A COMPOSITE IMAGE

How, specifically does all this talk of taking images with a digital camera fit into Photoshop? Generally, the point is to plan for the result of a composite image, rather than just attempting to let it happen from randomly generated shots. Although the latter can happen with much to-do and some incredible luck, you can create easy results by considering how you take the parts intended for the composite. The following example shows how to create an improbable result with a composite that looks fairly natural.

The idea for this example came directly from a six-year-old who wanted to balance on a baseball bat. It apparently couldn't be done in real life, but in Photoshop it would be fairly easy. All it required was a simple composite of two different images. The first image would be of the bat in the field, and the second would be of the child, preferably in a similar scene, yet the child would have to be raised off the ground for the sake of retaining what the camera would normally see.

The two images (see Figures 19.3 and 19.4) were taken with the camera facing in exactly the same direction, about five minutes apart—one in the field with the subject assisting by holding the bat, and the other—for lack of a better stable device—the subject posed as if balancing on the bat, on top of a parked car.

Figure 19.3
These images will be the source of the later composite. Although attention to detail here is good, there could be more to do to make the results end up right on. Do you see what else needs to be done?

Caution

If you ever try a similar simple composite that requires elevation of the subject, be sure the subject is on something sturdy. No image is worth hurting or even endangering someone.

Figure 19.4
Putting together the two sources is as simple as selecting the child from on top of the car and pasting her into the other image, and then touching up the foreground and background to match the desired result.

Several things could be improved with the source images. First the incident angle might have been better prepared, using the tripod to hold the camera at a level exactly even with the top of the bat bottom rather than slightly above. The original setup was for a broom and the settings were not changed. Also, more room could have been left for casting the shadow. On the other hand, the capture of the camera is limited, so cropping tightly is an advantage when it comes to resolution in the subject and scene. There will be trade-offs to make when shooting images.

A third image (and possibly more) could be taken to improve the results. For example, a shot of just the shadow of the child in the intended pose standing on the grass would have given a very accurate rendition. As it was, this shadow had to be created from the elements and cannot be as accurate. The subject could be placed in the same pose right where the shadow of the bat ended, and another image could be taken to record the exact shadow. This would allow you to copy and paste the segment of grass where the shadow falls directly to the result without much to do in the way of alteration or blending.

Paying attention to the elements and angles as you shoot will help to simplify the process and achieve the results you want.

TROUBLESHOOTING

MY CAMERA TAKES PICTURES THAT PHOTOSHOP CAN'T SEE!

I have been trying to open images I downloaded from my digital camera using Photoshop and it isn't working. What am I doing wrong?

The images you are trying to open in Photoshop may be a type of proprietary format or may have some compression, which Photoshop will not be able to read. Compression is very common with these files, because the idea is to save space on the camera's memory in order to allow you to take more pictures. There are a few things you can try.

First, take a look at the manual that came with the camera and see whether there is any specific procedure they suggest for working with images. There may even be a plug-in or some type of conversion utility to help the camera work more closely with Photoshop. It is unlikely that a company would create a camera that made digital images that could not be configured for use with the world's most popular image-editing software.

If the manual doesn't clarify a solution to the problem, the answer may be in proprietary software that was included with the camera. Usually, a digital camera has some type of image-correction software included—either a known editor or one created for the manufacturer. File types for these cameras may be unique to the camera (this may be done to save file size, improve capture, and so on). What you will have to do is open the images in the software and save them as a more common file type (TIFF, for example). If the option is offered to save with or without compression, save the file without compression.

If the software does not allow export to a familiar format, you might try decompressing the file using a general decompression utility. It may be that the camera compressed the file to save space, and a utility may be able to decode the file (if it is a common compression type). If the file still doesn't work after decompressing, try the decompression a second time; some compression structures will compress parts of the file in more than one stage. You might try Aladdin's Expander, available for free on its Web site: http://www.aladdinsys.com/expander/index.html. This is available for Mac, PC, Linux, and DOS.

For Windows users, a missing or improper file extension could also be a problem, forcing Photoshop to look at the file in the wrong way (you may get a parsing error, for example). Although you can use Open As and try file types until one works; it may be best to use a utility to determine the file type. Debabelizer has a demo product that you can use to determine the file type. If you are on a Mac, Debabelizer Lite is a free download. Look for it here: http://www.equilibrium.com/index.html. After you know the file type, you can change the extension to the appropriate set without the trial and error.

If none of this works, contact the camera manufacturer and request an explanation.

PART **VI**

COLOR HANDLING: USE, EVALUATION, AND CORRECTION

CHAPTER 20

EVALUATING IMAGE COLOR

In this chapter

AN OVERVIEW OF COLOR AND TONAL CORRECTION

Image color and tonal correction is more of an art and preference than a science. The idea that image color is correct is like measuring a swan: Do you measure from the head to tail, or from the feet to the head? Do you measure with the neck extended or with the natural posture? Measuring color is similar in that there are choices of what to match: Do you match the natural color? Do you match the color in the source slide or image? Or do you just plain make it look good regardless of the source or nature? These decisions need to be made image by image. However, the general technique for getting the results will often be the same (or very similar) for various images. Understanding how to use Photoshop's color and tonal correction tools and following some basic principles can take even an inexperienced user through making general corrections for tonality and color. Getting the color "right" is dependent on mastering the tools and knowing where you want to end up. Although there are more scientific ways of going about correction and matching, such as using calibration and matching devices, the final result with color is in the experience of the people doing the corrections and the decisions and choices they make during that process. Evaluation starts with the appearance of the image on the screen.

It is expensive to practice working on color for print, and the process is often shrouded in mystery. Color correcting work for printing can save or lose thousands of dollars and hours or days of work; if you work at color to get it right the first time, you can ward off unnecessary reprinting, save on additional proofs, and save time spent reworking the corrections and rescanning. Additionally, if you learn to do color correction—rather than having technicians do it—you can save correction fees that can run quite high, and you will have more control over the final results in your images.

Color correction may be most useful for correction of scanned images rather than computer-developed graphics, but learning to use the tools of correction will help when you're using electronically developed graphics in print media, or when other changes are desired in tonality and color. Although there is less immediate potential damage in dealing with Web graphics, it is nice to get images looking as good as possible across as many systems as you can.

Color and tonal correction involves many variables, and almost always trade-offs, but better color and tonal results can be achieved first with basic techniques, and then with studied practice. There are reasonably easy ways to achieve decent results in image tone and color with proper evaluation and steps in correction. But there will be decisions to make that experience will help overcome, such as knowing which colors you can and can't get in CMYK process, and when it is a good time to replace a color for more vivid results rather than just living with it the way it appears. Most texts on correction tell you which tools to use rather than how to evaluate the image. Those same texts might tell you the tools to use but not exactly how to apply them. Here you will learn the tools and how and why to apply them.

It is best to learn black-and-white correction before jumping into color because this helps develop the skills and understanding necessary for image evaluation and the use of the tools in correction. It is easiest to do basic color corrections in RGB, and the methods here mostly deal with RGB techniques. Although it is possible to correct in CMYK and LAB, the results are, perhaps, a little more difficult to intuit. When you are more experienced with RGB corrections, it will be time to explore other means of correction, although techniques here will use additional color modes as appropriate. For example, an image corrected in RGB can then be prepped for conversion to CMYK, and final separations can be made in CMYK for image printing. This allows you to use the ease of correction in RGB and tweaking in CMYK to get the most from the potential in the color following the conversion.

For the most part, this chapter flows in order of what you will actually have to do with images: viewing the image, evaluating the image, correcting the image, and finishing the image. This is a fine general procedure, but every step of the process isn't written in stone; you might find that you want to work in a slightly different order, or that you need to revisit certain steps in the process to get an image just right. You may finish an image more than once (for more than one purpose). The important thing in working through the steps is not how many times you have to go through them, but how you develop your sense and ability with color correction.

Tip

One general tip for all color and tonal correction: Make changes in small increments rather than fell swoops. Broad, sweeping changes that seem to accomplish what you want might actually damage information in the image irreparably (except by reverting to the original). As with soup, you can always add more salt, but it is far more difficult to take it out. Add a little image change at a time.

EVALUATING COLOR IMAGES ONSCREEN

Visual evaluation is one of your best tools in deciding what needs to be done with an image. Other tools can aid along the way in evaluations of color and tonal integrity, but using a good monitor that is properly calibrated, testing output and comparing results, and going "by eye" are the best ways to achieve good image quality. Your eyes are the best judge of whether color is natural and realistic, and no automatic setting will correct an image and do it justice (at least not with any consistency). With Photoshop's improved onscreen color proofing, potential for more accurate color increases, while making it easier to make fine adjustments or quickly change preset views.

Images can be high key (see Figure 20.1), low key (see Figure 20.2), high contrast (see Figure 20.3), or low contrast (see Figure 20.4), and each requires different evaluation. The real trick in correction comes when images are intended to have a certain color cast (like sunsets). You need to be able to rely on what you see, and know what you want to keep and how to change it without ruining what is already on target.

Figure 20.1
A high-key image is an image that displays with natural brightness, rather than appearing overexposed. High-key images are not absent of darks, but luminosity averages in the lighter tones.

© PhotoDisc, photodisc.com

Figure 20.2
Low-key images have a tonal tendency toward dark colors and blacks. Images appear dark, but naturally so, with lights and whites that would be overexposed with more brightness.

© PhotoSphere Images, Ltd., photosphere.com

→ For more information on image qualities and how they appear in image measurements, **see** "Measuring the Need for Color Correction," **p. 433**.

From simply looking at an image on a well-calibrated monitor, you can tell more closely whether it needs general color correction or whether a simple spot-checking of target points (white and black points, for example) and minor corrections will do. If you have accurately calibrated the monitor and checked physical proofs against screen proofs for matching, you can be even more sure of your ability to match the final results. Almost any image can be improved with some correction—either to suit your tastes better or to match the image to your method of output. If an image looks good, it is a sign that any correction you make should be minor or perhaps controlled by selection. If something definitely looks wrong, it is an easy choice to turn to correction tools.

Figure 20.3
High-contrast images have a decided lack of medium tones. This may make them somewhat dynamic.

© Seattle Support Group, www.ssgrp.com

Figure 20.4
Low-contrast images are weighted toward the middle tones. This may make them appear flat, but somehow they should be naturally so.

© PhotoSphere Images, Ltd., photosphere.com

Note

Visual inspection is a general guide to seeing how the colors work together. This should not be your only basis for determining whether an image needs color correction, but it certainly helps. Understanding how to measure color and what those measurements mean is essential to really getting the color right.

Before relying on visual inspection, you must first calibrate your monitor. Ideally, calibration sets the display so that it presents colors and tones as they should appear—at least from the standpoint of how the display should present them. The purpose is to balance grays so that they do not appear to have shifts (they appear neutral across the spectrum from light to dark) and to set white and black points—not merely as absolutes in what the monitor is capable of, but as practical light and dark values. There are quite a few factors to balance, including screen color, contrast, and brightness. Getting the settings right is not as easy as making the screen look good with manual controls and leaving it at that.

When a reasonably good monitor is set correctly, and you view images in the proper soft-proofing mode, you can be fairly sure that you will approach WYSIWYG (pronounced wizzy-wig: What You See Is What You Get)—at least within reason. When you are reasonably sure you can rely on the screen, identifying color casts, bad contrast (low or high), tonality shifts of highlights and shadow areas, and even some banding and separation problems will be simplified. When the problems are apparent and you can reasonably trust what you see onscreen, the problems are much easier to fix.

Setting up your system for onscreen evaluation involves four steps:

1. Calibrate the monitor.
2. Make appropriate settings and complete the color setup in Photoshop.
3. Create a test image to use in evaluating calibrations.
4. Compare the output of the test image to the way the image views on the screen, and make adjustments accordingly.

CALIBRATING YOUR MONITOR

Calibration of your monitor and system is essential to getting good results with color or black-and-white images—on the Web or in print. Calibrating is a several-step process that involves more than just selecting generic settings in the preset menus of various preferences. You need to interact with the computer by viewing the screen and making selections that appear correct.

Tip

A monitor is not the only device on your system that will require calibration. For best results, you should calibrate your scanner and probably your printer as well. See your manufacturer's instructions.

A careful run-through of the initial steps of monitor calibration gets you in the ballpark; follow-through with comparison to output results and adjusting for that will yield relatively consistent color—usually across devices and outputs if all goes as planned. When it comes to printed color, nothing is exact, although some processes are more consistent than others. For example, output to a film recorder will probably be relatively consistent, but print to paper will vary considerably, simply because there are more variables. Being able to trust what you see on the monitor gives you a common ground to work from in adjusting for known variations.

Why calibrate the monitor? If you are looking at a screen that is shifted green, you will tone down the greens when looking at the screen to make the image look right. This will cause output of any kind to be shifted toward reds. Calibration will help compensate for shifts by flattening the response of your screen.

Before you begin, you should know several things about your monitor, including color temperature (usually 5,000°, 6,500°, 7,500°, or 9,300°), gamma (often a number with two decimals between 2 and 3), and phosphors (a set of six numbers with x and y coordinates for red, green, and blue; these numbers can be up to three decimal places). Do not copy a friend's settings because the settings are specific to your monitor (brand and model).

Note

For some reason, monitor manufacturers never seem to want to put monitor specs for phosphors, white point, and gamma in the manuals. You may have to check with your monitor manufacturer for the settings specific to your monitor. This information can sometimes be found on manufacturers' Web sites. When you find the information, write it down and keep it both with your Photoshop manual and in the hardware manual for the monitor. I usually write the settings right on the cover of the manual for easy reference.

Tip

I use my Rolodex as a reference for certain information that can get lost on the computer. I use it to gather serial numbers for all my software, and to keep certain specific information—like the phosphors for both of my monitors. I list the phosphors on the card with the manufacturer name, along with a tech support number, Web site address, and email contact. This is better than trying to find the manual if anything ever goes wrong.

Before attempting calibration, turn on your monitor and system, boot up, and let it warm up for at least a half-hour. It is important to let the monitor warm up and stabilize or your calibration results will not be accurate. While you are waiting for the system to warm up, read the owner's manual for the monitor and Adobe's suggestions about calibrations before doing anything. This is your best resource to find specific information about your equipment and software. Reread these things as your monitor warms up every time you calibrate: You will likely not have to do this very often, and you will tend to forget the right procedure.

Use the following steps to calibrate your monitor:

1. After reading and waiting at least 30 minutes, open Adobe Gamma by double-clicking the icon in the Control Panels folder. On a Mac you can select Adobe Gamma right from the Apple menu. On a PC you can go to the Start menu, click that, choose Settings, and then Control panel. This will open the Control Panel window where you can find the Adobe Gamma icon. Double-clicking the icon will open the Adobe Gamma screen (see Figure 20.5).

2. Choose either the Control Panel or Step By Step option from the Adobe Gamma screen before clicking the Next button. The Step By Step option will lead you through the process of creating an ICC profile for your monitor. Unless you are familiar with the process or have a specific purpose in mind, choose Step By Step. Follow the instructions as you are led. Steps 5 through 12 discuss each step and what you need to do.

3. Select a name for the Profile you will be creating by typing it in the Description. Although there is room to type quite a lot in here, keep it short, and use abbreviations.

I find it handy to name the monitor, add the date, and leave it at that. Click the Next button after you have entered the description.

Figure 20.5
Adobe Gamma functions outside the Photoshop interface. Following the screens and instructions will lead you through creating an ICC profile for your monitor. You can then use this setting for color management.

Note

If you work with the same Profile each time, chances are your evaluations will not change very much, and you will get closer to optimal each time you calibrate. Dating the profiles in the name will help you identify them.

4. The screen that follows is for adjusting brightness and contrast on the monitor. There is a set of three concentric boxes to the right of the screen, which you will use to make a visual adjustment using the monitor's Brightness control (see Figure 20.6). Set the contrast on the monitor all the way up and then adjust brightness until the box in the center is just discernable from the black box surrounding it. If you notice the white frame becoming dark as you darken the center square, do not adjust further. When you have finished, click the Next button.

Figure 20.6
Optimally, the white should stay as white as possible; the center box and black box surrounding it should almost meld. Some compromise and judgment may be necessary.

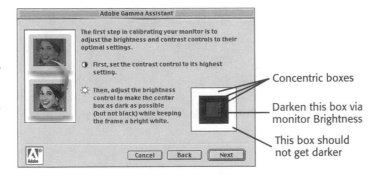

Concentric boxes

Darken this box via monitor Brightness

This box should not get darker

5. The next screen that appears enables you to enter or select Phosphor settings. Select Custom from the pop-up and enter the six values obtained from the manufacturer of your monitor (see Figure 20.7). When you have finished, click the Next button.

Figure 20.7
Enter the X and Y phosphor values for your monitor in this screen. Be sure to enter them correctly and to use numbers specifically for your monitor. If you change monitors, you will have to build a new profile.

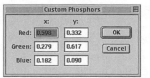

6. The screen that follows has an adjustment viewer, slider, and a View Single Gamma Only check box. Adjust the viewer by squinting at the screen (try to do so to blur the box slightly in your vision) and then moving the slider so that the viewer square seems to be a uniform tone. If the screen color seems to have a distinct hue, uncheck the View Single Gamma Only box and shift the individual sliders for red, green, or blue individually. Look specifically at the gray area of the dialog box to note any color in the grays. Don't make wild adjustments here. This is strictly a visual check.

→ For more information on what you are trying to accomplish with these changes, **see** "Evaluating Color Images Onscreen " **p. 411**.

7. Enter the Gamma value you got from the manufacturer in the Gamma field. You will be able to enter a two-decimal value, but Photoshop will round the value off when you save the entry. When you have finished, click the Next button.

8. Set the monitor's white point by choosing the white point value in the list that corresponds with the number you got from the manufacturer. A second option allows you to measure the white point. Select this option to fine-tune the adjustment of your screen. Dim (or shut off) the lighting in your work area and select the squares that seem most flatly colored as they appear on screen. They appear in sets of 3. Photoshop will automatically lead you through the process and generate appropriate values based on your selections. When you have finished, click the Next button.

9. The following screen may seem redundant in that it allows you to select the white point again. This selection should be based on the color temperature of the intended output media—for example, paper white. If you are unsure, or are creating images for the Web, display, or digital output to a film recorder, use the Same as Hardware setting. When you have finished, click the Next button.

10. Compare the Before and After settings by toggling between the Before and After option buttons. Specifically, note the grays in the dialog box and see whether the color appears neutral. If you're satisfied that the results are an improvement, save the settings. If you're not satisfied, restart the process. You can choose to save and go through the process again just to be sure that the settings are as close as you can make them. Saving will create the ICC profile for the current settings.

PART
VI
CH
20

Tip

Although I wish I could, I never calibrate one time and sit back satisfied—even when using a calibration device. I run through the process a few times, saving the settings by different names to compare them later.

Tip

Naming the ICC profiles with date and color temperatures can help you locate profiles to use for specific purposes without having to recalibrate each time. For example, 060900_7500_S would be a calibration done on 6/9/2000 using 7500° for hardware and the same (S) for output temperatures. Your method of coding can, of course, be different. Keeping track by naming profiles appropriately can provide information about which color settings you used when an image was created, and which proved to have successful results.

Be sure the lighting where you work remains the same as when you calibrate the monitor. The monitor can be calibrated to different light conditions, but it is easier to maintain the room lighting than to add it as a variable in color corrections. Extremely bright or overly dark rooms might cause some problems with calibrations and monitor viewing. Optimally, room lighting should be bright enough that you can read and view materials that are not on the screen, yet not so bright that it causes glare or washes out the display.

If lighting conditions change, recalibrate. If you don't use any calibration and you keep your monitor at one setting for all different types of output, your results can vary from what you see onscreen and might tend to be unpredictable. Using onscreen proofing to mimic the look of various output devices can help improve your results.

Color calibration by eye is not foolproof. You may have a certain color blindness, to whatever degree. Also, your eyes will adjust to the screen brightness, and this will affect how you calibrate. The point is to get close to optimal calibration—there really is no way to calibrate exactly by eye.

It is possible to create a custom ICC profile for your monitor with hardware calibration as well. Although Adobe Gamma is an adequate tool for visual calibration, calibration devices (see Figure 20.8) can measure more accurately than your eye, and will probably measure a greater number of gray levels. Measurements are taken directly from your screen, and create a profile based on actual measurements. This can ensure that your monitor is calibrated properly, and it may actually save some time during calibrations. Color onscreen varies with the age of the monitor and changes in lighting conditions, so recalibrating periodically is suggested; and these devices can help you recalibrate with ease. If you're using a calibration device, there may be no reason to use Adobe Gamma, because the work will be done for you. However, you may want to use Adobe Gamma to create additional profiles.

Figure 20.8
This monitor calibration device by Sequel Imaging (www.sequelimaging.com) is relatively inexpensive. It measures color shifts over 16 levels of gray and creates ICC profiles.

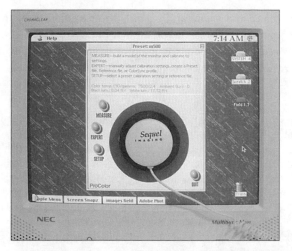

> **Note**
>
> The main problem with hardware monitor calibration devices is that they may not seem readily available. That is, they are not carried by most major computer-store outlets. If you are in need of a device, search around online for manufacturers. These devices can be expensive, but a poorly calibrated monitor can be far more expensive, because it may cost additional money in associated printing costs if jobs need to be re-created or reproofed because of a poorly calibrated monitor.

Even more important than the type of calibration is to choose one method or another for creating the standard profile you will be using, and stick to it. Calibration by committee is only a high road to eventual disaster. To obtain consistent results, you need to practice and maintain a color standard. With every change, even if it is eventually a positive one that will yield more consistent results over the long haul, expect to experience some problems and pitfalls. Until you get the hang of how a new system works, be meticulous about testing output and checking against your display. With any change in color management, retest the output. If you don't test, you are taking a chance and might potentially run into some costly printing problems if you have to redo a job.

> **Note**
>
> If you rely on default calibrations, results for your images and color will probably be inconsistent. If you input calibrations based on factory recommendations for your monitors, results might be better than with default settings, but they will not be optimal. If you use Adobe Gamma, results should be notably improved over using defaults or factory settings. If you use hardware for calibration, results will be the most accurate of any of these options.

PART

VI

CH

20

Color calibration is involved and tricky, and making it more complex by involving extra elements along the way is simply a mistake if you are not prepared to work through the difficulties. For example, even changing paper at the printer will change your result. If you are getting decent color results, there is almost no reason to change what you are doing.

Paper Variations

Paper has several variables that can affect the final look of images in print—even when you're using the same process and the same images. The outcome of printing can be affected by paper absorption (the rate at which the paper takes in and dissipates ink), the color of the paper (white paper is not 100% white, and papers are color rated), the thickness of the paper (which affects both absorption and opacity—or separation of inks as applied to two sides of the page), and the density of the ink. Papers with coatings, lower absorption, and greater thickness tend to hold printer dots better, whereas thinner, uncoated papers bleed dots together and lose image crispness. Adjustments can be made in Photoshop to greatly improve the final print quality as long as the factors are taken into account before images are submitted for printing. However, without accurate monitor calibration, it is not likely that adjustments will be anything more than guesses, because there is no real visual basis for comparison.

ICC PROFILES AND COLOR MANAGEMENT

Color management in Photoshop 5 made a leap that perhaps not everyone understood or embraced. The purpose was to improve portability of images to other machines, other monitors, and output devices by providing a color reference that can be embedded in the image. The embedded profile (ICC) describes information about the system on which the image was originated. If the technology is supported on the current system, the system can compensate for differences in the originating system and the current system by using the profile. Using ICC profiles is not essential to getting results, but it can help in certain situations (such as when you print to various media or use several vendors). In any case, setting up this feature will give you the option of choosing whether to use it.

> **Tip**
>
> Regardless of whether you make a change in the settings, it is a good idea to consider each possibility and what it means to your workflow. Don't feel that you necessarily have to make a change to manage your color "correctly." Make changes only when you have a purpose in mind.

You can manage the way color is handled in Photoshop by using the Color Settings menu (Edit, Color Settings). The new Color Settings dialog box (see Figure 20.9) combines several color management areas from version 5 into one convenient location in version 6. These areas include options for managing Working Spaces, Color Management Policies, Conversion Options, Advanced Controls, and Description.

Figure 20.9
Here the Advanced check box is checked, revealing the full options for the Color Settings palette. With the Advanced box unchecked, the Conversion Options and Advanced Controls sections of the screen do not appear, and the palette resizes accordingly.

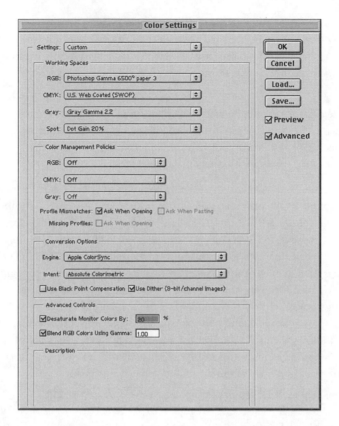

DEFINING WORKING SPACES

Working Spaces is the uppermost section in the Color Settings dialog box. It is used to define display options for RGB, CMYK, Gray, and Spot (or spot color). Selections on this portion of the dialog box define the means of handling those color spaces in your workflow. A definition of what each selection is used for is described in the following bullet list:

- RGB—Enables you to set up the monitor display, or the RGB color space you want to use for display.
- CMYK—Helps set adjustments for color separations and printing.
- Gray—Enables you to choose a specific dot gain or gamma for onscreen compensation of grayscale images.
- Spot—Lets you control the appearance of spot colors.

The initial setting for the RGB Working Space when you open the dialog box will be based on the choices you made in the Color Management Assistant. Generally, these are intelligent choices made according to the setup, and they should not be changed unless you really know what you are doing and why you need to change them. Any changes will directly

PART

VI

CH

20

affect display on your monitor and, therefore, output. Unless you have a reason for overriding this setting (such as changing monitors—although you should rerun the Color Management Assistant if this is the case), select the ICC profile you created and leave it at that. Of the color settings in this section, this should be the one you have the least reason to change.

The CMYK Working Space reflects the destination of CMYK image products. Generally, you will choose U.S. Web Coated in the U.S. if you're printing to press. You may be able to get a more specific profile from your printer, and you may want to change this setting if you're creating images for specific output devices.

The settings in the Gray Working Space can help you get better results with grayscale images by selecting RGB compensation for their display. This choice should probably be based on whether you use RGB or CMYK more often for final products. In other words, if you do a lot of grayscale for Web images, use settings for Gamma (1.8 for Mac and 2.2 for PC); if you use grayscale more for printing, use dot gain settings. This may save you from creating a separate color setup for projects requiring printed black-and-white images. However, in any of these cases and as mentioned earlier, you will need to check any changes in these settings by comparing the printout to the display. This setting may need to be varied for changes in paper types and processes. Spot-color compensation functions much like Gray in that it allows the user to adjust the intensity of the appearance of the spot color by adjusting the dot gain. This should not be readjusted without physical testing and comparison of results to how a printed image appears onscreen.

→ For more information on CMYK setup, **see** "Printing Considerations," **p. 558**.

MANAGING ICC PROFILE HANDLING

The Color Management Policies section of the Color Settings screen allows you to choose a method for managing image color profiles. RGB, CMYK, and Gray handling can each be defined as Off, Preserve Embedded Profiles, or Convert to Working (RGB, CMYK, or Grayscale) in scroll-box lists associated with each. When an image is opened, Photoshop checks the preferences, and then checks to see whether there is a profile and applies the selected rules while the image is opening. See Figure 20.10 for the scroll-box list options.

Figure 20.10
All three of the Color Management Policies scroll boxes have the same options pictured here (with the appropriate color space name in the third item).

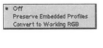

If Off is selected for the Color Management Policy and the Ask When Opening Profile Mismatches box is unchecked, Photoshop will not use color management profiles. The image will simply be opened without profile management. If the Ask When Opening

Profile Mismatches box is checked, the user will be given an option to handle the color profiling for each image that is opened (see Figure 20.11). Selecting Preserve Embedded Profiles for the Color Management Policy means Photoshop will open the image retaining the currently embedded profile. Selecting Convert to Working means that the file will be converted to the currently selected Working Space profile for the color mode. If either the Preserve Embedded Profiles or the Convert to Working profile selection is made for any of the color spaces in the Color Management Policies section of the screen, the Ask When Pasting option for Profile Mismatches and the Ask When Opening option for Missing Profiles will become available. If the Ask When Pasting box for Profile Mismatches is checked, Photoshop will compare the color management of a Clipboard item with the image it is being pasted into; if there is a mismatch, Photoshop will enable the user to manage the profile conversion using the Embedded Profile Mismatch screen. If the Ask When Opening option for the Missing Profiles is checked and an image is opened that does not contain a profile, Photoshop will enable the user to manage the profile conversion using the Missing Profile screen (see Figure 20.12). The options include not managing the profile, converting to the current Working Space profile, or selecting any profile available in the current ICC list (in order, as pictured). If you're using the last option, the ICC profile can be assigned and then converted to the current working space when the "and then convert document to working [colorspace]" check box is clicked.

Figure 20.11
The Embedded Profile Mismatch screen appears when Photoshop opens an image whose profile is different from the Color Setting for the current Working Space. The user can choose to use the embedded profile, convert the image profile to the working profile, or ignore profiling (in order, as pictured).

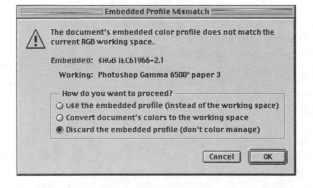

Figure 20.12
The Missing Profile screen allows the user to choose how to handle the profiling of an existing image that does not currently have a profile embedded.

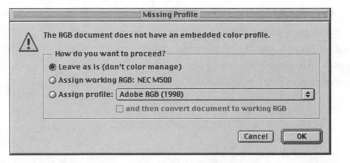

There is no definitive way to handle conversions, which is why Adobe gives you choices. There may be some images you will want to convert, and some that may be fine as is. With the choice of options, you can set up the process to occur as per your preference for color handling, and hopefully streamline some of the choice making. If you choose None on all the options and never embed profiles, it is not necessarily better or worse than choosing to embed profiles every time and having automatic conversions for every possibility (although the latter choice may prove to have worse results than the former). The decision as to how to work with color depends on what you get used to and how you like to work with images, as well as what your workflow is. If you always get images from the same source, choosing defaults is far easier because the workflow is consistent. If your source often varies, you will probably want to use Ask When Opening, which will be easier than changing the defaults every few images.

Again, the key to consistency here seems to be making a choice and learning to work with it. No system is foolproof. Embedding your profile (as long as it is accurate) will not hurt your images. However, if you never use an image anywhere but on your own system, embedding profiles isn't necessary. On the other side of the coin, converting images without knowing why or at random can lead to unexpected results. Understand the choices you are making, and when in doubt, leave the settings at the Adobe defaults—they have done some of the preliminary thinking for you.

Note

I like Photoshop to ask about conversions before going ahead so that I know what the information is coming from and going to. This can give me a hint as to how to handle the change. Making the selection to Ask When Converting really applies only to mismatched profiles, because images with no profile will probably always get the same response: There is nothing in the profile to base an adjustment on.

Note

It confounds some people why images created on their own system require conversion. If you have previously created images with color profiles and you change your color settings, opening those images may invoke the Embedded Mismatch handling because your profile will no longer match. If you have a setting that's set to Ask When Opening for the color mode of that image, you will be asked about conversion every time you open the image. This may be annoying, but it is necessary if you want that type of control.

 When you have finished adjusting the Color Settings, save the configuration you have created. This will make it easy for you to return to the settings should you change them for any reason, or it can allow you to have several different settings that you switch between for specific purposes. Although you will probably use one configuration most often, there may be good reason for you to have several different sets—all depending on your workflow.

Tip

Although you may save as many Color Settings as you like, it is probably best not to save a bunch of configurations that you will really never use. Gluttony in several areas (too many actions, too many fonts, and so on) may actually lead to slowing Photoshop down. When possible, run lean instead of offering too many choices.

CREATING A TEST PATTERN AND TESTING OUTPUT

The only true test for examining output is to do a test with the equipment you are going to use for output. This can certainly be costly, especially if you use various media and several sources for output. Testing is a necessary evil. Matching the output to the screen is the final word in achieving WYSIWYG.

The following steps assume that you have already set your profiles and created and loaded ICC profiles as discussed in the previous portions of this section.

1. Set up a file to test output. The file should be created using your normal output routine. That is, if you usually output by placing Photoshop images in Quark, create the Photoshop image and place it in a Quark file to output the test.

2. Send the file to your service bureau or output it to your printing device.

3. Compare the output to the screen and make adjustments to the monitor to compensate for the differences.

Tip

The assumption here leans toward getting output done at an external service, and using the home printing device as a personal proof in preparing for this type of output. I make this assumption because home users generally do not have access to the type of expensive, quality printing devices available through services. If your method of output is home use and you have a new photo-quality printer, these tests are just as important, but less costly. If you plan to use outside services, it makes sense to calibrate for the endpoint, not the proofing device.

Output on the machine you will use in the end is the only true test for seeing exactly what you will get. Although it is good to use other testing means to assure that you get the printed results you want, such tests (proofs) should be considered only approximations. Fine-tuning your monitor to the look of the final output is the best way to get output results that match the screen.

Tip

It might be necessary to have several different monitor settings to compensate for different output devices. Be sure to save and load the appropriate settings in the Color Settings screen before working on any image. Being careful, accurate, and consistent about color management will yield the best results.

SETTING UP A TEST FILE

Plan on testing at least a single 8.5×11 page using the full process you will generally be using for output. The size of the output may vary if that is impossible, or if it is not a native size for the output method (for example, a film recorder might print in 8×10). When I say "full process," I mean that you should print your proof at home and allow the service to print a proof and a final as well. This way, you can check the compatibility and accuracy of their proofing with yours and make a comparison. Checking both proofs against the final will let you know whether your home proofing device is adequate or may need some adjustments; the test also lets you know whether the proofing device that the service uses adequately matches the output that they get.

Set up a test file using the following: a sample color swatch of at least 14 colors (including color standards of 100% C, M, Y, K, R, G, B and several mixed pastels), a sample grayscale in 5% steps (0% to 100%), a grayscale blend (0% to 100%), a rainbow blend, and several colorful sample images. You can lay this out in any configuration. Each portion of the file can be created separately and placed in a final output file created in a layout program, or the entire image can be created in Photoshop. Be sure to convert the colors to the appropriate output for your tests. Generally, this will be CMYK, but ask your service which way they prefer the files. As far as format is concerned, it is probably best to save the images as uncompressed TIFF files, but again, check with your service as to what they prefer.

→ For more information on file types and making file type choices, **see** "Selecting a File Format," **p. 319** and "Choosing an Image Mode," **p. 309**.

The grayscale test strips can help you pick out tonal and color shifts in your monitor and in the print process. Note the color shifts in the grays using the monitor only, and use the print to match the monitor to the look of the tonal result. Before you get the proof back, use the gray strips, viewed in Photoshop, to see whether there is anyplace where the monitor appears to get out of color sync in display. The steps in the grays on the test image should appear to be even onscreen, each step easily discernable from the previous. For example, if the lighter grays seem a little red whereas the darker tones look flat, you might have a problem with the calibration (the color of the grays should be the same throughout). The tones on the print should be flat in color as long as only black ink is used. Color appearing in the grays in the print will probably be only a reflection of the color of the black ink or the paper, rather than a problem in matching the display.

Black Ink in Color

Although you'd think at least this would be simple, black ink is not always just black. Although tones should stay relatively consistent, black inks actually come in a variety of shades. How the ink takes to the page affects the density and coverage, and the ink itself will vary depending on the press person or whoever is mixing it. You can get prints from a service's offset press where the ink will look a deep, balanced black one day; and the next day another pressman might dilute the ink a little more than the first, and the ink may not cover the same or may change slightly in shade with dilution. The effect of this, although perhaps not expected, can sometimes be pleasant. For example, a warm black ink might give the printing a slight sepia toning. This is more something to be aware of than to attempt to compensate for.

Color swatches on the test should provide a good basic color test. Having at least 14 colors is somewhat arbitrary, but that number provides at least 7 other colors beyond the standards for comparison. The idea of using pastels is that these colors are more often in a delicate balance: A salmon pink can quickly turn to an unseemly orange with a few degrees' difference in the appearance on your display and the way the colors actually appear in the output.

To set up the RGB portion of the test, you will have to create an RGB document and create the red, green, and blue swatches. You can convert to CMYK or leave as a separate RGB image to place in the layout file (if the service will handle the conversion; check with your service beforehand). This will give you an idea of how the RGB file would be separated, and it shows some of the limitation of the CMYK color space. *Do not* expect that the RGB will look exactly like the RGB on your screen before converting to CMYK. Color images should be corrected to the best of your ability. If you are a newcomer, it may be best to place an image on the test in two versions: the original scan and the corrected version. This will help you judge whether the corrections you make are actually an improvement.

Images should be placed on an 18% gray background to provide a neutral background for viewing the test. I have included a test image for download on this book's companion Web site at www.ps6.com. You may want to use that, or just use it to get ideas as to how you might like to set up your own test.

SENDING THE TEST FILE

Pack up the test file and forward it to your service bureau. This should include the layout file (if any) and the images you included in the layout test. Be sure to request a proof and final (along with film and whatever else may be required). You may need to provide a color separation printed from your file. The finer points of submission are covered in Chapter 40, "Prepping for Printing: Prepress."

➔ For more information on what to do when completing a job to send to the printer, **see** "Prepping for Printing: Prepress," **p. 869**.

EXAMINING THE TEST PROOF

When the proof comes back from the service, you will want to check the result primarily against the monitor. To do this, first take a good look at the print in some balanced daylight. Use a window with white curtains in somewhat-direct sunlight, or any bright room on a reasonably sunny day. The conditions don't have to be perfect, but the idea is to get a good look at the proof in light that is not going to affect the appearance much. When you get in front of your monitor, your lighting might not be as bright, evenly balanced, or consistent as sunlight. Try to note areas of the image that don't appear as you would have thought. Pay close attention to those pastel swatches. Note any hue in the grayscale (as long as you have used only black ink for the grays, this will reflect the color of the black ink used).

Bring the proof in front of your computer and take a good look at the Photoshop files that made up the result (looking at the Photoshop files in the layout program won't do you any good). See where the proof fails to match what you see onscreen. If the proof is generally too bright or has too much contrast, you can make slight adjustments in the screen settings using the monitor controls to bring the proof and the screen closer using the onscreen (or external dial) controls for the monitor. Don't go fiddling or adjusting a lot because that may require that you recalibrate. You may try slight RGB color adjustments to the monitor as well.

Another method of working with the matching is to go back to the Color Settings and change the Working Space for RGB. Before you do, be sure to save the current settings so that you can revert to them if necessary. You may want to go back to them if experiments with changing the preferences don't work out and this proof seems better than the next one you do. In cases in which the proof and the screen are miles apart, it may be reasonable to recalibrate the monitor and start again. You can change the monitor settings by selecting a different ICC profile or creating a new ICC profile.

Whatever you do, *do not* correct the images to make the proof match. In your hands you hold the key to knowing what to expect from images and output, and it was expensive—to both prepare and output. Keep it for reference, and use it as a check for further calibrations. In fact, you can use those same images to work with calibration on other monitors. Simply load the original images in Photoshop and compare to the printed results.

 If you have examined the proof and compared it to the monitor and are still not sure you have the right result, see "Adjusting to the Proof" in the Troubleshooting section at the end of this chapter.

Tip

Sometimes it is better to simply note a color behavior and compensate for it without changing the color of the monitor. For example, if you know that your blacks appear with a slightly reddish cast onscreen, you might find that adjusting the black color ruins the appearance of the mid- and quartertones. You will be far more likely to ruin an image by correcting for the cast caused by fixing your blacks in this case than just ignoring the black. However, if the shading is so extreme, it may be time for a new monitor, or a calibration device.

EVALUATING AN IMAGE BY EYE

Visual inspection on a properly calibrated monitor should imitate what you see in print. It is far better to trust the eye than to attempt to check out all the variables and possibilities of color and combinations and how they interact in an image. In other words, there is no reason to get in and check every pixel. Complex colors and tones are the result of variations that are hard to evaluate concretely, and an overall visual check lets you determine whether the colors look right. Hundreds of tones and colors might make up an appearance, whereas single pixels might vary tremendously within the same area of the image (see Figure 20.13). If the image looks good, make only minor corrections based on other evaluations. If you can learn to trust your eye and the equipment for the bulk of correction, everything becomes simpler in color and correction work. Here, simple inspection and checking a list of pertinent points lets you know whether the image is in need of more intensive, radical correction.

Figure 20.13
The subject in the source image at left seems to have relatively even skin tone. The center swatch is filled with a tone that averages a selection of the forehead area of the subject. The right shows the actual quality of that same patch of skin at 800%. Note the variation in the tonality.

Some general concepts can be used in evaluating the need for general tonal and color correction based on visual inspection. These evaluations are based strictly on what you see onscreen. The idea here is that your vision will help you see what may need to be measured and considered for correction.

The following questions can help you make a good decision as to what needs further evaluation in any given image:

- What are the general key tones of the image (high, medium, or low key)?
- What is the image contrast (high, average, or low)?
- Is the color integrity good?

Although these elements are good to keep in mind, serious evaluation of an image will require always checking certain areas of an image to be sure it is as good as it can be. These checks should be completed with Photoshop's measurement tools after these questions have been answered.

→ More information on evaluating images with Photoshop's color tools follows; **see** "Measuring the Need for Color Correction," **p. 433**.

HIGH-, MEDIUM-, AND LOW-KEY IMAGES

High-key images have an average tonality that is shifted toward the brighter end of the spectrum. Beach-area shots with lots of light sand or winter scenes are good examples of high-key images (see Figure 20.14). Low-key images are shifted toward darker tones (see Figure 20.15). An example might be a group of faces around a birthday cake lit only by the candles. Noting that an image is tending toward brightness or darkness should give hints as to what not to correct. You might not want to simply balance a low-key image or you will risk ruining the image information as well as the natural appearance of the image. If it seems that shifts in the image are not natural and may be due to being exposed incorrectly, correction should be considered.

PART
VI

CH
20

Figure 20.14
A high-key image in which the brightness is really part of the overall mood.

© Seattle Support Group, www.ssgrp.com

Figure 20.15
A low-key image in which the tonality is generally dark—yet certainly the darkness of the image is not a mistake.

© PhotoSphere Images, Ltd., photosphere.com

IMAGE CONTRAST

Harsh lighting in direct sunlight can create a chasm between lights and darks, which is undesirable. However, high contrast can help separate subjects from the background of an image if used properly and may be desirable (see Figure 20.16). Low-contrast images may appear to be flat and lacking dynamics. However, at times low contrast is perfectly natural for the appearance of an image, depending on what it is displaying (see Figure 20.17). If the contrast is not desirable, the image may need correction (see Figure 20.18).

Figure 20.16
This is a high-contrast image that makes the subject stand out from the background.

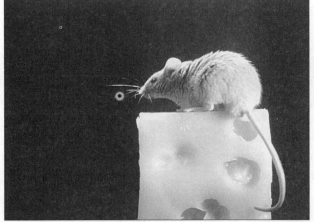

© Seattle Support Group, www.ssgrp.com

Figure 20.17
Even tones in this image lead to a low contrast, but the contrast is natural for the image, which was simply shot on an overcast day.

© PhotoSphere Images, Ltd., photosphere.com

Figure 20.18
High contrast in this image obscures the subject in this image, whereas a more even tonality would make for a more natural appearance. This can be corrected and improved.

PART
VI

CH
20

COLOR INTEGRITY

Color casts can also be perceived as natural or unnatural in an image. A photograph taken at sunrise or sunset, for example, will be affected by the warmth (redness) of the light at that time of day. The color of the resulting image can shift quite dramatically toward red (or warmer colors). Correcting this out of an image can shift the spectrum of color in the sunset so that it becomes unnatural. In other words, recognizing a desired shift can help keep you from making a mistake in corrections.

In a similar way, photographic filters might have been used to attain special effects. If the goal of correction is to remain true to the original image—as it is in many cases—be careful not to correct the color shift out of the image by tonal and color adjustments.

On the other hand, man-made lighting, such as fluorescent light, will often give images an unnatural coloring. In the case of fluorescent light, it will cast greenish. If the shift is not natural or desired, the image should probably be corrected.

Specifically, you may want to look at the following things, and if any has an unnatural or unexpected coloration, it may suggest need for correction:

- Is the color generally unnatural? Do any of the known colors of image elements present the wrong color? For example, does a photograph show a blue car as decidedly purple? Generally, we note this in expected colors, such as skin tones; we know what they should look like, even if they might be hard to describe. You may note any number of colors that simply don't look right in an image. These demand further inspection of color.

- Is there a color shift at the edges of the shadow areas? Sometimes this can just be a calibration issue, but in the earlier days of digital imaging, this often had to do with bad color setup and worse separations. If the fringes of shadows often appear to have a hue that cannot be accounted for from what you know of the monitor calibration, this would suggest that the image needs some help.

- Do the highlights show a definite undesirable hue? This may suggest the need for a shift in the image white point, but it is really impossible to tell without evaluating the image further. Light colors are often the most difficult to evaluate without measurement using Eyedropper tools.

- Are there broad areas of light pastel or complex colors? Even if these appear correct onscreen, it is a good idea to slate these areas of an image for checking. For example, areas of a sunset may lend a little too much blue (Cyan) to the mix, and in print what seemed to be a very warm sunset will have unnatural greenish hints near the sun. Correcting this before it gets to print and has to be redone will save money. Give pastels a check because they can easily shift when images go to print.

MEASURING THE NEED FOR COLOR CORRECTION

Regardless of the outcome of visual inspection, it is recommended that you check certain key points of images using Photoshop's diagnostic tools to optimize every image for print output—even if you are fairly confident in the color and tonal integrity. Completing these checks will include examining the black and white points and spot-checking for good color and matching just to be safe. Highlights, shadow transitions, and pastel colors should probably be checked regardless of how good an image looks onscreen. The combination of evaluation by eye and quick checks with Photoshop's tools enables you to know how to proceed in correction.

For example, Histograms show a chart of the image, reflecting overall tonality. Knowing what key and contrast types look like in Histograms will help you see the correlation between the image and results with Photoshop's measurement tools. Recognizing the general patterns may help keep you from overcorrecting an image so that it doesn't lose desired qualities.

On the micro side of evaluation, Eyedropper measurements can note exact color values of individual pixels and pick up slight variations that a quick visual inspection might miss. Both tools provide valuable information in assessing the need for image corrections.

Color Correction for Web Graphics

Correction implications are heavily weighted toward print imaging in these sections because it is quite a bit more tricky to deal with print because of conversion. The fact is that you can readily proof your Web images fairly well on your own monitor, whereas print is another process entirely. Although there are variations in monitor screens, number of colors, and monitor control settings, regrettably there is no way to adjust for all the possibilities—as of yet. The best method for working on Web graphics and checking color for them is to work on a neutral screen, or one reverted to factory settings. This usually helps put your Web graphics in the middle of the road as far as brightness, contrast, and color are concerned and makes the resulting images more compatible with a variety of monitors. Use color proofing to check how images will appear on Mac and PC environments.

EVALUATING IMAGES WITH HISTOGRAMS

PART

VI

CH

20

A Histogram charts the number of pixels for each color level throughout the entire range of the image. Looking at a Histogram shows important information about the color and tonality of an image. Evaluating the graphs can show decided color shifts and abnormalities that help in making a decision as to what might need to be done to an image to correct it.

Note

Most Histogram evaluation of an image is discussed here in terms of RGB, where most basic color corrections will occur.

It doesn't matter what the machine or the scan costs; scans might not turn out well if the skill of the person operating the scanner is less than adequate for doing the scanning. PhotoCDs can yield results comparable to drum scans—if worked on carefully to achieve the best results. The information has to be in the scan for the scan to have the potential of excellent color or tonality. Basic use of Histograms lets you take a look at and evaluate some basic parameters of an image including key and contrast types, but it also lets you see whether an image has been damaged in processing or is limited by the information provided. Knowing whether you are in the ballpark gives you hints as to what needs to be done to an image or how to assess damage.

Tip

For more accurate image information in the Level and Histogram displays, deselect the Use Cache for Histograms check box in the Image Cache preferences by choosing File, Preferences, Image Cache.

Use the following steps to evaluate an image using the Histograms:

1. Open the image you want to evaluate.

2. Open the Levels Histogram (Image, Histogram or Image, Adjust, Levels).

Tip

It is possible to evaluate a section of an image by selecting it with the selection tools. The Histogram charts the results only for the active or selected portion of an image.

Note

Histograms and Levels show the same representations of the image information. The advantage to using the Levels is that the tools you need for some corrections are right there. Histograms are more or less strictly for evaluations and measurements.

3. Evaluate the information provided about the image in the Histograms by noting the image key, contrast characteristics, tonal shifts, and image integrity (scan density).

The Histogram displays an accurate representation of the image as a graph of pixel densities. The height of each line in the graph represents the number of pixels with particular color value or luminescence.

Evaluating a Histogram is as easy as looking at it. Switching through each channel, you will want to note aberrations that are not explained by the visual nature of the image. These aberrations can present themselves as uncharacteristic shifts or lack of balance, and gaps in the information. A Histogram that contains many peaks and valleys, gaps in information, and/or clipping (spikes in information that run off the chart—usually at the extreme right or extreme left of the graph) may represent some form of image damage, limitation, or loss of image information. These images might have insufficient tonal range for manipulation, correction, or use.

Do not be overzealous in accepting the appearance of the Histogram as an absolute judge of the image; be sure to make the visual assessment as well and use the two assessments in tandem. The visual assessment should always override the digital one, especially if you get good results in tests and can trust the view of your monitor.

The following examples are provided to show a basic blueprint for specific image types, such as high-key, low-key, high-contrast, low-contrast, or even-toned images, and images with damaged information (see Figures 20.19 through 20.27).

Figure 20.19
A lopsided or skewed composite Histogram that is weighted toward the blacks or dark end of the spectrum, and that does not have gaps in tonality at the light end of the spectrum, represents a low-key (dark) image. This Histogram is from the image in Figure 20.14.

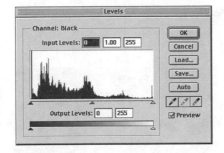

Figure 20.20
A Histogram that is skewed to the light or white end of the spectrum, and that does not have gaps in the dark end of the spectrum, represents a high-key (light) image. This Histogram is from the image in Figure 20.13.

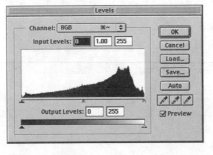

Figure 20.21
A Histogram that peaks in the dark and light areas while having lower pixel density in the middle of the spectrum is representative of a high-contrast image. This Histogram shows a mapping of information from Figure 20.16.

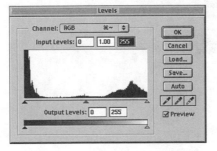

Figure 20.22
A Histogram that shows a relative density (peak) in the center is low contrast and medium key. This Histogram represents the image information in Figure 20.23.

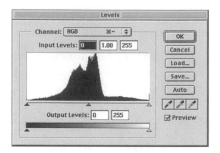

Figure 20.23
This medium-key, low-contrast image is described by the Histogram in Figure 20.22.

© PhotoSphere Images, Ltd., photosphere.com

Figure 20.24
An image with even tonal range displays as a flattened graph with few peaks and valleys across the spectrum in the Histogram. This Histogram describes the image in Figure 20.25.

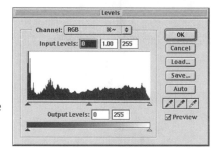

Figure 20.25
Images with full tonal range can have quite a bit of local contrast as opposed to high total contrast. This image is described by the Histogram in Figure 20.24.

Before

Figure 20.26
This Histogram shows image information from the image in Figure 20.27. The image has been altered by changing to a limited number of colors in Indexed Color mode.

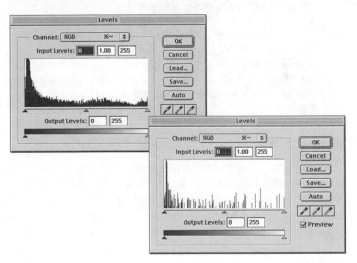

After

Figure 20.27
A close-up of a section of the original image at 500% reveals the difference in the tonality before and after the change in image information. Depending on how severe the damage is, the process and paper used to print, and so on, damage may or may not appear in the final print.

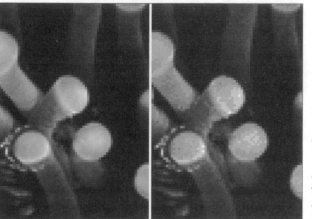

> **Tip**
>
> If the Histogram presents as damaged (missing information), you might consider getting the image rescanned. Rescanning with appropriate changes in the scanning parameters might yield far better results. If the damage is inherent in the image (for example, it might be the result of changing the color mode to indexed color for Web graphics), it might be necessary to go back to the original image. In the worst cases, when the original is not available and rescanning the image does not help, it might be wise to choose another image because repairs might be far too time-consuming to justify.

EVALUATING AN IMAGE WITH THE EYEDROPPER

Using the Eyedropper to spot-check various areas of an image either assures you that the image is ready to be saved or lets you know whether the image needs some further, perhaps subtle, correction. The Eyedropper and Color Sampler can be valuable tools in assessing an image and evaluating and correcting the color throughout the process of correction. Knowing the values for target areas and checking them against swatches (and with more experience, just knowing what the values mean) give you a good idea of the color integrity of the image and what needs to be done in correction, and it can speed those corrections by showing you where you need to get to. Use the sampling tools to your advantage throughout color changes and corrections for spot-checking (Eyedropper) and consistent anchored checking (Color Sampler).

> **Tip**
>
> Check colors that you find notoriously difficult. For example, I habitually check yellows for cyan casts that will turn them slightly green when images go to print because I got into the habit on a system whose monitor shaded light greens toward yellow—a situation that could not be corrected. When found, such aberrations are easily removed, but without spot-checking, they may not seem apparent. Various nuances might occur in your color work, and being aware of them can help you compensate.

ULTIMATE LAYER EFFECTS

Layers are the ultimate tool for creating image effects. Here various masking techniques are used to emphasize the patriot in this patriot. See Chapter 3, "Creating Images in Layers," for more on layer effects.

Original image Copyright © 1999 PhotoSphere Images Ltd. http://www.photosphere.com

Changing Colors in Channels

Rearranging RGB channel information leaves tonality the same while delivering very different color results. See Chapter 4, "Working with Channels," for other helpful hints on making the most of channel information.

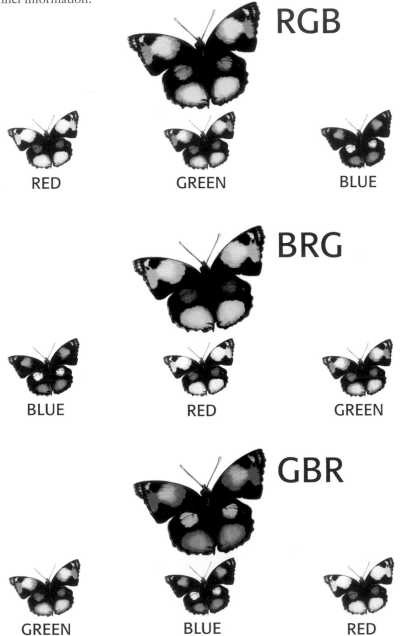

RGB

RED   GREEN   BLUE

BRG

BLUE   RED   GREEN

GBR

GREEN   BLUE   RED

Making Magic with Selection and Masking

Replacing the sky with a fireworks shot and working with color and tonality existing in the image changes this day scene to a nighttime promo shot. See Chapter 5, "Selection and Masking," for more on working with selection.

MODELING IMAGE SHAPE WITH LIGHT

Emphasizing texture and lighting by careful blending help reclaim much of this image from a scan of the original print. For more on working with shaping image objects, see Chapter 30, "Working with Shadow and Light," for other great examples.

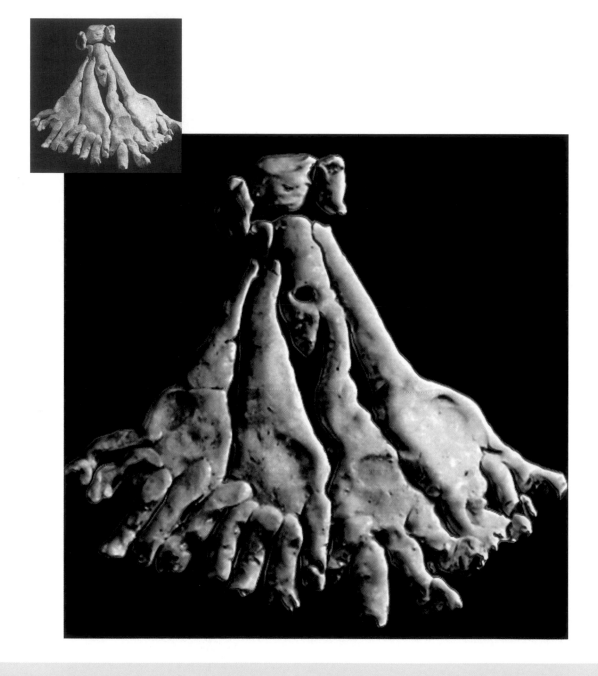

FINDING SATISFYING COLOR

Any of these images could have been the original. Careful manipulation of color can change your results to match particular color schemes, enhance existing color, or just get the best results from CMYK printing. See Chapter 23, "Color Conversions."

FILTERS THAT FIX

Understanding Blur, Noise, and Blend If gives you the opportunity to adjust and improve image information selectively and without losing the desired details. Subtle changes can improve the look of images and the models in them. See Chapter 29, "Applying Filters to Improve Images," for more on how to use these filters and others.

ORIGINAL

BLURRED

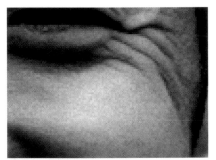

SIZED NOISE

BLENDED NOISE, BLUR, AND ORIGINAL

EXACTING COLOR CORRECTIONS

Color correction is not best handled by eye in every instance. Here, a gray card is used to target color zones at 25%, 50%, and 75% gray to help accuracy and to speed color correction results. See Chapter 22, "Color Corrections," for more information.

Extracting the Most Detail in Grayscale Conversions

Images can go from color to black-and-white to color again while improving the results. There are many opportunities for changing a color image to black-and-white besides straight color conversion using Modes. See Chapter 23, "Color Conversions," for more of these options.

Original image Copyright © 1999 PhotoDisc http://www.photodisc.com

THE ART OF HANDCOLORING

When an image has color that you think could be better, it may be an opportunity to practice handcoloring. Take the color out of the image by converting to grayscale and then add it back in. You don't need to be an artist (the rough painting here shows you that!). Chapter 23, "Color Conversions," will give you more on this topic.

Out-of-This-Gamut Color!

There is no reason to stay with original color if you want something else. Creative replacement can have dynamic results. See Chapter 24, "Using Duotones and Spot Colors," for additional information on using colors to their fullest.

Original image Copyright © 1999 SSGRP, http://www.ssgrp.com

In this case, the car was recolored and the background was replaced with the sky (see insert image). Spot color and varnish add special effects to printed images for more dramatic results. See Chapter 24, "Using Duotones and Spot Colors," for other examples of how to get great results from your printed images.

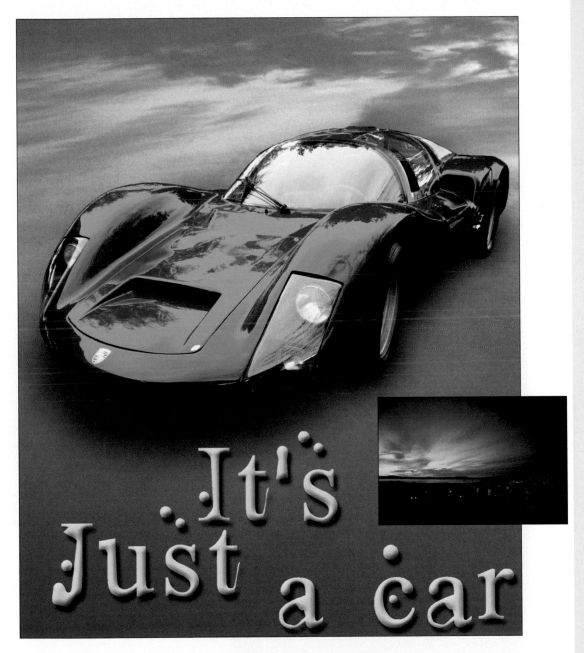

JUST FILTERS

It is possible to create a snake by applying filters with almost no manual intervention. See Chapter 34, "Using Filters and Plug-Ins," for more on how to make the most of Photoshop's filters. Filters are also useful in creating text effects like fire, as you'll see in Chapter 33, "Type Effects."

Borrow elements from one image to dress up another, and then use these results in yet other images to create unique images (such as for your own alternative band's CD). For more on selection, see Chapter 5, "Selection and Masking," but for putting images together, see "Composition Changes and Improvements," in Chapter 28, or "Combining Images: Collage and Composites," in Chapter 32.

Original images Copyright © 1999 PhotoDisc http://www.photodisc.com

Reflecting on Your Images

Working with highlighting, shadows, and reflection to create dimension can give your image some added dramatics and depth. See Chapter 30, "Working with Shadow and Light," for more on working with these elements.

CREATIVE COMPOSITES AND IMAGE MORPHING

This image is really a collage of five different scans of objects, not images. Fitting image elements together so they work is one of the most challenging aspects of Photoshop. See Chapter 32, "Combining Images: Collage and Composites" for more on creating this type of composite.

UGLY CONCEPTS: MORE THAN PRETTY TECHNIQUE

LAB

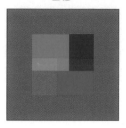

CMYK CONVERSION

GRAYSCALE CONVERSION

When converting from the Lab swatch above to CMYK, you get the same colors, or a very close approximation. When converting to grayscale, these distinct colors blend because they have the same tone. This is a problem when making grayscale images, but there are solutions. See Chapter 23, "Color Conversions," for more information and examples.

C: 0%	M: 0%	Y: 0%	K: 100%
C: 0%	M: 0%	Y: 100%	K: 100%
C: 100%	M: 100%	Y: 0%	K: 100%
C: 65%	M: 55%	Y: 53%	K: 97%

Does black always look the same in print? These black swatches are printed with varying ink combinations. The color of your black ink might influence your results. See Chapter 24, "Using Duotones and Spot Colors," and Chapter 25, "Handling Color: For Print and the Web," for details on how to make your images come out right—the first time.

UNIFORM

GAUSSIAN

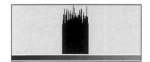

When applying noise on a color image, Uniform and Gaussian settings perform very differently. These differences can help you fix or ruin your images unless you know what to do. See more in Chapter 29, "Applying Filters to Improve Images."

Eyedropper Versus Color Sampler

The Eyedropper and Color Sampler function in different ways although they can both be used to evaluate color. The Eyedropper is a mobile, floating checker, and the Color Sampler is an anchored checker. The Eyedropper shows values in the Info palette for pixels within the radius defined in the Options. Clicking the mouse with the Eyedropper over the image makes a single selection of color, which is introduced into the foreground color swatch. Holding down the Option key while clicking replaces the background color. Neither selection can be reverted with undo or histories. The Eyedropper tool toggles to the Color Sampler when you hold down the Shift key. The Color Sampler allows up to four markers to be placed in the image that will show current values for the selected spot(s) in the Info palette. The selections save with the image and are not deactivated until they are removed (they will be removed if the image is opened and saved in an earlier version of Photoshop that does not support anchored sampling). You can move the selections by clicking over them and dragging; you can remove them by holding down the Option key and clicking.

In the end you will find that you need to use both tools: the Color Sampler for checking consistent areas, and the Eyedropper tool for spot-checking.

1. Open the image you want to check with the Eyedropper.

2. Double-click the Eyedropper or Color Sampler tool. This opens the Preferences for the sampling tool.

Tip

Using too small of a sample size might only make confusing samples; point samples might change too rapidly to make sense of as you move the sampling tool across an area that seems evenly toned to the eye. This makes the values for the sample hard to interpret, let alone read. A point sample on a skin tone can range broadly point to point (pixel to pixel) but shows more consistency with a larger sampling range. In certain cases, such as skin tones, it is better to sample with a broader sample size to get a better average reading of the tones you want to measure.

3. Choose the radius for the sampling area. If the radius is 1 (point sample), the sample will reflect the pixel that the dropper is over; if it is greater than 1 (3×3 or 5×5), a square with the dimensions selected will be sampled and averaged for the result.

4. Bring the Info screen to the front by selecting it from the Window menu, or by pressing the F8 key on your keyboard.

5. Spot-check with the Eyedropper by passing the Eyedropper icon over various areas of the image that you want to check and noting the values. (See Table 20.1 for areas to check.)

6. Use the Color Sampler to set sample points that reflect the areas of the image you feel are typical of the color points you want to monitor during any color changes. For example, if your pastels look good and you don't want them to change much from their present values, yet you have general corrections to make, you might set a marker or two in the pastel areas so that you can monitor the effect your changes have on those parts of the image. If you are making general changes, you might place a marker in each of the following: shadow transitions, highlights, medium grays, and pastels or skin tones. This enables you to monitor the effects your changes have across the spectrum and key points of the image.

Tip

Check the values of the areas selected with the Color Sampler frequently in the Info palette during image changes to be sure you remain within the target values. Spot-check with the Eyedropper in and around the Color Sampler anchors to be sure you get readings that are a good representation.

TABLE 20.1   IMAGE AREAS TO CHECK WITH THE EYEDROPPERS

What to Check	What to Look For
Highlights	Check the lightest areas of the image. Images should have different highlight values depending on the use. For print, extreme highlights should maintain a slight dot (4,2,2,0) or they will appear to blow out (have no dot). Specular highlights in Web materials should go all the way to the brightest white (255,255,255).
Blacks	Black should take advantage of the available tonal range to allow for more contrast and total color depth. This would vary based on your CMYK separation settings for print and should be absolute black (0,0,0) for Web images.
Shadow transitions	The fringe areas of shadows can be tricky when you're converting to CMYK from other color modes, and they are notorious in some other conversions. This might have to do with your UCR (Under Color Removal) or GCR (Gray Color Removal) settings, or it can be because of oddities in scanning. Shifting to red or blue is rather common and should be checked and corrected.
Grays	Gray tones should measure with relative flatness; that is, the RGB or CMY values should be fairly even (the Cyan value may tend to be slightly higher). If one or more of the measurements show a decided and persistent shift, the image color probably needs some balancing.
Pastels	Pastel mixtures are generally very fragile, and a change of a few percentage points in any channel can show a decided shift in color. Check a printed color swatch if available for the color you hope to see, and be sure that the CMYK breakdown is not very far off. A shift (especially if matched by a corresponding gray level) should be corrected.
Skin tones	Skin tones are a visual color marker. If a skin tone is off, the image won't seem realistic. Skin tones are also one of the toughest areas of an image to get an accurate reading of because of texture and tonal variation. They run the tonal range from specular highlight to shadow, and vary from person to person, so there are no set values to attach. You need to be diligent in checking skin tones for color range to be sure they are acceptable—especially when they will appear in print.

→ For more information on all issues of correcting black-and-white images, **see** "Basic Tonal Correction: Channels and Grayscale," **p. 445**.

→ For more information on all issues dealing with correcting color, **see** "Color Corrections," **p. 465**.

→ For more information on Web-specific color issues, **see** "Web Graphic Color Considerations," **p. 563**.

→ For more information on using images in print, **see** "Prepping for Printing: Prepress," **p. 869** and "Printing Considerations," **p. 558**.

Tip

If you're doing color correction for print, use the values of the areas you sample to check against printed color swatches. Various color books are available through manufacturers, and some printers make them available to customers directly from their own presses.

Note

While floating over the image, the Eyedropper will sample the composite of the visible layers. Note the readings at several areas before coming to any color conclusions and making changes based on samples.

Color samples can also be done in several modes at once in exactly the same spot. Using the Color Sampler, place two, three, or four sampler targets near the spot you want to see in more than one mode; then drag them on top of one another. When they are all aligned in the same spot (they don't necessarily snap to one another; but they seem to snap to a pixel, so placement is pretty easy), set the color modes you want to sample from the spot (see Figure 20.28). This can be handy for checking an image that will be used for multiple purposes, such as in color and black-and-white printing and Web applications.

Figure 20.28
This Info palette shows the result of placing several markers in exactly the same spot, but using different measures for each marker.

Tip

A very handy pop-up menu to the Info palettes is right in the info boxes, so you can choose or change color references at any point without having to go to a dialog box or switch image color modes (see Figure 20.29).

Figure 20.29
The Info palette pop-up menus are handy for switching to desired color mode measurements quickly.

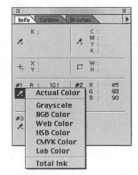

TROUBLESHOOTING

ADJUSTING TO THE PROOF

I have looked at the proof and compared it to my monitor and they are not exactly alike, even though I have made some adjustments. Is there something else I should be doing to improve the correlation?

As long as the image onscreen and the result are very similar, that may be the best you can do. What is "similar" to some may be unacceptable to others, and this may depend on the end product. If you are proofing images for magazine covers rather than images to share with friends, the accuracy in matching proof to screen will need to be higher. At that point it comes down to equipment and the ability to adjust your display. Serious work requires serious equipment; a more expensive monitor is not just more expensive because of the brand name. Usually, along with that expense go increased accuracy and integrity in the image projection, as well as improved controls. If you cannot get the results you need, it may be that you have outgrown your equipment. On the other hand, you may have outgrown current technology. The cure for the former may be to upgrade; the cure for the latter is to note the exceptions and compensate as you work.

PHOTOSHOP AT WORK: DON'T PUT OFF PROOFING

The logical conclusion to this chapter is to suggest that you go through the steps of calibration and proofing. This is suggested procedure, because it will be most accurate for your situation. However, and because this is a costly proposition depending on the output, another option is made available here for performing at least a preliminary calibration. You will need this book, which contains printed color images, and the workbook, which contains copies of several of the original color images used to print that color. The images have been collected on page 20 of the PDF workbook (which you can get on the companion Web site for this book—www.ps6.com).

Use the following steps to perform basic color management and calibration for your system:

1. Build an ICC profile of your monitor to use in Photoshop.

   → For more information on creating the ICC profile, **see** "Calibrating Your Monitor," **p. 414**.

2. Check the Color Settings to be sure that the RGB Working Space is set to the profile you created in Step 1, and that the CMYK Working Space is set to U.S. Web Coated (SWOP).

3. Check the Ask When Opening check box for Profile Mismatches (if it isn't already checked), and save the changes. You may want to save these settings as a preset by choosing Save before exiting the screen.

4. Open page 20 from the PDF workbook (www.ps6.com) in Photoshop (opening the page in Acrobat Reader or Exchange will not get the desired results). When Photoshop is opening the image, the dialog box for the profile mismatch should be displayed. In this case, choose Convert Document's Colors to the Working Space. This will convert the image from the profile I used when creating the image to your current one.

5. Compare the images from the color section against the images you have onscreen in Photoshop.

6. Make adjustments to the monitor (brightness, contrast, and color) to fine-tune the matching between the monitor and the printed image.

This comparison and calibration will do in a pinch. The point is that you have the original image with the embedded profile (these are now retained by images saved in the PDF format), and that will help you convert the image to the profile of your machine. After the profile is exchanged, the image you have is essentially the same one that was printed. In comparing the proof (the printed image in the book) to the original (the image you have converted to your color space), you will have a reasonably accurate test for the output with which to test the matching on the monitor.

Remember that various factors in your workflow might make this somewhat inaccurate for your situation. For example, unless you are printing your color work in the same fashion as the test image (using the same press, paper type, and the like), actual results may vary. If you use a wildly different process (for example, printing to newsprint on a WEB press), your results may vary widely. For the most part, this should create a reasonably accurate base, but it is accurate only for four-color offset printing. Other output will require other tests directly to that type of output.

CHAPTER 21

BASIC TONAL CORRECTION: CHANNELS AND GRAYSCALE IMAGES

In this chapter

BASIC TONAL CORRECTION

The basic techniques used to correct black-and-white images provides the foundation for all tonal and color corrections. This chapter focuses on providing that foundation by giving you step-by-step procedures for correcting black-and-white images with Curves and Levels. After you have mastered the techniques on black-and-white images, these same techniques can be used to correct color channels—which are grayscale representations of the color elements in the image. Learning black-and-white correction is somewhat less complex than manipulating color because you need deal with only one channel at a time. So, mastering the techniques here is imperative to your success in all tonal and color correction.

Even if you have evaluated a need for correction, that doesn't tell you where to begin or what to do to make the corrections. The next task is to define what to do and how to accomplish it. Following a simple order in corrections gives you more direction and a conditioned approach, while making sure you accomplish everything you need to get done. Using the same method each time ensures that you get results consistently and that you have a means of approaching any image.

> **Caution**
>
> For corrections to improve your images, you need to calibrate your monitor and test your output. Unless you perform those steps, any action toward correction may alter images in unexpected ways.

→ For more information on calibrating your monitor and testing output, **see** "Evaluating Image Color," **p. 409**.

→ For more information on evaluating the image, **see** "Evaluating Image Color," **p. 409**.

→ It may be best to correct images for dust before making corrections. For more information on dust correction, **see** "Correcting Image Damage: Restorations," **p. 579**.

The following steps provide the basic procedure you should follow in making corrections for your black-and-white images. These guidelines are general and can be altered as you develop your own style.

1. Be sure that your monitor is calibrated and that you have set up Photoshop preferences and tested output.

2. Crop the image so that you are working with what will become your final output.

> **Tip**
>
> Cropping the image first will save time in corrections. However, if the image will be used for many purposes, it may be best to correct the whole and save a copy before cropping.

3. Make general dust correction to the image.

→ For more information on dust correction, **see** "Remove Dust from an Image," **p. 580**.

4. Evaluate the image using visual inspection, Histograms, and the Eyedropper.

5. Make general levels corrections.

→ For more information on levels corrections, **see** "Corrections with Levels," **p. 447**.

6. Use curves to improve contrast and tonality.

→ For more information on using curves for tonal correction, **see** "Corrections with Curves," **p. 456**.

7. Make specific changes by controlled selection.

→ For more information on controlling images with selection, **see** "Selection and Masking," **p. 93**.

8. Use Unsharp Mask to sharpen an image or increase local contrast.

→ For more information on using the Unsharp Mask, **see** "Sharpening with Unsharp Mask," **p. 618**.

9. Consider overall brightness of the image, and make adjustments using Levels and/or Curves a second time.

10. Set black-and-white points, as appropriate.

Your work method and experience, and in some cases the image itself, might dictate a different workflow. However, following the order here will ensure that you touch on all the corrections you might need to do. After working with this method for even a short time, you may develop other preferences because there are many ways to accomplish similar ends.

Steps for correction can be saved as actions with appropriate stop points for adjustment. The actions will not do the corrections for you, but they will help lead you through and will make sure you touch on all the necessary steps. This will not only speed your corrections by automatically opening palettes and tools but also ensure that you make appropriate assessments and cover all the steps so as not to leave anything out.

In some cases, actions can be very helpful in loading defaults. For example, your printer or service might suggest that you use at least a 2% dot in the whites to keep from blowing out the highlights. A curve can be loaded to automatically correct whites to 2% using the action, and you never have to check to see that you remembered the step. Develop correction actions around the steps as previously listed or according to your preference.

→ For more information on using actions, **see** "Creating Effective Actions," **p. 263**.

CORRECTIONS WITH LEVELS

Tonal correction will give black-and-white images broader tonal range and stronger overall contrast. After you dust-correct and evaluate the image visually and with Histograms, the first step in correction should be to open the Levels dialog box to make a general tonal correction. Basic tonal correction is rather simple if an image is supposed to display a full tonal range. Proper use of the levels can quickly fix tonal range and the general brightness and contrast of an image.

Note

Be sure the Preview box is checked in the Levels dialog box when you're making any changes so that you can preview the changes before accepting them.

PART

VI

CH

21

1. Open a black-and-white image for corrections (see Figure 21.1).

Figure 21.1
This image was originally in color, and the color made the low-key appearance interesting. However, in black-and-white, it seems a little too dark, although with some contrast potential.

1999 © PhotoSphere, www.photosphere.com

2. Complete dust corrections, cropping, and minor alterations.

3. Make a visual inspection, noting whether the image is high-key, low-key, or average-key.

4. Open the Levels dialog box by selecting Image, Adjust, Levels.

5. Inspect the Histogram (black will be the only channel available), looking for confirmation of the visual inspection in Step 3 and abnormalities in the Histogram. If there are no concerns about the Histogram, skip to Step 8.

6. If the Histogram seems out of character with the image or shows hints of damage, consider rescanning or replacing the image.

7. Correct shortened tonal range by adjusting the Levels sliders.

8. Adjust the middle slider for the Levels graph. This can adjust the brightness level of the midtones and shift the entire image toward lighter or darker tones. No adjustment is necessary if the image seems in good balance.

MAKING CORRECTIONS BASED ON INSPECTION OF THE HISTOGRAM

Recognizing abnormalities in a Histogram is fairly simple. The most common tendencies you will discover in image Histograms are shortened tonal range and clipping. Any abnormalities might not always represent problems, but they are certainly good indications of unusual conditions.

CORRECTING A SHORTENED TONAL RANGE WITH LEVELS SLIDERS

Shortened tonal range is represented by a Histogram that does not have information across the entire 256 levels of gray. In other words, the Histogram graph should have some information for every level from the right to the left of the graphing, or the tonality is not covering the potential. A shortened tonal range in a Histogram for a color channel may indicate color and tonal shift (see Figure 21.2). In a black-and-white image, shortened tonal range means that the image is not taking full advantage of the shades of gray available (0% to 100% black). Although sometimes it is a mistake to drastically alter tonal range, more often than not shifting the range works to the benefit of the image. Generally, the images will appear to have more life. Even though this may seem like a deliberate misinterpretation of image information, it can help overcome some of the limitations of printing images caused by the printing process.

Figure 21.2
This Histogram represents the image in Figure 21.1. It shows some potential for stronger contrast, and a shortened tonal range, confirming the visual inspection. The tonality of the image can be redistributed to make the image more dynamic using levels.

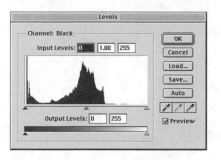

CORRECTING CLIPPING OBSERVED IN HISTOGRAMS

Clipping is similar to a shortened tonal range that occurs in the extreme highlights or shadows of an image. Clipping happens when Levels of image detail get combined as pure white or black. This suggests that information has exceeded the digital capacity to retain the image information (see Figure 21.3). The result is usually that some of the highlight or shadow detail is lost. This may be caused by any number of processes that occur in obtaining, opening, and resaving an image, such as getting a bad scan, overfiltering, bad handling of levels or curves during correction, changing color modes, and so on. Clipping can usually be considered some type of image damage.

However, clipping may not always interfere with or otherwise disturb the performance of an image. For example, after correcting tails on a Levels Histogram, information may suggest that the highlights have been clipped. If this is image noise, rather than detail, the image may improve. The key to keep in mind is that when the Histogram confirms the image damage, or makes image damage apparent, it is time to recapture the image rather than waste time in correction. If the original image is damaged, it may be best to choose a different image to work with.

Undesired clipping can be reduced or eliminated by using adjustments to the tonal range in the scanning software if such adjustments are available. If the image is from a scan, consider adjusting tonality settings to be sure you are scanning a full range, or to get better detail.

PART
VI

CH
21

Scanning Software
A lot of what sets a good scanner apart from a mediocre one is the software that comes with it. The same scanner with a better interface becomes a stronger tool, capable of producing better results over a broader variety of images. When considering a scanner, be sure to consider the software that comes with it. For example, LinoColor Elite gives you a broad range of options for correction (see Figure 21.4).

Figure 21.3
This Histogram represents an image that was scanned with a low-end, unsophisticated scanner that had a damaged motor drive. The tonal integrity of the image is inconsistent, and the resulting scan is streaked, noisy, and uneven.

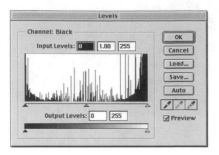

Figure 21.4
LinoColor Elite's adjustment tools allow the user to fine-tune how image information is incorporated by changing detection for each color in making a CMYK-compatible scan.

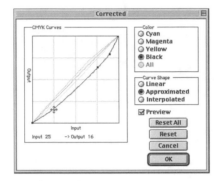

→ For more information on scanning, **see** "Scanning to Create Images," **p. 361**.

If these are possibilities, you might want to consider returning to the original image and changing the conversion settings. If adjusting the scanner settings, reopening the image with a different conversion, and opening the original image do not produce better results, consider using another image.

CORRECTING A SHORTENED TONAL RANGE WITH LEVELS SLIDERS

Shortened tonal range can be a sign of flattened tonality. You must evaluate if this is desirable by looking at the image. Such shifts are easily corrected by moving the sliders to the ends of the range represented in the Histograms.

To correct a shortened tonal range, simply move the end sliders (black or white) to the absolute ends of the tonality graphed on the Histogram. When you commit your changes by choosing OK, Photoshop automatically redistributes the tones over the total available range (0 to 255 levels of gray), depending on the settings you have set for the sliders. This change is one you can make strictly by looking at the appearance of the Histogram and adjusting accordingly. The purpose is to take full advantage of the tonal range. For example, if the Histogram defines an image that shows a tonal range of 14 to 145 levels of gray, it is using only 51% of the available grays. Redistributing the image information by moving the black and white level sliders to the ends of the available information (black to 14, white to 145) makes use of the whole range of tonal levels (see Figure 21.5). The result is greater tonal depth and stronger contrast.

Figure 21.5
Moving the white Levels slider to the left will lighten the image. Here the slider is moved to the edge of the solid portion of the graph, changing lighter elements from the original into genuine highlights.

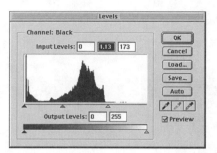

Where exactly to place the slider is a matter of what you want to accomplish. Changes can be conservative or quite radical. Going lighter on the changes and making them in increments will often yield better results, so taking the incremental route is probably the best course of action (see Figure 21.6). This does, however, depend on the size of the change. If it is a change of only five levels or so, there is no need to make it in increments (see Figure 21.7). As a guide, make incremental changes in a maximum of 15 to 20 levels.

Note

Redistribution of the tonal information in an image from a thinner to a broader band will necessarily create some gaps in the presentation of the image information as a history.

Figure 21.6
This Histogram represents a change in the Histogram shown in Figure 21.5 when the Level adjustment is applied.

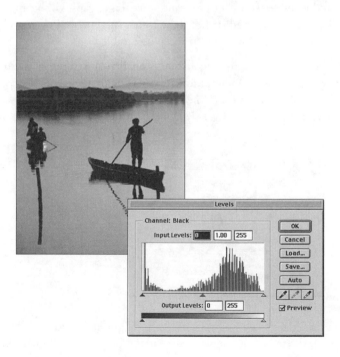

PART

VI

CH

21

Figure 21.7
This Histogram is notably different in character from the Histogram in Figure 21.6, yet the effective change is the same. The result here was accomplished by implementing the levels change in five steps.

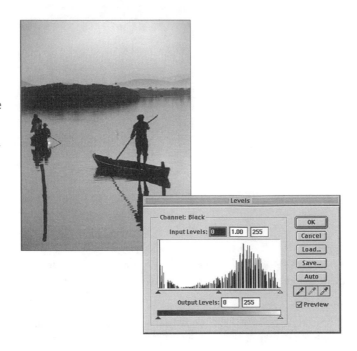

If the tonal band is increased by a significant percentage, gaps will be apparent in the Histogram when Photoshop redistributes the tones. Incremental changes have different results due to fractions and rounding to acceptable values.

One possible means of smoothing inconsistent tonality caused by redistribution is to apply a slight (less than 1-pixel radius) blur and sharpen to the image (see Figure 21.8). This can smooth out the tonal information to the benefit of the image in some cases. This will, however, blur fine detail and soften edges depending on the severity of the application of either filter.

Figure 21.8
This shows the Histogram from Figure 21.7 after blur and sharpen have been applied. Although this results in a more even Histogram, it may not have desirable effects on the image.

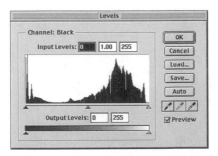

Using the Levels sliders to clip off tails in the highlight and shadow portion of the Histogram graph for the image might contribute to better overall image contrast. *Tails* represent scattered highlight or shadow information, generally attributable to image noise rather than actual image detail. Snipping the information turns it to absolute white for a highlight, or absolute black for a shadow. Generally, you will want to cut scattered pixels in a tail; however, it is sometimes desirable to cut all or a portion of a solid line.

The longer the tail, the less—proportionally—you should cut off. For example, whereas you may completely remove a tail that covers 15 levels, a tail that covers 50 to 100 levels might only be cut in half. If you are cropping tails on a color image, usually you will want to cut the same proportion on each channel (see Figure 21.9).

Figure 21.9
Here's an example of an extended tonal tail that most probably represents image noise. Cropping this off using the sliders will increase the tonal range of the image and improve contrast.

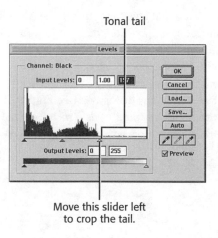

Tonal tail

Move this slider left to crop the tail.

If you have cropped the image tail and the visual appearance of the image suffers, see "The Do's and Don'ts of Cropping a Tail" in the Troubleshooting section at the end of this chapter.

CONTROLLING MIDTONES WITH LEVELS SLIDERS

The final general tonal correction to make using Levels is for overall brightness. A black-and-white image that appears too dark or light can be corrected by using the middle slider in the Levels tool. Moving the slider to the left lightens midtones, whereas moving it to the right darkens them (see Figure 21.10). This may seem slightly counterintuitive; however, it makes a lot of sense. The idea is that you are moving the median so that more levels of tone fall within the lighter or darker half of the tonal range.

Figure 21.10
Moving the middle slider right will darken the image by shifting more of the light levels into the dark range. Moving the slider left will lighten the image by moving the dark levels into the light range.

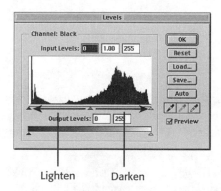

Lighten   Darken

Be careful not to abuse this tool—there are other, and perhaps better, ways of controlling the midtones (using curves, for example). As a guide, try not to move the slider more than 25 levels in any direction when making midtone corrections. This keeps the redistributions small and more forgiving. You can always come back and lighten or darken an image more later in additional steps.

AUTO RANGE

Another way to accomplish general changes in levels is by using the Auto Range Options in the Levels palette. To invoke the function, simply click the Auto button. This will redistribute the levels according to the image information and the settings in the Auto Range Options. To look at or change the settings for Auto Range, open Levels, hold down the (Option) [Alt] key, and the Auto button changes to read Options (see Figure 21.11). When the Options button appears, click it to open the Auto Range Options dialog box (see Figure 21.12). The settings for Auto Range are used for the Auto button on the Levels screen, on the Curves screen, and in adjusting Auto Levels (Image, Adjust, Auto Levels).

Figure 21.11
The Options button in the Levels dialog box allows you to enter a percentage of pixels to clip (works according to an actual pixel count). The Auto button turns into the Options button when you hold down the [Option] (Alt) key.

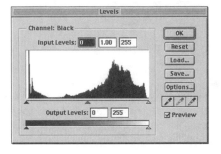

Figure 21.12
Clicking the Options button calls up the Auto Range Options dialog box. Entering Zero (as in this figure) will not remove pixels from the image but will redistribute the levels to cover the entire range available.

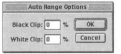

Clicking the Options button opens the Auto Range Options dialog box. To select no clipping (in other words, no removal of the tail or other image information), set the values for clipping in each box to 0% (see Figure 21.12). Close and save the settings by clicking OK.

Tip

The Auto Levels control might give quick-and-dirty results, but it might do unacceptable things to an image and damage the image information.

LEVEL EYEDROPPERS

The third way to accomplish tonality adjustments in the Levels dialog box is to use the Level Eyedroppers. The droppers can set values for selected pixels at preselected values and redistribute the tonal range accordingly. These tools offer a different type of control based on targeting black points and white points directly in the image (much like setting black points and white points for scanning).

Use the following steps to set values for the black points and white points using the Levels Eyedropper:

1. Be sure the Info palette is visible so that you can use it to pinpoint the areas you want to select using the Eyedroppers. If you don't see the Info palette, it may either not be shown, or it can be hiding behind other palettes. Choose Show Info from the Windows menu—you may need to do this twice to get the palette to come out of hiding if it is behind another palette.

2. Double-click the Eyedropper tool on the Tools palette and select a sampling size. For exact control, use point sampling; for broader tolerance and sampling a range of pixels, use a 3- or 5-pixel sampling size. Point sampling will give an exact reading of the value being selected (see Figure 21.13).

Figure 21.13
In the Eyedropper dialog box, you can select a range for sampling the image from the pop-up menu. This can be an exact point, a 3×3 square, or a 5×5 square.

3. Access the Color Picker from the Levels dialog box by double-clicking the black Eyedropper.

4. Enter values you want to use for the black point you select. These values will be assigned to the pixel you click in the image, and other levels for the image will be redistributed accordingly.

> **Note**
>
> If you are using the levels for tonal corrections of an image that will be printed, check with your service bureau or printer before making any final decisions on white and black points. Depending on the type of digital output (film, poster plotting, image recorders, and so on), needs will vary.

5. With the Level's Eyedropper, using the Info palette as a guide, select the darkest pixel that you want to be your black point.

6. When the black point is selected, the curve redistributes according to the information in the image, the selected point, and the tonal (or color) value assigned to the black point.

7. Repeat Steps 3 through 6 for white point selection using the white Eyedropper from the Levels dialog box. You can use the Median Eyedropper to reassign a median value for the slider. These settings also affect operation of the Auto correction functions.

Note

None of the Levels correction methods is a cure-all to selecting white and black points, and none can be expected to work in every situation. Often a combination of tool use accomplishes the best results. For example, you might use the Auto Range control to do the initial selection of black and white points with zero clipping, and then use the Eyedropper tools from the Levels palette to help you achieve a flat black in the image. Then, you may want to eyeball the median setting. Again, this depends on how you like to work.

The Output Levels Slider

The lower slider on the Levels screen is the Output Levels slider. This helps you shorten the tonal range of the image, essentially serving a purpose that is the opposite of the upper slider (see Figure 21.14). For example, if you want the current range of levels to be shortened so that brightness runs from 2% black to 98% black rather than 0% to 100%, you could accomplish this with the bottom slider. Simply set the black slider to 5 and the white slider to 250. This will squeeze the current levels into the range you select.

Figure 21.14
The Output Levels slider limits tonal range extremes and also redistributes image information. For every 2.5 levels you move the slider, there will be a 1% change in the available levels of black.

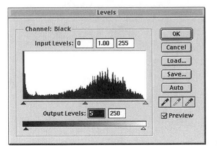

CORRECTIONS WITH CURVES

Curves can accomplish results similar to what can be done with levels, but using curves for this type of correction requires a little more savvy. Curves are both a more versatile correction tool and a more dangerous one than levels because of their power. However, using curves for corrections can help remove a step in corrections because you can make specific tonal-range and white-point corrections while making contrast changes over specific levels—all at the same time. It is like having levels with many more slider points.

Curves are the ideal tool to help fine-tune and reshape the tonal distribution of an image. Whereas levels have only three slider points to change, curves can have many and can help control different tonal levels separately.

Use the following steps to apply curves to your image:

1. Open your image and determine through inspection and measurement what needs to be altered.

2. Open the Curves (Image, Adjust, Curves).

Consider the contrast across shorter tonal ranges as well as overall. For example, does a face or skin tone appear to be flat? Does a white garment lack detail? Fine adjustments in the curves can help bring out these details. See the example later in this section.

3. Set points on the curve to redistribute image information. To increase contrast, increase the gradient of the curve; to decrease contrast, decrease the gradient of the curve. To darken an image, increase the volume under the curve; to lighten, decrease the volume under the curve. General tonal corrections can increase or lower contrast, darken or lighten, and/or distort image information over the whole of the image or in specific areas. (See Figures 21.15 to 21.20 for more on how to adjust the curves.)

4. Choose OK from the Curves dialog box to accept the changes and close the dialog box.

Figures 21.15 through 21.20 show some general changes you might make in curves to accomplish slightly more specific changes in general tone distribution than you get using levels. Confidence in using the tools without Histogram data is necessary for working with curves because the curves have no Histogram display; you have to adjust the image according to the preview and Info palette. The dialog box numbers for curves work as shifts in percentage of black (0% to 100%), not as in the Levels dialog box, where the numbers are noted in levels of gray (0 to 255).

Figure 21.15
Lowering the light quartertone and raising the dark quartertone increases contrast in the midtones. Quartertones are marked by the grid on the dialog box.

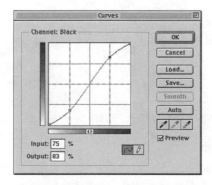

Figure 21.16
Raising the light quartertone and lowering the dark quartertone decreases contrast in the midtones.

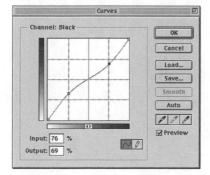

Figure 21.17
Anchoring the light quartertone and adjusting the curve to run steeply in the shadows increases shadow detail. Here, placing the curve handle at 25,25 keeps the information at the quartertone from changing.

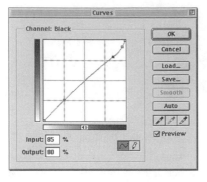

Figure 21.18
Anchoring the dark quartertone and adjusting the curve to run steeply in the highlights increases highlight detail. Anchoring the dark tone would require placing a marker at 75,75 to keep the darker image information at that level from changing.

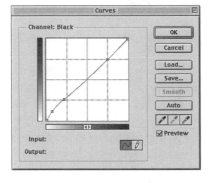

Figure 21.19
Inverting the vertical positions of the light and dark points on the curve inverts the image tonality.

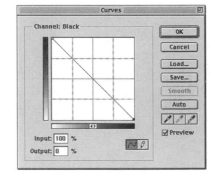

Figure 21.20
Wild distortion of tonality is also possible by applying curves to displace tonality radically.

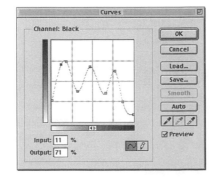

Corrections in contrast over shorter ranges should be evaluated with the Eyedropper to help limit the correction to that range. For example, if a face seems somewhat flat, or highlights lack detail, there might be a reason to strengthen the contrast just in those ranges. To measure the range, select the Eyedropper and measure the brightest and darkest areas of the tonal range you want to include using a sample of 3 or 5 pixels rather than a point sample. The idea here is to correct to a range rather than an exact point. Test samples of areas near the light and dark side of the range, and note what the values are to use as anchor points in changing the curves.

Caution

For every action, there is a reaction. Increasing the gradient of a curve at one point affects the gradient of the curves at other points. This can cause unwanted compression of tonal values in other parts of the image.

The following steps show how to use curves, sampling, and anchors to shift contrast effectively:

1. Open the Image you want to correct (see Figure 21.21).

Figure 21.21
This image was taken in direct sunlight and shows harsh shadows. Careful use of curves can help soften the effect and improve the image.

2. Set the Sample Size to a larger averaging area. You will most probably be looking for an average in this case rather than a specific value.

Tip

(Ctrl-click) [Right-click] will bring up the Sample Size menu when you're using the Curves dialog box.

3. Sample the bright end of the range you want to correct, and note the value in % black (see Figure 21.22). (Use the K value in the Info palette to view this.)

Figure 21.22
The highlight area of the cheek is the lightest portion of the area that will be changed. It measures about 15% black.

4. Sample the dark end of the range you want to correct, and note the value in % black (see Figure 21.23).

Figure 21.23
The transition area of the shadow moves sharply from light to dark. Softening this band will help soften the hard contrast of the image.

5. Place anchors at the measured highlight (Step 3) and measured shadow (Step 4). Shift the point positions to adjust the tonality as desired (see Figure 21.24). You might need to place other anchors along the curve to smooth it out and maintain the integrity of the rest of the image (see Figure 21.25).

Be aware of the effect your changes have on the other portions of the curve. For example, increasing contrast in the midtones loses some highlight and shadow detail; decreasing contrast increases highlight and shadow detail. Be sure an image can withstand these changes, and be highly critical in all visual evaluations. The tonal values outside the range of the anchors are affected by the changes. Make constant visual checks on the changes you make to be sure you are not damaging the image information irreparably. To avoid altering the image information while applying the curves, use adjustment Layers.

Figure 21.24
This curve should effectively increase detail in the highlights where it was washed out, and help lower the overall contrast of the image.

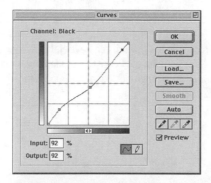

Figure 21.25
The result has improved the tonality of the image by lessening the harsh contrast. Curves might be applied again to attempt to improve the image even more.

Adjustment Layers

Adjustment layers enable you to make some image adjustments without altering the information in the image (until the layer is applied). The adjustment can be controlled like any other layer using Blend If, Opacity, Modes, layer order, and grouping. You can make adjustments with 10 of the 16 image adjustment controls that appear on the Adjustment menu (Image, Adjust); see Figure 21.26 for the list. To invoke an adjustment layer, select Layer, New, Adjustment Layer, or select New Adjustment Layer from the pop-up menu on the Layers palette. Adjustment Layers are handy for creating special effects (using Layer Options) or viewing changes without affecting image data.

Keeping curves smooth is more likely to create good results. If changes seem extreme, make them over the course of several applications of the curves rather than just in one shot. Check your results visually by undoing the curves (using Histories) or shutting Adjustment Layer views on and off. If the change is positive and what you want, it will commit when you flatten the image.

PART

VI

CH

21

Curves can also be used with Auto functions, which are adjusted in the same way as with the Levels palette. It seems, however, that Auto functions have somewhat limited appeal when one is using curves, because the nature of the tool suggests a desire for manual control.

Additional Curve Features

You can save and load curves for use in correcting images, which can be useful in making batch corrections or adjusting curve actions. The Smooth button is for use with the Pencil tool in the Curves dialog box. The Pencil allows you to manually draw curves (which may be incongruous), and the Smooth function reshapes them to smooth out bumps and the like, forming Bézier curves.

TROUBLESHOOTING

THE DO'S AND DON'TS OF CROPPING A TAIL

I have cropped the tail from my grayscale image and the results seem too drastic. Is there some other approach I should take?

If the results seem too drastic, they are. Put simply: Do crop a tail that improves the image; don't crop a tail that compromises the image. When cropping a tail, be sure it is just a tail and not important image information. Most of the time important information will be fairly evident by the Levels graph, but that is not an absolute judgment. Tails should not be cut when doing so will lop off clusters of information along the tail. Such clusters suggest that the information is important rather than disposable. See Figure 21.26 for an example.

Figure 21.26
The cluster of information to the far right on the Levels graph probably represents some highlight detail; this is an example of information that probably should not be ignored and removed—even though there is a seemingly significant tail and even areas where the tail breaks up.

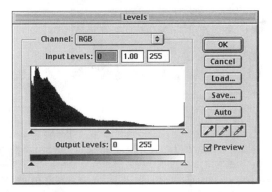

In the case of Figure 21.26, it is probably better to adjust the Levels center slider to the left than to remove the tail and associated image information. Probably even more fitting for this image would be an adjustment using the curves—if an adjustment is necessary or desirable.

Don't feel that you have to crop a tail in the image just because it exists. Be aware of the image type (high-key, low-key) and other options, and use that information to help with your decision in corrections. In the long run, everything should look good onscreen, and you should not be automating your response to an image based on measurements and theory alone. Use your monitor and your perception of the image as the final call. If the image still seems as though it could be better, you may need to make a different type of correction. The following "Photoshop at Work" section provides an example that attempts to illustrate the choices behind clipping.

PHOTOSHOP AT WORK: FINESSE IN CLIPPING A TAIL

Page 21 of the PDF workbook (get the workbook on the companion Web site, www.ps6.com) has an image that was altered so that it would need correction (see Figure 21.27). Because of the nature of the original shot, which required high-speed film, the image is grainy and a little delicate when it comes to sweeping changes in tonality.

Figure 21.27
The graininess of the image may not be visible here in print, but the quality will be visible in magnification onscreen and/or after levels correction. The graininess might become very apparent if you are not careful with the corrections.

Although the initial Levels reading (see Figure 21.28) might suggest that you should just cut the highlight and shadow tails completely, the grainy nature of the film may cause the image to break up a little (in particular, you will want to watch the shadow under the wing). The visual effect of this may be more pronounced depending on the sensitivity of your monitor, color settings, and so on. In fact, what you see may be inaccurate when it comes to the representation in print. You need to meter the correction to your purpose, and approach this according to your workflow and understanding of your equipment.

→ For more information on establishing color settings for your workflow, **see** "ICC Profiles and Color Management," **p. 420**.

It may be best with this image to use fancier techniques (layering, blending, despeckling, and so on), but for this exercise, simply open the image and use the sliders to achieve the best image in appearance without using other techniques. The settings I arrived at (which may be different than yours) can be found in my answer box on the PDF page. Simply copy the gray box to its own image, open the levels, and click the Auto button. My answer will appear. The final image should appear something like what's shown in Figure 21.29, with increased contrast and improved separation. Additional attention to details and smoothing can yield even better results.

Figure 21.28
The tail to the right (highlights) and the space to the left (shadows) would most often be cropped away by setting the sliders as shown. However, this image may require finer adjustment because of the image quality.

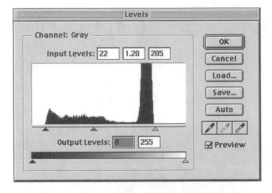

Figure 21.29
The straight Levels correction yields a rather harsh correction, perhaps a little too dark and insensitive to the image. Going a little softer with the Levels correction in this case yields the result to the right, which can still be improved, but leaves more to work with and a better result.

CHAPTER 22

COLOR CORRECTIONS

In this chapter

BASICS OF COLOR CORRECTION

Color correction is simply making changes to the color in an image. Generally, this is done to improve the perception of color in the image. Correction can be necessitated by weakness in the capture (for example, poor film exposure or a poorly executed scan), poor lighting conditions, or a simple desire to change the color to match a color scheme, hue, or so forth. Most often, color correction will be done in an attempt to make the color as realistic as possible.

The same techniques used in basic tonal correction are used for color correction. However, because there are additional channels to consider in a color image, the interplay in the corrections and manipulating the tools for the corrections themselves become somewhat more complex. For example, mode shifts might be necessary to accomplish your goals in correcting a color image for CMYK conversion. In extreme cases, it might be necessary to rebuild, re-create, or alter an image to fix the problems. Gauge the amount of work to the relative importance of the image.

Generally, you will want to use RGB for color corrections. This is not an absolute, and, in fact, there are certain advantages to correcting in other modes. RGB simply has the easiest, most intuitive means of correction in a broad color space. Although it may require shifting color modes, RGB will generally be the color mode of choice for correction. Lab will be discussed in the context of changing specific color without affecting tones. CMYK is important to color correction in two ways: as an input and an output mode. First, scanning into CMYK as a means to get color close to what you can output will often save you from complex corrections and abundant frustrations. Second, you must make final image corrections to images going to print in CMYK so that they can attain their best performance. Corrections should move from the general to the more specific.

This section explains how to adapt black-and-white correction techniques to correcting color images and expands on the tools that are specific to color corrections.

Note

By "scanning into CMYK," I mean using the direct conversion created by a higher-level scanner whose conversion you can trust. Scanners that do not retain a high level of quality in CMYK conversion generally will not claim to be able to do it.

SIMPLIFIED COLOR CORRECTION TECHNIQUES

Even though there are more variations and possibilities, the actual basic procedure for correcting color is very similar to correcting black and white.

Use the following steps to make corrections for your color images. Again, these are guidelines to use and can be altered as you gain confidence and a style of your own.

1. Open the image you want to correct and switch the image to RGB color mode if it is not RGB already.

2. Crop the image.

3. Make general dust corrections to the image.

→ For more information on dust correction, **see** "Removing Dust from an Image," **p. 580**.

4. Save the image. This is a good spot to save the image in a clean version. If you have to return to the beginning of the corrections (for example, because of a crash or you want to take a different approach to the corrections), you won't have to do the basics (Steps 1 to 3) all over.

5. Evaluate the image using visual inspection, Histograms, and the Eyedropper. Pay specific attention to the gray values and skin tones (if any) because these can be used to get a general sense of color. Place sampler anchors with the Color Sampler at points that you consider important for the image correction.

→ For more information on evaluating the image with the Histogram and Eyedropper, **see** "Measuring the Need for Color Correction," **p. 433**.

Tip

From here on out in the color correction, check Color Sampler readings frequently in the Info palette to see where your corrections are headed. If color seems to get worse or move from target values, consider returning to the previous step and trying a different application of the tools. Things may get worse before they get better, and you might just keep going in your correction if you know that later steps will correct a problem that seems to arise. You can always step back to an earlier state using Histories.

6. Make Levels corrections for each channel to extend the dynamic range of the image. This should correct most of your color cast and strengthen contrast. Be careful not to remove desired color casts.

→ If you're not familiar with doing Levels corrections, **see** "Corrections with Levels," **p. 447**.

7. Consider the overall brightness contrast of the image. Make brightness corrections with Levels, Curves, and Unsharp Mask.

→ For more information on controlling tone with Levels and Curves, **see** "Basic Tonal Correction: Channels and Grayscale Images," **p. 445**.

→ For more information on working with local contrast using the Unsharp Mask filter, **see** "Sharpening with Unsharp Mask," **p. 618**.

8. Use Color Balance, Channel Mixer, and Variations to do general visual color corrections.

→ For more information on using color correction tools, **see** "Basic Color Correction," **p. 468**.

Note

By this point, most of the color correction should be complete. Steps 8 to 10 and 12 consider issues that mostly apply to CMYK. Be sure to measure and to have good reason for making any of the more specific corrections that follow. You may want to save a copy of the image at this point before continuing.

9. Employ Curves after completing global corrections to alter specific tonal ranges that do not improve with general corrections. Focus on skin tones and grays, which are visual anchors. Correct using selections if necessary.

→ For more information on correcting for skin tones, **see** "Correcting Skin Tones," **p. 475**.

10. For CMYK Images: If switching to CMYK, check the CMYK preview to define elements that might reproduce better in other colors and consider changing the color of the elements. This may require selection and maybe even a switch to Lab mode.

> **Tip**
>
> If you switch from CMYK to RGB to make corrections, it is probable that color will most likely remain CMYK-compatible even after corrections. It is good, however, to check for color compatibility before blindly shifting over to CMYK.

→ For more information on Selections, **see** "Using Basic Selection Tools," **p. 95**.

→ For more information on making selective color corrections, **see** "Layering and Selective Corrections," **p. 479**.

→ For more information on reasons for working with Lab mode in corrections, **see** "Choosing an Image Mode," **p. 309** and "Converting an Image from RGB to CMYK," **p. 506**.

11. For CMYK images: Save the image and make a conversion to CMYK. Save as a separate image so that you can go back for additional corrections.

12. For CMYK images: Adjust black in CMYK for better contrast and tonal range.

13. Use Unsharp Mask to define an image if desired or necessary. Consider sharpening individual channels to reduce or eliminate any halo effects.

14. Set black and white points.

→ For more information on working with and setting black-and-white points, **see** "Setting White Points," **p. 558**.

The reason for proceeding in this order is to go from broader changes to the more specific. The further you go on through the corrections, the less drastically the changes should affect the entire image. Weight is given to corrections for print because getting good color in print is tricky due to the limited dynamic range.

This step by step is a simplification of the broader process, which can actually be very involved. The following sections explain some of the finer points and details, which have not been fully discussed here.

BASIC COLOR CORRECTION

You can take some very simple steps to go a long way toward great color using the tonal correction techniques described in "Corrections with Levels" in Chapter 21. The basic step of employing tonal correction techniques will not correct color perfectly for every image but can often perform near miracles in a few minutes, making a seemingly hopeless image spring back to life. Several other tools will probably be necessary to fine-tune your corrections, but the Levels can solve most of the basic problems quickly. Simple RGB Levels corrections are the easiest way to get decent color fast. You can make this type of correction almost without checking the image visually first (although it is always a good idea to make a visual check of any image you are correcting). The exceptions to going ahead with Levels corrections are images that you know have color casts, such as sunset or sunrise pictures where there will be a decided and necessary color shift. Doing Levels correction to images with desired color casts will probably ruin tone and color. In some cases, it performs some rather unexpected and miraculous retrievals. For example, the Levels technique corrects quite nicely for fluorescent and most other man-made lighting. It is really a mistake not to apply the Levels correction technique to every color image and see what happens. If you don't like the results, simply close the Levels dialog box by clicking Cancel, which will return the image to what it looked like before you opened the Levels dialog box.

Note

Levels correction is so easy to do that it may seem like an accident or coincidence. It isn't. Adjusting the RGB levels as described balances the image because the three colors work together in a balanced fashion to produce what you see. The relationship in CMYK and Lab does not correlate as simply.

Use the following steps to do Levels color correction for any color image:

1. Open the image you want to correct.

2. Open the Levels dialog box by pressing (Cmd-L) [Ctrl+L].

3. Switch to the Red channel using either the pop-up menu or (Cmd-1) [Ctrl+1]).

4. Using the sliders, crop the Histogram. You might want to use the Eyedropper or Auto options to help you with this selection and correction. To do the correction manually, move the right and left slider in to the edge of the solid area that registers on the graph.

→ For more information on cropping Histograms, **see** "Corrections with Levels," **p. 447**.

5. Repeat Steps 2 and 3 for the Green (Cmd-2) [Ctrl+2] and Blue (Cmd-3) [Ctrl+3] channels.

6. Return to the composite RGB (Cmd-~) [Ctrl+~] to see whether the image seems to need lightening or darkening. Test by running the middle slider between 120 and 80, according to the slider value in the dialog box.

Tip

When in doubt about how light to go with an image, go lighter rather than darker—but don't go very far. A shift of more than 10 levels without certainty that you are making a positive correction is going too far. You have less of a chance of making an image too light (unless you are dealing with something very delicate such as a soft, high-key image) than of making it too dark. Dark print oversaturates and tends to get a little murky, and dark Web images are not often as lively as light ones. Lighter/brighter images are generally easier to see.

7. If everything looks okay, save the image. If additional correction is needed, continue to work on the image color using the other correction techniques that follow in this chapter.

Levels corrections should really need to be done only once per image. Be careful using this technique when encountering unusual Histograms, or images where one or two of the three colors seem extremely compressed (a lot of the image falls into a very short tonal/color range). Compression might suggest some intentional distortion (such as use of a filter by the photographer). It also might suggest that you have a bad scan. The more extreme the changes you make, the more chance you have to damage the image, so go a little at a time. Some experience doing color corrections helps you know what to do.

Correcting Level Histogram Tails

Tails on the Levels graph are handled pretty much the same way here as they are in black-and-white corrections. Correcting for a lengthy tail in any Histogram might produce poor results if you choose to cut off the tail completely. As a general rule, the longer the tail, the less you should be apt to cut off percentage-wise. Cut half or a quarter if the information in the channel seems compressed. If the information in the channel is very compressed, meet the tail only partway. If more than one channel has a tail, cut the tails by the same percentage (for example, if you cut 50% of one tail, cut 50% of the other tail). If all channels look very different, you will have to make a judgment call based on visual examination of the image.

➔ For more information on working with Level Histogram tails, **see** "Corrections with Levels," **p. 447**.

If only one channel has a tail, be more conservative—especially if the image has an apparent color cast you need to retain. Again, you always have the chance to go back and cut more.

If you lose important highlight or shadow detail, you can actually paint that back in from the original image scan or from a snapshot. Often the information you cut in a tail is more or less image noise. However, there are some images (such as wedding shots of the bride and groom) where the highlights and shadows in an image become both critical and hard to come by. The key is to watch the preview and evaluate the changes as they are being made (visually and with Color Sampler markers). Even if you choose OK, you always have a chance to go back using Undo or the Histories.

➔ For more information on painting back lost detail, **see** "Blending Back Lost Details," **p. 471** and "Creating with Image Histories," **p. 251**.

Caution

If changes you are making to the image seem extreme, they probably are, and you might be doing damage to the information in the image. Better to make more than one correction than to make one that is too strong and damages the image information.

You can make corrections similar to Levels corrections using the curves. Curves may have an advantage because you can correct specific color casts as well—all in one shot. However, unless you are extremely confident in the view of your images onscreen or your ability to use color samples, curves might end up causing more trouble than they solve. As long as the device used to collect the image information (scanner, digital camera, and so on) is not defective or prone to collecting bad image information, Levels can accomplish most basic correction tasks. In other words, if the device has a relatively linear behavior, the linear ability of levels should be a fairly even match in making the desired basic corrections. Basic rule of thumb: Use the Levels correction first, and then, if needed, use the Curves techniques.

→ For more information on making color corrections with Curves, **see** "Correcting Skin Tones," **p. 475**.

BLENDING BACK LOST DETAILS

One consequence of using Levels correction techniques may be loss of highlight or shadow detail. If you are gentle with your tail snipping, this should not often be a problem. However, if it becomes a problem, there are a number of ways to restore highlight and shadow detail while retaining the corrections you have made.

One simple solution for quickly re-creating a detail lost by cutting a tail is to use the power of Histories. You can spot paint the details back using the History brush. Switch to the History brush and click the Snapshot for the original. Create a new layer and paint the detail on the layer. This will allow you to blend with Modes, Opacity, and Blend If to achieve the effect you want.

→ For more information on using layers for corrections, **see** "Layering and Selective Corrections," **p. 479**.

CORRECTING COLOR CASTS

Color casts result in image flatness and unnatural or plain old bad color. The cast might be a result of poor image processing, varied lighting conditions (photos taken under fluorescent bulbs, for example), aging of the medium (such as paper yellowing), or any number of other natural and unnatural occurrences. Basic color correction often takes care of this. However, basic color correction might also remove intentional casts. The obvious premise here is to know what you want to correct before making the corrections.

Color casts and shifts (such as a color shift in a shadow transition) are often a little more complex than looking at a Histogram or doing a basic slider correction in Levels. Tools such as Variations, Channel Mixer, and Color Balance can help with such corrections by providing visual feedback and an easy interface.

Use the following steps to make general tonal corrections with the Variations, Color Balance, and Channel Mixer.

1. Open the image you plan to correct. It can be in RGB, CMYK, or Lab for these corrections—only the Channel Mixer is affected by the mode. If the final image will be for print, it is suggested that changes be made in CMYK mode.

2. Select Image, Adjust, Variations to open the Variations dialog box (see Figure 22.1). Depending on how large the image is, it might take a moment to display.

Figure 22.1
The Variations dialog box shows you an array of possible choices. Select the choice that looks the best by clicking it. Continue clicking until the best choice is in the center of the screen.

beetle © Seattle Support Group, www.ssgrp.com

3. When the dialog box appears, the default selections will be Medium Coarseness and Midtones. View the choices and simply select the variation you like best by clicking it.

> **Tip**
> Use the slider to your advantage in choosing the coarseness of Variations. The default is in the middle of the slider. It might be difficult to see a change there depending on the color mode and configuration of what you are working on. For example, if you use pure RGB colors (100% red, green, or blue), the midtones will not be affected by any changes in the slider, unless you work with highlights, shadows, or saturation. If the changes are not apparent, try increasing the coarseness on the slider. When you see a change, visually determine whether it is a positive one. Lower the coarseness level on the slider a notch or two before clicking the change and choosing OK. This will keep the changes in small increments, which is desirable.

4. Repeat Step 3 until optimal color is achieved visually.

5. Repeat Steps 3 and 4 for Highlights and Shadows.

> **Tip**
> If you have color-corrected the image using Levels, it is almost redundant to consider the saturation of the image unless you want to reduce it. With proper correction in the Levels, saturation should be fine.

6. Accept the changes and close the Variations dialog box by clicking OK.

7. Choose Image, Adjust, Color Balance to open the Color Balance dialog box (see Figure 22.2).

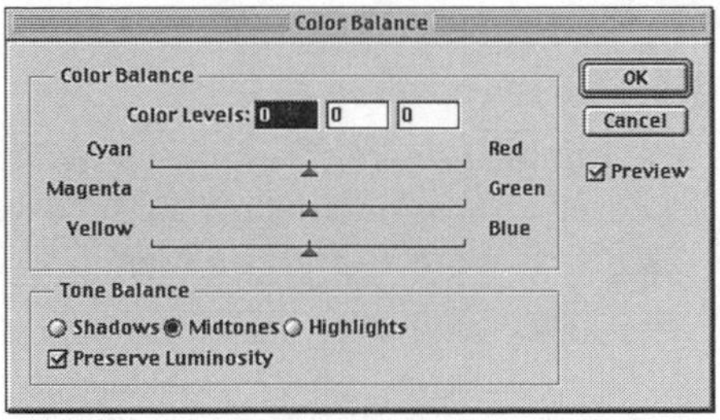

Figure 22.2
The Color Balance dialog box allows you to alter the balance of color between opposites using slider adjustment. This functions in a similar way to the variations, but uses the actual image as a singular preview and offers more flexible control of the Variations.

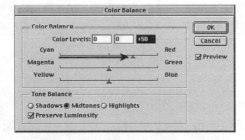

8. Starting with the Midtones checked, make a radical shift in the top slider (Cyan/Red). Slide from approximately –50 to +50 and watch the effect on the image. Like using the coarse variations, this gives you an idea as to whether a move with the slider makes a change that seems visually pleasing in the color of the image overall (see Figure 22.3). If so, consider the difference between the center (0) and the point you shifted to by moving the slider between those points (–50 to 0, or 0 to +50). Continue dividing the field in half with each successive swing of the slider until you arrive at the best choice (see Figure 22.4).

Figure 22.3
To test the possibilities, shift the slider 50 points in either direction to the left and right of center. If anything looks interesting, you can examine further.

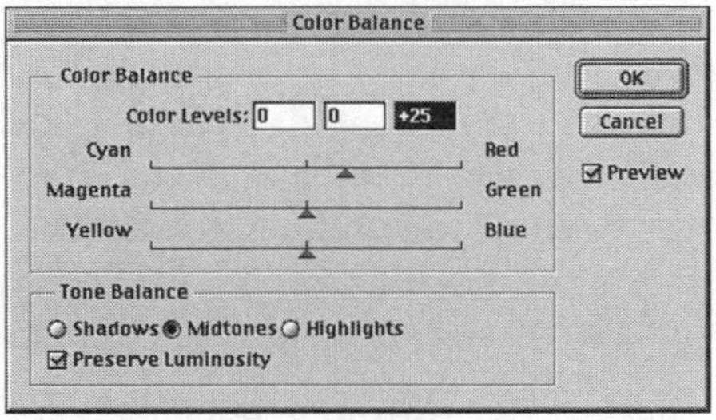

Figure 22.4
After determining that a change might have a positive effect, place the slider halfway between the points you have tested that look best. Continue moving the slider between the two best points to narrow the range and decide on the best position.

9. Repeat Step 8 for the Magenta/Green, Yellow/Blue sliders.

10. Repeat Steps 8 and 9 for Highlights and Shadows.

11. When all sliders have been set, click the Preserve Luminosity check box and compare the image with luminosity preserved or not. You might want to leave this checked or not checked as per visual inspection as this will affect different images differently according to the image type and changes you have made.

12. Click OK to apply the changes.

13. Open the Channel Mixer by selecting Image, Adjust, Channel Mixer (see Figure 22.5).

Figure 22.5
The Channel Mixer allows you to target a specific channel and redefine it based on other color channels or itself. This is very handy for fine-tuning CMYK colors.

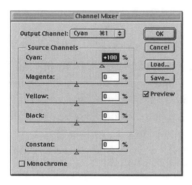

14. Identify tones and colors you find to be visually off and mix to alter casts. There are numerous combinations you can use with this tool. Generally, the changes you make are those you specifically identify through visual inspection.

→ For more information on working with the Color Mixer, **see** "Channel Mixer for Color Balance," **p. 475**.

15. When you are happy with the corrections, click OK to apply the change.

Variations, Color Balance, and Channel Mixer offer immediate visual confirmation of image corrections. Variations and Color Balance offer broad control over the entire image and effectively redistribute color levels in the Highlights, Midtones, and Shadows.

You can accomplish similar things in the curves, but the Variations, Color Balance, and Channel Mixer tools accomplish this much more quickly and intuitively. Some will argue that curves enable far more control, and they do, but in dealing with color shifts and casts—unless you are trying to create specific effects, or proceeding with extreme confidence in color fidelity—these tools will do most or all of what you need. Work with the curves for color correction only after you are very competent in correcting with these tools.

At the point where you have completed color correction using the Levels, Variations, Color Balance, and Channel Mixer, the image should be 95% correct. This does not mean that things get easier from here—only that the image should be correct for a variety of purposes. Spot-checking the white points, highlights, skin tones (or pastels if there are no skin tones), and black points completes the corrections.

⚠ *If you have made color corrections using all the techniques described previously and the image still looks bad, or has gotten worse, see "When Color Correction Goes Nowhere" in the Troubleshooting section at the end of this chapter.*

CHANNEL MIXER FOR COLOR BALANCE

Channel Mixer offers a rather unique opportunity to balance colors based on existing channel densities. Colors can be neutralized or strengthened in specific areas. Using the sliders you can reduce the effective color in a channel, or strengthen opposite colors using a channel as a key. Alterations can be targeted by sampling areas of the image where you want to change the color. You can adjust color saturation in proportion to other colors in the same area of the image.

Although experimentation can work with the Color Mixer, try to determine what you want to change before considering every possible configuration, or you will be at it for a very long time. Essentially, this is a more complex tool for color balance. You may want to add or subtract individual colors, or make more complex mixtures between colors. The advantage to this adjustment is it allows you to make tone and color-based adjustments. What you want to do is add or subtract color by working with the color and its opposites. Add opposites to neutralize the color; subtract opposites to purify the color. Adjustments can be used to lighten or darken the color areas as well.

For example, if there is too much red in a CMYK skin tone, adding magenta and yellow (effectively red) to the yellow and cyan (effectively green, or the opposite of red) can help boost the opposite color in proportion to the red. Boosting the opposite will help neutralize the color. In RGB, if there is a bad transition in the shadow where red surges in density, you can increase green and blue in those areas by mixing the red channel into the blue and green by a few percentage points. This will blend and neutralize the red.

CORRECTING SKIN TONES

Proper correction of skin tones is a relatively hot point in corrections because skin tones provide a strong marker as to what people perceive as realistic. Most people can tell right away if skin color is off because it is so familiar. Because of this, it is imperative that the skin tones fall within a reasonable range so that they look realistic. However, and at the same time, they are nearly impossible to measure because tones run from the brightest highlight to the darkest shadow, and hue is all over the map. For some reason, and probably because it is more an art than science, this part of color correction is kept a mystery.

In any case, there are methods you can use to get natural skin tones. What's the solution? Don't correct them. In fact, correct everything else and just give them a quick look to be sure they appear normal and fall within a range of possibilities—then be on your way.

To correct everything else, your best reference points are grays. This is because they are easy to measure; they will have even amounts of red, green, and blue in RGB (as measured with the Sampler set to RGB). If you can find 25% (64,64,64), 50% (128,128,128), and 75% (192,192,192) gray references in your images, and set accurate white and black points, your images will balance nicely. It usually isn't too easy to find these references unless you place them right in your image—which you can do using a reference card. If you have an image in which you couldn't place a reference to correct to, look closely for something that should be a flat shade of gray, such as steel, something silver, asphalt—anything that should be flat gray can be useful for evaluation.

EVALUATING SKIN TONE VALUES

Like calibrating your monitor, the 25%, 50%, and 75% grays (or really any reference for which you know the color values) can serve as a reference in correcting images. You can complete the color correction by simply evening up the levels of Red, Green, and Blue for the point selected to be the gray. To do this, just mark your reference tones with Color Samplers, and then open the curves and make adjustments with the RGB (CMY) curves to even out the colors.

Use the following steps to color correct your image with Curves:

1. Open the image in which you intend to correct skin tones.

2. Select the Eyedropper tool and double-click it to open the Options palette. Set the appropriate sampling area. A lower dpi might require a lower sample size, but generally, sampling skin tones with the broadest setting is best.

3. Make samples in medium skin tone areas. Medium might be defined as somewhere visually where the tonality seems to be in the midrange, or halfway between the lightest and darkest skin elements—not necessarily the skin shadows or highlights.

4. Note any obvious difference between the measured skin tones and the desired range. The measurements should fall approximately within a particular zone (see the "Probable Skin Tone Values" sidebar). A variation might suggest a necessary color correction. However, make no corrections at this point.

Probable Skin Tone Values

Skin tones for various ethnic groups are hard to determine concretely. Tans, skin conditions, lighting, and relative tone might throw off your color correction. However, after making a general Levels color correction to remove color casts, the following generalities usually apply. For Caucasian skin, magenta is equal or up to 10% less than yellow; cyan is 15%–25% of the magenta value. Asian skin might have a yellow content between 15% and 30% more than Caucasian measurements (with yellow roughly equal to 20% more than magenta); cyan 10%–50% of the magenta. Black skin has a higher level of magenta than Caucasian skin (between 10%–20% more than the yellow), and cyan runs between about 60%–100% of the magenta.

---

5. Using the Color Sampler, set markers in one or two areas that represent general skin tone.

6. Look for a solid gray somewhere in the image. Gray tones vary, but not by much. Depending on the color mode you are working in, the measurements for a flat gray target are different. RGB grays have equal RGB values; in CMYK, grays, yellow, and magenta should match, and the cyan should be within a few points of the same percentage, preferably on the high side (plus 5%–10% of magenta).

7. If a discrepancy exists between your measured values for the grays and the preferred levels, and the skin tone shows a cast of similar proportion, make corrections in the curves to correct the values. Otherwise, correct for the grays as per values noted in Step 6.

→ For more information on how to make the curve corrections, **see** "Curve Corrections Using Gray Values," **p. 477**.

In this case, knowing the approximate skin tone value that you want to achieve (see the "Probable Skin Tone Values" sidebar earlier in this section) helps get you in the ballpark; registering the skin tones against the grays confirms the need for correction. When you know the approximate values you want and can confirm the discrepancies, correction is easy. Be sure, however, that correction doesn't visually throw an image out of whack. Always inspect the results of changes on a calibrated monitor.

The fact is that it might be far better and easier to correct the grays than to attempt to figure out the nuances and variations in the skin tones. Although it is nice to know acceptable limits in skin tone and ranges for that, it is far less practical to try to practice correction from that standpoint. In fact, unless you want to match an original and have access to some expensive spot-checking color devices, correcting for gray might be your only practical color correction tool for making skin tones look right.

CURVE CORRECTIONS USING GRAY VALUES

When you are making corrections to grays, the curves offer the best option because of their flexibility. Curves are easily adjusted to an exact point. Because of this level of control, your choice in selection of a gray reference is very important to the outcome. For example, if you choose a gray that in reality is supposed to be slightly green and you don't allow for that in the correction, your final corrections will end up somewhat warm. Again, visual inspection and the numbers have to work hand in hand to achieve the best result.

Use the following steps to adjust the curves according to your gray selection.

1. Measure the gray. For this example, let's say we found a steel pole in the image background with a measured value of 114,122,129 in RGB.

Note

These corrections can be done in RGB or CMY, but the CMY will have to discount the K value for the calculations, and the calculations get quite a bit more complicated. Because of this, CMY corrections may not be as accurate, and the two methods will lead to different conclusions.

2. Average the gray value (add the RGB values and divide by 3). Total of the values: 114 + 122 + 129 = 365. The average value: 365/3 = 122.

3. Determine the target values for a flat gray. Because we are using RGB, this is simply 122,122,122.

4. Open the Curves dialog box and go to one of the color channels. Click the curve to create a point, and then enter the current value (Input field) and target value (Output field) (see Figure 22.6).

Figure 22.6
For the red value in the example, you want to shift the point on the curve that is currently at 114 to 122. These values can be entered directly into the input/output fields in the Curves dialog box to quickly set the point.

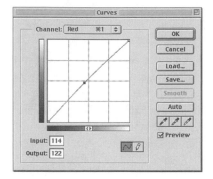

5. Repeat Step 4 for each of the color channels.

When you are done, the pixel you have chosen will be corrected to a flat gray, and this correction will affect colors for the entire image. If you measure several gray key spots, make the corrections all at once by placing as many points on each curve as you have key spots. Do this instead of returning to the process several times. This will make sure that you are changing the measured spots relative to one another; if you change the values sequentially on separate curves, the changes will occur independently and simply won't work right. If measuring one level of gray, try to make it a midtone; if measuring two, use a lighter and darker gray; if measuring three, use quartertones. The more evenly you divide the gray levels used for the correction, the better. The more levels of gray you correct for, the more accurately your correction will appear (see Figure 22.7).

Figure 22.7
The corrections for this image are being made based on a gray card that was inserted to the fringe area of the image. Measurements taken from the card in the image allow quartertones to be corrected easily.

Because there should be 5%–10% more cyan than magenta in CMYK grays, the math becomes a little sticky. You can work with the CMY directly, but it is probably easier just to make adjustments based on the RGB measurements. To make corrections using RGB values on a CMYK image, switch the Color Sample display by clicking the Eyedropper on the Info palette (see Figure 22.8). This will open the Eyedropper display menu.

Figure 22.8
The pop-up menu for the Color Sampler menu on the Info palette will allow you to switch the color space in which the sampled colors will be displayed.

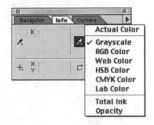

When you have determined the RGB target values, you will have to convert those numbers to CMY, or convert the whole image to RGB to apply them. The reason for that is the Curves will appear for you only in the current mode. Although you could adjust the curves manually, watch the values on the Info palette until they match the target values.

Tip

You can convert RGB and CMY values by opening the color picker and entering the known values in the CMY or RGB fields. Photoshop will calculate the equivalent in the other fields for each of the other potential color values.

LAYERING AND SELECTIVE CORRECTIONS

Using layers to perform correction gives you an opportunity to compare before and after applications of tools and isolate image changes, and it creates the opportunity to apply a variety of tools together. Essentially, you use layers to stack your corrections. There is a whole range of potential from spot corrections to applying color tool effects as layers that can be removed and reordered at will. The best thing about layered corrections is that you can make the corrections and changes without altering the original image information, which remains untouched below the added layers.

Layered and selective corrections can be used to alter individual colors and image areas without affecting color in other portions of the image. To pick on an old foe of many casual photographers, say you correct an image you took at a party. The lights were dim and the shot was great. Your initial corrections give you great skin tones and color and everything looks very natural, except for the fact that everyone in the picture has redeye. In this case you don't want to apply a change across the whole image to attempt to correct the redeye.

Redeye

Redeye is a reflection on the back of the subject's eye. This occurs almost exclusively with a flash in dark situations where the subject's pupils have had the chance to dilate. When the flash goes off, it enters the eye and reflects off the blood vessels in the back of the eye, and the redness is captured on film (or digitally). This effect can be reduced with preflash, which helps constrict the pupils before the shutter kicks open, and placing the flash off-axis from the camera and lens.

To correct the redeye, select the affected area and copy it into its own layer. When it is in its own layer, you will have more options to play with the isolated portion of the image until you find a solution. The solution can be inverting the layer and using color mode and opacity to average out a change, or it can be to colorize the layer or make a change in the selected information using correction techniques. Yet a third possibility would be application of another layer of correction above the current layer that you have just selected and moved. In that last case, layers can be grouped so that the effect of an added layer applies only to the lower layer it is grouped with. If necessary, you can even separate a layer into a new document so that you can change color modes and apply a color change technique without converting the entire image. This will save the rest of the image from an unnecessary color change and potential distortion and remapping of color information.

Note

This application for redeye is a simple application. You can use Layers corrections to select out multiple portions of the image to isolate and work on selectively.

The abilities presented by layering corrections offer unlimited potential in making spot corrections and adjustments for an image. They also offer opportunity to make seamless and integrated color overhauls where you can, for example, replace an unprintable color in Lab without altering anything but that color, and leaving the current CMYK intact.

→ For a little practice with spot correction, **see** the "Photoshop at Work" section, **p. 481.**

TROUBLESHOOTING

WHEN COLOR CORRECTION GOES NOWHERE

I have used the Levels, Color Balance, Channel Mixer, and Variations to attempt to correct an image I am working on and the image actually got worse. Where do I go from here?

If the image doesn't improve using the techniques described, there can be a number of things going wrong—from poor implementation of techniques to applying great technique to a poor image. I would suspect the latter more often than the former.

To check, reopen the original image (or hopefully the version saved in Step 4 of the steps at the beginning of this chapter) and apply Auto Levels (Shift-Cmd-L) [Shift+Ctrl+L]. If you see more improvement in that than in the corrections you made, you will need to review your technique, and refer to Chapters 21 and 22.

If the Auto Correction and your correction both produce absolutely horrible results, check to see that you are making corrections in RGB and not CMYK, Lab, or Indexed Color. If the corrections are being made in one of the other color modes, shift to RGB. If the image is in RGB, consider using another image.

If the image is not as good as your final corrections (and it shouldn't be), you might want to continue with the correction. Go through another round of tool use as described in this chapter. Try to evaluate what you believe needs to be improved. If you have not yet used the curves to make a final correction, try using those.

→ For more information on evaluating what to do in color corrections, **see** "Measuring the Need for Color Correction," **p. 433**.

If the correction seems nearly the same as the Auto correction, and there is no image damage causing your dissatisfaction (you might evaluate damage visually or using Histograms), approach the correction again and in a somewhat different manner. Set out to color correct the image from scratch and try tools that you did not use in the first set of corrections; for example, if you used Color Balance and not the Channel Mixer or Variations, use the Channel Mixer and Variations this time. If you get the same, or nearly the same unacceptable results, chances are there is something wrong with the image itself.

If the image is obviously bad as a result of damage (missing image information, bad scanning, bad initial lighting, or any of a number of other problems mentioned throughout this book), consider rescanning the image.

Note

Just because a service scanned your image does not mean that the scan is perfect. If you are suspicious of a scan that you had done, and don't believe it matches the quality of the original it was scanned from, have the service redo the work. Point out the problems to them with specific comparisons of the differences in the original and the result. In some cases the equipment may have malfunctioned or the operator may have made a mistake.

If your dissatisfaction has to do with the image simply looking bad by the time the correction is done, it is probably either a bad image or one slightly above your current ability and experience with correction. Put the image aside and use another. It may be good to save the image in a special place so you can come back to it for practice as you gain more experience in color corrections.

PHOTOSHOP AT WORK: MAKING A SELECTIVE COLOR CORRECTION

This exercise will help you get your hands dirty in color correction. The clown image seen in Figure 22.9 has colors that are impossible to reproduce in CMYK. The costume has vivid reds, a deep blue, and a pistachio-flavored green that are all out of gamut. The image can be corrected using Levels and Curve color correction, but that still leaves much of the image out of gamut for CMYK. If the image were converted to CMYK without further alterations, that would leave colors that would be drab.

Figure 22.9
This clown's suit is brightly colored in the RGB representation, but the color conversion to CMYK kills the gaiety of the color. To preserve some of the intent of the color, a complete shift to colors that will appear more vibrant in CMYK might be a good idea—even if these are not the original colors of the suit.

© PhotoSphere Images, Ltd., photosphere.com

A possible solution is to do the general corrections and then select the clown's suit and move it to its own layer (see Figure 22.10). You can do that, or even select each of the colors one at a time to move them to their own layers. This allows you to work on the colors independently, using different methods and modes as you go.

Tip

Many of your color changes are best accomplished using Lab mode and a variety of layering techniques, including splitting out the layer into its own document, and masking layers separately for particular color areas and different layer modes.

Figure 22.10
This mask can be used as a Layer Mask to limit the effect of color changes made with newly created layers. In this case the effects would be limited to correcting the red in the clown's suit.

Tip

It is often best to consider colors in groups, according to original color. As mentioned earlier, changing the color of an entire bathing suit rather than a few out-of-gamut colors may actually retain better color harmony (depending on the colors selected for the suit). In the case of the clown, altering the colors together can potentially work better to keep the harmony of color as originally designed.

The image seen in this example is included in the PDF workbook on page 22 (find the workbook on the Web site—www.ps6.com). I have included my selections and corrections to the image for you to look at, but best to try out the techniques on your own. Start with the uncorrected image by highlighting Original Layer, and duplicate the layer to a new document. Then, follow these steps:

1. Evaluate the image color, considering color harmony and Color Proof the image in CMYK. This may be a good time to set up additional views if you plan on using them. Two views at this point would work well: one a view of the image with no review, and the other with your working CMYK.

2. Crop the image and clean up any dust or damage.

3. Make an initial color correction using Levels.

4. Make other general color corrections.

5. Consider the color result and out-of-gamut colors by switching on and off the Gamut Warning (Shift-Cmd-Y) [Shift+Ctrl+Y]. Compare the RGB to the CMYK result using Color Proof and note the areas of drastic change in color (if you already have two views of the image, there will be no need to create a new view or apply the Color Proof as it will already be visible onscreen).

6. Decide on a course of action based on the evaluation in Step 5. This will probably require making various selections of color areas and application of a broad variety of techniques.

If you are not sure what to do at this point, take a look at the image provided in the PDF workbook and note my solutions. You might want to borrow one or two of the alpha selections to speed up the process and get right to the corrections. However, this is a great opportunity to practice selection skills. Your result might end up quite a bit different than mine, depending on what you choose as a color scheme. The important thing is that you understand how to do the corrections and that the end result is satisfying.

CHAPTER 23

COLOR CONVERSIONS

In this chapter

OVERVIEW OF COLOR MODE CHANGE

The basics of color mode changes are fairly simple: You choose from a list on the Color Mode menu (Image, Mode) and Photoshop does the rest. However, some changes can damage image information. For example, changing from RGB to CMYK or Indexed Color will limit the colors in an image and will throw out digital information. There are ways to make better and worse conversions, and concepts to use before, during, and after conversions to be sure you get the best possible results. These more complicated color changes and conversions are covered throughout this chapter.

Often conversion is a necessary evil in saving a final file for use. The problem with color conversions is that all color modes are not alike—otherwise, there would be only one type of conversion. Although Photoshop does an excellent job of automating most of the conversions, mathematical conversion cannot account for artistic choice and realistic qualities of an image. RGB images can simply reproduce more colors than CMYK, and Indexed Color images are severely limited by a maximum of 256 colors for the sake of keeping file sizes small. Even the change from color to grayscale is not an automatic shift. Before you switch to grayscale, compensation for tonality and color can help make the image as clear to the eye in black and white as it was in color. In short, a conversion requires not just selecting a color mode, but rethinking all the parts of an image and appearance to get the most out of the conversion. The more extreme the shifts in color mode are, the more likely it is to produce undesirable results. With a clear understanding of the process, you can avert or offset many of these problems, and use the conversion as an opportunity to improve the image.

For example, you just can't get a bold rich blue in CMYK. This is not to suggest that you throw up your hands every time you see a blue in an RGB image that you want to use in CMYK, but you need to be aware that there are limitations to what you can achieve. The techniques and tools in this chapter will help you achieve the best possible or most pleasing results.

Note

Conversions to Lab are not addressed in this chapter because Lab is the broadest of the color spaces. It should absorb colors from any other space readily. However, conversion of an image from any space to another is a conversion. Just because the appearance of the image essentially remains unchanged does not mean there is no change in the image information. Each change adds onto the alteration and changes more of the original image information. Make as few conversions as possible and try to select your color modes carefully to avoid extending your conversion chain. The fewer conversions of any sort, the better.

CONVERTING AN IMAGE FROM COLOR TO GRAYSCALE

There are tricks to getting better tonality in grayscale images than what the automated conversion produces. These advantages cannot be considered by Photoshop when you select the Grayscale mode to convert a color image; you have to make the considerations yourself. A good conversion will keep the elements of a color photo intact after conversion to grayscale, and it will attempt to improve them for grayscale representation. This might require essentially ruining the color to get a better grayscale conversion result. Actually, it is ignoring the color to get a better conversion, not ruining it; when you are converting from color to grayscale, the colors themselves no longer matter.

Knowing what to look for and where to look will give you more options for the conversion. With more options, you can trick the image into looking like you think it should. Although you will often get a fairly good end result by just converting to grayscale, the tips and techniques in this chapter prove very useful in difficult conversions. Many of these same techniques can be applied to individual channels in doing complex color work as well. As each separate channel in a color image is essentially grayscale, understanding and mastering this type of grayscale adjustment is invaluable for color control.

TONALITY IN CONVERSIONS FROM COLOR

Grayscale success depends on having contrast in an image—contrast in light and dark rather than just contrasting colors. If an image doesn't have contrast, the tones will stay flat and a relatively colorful scene (for example, a field of multicolored flowers) might lack character or dramatics when switched to grayscale, especially if the color contrast is high while the tonal contrast is negligible. Taking precautions before you convert will result in better, more dramatic grayscale images. This usually means making color and contrast corrections before switching the color mode to Grayscale, and borrowing the best attributes you have to work with in different color plates. The idea is to look at the possibilities, and steal, or exchange, the parts that will look best—always keeping the endpoint of the grayscale result in mind.

CONVERSIONS FROM DIFFERENT COLOR MODES

Color mode will have an effect on switches to Grayscale as well. Sometimes the unexpected will happen. In Figures 23.1 to 23.4, what should be a simple conversion from color to Grayscale mode is not: Conversion from Lab to Grayscale, Lab to RGB to Grayscale, and Lab to CMYK to Grayscale lose information from the original image by merging colors which have the same tone in those color spaces. The result is that the gray representation of the RGB or Lab image shows at least two distinct colors as exactly the same gray.

PART

VI

CH

23

Figure 23.1
In converting this simple image to Grayscale mode, you would expect that each of the squares would remain visible. The L, a, and b channels that make up the image color are shown here as evidence of color content and difference.

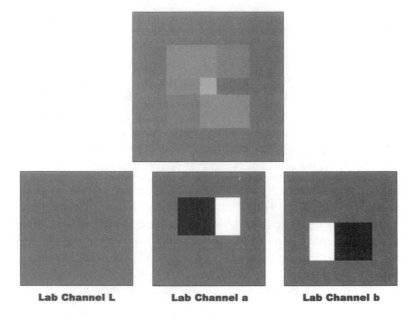

Lab Channel L   Lab Channel a   Lab Channel b

Figure 23.2
Changing the image in Figure 23.1 to Grayscale mode directly from Lab flattens the image completely, as the conversion considers only the L-channel information.

Obviously, the simplest conversions don't work in retaining the integrity of what is apparent in the color in this case, and it is good reason to look for another solution. Although the CMYK conversion is okay, it is dark and there are yet a number of other possibilities to consider, which might yield a better result. These possibilities include

- Manual manipulations (selecting colors and using those selections to change tones)
- Employing other, more complex conversion routes
- Examining image information through the channels (rather than color)

- Using custom calculations
- Using filters to create the result

Figure 23.3
Converting to RGB from Lab before the conversion to Grayscale produces slightly better results, but some color information still blends together as the gray result.

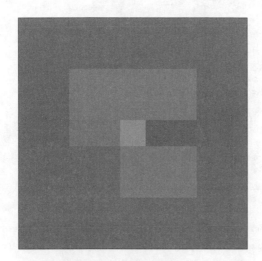

Figure 23.4
Converting to CMYK from Lab before the change to Grayscale mode seems to produce the most likely match. Here it is shown with no correction (left) and simple Levels correction (right).

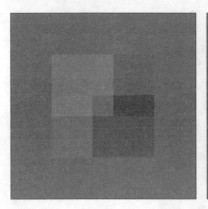

As tone is the key to the result here, looking at the channels (which are grayscale representations of color) can prove most helpful. Channels can be looked at alone or in various combinations. Employing Calculations after a switch to RGB offers many options (see Figure 23.5).

No matter what initial conversion you use, you still have the opportunity to make changes and improvements to the image after making the change to grayscale. Taking full advantage of the extra information in the color image first will help get the best results. The test image in the previous example is abstract, so there are a lot of possibilities that will not be available to a recognizable image.

Figure 23.5
The left is the result of Screen with Red as Source 1, Green as Source 2, and Blue as a Mask. The center was a result of the same except with Difference applied. The right is a result of the left image with a Levels correction.

Figure 23.6 looks drab when switched to Grayscale from RGB with no corrections. Several easy changes can make the end result quite a bit more dramatic. There are many possibilities.

Figure 23.6
This image has been converted to Grayscale from RGB with no correction. As a low-contrast, medium-key image, it appears flat and a bit muddy. It can be improved by properly preparing for the switch to Grayscale and considering other options for the conversion.

Use the following steps to evaluate the possibilities in making a conversion from RGB mode to Grayscale mode:

1. Change the image to RGB if it is not already in that color mode.
2. Make basic color corrections with Levels as outlined in the last chapter.

3. Take advantage of existing color to make obvious and easy color selections, and save these selections as channels. For the sample image, a quick selection of the sky seems appropriate (see Figure 23.7). Not only will this give you control over the sky area at any point in the conversion, but an easy inversion of the selection will let you work specifically on the lizard and tree—before and/or after the conversion. This might come in handy, for example, if you want to sharpen the image without changing the appearance of the sky, vary the sky tone, and so on.

Figure 23.7
Selection of the sky in the color image is easy because nothing else is blue. This would be much harder to accomplish in Grayscale.

Note

The reason you want to make selections at this point is that the selection will carry to other steps in the process. As you will be creating different snapshots by different processes to compare versions of the same image, each version might benefit from adjustments you make that require the same selection. If you make the selection before moving on in the process, the selection will be available to all the versions you create, rather than having to re-create the selection for each version you want to apply it to.

You might not know what will come in handy until later in the process, but some selections (as in the example) might be obvious choices. If you wait to make this selection, you will have to go back to the RGB, make the selection from the color version of the image, save it as an alpha, and then copy the alpha to the image versions that need it—which is a lot more work and bother. Your other choice is to start over. If you create a new alpha and apply it to image versions, be sure to retake snapshots you are using for the comparisons to save the changes.

4. Take a snapshot of the color before you proceed by selecting Histories, New Snapshot. With a snapshot, you can return to this image state to make comparisons, additional selections, and changes, or just revert to examine other possibilities. The name for this first snapshot will default to Snapshot 1.

→ For more information on Snapshots, **see** "Creating with Image Histories," **p. 251**.

5. Preview the grayscale change by converting to the Grayscale mode. The basic levels correction might have made a significant difference and might be enough to achieve what you want (see Figure 23.8). If so, skip to saving the image (Step 16). However, it is probably best to explore other possibilities by continuing with the following steps.

Figure 23.8
Basic levels correction to the color image before converting to Grayscale mode does a lot to improve the tonal range of this image, and it is a good place to start. However, there might still be better options for the conversion.

6. Take a snapshot of the grayscale image created by the conversion in Step 5. This will allow you to view and compare the simple grayscale to other image states as you create them. The name for this snapshot will default to Snapshot 2.

Tip

To help viewing, be sure to switch off the Color Channels in Color option in the Display & Cursors Preferences (Edit, Preferences, Display & Cursors). With that box unchecked, the channels will appear onscreen in grayscale rather than the color of the channel.

Note

You can rename the snapshots as you go to identify them. Just double-click the snapshot and the Rename Snapshot dialog box will appear (see Figure 23.9).

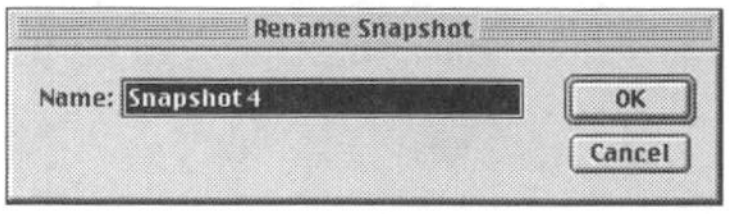

Figure 23.9
Double-clicking a snapshot in the Snapshots palette brings up the Rename Snapshot dialog box.

Rename Snapshot

Name: Snapshot 4   OK   Cancel

7. Switch back to RGB color from Grayscale by clicking the snapshot created in Step 4 (Snapshot 1).

Tip

> If you were to change the color mode again rather than use the Histories to backtrack, your image would appear as grayscale with three even channels. The snapshot will retain the Levels corrections made in Step 2. When you want to revert, always use Histories or Snapshots. This will save time and prevent potential changes in the image information because of multiple conversions.

8. Check the red, green, and blue channels for the image by clicking each in turn in the Channels palette. Each will be in grayscale and will appear as different representations of the image. If any are interesting representations, take Snapshots of each. Feel free to make Curve and Level corrections to the individual channels. For example, you might want to lighten or darken midtones, or change areas with selection.

Note

> At this point, don't even look at the color composite. It is meaningless. You are looking to improve the grayscale possibilities, and the color just doesn't matter.

9. Click the snapshots you have taken one at a time and compare the results. If there are any to eliminate, do so by highlighting the snapshot with a single click, and then either drag it to the trash or click the Delete button (see Figure 23.10). You might want to keep snapshots that have a good part or parts; these can be combined with other options sometimes to get the results you want.

Figure 23.10
Removing unnecessary Snapshots can free up memory. Trash the ones that aren't really an improvement or that don't offer a unique opportunity with the image.

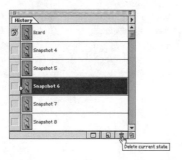

10. Switch to Lab mode and look at the lightness channel (the other channels will most probably be useless to you in the case of switching to Grayscale mode, although it doesn't take much time to take a look). Make any adjustments or corrections, and take a snapshot if this version appears to be an improvement or shows promise. This will often be one of the best representations of the image in grayscale.

The Role of CMYK in Grayscale Conversions

Individual CMYK channels tend to be far from representative of an image as you would like it to appear in grayscale when each is viewed alone. However, the channels might be useful in creating additional selections or for creative rather than representational purposes. On the off chance that they might offer some options, it is good to take a look at them, considering there is nothing to lose.

Note

There is an action on the Web site (http://www.ps6.com) called BW Channel Views that takes your original image and makes a gallery of the plates possible with RGB, CMYK, and Lab separations. This can create the possibilities to give you an overview without having to go through the tedious steps of creating all the possibilities yourself. It would be good to run this action on a small version of your file to save space and time, but it works with full-size images.

11. Switch back to RGB (using the History snapshot created in Step 4).

12. Select Image, Calculations, and do some experimentation with the channel that appears to have the most promise. There are a number of combinations (this can change depending on the available channels and if you select to use the mask or not). The possibilities are endless: If you open the image in several color modes, you can mix and match layers from different color modes and documents. Accept the calculations and take snapshots as you find interesting combinations.

→ For more information on the Calculations, **see** "Combining Selections," **p. 140**.

Note

A good suggestion is to name snapshots to help identify how you achieved them. For Calculations, I created the name using the image source, the channels (in order for Source 1 and 2 and the mask—if any) and the process, each separated by periods. For example, ORG.calc.rgbscreen would be the original image corrected with a calculation using red as Source 1, green as Source 2, and blue as a mask with the Screen mode setting.

Tip

You could run the Calculations Generator (an action described in Chapter 5 and available on the Web site at www.ps6.com) for Step 12, but it doesn't cover all the numerous possibilities—and covering all those possibilities will present many options that won't work for this type of conversion. Several options always seem most interesting to me. Try screening the red and green channel with the blue as a mask. Also, try screening the most interesting channel by itself. For example, use the green channel as both Source 1 and Source 2.

Channel Mixer

As an option, you could use the Channel Mixer to work with channel combinations in Step 12. Although it has fewer options and modes, it can also offer a different kind of control (see Figure 23.11), and might be less intimidating. For this type of correction, select the channel that seems most representative of the original from the Output Channel pop-up, and then click the Monochrome box. This will show you a grayscale representation of the channel you have shown in the Output Channel onscreen, and will preview the changes for you as you move the sliders.

Often I use the Channel Mixer after the Calculations to play with mixtures that seemed to have worked especially well. This allows you to work with similar combinations to build different results.

Figure 23.11
Channel Mixer is available for CMYK or RGB only. The Initial Output Channel pop-up will reflect the channels in the current color space (shown at left). Checking the Monochrome box will change the Output Channel to and change the response in the image to grayscale. In an RGB image this will mean even values for each channel, and in CMYK the result will affect the black channel only.

Outout channels
for CMYK

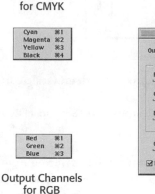

Output Channels
for RGB

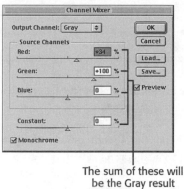

The sum of these will
be the Gray result

13. Compare the Snapshots you have taken again (see Step 9). Eliminate all but the best representation and any improvements you would like to use for enhancements.

14. Make the Channel you have chosen a new document. To do this, select Duplicate Channel from the Channels pop-up (on the Channels palette), and select New as the destination (see Figure 23.12).

15. If there are enhancements you want to try, go to the individual snapshots and save the Channel to a new document. You will be able to manipulate this channel separately or add it (in whole or part) to the conversion you have selected, using techniques of selection, layering, and so on.

→ For more information on manipulating image information, **see** all of Part VII, "Cleaning, Repairing, and Altering Images," **p. 569**.

Figure 23.12
Selecting Duplicate Channel from the Channels palette pop-up will open the Duplicate Channel screen. You can select the destination and name the new document.

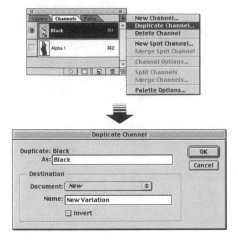

16. Save the final version of the image and proceed with grayscale corrections as necessary.

→ For more information on correcting grayscale images, **see** "Basic Tonal Correction: Channels and Grayscale Images," **p. 445**.

Exploring the options already present in an image might save you from spending too much time making radical corrections in order to get something to look good in black and white. Certainly, unless it is a very important image, you will not want to go through this type of depth in exploration every time. The changes can be subtle, and the end results of the changes are more of a preference than a clear result.

Note

Gauge the importance of the image against how much time you will spend in correction and exploring your options. There is no good excuse for leaving an image looking dreadful when you know a quick fix, but there is no good reason to make a simple switch into a major project.

Some of the possibilities I came up with as interesting conversions for this example are shown and described in the following series of images (Figures 23.13 to 23.18). As I write this, the calculation screening of the green channel with green seems to produce the best results (see Figure 23.16), but that is in consideration of my target, knowing the paper quality and absorption. However, for other purposes, different choices in this same series might be better. For example, output to a film recorder, which has no dot gain, will probably look best with the original green plate leveled and lightened (see Figure 23.15). That image has lower contrast, but better subtle details, and will make better photographic prints. It does not, however, print as well on press.

Figure 23.13
The original image, after Levels corrections in RGB, was desaturated, switched to Grayscale, and then altered with levels by lightening the mid-tones. In this case, it helps the lizard stand out against the light background.

Figure 23.14
The original image, after Levels corrections in RGB, was switched to Lab, and then the Lightness channel was altered with the Levels by lightening midtones. A similar result to Figure 23.13, but with more local contrast in the subject and a slightly darker sky.

Figure 23.15
After original image Levels corrections in RGB, the green channel was altered with the Levels by lightening midtones. Similar to the result in Figure 23.14, but with less contrast, which might reveal more detail in the subject.

Figure 23.16
After original image Levels corrections in RGB, a calculation was applied. The green channel was used as both Source 1 and Source 2, and the mode was set to screen. This gives a lighter representation of the subject while utilizing the contrast.

Figure 23.17
After original image Levels corrections in RGB, a calculation was applied. The red channel was used as Source 1, the green as Source 2, the blue as a mask (inverted, using the check box), and the mode was set to screen. The whole has a closer resemblance to the darker nature of the original tones.

Figure 23.18
The background of the image in Figure 23.17 was lightened using the selection of the sky (created in Step 3). This allows the subject to stand out against the background a little better than in Figure 23.17.

When switching from color, you have many options for exploring the subtle differences in black-and-white images. The previous steps show only a few of these options. You might find conversion variations that you feel are very effective that were not mentioned. For example, I sometimes like to increase contrast by using CMYK black as a Layer Blend over the Lab mode L layer. This is clearly a personal preference, and might be important only for some print work where high contrast is important to getting good results.

Having a good idea of what you expect to accomplish can save work that is potentially unnecessary. Don't overcomplicate a correction where simple examination and levels correction can get you a good end product. Keep the techniques in mind, but don't use them on every image—it simply isn't necessary.

PART

VI

CH

23

Why Concentrate So Hard on Black-and-White Results?
If you can master getting the kind of results you need to get in black and white, working with color and realizing the potential and possibilities becomes easier. Black-and-white work is simpler, and grasping the concepts behind the strength and weakness of tone and resulting contrast can help you understand the workings of color channels. Not only that, you can get great black-and-white results as well.

CONVERTING AN IMAGE FROM RGB TO INDEXED COLOR

Going from millions of potential colors to 256 is indeed limiting your color potential. Changing to a Web-safe palette of 216 colors—unfortunately—offers even fewer colors and more of a trade-off in color integrity. However, for GIF images and Web graphics, the conversion is one that needs to be made all the time if you work in RGB. There are better and worse ways to approach scrunching your images into the tiny GIF color space, and if you look around the Web at all, you will see a variety of successes and some pretty terrible failures.

This conversion is one of the more unforgiving color mode switches. Continuous tone images (photographs) suffer somewhat more from the limitation on color than simple graphics (such as plain type over a single color background). The complex image posterizes in a nondithered conversion. With dithering, the image might become somewhat soft and speckled or grainy, depending on the size of the image, the dithering you choose, and the number of colors involved. Larger images seem to fare slightly better—mostly because there is more room to dither. Either method compromises the complex image somewhat. For the most acceptable conversions (if acceptability is retaining the look of the original), use dithering for images with complex tone and color and no dithering for unblended colors and tone.

Besides the look of an image, the size of the file is also a concern. A smaller file will download more quickly, and a file with fewer colors will be smaller. You can toy with and limit colors in the color table based on a selection, or just do it manually. In cases where you are looking to maximize the speed of downloads, every color you shave from an image will shave some time from the download.

As Indexed Color is not really desirable for working on images (the tools and functions will be limited, and somewhat unpredictable—although consistent), there is no real reason to store an image in Indexed Color. In other words, this is really an endpoint, and you should not consider Indexed Color images to be working models. Because of this, you should save the image in RGB prior to the switch to Indexed Color.

Tip

For any corrections and changes to the image, go back to the RGB image and then reconvert for best results.

Use the following steps to make a conversion from RGB to Indexed Color:

1. Open an RGB image that you want to convert to Indexed Color.
2. Save a copy of the image including all the layers so that you can go back to it at a later time to make corrections and changes or use for other purposes.

Saving File Format Extensions

Three-letter file format extensions can be lifesavers when it comes to images that you use in multiple formats. For example, it can keep you from saving a dithered GIF over your original PSD. Saving the file format extensions can be automatic, semiautomatic, or completely manual, but in any case, it might save you heartache and can make finding and filing images easier. See the following sidebar for information on automating extensions.

You can save file format extensions automatically, semiautomatically, or manually. The Saving Files preferences (Edit, Preferences, Saving Files) have an Append File Extension pop-up menu that enables you to save files with the appropriate extension. You can choose to save automatically (Always), in the Save File dialog box (Ask When Saving), or you can choose not to alter the filename (Never). There is also an option for saving the extensions in upper- or lowercase letters. Yet another option is to add extensions using the (Option) [Alt] key at the time of saving. This is useful if you occasionally want to save only file extensions and have Never selected in the Append File Extension pop-up menu. Simply hold the (Option) [Alt] key down while selecting the file type in the Save File dialog box, and the extension appears in the filename per the choice you make.

3. Flatten the image, and remove extraneous elements (alpha channels and paths). See Alternatives for Saving in the next section for help.
4. Choose Image, Mode, Indexed Color and the Indexed Color dialog box will appear.
5. Select the Palette (on the Color Table dialog box) and dithering method. (See "Color Table Options" and "Choices for Dithering" later in this section.)

Tip

Use the Web palette for the best compatibility across systems.

6. Save as a CompuServe GIF (File, Save As).

 If you are having trouble saving your image as a GIF, see "Removing Extraneous Elements from an Image" in the Troubleshooting section at the end of this chapter.

ALTERNATIVES FOR SAVING FOR THE WEB

It is also possible to save the RGB to a browser-compatible file by choosing Save a Copy or Save for Web, or by creating a new document and saving that (for example, by using Copy Merged (Shift-Cmd-C) [Shift+Ctrl+C]). Some of the options might be easier than fishing out all the extraneous stuff in an image. Also, these options will help keep you from saving over the original image by accident.

→ For more information on options for saving images as GIF files and controlling conversions, **see** "Saving for the Web," **p. 783**.

PART

VI

CH

23

Tip

Copy Merged enables you to make a copy of visible layers as they appear on the screen, minus spot colors. The Copy Merged command is available only if a selection is active in a multiple-layered document. The command copies effects and adjustment layers and converts them into one flattened layer, which is stored in the Clipboard.

COLOR TABLE OPTIONS

You can choose all the colors used in your Color Table and limit them as you see fit. These are selected using options on the Palette drop-down menu on the Indexed Color dialog box (see Figure 23.19).

Figure 23.19
The Palette drop-down menu includes options for selecting colors to include in the Indexed Color table, which will be created during the conversion to Indexed Color.

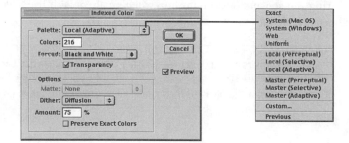

An easy way to limit a color table to a specific set is to create a subsampling from the image. To do this, select an area of your image that contains the colors you want to target and include in the table. Switch the color mode to Indexed Color, and choose Adaptive. This will weigh the colors in the selected area more heavily, as Photoshop automatically selects the best colors to include in the table.

For yet more control, you can isolate a portion of the image before the conversion to base the color selection on. To do this, follow these steps:

1. Copy an area of the image and paste to a new document.
2. Switch the color mode to Indexed Color.

3. Choose a Palette option from the dialog box, which allows selection of the number of colors and bases selection on the existing image (these include Perceptual, Selective, and Adaptive). Enter the desired number of colors, and allow the conversion. Photoshop will select the colors based on the selection only (see Table 23.1 for more information concerning criteria for color selections).

4. When the conversion is complete, save the Color Table. To save the table, open the Color Table dialog box (Image, Mode, Color Table), and choose Save.

5. You can then load Color Table into the original image by activating the image, selecting Indexed Color mode, choosing Custom in the Palette pop-up, and clicking Load. When the browse dialog box opens, find the Color Table saved previously and open it. This will be used to limit colors in the image during the conversion.

NEW TO PHOTOSHOP 6 A new Indexed Color Palette option, Master (Selective, Adaptive, and Perceptual), enables the user to choose colors for the palette from all open documents. This is good for building and optimizing a color table among several different images simultaneously. Simply open all the images you would like to use with the same Indexed Color table and convert one of the images to Indexed Color while selecting one of the Master Palette types (for a description of Selective, Adaptive, and Perceptual, see Table 23.1). This will look at all the images that are open to make color selections. To use the same color table in converting the rest of the images that are open, simply choose Previous from the Palette pop-up in the Indexed Color dialog box during the conversions (Photoshop will actually default to Previous for you, after Master has been selected).

Note

The same colors will be chosen for the color table if converting any one of the open images. However, the colors might appear in a different order in the compiled tables, depending on which image is used for the initial conversion. This in no way affects the utility of the function.

TABLE 23.1 THE INDEXED COLOR PALETTE OPTIONS

Palette Option	User Specifies Number of Colors? (Yes/No)	Web-Safe Colors?	Color Selection Criteria
Exact	No	No	Automatically selects the colors if there are 256 or fewer in the image.
System (Mac OS)	No	Safe on Mac OS	Uses the Mac OS set of 256 system colors.
System (Windows OS)	No	Safe on Windows OS	Uses the Windows OS set of 256 system colors.

TABLE 23.1   CONTINUED

Palette Option	User Specifies Number of Colors? (Yes/No)	Web-Safe Colors?	Color Selection Criteria
Web	No	Yes	Uses 216 colors that are common to the Mac OS and Windows OS system color sets.
Uniform	Yes	No	Uses evenly graded colors that reflect color palettes that would result from cubes of numbers 1 to 6 (1, 8, 27, 64, 125, and 216 colors). Can make Unix-compatible color (for example, the 125-color palette) or the broadly compatible base 8-color palette.
Perceptual	Yes	No	Gives priority in color selection to colors to which the human eye has greater sensitivity.
Selective	Yes	No	Chooses frequent colors in the image and favors Web-safe colors.
Adaptive	Yes	No	Chooses colors based only on most frequent colors in the image, ignoring Web safety and perception qualities.
Custom	Yes (manual)	No	Allows the user to build and/or alter any other color palette by adding and subtracting colors by choice.

Tip

Although some results might look good onscreen, this does not always mean they are the best or most highly compatible. For example, selecting Local (Adaptive) palette, 256 colors, Diffusion Dither, None for Forced, and Preserve Exact Colors might produce good results in the conversion, but the results will not be as likely to view well on the broadest number of computer systems.

DITHERING OPTIONS

Choices for Dithering on the Indexed Color dialog box include None, Diffusion, Pattern, and Noise. Dithering will blend colors more effectively than nondithering, but might not be good for areas of flat color (unless you are looking to simulate a color that is not in the 216-color palette). Figure 23.20 is used as an example to compare to the results of each of the dithering types.

- **None**—Provides no dithering and is best used with images that are solid colors with no blends or shadows. Undithered images can tend to posterize (see Figure 23.21).

- **Diffusion**—Probably the best all-purpose dithering. It randomizes pixels somewhat, so there is no noticeable patterning in the dither. This is the only control that allows the user to pick a density or strength for the dithering (see Figure 23.22).

- **Pattern**—Creates the dither in a pattern that is consistent, and will be noticeable. This seems more useful for creating effects than for general use (see Figure 23.23).

- **Noise**—Less subtle than diffusion and seems more or less insinuated at a constant rate across the image, but in no particularly noticeable pattern. The effect is stronger than Diffusion, but less obtrusive and rigid than Pattern (see Figure 23.24).

Figure 23.20
This image is convert-ed from RGB using 256 colors and an Adaptive color table with diffusion dither-ing. In a casual glance at this, it is passable for the original image. Restricting the image to Web-safe colors will have a more dramatic influence on the appearance.

Figure 23.21
Using no dithering, even 216 colors are not enough to keep the colors from banding. Dithering is really necessary with any type of image with blended color.

Figure 23.22
Introducing Diffusion dither to the 216 colors helps, but you will notice that the tone is not nearly as even as using 256 colors.

Figure 23.23
Patterned dithering creates a graininess or screening like newsprint. It seemingly has special-purpose application in creating special effects.

Figure 23.24
Noise can create an interesting effect and can offer more of a stylized effect than pattern dither.

Deciding whether to dither image information depends on the tonal and color complexity of the image. An image with complex color and tone should probably be dithered for the best results, whereas an image with flat, solid colors (no blends or shadows) converts better without dithering. Because Photoshop offers a preview (for example, in Save for Web), you can check the image both ways before making a decision.

> **Tip**
>
> If you use an image with flat colors and tones, stick with no dithering (select None in the Dither pop-up menu).

The result of simply loading the 216-color palette into a complexly colored RGB image without dithering leaves the image smooth but the color distorted or posterized, and quite untrue. Conversion with or without dithering leads to some distortion unless the image is built in Indexed Color. This is a severe limitation from the outset; Indexed Color mode is difficult to work in because there is limitation not only on colors, but available functions.

> **Tip**
>
> If a quality loss is undesirable, you might consider saving the images as JPEGs, which retain far more of the original color content and integrity. JPEG files might prove somewhat larger depending on the level of compression you choose, but they generally look better for continuous tone images that contain blended color than GIF images.

→ For more information on JPEG files, **see** "JPEG," **p. 329**.

CONVERTING AN IMAGE FROM RGB TO CMYK

You can often get a satisfactory conversion when switching from RGB to CMYK, but certain stubborn colors never appear to have the "pop" in CMYK that they do in RGB. Specifically, images that are very vivid in RGB lose some luster in CMYK, and notably greens, blues, and reds are worst. You cannot retain all the color in a conversion from RGB to CMYK, as RGB simply is capable of producing more colors than CMYK. The difference can be quite dramatic, and you might be discouraged by the image appearance after a straight conversion.

Careful color alterations before and after making a conversion help retain as much of the color as possible. Correction after the conversion helps make the most of what you get. These changes include general as well as selective changes. For example, color replacement is a broader option to consider, where you will actually exchange an existing color for one that will print better.

In many cases, there will be some fairly significant trade-offs in image color. Practice helps, and strong color correction and alteration skills can lead you to opportunities to shift the color to your advantage. Separating the areas of the image that will experience the worst of the color change can give the most versatility in getting the best results. You will need to be adept at selection and use of layers and channels, and know color correction and image manipulation thoroughly to get the most out of an image.

→ For more information on selection, **see** "Selection and Masking," **p. 93**.

→ For more information on layers, **see** "Creating Images in Layers," **p. 53**.

→ For more information on channels, **see** "Working with Channels," **p. 79**.

→ For more information on color correction, **see** "Color Corrections," **p. 465**.

→ For more information on altering images, **see** Part VII, "Cleaning, Repairing, and Altering Images," **p. 569**.

Tip

Pay attention to color harmony when making color changes. Don't just make changes to get a color inside the gamut or your image might end up looking worse. Use Proof Colors previews to your advantage (Cmd-Y) [Ctrl+Y]. By setting up multiple views of your image, and previewing RGB and CMYK side by side, you can immediately see both what you are working on and the end result.

→ For more information on working with multiple views, **see** the "Practical Use of Multiple Views" sidebar on **p. 511**.

Use the following steps to convert an image from RGB to CMYK.

1. Open the image that you want to change from RGB to CMYK.

2. Be sure the Proof Setup is set to Working CMYK.

3. Select Proof Color by choosing View, Proof Colors (Cmd-Y) [Ctrl+Y] for a quick survey of the color change without making the conversion. Switch the Proof Colors on and off several times to note which colors go through the most drastic, visible changes. When finished, switch off the Proof Colors (the Proof Colors menu item should be unchecked).

Note

You will want to repeat Step 3 several times throughout the process to check your progress (or lack thereof). This is not a conversion in that it does not change any image information, so use it freely and don't worry about damaging image information.

4. Select <u>V</u>iew, Gamut <u>W</u>arning (Shift-Cmd-Y) [Shift+Ctrl+Y] to see specifically which colors are outside the CMYK gamut.

Tip

The out-of-gamut colors will be overlaid with the Gamut Warning color, which is set or changed in Transparency & Gamut Preferences (<u>E</u>dit, Pre<u>f</u>erences, <u>T</u>ransparency & Gamut). The gamut warning is covered in more detail in the section that follows.

5. Compare the results of Steps 3 and 4 to get an idea of what needs to be altered to get better results from the conversion. If an area of color is both adversely affected by the change visually (Step 3) and appears in the area of the Gamut Warning (Step 4), you will need to concentrate change on those image areas to improve conversion results. If colors are in the Gamut warning but do not appear as problematic in the visual assessment, don't worry about them very much. This means the conversion will choose colors that are acceptable to your visual cues—although they are not exactly within the CMYK gamut.

6. Take steps to change the areas of image color identified in Step 5 to get them in gamut for CMYK. This step will vary in complexity and length of time required to complete it, depending on the level of difficulty. You might need to alter color in selected (isolated) areas on top of general color corrections. It might mean shifting the color slightly or altering it completely, depending on what you want to achieve.

Tip

Consider separating difficult colors into their own Layers for corrections. Use your knowledge of everything in the color correction arsenal from Chapter 22 to alter colors as needed. Layers and Adjustment Layers will probably be important tools in spot corrections.

→ For more information on how to achieve color corrections, **see** "Color Corrections," **p. 465**.

6. Save a version of the unflattened image (.psd) so you can go back to it for changes if you need to; be careful to not save it over the original, which you might want to retain for RGB applications.

7. Flatten the image (<u>L</u>ayer, <u>F</u>latten Image) and convert to CMYK. If you do not flatten before conversion, Photoshop might warn you that some of the adjustment layer effects might be lost, or that Layer compositing will be affected.

8. Save the CMYK version of the image using a different name.

Following the previous series of steps will help you identify and change areas of color in an RGB image that simply will not convert well to CMYK. You want to take care of the color adjustments before the change, as the problems will be easier to remedy before the change occurs.

SELECTIVE COLOR CHANGES

Some of the most useful color tools for spot color changes will be adjustment layers using Hue/Saturation and Color Balance in Color and Hue modes. Adjustment layers work well when making color changes to selected image areas because you can change the color specifically by grouping the adjustment with the layer you are working on in an isolated portion of the image. Working areas of the layer can be limited further by selection.

You might need to make intermediate color-mode changes to get the results you want. For example, many of your more specialized color changes are best accomplished using Lab mode and a variety of layering techniques, including masking layers separately for particular color areas and using different layer modes. Before switching Lab to either RGB or CMYK (you can take either route: RGB if there are more corrections to make, or CMYK if you have finished the image and want to convert without an additional step), you will need to merge adjustments to keep the effect of the current view.

By working with the color independently of trying to accomplish or imitate the exact result you see in RGB, you can get more interesting and better color for CMYK images. Getting good results might require a number of different steps and a lot of manipulation. Pay attention to the most needy portions of the image and allow some colors to remain out of gamut if the color changes are acceptable. (Some examples of color alterations appear in the color section—ColorPlate 5.) ColorPlate 5 shows a picture of bottles that was unaltered in conversion. The RGB version of the color showed more vivid blues and reds, and although the converted effect is not horrible, it is not as exciting. Of course, it is impossible to show this in print. The blue and green were adjusted and brightened slightly, the red was altered toward magenta, and the yellow was made more opaque to make the color somewhat spunkier. The final example changes the bottle colors completely and attempts to correct some of the interplay between the results while working with the contrast. None is necessarily better than another in this case; this was meant as a demonstration of possibility.

You can do almost anything with color, but you will have to work with the limitations posed by the possibilities of CMYK in order to get good color print results. The only other alternative will be to spend a fortune on color print methods. For example, hexagraphic color or intensive spot coloring might offer costly solutions to improving color print. Be aware of what is important in the color you want to achieve. If you want accurate reproduction, work with the color to get it as close as you can to the original; if you are just looking for good, strong color, test the possibilities before accepting a mediocre, color-flattening conversion.

If all else fails, you can consider coloring the image from scratch.

→ For more information on coloring a black-and-white image, **see** "Colorizing a Grayscale Image," **p. 514**.

GAMUT WARNING

The Gamut Warning view overlays the image with a map of color that marks all the pixels that are outside of the CMYK gamut. You can change the opacity and color of the overlay using the Transparency & Gamut Preferences (Edit, Preferences, Transparency & Gamut), as shown in Figure 23.25. Using this view does not affect the image in any way; it is merely a visual clue as to where, specifically, you might need to work on image color. To change the Gamut color, double-click the color swatch and choose a color using the Color Picker. In most cases, this color should be one that stands out from or opposes color in the image. You can also set the opacity in percentage. This should probably remain at greater than 80% in most cases so that it is easy to discern.

Figure 23.25
The Transparency & Gamut Preferences dialog box allows you to change the gamut color and opacity for the Gamut Warning. Change the color as necessary to stand out from the original image.

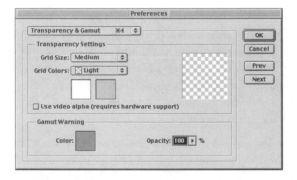

Caution

Keeping opacity on the Gamut Warning too low can cause problems. To avoid accidentally looking at the image with the Gamut on and making improper visual corrections based on that, keep the gamut opacity high. A stiff Gamut Warning color (very vivid, with high opacity) is recommended.

Some colors that are mapped as outside of the CMYK gamut will be drastically affected in a conversion; others will be only slightly affected, and others will alter unnoticeably. Don't expect to make the image a perfect Gamut match before the conversion: It won't always happen and isn't always necessary. Your goal is to make the image look as good as it can and limit the severity of the change. Pay a lot of attention to areas that promise to go through drastic conversions because they might end up mapping badly, and conversions might yield blotchiness, gritty color, or bad/unexpected color mixes. Use the CMYK preview often as you work to check on results. If your screen size permits, use two views of the image as you work, one showing the CMYK preview and the other showing the image in RGB. This can help to show how close you are coming to a clean conversion.

Practical Use of Multiple Views

The image you work on can be viewed in more than one way simultaneously—if you have room on the screen. Multiple views of an image will allow you to visually monitor details at different magnification and with different previews (see Figure 23.26). Previews for each image view are controlled from the selections on the Preview menu (View, Preview). To create a new view, choose View, New View. Views can be magnified separately to zoom in on particular areas of the image, and different Proof Color settings can be applied for each view.

NEW TO PHOTOSHOP 6 Content of all views of the image change simultaneously as you make changes to any of the views as the changes affect the current color space for the image. The new Proof Color function (see the menu in Figure 23.27) is an improved version of the Preview from an earlier version of Photoshop, which allows more flexibility and control over the matching that appears on screen. Lab, RGB, Grayscale, Indexed Color, and CMYK images support Working CMYK, Working Cyan Plate, Working Yellow Plate, Working Magenta Plate, Working Black Plate, and Working CMY Plates views. These views show a preview of the image in the plates selected using the CMYK settings for the Working CMYK color space in the Color Settings (Edit, Color Settings). RGB, Grayscale, and Indexed Color have additional compensation settings for Macintosh RGB, Windows RGB, and Monitor RGB, which show Macintosh system color, PC system color, and uncompensated color. CMYK has additional adjustments for Simulate Paper White and Simulate Black Ink. These simulate the effect of the paper color on the printing and the press result of absorption of black ink, respectively. Custom settings are available for CMYK, RGB, Lab, Grayscale, and Indexed Color. These can be used to adjust the Proof Color views to other color-matching situations.

Figure 23.26

This image is split into five views. The large view is the image in RGB. The smaller views show the image at 50% with Gamut Warning (top left), a closeup at 169% of a portion of the image (upper right), the black plate at 50% (bottom left), and the image at 50% in CMYK. This would help monitor the CMYK color, black generation, out-of-gamut color, and affected details all at once.

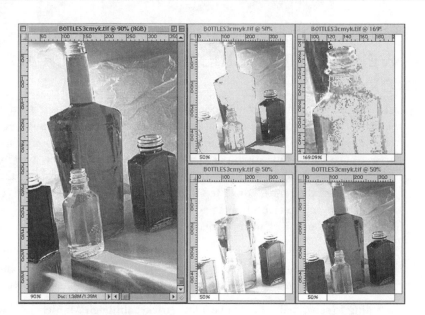

Figure 23.27
The Proof Setup menu is accessed on Photoshop's View menu. Simply select the proof type you would like to use with the current view, and when Proof Colors is active (selected from the View menu as well), the setting affects the view of the image.

Be careful when using the Color Range to make selections of out-of-gamut colors. Although this will target colors that are out of the gamut of CMYK, it might not select whole areas of color. Areas of color that end up only partially selected will probably show bad transitions at the edge of selections if any type of correction is made and might cause more damage than a straight conversion. Be sure to feather and alter selections made with out-of-gamut selections to blend corrections as appropriate.

CONVERTING FROM DUOTONE TO GRAYSCALE OR COLOR PLATES

When switching from Duotone mode to Grayscale mode, Photoshop ignores the effects of the curves and reverts to the original grayscale. Reverting makes sense because the original image information is not changed; the duotone effect is merely a digital application of curves (much like an Adjustment layer), which does not change the pixel information directly. When you're switching to RGB or CMYK (or any other color mode than Multichannel), the color of the duotone is converted to the color space you choose. This can be quite frustrating if you want to take advantage of duotones to work on the tonality of your images, or expect to be able to work with the plates as you created them for the duotone.

To make duotone changes stick when switching back to Grayscale mode, you have to trick the image into accepting the changes by moving to another color mode and then switching to Grayscale. RGB or Lab mode switches will quickly accomplish what you need.

Switching to separated color can be a little tricky; although Multichannel will create the channels for the color separation, it will not save as anything but a PSD. You can save the Duotone as an EPS (Photoshop EPS only) and use it that way for layout, but there might be reasons why you need to alter the image (such as to add type). You will have to gather the channels from the Multichannel document into CMYK as spot channels. Procedures for changing to black-and-white and creating separations follow.

DUOTONE TO GRAYSCALE

Use the following steps to save duotone corrections for a grayscale image:

1. Open the image you want to change to grayscale from duotone.

→ For more information on working with duotone images, **see** "Creating a Duotone," **p. 528**.

2. Switch to Lab or RGB mode. The duotone colors will convert to that mode, and separate to the proper channels.

3. Switch to Grayscale mode from the RGB or Lab mode. The image will retain the tonality imposed by the duotone curves.

Changing the color mode applies the curves to the image by forcing a color separation. This changes the information in the image, and conversion to grays from that point will reflect the duotone changes.

This is useful when using duotone curves to fine-tune black-and-white images. The conversion is rather simple but certainly roundabout. Included in the actions on the Web site (www.ps6.com) is an action for making the conversion (converting duotone to grayscale).

DUOTONE TO COLOR PLATES

Use the following steps to split the channels for the duotone file into separate editable channels:

1. Open the image you want to change to separate channels from duotone.

2. Select Image, Mode, Multichannel to convert the image to Multichannel. This will create one channel for each color and apply the appropriate curve. The Multichannel preview might not appear as expected, but the conversion will produce the proper channel results.

3. Add channels to the current image, one for each of the channels of the new color mode. If you are switching to CMYK, add four channels; if switching to Lab or RGB, add three.

PART

VI

CH

23

Note

If any of the colors you used for the duotone is a color from the color mode you will be switching to (for example, you used a Cyan, Magenta, Yellow, or Black ink and are switching to CMYK), you can add one less channel for each match. In other words, if the duotone was made with Magenta, Yellow, and Black and you are switching to CMYK, you need to add only one channel to the Multichannel image before the conversion. The existing channels will be used for the M, Y, and K channels. If the colors for the duotone are Black and a PANTONE color, you would need to create three channels because only the Black channel would be assigned as a CMYK channel (the K channel). The PANTONE would be assigned as a spot channel. (See Figure 23.28 for more on the setup.)

Figure 23.28
The order of the channels in the Multichannel document will correspond to the channels in the color mode you convert to. The color channels necessary to the color mode will be renamed during the conversion.

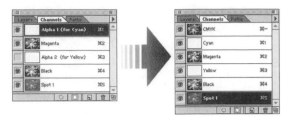

4. Order the list of channels as you want them used. For example, if switching to CMYK, place the channels in order C, M, Y, K, spot 1, spot 2, and so on. See Figure 23.25 for an example.

5. Change the color mode to CMYK. The channels will be renamed and the composite for the color mode generated.

Using Duotones in Layout Applications
Duotones can be used in most layout applications without other color conversion if they are saved from Photoshop as Photoshop EPS files. Be sure the target colors are named and assigned properly, or there might be difficulty with the separations generated from the layout program. Converting, as per the instructions in the preceding steps, will solve some potential problems in output and printing.

 If you are having trouble outputting a duotone job, see "Outputting Duotone Images" in the Troubleshooting section at the end of this chapter.

COLORIZING A GRAYSCALE IMAGE

Colorizing grayscale images is very difficult if you go about it in the wrong way. Using advantages offered by Photoshop's layers, you can make relatively short work of even difficult coloring and create some amazing effects in very little time.

You can paint with any number of available tools, and apply blends and filters to create better and more realistic tonal qualities. You need to convert the image from Grayscale mode to a color mode. Depending on the use for the image, you might want to choose RGB, Lab, or CMYK. Again, Lab will probably yield the best color change. Next, you can create layers to paint and blend color into the image. Depending on the image and what you want to accomplish, you can use Layer properties (Opacity, Mode, Advanced Blending/Blend If) in Layer Styles to make the color work with the information in the Grayscale mode, or you can use painting tools in different modes (usually Color). Although there are other possibilities, using a combination of the Layer properties is the most versatile in applying color, as it can target and separate changes so they can be altered if necessary; whereas, paint tool applications are hit or miss and are far more difficult to alter.

> **Note**
>
> To access Layer Styles, double-click the layer you will be using to make the application. The Layer Styles will be available only for layers, it is not available on background layers.

Advanced Blending/Blend If functions for layers can act as a selector for tonal range and targets colorizing to a specific area. Using Blend If sliders to help control the application of color to an image is an effective way to confine colorization quickly. It requires careful sampling to keep colors confined to the area you intend to paint.

STEPS FOR COLORIZATION

Use the following steps to colorize a grayscale image:

1. Open a grayscale image that you want to colorize.

2. Change the image to a color mode. Use Lab or RGB for an image you won't be using in print, and use CMYK for print images in order to simplify color choices and remove the need for correction and conversion.

3. Add a layer to the image by choosing New Layer from the Layers palette pop-up, or press (Cmd-Shift-N) [Ctrl+Shift+N] on the keyboard.

4. Switch the new layer to Color mode.

5. (Option) Choose an area of the image you want to color. Measure the tonal range of the area you want to affect. Use the measurements to set the blend of your layer using the Advanced Blending/Blend If function.

→ For more information on measuring tonal range and setting up the Blend If function, **see** "Assigning Blend If Ranges," **p. 516**.

6. Choose the color you want to apply by double-clicking the foreground color swatch and selecting with the Color Picker.

7. Paint the area roughly with the color you selected, using the paint tool of your choice. If you have selected the tonal range properly, the only areas affected by the color will be those you measured for the application.

8. Use the opacity of the layer to get the color saturation you want.

9. Optionally, you can apply a color-correcting Adjustment layer to the color to adjust it to the way you prefer it to appear.

10. Repeat Steps 3 through 9 for each color you want to apply.

11. View the results closely and adjust the painted areas, blends, and adjustments as necessary to achieve the best results.

12. Save the image with all layers, channels, and adjustments so that you can go back to them later and make any necessary changes.

13. Flatten the image and save it in the format you will use it in. Be sure to use a unique name so you don't save over other versions of the file.

You can make the color as simple or complex as you want, and this technique lends itself well to any number of special effects. Be willing to try color layering, and apply color into and around image areas. Experimenting with color modes, layer order, and Blend If sliders will help you to realize the possibilities of confining the application of color. Color can also be applied by blending images and sketches for some very unusual and interesting effects (see ColorPlate 8 and 9 in the color section of this book).

The possibilities are tremendous for a variety of grayscale and line-art images, and offer almost infinite flexibility and very tight control.

ASSIGNING BLEND IF RANGES

Blend If, used properly, can help you target areas of an image to which you want to apply color by limiting application to a specific tonal range. The values of the image (the underlying value) can be set according to specific measured values in the image you select.

You will have to carefully measure the tonal range for each color you intend to apply and each area in which you want to confine the application of that color. To measure the tonal range, use the Color Sampler tool. Select four points on your image that reflect the following criteria for the area you want to color: the darkest point you do not want to color (sample 1), the lightest point you do not want to color (sample 2), the darkest point you want to color (sample 3), and the lightest point you want to color (sample 4). Take the L measurements of each and multiply by 2.55 (see Figure 23.29).

Figure 23.29
The measurements here are made to apply color to the dark scales on the lizard's back. The L values for the four selected points are: darkest tone not colored, 71; lightest tone not colored, 93; darkest tone to color, 4; and lightest tone to color 60.

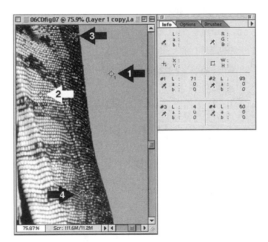

If the area you want to color is darker than the area you do not want to color, set the blend sliders as follows: Split the black slider and set at 0 and the converted value for sample 3. Split the white slider and set at the converted values for samples 1 and 4. Sample 1 should be lighter (greater numeric value) than sample 4 (see Figure 23.30).

Figure 23.30
This figure shows how you would set up the sliders to make the color application only to the desired dark area of this image. The Blend If should be set up in this fashion if the area of the image you are attempting to color is the darkest area in the portion of the image you are working on.

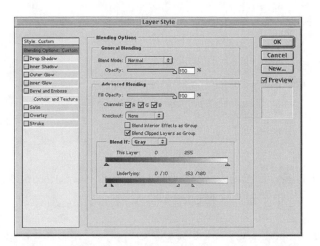

Note

To split Blend If sliders, hold down the (Option) [Alt] key, click the left of the light or right of the dark slider, and drag.

If the area you want to color is lighter than the area you do not want to color, set the blend sliders as follows: Split the black slider and set it so it reflects the converted values for samples 2 and 3. Sample 3 should be lighter than sample 2. Split the white slider and set it to sample 4 and 255 (see Figure 23.31).

Figure 23.31
This figure shows how you would set up the sliders to make the color application only to the desired light area of this image. The Blend If should be set up in this fashion if the area of the image you are attempting to color is the lightest area in the portion of the image you are working on.

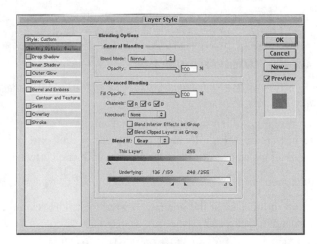

If the area you want to color is between light and dark areas, set the sliders as follows: Split the black slider and set the points to the converted values for selection 1 and 3; split the white slider and set to the values for samples 2 and 4 (see Figure 23.32). Sample 1 should be darker than sample 3, and sample 2 should be lighter than sample 4.

Figure 23.32
This figure shows how
you would set up the
sliders to make the
color application to
the desired area, if it
is between the lightest
and darkest areas of
this image.

Tip

To move or change samples made with the Color Sample tool, hold down the (Option) [Alt]
key and click the sample you want to change.

With the sliders properly set, you will be able to apply color so that it affects only those
areas of tone that you have defined. Using this technique allows greater flexibility with
Layer modes as it more effectively confines any application of color. For example, although
you can set the layer you are using for the application to the Color mode, you might get
better results by applying the color in Normal mode and adjusting the opacity to blend the
applied color with the area you are coloring.

Note

Applications of color do not have to be solid colors only. Blends, patterns, fills, and images
can be used in this way with Blend If to create complex image effects.

TROUBLESHOOTING

REMOVING EXTRANEOUS ELEMENTS FROM AN IMAGE

*When trying to save my image as a GIF I do not get the CompuServe GIF option on the Save As
menu. Is there something I can do to remedy that?*

To be sure there is nothing hidden in your image that might be causing this problem, it
might be easier to just create a fresh document and paste in the content from the image you
want to save as a GIF. This can be accomplished easily with the Copy Merged command.

To make a new document with Copy Merged:

1. Make a selection of the area of the image you want using the rectangular marquee or
just select all (Cmd-A) [Ctrl+A].
2. Choose Edit, Copy Merged (Cmd-Shift-C) [Ctrl+Shift+C].
3. Select File, New to open a new document. The image size will default to the size of the
area you have copied.
4. Paste the area you copied to the new document.
5. Flatten the image with Layers, Flatten Image.

With the new document created, you can Flatten it and be sure there are no hidden elements keeping you from doing what you'd set out to do. Follow the steps under "Converting an Image from RGB to Indexed Color" and you should be all set.

OUTPUTTING DUOTONE IMAGES

When trying to output a duotone with my service bureau, I have been charged extra for creating separations of my duotones. How can I avoid these charges?

When sending duotones to print, you can save money in several ways. First, if you are using a four-color process, you can get decent results in many cases by turning the duotone to CMYK color. This is a simple conversion. Simply open the duotone and change to CMYK mode. The colors will separate into CMYK even if you have used duotone colors. Incorporate the new image into your layout program rather than the duotone, and the job will need to print with only four colors (rather than four plus the number you have added for the duotone). This will save cost on running another custom ink in the printing, and that can be a significant savings. The conversion might not be exact if you use spot colors that are clearly out of gamut for CMYK, but it is worth looking at the conversion to see whether the trade-off is worth the savings.

If the service is separating the duotones before printing a spot color job (for example, something you are printing in two colors), that might really be unnecessary. However, to avoid the charges, separate the duotone and create a new CMYK or grayscale file (described in "Converting from Duotone to Grayscale or Color Plates" in this chapter), and save it as a Photoshop EPS. If you do this correctly, the plates should separate with no problem.

If you have a PostScript printer, you can test the color output and the separations by printing a sample of the plates. This is really a good idea to do whenever doing color separations to ensure that nothing goes wrong press-side when the film is output. Proofing the plates will let you know whether you have removed extra colors and created separations properly—if it works on your machine, it will work on theirs.

→ For more information on printing color separations, **see** "Prepping for Printing: Prepress," **p. 869**.

PHOTOSHOP AT WORK: WORKING WITH COLORIZATION

Colorization can use a number of the techniques described in this chapter. In the PDF workbook (see the Web site at http://www.ps6.com), open page 23 in Photoshop. There are several layers to the image (these will appear only if the image is opened in Photoshop, not Acrobat). The bottommost layer is the original image; the next layer up is the original image converted to black and white. The additional layers are my rather simple targeted corrections. Although these can still use some further adjustment (and completion over the rest of the image), they should give you an idea of what is possible.

My objective was to colorize the object to get close to the color of the original. The colorizing was done using layers and Blend If to selectively target tonal areas for the application of color and multiple modes layers.

Follow these steps to colorize the image:

1. Open the PDF from the workbook.
2. Look at the original by clicking off the view for the black-and-white layer.
3. Switch back to the black-and-white layer by turning the view back on.

Tip

Before doing Step 3, you might want to cheat a little and sample the blue and yellow colors from the original, just to simplify the process of color selection. However, it is more challenging to do the example without making those samples.

4. Add a layer to adjust the general color of the image. This might require selecting a Layer Mode, Opacity, or Advanced Blending settings.

Note

In this case, it seemed like there was a general reddish hue in the original, but it seemed inconsistent. To match what I thought should be there, I created a rough pattern using several filters. I filled the channel with 50% gray, added noise (Gaussian, Monochrome), blurred the result (Gaussian, .5-pixel Radius), scaled it 300%, and then applied Hue/Saturation with the colorize box checked to create the color I wanted to apply. The result was applied to the original image, using Blend If settings which targeted a broad range of tones and the application was adjusted with opacity.

5. Add a layer to target the yellow and light blue colors on the nodes.

Note

These colors could be applied separately on different layers for better control. You will want to target mid and light tones, and adjust the intensity using opacity.

There is still much to be done to complete the sample. You can use either the corrections I made or your own corrections as a basis to complete the colorization. Although attempting to match the color in the original gives you a tangible goal, there is no need to limit yourself to matching the original color. Such experimentation can help you understand how the process works a little better.

USING DUOTONES AND SPOT COLORS

In this chapter

UNDERSTANDING DUOTONES AND SPOT COLOR

Creating duotones and using spot color are different things; however, they are usually concerned with the printing process. Each is a different means of adding or manipulating color in an existing image. This can be done both to augment and improve color, and attain color beyond the capability of the current working color space. As color addition is more useful in color spaces that have greater limitation, these processes are most often used with CMYK or grayscale images—although they can be used for special effects and color matching in other color spaces as well.

Duotoning is the application of two or more inks based on the grayscale tone of an image. The purpose of duotones in printing for publications is usually to improve printed results of black-and-white images by creating more refined prints. This is accomplished by enhancing tonality and using smaller dot sizes. Because there are more inks, each prints in a screen with smaller dots (see Figure 24.1).

Figure 24.1
This is a magnification of printed screens. The upper sections are the screens that are used to achieve the results at the bottom. The result of the two plates of smaller black dots when combined and the larger gray dots plates when combined is approximately the same as the larger black dots alone. The finer dots or the larger gray dots will be more difficult to see with the naked eye, and prints will look smoother.

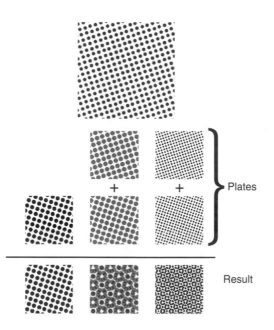

Plates

Result

The use of one ink is monotone, two inks is duotone, three inks is known as tritone, four as quadtone, and so on, but each of these processes is generally referred to as duotone process.

Smaller printing dots create finer ink coverage, and substituting tones can help even the coverage even further. The ink is adjusted using a special dialog box in Photoshop which allows the user to target and blend individual colors based on levels of gray. Adjusted with care, this can render a subtle toning for the image (such as sepia toning). Toning is most often used with grayscale images to impart a sense of color.

Spot coloring is the application of a specific ink color to a specific spot (or spots) in an image. The most effective use of spot color is to attain colors outside the gamut of the current color space; however, spot colors can be used to reduce or eliminate printer dots in light colors that are within the gamut of the current color space. Spot colors might actually be CMYK process equivalents, meaning that the colors are a mixture that can technically be achieved by using only CMYK inks. Again, the reason you would use these colors is for the effect on the resulting print. For example, you might not want printed dots to be visible when working with lighter tones of ink.

The application of spot color is done in a spot color channel, independent of tonality that currently exists in the image and without a separate tool or interface, unlike duotones. And, unlike duotones, spot colors are often used with color images. A readily identified use of spot colors is found in packaging. Products often use spot color to attain brighter packaging than you would get in a standard CMYK process.

Duotones and spot coloring often add cost to print jobs, although smart use of duotone and spot color can actually help reduce printing cost by reducing the number of inks used on press compared to CMYK.

Color Printing Costs

Costs for printing increase as the number of inks rise. For example, printing duotones (two inks) might be cheaper than CMYK (four inks) but not if you are doing both CMYK and duotone printing in the same project (at least five inks, by count, if you use a spot color and black for a duotone in the same project). Count the total number of inks per project, not per image. If you counted only colors per image instead of total number of inks for the project and you vary your duotone inks from image to image, your final cost on the print job might be a huge surprise.

The additional colors used in duotones or spot color applications are often called spot colors or PANTONE colors, although there are other actual names for the color books (TRUMATCH, FOCOLTONE, and so on). To see a list of available ink books, double-click a color swatch in the Color Picker, and then click the Custom button to open the Custom Colors dialog box. The Custom Colors dialog box has a Book drop-down menu (see Figure 24.2) that lets you pick from any of the color swatch book standards. To use one of the colors, simply choose a color from the swatches. These colors are standards and can be matched by your printing service.

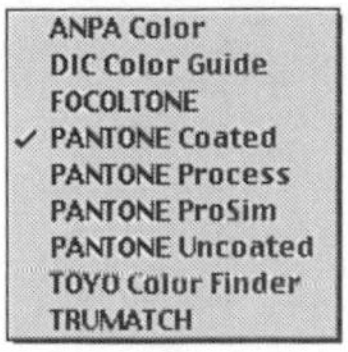

Figure 24.2
These choices represent standard color sets that your printer should be able to match.

ANPA Color
DIC Color Guide
FOCOLTONE
✓ PANTONE Coated
PANTONE Process
PANTONE ProSim
PANTONE Uncoated
TOYO Color Finder
TRUMATCH

Many duotone and spot color effects are used only in print media and are effective only in the originally specified colors. That is, out-of-gamut colors will not be reproduced without using the spot color inks at an additional cost. However, effects can be created with spot colors and duotone curves and then converted to CMYK to approximate effects while keeping color printing costs down. This will only create an approximation of any effect achieved. Again, you will need to judge whether the added printing costs will be justified in the results.

Although usually a printing effect, images created with spot color and duotone curves might be used for other purposes. For example, sepia toning is sometimes a desirable effect independent of its effect on printer dots; it can add warmth to the tone of a black-and-white image without changing the image. You can use this effect in creating images with limited color for a Web page in RGB, or to add color qualities to the tone of photographic prints. Some aspects of spot coloring are convenient for controlling color, such as in making selective color changes. Both can give the user an interesting level of control in correcting and altering images. Duotone and spot color effects range from the subtle to the extreme.

→ For more information on selecting areas for application of spot color, **see** "Layering and Selective Corrections," **p. 479** and "Selection and Masking," **p. 93**.

In this chapter we examine the basics, and not so basics, of making and applying ink choices.

Spot Colors

Spot coloring is used to change a specific area of color in an image. Usually, these are colors outside what you can attain in CMYK process (for example, PANTONE colors), but some colors are CMYK equivalents. Spot colors are often used to brighten packaging (laundry detergent boxes are a good example), or CMYK colors can be used without screening. In other words, instead of printing a warm gray with a CMYK setting of 0C, 11M, 11Y, 34K, you might choose to use a PANTONE 408 at 100%, which you can print with no dot or screen; it appears as a solid color rather than a collection of dots. Commonly, spot color inks are not used to blend with other inks, although they don't need to be kept separate. Essentially, when they do blend, they act somewhat like duotones and process color, but control of the application is completely manual, compared to separations, which Photoshop creates automatically. This makes application somewhat more challenging. Good technique often involves selection and borrowing from other portions of the image.

An example of spot color use appears in Figure 24.3. Although you cannot see the effects directly in black and white, this image appears on page 24 of the PDF workbook (download the workbook at www.ps6.com), and the spot color plates are included here so you can see how the image was put together.

Figure 24.3
This product bag is printed on clear plastic to allow a view of the contents (the window at lower left). All colors are printed at full strength except in the area of the flame (see plate separations in Figure 24.4).

PART
VI
CH
24

Figure 24.4
The separated plates show the density that each color will print. Where the plate appears dark or black (100%), the ink is denser; where it appears light, it is less dense or absent (0%). The most confusing plate here is probably the white ink, which appears as black on the plate at 100%.

1788CVC

Black

Yellow

Cyan

White

The image in Figure 24.3 was a CMYK process image, yet the magenta plate was replaced by PANTONE 1788, which is similar but a little redder (see Figure 24.5). A white ink had to be used for the type on the bottom because the printing was done on a clear plastic bag.

Use of white ink in most cases is unusual in printing, as paper is considered white. The black is warmed slightly by printing it with the yellow and PANTONE 1788, warmth having a great deal to do with the content of the bag.

Figure 24.5
The image has six plates here, but only five will be used. The magenta plate is unused. This could be thrown out, and the image would convert to a multichannel image. It would have to be saved as a Photoshop DCS 2.0 file to go to the printer.

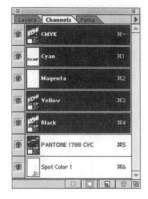

→ For more information on using and selecting spot colors, **see** "Selecting and Using Spot Color," **p. 540**.

DUOTONES

Monotones (one ink), duotones (two inks), tritones (three inks), and quadtones (four inks) are all referred to as duotones in Photoshop. With duotones, the inks are separated depending on the tonality of the image. Generally, the greater the gray density of the tone, the higher the application of the individual duotone inks—although this is completely dependent on the application of the duotone curves. The result of each ink uses the grayscale as it would look with the corresponding tonal curve applied. That is, each ink in the duotone contains the same original image information; if you change the grayscale for one, you change it for all.

Skilled use of duotones can bring out better richness and image detail and more consistent tone by letting inks play to their strength. For example, a light ink can be run at a higher percentage in the lighter tones to reduce the appearance of dots—both by using larger dots and blending inks (see Figure 24.6 for a sample of what the curves might look like). This can give the image more of a continuous tone or photographic appearance (rather than appearing to have dots). Even using two black inks can improve a printed image because the two sets of dots will be offset and screened differently for better application of inks. There is also an interesting subtlety in controlling tone, which can actually be useful in some tonal corrections even if the final application will only use one black ink. See Figure 24.7 for an idea of how curves might be applied for this effect.

Figure 24.6
This set of duotone curves shows a 45% gray ink and a pure black ink and how they might be used together to extend the tonal range of an image. Note that the ink applications overlap somewhat, so they blend with no harsh transitions.

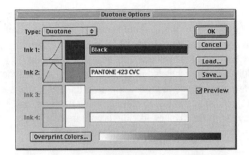

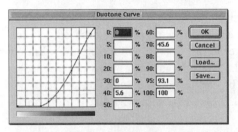

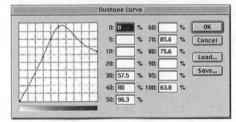

Figure 24.7
Two black inks (they could be plain black, but here a process black and a warmer black PANTONE were chosen) can smooth the image dots and interact to generate a smoother print. Note that the warmer (colored) black ink is used with more strength in the midtones. This lends a slight colored tone to the resulting image.

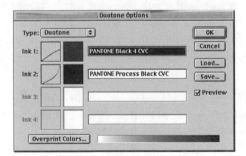

Caution

There is an additional charge at the printer for using special inks, and this usually includes PANTONEs. The printer's stock black ink will be cheaper for them to use because they can buy it in greater bulk, and they will probably pass that savings on to you. Also, some non-process ink colors cannot be imitated well using standard proofs. Proofing spot colors properly might require press proofs—a process that uses the actual colors on the press. Press proofs can run significantly more than other proofing methods, and it gets more costly if you find you have to make changes after the proofs are run. The cost of testing is always worth saving you from an absolute printing disaster.

Setting the curves or ink densities in a duotone is usually done to enhance the tonality and local contrast of the image. The inks work together to orchestrate a subtle tonal effect. Blacks will be richer and darker in print because of mixing the inks than they would be if printed with a single black ink. The printed effect is that there actually is a greater tonal range because the blacks will be darker—even though you are dealing with the same number of levels of grays in the image. This works somewhat like putting on a second coat of paint.

CREATING A DUOTONE

Using duotone curves is the key to making an effective simple duotone. The curves give optimal control over the tonality of the image and the mixture of the inks. Creating a duotone in Photoshop is easy after you get the hang of what you need to do with the curves.

You have several options for putting together a duotone effect. The easiest method is to simply convert the image to Duotone mode and use the Duotone curves to create the effect. The second method is a manual process using Multichannel or Grayscale mode, which is typically used only in special situations in which you want a little more control over the image color plates than you can get in a straight conversion. For example, you might use the second method if you want to use more than four inks in your image, or if you want to apply filters to different channels as you go (such as spot sharpening—sharpening one of the individual layers, but not all).

Note

Duotoning does not change the information of the original grayscale of the image, but changing the channel information in a multichannel image will. You can go back and repeatedly change a duotone without affecting the original grayscale information, but you will have to rebuild or revert multichannel duotones to reverse changes or revert to the original information.

There is no absolute way to approach setting the duotone curves. A lot of how you set the curves depends on just what you want to achieve. Photoshop presets may offer a clue as to what you want to do generally (you can load these into the Duotone Curves from the Duotone Presets folder in the Photoshop program folder). Additional guidelines are provided here to assist you with what you are trying to accomplish specifically.

Curves often require a little manipulation to best fit the effect you want and the image you are applying them to. Preview the effects on the screen and make adjustments with the curves; then preview again. Use Undo/Redo and Histories (and Snapshots) to compare versions and subtle differences. You can learn a lot about setting duotones while using the curves, and the skills you develop in manipulation will be applicable to color and tonal corrections as well. The more you use duotones, the more confident you will be approaching them.

The goal for creating a duotone is to achieve a balance that makes the most of the image tonality and ink depth, while improving the look of the image. The following sections look at how to make a duotone by using each process.

CREATING A DUOTONE USING DUOTONE MODE

This method is the simpler of the two options for creating a duotone. It relies directly on the Duotone mode for creation of duotone effects.

Use the following steps to create a duotone using Duotone mode:

1. Open a grayscale image that you want to change to a duotone. If you want to use an image that is in color, you must first convert it to grayscale. Duotones are effective only on grayscale images.

   → For more information on converting color images to grayscale, **see** "Converting an Image from Color to Grayscale," **p. 487**.

2. Change the color mode from Grayscale to Duotone by selecting Image, Mode, Duotone.

Note

The Duotone dialog box will default to your previous settings. The original default will be monotone (one ink), and you can return to that by holding down (Option) [Alt] and clicking the Reset button when it appears (changes from the Cancel button). If you want to create a duotone, tritone, or quadtone, these options appear in the Type pop-up menu in the Duotone Options dialog box.

Note

If you want to include more than four inks, consider using the Multichannel mode.

   → For more information on using Multichannel to create duotones, **see** "Creating a Duotone Using Multichannel Mode," **p. 530**.

3. Select a color for each ink by clicking the color box. This will open the Color Picker. You can use the Color Picker to select CMYK, Lab, HSB, or RGB colors, or select from a number of book color sets such as PANTONE colors from the Custom Color menu (opened by clicking the Custom button).

PART

VI

CH

24

Color Books

Although there are book colors onscreen that attempt to replicate the color of the actual swatches, when doing spot color work you really need to check against a printed swatch book to be sure the color is exactly what you want. The books themselves are often fairly expensive—it is probably not practical to get all of them unless you are very, very serious about spot color. If you have a favorite service, ask them what they recommend as they may not match all of the color books as standard practice.

---

4. Set the Curves for each ink by clicking the Curves swatch. When the Duotone Curves dialog box opens, you can alter Curve gradients by placing and moving guide points with the mouse, or you can enter numeric values in the percentage as you would when using the Curves dialog box.

Tip

Naming channels properly is helpful in keeping track of plates, especially if you are planning to split the channels (using Multichannel). Some will already be named. Names you enter will be assigned to the channels, and when the channels are separated, the documents are named based on the name(s) of the channels. Custom Color selections from books automatically register the color name in the channel, but at times you may want to name these yourself (for custom colors) or augment the names. For example, it might be helpful to show the percentages of the CMYK colors in naming a color if a spot color ink you create is set up as a CMYK mix. When you split the channels, each plate will be easy to identify by the name, and you can re-create color associations (split channels will become simply Black as a channel ink, although the name of the color will be retained as the filename).

5. Compare the results of the change with the original by checking and unchecking the preview box.
6. At this point, you might want to save the duotone in presets, if you are confident that it achieves an effect that you might like to repeat.
7. When you are satisfied with the appearance of the duotone, save the image.

A simple duotone (with no alpha channels) will allow you the option to save as a Photoshop, Photoshop 2, Photoshop EPS, or RAM image. For use with other applications, choose Photoshop EPS. You might need to consider other options for saving and getting the right output from the file.

 If you are having trouble getting a duotone to print when saved as a duotone image, see "Printing Duotones" in the Troubleshooting section at the end of this chapter.

CREATING A DUOTONE USING MULTICHANNEL MODE

The duotone effect can be created in the Multichannel mode, but it is somewhat more complicated than just using the Duotone dialog box. Also, the changes in the Multichannel mode are more permanent and difficult to manage than in the Duotone dialog box; the changes to the multichannel image actually alter the pixel information in the channels as they are applied, unlike Duotone Curves.

Note

A similar effect can be achieved using Grayscale mode and adding a spot color, but as of this writing, the preview in Grayscale mode is not as exact as the preview in Multichannel mode.

Use the following steps to create a duotone effect in Multichannel mode:

1. Open a grayscale image that you want to change to a duotone. If you want to use an image that is in color, convert it to Grayscale mode (unless you plan to use the color channels to create the duotone; in that case, you would convert directly to Multichannel).

Note

You can use multiple source images for creating duotones in Multichannel mode. To do this, repeat Steps 1 and 2 for each image to be included, and move the images into one file as separate channels.

2. Change the color mode from Grayscale to Multichannel by choosing Image, Mode, Multichannel.

3. Duplicate the Black channel by dragging the channel to the Create New Channel button on the Channel palette. Do this once for every additional color you want to use. For example, if you want three colors, you need to duplicate the Black channel twice. This step may be unnecessary if you are using multiple images.

Tip

When completing Step 3, duplicate an extra alpha channel so that one channel remains untouched should you need to revert or add another channel. This can save you from having to reopen the original. If you use a duplicate channel, hide the duplicate by clicking off its visibility.

4. Select a color for the color channels created in Step 3. To do this, double-click one of the channels you intend to use as a color in the Channels palette. This will open either the Spot Channel Options dialog box (if the channel is already assigned as a spot color) (see Figure 24.8) or the Channel Options dialog box if the channel needs to be changed to a spot color (see Figure 24.9). If the channel is already a spot color, you can click the color swatch to bring up the Color Picker dialog box and select the color you want to use. If the Channel Options dialog box opens when you double-click a channel, the Spot Color indicator must be checked in order to select a Spot color. Repeat this for each color channel in use.

Figure 24.8
Double-clicking the channel will open the Spot Color Options dialog box if the channel is already a Spot Color.

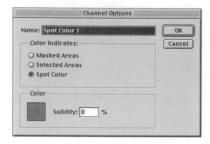

Figure 24.9
When you're duplicating a channel, the result may be a Spot Color or mask, depending on previous settings. Double-click the channel in the Channels palette to open the Channel Options dialog box, and be sure the Spot Color indicator is checked if it is to be used for a spot color.

5. Manipulate the channels with the Curves to create the duotone effect you want. It is probably best to start with the darkest ink for the greatest control of the tonality. Use of the Curves should be identical to your method for using Curves with duotone inks. Repeat this step for each color you created in Steps 3 and 4.

6. Manipulate channel information as desired to add other effects. The effects will be applied to only the currently selected channels (using Duotone mode, this is not possible; there is only one channel, so all colors are affected by changes to the channel). For example, you may want to create type in one of the pure spot colors, rather than a duotone mix, or you may want to apply sharpening or other effects to a single channel. To apply effects to more than one channel at a time, hold the Shift key down and select the channels you want to work on.

→ For more information on how to manipulate individual channels for spot color control, **see** "Using Selection to Apply Spot Color," **p. 542**.

7. Set the name of the channel so that you can readily recognize the colors if you plan to split the channels. (Custom Color selections automatically register the color name in the channel.)

8. Compare the results of the change with the original by checking and unchecking the preview box.

Note

As of this writing, Multichannel previews are more accurate than Grayscale, but they are not 100%, and do not have the advantage of adjustment like Overprint Colors in Duotone mode. For this reason, it may be best to define the duotone colors and Curves using Duotone mode (which has more accurate previews) and then switch to Multichannel mode for Step 6.

9. When you are satisfied with the results, save the image.

This method offers possibilities that cannot be duplicated in Duotone mode because the channel information can be treated separately. It also allows you to use completely different tonal sources for the duotone (Duotone mode can work with only one tonal source). It is an option for flexibility that you can use alone or in conjunction with the Duotone mode functions.

Split Channels

An option in the Channels pop-up menu enables you to split your color channels into separate documents. This has a variety of uses, from helping with changes and corrections to doing color and grayscale conversions, to creating special effects. Split channels appear only as grayscale separations, but the documents take the name of the channel (color) they are separated as. Split channels are easily reassembled using Multichannel options (the Merge Channels on the Channels palette pop-up menu, which is available only when more than one single channel document is currently open).

ORDERING INKS IN DUOTONES AND OVERPRINT COLORS

If there is no other scheme that you are following (CMYK, RGB, and so on) for which there is a predefined order, it is suggested that the darkest color be placed as the first ink in the Duotones Options and that the tones get lighter as the ink number goes up. For example, if you are using a light blue, dark blue, and black, black would be Ink 1, dark blue would be Ink 2, and light blue would be Ink 3. This represents the stacking order in which you will want the inks to print to the page. There may be subtle differences in printing a blue over a black, for example, which depends on the opacity of the ink, absorption, printing method, and a variety of other factors.

An opaque ink will cover the inks it prints with and will probably not mix well (a good example of this is metallic inks). For this reason, opaque inks are usually put down on the paper last (and appear at the top of your ink layering). Creative use of ink layering can produce some interesting effects, depending on ink opacities, paper, and so on. Unless you specify that the inks should be put down in a specific order, most printers would probably decide the order in which to put the ink down for the best results. (The order is usually a matter of standard practice, although it can be a matter of convenience; an expert pressman knows when it will make a difference). However, failing to order opaque inks correctly (and making these intentions clear to your service or printer) may lead to unexpected results.

When you're viewing onscreen, the ink order seems to matter slightly less than properly setting the opacity of the ink and the way that ink mixtures actually appear in print. You can view and control the appearance of ink mixtures using the Overprint Colors dialog box.

Tip

If you know an ink might have a certain solidity (that is, an opaqueness where it simply covers other inks), it might be best to use Multichannel rather than Duotone mode to build your duotones. Grayscale mode with spot colors would also work. Duotone mode deals best with inks that mix (0% opacity).

To open the Overprint Colors dialog box, click the Overprint Colors button on the Duotone Options dialog box (see Figure 24.10). The Overprint Colors dialog box (see Figure 24.11) shows swatches of how you should expect ink combinations to appear in print when mixed at 100%. It is recommended that you check these against actual results (press proofs). Without a prior test print of the results of your duotone settings, it is not possible to set up the colors accurately. The Overprint Colors dialog box can, however, give you a quick idea of what the colors will look like when combined at full density if there are no ink opacity issues.

Figure 24.10
Overprint colors button can be selected from Photoshop's Color Picker using any of the swatch books and color picker controls. These are settings that you will control by eye. The changes do not affect the color of the ink, only the way those inks appear in the image onscreen.

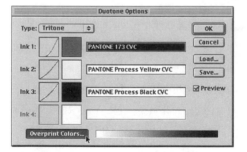

Figure 24.11
The swatches in the Overprint Colors dialog box show the color that inks will print in combination at 100%. To alter the appearance of the color mixtures, double-click the swatch and select the color in which the ink mixtures should appear.

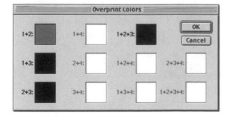

You can change the appearance of the swatches by double-clicking to open the Color Picker. You can then use the Color Picker to select the proper result. This will, in turn, affect the appearance of the image on the screen. It will in no way affect the image pixels or output of the image information.

Caution

You can do more harm than good if you get into the Overprint Colors dialog box without knowing very well what colors you need to change and match. You need a real understanding of what the result will look like, and the best way to obtain this result is with actual testing in print. Changing the overprint values by clicking a swatch and altering the color does not change the output; it changes only the way the inks present onscreen. Do not use this method to set or alter color to the way you want it to appear.

SETTING THE CURVES AND CHOOSING INKS

The goal of setting the duotone curves is to manipulate the image information to benefit the image. This might take the form of developing better tonality, adding hue to the image, or creating special effects. In a simplistic view, the lighter blends emphasize the contrast in the brighter or highlight/midtone range of the image, and the darker blends emphasize the shadow details. To reflect this in the curves, darker inks are often steeply graded in the shadow tones, whereas lighter inks are more steeply graded in lighter tones. Throughout the tonal range, the inks blend to form shades and tones, which can be finessed to the advantage of the image. A little experimentation and preview in a color-calibrated workspace enables you to see what combination you prefer before committing to it.

Although there is a little art to the experimentation, there is science as well. A 50% gray ink at 100% strength still shows at 50% gray when printed; it can never get darker unless mixed with another ink. With this in mind, any ink affects an image most strongly in tonal areas that are lighter than the 100% value of the ink. The effect is almost strictly on the lighter tones because of the subtractive nature of ink (the more you put on the page of various colors, the darker it gets), yet a very light ink may appear to actually lighten the tone of a black ink slightly—this effect can be heightened or lessened depending on how those inks are put down.

Grade an ink steeply in its effective range, perhaps going to 100% of its gray value. Concentrate the ink in its effective area, and remove its density when it gets out of bounds to lessen the chance of any unexpected effects (such as having too great a total ink density or adversely affecting darker inks).

Tip

To find out the effective tone of an ink, you may have to test it. Create a new, small document (say 100×100 pixels). Set the color as the foreground color and fill the color at 100% into a new document with the Paintbucket tool or (Option-Delete) [Alt+Delete]. Take a reading with the Eyedropper set to measure grayscale (K). The Info palette will show the sample as a measurement in percentage of black. Use that measure to determine the maximum effective point for the ink, and be sure to have another ink take over and/or augment the tonality from there because the ink will not appear any darker than the measurement you make.

Be sure to blend inks and overlap gradients so that one ink can pick up where the next leaves off. Finally, use the gradient bar at the bottom of the Duotone dialog box to judge the quality of the gradient you are creating. Although you could take a screenshot and measure the tonal blend for accuracy, eyeing the result is probably as good. The gradient should appear relatively smooth and even, unless you are using the duotone for some type of image correction or special effect. Figures 24.12 to 24.14 demonstrate the effects you get from applying curves.

Figure 24.12
This set of curves was created for a quad-tone using three grays and black, using the theory that inks should be heavily graded in their zone. The results of application are surprisingly good on a wide variety of images (although it may not be your least expensive or best solution).

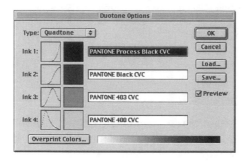

Figure 24.13
The detail of the curve settings shows how the inks are inter-twined. Note that the lightest ink never goes below 10%, even at white. The lightest ink is a PANTONE 400, which appears with about 17% black when at 100%. At 10%, this ink appears as 2% black; however, it still uses a 10% dot, so it covers the page better.

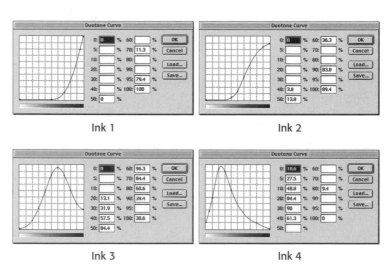

Ink 1   Ink 2

Ink 3   Ink 4

Presets for duotones provided with Photoshop almost all show curves that emphasize the mid to dark tones by increasing the contrast with the inks in the upper portion of the curves. This works fine for normal and low-key images; however, it would not work as well for high-key images, which would probably suffer from the attention to shadow detail. With attention to shadow detail, the highlights would flatten out, which would do damage to the appearance of a high-key image. Generally, curves need to be set dependent on the overall tonality of the image; high-key images should be set to emphasize detail in the highlight areas and low-key images should be set to emphasize detail in the shadows.

Figure 24.14
The results of applying the curve set to a black-and-white image separated as color plates. The original image appears as comparison to the four plates generated from it.

© Seattle Support Group, ssgrp.com

Black

PANTONE 400

PANTONE 403

PANTONE Black

Tip

When saving duotone presets for use with other images, give them meaningful names. For example, use the PANTONE numbers, process letters and low, norm, or high, to indicate the image key. For example, duonorm2597K would be a duotone setting for a normal key image using PANTONE 2597 and black (K). Putting the tone type first (duo, tri, quad), and following with the key (low, norm, high) can help you select from your duotone list by picking from easy groupings as they will list alphabetically.

The choice of inks plays an important part in deciding how to set the curves. If you use two shades of black ink, for example, you probably want to de-emphasize the total density of the inks or you will darken the image (see curve settings of this type in Figure 24.7). If you use two lighter color tones (nonblack), you probably want to emphasize the total density to compensate as much as possible or the overall tonality of the image will compress. If there is no compensation, the image might lighten considerably, depending on the inks and curves you choose.

When choosing inks, being aware of what you want to accomplish is important. Although some of the choice is subjective, a lot of it is using good color sense to accomplish a goal with the duotone. A rule of thumb should be to use at least one dark or black ink: A dark ink can represent lighter tones, but the opposite can never happen. Evenly distributing the color tones can help improve ink coverage. For example, if using three inks, you might consider using a black, another color which represents a midtone and a light color. This can maximize coverage. When choosing color, also try to work with harmonious color, meaning color that will blend along the tonal scale effectively. For example, you might choose a black, red, and light yellowish-orange, or a black, a blue, and sky blue to choose tones in the same family. The harmony will make it easier to set up effective curves. If you chose a combination of, say, dark red, medium-light blue, and yellow, you may be able to wrangle a result out of the image, but it will depend on the image. A more abstract image may deal with unusual color selection better than a familiar setting. It would probably be a struggle to balance the color mixtures to create a curve set for a normal image, unless you leave the tonal response of the inks with the default curve settings or make only slight variations. However, if you are going to practice the latter, you may not be making best use of the duotone advantage. Save the wilder experiments for when you have a little experience with duotones and are confident with them.

Using the plan of attack for shaping your duotone curves can help you create the duotone that is best for your image. Setting the curves without some sort of technique or method might prove quite fruitless. First look at the image to decide the goal, select inks compatible with that goal, and apply curves to make the most of the inks you have chosen in the image you have.

Using Duotone for Tonal Corrections

Duotone curves can be used to make subtle changes and corrections in difficult black-and-white images. Although the images will not retain the richness of duotoning or the effect of multiple inks, creating duotone effects to correct grayscale images can help strengthen subtle detail, and some of this can be retained in switching back to Grayscale mode. Consider the duotone curves as part of your grayscale correction arsenal.

For example, if you have an image with subtle highlight detail (such as a wedding picture where dress detail can become somewhat washed out or faded due to harsh flash lighting), you can separate the highlights from the medium and darker tones in the image and make subtle adjustments. To do this, open the image in black-and-white, and then switch to duotone and pick a black and light-gray ink for your colors. Use the light gray to emphasize the highlight area of the image (see Figure 24.15), and then separate the channels into a Multichannel image. This will give you separate plates/channels for the black (as a general tonal anchor), and the highlights (somewhat isolated from the rest of the darker image tones in a separate channel). You can then work on the subtleties of the light tones independently of the darker tones in the image without really having to be concerned too much with the repercussions your changes will have across the darker tones. Work with both channels visible but with only the lighter ink active. Generally, you will want to accomplish your changes using the curves—although other methods of alteration and change that you are comfortable with may come in handy. It depends on the image.

Figure 24.15
The curves here slightly de-emphasize the black ink in the highlight while emphasizing the gray in the lighter tones. This serves to take a fingerprint of the light tones. As the ink is only 25% gray, it will be effective mostly over the lighter tones in the image.

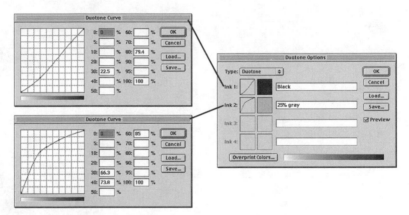

When the channels are separated in the multichannel image, they will look something like the examples in Figure 24.16. Keep in mind that although the Gray channel is darker, it only has about 25% of the effect of a black ink.

→ For more information on measuring tonality and adjusting tone, **see** "Corrections with Curves," **p. 456**.

Tip

Currently, there is no option to convert from Duotone mode to Grayscale while maintaining the effect of the curves. To do this, first convert to RGB mode from Duotone and then to Grayscale.

→ For more information on making a conversion from duotone to grayscale, **see** "Converting from Duotone to Grayscale or Color Plates," **p. 512**.

Figure 24.16
Work with only the 25% gray plate to adjust the highlights. These changes can be made visually, or by using methods discussed earlier to adjust image tone.

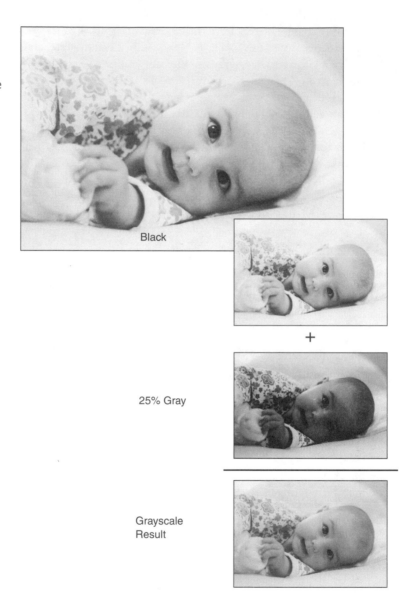

Black

+

25% Gray

Grayscale
Result

SELECTING AND USING SPOT COLOR

Spot coloring uses additional ink color(s) to achieve color that is not possible in CMYK printing. The application might be truly spot coloring (that is, application of a special color in a particular spot such as to fill type), or it can be used as additional color to broaden the range of color print possibility by either using a color outside the attainable gamut of CMYK or choosing a CMYK equivalent to print in a solid tone. In other words, spot coloring can help attain colors that are impossible in traditional CMYK prints.

Determining whether you need a spot color to match a color in an image is a lot trickier than assigning and using them as spot or fill colors. There is currently no way to automate that type of separation, so the application of spot color to improve an image would need to be done manually, very carefully, and by quite a skilled hand. Also, proofing methods are lacking in accuracy, so expensive press proofs are the only dependable option.

Some uses of spot colors, such as for varnishes and bold packaging colors, are rather obvious and easy. Using the CMYK preview, knowing what is attainable in CMYK conversion, and deciding on the importance of color matching are key factors in making spot color decisions.

Use the following steps to incorporate a spot color in your image:

1. Open the image in which you intend to use the spot color.

2. Create a new channel by selecting New Spot Channel from the Channel palette's pop-up menu.

3. Choose the color for the spot channel by selecting the color swatch from the New Spot Channel dialog box. While it is open, select the appropriate Solidity (opacity) for the ink you plan to use. Choose OK to accept your selections.

PART

VI

CH

24

Solidity

The *solidity* of an ink is its opaqueness or capability to obscure other inks as it is applied. Generally, the opaqueness of an ink is 0% (even with black) unless it is a special purpose ink. Metallic inks, for example, will often cover everything underneath them with 100% opacity, so their solidity should be 100%.

---

4. Apply the spot color as percentages of black in grayscale in the channel (not the Layers). 100% black applies 100% of the color, and 0% black applies no color. You might want to use selections from the image to create an area or areas to apply the spot color.

→ For more information on using spot colors with selections, **see** "Using Selection to Apply Spot Color," **p. 542**.

5. (Option) Remove other colors from the mix in the spot color by using the spot channel as a selection (Select, Load Selection) and desaturate (Shift–Cmd–U) [Shift+Ctrl+U].

Tip

You may need to adjust the tonality, depending on what you are trying to achieve with the spot color application. To do this, keep the selection active and use the Curves or Levels to adjust the tone to suit the spot application.

→ For more information on techniques for accomplishing this, **see** "Using Selection to Apply Spot Color," **p. 542**.

6. Save the image when you are satisfied with the effect.

Test the possibility that you can avoid using the spot color by converting to CMYK and merging the Spot channel(s). Be aware that the change will rely on screening rather than using the spot color as a more solid tone. So, even if it appears okay on your monitor, the switch can have detrimental effects on the appearance of images in print, especially if the spot color is light.

Halftone Screening

Screening is the process by which inks are distributed in printing. Ink densities are broken down into dot sizes in a series of rows. The screens for individual inks are angled so that colors mix with less chance of forming a noticeable pattern. You can see a quick example by applying the Color Halftone filter (Filter, Pixelate, Color Halftone) to an image. Use a radius of 4 along with the default screen angles. After applying the filter, view the results by looking at the channels individually. Note that lighter image areas use smaller dots that will not blend together to form a solid area of color, and as such are more apt to be apparent to the naked eye.

Spot color acts as an added color, giving you more possibility and selectivity in color choice and control for printing (although some of the techniques may be useful in graphics with other purposes). For example, using a varnish is an effective spot coloring to add luster to an image—either the whole thing, or selectively. Varnish is applied just like any other spot color with the specific use of adding shine or glossy overlay. For example, a ring printed with CMYK colors might appear reasonably close in color representation, but a varnish added to it can make it sparkle more like metal and stone, and will help it stand out starkly from a flat background (see Figure 24.17).

Figure 24.17
The ring at left is selected and then the selection is saved and converted to a spot color. The spot color in this case will be an applied varnish. The resulting varnish plate appears to the right.

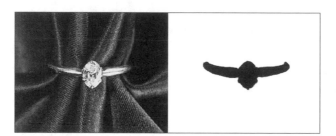

This example is somewhat of a special case where the ink is considered 100% opaque and is simply applied to the image. In some instances where you want pure spot colors, you will have to apply the ink and then remove other colors that will otherwise mix with the spot color that you apply.

USING SELECTION TO APPLY SPOT COLOR

Spot color will often be applied in an area defined by selection. The selection can be created in any fashion, but the technique for applying color depends on the final purpose. In a spot replacement, you will be applying a nonprocess color to specific areas of an image; generally, you will want this application to be pure color—not mixed with CMYK process. You can use careful selection and replacement to change color in an image, and even mix spot and process colors if you do so wisely.

Caution

It is not recommended that you mix spot color and other color unless you are very confident that you know the ramifications of what you are doing. Simply introducing color without a clear direction or plan can have costly side effects--both in the cost of the printing and cost of redoing what came out wrong. Knowing how colors will mix comes with experience. After careful experimentation you will find that you can use selection and replacement to color in an image, and even mix spot and process colors.

The trick to spot coloring is neutralizing some or all of the other colors in the image so that only the spot color shows. In effect, the spot color will knock out the background. Make a selection, use it to fill in the spot color area on the spot color channel, and then use the same selection to delete ink application in all the other channels. Another method is simply to fill the selected area with white, and then use the same selection to create the spot color fill for the channel. The following example shows how to use type for application of a spot color.

Knockout Colors

Knocking out color refers to the action of one color overriding the others so that there is no blend between them. When a color is applied to knock out other color, it is like deleting that color area in the other channels. In this case, inclusion of the spot color knocks out the background so that the tonality and color are removed.

Use the following steps to create type in a spot color:

1. Open the image to which you want to add the spot color type.

2. Choose the Type tool and click an appropriate area of the image to place the type.

3. Select the spot color you want to use for the type by clicking the color swatch in the Tool Options bar and choose the color in the Color Picker when it opens. When you find the color you want, make note of the choice for use in Step 12.

Note

Step 3 will not be used to apply the spot color. Instead, it will be used as a preview for placement and viewing.

4. Input the type, and place it as desired.

→ For more information on using fonts, **see** "Type Control, Placement, and Settings," **p. 221**.

5. When the type is set as you want it, switch the type color to pure white (255,255,255 in RGB, or 0,0,0,0 in CMYK). To do this, highlight the type layer, change the foreground color swatch to white, and click (Option-Delete) [Alt+Delete].

Note

The purpose behind this step is to remove the color so that it will not affect the application of the spot color ink. It will also not affect the color plates for the image below, so there is still a chance to make alterations in placement.

6. Accept the changes by clicking OK on the Type Tools palette.

7. (Option) Add effects to the type layer using Effects (Layer, Effects).

8. Duplicate the type layer.

9. Remove any Layer Effects by selecting Layer, Layer Style, Clear Layer Style.

10. Make a selection of the text using the Magic Wand with Tolerance set at 1 and Contiguous unchecked in the Magic Wand Options palette. This will create a selection of the type only, and should do so with a single click. Another way to make this selection is to press (Cmd) [Ctrl] click on the layer in the Layers palette.

11. Create a New Spot Channel by selecting New Spot Channel from the Channels palette pop-up menu.

12. Choose the color selected in Step 3 for the channel color, and change the ink opacity to 0% (unless using an opaque ink, such as a metallic).

13. Remove the duplicate layer created in Step 8.

Steps 10 and 11 will create a channel that makes the spot color full strength (100%) over the type. As long as the ink is not opaque, the effects added to the type layer (Step 7) will affect the shading for the spot color. These steps essentially create a layer mask, which allows you to apply spot color to the image. Figures 24.18 to 24.20 diagram the effect, showing the interaction of the layers, the result of the steps, and the final result.

Figure 24.18
The type is set in its own layer and then is used to make a selection that is filled with the spot color in a separate channel. The color appears to be applied to the text layer, although it is really independent.

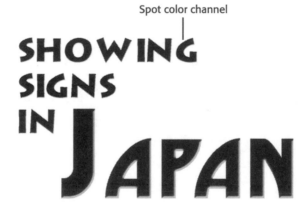

Spot color channel

White text layer with bevel

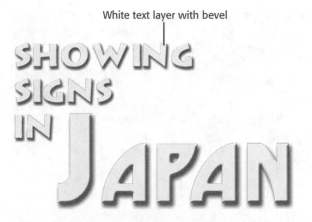

Background

© PhotoSphere Images Ltd.,
www.photosphere.com

Figure 24.19
When you have completed the steps, there are two layers and five channels, as pictured here. You can flatten the image to accept the changes and save in a print-compatible format (TIFF, EPS, and so on).

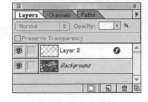

Figure 24.20
The flattened result knocks out the background with the white, and then fills in the spot color. To stand out in this image, the type needs all the help it can get. Considering the image, a metallic ink might make this work the best.

As long as the ink is not opaque, you can change the spot color by mixing it with other available colors (for example, Cyan, Magenta, and Yellow). To mix the colors, highlight the type layer and select the channel you want to mix with the spot color. Choose Image, Adjust, Levels to open the Levels dialog box, and use the bottom sliders to add color to the type (see Figure 24.21).

Figure 24.21
The Output slider enables you to selectively darken the tone of any ink in an active layer. Here the type layer and the Yellow layer are made active, and Yellow is brought up to 50%. This will result in the Yellow mixing at 50% with 100% of the spot color.

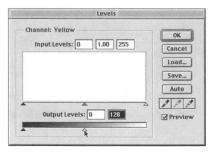

Selections used for this type of color application can be quite a bit more complicated. For example, say you have an image with flowers whose color was unobtainable in CMYK. The image is to be used in a color cover, and the subject is color correction and enhancement. Well, you could just switch to CMYK and hope it was good enough, but using a spot color would probably improve the effect of the color (and would prove more fitting to the subject). However, when using the method described in the preceding paragraph, the flowers come out flat, and without detail. What you have to do is work with more complicated selections and be more selective in color removal so that the tones blend better.

For example, the following image (Figure 24.22; page 24 in the PDF workbook downloadable from www.ps6.com) has bright red flowers, well out of gamut for CMYK. To print this right, you have to put in a little more effort than making a knockout or straight exchange of color. You have to make a selection of color to replace or augment, and use that selection to alter the image.

Figure 24.22
This image has reds that are clearly out of the CMYK gamut. The red is close to a PANTONE 172, and with careful selection of the flowers, the color can be replaced with the PANTONE as a spot color.

© Seattle Support Group, ssgrp.com

PART
VI
CH
24

My choice here would be to make a color selection using Color Range, use that selection to create a new spot color channel by duplicating the saved Color Range selection, and then selectively desaturate color in that area using the same selection. In this case, because you are adding red, you would want to desaturate yellow and magenta in proportion, or you might find (regardless of the preview) that the color in the print gets darker. In other words, as you add the replacement color, desaturate the color(s) it is replacing. See Figures 24.23 to 24.25 to see some detail of the methods that would be used here.

Figure 24.23
This selection was made using color range. The Add (+) Eyedropper was used to sample a broad range of the reds in the flower. Then the selection was saved (Selection, Save Selection).

Figure 24.24
While the selection was active, a spot color channel was created by selecting New Spot Channel from the Channels pop-up menu. This will automatically fill in the area where the spot color is to be applied. All you have to do is choose the spot color.

This effectively combines blending and knockout techniques, and is a more complex use of spot coloring. It is, perhaps, the most complex you will ever use. The selection does not completely remove all color behind the spot application so the application blends somewhat with the surrounding CMYK. This leaves a delicate balance of blended edges and a spot color application that improves on the potential of the color available in the CMYK space without flatly involving it as a knockout.

Magenta Before

Magenta After

Yellow Before

Yellow After

Figure 24.25
The yellow and magenta channels were desaturated using the same selection because these two colors in CMYK will make up any reds. Simply go to each of the channels and delete the area with white as the background color.

TROUBLESHOOTING

PRINTING DUOTONES

When I send a Photoshop Duotone to print as an EPS, I do not get the results I expect. How can I make sure that this works as desired?

Several things could cause this. First, if you are not printing to a PostScript printer, the results will print from the screen preview rather than the image because EPS files are meant to print to PostScript devices only. Second, if you are printing to a PostScript device, it is possible that there is some incompatibility with the Photoshop Duotone, making it necessary to make adjustments either in the layout program you are using, the output method, or both. An easy solution in either case is to change the duotone into a different type of file for printing.

The best choice for conversion will probably be converting the image to a TIFF. To do this, change the duotone to a multichannel image to split the channels. Next, prepare the image for conversion to Grayscale mode. For this you have to have at least the Black channel. If you are not using a Black ink, add a channel, call it Black, and leave it blank (if you don't do this, Photoshop will take the uppermost Channel and rename it Black). Make the conversion to Grayscale mode. Check to be sure that the names are right for the colors, and resave as a TIFF. Then replace the image in the layout application with the file you have just created.

→ For more information on output options for duotones, **see** "Outputting Duotone Images," **p. 519**.

PHOTOSHOP AT WORK: REPLACING OBJECT COLOR WITH A SPOT COLOR

This project section takes all of the spot color and duotone theory provided in this chapter and puts it together in one project. Your goal will be to make a hextone (six-color channel) image to change and emphasize the color of the source image.

A hextone uses six colors or, in this case, six printing channels. There are many options for putting together complex color documents, and this may include working in multiple color modes. It is sometimes best to build an image in separate parts and then put them all together. This not only allows you to save the independent pieces but will probably speed working with the documents, especially if they are large. Also, if portions of the image require color mode change and others don't, working separately can keep color changes to a minimum.

Start with the image in Figure 24.26 (see page 24 in the PDF Workbook file downloadable from www.ps6.com).

Figure 24.26
This Porsche would probably print okay in CMYK, but spot color will allow enhancement or alteration of the color, and varnish can make the polish stand off the page.

© Seattle Support Group, ssgrp.com

The basic problem here is to color a car with a spot color, both to change the color of the car and allow good ink coverage. Next is to add a varnish plate for luster. In the final image, I also replaced the background and added type in the spot color, with layer effects.

APPLYING SPOT COLOR TO THE IMAGE

There are a number of different ways to color the car and incorporate the spot color. However, considering the varied tone of the car, duotone curves can help control application of the paint. If you try to apply the color with color selection alone, it might prove very difficult to get a mix that makes the car appear to have a sheen. Using duotone allows several things: It limits the colors (removing potential color casts) and adjusts ink and color according to tone. These are great advantages in this case.

Use the following steps to apply a spot color to the car:

1. Open the image from the workbook on page 24.

2. Make any necessary color or levels corrections.

3. Make and save a selection of the car. This will allow you to isolate the object in its own layer. See Figure 24.27.

Figure 24.27
To create the selection, I used a hard-edged airbrush and shift-clicked between points along the outline. Holding the Shift key down draws straight lines from point to point as you click.

→ For more information on selection, **see** "Selection and Masking," **p. 93**.

4. When the selection of the car is complete, cut and paste the car. This will isolate the car on its own layer.

 5. Next, you will want to create a selection for the painted portions of the car only. Duplicate the current selection and erase those areas where there is no paint. To view the image and selection you saved previously at the same time by clicking on the channel view, be sure the Adobe eyeball is on for the color composite and the channel you are using to shape the mask (see Figure 24.28).

Figure 24.28
To get the results, I created a new channel and used Quick Mask to paint in areas over the tires and glass. After these areas were filled in, I did a calculation and subtracted the new selection from the selection of the whole car.

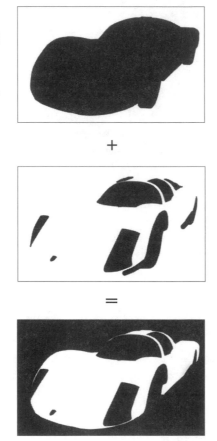

→ For more information on calculations, **see** "Converting an Image from Color to Grayscale," **p. 487**.

6. A third selection can represent the varnish (see Figure 24.29). Load the original selection of the car, switch to Quick Mask, and remove the areas where there should be no luster to the car (the tires, the windshield wipers, the open window, and so on). Save the selection as a channel, and name it Varnish.

Figure 24.29
The selection for the varnish was created by removing areas that would not have varnish applied from the original selection of the car.

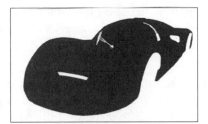

7. Load the selection created in Step 5 and copy and paste the isolated car.

8. Copy the layer and desaturate (Shift–Cmd–U) [Shift+Ctrl+U]. This serves more than one purpose, but in the original document, it removes the color of the car so that the spot color can be applied without interference from other inks.

9. Copy the desaturated layer to a new document using the Duplicate Layer command on the Layers palette pop-up menu.

10. In the new document, change the mode to Grayscale and then Duotone.

11. Select the duotone colors for painting the car. One should be Process Black, and the other whatever color you want to paint the car. I chose FOCOLTONE 3394.

12. Use the duotone curves to apply color. I used a rather heavy-handed application of the color because the tone will be affected by information in the original image as well as by the duotone separation. See Figure 24.30.

Figure 24.30
The goal here is to make the color prominent, yet add some variance to the applied tone so that highlights appear shiny.

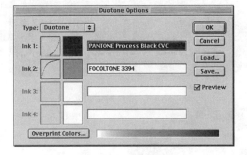

13. Separate the duotone by switching to Multichannel mode. This will separate the image into the FOCOLTONE and process black channels.

14. Copy the channels to the original image. You can do this using the Duplicate Channel command on the Channels palette pop-up menu.

15. Save and close the duotone image.

At this point you need to work with some of the settings until you get the result you want. The layers can all be on, and so should the additional spot channels, except the varnish (there is no way to make the varnish appear properly onscreen). You may prefer the extra black channel on or off for greater contrast in the paint. If it's on, you will want to merge the black back into the other plates before you finish the image.

ADDING FINISHING TOUCHES

With the car separated, it was easy to replace the background and alter other portions of the image independently (see Figure 24.31). Here the background ground was replaced using the sky from another image (see Figure 24.32). The shadow for the car was drawn in its own layer manually using a soft airbrush and Overlay mode. The type was added as described in the section "Using Selection to Apply Spot Color," earlier in this chapter. For more even color matching and theme, portions of the Cyan were replaced with the spot color. In the end you should have a collection of some nine or ten channels (see Figure 24.33). The final result appears in the color section using CMYK separation.

Figure 24.31
The sky was used from this image by simply rotating 180 degrees and copying it to the other document above the background.

© PhotoSphere Images Ltd., www.photosphere.com

Figure 24.32
This upside-down sky makes an unusual landscape for the newly colored car.

Figure 24.33
The end result of your channel collection should look something like this, with six color channels and three or four selections that helped you achieve the effect. The selections can be deleted for the print version of the file to save space.

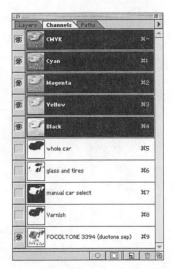

Caution

When using spot colors, be sure to keep account of the total ink. Some presses will be able to put down all six inks at once, so be sure you are not oversaturating the result. It may not be wise to mix spot color too heavily into darker areas of an image without careful scrutiny of the ink totals, or you will risk oversaturating the inks. This can cause press problems or additional costs for adjustments.

CHAPTER 25

HANDLING COLOR: FOR PRINT AND THE WEB

In this chapter

PRINTING CONSIDERATIONS

There are numerous printing considerations and options brought about by the printing process. These include spot coloring, duotoning, and CMYK conversions and corrections. Several additional finesse areas of print jobs occur in highlights and shadows. Specifically these are setting white point, setting black point, using UCR/GCR (Under Color Removal and Gray Color Removal), and considering total ink.

In printing, a *white point* should never be completely void of ink or it will be apparent in the printing. A spot in a print that is completely absent of ink is known as *blowout* and will seem like an imaging mistake. It is simply the visible area where printing goes from a 1% dot to 0%, or no dot. Although this can consciously be used as an effect with a specular highlight, generally it is something you want to avoid in printing and can avoid rather easily. Knowing what to do to correct for white points keeps images from running out of dots and blowing out on the press, as well as making the most out of image contrast.

Black points, UCR/GCR, and ink total are the opposite concern of white point. *Black point* is the area of the image where shadows become densest. At times the density, if left uncorrected, might either be too light to take advantage of the potential contrast, or too dense. When too dense ink may not be properly absorbed in printing. This can lead to a number of problems on the press including streaking, effects on drying time, and so forth. Generally, failure to correct this adds a prepress charge as the prepress person goes back to set the limits for you. Again, this is something that is easily controlled by setting your own black points, using UCR/GCR controls and ink limits.

UCR/GCR stands for *Under Color Removal and Gray Color Removal*; these are really sets of curves that control the proportional density of C, M, Y inks to black (K). The Total Ink Limit (and Black Ink Limit) enables you to set specific percentages for the maximum total ink in any color breakdown. Done properly, making settings and making the correct settings can save prepress charges and can improve your press results and the appearance of images printed in CMYK.

SETTING WHITE POINTS

Highlight white should be an actual color, measured at, or very close to, 4%C, 2%M, 2%Y and 0%K. This will keep a dot in the image, and produces a visually acceptable equivalent to white. This works two ways: First, it helps keep images from having areas that blow out (no printed dots), and it can help extend the dynamic contrast of the image (if it has not been corrected properly).

Note
As correction for white points and blowout is important only for images being printed, images should be in CMYK when performing this evaluation and correction.

Use the following steps to check and correct white point in your images before sending them to the printer.

1. Open an image you are ready to send to the printer (make sure it has been corrected for color as per the steps in Chapter 22).

→ For more information on color correction, **see** "Evaluating Image Color," "Basic Tonal Correction," and "Color Corrections," **pp. 409, 445,** and **465**.

→ For more information on color conversions, **see** "Color Conversions," **p. 485**.

2. Set the Eyedropper tool to sample a point, and then examine the highlight areas of the image, checking the readings for the samples in the Info palette. If you find that much of the highlight area gives consistent readings of no color information (255,255,255 for RGB, 0,0,0,0 for CMYK, or 0 for K), go to Step 3; if there are generally measurable tones (anything other than the previous readings), go to Step 4.

3. If you find areas of the image in which there is no color (as per measurements in the previous step), consider restoring the highlights from an original scan or image. Abundant areas that are blown out suggest an image might have been damaged by corrections or that it was not obtained properly.

Tip

If the highlights are absent in an original scan, consider changing the scanner settings and redo the scan. If the highlights are missing in the original image, you might want to consider another image unless this is being used for a special effect.

4. Take note of the lightest highlight setting you can find.

Tip

Take some time making the measurement in Step 4. There is no need to painstakingly sample every possible point, but check generally in apparent highlights. You can use the Threshold function to identify the lightest and darkest areas. Simply open Threshold (Image, Adjust, Threshold), and push the slider right to identify the lightest areas of the image (white on a black background) or left to identify the darkest areas (black on a white background).

5. If the values noted in Step 4 are 4,2,2,0 in CMYK, consider the white point corrected and go to Step 12. If the numbers are below this (0,0,0,0, to 4,2,2,0), go to the next step. If the numbers are higher than 4,2,2,0, you might need to revisit the section on levels corrections. If the values seem acceptable (considering the image), go to Step 12.

Note

It might be that values higher than 4,2,2,0 are desirable and do not require correction. For example, a low-key image might not have any strong highlights, and the numbers might be substantially different. However, this would be more the exception than the rule.

6. Open the Selective Color dialog box by choosing Image, Adjust, Selective Color.

7. Click the pop-up menu and select Whites (see Figure 25.1).

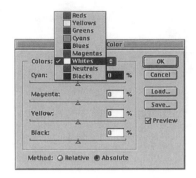

Figure 25.1
Choose Whites in the Selective Color dialog box to limit new changes to the white portions of the image.

8. Select the Absolute option button on the Selective Color dialog box.

9. Enter numbers in the Selective Color dialog boxes to make the totals for the lightest point 4%C, 2%M, 2%Y, and 0%K; for example, if the lightest point measured in Step 4 was 2C, 0M, 1Y, 0K, type 2 in C, 2 in M, 1 in Y, and 0 in K. This process adds these amounts to the absolute value you measured and adjusts the image globally.

10. Accept the changes by clicking OK on the Selective Color dialog box.

11. Make spot-checks with the Eyedropper tool to be sure you have achieved acceptable values.

12. Save the image.

As you have checked the image and determined (within reason) an absolute white value, the values you enter in Step 9 will add to the current white values in the image, raising the total of the brightest point to the desired, target level.

A similar effect can be accomplished using several other techniques. The best of these is using the eyedroppers from the Levels dialog box. In some cases this might be more convenient as the dropper can sample and apply the changes simultaneously. The eyedropper can be set to the desired CMYK value for white (double-click the white Eyedropper to open the Color Picker for setting the value). When the eyedropper clicks on a point, it changes that point to the value set for the dropper and reassigns values in the image accordingly. If you substitute this method for the Selective Color command used in Step 9, it should produce similar results.

Other methods might seem right but end up less accurate. For example, setting the curves to an absolute 4%C, 2%M, and 2%Y would change the entire image so that no pixel falls below the desired white value, but this can affect other colors, and is less accurate than either of the other two methods. The other methods attempt to confine the adjustments to white areas of the image, whereas this affects a global change regardless of color value.

White point is also important in black-and-white images. Generally, you can trust presses to hold about a 2% dot, so limiting the blacks to higher than 2% will save the image area from blowout in most cases. You might need to consult with your printer or service for their recommendation.

SET BLACK POINTS FOR PRINTING COLOR

Although it might initially seem like a good idea, print black should not be composed of 100% of all four CMYK inks. Printing at 400% total inks *oversaturates* image areas, and might cause the ink to run, streak, dry incorrectly, or just otherwise turn into a total disaster. You might be charged to fix it, or worse—the job might be run at your expense. Knowing what to do to correct for black points and how to use UCR/GCR makes images more stable on the press and saves time and money.

To correct for blacks in CMYK, it is first necessary to set up GCR/UCR settings including ink limits (see Figure 25.2). These are set up in the Color Settings dialog box by choosing Edit, Color Settings (Shift-Cmd-A) [Shift+Ctrl+A] and choosing Custom CMYK from the Settings pop-up menu. The settings here will affect the curves Photoshop uses to separate the inks in the image. GCR and UCR are different curve sets that accomplish similar things: Both are used to limit ink totals based on the total allowable percentage entered. You can get these values from your printer or service. By default, I use UCR, 270% and 98% Black.

Figure 25.2
The Custom CMYK dialog box allows you to adjust total ink limits.

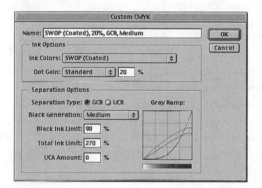

Note

Always consult with your service bureau and printer before correcting color on a job if you are unsure of anything, if printing in color is new to you, or if you are using a different process or service. Different machines and different processes (as well as different papers and other media) require changes in color settings to get materials right—or at least very close to what you expect. Consulting first saves cost and time. Always do proofs, and see whether you can get samples or a test run before doing the final output.

The UCR/GCR sets the total allowable inks, and using the Levels command and the black Eyedropper enables you to choose which pixel is assigned absolute black—that separation which represents the darkest possible values of inks based on your setup. The selection redistributes the color information in appropriate channels in consideration of the selected sample. This technique is great for eliminating undesired shadow detail, or to create flat black expanses for backgrounds as well.

Use the following steps to set black points using the Levels eyedropper:

1. Be sure a total ink limit is set in the UCR/GCR setting by selecting Edit, Color Settings to open the Color Settings dialog box. From the pop-up menu at the top of the dialog box, choose Custom; then, choose Custom CMYK from the CMYK pop-up menu in the Working Spaces area. Check with your printer or service bureau for the proper GCR/UCR setting for your output.

2. Open the image you want to correct.

3. Open the Levels dialog box by selecting Image, Adjust, Levels.

4. Double-click the black Eyedropper and when the Color Picker dialog box opens, the totals from the CMYK boxes should add up to the Total Ink Limit as set in Step 1. These values can be changed only within the limits allowed by total ink and GCR/UCR curves.

6. Use the eyedropper to select a pixel that represents the darkest portion of the shadow areas. Click that pixel to set the black point. Photoshop redistributes the levels according to the pixel selected and the settings for black and total ink limits.

This technique might cause undesirable color shifts, depending on the extremity of the shift. Although this method is quick and easy, I often use another technique. I usually just have a look at the black levels (Image, Adjust, Levels) and make a correction there after converting to CMYK. I simply move the left slider on the Histogram graph to where black information seems to start, as if doing an RGB levels correction (see Figure 25.3). This makes the image come solidly to black. There might be some darkening with this method, but shifting the middle slider to the left can counteract that. Overall, shifting the black does less to the image information than depending on the Levels eyedroppers, and it seems to retain more shadow detail.

Figure 25.3
A Levels correction for the black channel after CMYK conversion can set the black point as well.

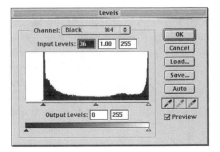

The eyedropper correction method is very useful in clearing out unwanted noise from black backgrounds that are supposed to be flat. In such examples, the black background is quite varied even though it might appear to the eye to be relatively flat. Successive mouse clicks in progressively lighter areas flatten out the darks so they will print with a more even tone. See Figure 25.4 for an example of this type of change (see also ColorPlate 4 in the color section of this book).

Figure 25.4
This image was scanned from a screened print in a book of photos of clay sculptures by blind children. The dark tones throughout suggested a flat black background was used for the images. After adjustments to remove the screening (left), adjustment to a flat black was completed using the Levels and black Eyedropper (right).

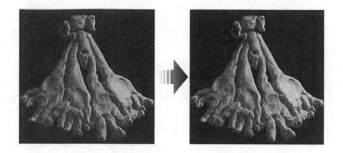

Tip

When creating flat black tones for printing, they can sometimes appear too flat. You might want to add a few points of noise (Filter, Noise, Add Noise) to the final black area to give it a more realistic appearance.

Note

Do not add noise to black expanses intended to blend on Web pages that are flat toned. It will ruin the effect.

 If you have done everything you can think of, including calibrating your monitor, color correcting the image, and setting the black and white points for printing yet you don't get the right color, see "I Still Don't Get the Right Color!" in the Troubleshooting section at the end of this chapter.

WEB GRAPHIC COLOR CONSIDERATIONS

Web graphics function differently than print graphics. Colors in Web graphics can go from the purest white (100% red, 100% green, 100% blue) to the purest black (0% red, 0% green, 0% blue), unlike print that can have too much white or black. A calibrated monitor gives the most reliable Web graphic results, and using a Web-safe color palette (216 colors) ensures that colors you see on your screen appear at least similar on other computer screens (Mac and PC). Knowing Web color potential is imperative to getting good blends and color matching. Color matching is best done using exact hexadecimal colors. The reason for this is the coded color selections (those colors created with HTML) will be interpreted by any system. If they appear only the same (in view onscreen), the conversion might not be the same on all machines unless the 216-color palette and hexadecimal color matching are used.

Part
VI

Ch
25

Generally, color in Web graphics can be controlled by eye—that is, the color of the image should be created as you want to see it considering your monitor is properly calibrated. If you are trying to make a blended graphic (one in which the edge color matches the HTML background color and appears to blend in with the page), it is important that the graphic's edges match the background color exactly. If not, the colors might show variance depending on which system they are viewed on, and the effect you are looking for will be lost. The solution is to know how to use hexadecimal colors, which colors to use, and to be sure your assigned image colors match your backgrounds numerically. Also, do not make color corrections and changes to the image overall after the background color and foreground image edges have been matched.

Figure 25.5 shows a bad blend. The button was meant to go over a white background (in this case, the paper in this book), and should have looked like an oval button. It is close, but the area around the button is shaded (is not 255,255,255 in RGB), so it doesn't blend, and the effect is ruined. It would be easy to eliminate this, but it need not be there in the first place with a little extra care.

Figure 25.5
This button was meant to appear as a simple oval in a white background. However, because the edge of the graphic was not matched to the HTML white (#FFFFFF), the slight variance causes the graphic to appear as a mistake.

Note

The solution in this case could also be accomplished with transparency depending on the complexity of the color in the graphic, but matching is still a good practice and it offers more flexibility with other effects, such as creating drop shadows with JPEG images.

Use the following steps to remove the bad blend.

1. Find out the hexadecimal value for the background on your Web page. This will be in the Body tag, and should look something like: <BODY BGCOLOR="#FFFFFF"> (the color '#FFFFFF' is only an example, and can be any of the Web-safe colors, depending on your preference).

Tip

If the color in the BODY tag for the Web page is not a Web-safe color, consider changing that to a Web-safe value for greater color consistency across systems.

→ For more information on hexadecimal colors and the 216-color chart, **see** "Hexadecimal Color Equivalents for Web Creation," **p. 917**.

2. Make a selection of the image area that will be replaced. In the example, it would be the area around the button that is giving the button the appearance of being rectangular.

3. Set the foreground color to the background color of the Web page using the hexadecimal value from the HTML (see Step 1) to determine the color exactly.

Hexadecimal Numbers

Hexadecimal is a base-16 system, numbered 0, 1, 2, 3, 4, 5, 6, 7, 8, 9, A, B, C, D, E, F, where A–F stands for 10–15. The first number in the set (H1) stands for the number of 16s in the total; the second number (H2) stands for the number of 1s. CE, for example, would be 12(16)+14, or 206. To convert the other way is a bit more complicated. Where X=your RGB value: |X/16|=H1 and X-(|X/16|)16=H2. For example, an RGB red value of 245 would be used in the equation as follows: H1=|245/16|=|15.3125|=15 or H1=F; H2=245-(|245/16|)16=245-(|15.3125|)16=245-(15)16=245-240=5 or H2=5; H1H2=F5. Green and blue hexadecimal pairs also need to be converted to complete the hexadecimal set. Things have gotten easier: Photoshop allows you to choose hex colors in the color picker by typing in a value. A simple conversion chart for 256 permutations is also presented in Appendix D for your convenience.

---

4. Fill the selected area with the foreground color.

5. Test the blend by loading the HTML and image into your browser (see Figure 25.6).

Figure 25.6
With the color replaced to match the background color for the Web page, the button will appear to blend with the page as intended.

All you are doing here is replacing the peripheral portion of the image so that it matches the background. You could do this the other way around as well (replace the background color for the page), but check to see that the color you are matching at the edge of the graphic is in the 216-color palette. Matching the colors exactly is important to getting the blend right, and it won't just happen by guessing or trial and error—even when using black or white. Close enough just isn't good enough considering the broad variation of systems and settings, especially when hitting it right on is easy enough to do.

Adding a drop shadow works better this way than when using transparency. Transparency can end up looking blocky and might not blend well (again, depending on the makeup of the background in both the HTML and the graphic that is intended to blend with it).

To make a drop shadow, use the selection created in Step 2 to select the button and copy/paste it into its own layer. (Next, use a Layer Style (Layer, Layer Style, Drop Shadow) to put in a simple drop shadow. Expand the canvas size if necessary (Image, Canvas Size) to accept the shadow area without clipping. Be sure, if expanding the canvas, that the background color is set to the background color of the Web page. When complete, flatten and convert the image. Figure 25.7 shows a comparison between a drop shadow created with this technique and one done with transparency and a mismatched background. The point is, you have to match the background color for transparency to work properly with a drop shadow anyway.

Figure 25.7
The upper version of the drop shadow was completed after matching the background color for the Web page; the lower version was completed without matching and using transparency. Here the effect is somewhat muted, but still it is apparent and undesirable.

TROUBLESHOOTING

I STILL DON'T GET THE RIGHT COLOR!

I have calibrated my scanner and my monitor, set up the color management, color corrected the image, and set the black and white points, but I am not satisfied that the results of my prints match what I see onscreen. Is there anything else I have to do?

If you have followed all the rules and still aren't getting the right color, there are a number of things that can be affecting output—although I would suggest that calibration is probably the most likely cause. Use the following points to determine the cause and find a solution if you are using a service for printing.

1. Be sure that you are working with an image that is in the right color mode when you send it to print. If you use an RGB image in CMYK process, no matter how you have the color management set, you may end up with unexpected results.

2. If you are new to this or haven't done it in a few months or more, go back through the calibration process one more time—just to be sure nothing has changed on you. Do a complete test, including running a proof and matching it to the monitor. Note what, in particular, you think is wrong with the output (which colors are too dark or too light, and so forth).

→ For more information on getting what you see onscreen and testing output, **see** "Evaluating Color Images Onscreen," **p. 411**.

■ With the test in hand, consider your output device. If you are printing with a printer or service, you have to assume the results are accurate and stable—meaning you will get the same thing pretty much every time. If you repeat a printing on the same files and get markedly different results (compare your test proofs), it is time to confront the service, or use another one. It is natural for things to vary somewhat (even humidity can affect the printing results). Be sure you are printing to the same printer and using the same paper.

■ If you are satisfied that results are close enough, and that the system is optimized, try using a transfer function. You create the Transfer based on the test proof, not what you see onscreen. A good way to do this is to note the differences you saw in the proof when you evaluated it, look at the print, open the Curves (Image, Adjust, Curves), and correct the screen image as if it were the print. This will probably make the image look a little off onscreen—the opposite of what you have in the print. For example, if the image is red overall, the image onscreen should be a little green when you have set the curves. Note the settings you used and close the curves without saving. Open the transfer function by selecting (File, Print Options) [File, Page Setup] and clicking the Transfer button. Apply the curve settings in the Transfer Function dialog box. Save the settings (you should probably use the service's name and date in the name of the saved settings), save the image, and send it for output again. Although you might have to adjust to fine-tune, if the transfer function gets what you want, use it for the images you send to the service.

■ Home color printers should be calibrated as well as your monitor. If your manufacturer has provided steps for doing this (see your owner's manual), calibrate the monitor and perform maintenance (for example, ink jet printers will probably have a process for clearing the ink nozzles). If you print to both your home printer and use a service, it is more likely that the results at home will vary. Be sure, again, that you aren't printing to varied papers. If using a photographic-quality printer, be sure you are using a high-grade paper meant to work with photographic-quality prints, as these will offer the most consistent results. Other papers may absorb ink differently and can cause some of the problems you are experiencing. Create a transfer function for your printer using the same steps as previously, but running the proofs and tests on your printer. You may have to set up different transfer functions, depending on the different kinds of paper used.

■ Be sure you are assigning the proper transfer function to the proper image for output. You should not have to set up a transfer function for everything. Really, you should set up your system so that images view as closely as possible to the output you use most frequently and use transfer functions for other devices. Be sure to remove the transfer function when sending the image to print on other devices. It is probably best to save images with embedded transfer functions separately, so you can tell them from the original—although you can remove the function, it is likely you may forget the transfer function is there, and the output will suffer if the image goes to the wrong device. You can use an action to set or remove transfer functions from images via batch processing, if you find you use them a lot.

→ For more information on batch processing, **see** "Batch Process Images," **p. 286**.

PART **VII**

CLEANING, REPAIRING, AND ALTERING IMAGES

CHAPTER 26

APPROACHING IMAGE CORRECTIONS

In this chapter

AN OVERVIEW OF IMAGE CORRECTION

Cleaning, repairing, and changing a digital image is where Photoshop excels in tool variety, options, and capability over other image editors. You can do things with photographs in Photoshop that are just impossible in the darkroom—or are too time-consuming to consider.

Decisions that you make in correcting and changing images are probably 70% artistic and 30% application of tools. That is, you have far more control over the appearance of the image using the tools to do the job than you have over the available image information. If all the sky in a photo is damaged and dust-ridden, there might be no way you can use it to fix the image. In this case, you have to decide whether you have a proper substitute—either in the image you are working on, or whether you can replace it using another image.

A more dramatic example might be needing a second hand for a subject—say a hand was cut off in a photograph because of framing. You might replace the missing hand with the other hand just by copying, flipping, and maneuvering it into position with a few alterations. However, the lighting will be backward. If the hand you have is palm down, and you need one palm up, you are going to have a hard time finding a replacement with the same light- ing conditions, or one that can be altered to look natural—unless you have another shot of the same subject in the same place, lighting, and so on. In this case, knowing that you might be missing some elements and shooting a second or third shot might make the difference in having the image elements you want to use, rather than fabricating or copying from another, less-compatible image. In the case of the missing hand, you will have to re-create or extend the image background to fill the area of the frame where the hand was cropped out. All this is possible, although, at times, time-consuming. And none of it will be done for you by a magic plug-in. It is meticulous work.

WORKING WITH WHAT YOU HAVE

More often than not, the elements that need minor corrections are right in the image you have. You can duplicate image areas, elements, and patterns in such a way as to make them unnoticeable in the repairs. A little creativity and attention to technique and detail will go a long way toward making the image not only better, but actually restored with the original look, feel, and quality. You can use elements from other images, but you might have trouble matching the qualities of the rest of the image (paper qualities, grain, focus) without a lot of work. Using the elements from the image you are working on reduces this concern.

PLANNING CORRECTIONS AHEAD OF TIME

A slightly higher level of correction is really planning: correction by design rather than as a serendipitous event. You might get lucky in finding just the image information you need in two photos, but you will get better results consciously shooting several pictures to get one good image of several image elements that you plan to merge together. You might know an effect you'd like to create that is currently impossible: for example, something like balancing a girl on a broom. You could take this from two completely separate photos taken at differ- ent times and in different conditions, or create the shot in different images and put it together. This same technique can be incorporated in different ways throughout your corrections if you consciously plan your corrections while gathering the elements for your images, keeping the end result in mind.

For a less extreme example, in taking a group shot of several people, you will have more opportunity to get the best expressions over the course of several photos. Regretfully, the best expressions will invariably be in different photos. Good Photoshop technique enables you to take the best expressions from each of a number of different images and marry them together for a better final image (a technique that can be used with much success in studio family portraiture). Likewise, you can solve problems of depth of field. There are times when it is virtually impossible to get everything sharp within a single frame. Taking several photos of the same subject, selectively focusing on different parts, will give you the image information you need to fit together the parts that are in focus.

Plan an approach to corrections and use the advantages Photoshop has to offer. If you have the opportunity, preplan an image as you are shooting to have what you need when you sit down to the computer.

THE ADVANTAGE OF LAYERED CORRECTIONS

Layers are indispensable in making corrections of all kind. Layering corrections from the moment you start work is the best way to progress through image changes in Photoshop. On some images, I will even make dust corrections on a second layer (usually an immediate correction) just to be able to compare before and after results using different methods. Working on a second layer all the time offers the convenience of quick before/after comparison by simply hiding the layer (turning off the eye icon on the Layers palette). It also offers options for selective blending in the Layer Styles dialog box, such as using Blend If, blending modes, and opacity. These layering options can help you reduce the visual presence of your corrections so you have the opportunity to make changes that are far more difficult or impossible with any one tool alone. In fact, you might want to make corrections to your corrections before committing them, and layering will allow the flexibility you need.

PART
VII
CH
26

Built-In Layer Protection with Histories
With the introduction of Histories, Photoshop has done away with what used to be my initial step in working with an image—duplicating the background. Leaving the default setting for Automatically Create First Snapshot in the History options (in the History palette menu) enables you to retain the original image information in all existing layers of the image as you work on it. This lets you work with the potential of reverting all or portions of the image at any time, by either stepping back in the History, or using the History to revert selected areas of the image. This History feature acts to duplicate your initial set of layers.

The only drawback to layering is that each layer increases the size of the image. If you are working on large images that require a lot of changes, performance might start to stall, depending on how much memory your system has, how it is allocated, how you like to work, and so on. Know which layers are important and which you might want to change or experiment with. If corrections are immediate and obvious (for example, there is a small but obvious dust speck on the end of your subject's nose), correct it directly. If they are more subjective, use layers for manipulation and comparison, and then commit changes only when you are sure there is nothing else you want to change. Separate alterations to different areas of the image in different layers. This gives you maximum control. If performance seems burdened and you are not ready to commit changes, yet you want to go on, save the image with the layers, then flatten (Layer, Flatten Image), and go on with your changes. This will save image size, and you will be able to copy the new layers to the saved image at a later time by stacking them on top of what you've already done. Barring cropping, the stacked effect should be the same as if you were working only on one image.

SECTIONING AN IMAGE FOR CORRECTIONS

Onerous tasks are often best approached in small detailed segments. Likewise, particularly difficult image corrections can be worked on by sectioning an image. That is, you can set up a grid to help you in navigating the image, and actually use the grid to cut and paste image segments to work on them as separate documents if there is reason.

For example, say you had a particularly difficult image that needed repairs. The image had been carried in pockets, written on, scratched, and is cracked with age (see Figure 26.1). You might have to zoom in to work on the image, and clearly defining where you are—or where you have already corrected—might be an additional headache, involving interminable scrolling, view changes, and so on. After you get started on the image, you might find you get lost following various problems rather than making specific progress on the image. Placing guidelines on the image can help you keep a handle on what has been done and where you have to go. You can more easily scroll the image in even columns and determine where you have been and where you need to go.

Figure 26.1
This image is well worn and needs quite a bit of work for the image to be restored. Sectioning the work areas into smaller segments can make the job of cleanup more orderly.

To determine where to place the guides, zoom in on the image to a percentage you would like to work at. This will vary depending on the image size and resolution. Once zoomed in, set the document palette comfortably on your screen, with space for your other palettes. Move to the upper left of the image (using the navigator palette or the scrollbars), and place guidelines about a 1/4–1/8 of an inch from the right and bottom of the screen. Next, note where the guides are placed according to the rulers. If the rulers are not showing, press (Command-R) [Ctrl+R], or select View, Show Rulers. Place additional guidelines in increments according to the measurement on the ruler. For example, if the right guideline falls on 280 pixels, place a guideline every 280 pixels to the right until you run out of image (560, 840, 1,120, and so on). When you have done this both horizontally and vertically, you will have set up a simple grid to follow for your corrections. See Figure 26.2.

Figure 26.2
After you have sized the image comfortably for your work area and placed the first two guidelines, use their placement to set up a grid for the whole image. This will leave you with neat rows and columns to follow when making your corrections.

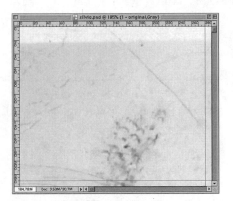

→ For more information on rulers and navigation, **see** "Using the Interface," **p. 25**.

When the grid is set up, zoom back and get to work following the image in rows or columns. When a box is complete, move on to the next. If you have to go do something else or shut down and don't have time to finish, you can come right back to your square and get to work again.

PART
VII

CH
26

This can be particularly useful when correcting dust in images intended for high-resolution output.

WHEN TO STOP MANIPULATING

There isn't really a question as to what to correct: Correct anything you want to correct. And don't consider correct as a connotation which means fixing with the purpose of correctness or being proper. Corrections are all subjective; you don't even have to remove dust from an image if you like it there. What to correct is simply what you want to correct. Developing the skills of correction and observation is the only obstacle in overcoming limitations in making the corrections.

What is more difficult to consider than what to correct is when to stop correcting. For example, how small a dust speck is one that is too small to notice? What changes are you making that are merely pushing insignificant pixels around the image with no real purpose?

The temptation to make alterations is great—especially when presented with such a powerful tool as Photoshop. At some point, however, you need to decide that an image is complete—sometimes you need to put it aside even if you can do more to perfect it. Consider the amount of time and effort needed to make the changes you want to make, as well as the use of the image and the importance of the presentation. For example, a cover shot for an art magazine justifies more work than a thumbnail image in an informal flier. Unless your sense of perfection gets in the way, an image you are creating for fun need not be as detailed and exact as something you are creating for your résumé, a client, or as a display product.

When it gets down to the image, consider whether you are making changes for gratification or whether the changes are important to the impact of the image in the context in which it will be used. When the changes are no longer affecting the purpose of the image, you are done.

However, it is often best to learn all you can during a correction, so consider learning a value to your work on an image. If a few moments more, even if just working for fun, help you to understand a tool or function better, spend the time. Likewise, you will make changes that just don't work, even though the idea might have been great. Don't force the image and keep the changes if the original is better, no matter how much time you have invested. Learn from the experience of the manipulation. Chances are you will have learned something more about Photoshop and how to use it better. You'll use that tool with more proficiency in future Photoshop projects.

To avoid losing time making complex image changes, especially in larger images, consider working on a rough draft of the image first in a smaller size before committing to making the image at full resolution. Use rougher selections and less fine-tuning in the draft. This will give you an idea whether the image will work the way you envision it before you invest the time to make the full-resolution version. If it works, jot some notes down about what you did, and start to work on the image at full size and resolution. You might even take a screenshot of the History, Layers, and/or Channels palettes to remember how you accomplished your ends in the draft. Predeveloping an image can save time in processing, and can be considered a learning experience or dry run for working with higher resolutions where you can waste a lot of time on something that just is not going to fly as it is.

→ For more information on screenshots, **see** "Obtaining Source Images," **p. 355**.

If manipulations fail, you might try them another way; go back and plan your images again, or find the elements you need to make them work. But always make the effort to take away something you've learned.

CHAPTER 27

CORRECTING IMAGE DAMAGE: RESTORATIONS

In this chapter

REMOVING DUST FROM AN IMAGE

Basic tidiness in picking the dust out of your images is necessary for just about any image you use. Even in climate-controlled environments used for scanning that are built with dust suppression in mind, dust is merely kept to a minimum and not completely eliminated. Dust can appear on the scanner glass, on the surface of the print or negative, in the print or negative, or on the subject you are capturing—essentially at any point where the image makes a physical rather than electronic transfer. You will want to remove this from your images to have the final images look their best. Luckily, this dust is usually very easy to take care of (even if at times it is a bit tedious to do so). Using some care before making scans can help keep some dust out of the electronic samples. Care in touch-up after the image or object is in digital form permanently removes the dust from later uses of the image.

→ For more information on scanning techniques and suppressing dust in scans, **see** "Scanning to Create Images," **p. 361**.

You can use a variety of techniques in correcting dust, but the simplest and most to the point is to clone image areas over the dust. *Cloning* substitutes information from other parts of the image that might be damaged or missing, and is really just another name for copying and pasting a selected area of an image to another area. Cloning is most often done with the Rubber Stamp tool (also referred to as the Clone Stamp tool). The Rubber Stamp has several cloning options built in. Using care and proper technique—good sampling, aligned application, a conscious effort to avoid patterning, and selection if necessary—you can make dust corrections that are imperceptible. The same technique used for dust correction can solve any number of minor problems (dings, dirt, damage, and tears) that can afflict your images.

The goal of any good correction is to improve the image—but not create noticeable patterns or duplications with the substitutions—and fit replacement elements seamlessly into the surrounding image. Some areas of an image, such as skin tones, prove the most difficult to correct for dust and minor damage tonal and color gradients may be difficult to reproduce from other sections of an image. Carefully select the points you will clone from to make the best match.

Tip

Be aware of the potential of the elements already in the image. Often what you do not have can be rebuilt with what is already there. Look carefully at images to find matching patterns and pieces or parts of other image elements that will make good substitutes for damaged image areas.

For very difficult areas, you might have to consider smaller applications of techniques described in later sections of this chapter, which are generally used for replacement of larger image areas. For example, these techniques would be used for replacing a missing slice of pizza in an image if there were only a single slice missing from the whole. Whereas it would be ridiculously tedious to attempt to clone the slice using the Rubber Stamp tool, it would be easy to select one of the other slices, copy it, paste it, and then rotate and scale it so that it fits in place. The trickiest areas of your dust correction might require similar technique.

To simplify making corrections, especially in images that contain a lot of damage (for example, restoration of older photographs), you might want to break the image down into sections, so you can work on it a little at a time. This allows you to attack the problems in smaller chunks, reduce larger visible patterning, and simply gives you less to think about all at once.

→ For more information on sectioning your image to create smaller working areas, **see** "Sectioning an Image for Corrections," **p. 574**.

GETTING STARTED WITH BASIC CORRECTIONS

Use the following steps to make simple dust corrections.

1. Open the image you want to remove the dust from (for this example, we will use the image from Figure 27.1).

Figure 27.1
Grit, dust, scratches, and cracks galore make this a perfect image for the demonstration of what you can do with dust correction.

2. Zoom into the image several times the size it will actually appear. The greater the dpi, the more you should zoom in. A good rule of thumb is to zoom in to the point where you can just begin to see pixels, or "jaggy" edges.

Screen Displays in Photoshop
Images display on screen in Photoshop with a percentage based on pixels you actually view. That is, an image that is 288dpi at 5×5 inches will actually display at 20×20 onscreen when the viewing percentage says 100%—four times the dimension in inches. This is because Photoshop viewing is based on the user's view of pixels, not just the image dimensions. There is a strong rationale behind this. Because screens display at a low dpi (usually 72dpi), some image information cannot be displayed and would have to be compressed if a 5×5 288dpi image is displayed at 5×5 on a 72dpi screen. Basing the view on screen dpi ensures that you know what percentage of the available image information you can actually see. So, when viewing the 5×5 288dpi image at 5×5 onscreen, you can see only 25% of the image information, and that is what the percentage tells you. You will want to view any image at 150%–200% onscreen to check for dust and make corrections. At this magnification, you will be sure to see all the dust that affects the appearance of the image.

Select Rubber Stamp Options by clicking the Rubber Stamp tool (see Figure 27.2).

Tip

For most corrections, you will use Aligned cloning, which will align the clone-from point to point and keep that as a set distance and angle (see Figure 27.2 for an example of how that works).

Figure 27.2
Normally, you will use the Rubber Stamp in Normal mode, but there are instances where other modes can serve a purpose. For example, using Lighten when stamping from slightly darker portions of an image will still lessen the impact of black spots while not darkening lighter areas as Normal would.

4. Choose a brush and brush options appropriate for correction. To select the Brush Options, click to open the drop menu for the brushes and double-click any of the brushes in the Brush floating palette (see Figure 27.3). You may want to be sure the view for brushes is set to Brush Size in Display & Cursors (this is the default).

→ For more information on sizing brushes for correction work, **see** "Brush Options for Dust Correction," **p. 585**.

Figure 27.3
Brush size for dust correction should be set slightly larger than the width of most of the specks (usually threadlike particles). Use a fairly hard brush so that corrections feather, slightly, into the surroundings.

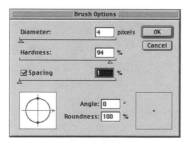

→ For more information on brush options, **see** "Freehand Painting Tools," **p. 203**.

5. Choose the spot you would like to clone from and set it as the clone-from point. To do this, hold down the (Option) [Alt] key, and click the cursor in the area you have chosen as the source (see Figure 27.4). The area you clone from should be clear of damage and dust, or you will just copy that damage to the spot you are cloning to.

Figure 27.4
When you hold down the (Option) [Alt] key, the cursor will change to the sampling cursor (pictured here) or the Precise cursor, depending on your setting for Other Cursors in the Display & Cursors Preferences.

6. Choose the spot you would like to clone to (the dust or damaged area) and set it as the clone-to point. To do this, move the brush over a damaged spot in the image and click the mouse, and then drag across the damage while holding the mouse button down. When you're using Align, clicking the mouse sets an alignment between the clone-from and clone-to areas, and then applies the clone between those points (see Figure 27.5).

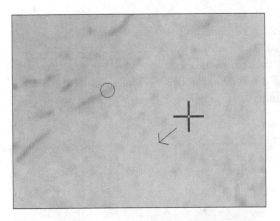
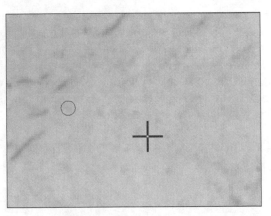

Figure 27.5
Both the clone-from and clone-to areas show on the image while you hold down the mouse button. This way, you can monitor accurately what area will be copied as well as the result.

The Rubber Stamp tool samples from the original state of the image as if a snapshot is taken each time you click the mouse. The snapshot lasts for as long as you hold down the mouse button. Continue applying clone areas to remove dust and minor damage. For the best results, hold down the mouse button only as long as you have to; click over the damage, release, and move. Holding down the button too long can lead to undesirable results. Spot retouching like this keeps excess cloning to a minimum and helps reduce the chances

PART
VII

CH
27

of creating noticeable patterning. Click often, and change the angle of the sample frequently (by repeating Steps 5 and 6).

The most common mistake in using the Rubber Stamp tool for cloning is creating bad patterning and redundant image areas. This shows carelessness with the tool and is plainly bad technique (see Figure 27.6).

Figure 27.6
One type of undesirable patterning is copying an image area in a series. This figure shows a rather obvious example of cloning to inadvertently develop an undesirable pattern.

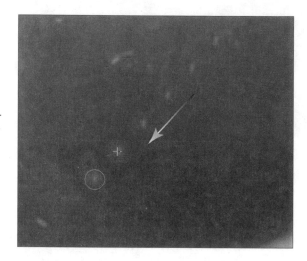

Bad choices in using the Rubber Stamp tool for cloning can also take the form of duplicating obvious image elements in a larger sense. The example in Figure 27.7 is a straight duplication of an image element. Although the result might be okay for some purposes, it is an apparent duplication. The appearance of duplication might be corrected with great care by shifting the insect's legs, antennae, position, direction, and shadow/lighting. Generally, you will want to avoid straight patterning.

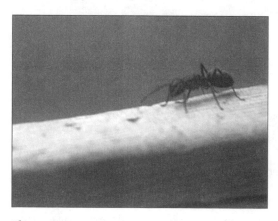 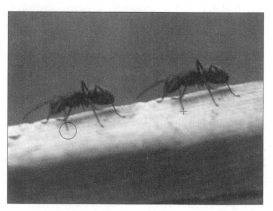

Figure 27.7
Duplicating the image element in this case looks okay in that it has been fit into the image and surroundings, but the duplication is apparent. Putting more work into the application of the duplicated element would help make the duplication less obvious.

It is possible to do your corrections by selection, but mastering the basic control of spot correction without selection is paramount to using the Rubber Stamp tool effectively and making good, fast dust and damage correction. Although selection will sometimes be necessary or desirable, not having to make the selections can save time.

⚠ *If you have taken all the steps in dust correction and you're still having trouble getting smooth results, see "Clearing the Way for Cloning" in the Troubleshooting section at the end of this chapter.*

BRUSH OPTIONS FOR DUST CORRECTION

Select a brush size for dust corrections that is about double the width of an average dust speck in your image. This will ensure that the specks are covered easily. If in doubt about the size, go a little smaller in diameter, but don't go so small with brush size that it takes several swipes to remove little pieces of dust.

A brush with a hard center can help make sure you cover the damage in one stroke. Usually, this will mean using a brush that has greater than 50% hardness, but less than 100%. Hardness will assure good coverage, but a slightly soft edge acts like a dither or feather to help blend corrections better. I often use settings of 85%–95% hardness in the Normal mode to assure good coverage and slight blending. You might need to vary the hardness depending on the Mode you have selected for the application of the Rubber Stamp tool to get the best results.

Using Spacing settings for the brush of more than a few percentage points is more or less a special effect and should probably not be used for dust and minor damage correction. Space at 1% if you like to use the Shift-click option for paint tools to draw straight lines from point to point. If you shut off Spacing by unchecking the box (see Figure 27.8), that feature will be disabled. Shutting off the spacing totally is not a great idea in most cases because the brush will be applied and spaced according to the speed you move it; the faster you go, the more likely it is that there will be gaps in the brush application.

Figure 27.8
Check the Spacing box in the Brush Options dialog box to control the spacing of the brush application. Keep the spacing low so that strokes with the brush will be smooth and even.

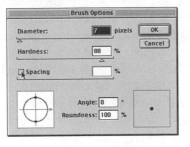

RUBBER STAMP TOOL OPTIONS FOR DUST CORRECTIONS

Generally, you will choose Clone Aligned and check the Sample All Layers box if you are correcting a multiple-layer image. Using these options, it is also very easy to use another layer to hold the corrections. Simply create a new layer, sample, and stamp. Any changes will be applied to the new layer, and you can view before and after by toggling on and off the Adobe eye for the Layer. Again, there are advantages for blending and modes when using a separate layer to hold the corrections. For example, if you're blotting out some dark specks on a light background, using the Lighten mode may confine corrections to only the area of the specks. This will also isolate the corrections so that there is opportunity to apply other effects to the corrections only (such as blur or noise to help with the blending— depending on the application).

To set the Display & Cursors Preferences to show a brush size, choose File, Preferences, Display & Cursors. What you actually see onscreen as the brush size is the area of application of the brush that is 50% opaque or greater. If your brush has a soft edge, keep in mind that the actual effects of the brush application extend outside the size shown onscreen.

USING APPLICATION MODES IN DUST CORRECTIONS

If you use Lighten or Darken mode to make your dust corrections, you still need to clone from areas with similar color and tonality. If you are stamping with Lighten to try to lighten dark dust in a light image area, try to clone from an area 1%–2% darker than the area you are cloning to. If you are stamping with Darken to darken light dust specks in a dark image area, try to clone from an area 1%–2% lighter than the area you are cloning to. This will make the corrections affect only the specks while keeping the general tone of the area unchanged. Measure the percentages in grayscale using the Info palette. Doing this keeps you from overcorrecting and making dark or light spots around the corrections.

Note

Using modes for correction is not necessary, and sometimes not desirable. It might be best to control this type of application with Layer mode controls rather than tool controls.

FIXING DENTS, SCRATCHES, AND LARGE DUSTY AREAS

Corrections for larger damaged image areas can be handled with the Rubber Stamp tool and a larger brush, but this is often not the best way to produce optimal results. Although corrections could be done with the Rubber Stamp tool alone, the process might be arduous. Combining selection with cloning gives you more control over the exact area where you will make cloning applications, regardless of the size of your brush. Cloning large portions of an image to apply sweeping changes can also be controlled and confined to large image sections with selection and masking. There are sometimes advantages to making bulk corrections by simply replacing larger areas of an image rather than painstakingly removing each speck of dust one at a time.

The first thing you should always do is to prepare your image so that you start with the least amount of dust to correct in the first place. The possible routes for correction in Photoshop encompass quite a range as far as use of tools is concerned, from using the Dust & Scratches filter to filling image areas and re-creating textures, to replacing image areas using parts of other images, to using selection techniques that pick out the dust, to applying a combination of techniques. This discussion cannot exhaust all the possibilities.

Some of the techniques discussed here are good for large areas with one dominant color (a red dress, for example) or light gradient blends (such as cloudless skies). You can apply these techniques to more complex image areas, but you need to be careful that you don't do more harm than good and damage image information. The method you pick depends on how badly damaged the image is, what the complexity of the image area is, and what your plan is for the end product. Some changes will be fairly simple: You can select the area where the damage is, feather the selection, and fill with information borrowed from other portions of the image (as you did for cloning out dust, but on a much larger scale). Other corrections will be far more complex and involved where you have to borrow from several different images to get a good result.

If you want to restore an old photo, and you want to keep the feel of the image, you need to be aware of the image texture and tone before simply replacing image areas with samples from new images. Because there will probably be a quality and texture difference between the new image(s) and the old, you can get a rather stark and unrealistic effect if you are not careful or selective. In such cases, use care in doctoring the replacement elements so that they match the original feel of the image. Strike some sort of pleasant medium between replacing the elements and matching the original.

Making a selection of damaged areas that need sweeping corrections gives you many options for making the necessary changes. Options and solutions will vary from image to image, but the order of your approach and some basic techniques will remain the same.

The following steps give you an order to follow in making larger corrections.

1. Open the image you want to correct.
2. Make a selection of the general area of the image you want to work on.

→ For more information on making selections, **see** "Selection and Masking," **p. 93**.

3. Feather the selection (usually only a pixel or two) and save it.
4. Copy the selected area to another layer using New Layer Via Copy (Cmd-J) [Ctrl+J]. This keeps the original intact but separates the image area you need to work on.
5. Decide which method(s) to use in correcting the area and apply corrections. Information on specific methods for correction appears in the following sections.

→ For more information on correction methods, **see** "Dust and Scratches Filter," **p. 588**, "Gradient Fills," **p. 590**, "Copy and Paste for Small Area Fills," **p. 591**, "Selectively Replacing Dust Damage," **p. 593**, and "Repairs Using Additional Images," **p. 598**.

6. Repeat Steps 2 to 5 as per the needs of the image. Try several different solutions to the same problem areas if time permits, and compare by turning the appropriate Layer views on or off.
7. Before saving the image in a native Photoshop format for storage, remove extraneous layers and unnecessary channels used in experimentation.

You'll want to create several different selections for Step 2 because you might want to approach different areas of the image in different ways. You might even want to work on an image area in stages; that is, first remove the smaller problems and work to the larger. The reason for working first on the small damage is to remove minor problems before using those image areas to repair other areas of the image. This way, you can correct minor damage before duplicating that damage to other areas of the image.

Generally, you will want the selections that you make to cover whole image elements, such as sky or water as seen in Figure 27.9. However, you can combine selections and alter them (as with using gradients) to mask tool or layer applications further.

Figure 27.9
Selecting the sky and water in this image serves many purposes. Generally, it helps isolate image elements so one can be worked on or replaced without affecting the other.

The image shown in Figure 27.9 will be used in all the following sections to discuss options for reclaiming, repairing, and replacing image elements.

DUST & SCRATCHES FILTER

The Dust & Scratches filter can reduce problems in image areas that are speckled with fine dust or abrasions. This works especially well when the damage is in high contrast with the surrounding image—for example, where the damage appears very light on a dark background or dark on a light background. With the area you want to correct selected or isolated in its own layer, application of the Dust & Scratches filter will be confined to the selected area. Isolation can be desirable when using Dust & Scratches as the filter may damage detail information in an image.

Figure 27.10 is a section of Figure 27.9, which presents a number of challenges that can be solved in a variety of ways. Applying the Dust & Scratches filter to the area of the sky can help clear up a number of the smaller specks and damage. The goal of the correction will not be to solve every problem, but to use Dust & Scratches for what it does well.

On this image, I used a Threshold of 5 to 10 levels and a Pixel Radius about the width of the damage (3–5 pixels in this case; you will have to adjust this as per the dpi of your image). The Threshold keeps the effect limited to high-contrast areas, which will help keep some of the image texture. Those precautions should keep the filter from damaging the image. Greater pixel radii or lower Thresholds might tend to make the image blurry and can soften detail.

Figure 27.10
This image area presents a number of challenges, including missing information, alongside textures and detail that should probably be retained, and a plethora of minor damage.

Figure 27.11
This image shows the result of applying the Dust & Scratches filter. There is a significant improvement in minor damage and retention of much of the tonal detail.

Dust & Scratches may prove to have the best results if used in combination. For example, it can be very helpful in modifying an area that you plan to use as a substitution in a later correction, or in removing minor damage in an area and then applying that area in Lighten or Darken mode (depending on how it would do the most good). You may want to use it in combination with the History brush, as well. For example, you can apply dust and scratches to the image, take a snapshot, revert, and then paint with the History brush over the damaged areas only.

→ For more information on using the History Brush, **see** "Creating with Image Histories," **p. 251**.

PART
VII
CH
27

Application of the Dust & Scratches filter to the masked section of the sky in the sample image and using Lighten mode for the layer might supply better image information than a straight application of the filter (see Figure 27.12).

Figure 27.12
Although the results are very similar to the results in Figure 27.11, there are notable differences, especially around the ribbon on the subject's cap where the previous correction tended to blur somewhat.

GRADIENT FILLS

Gradients can fill a selected area quickly and create adequate tonality if it is a simple image area, such as a cloudless sky. You might choose to fill with the gradient at a percentage by selecting an opacity of less than 100% from the Gradient Options, or by changing the mode to Lighten or Darken depending on the image the gradient will be applied to. To apply a Gradient, choose the Gradient type that you believe will be fitting for the image area, and then sample the beginning and end areas of the blend to match the tonality. Set one sample as the foreground and the other as the background.

When the blend is applied, it will have a similar tone to the original. Use filters to rebuild texture while the area is still selected. For example, Add Noise, Blur, and Texturizer filters might be some of the most frequently used in replicating the feel of an original photo, but many filters and combinations might come in handy in rebuilding textures.

→ For more information on using Gradients, **see** "Color Fills and Gradients," **p. 159**.
→ For more information on using and creating textures, **see** "Creating Seamless Textures and Tiling Backgrounds," **p. 667**.

In Figure 27.13, a Linear Gradient was used to fill the sky and remove all the damage in one fell swoop. After the fill, the Add Noise filter was applied to roughen up the flatness of the blend, a slight Sandstone texture was added using the Texturizer, and then finally the layer was blurred. This may be good enough to complete the correction for the sky.

Another option is to again use the gradient as a partial solution, rather than a one-step correction. Using layer Opacity, Blend If functions, and the Darken mode for the layer, the gradient was blended into the lighter areas to fill the holes left after corrections to the figure as it appeared in Figure 27.12 (see Figure 27.14).

Figure 27.13
Depending on your goals in correction, this simple gradient fill of the sky produces reasonable results, and light application of filters to the gradient supplies enough texture to make the substitution seem realistic.

Figure 27.14
Instead of flatly applying the gradient to fill all of the sky, here Layer Mode, Opacity, and Blend If settings are used in Layer Styles to limit the application of the gradient to the areas where image information was missing after corrections leading to the result in Figure 27.12.

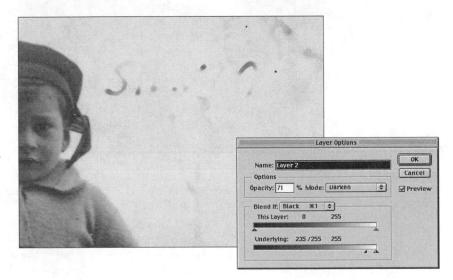

COPY AND PASTE FOR SMALL AREA FILLS

An alternative to using the Rubber Stamp tool for larger areas of damage is a straight copy and paste of image information. The benefit to this is that you can duplicate areas of texture and tone within the image to provide a better match to the existing areas than by re-creating image areas using fills and filters. The series of images in Figure 27.15 shows first an area that was selected to use in patching the image, and then two applications of the same patch, overlapped to fill a badly damaged portion of the image. The pieces were fit in place then adjusted slightly using the center slider in Levels.

PART

VII

CH

27

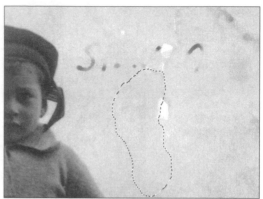

Figure 27.15
A patch was selected from a reasonably clean area of the image, and it was duplicated and applied two times to fill and repair a damaged area. Here, some overlap is used to lessen the appearance of any patterning.

More can be done to lessen the possibility of patterning by rotating the patches at various degrees, or flipping them horizontally or vertically. To fit selections to a defined area, you can make a selection of the area you would like to fill and then fit it to an available "donor" portion of the image. In Figure 27.16, the remaining damaged area on the right of the image was used to create a selection. The selection was drawn with a lasso over the damage that needed to be covered, and then the selection was moved over the donor portion of the image, and the donor area was copied and pasted and then moved into place for a perfect fit over the damage. This technique can be used for large- and small-area corrections. It can be very useful for tight spots and use in areas that are simple to select.

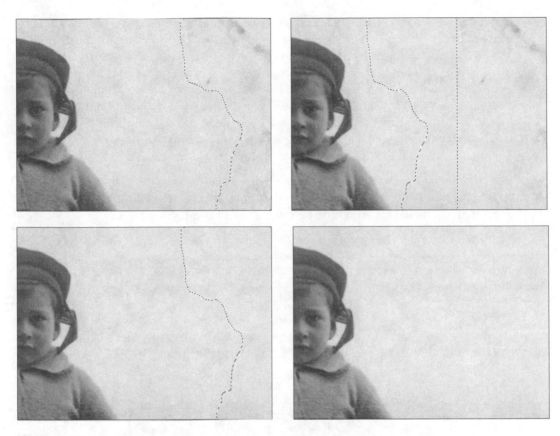

Figure 27.16
Preselecting an area will allow you to take the selection and find the best available replacement area to make quick work of repairs in a large area of damage.

Although there may be still more to do to the area of the sky to soften any patterning, the result in Figure 27.16 is a significant improvement over the original, and it retains much of the feel and texture of the original.

SELECTIVELY REPLACING DUST DAMAGE

Picking out the damage with selection can be a creative endeavor, but sometimes it is possible to make quick work of damage correction using selection as a means of identifying and replacing damaged image areas. The idea is to separate the damage by creating a selection around it, and then make a blend, fill, or clone of the image to fix the damage. This works best in relatively flat image areas, such as the sky in our sample image.

PART

VII

CH

27

You can use a range of creative techniques for selecting just the damaged areas of an image. For example, in the case of dust, duplicating an image area and applying Threshold, Find Edges, selection by Magic Wand, oversharpening, or a combination of these can help pick out the damage. These selections may be made from the composite or from information in any of the color channels if they prove to show an advantage for the selection. After the damage is identified by the selection, cut and paste (as described in the previous section) can be used to paste replacement information into the areas of damage only. This is effective in confining the changes, and can potentially reduce patterning that might be created by well-intentioned repairs if they are done without this selective limitation.

Use the following steps to selectively replace image areas over just the dust and damage in a larger image area. These steps may need to be altered depending on the image and use, but as an example, these basic steps can give you a good idea of how to proceed.

1. Open the image you want to correct (see Figure 27.17).

Figure 27.17
This image has some grit apparent in the sky. It can be isolated and eliminated with selection and replacement without affecting the subtle shading of the clouds.

2. Identify and isolate the image area that needs correction. To isolate the area, make a broad selection and copy and paste the area to place it on its own layer.

3. Sharpen the layer using the Unsharp Mask filter to define the dust and damage better (see Figure 27.18). You might use other techniques to make the damage stand out better, such as Level or Curve manipulations. This is one of the few times you will actually want to see the dust a little better.

4. Use Find Edges (Filter, Stylize, Find Edges) to pick out the damage more clearly, giving the damaged areas stark contrast (see Figure 27.19).

5. Select Image, Adjust, Threshold to eliminate any lighter noise created by application of Find Edges. This will allow you to target the damage (see Figure 27.20).

Figure 27.18
Sharpening after a slight curve adjustment (Curves were used to darken the grit) makes the grit stand out from the image more starkly. Here you are using the image area to create a mask, not to fix the image directly, so damaging the information doesn't really matter as long as you achieve the goal of the selection.

Figure 27.19
The Find Edges filter will pick out the high-contrast areas and highlight them. Here it helps to selectively identify the damaged areas. There are other means of producing similar effects and ends.

Figure 27.20
Threshold can eliminate some of the noise generated by the Find Edges filter that you will not want included as part of the final selection.

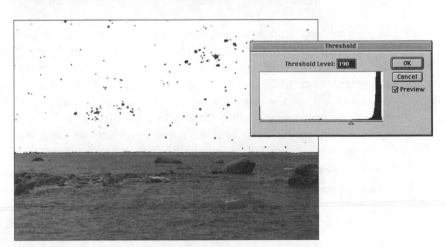

6. Use the Magic Wand tool with low tolerance (0–5) to select the white area outside the damage. If you have isolated the damage as suggested using Threshold, Tolerance can be zero as there will be only black and white pixels (no levels of gray). Leave Contiguous checked in this case because the application of Find Edges may leave some holes, particularly in larger bits of debris.

7. Invert the selection inverse using the Inverse command for Selection (Cmd-Shift-I) [Ctrl+Shift+I] (Select, Inverse).

8. Save the selection (Select, Save Selection).

9. Deselect (Cmd-D) [Ctrl+D], and then blur the channel created by saving the selection using the Gaussian Blur filter. Blurring helps corrections blend when the channel is loaded as a selection. The result of creating this mask following Steps 2 through 9 appears in Figure 27.21.

Figure 27.21
The final selection of the damage should look something like this. The white specks here correspond to the areas of damage in the image.

10. Load the Mask (Select, Load Selection) and apply correction to the damaged areas.

For the final result in this example, I made a copy of the sky and applied Dust & Scratches to that. After making the Dust & Scratches correction, I copied the sky to the buffer by selecting the whole Layer (Select, All) and copying. With the patch sky in the buffer ready to be pasted, I loaded the damage mask and copied the sky into it using Paste Into (Edit, Paste Into). Using Paste Into with the selection still active creates a Layer Mask from the selection. After the paste, I offset the layer by a few pixels (8 pixels right, 10 down) with the mask unlinked (see Figure 27.22). This moves the patch that was pasted a few pixels so that the damaged area is not at the center of the damage mask; a precaution in case the Dust & Scratches didn't take care of some problems.

→ For more information on Layer Masks, **see** "Layer Masks," **p. 64**.

Figure 27.22
In many instances, you will want to link the layer and mask so that you can move them together. To create the link, click the space between the layer thumbnail and the mask, and a chain will appear signifying the link. To move image areas independently of the mask, break the link by clicking the chain.

Because of the offset, the left and upper edge of the image will reveal damage if there was any there in the original. To fix that, you can use the rubber stamp to fill in, either directly in the masked layer, or in a new layer above that. You can also go back to any of the damage areas and touch up as necessary, although you should find that the damage is significantly reduced. Be sure when making the additional changes that the selection is not active so that the Filter effects apply to the whole image in the layer. Using selection confines the changes to the active areas of the selection, and the intent is to apply the change to the whole layer, in case you decide to move it again. The final result of the example image appears in Figure 27.23.

Figure 27.23
Here the image is clear of the grit and damage without having to go through the painstaking correction with the Rubber Stamp tool to cover every dot. This image is now ready to be used as a background.

PART

VII

CH

27

Tip

Depending on the image, you may be able to simplify the series of steps outlined for this damage correction. It might be possible to simply make the selection using the Magic Wand, skipping the steps of creating the new Layer, and applying Sharpen, Find Edges, and Threshold. This works only if the image noise stands out starkly. If you make this type of correction often, create an Action to walk you through the steps. It will help keep you on track and speed up corrections.

REPAIRS USING ADDITIONAL IMAGES

Entire image elements can be replaced to solve nagging problems in areas of an image where correction either seems impossible or just too difficult to undertake. Although this may seem very difficult, the most difficult part of this type of correction is finding an adequate replacement that matches the tone and flavor of the image. The replacement itself— if a good match is found—is as easy as pasting the element into the area you have selected.

Use the following steps to replace an image area:

1. Open the image in which you would like to make the replacement.
2. Select the area that you would like to replace.
3. Save the selection.
4. Open the image you would like to use for the replacement.
5. Copy the image area you want to use from the image. This will place the image area in the buffer.

Tip

The selection for Step 5, as it will be masked by the selection you saved in Step 3, does not have to be accurate. Often Select All (Cmd-A) [Ctrl+A] is fine, unless you are trying to conserve memory.

6. Activate the image opened in Step 1. You can select it by name from the Window menu.
7. Load the selection created in Step 3 (Select, Load Selection).
8. Paste the image you copied in Step 5 into the selected area (Edit, Paste Into). This will place the copied replacement area into a Layer with a Layer Mask defined by the selection you loaded.
9. Adjust the replacement image area as desired. This may include using corrections, applying Textures, using the Transform function, or any number of things in order to get the image area to match with its surroundings.

Using the image from Figure 27.9, and the selection of the sky and water area, it is very easy to replace the background of the image. Figure 27.24 shows the image using the image in Figure 27.23 as the replacement for the sky and water. With a few additional adjustments, such as removing most of the rocks and slightly quelling the waves, the replacement gets even closer to looking like the original.

Figure 27.24
The straight replacement of the image area is somewhat of an improvement. When the image area is replaced, you can fine-tune the image to fit better with the surroundings and do more to make it look like the original by comparison (by turning on and off the view for the layer it has been pasted into).

Choosing the image for the replacement is important. Although it isn't necessary to absolutely match the image area on the replacement, making a haphazard replacement will just make for a bad image. Considering that the image in Figure 27.9 was taken around 1930, the replacement used in Figure 27.25 is just unconsidered, and it becomes a distraction in the image.

Figure 27.25
It would probably be better to work with the damaged background and hope for the best than to make a replacement that is so poorly considered.

TROUBLESHOOTING

CLEARING THE WAY FOR CLONING

I am trying to complete dust corrections on my images using the Rubber Stamp tool, and I am not getting the results I expect by following the steps as outlined. What might be causing the difficulty?

Several things might be interfering with application of cloning, including tool selection, brush settings, Layer settings, and Layer grouping. The simplest thing to check is whether you are using the right tool. The Pattern Stamp and Clone Stamp look very much alike so it is easy to overlook the difference. The Pattern stamp has a screen on the stamp around the icon's pointer. To check which tool you have selected, click the Stamp tool in the toolbar and hold the mouse button down to open the menu. The tool currently selected will have a bullet at the left of the tool name. The bullet should be next to the Clone Stamp tool.

The brush for the Rubber Stamp tool will retain the previous settings you used for it—even if it was in a previous session using the program. To check whether the brush settings are the problem, set the Brush mode to Normal, be sure the brush hardness is 90%, check the Use All Layers box (if it isn't already), and set the Brush Opacity to 100%. Test the changes by attempting to make some corrections. If this resolves the problem, change the settings back one at a time to note which was stalling your corrections, and adjust accordingly.

If you are still having problems, reset the clone-from and clone-to points for the application of the clone. If this suddenly fixes the problem and you have changed the Use All Layers check box to on, the problem was probably that you were cloning from a layer with limited opacity. As you changed to Use All Layers, the clone-from point is now using all the visible information, rather than just information from the layer that was active when you made the selection. If this resolves the problem, change the settings for the brush back to what they were before, except for the Use All Layers box, and continue with corrections.

If none of this has worked thus far, check Layer Opacity, Mode and Preserve settings. To do this, create a layer to clone to above all the other layers in the image. Be sure the opacity for the Layer is set to 100%, Mode to Normal, do not group the Layer, and be sure the Preserve is unchecked. If this corrects the problem, the Layer you were cloning to may have had an Opacity, Mode or Preserve setting that was getting in the way. The least apparent of these would be if you were previously cloning-to a layer in a clipping group which was above another layer in the group where you had changed the opacity. In this case, the grouping effectively reduces the opacity of every layer above it in the group, but the opacity of the layer you were working on might still have been 100%. You can continue cloning on the new layer you have created, although you may want to move it to an appropriate spot in the layering of the image. You may also want to check layer styles to be sure your default did not somehow change to settings, which obscure added layers.

If cloning still doesn't work, be sure you do not have a hidden selection lurking in the image. To do this, Deselect (Cmd-D) [Ctrl+D]. Test the application of the tool. If you still have problems, restart.

This set of checks can be used when application of any freehand tool is stalled.

PROBLEM: CORRECTING IMAGE DAMAGE

On page 27 of the PDF workbook (from http:\\www.ps6.com), you will find the image from Figure 27.9 as well as Figure 27.17, the image used as a replacement for the background.

Following the steps listed here, you will be able to practice most of the techniques shown in this chapter.

Use the following steps to fix the damage in the sample image.

1. Open page 27 of the workbook in Photoshop.

2. Crop or copy the two images to separate documents.

3. Activate the image of the boy, and make a selection or mask of the sky and sea area.

→ For more information on selection, **see** "Selection and Masking," **p. 93**.

4. Save the selection when it is complete.

5. Use the selection to copy the boy to his own layer. To do this, load the selection (<u>S</u>elect, <u>L</u>oad Selection), and choose to Invert the selection by checking the box on the Load Selection dialog box. When the selection is loaded, Copy and Paste the boy or create a new layer via copy (Cmd-J) [Ctrl+J].

6. With the boy in his own Layer, begin making corrections to the boy using the Rubber Stamp tool. Make the corrections on a new Layer and be sure the Use All Layers box is checked in the Rubber Stamp Tool Options palette. Completing these corrections may take some time.

7. Activate the donor image.

8. Remove the damage from the image using the techniques outlined in "Selectively Replacing Dust Damage" earlier in this chapter. The results should look like Figure 27.23 when completed.

    After completing the corrections in Step 8, copy the whole image to the buffer using Select All (Cmd-A) [Ctrl+A] and Copy (Cmd-C) [Ctrl+C].

10. Activate the image of the boy.

11. Paste the replacement background into the image of the boy. This can either be done by loading the selection of the sky and water and using Paste Into to create a Layer Mask, or by pasting into a new Layer created between the background and the boy.

Note

Creating the Layer between the boy and the background isn't as important as that the Layer end up there. If you paste the image and it ends up in the wrong place, just move it by dragging it in the Layers palette.

12. Size and place the replacement image area as desired. It may be helpful to temporarily reduce the opacity of the layer so that you can match the horizon line.

13. Make adjustments to the tonality to attempt to make the replacement match the original as closely as possible. If you have reduced the opacity of the layer for Step 12, be sure you increase the opacity before making other corrections. This step may require using selection, Curves, Levels, and a number of other general correction tools.

14. Remove undesired image elements in the replacement. For example, there are more boulders in the replacement than in the original, so you may want to remove those.

When the corrections in Step 14 are complete, the image is essentially done. One final touch I applied in my corrections was to adjust the contrast in the upper portion of the boy—it seemed a little flat. The correction was applied to the boy in his own Layer, by making an oval selection with broad feathering and applying Unsharp Mask (Filter, Sharpen, Unsharp Mask) with a broad radius and low percentage. This technique with Unsharpen raises local contrast (see Figure 27.26).

→ For more information on using the Unsharp Mask filter, **see** "Sharpening with Unsharp Mask," **p. 618**.

Figure 27.26
This application of Unsharp Mask will increase local contrast to help bring out some detail in the boy's face that seems to have faded with the age of the image.

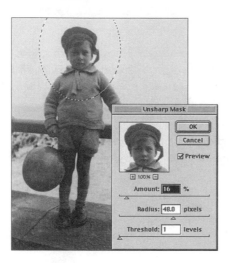

These 14 steps suggest you use a number of techniques to complete the restoration of the original image from basic dust correction through matching and replacement of image elements. If you can complete this restoration successfully, you have the tools you need to restore just about any image, so long as you can identify the damage and recognize suitable replacement elements (either within the image or in another). To practice restoration and expand your understanding of corrections, apply the techniques from this chapter to your own images.

COMPOSITION CHANGES AND IMPROVEMENTS

In this chapter

REMOVING DISTRACTIONS FROM AN IMAGE

Some image problems are compositional rather than being a result of damage. Compositional problems can prove distracting and can detract from the impact of an image just as damage can. An example of a compositional problem was created in the last chapter in the example where a bad choice was made for image substitution (see Figure 28.1). The only real difference is that the image element causing the problem is part of the original image.

Figure 28.1
The background in this image is distracting and noisy and can be replaced with a more tranquil scene to benefit the image, helping the subject stand out more.

Changing or replacing these image areas to improve the composition can help focus the image better on the subject and improve the image overall. Such corrections follow similar techniques to those used for correcting damage, but the purpose is somewhat different; here the idea is to change an image with the purpose of making the image better, rather than simply repairing or replacing what is already there.

The solution for composition problems is often right in the image you have, but techniques can range from duplication of image areas to replacement from other images. The solution to this type of problem is often very similar to fixing large damaged areas. Changes in composition will probably prove to be more radical because your purpose from the outset is to change the image rather than to restore it. The steps for any alterations will be highly specific to that image, and can be summarized as follows:

1. Identify the compositional problem(s) within your image.
2. Isolate the areas that will be replaced from the areas that will remain.
3. Identify replacement elements (from this image or other images).
4. Combine the image elements to produce the final result.

As the process is highly specific to an image, an example is provided here to show how the process might proceed. Figure 28.2 shows an image taken of a statue in progress at the artist's studio. It was not really an option to move the statue when the image was taken. As such, the photographer did what was possible—and did an excellent job—using available light to help bring out the statue's detail. Although the window provides some of the lighting and is integral to the image in that way, it proves to be a potential distraction from the statue. There are any number of solutions to the problem, but one of the most interesting and effective is right in the image: borrowing the wall from the right of the photo and rebuilding it to cover the window on the left.

Figure 28.2
The image of this plaster statue by Mihail Chemiakin (photo by Arkady Lvov, courtesy of Mimi Fertz Gallery, NYC) was created in the artist's studio.

The goal of the change in this image will be to isolate the statue and alter the background, much like the correction for the restoration of the image of the boy in the previous chapter. The background will be rebuilt using existing image elements.

This preliminary evaluation takes care of Steps 1 and 3 in the general procedure noted previously as the problem and solution are found in the same image. The following steps were used to complete the task of removing the window from this image and satisfying Steps 2 and 4 of the general procedure, which require isolating elements and fixing the composition.

1. After the image was scanned and opened, the first move was to make a selection of the statue in order to isolate it.

PART

VII

CH

28

Note

This selection will be used to isolate the statue, as well as for masking and copying background image areas. To make the selection, a quick selection of the black background was made with the Magic Wand. Then, the selection was turned to a quick mask and altered using the airbrush to paint in additional masking around the statue's fingers where they crossed into the window area. When the alteration to the quick mask was complete, the Magic Wand was used to create a selection inside quick mask over the statue. A single click with the Magic Wand inside the statue area trims the noise from the area outside the statue, and selects only the statue and floor. The noise in the quick mask—the window and bricks—is quickly eliminated in this way. The new Magic Wand selection was then saved to a channel to use in isolating the statue in later steps. See Figure 28.3.

→ For more information on creating selections to help isolate areas, **see** "Selection and Masking," **p. 93**.

Figure 28.3
The three steps used in creating the selection are shown here. A rough selection is made with the Magic Wand, and then that selection is retouched to shape the selection around the statue (the element you want to isolate). Finally, clicking inside the area that has been refined selects it neatly from the rest of the Quick Mask. That result is saved.

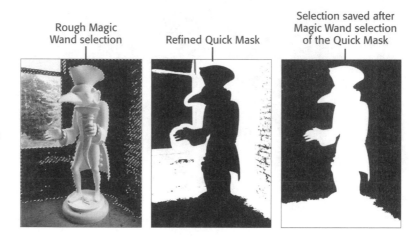

Rough Magic Wand selection

Refined Quick Mask

Selection saved after Magic Wand selection of the Quick Mask

2. The selection created in Step 1 was loaded and used to copy and paste the statue to its own layer. This effectively isolated the statue; the background could be changed without worrying about the image of the statue being affected.

3. The selection was inverted and the background was copied to its own layer, and then the layer it was pasted into was flipped horizontally (see Figure 28.4). This is the start of substituting the wall at right to cover the window.

4. The extraneous areas of the duplication were removed. Here it was easy to make a quick selection of the entire right side of the image using the lasso. Removing the extra simply leaves less to juggle—for this correction the extra would not prove useful anyway. After the selection was made, the area was removed by pressing the Delete key.

5. The replacement area was resized using Perspective and Distortion from the Transform function. The goal was to better fit the perspective of the wall and the size of the area that needed to be filled (see Figure 28.5).

Figure 28.4
This area of the right wall will be distorted and extended to make the bulk of the replacement for the window on the left of the original.

Note

To work with the Transform functions, select the image area you want to transform. If no selection is active, the tools will not be available. After the selection is made, call the Transform function by pressing (Cmd-T) [Ctrl+T]. Change perspective (Shift-Cmd-Option-Drag) [Shift+Ctrl+Alt+Drag] and distort (Cmd-Drag) [Ctrl+Drag].

Figure 28.5
After removing the unnecessary informa-tion in Step 5, the result is resized using Transform functions to fill the space and con-form to the new per-spective as the left wall. The background has an adjustment layer applied to tem-porarily lighten it and lower contrast so it is easier to tell the parts from one another.

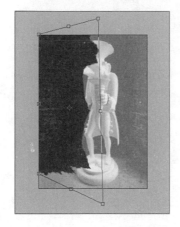

6. The Eraser and Stamping tools were employed to help work the layer into the surrounding image by blending and softening edges.

Note

To do this, the foreground layer of the statue was toggled on and off many times to view how the elements were blending, both with the background and with the presence of the statue. For example, parts of the bottom of the replacement wall are erased to blend with the floor, and some of the wall is extended by cloning to cover background noise near the statue. The result is not pretty when viewed by itself, but it works well in the image (see Figure 28.6 to view the replacement layer by itself). The important idea is to cover the window and blend with the background to create the appropriate fix.

Figure 28.6
Because the statue will act like a mask over this replacement layer, the edges that end behind the statue can be rough—no one will see them, as they will be covered by the statue.

7. Finally, the right wall itself was extended by duplicating the right wall again, inverting vertically, and using Select, Transform Selection to adjust the perspective. Similar steps as those taken in Step 6 were used to blend the bricks. This was meant to center the statue, but also helps to hide any overly apparent duplication in the bricks. The result of all the changes appears in Figure 28.7.

Selecting the area you don't want to change allows you to use the element itself as a mask to block out the layers below. This gives you more leeway in moving, distorting, and arranging elements behind the key element, so that they don't affect the elements that you want to keep intact. This type of replacement and alteration has numerous uses; you can alter and improve images in an almost limitless way.

 If you have identified a problem area in an image and are not sure as to how to proceed, see "Finding Image Elements" in the Troubleshooting section at the end of this chapter.

Figure 28.7
The final image combines the changes made to extend the right wall and cover the window, leaving a fairly stark representation of the statue with almost no distraction from the image background.

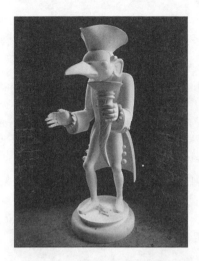

CONTROLLING COMPOSITION WITH SELECTIVE FOCUS

Throwing image elements into or out of focus in comparison to their surroundings can help image elements stand out. Focus can be manipulated in circumstances where it is impossible to focus on foreground and background elements simultaneously. For example, in a low-light or close-up situation, it may be impossible to take the entire image area in focus. In this situation, two photos can be taken, each selectively focused on different image elements. The sharp areas of the two photos can be combined into a composite that contains both sharp elements. On the other hand, selective blurring of elements from sharper images can bring the viewer's eye to the subject or area of an image that is left in focus.

SELECTIVE SHARPENING

Selectively focusing on elements in an image can make individual elements stand out in a photograph. Selective focus is usually accomplished photographically by reducing the depth of field. With a shorter depth of field, fewer items in an image will be in focus, and those that are in focus stand out from those that are not. It is, however, not always easy or possible to control focus when taking an image, depending on the type of lens you are using, lighting conditions, and so on. In some cases, you will want more of an image to be in focus than you can actually get in one shot. In this case, you can use more than one shot and Photoshop to achieve the results you want.

Depth of Field
Depth of field is the distance a camera will see in focus. The depth changes, meaning that a deeper or shallower field will be held in focus, depending on aperture and type or focal length of a lens. Greater depth of field captures more in focus in the foreground and background of an image, whereas short depth of field tends to isolate image elements that are focused on.

PART
VII

CH
28

Much of this effect is in the preparation. Essentially, it is most useful when there is a technical reason why you can't focus on all the elements in an image. You will have to take two images of the same scene: one focused on each of the main elements. It is probably best to use a tripod to keep the camera in exactly the same spot when attempting this. First focus on one element and take a picture, and then focus on the other and take a second picture. These two pictures will be used as source images for the final image.

If you'd like to try this out but are having difficulty defining the depth of field for your images, see "Shortening Your Depth of Field" in the Troubleshooting section at the end of this chapter.

Use the following steps to sharpen an image selectively using two photos.

1. Open the images you have created and plan to combine. Figure 28.8 shows the source images chosen for this example.

Figure 28.8
In this scene, the camera was very close to the tulip in the foreground, and the camera was fitted with a macro lens. To get the whole image in focus, an image was taken selectively focused on the tulip in the foreground, and then one selectively focused on the tulip in the background.

2. Choose one of the two images to be the donor image. That is, look at the two images and decide which is better suited to the final image. Plan to leave that image intact while cutting the element you need from the other (the donor) image.

Tip

Most often it is easiest to select the image where the foreground element is sharp as the donor image, especially if the two elements you are working with overlap. However, careful selection can make either work. The selection of the donor image should be based on how you want the surroundings to look, not on ease of selection.

3. Activate the donor image by choosing it by name from the Window menu or by clicking on a part of the document palette to bring it to the front.

4. Make a selection of the area of the image that you want to copy to the final image (see Figure 28.9).

→ For more information on selection, **see** "Selection and Masking," **p. 93**.

Figure 28.9
Because of the framing of this image, it is not so important to select the stem of the tulip because that will not make enough difference to the new image to matter. In some images, it will be necessary to select several elements to complete the desired effect.

5. Copy the image area to the receiving image. This can be done via copy and paste, layer duplication (Layer, Duplicate Layer), and choosing, or you can create a new layer in the donor image (Cmd-J) [Ctrl+J] and drag the layer that is created to the new image.

6. Position the replacement over its likeness in the new image. You may need to adjust the size or distort slightly to make the elements fit and so that the donor portion of the image completely covers what it is replacing (see Figure 28.10).

Figure 28.10
The finished image shows both tulips sharply over a focused background. It is still possible to do more work on this image (such as blurring the wall in background a bit to soften it as an element), but the selective focus change accomplishes the purpose of creating the focus desired.

With the replacement in place, the effect is complete. The resulting image should look as if the elements are both in focus. The choice of the donor image is important. In the example, reversing the choices would have thrown the background out of focus, and might have provided more separation for the tulips. Decide what you want the result to be, and make the changes based on that goal.

This effect can be used to create special effects as well. For example, taking a shot of a subject in a noisy background and then taking another shot of the background out of focus will let you copy the subject into the image with relative ease. Although this simple effect can usually be accomplished in a single image photographically by controlling the equipment properly, additional combination effects based on this same principle are possible (such as blurring the background in a gradient from the left to the right of the image, and so on).

SELECTIVE BLUR

This technique works to pull the viewer's attention to a selected item in the image by softening the focus of the other elements. Selective focus on images can also be accomplished by adding sharp image elements to blurred images (as mentioned in the previous section).

1. Open an image that is relatively sharp (in focus). See Figure 28.11 for the image we will use for this example.

Figure 28.11
Because a number of sheep in this image are in focus, none really stand out to draw the attention of the viewer.

© PhotoSphere Images, Ltd., photosphere.com

2. Choose an element (or elements) that you want to have stand out in the image. It can be almost any element as long as it is already in focus.

3. Make a selection of that part of the image and copy it to its own layer (see Figure 28.12).

4. Choose the background layer from the Layers palette and apply a blur. This will effectively keep the element you have selected in focus while blurring the surroundings.

The effect can be improved from the rather simple effect introduced previously with more care in the blurring. Depending on the effect you want to create, you might mask the blur in one or more selections and blur in several steps. For the sample image, a blur was applied to the background two times. The first was an unmasked Gaussian Blur, and then a second Gaussian Blur application was masked with a simple linear blend (see the Mask in Figure 28.13). The purpose here was to mock a sort of depth-of-field effect.

Figure 28.12
In the example, one animal seemed to have more potential for this effect because it was facing the camera. The entire animal was selected (note the hooves).

Figure 28.13
This blend can be used to very roughly imitate a depth-of-field blur. Creating an exact imitation of the effects of depth of field and focus is not the purpose of this image.

Next, a soft Gaussian Blur was also applied to the sheep in its own layer, after a mask was created to keep the ears and face in sharp focus (see the mask for the application in Figure 28.14).

Figure 28.14
This mask was used to protect the animal's face, while a slight blur was applied to it in its own layer.

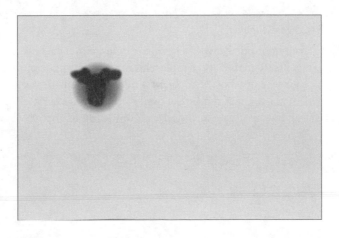

The purpose of this exercise was to make the depth-of-field effect seem more realistic, and also to focus starkly on the animal's face. Figure 28.15 shows the final results of the blurs.

Figure 28.15
The final result of blurring leaves the image with better focus on the lone image area apparently in good focus.

Depending on the effect you are trying to achieve, it might be desirable to use more control over the selections to make the effects more truly realistic. Generally, it won't be necessary to be precise using this type of effect. You might want to add emphasis to the selected image elements in other ways. For example, the sheep in the image was lightened slightly to brighten it and make it stand out slightly more. Lightening and darkening, or even adding a slight glow or shadow to image elements, can help achieve the separation to make the subject stand out better. Your goal should be to do what makes the image work by manipulating the composition to the advantage of the result.

TROUBLESHOOTING

FINDING IMAGE ELEMENTS

I've identified a problem area in the image I have, but there are no good replacement parts in the image itself. What are my options?

Replacement can require some heavy creativity at times, either in simple replacement or in using existing elements to manufacture replacement parts. Another option is to actually create photographic elements. For example, you might create patterns and textures to use in making filler materials such as the bricks used in the statue example. In fact, an example in Chapter 31 shows how to create a cinderblock wall without any photographic elements at all.

→ For more information on creating photographic elements from scratch, **see** "Creating Seamless Pattern and Texture Elements," **p. 668**.

SHORTENING YOUR DEPTH OF FIELD

I have been trying to shoot images with a shortened depth of field and can't seem to do it. Are there any additional camera adjustments I should be making other than focus?

Shortening depth of field in your images can be accomplished in a variety of ways. Some of these methods are not possible with every camera. There are three things that will probably be the most problematic in attempting to take images with a short depth of field: inexpensive cameras, automatic cameras, and proper control of aperture.

Aperture is important for letting the light into the lens to strike the film. The more light that is needed, the more you can open the aperture to let light in to expose the film. As the aperture opens, the light is drawn through a wider portion of the lens, and optical transmission is decentralized from the optimal point on the lens. The result is the depth of field suffers. The broader the aperture, the shorter the depth of field becomes. It is imperative to use wide apertures and/or long (telephoto) or short (micro) lenses to produce depth of field effects. Many cameras will limit your ability to control the aperture or lens you will be using.

Inexpensive cameras often come with a tiny fixed-focus lens. This is not an accident. Not only are they cheaper to produce, but a small lens leads to a small aperture (or lens opening) and one of the benefits of a small aperture is a greater depth of field. For example, pinhole cameras (which use a pinhole in the side of the camera box rather than a lens to guide light toward the film) have a tremendous depth of field. It is so great, in fact, that really everything captured by a pinhole camera is in focus. Essentially, if you have a cheaper camera with a smaller lens, you are forced to take images with a broad depth of field—making them consistently in focus, which actually may be a good thing for the casual snapper. It may seem strange, but it is only when you have a more expensive camera with more flexibility that you get to take images that are out of focus. The only solution here might be to upgrade your camera.

If you have an automatic camera and you are trying to adjust the depth of field, shut the automatic feature off. This should allow you to make aperture adjustments that are necessary to create a shallow depth of field. If the camera will not allow you to shut off the auto features, you can try taking the images in less light (this will usually force the camera to select a wider aperture setting), or trick the camera by changing the ISO/ASA setting for the speed of the film. Adjusting the film speed may not be possible with some smart cameras that either read the speed right off the film canister, or those that do not have a manual means of setting the aperture. If it is possible, knock the ISO/ASA down to ratings slower than the film you are currently using—perhaps to 1/2 or 1/4 the speed. For example, if using 400-speed film, change the ISO/ASA to 100. This should trick the camera into opening the aperture a bit, but it may not work if there is too much light, as the camera may just compensate by adjusting the shutter speed.

PHOTOSHOP AT WORK: IMPROVING IMAGE COMPOSITION

The PDF workbook (found at www.ps6.com) contains both the original statue image used in the first example in this chapter and the tulips used in a later example. The two tulip images will appear on separate layers within the document. Although ultimately you should be practicing this type of alteration with your own images, it will be more convenient to work with those we have already discussed here, just to get your feet wet. If you can complete the correction for the statue with reasonably good results, you should gain the confidence to be able to tackle just about any correction of this type.

In essence, the corrections to either image is the same: There is a problem with the image that can be improved with the replacement of an image element—when it comes down to it, it hardly matters whether the image element is in the same image or a second one. In this case, the tulips will probably be a little easier, but go for the statue if you feel like stretching your Photoshop muscles.

Follow the basic steps to make corrections to the image you choose to work on:

1. Identify the compositional problem(s) within your image.
2. Isolate the areas that will be replaced from the areas that will remain.
3. Identify replacement elements (from this image or other images).
4. Combine the image elements to produce the final result.

For more details on the steps for these specific examples, look back to the step-by-step for each image (page 605 for the statue and page 610 for the tulips). When you are done working through the corrections, a copy of the result appears on another layer for comparison. If you want to concentrate on just the correction, the selections can be loaded from an existing channel. It is, however, suggested that you use the opportunity to work on your ability with selections.

CHAPTER **29**

APPLYING FILTERS TO IMPROVE IMAGES

In this chapter

USING FILTERS TO FIX IMAGES

Many of Photoshop's filters can be used creatively to solve image problems. A few filters, however, will be most important in fixing your images, and you will find you use them often in making image corrections. At the same time, these may seem like the simplest filters in the bunch. The fact is, the more exotic the filter, the more exotic the effect, and probably the less use you will have for it—except in creating special effects. Simple filters can go a long way in developing your images and providing solutions to image problems.

The filters you will probably learn to use most often are the Sharpen, Blur, and Noise filters. I probably use at least one of these on every photograph I work on. Be sure you know what they can do and how they function most effectively. The following sections provide an overview to each of these tools and how to use them.

→ For more information on filters not noted here, **see** "Type Effects," **p. 721** and "Using Filters and Plug-Ins" **p. 755**.

SHARPENING WITH UNSHARP MASK

The sharpening filters in Photoshop are not magic. They will not take a wildly out-of-focus image and snap it back into focus. This is not to say that it is impossible to use filters to improve the appearance of an image. However, you should not expect a miraculous recovery. Although they do help the appearance of sharpness in the image, there are actually several uses for the tools.

What Sharpening (and specifically the Unsharp Mask) can do when used properly is to improve the appearance of image sharpness by working with contrast. It strengthens local contrast in an image based on the radius and percentage you select in the dialog box. This is useful not only for sharpening blurry images, but also for preparing images for print, adjusting images after resizing, and increasing local contrast in an image to help image elements stand out better.

Note

Although there are other sharpening tools (the freehand Sharpen tool, and Sharpen, Sharpen Edges and Sharpen More filters), I find them somewhat less valuable because they are preset applications and really do nothing that you can't do using the Unsharp Mask filter.

UNSHARP MASK OPTIONS

The Unsharp Mask dialog box (Filter, Sharpen, Unsharp Mask) has three sliders: Amount, Radius, and Threshold (see Figure 29.1). The Amount can be between 1% and 500%. This option determines how much effect neighboring pixels will have on one another; however, this effect is, in turn, affected by choices for radius and threshold. The higher the number, the greater the effect. The Radius can be from .1 to 250 pixels and works similarly to a feather radius. The Threshold option affects the way pixels work against each other based on their relative difference. For example, a low threshold (0) would allow neighboring pixels to freely affect one another; a high threshold (255) would keep pixels from affecting one another. The threshold notes the number of levels by which neighboring pixels must differ to have an effect on the pixel being looked at.

Figure 29.1
The Unsharp Mask dialog box offers preview and zoom buttons to go along with sliders for Amount of effect, Radius of the effect (in pixels), and Threshold of levels needed to measure where the effect is to occur.

SHARPENING AN IMAGE

The goal of sharpening is to improve, not reclaim, an image. The effect will work more or less effectively depending on the content of the image.

Generally, you will want to choose a setting with a low threshold. Threshold is measured in levels and you will want to stay between zero and five—usually keeping toward the lower end of this range. This means Photoshop will look at the number of levels of difference in the surrounding pixels, and if the number of levels is greater than the threshold, it will apply sharpening based on the settings for Radius and Amount. Often you will want to use zero tolerance, but some tolerance (one or two) will keep Photoshop from sharpening what is otherwise image noise. Sharpening noise will only make the image noisier. With that in mind, the noisier the image, generally the greater the threshold you should use. The only time when you will set the threshold higher than five is when you want to limit the effect of the filter to high-contrast areas of the image to play up contrast and separation of image elements. In these cases, you might actually apply the filter twice—once with a very low threshold (zero or one) for general sharpening, and once with the higher threshold for the contrast effect (how high you go depends on the relative contrast of the image).

Radius and Amount might be set quite differently depending on what you are trying to achieve and the dpi and content of the image. Although settings can vary depending on the type of image and desired effect, when sharpening you will probably normally keep the Radius low (.5% to 1.5% of the dpi on an average image) and the Amount between 50% and 100%. If the content of the image is busier, and lower-contrast, you can tend toward the high end of the radius range; if the image is not as busy and has high contrast, tend toward the low end. For example, a 300dpi image would have a target range for the Radius of about 1.5 to 4.5 pixels; a 72dpi image with the same content would have a Radius of about .35 pixel to 1 pixel. These are rough guidelines, however.

Tip

If you feel an image needs more sharpening than the guidelines suggest, try keeping within the suggested Radius while using the Amount to increase the effect. Better still, you might stay within the ranges and apply the filter more than once.

Tip

To repeat the last filter used, press (Cmd-F) [Ctrl+F]. To reopen the last filter used with same settings press (Cmd-Option-F) [Ctrl+Alt+F]. The latter will allow you to start from the previously used settings and make adjustments if necessary.

Figure 29.2 shows an image of an owl, which appears slightly soft. The correction uses a very strong application of the tool, which is tolerated well because of the relatively low contrast and busy nature of the image.

Figure 29.2
Usually, you will not be able to apply Sharpening so strongly with positive results. Although these settings are high, and beyond the suggested range, they are not radical or damaging for this image.

Figure 29.3 shows the owl with the same amount of sharpening; however, the original image was duplicated to a second layer before applying Sharpening, and Blend If and Opacity settings were applied to the new layer to soften some of the harshness of the Sharpening. See the settings that were used in the Layer Styles dialog box in Figure 29.3. The blending mutes the potentially detrimental effects of the sharpening (halation), and helps blend back some of the detail in highlights and shadows that can be lost during the Sharpening—without nullifying the effect. The Opacity should weaken (lower percentage number) and the Blend If should allow more of the original image through (movement of

white sliders to the left and black sliders to the right) to restore the original image information. These settings are subjective, based on what you want to achieve. A similar result can be obtained by using the Fade (Shift-Cmd-F) [Shift+Ctrl+F], here with a setting of about the same as the opacity (75%). The Layer Styles and Blend If function offer more flexibility, however. Here the sliders are split so that the blending occurs only in the highlight and shadow portions of the image, where the effect of the sharpening will tend to be most extreme.

Figure 29.3
To soften some of the negative effects of the strong sharpening in Figure 29.2, Blend If is used to retract some of the extremes that can occur. In this case, the sharpened image was placed over the original in a second layer.

Radical sharpening (or oversharpening) can damage images by creating a *halo* effect in high-contrast areas. The Blend If technique shown in Figure 29.3 is meant to reduce this halation somewhat. Halation occurs in image areas where larger, flatly dark portions of an image meet larger, flatly light portions of an image. In the owl image, this will be most apparent at the edges of the branch on which the owl sits. It is not very strong or overt in this image, but can become a problem (see Figure 29.4).

Figure 29.4 shows a very different type of image, which will tend to fare less well with extreme sharpening. It is of higher contrast and is far less busy than the owl image. The first image in the series is the original image (72dpi) with no sharpening. The next is the same image with sharpening applied well within the suggested range. The third image has sharpening applied at settings that might be used for a 300dpi image. The fourth has settings that are double the settings for a 300dpi image (or that are suggested for 600dpi).

Figure 29.4
Halation becomes
apparent when the
Unsharp Mask is
applied too strongly.
Not only will this tend
to blow out areas of
images, but the image
will distort and the
effect will become
unpleasant.

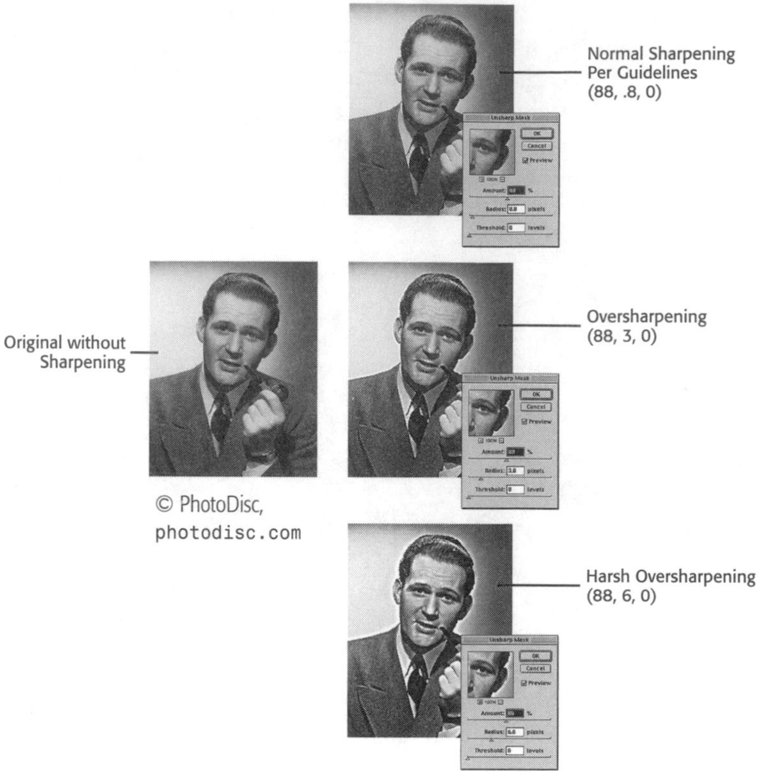

Normal Sharpening
Per Guidelines
(88, .8, 0)

Original without
Sharpening

Oversharpening
(88, 3, 0)

© PhotoDisc,
photodisc.com

Harsh Oversharpening
(88, 6, 0)

Staying within the guidelines helps you avoid the potential problems with oversharpening and creating halos in high-contrast areas of your images. Better to sharpen a little several times than to sharpen hastily and damage the image.

RAISING LOCAL CONTRAST WITH SHARPENING

Sharpening with Unsharp Mask can improve images by more broadly raising local contrast. It is a much different effect, which does less to sharpen the details than to distinguish image elements from one another. This effect works well with low-contrast images, or images that seem to somehow lack dynamics. This effect can really pick up a seemingly flat image.

When you are adjusting local contrast with the Unsharp Mask, the Radius might be much higher than suggested for normal sharpening (15% to 40% of the dpi), and the amount between 10% and 30%. Again, these are just suggested ranges. The goal of the settings is to get beyond the stage where halation is noticeable (hence the wide Radius), and to keep the effect from causing damage (hence the low Amount). Going wider in the radius at a certain point actually seems to do very little, but keeping the Radius low will speed the application. Set the Radius to determine the effective area, and then adjust with the Amount.

Figure 29.5 shows a somewhat low-contrast image of a biplane. By raising the local contrast, the image elements will have more separation from one another. In this case, the goal is to have the plane stand out from its surroundings better without making any type of complex selection. The first image in this series is the original image. The second is the result of raising the local contrast with the Unsharp Mask. The third is the result of applying Unsharp Mask to the second image in the series and adjusting slightly for Levels.

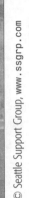

© Seattle Support Group, www.ssgrp.com

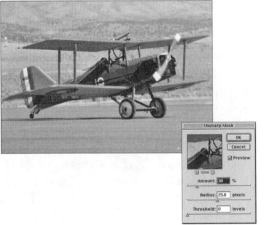

Figure 29.5
Two applications of the Unsharp Mask—one to build local contrast, and one to sharpen—make quick work of what would otherwise be an arduous task in masking to separate this plane better from its surroundings.

The original image lacks a little pop. After raising the local contrast with the Unsharp Mask (using a broad radius and low percentage), the biplane stands out better from the surroundings. With the Unsharp filter applied to raise the local contrast, the Unsharp filter is applied again, but this time to sharpen the image (short radius and higher percentage).

The radius and percentage need to be adjusted depending on the dpi and content of the image as described earlier. A slight adjustment to the left with the middle Levels slider lightens the entire image slightly, making it easier to view.

→ For more information on level adjustments, **see** "Corrections with Levels," **p. 447**.

IMPROVING REALISM WITH NOISE FILTERS

Using the Noise filters (Filter, Noise) can help both reduce and build surface texture in areas where texture is altered due to methods of repair. These same techniques can add some character to elements that you have created with paint tools from scratch, or areas you have created with blends. Often newly created areas end up flatly painted and they will almost always will look somewhat better—and fit better to their background—with a little noise applied. The Add Noise filter will remove that plasticized, absolutely flat look, or banding that occurs as one level of a color gives way to the next.

The opposite of introducing noise to an image area is noise suppression. Images can have noise levels of various type and size and several tools are available in Photoshop to help decrease these problems globally (or within selected areas). Noise can be reduced using Median, Dust & Scratches, and Despeckle filters. These filters can have a number of benefits in images where image grain is a problem, where sharpening introduces noise, or where images are damaged by grit, scratches, and dirt.

ADD NOISE FILTER

Simply put, the Add Noise filter generates *image noise* by randomizing color assignments for pixels. This may sound like an undesirable thing at first, because it would seem to be damaging the image. However, tones that appear even may not be completely so. The role of applying noise in most cases is to equalize the noise effects.

When applying the Add Noise filter (Filter, Noise, Add Noise), you have several choices in the Add Noise dialog box for controlling the effect, including selecting the Amount, the Distribution Type, and whether or not to keep the effect Monochromatic. The Amount is related to Percentage, and defines the range of variation possible in creating the noise distribution. Amount can vary between .1% and 400%. As the Amount goes up, the application of the noise is potentially more radical. Generally, noise applications will be less than 15%, and even at that strength can become somewhat of a special effect, depending on the dpi of the image. Images with higher dpi will be able to withstand stronger applications of the filter. Very strong applications of noise can tend to obliterate an image. Generation of noise will further be affected by the Distribution Type. Distribution Type can be Uniform or Gaussian.

A Uniform distribution changes color values of individual pixels by selecting a random number within the range defined by the amount. This number can be the original value plus or minus the amount for each channel of color. For example, applying an amount of 25 to a 50% gray image (128 levels) in Grayscale will result in gray values between 103 and 153 levels of gray for any pixel, each value generated at random. Applying the same Amount to a 50% gray image in RGB will affect each channel for the image (independently of one another if the Monochromatic box is not checked). That is, each channel could have a value of 103 to 153, each randomly generated, so the effect on the color image would be greater with the same settings. The point is that such randomized introduction of noise has the potential to make considerable changes in an image if the filter application is too strong, and the same settings will introduce more or less noise depending on the number of color channels. Figure 29.6 shows a breakdown of a typical application using Uniform distribution with Monochrome off.

Figure 29.6
Using Uniform distribution with an initial value of 50% gray (128,128,128), the value of each pixel in each channel can vary by the Amount. The composite is the result of applying noise to each pixel in each channel individually.

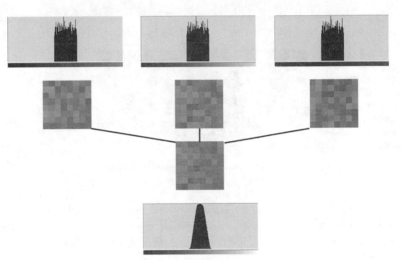

A Gaussian distribution changes color values of individual pixels by selecting a random number based on a Gaussian function. The function creates a tendency to select from the center of the range. This range is broader than the Amount, based on a Gaussian equation. Although the tendency is to select from the center of the range, deviations in individual color channels can potentially be broader, so this is a stronger effect than the Uniform distribution. The total effect will also tend to vary more between applications. In other words, it is less stable or predictable than the Uniform method. Again, when applied, each channel is assigned a value independently. Figure 29.7 shows a breakdown of a typical application using Gaussian distribution with Monochrome off. Figure 29.8 shows the difference between Uniform and Gaussian distributions.

Figure 29.7
In a Gaussian distribution, the individual channels have a more pronounced deviation using the same Amount as the previous example. The deviation is somewhat tamed in the composite. However, the composite effect is still more pronounced than the result of using Uniform distribution.

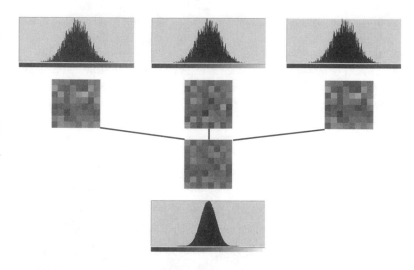

Figure 29.8
This side-by-side comparison shows the difference between the results in applying Uniform distribution (left) and Gaussian distribution (right).

Uniform Distribution   Gaussian Distribution

Selecting the Monochromatic option applies the filter to only the tonal elements in the image without changing the colors. That is, one value is selected according to the Amount, and the value affects each channel by the same number of levels in the same direction. For example, if the value selected for the pixel is 20 levels, and the original value for the pixel is 64,192,128, the resulting value will be 44,172,108 (a darker shade of a similar green).

Noise is generally best if applied lightly. In applying the Noise Filter, the goal is to help objects blend with the noise level of the surroundings. Figure 29.9 shows a repair in which noise was used to make an image correction blend better. The skin on the subject is not bad, but could appear much more youthful with gentler pores. A selection was made using the red channel as a mask (the Red Channel was simply duplicated). With the selection loaded, the area of the subject's skin was copied and pasted to its own layer (Cmd-J) [Ctrl+J], where Median (Filter, Noise, Median) was applied with a Radius of 3. The results smoothed the skin, but left it too flat. Noise was added with an Amount of 8, using Uniform distribution with the monochromatic box checked. This returns some of the texture to the skin without leaving it looking too flat and fake.

Note

Because the Median filter is applied according to a Radius, the dpi of the image will play into how the image is affected. In other words, a Radius of 3 used in this example will not necessarily produce the same result on an image with different dpi, size, and qualities.

Figure 29.9
The appearance of the pores is softened first, using the Median Filter to remove the noise. Next, the Add Noise filter is used to gently replace some of what was lost in the texture. The result is much smoother skin, and a somewhat more youthful smile. See ColorPlate 6 in the color section for a color version of this image.

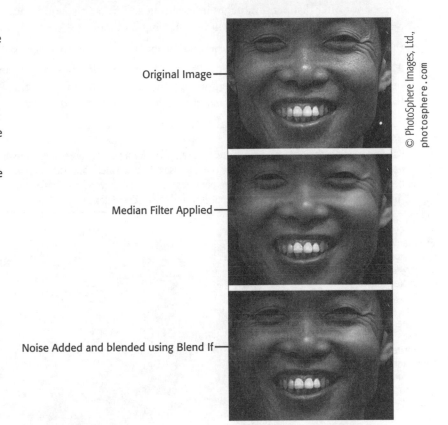

Original Image

Median Filter Applied

Noise Added and blended using Blend If

© PhotoSphere Images, Ltd., photosphere.com

After the application of Median and Add Noise filters, a Blend If (Layer, Layer Styles, Blending Options) was applied to the layer to define edges and features slightly more clearly. The settings for the blend made the blend effective only in the medium tones. Again, combinations of tool applications and functions generally work best in achieving goals in an image because no one tool can do it all. Additionally, you can use Add Noise to create graininess in an image overall to mimic film grain.

→ For more information on the Blend If function, **see** "The Blend If Layer Function," **p. 74** and "Colorizing a Grayscale Image," **p. 514**.

⚠ *If you apply noise and the noise isn't noisy enough, see "Applying Bigger Filter Effects" in the Troubleshooting section at the end of this chapter.*

REMOVING NOISE

The Median, Dust & Scratches, and Despeckle filters all remove or lessen the effect of image noise using a form of modified blurring. Despeckle, being a preset, is the least useful of these as you can't adjust the settings to control how the filter is applied to your image. As it does not offer distinct advantages in repairing an image, it is not discussed here. Dust & Scratches is discussed in the context of removing dust damage.

→ For more information on Dust & Scratches, **see** "Removing Dust from an Image," **p. 580**.

Median (Filter, Noise, Median) reduces noise by averaging tones over an area defined by the radius. As in the example from Figure 29.9, the application can cause blurriness or a sort of banding, and may not often achieve a desirable effect when used by itself.

Banding

Banding is a noticeable stepping in a blend that can occur for a number of reasons. One of the reasons for banding is a lack of noise in gradients or failure to use dithering when converting to Indexed Color. It is rarely a desirable effect, but can be used for some purposes, such as mock woodgrain and wood textures. Figure 29.10 shows an example of banding from an application of the Median filter.

Figure 29.10
Application of the median filter on this image area caused banding, or a stepped grouping of pixels. The appearance of banding (if any) will entirely depend on the content of the image and the intensity of your application of the filter.

The Median dialog box (see Figure 29.11) has a single slider to control the radius of the effect, and a preview. If the desired effect cannot be achieved in a single application, you can attempt additional applications, or combine applications with other tools such as the Blur tools for additional smoothing, or add noise as in the preceding example to restore a desirable range of noise.

Figure 29.11
The Median filter is used to smooth out noisy areas as per the settings for the radius. The Radius has a minimum setting of 1 pixel and a maximum of 16 pixels.

USING BLUR FILTERS EFFECTIVELY

Blur filters (Filter, Blur) effectively blur images or image areas by averaging the effects of pixels. This averaging is done over a range, and the effect is a softening of edges or smoothing of hard lines between areas of contrast. Essentially, this is the opposite of Sharpening, which builds existing contrast.

> **Note**
> As with Sharpening and Noise filters, the effects of the Blur preset filters (Blur and Blur More) can be duplicated by the Gaussian Blur, so they are not discussed separately here.

Blurring is effective for blending image edges, both to adjust focus (as seen in the previous chapter in the section on "Selective Blur") and to smooth edges created by compositing images—essentially a means of *anti-aliasing*, after the fact. Often you will want to use Blur along with Selection to confine areas that will be affected. After using Blur, you may need to use the Add Noise filter to fix the blurred areas so that they don't seem flat.

There are several Blur filters, which can be used for different ends. Gaussian Blur and Smart Blur are somewhat different versions of the same thing; each applies an omnidirectional blur based on dialog box settings. Motion Blur and Radial Blur are directional blurring tools. These latter tools are more specialized and best suited for special effects, so they are not covered in this chapter.

→ For more information on Motion Blur and Radial Blur, **see** "Using Filters and Plug-Ins," **p. 755**.

Nondirectional Blur filters (Gaussian and Smart) blur evenly in all directions by comparing adjacent pixels based on the selected Radius and averaging differences. The essential difference between the Gaussian Blur and Smart Blur is that Smart Blur has a Threshold control and options for Quality (Low, Medium, High) and Mode (Normal, Edge Only, Overlay Edge) (see Figure 29.12).

Figure 29.12
The Smart Blur has several additional controls that produce additional effects, and offer means of limiting the application of Blurs.

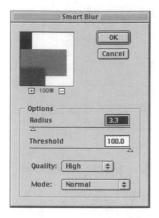

Either of these Blur filters could be used to accomplish an effect very similar to the effect created using the Median filter mentioned earlier in this chapter. You would simply substitute the application of the Median filter with application of Blur and proceed with the same steps.

APPLYING GAUSSIAN BLUR

The Gaussian Blur is applied simply by selecting Filter, Blur, Gaussian Blur, choosing a Radius in the Gaussian dialog box, and clicking the OK button. The radius can be any number between .1 and 250, using one decimal place. The Radius tells Photoshop how far to look when considering surrounding pixels for blurring, and the value for the target pixel (the pixel being looked at) is changed based on that average.

If you are blurring an image area that has been isolated on its own Layer, turn on Preserve Transparency for the Layer to confine any blurring to the existing area of the image information already on the layer. This is useful if you DO NOT want the element to feather into the surroundings. If you do want the element to feather based on the blur, leave Preserve Transparency unchecked (which is the default).

→ For more information on using Gaussian Blur, **see** "Feathering Selections," **p. 116**, "Threshold and Blur Techniques," **p. 118**, "Using Blurring and Curves to Define Selection Falloff," **p. 123** and "Shortening Your Depth of Field," **p. 615**.

WORKING WITH SMART BLUR

The Smart Blur is somewhat more complicated, and perhaps a bit less intuitive, than its Gaussian cousin. First, the Radius can be applied from .1 to 100 levels, using one decimal place, which is a notably shorter range than the Gaussian Blur. Threshold can be applied from .1 to 100 levels, using one decimal place as well. The application of Radius and Threshold work together within their own limitations to create a window of tolerance that defines where the blur will be effective. As the Tolerance can be set to only 100 maximum, high-contrast areas (black against white) are virtually excluded from blurs, whereas areas to either side of a high contrast line may blur freely (depending upon the settings). Lower Thresholds actually choke off the effects as Radius settings increase because more image information is considered. The more information that is considered, the more likely it will be to exceed the Threshold allowance.

Note

Smart Blur swiftly turns from a useful tool to one more suitable to special effects. More often, I would rather have considered control over the image using selection rather than Smart Blur when attempting to limit application of a blur.

The Normal mode simply blurs the image according to the settings for Radius and Threshold, whereas the Edge Only and Overlay Edge modes incorporate the areas defined as edges by the current settings. Edge Only shows only that edge, and Overlay Edge shows a combination of the Edge Only result set to Lighten over the Normal blur result (see Figure 29.13).

Figure 29.13
The Edge Only application defines edges across which blurring will not occur. This can be used as a sort of preview to gauge and understand the Normal effect—besides offering uses of its own.

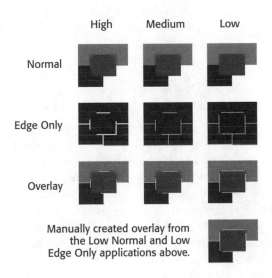

In either case and by using either Blur filter, the purpose is generally to reduce noise. You can use Smart Blur to your advantage where it is desirable to maintain existing image edges and boundaries that are defined by contrast, whereas Gaussian Blur will blur everything and might be better used in combinations (for example, with a selection or on isolated image elements). Depending on the application, you might need to reintroduce noise to blurred areas using Add Noise (Filter, Noise, Add Noise).

Spot Application of Filters

Application of filters (those above as well as others) can be controlled by a variety of means, including selection, Layer Modes, layer masks, layer clipping paths, clipping groups, Blend If, History Brush, and specific tools (Blur, Sharpen, and Pattern Stamp). These options offer variations for application and may produce similar or duplicate results. For example, if you want to apply a specific amount of blur to a spot on an image, you can apply the blur, Select All (Cmd-A) [Ctrl+A], Define Pattern (Edit, Define Pattern), to revert to the earlier state using Histories and then use the Pattern Stamp (Aligned) for spot application. Or you could apply the blur, take a Snapshot (using the pop-up menu on the Histories palette), revert to the earlier state, and use the History Brush to apply the spot application of the blur. Or you could use Quick Mask to paint in the area where you want to apply the blur, change the Quick Mask back to a Selection, and apply the blur to the selected area only. Or you can use that same Selection to copy and paste that Selection to a new Layer and apply the blur there…the list goes on.

The point is that you do not need to get trapped by a tool and how it is applied; using other combinations of Photoshop tools, you can command the application of filters to do what you want, rather than just what it appears to do in a flat application. Keep your options in mind, and use those options to attain the image goal.

TROUBLESHOOTING

APPLYING BIGGER FILTER EFFECTS

When I'm applying noise, the effect of individual pixels is too small. I need a larger application of noise, so that it affects several pixels at a time. Is there any way to do that?

Scaling filter effects can be done by applying them to other versions of the same image. For example, if you want a filter application to appear with noise that is four times as large as on the original, you can duplicate the image, Flatten if necessary, shrink it to one-fourth the size (Image, Size), apply the filter, and then increase the image size back to the original proportions (depending on the effect you are trying to achieve, you might use any of the Resampling methods). When that is done, copy and paste the scaled version back to the original (either using Copy and Paste or Duplicate Layer). When the result is back in the original, you can adjust the application using Modes, Opacity, Blend If, and/or spot application techniques. Figure 29.14 shows our smiling friend with application of noise at four times the original size. Note that this creates a pixelated effect in the replacement areas while leaving the rest of the image untouched. Certainly, this is a special effect for this image, but the application can work in reverse as well: If the filter effect appears too big, or dynamic, scale the image up, apply the same settings, shrink it back down, and copy that to the original. This will make the resulting effect subtler. See Figure 29.15.

Figure 29.14
This application of larger noise was accomplished by scaling down a duplicate of the image and applying identical noise settings. After the image was scaled back to size, Nearest Neighbor was used to retain the detail of the generated noise.

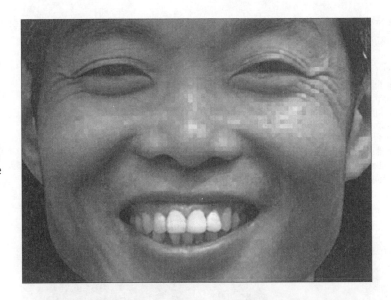

Figure 29.15
At 600× magnification, the difference is shown here between the original, the original with Median only applied, the solution with Median and unscaled Add Noise, and the solution with Median with scaled Add Noise. Applying an effect lightly might be important if, for example, you later want to sharpen the image using Unsharp Mask.

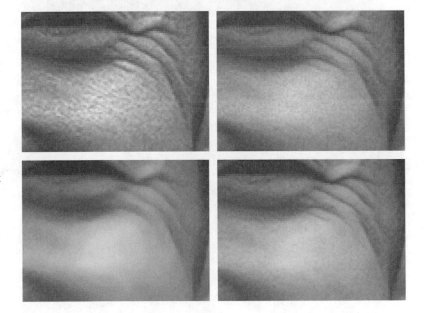

PHOTOSHOP AT WORK: FILTERING AWAY AGE

Using the filters and techniques described in this chapter, it is possible to quickly wash away some aging in subjects without losing detail. If you do this properly, you can simultaneously improve the end result of the image. Keep in mind that your settings and the series of steps you take may vary from image to image. In this problem, we will use the other half of the image used for much of the filter discussion in this chapter (see Figure 29.16). This image is available in the companion PDF workbook on page 29 (download the workbook at http://www.ps6.com/).

Figure 29.16
The goal for this half of the image is the same as the first half: to remove some of the aging and restore some of the skin. The end point will require using every tool discussed so far in this chapter.

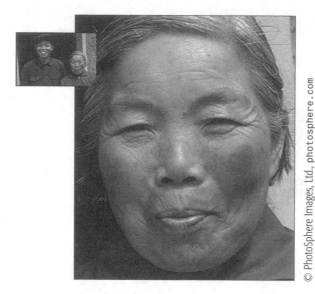

© PhotoSphere Images, Ltd., photosphere.com

Use the following steps to achieve the corrections:

1. Open the sample image on page 29 of the workbook.

2. Duplicate the red channel to create an alpha channel that will be used for the selection of the skin. To duplicate the channel, drag it to the Duplicate button on the Channels palette.

3. Load the alpha channel (Select, Load Selection). Alternatively, you can use the shortcut for loading channels: (Cmd-click) [Ctrl+click].

4. Copy and paste the selected area to its own layer.

5. Apply the Median filter (Filter, Noise, Median) to smooth out the area.

6. Duplicate the layer to a new document (Layer, Duplicate Layer; choose New for the Destination).

7. Use Image Size (Image, Image Size) to increase the size of the image 4×. Use Bicubic interpolation and check the Resample Image box. Note the current resolution, and then change the resolution to 4× the current dpi (for example, if it is 72dpi, change that to 288).

8. Apply Add Noise filter (Filter, Noise, Add Noise) to restore some texture to the Median effect.

9. Resize the image to the original resolution using the method in Step 7, but lower the dpi.

10. Copy the layer to the original image (using Copy and Paste or Duplicate the layer choosing the original file as the destination).

11. Apply Blend If, Layer Opacity, and Layer Modes as desired. Hint: You will probably want strong opacity because the layer is already feathered by the means of selection.

12. When all is as you want it, Flatten the image.

13. Use Unsharp Mask (Filter, Sharpen, Unsharp Mask) with a broad Radius to improve local contrast in the image.

14. Use Unsharp Mask with a slight Radius to improve sharpness in the image.

When all is said and done, the result should appear somewhat like Figure 29.17. A number of benefits should be realized including smoothing of general skin texture, smoothing of minor wrinkles, reduction of harsh highlights, general improvement of local contrast, and all this while retaining and improving the appearance of the subject. Similar techniques can be used on any image in which you would like to reduce various types of noise while retaining image detail.

Figure 29.17
Still more can be done to this subject to remove wrinkles and change the appearance, but those changes will clearly be spot corrections rather than something to take care of with filters.

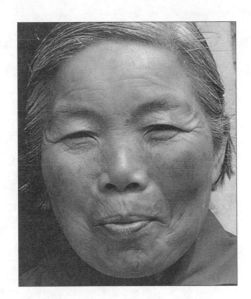

→ For more information on correcting images and details, **see** "Correcting Image Damage," **p. 600**.

PART **VIII**

ENHANCING IMAGES

CHAPTER 30

WORKING WITH SHADOW AND LIGHT

In this chapter

USING HIGHLIGHTS AND SHADOWS

With Photoshop, you can change the apparent dimensionality of images and the depth of objects in an image. Generally, this requires working with shadows and highlights to produce effects to enhance depth. Depth might appear as shadows and/or highlights on the object, as shadow behind objects, or manifest in reflection or texture. In any case, the use of shadow, highlights, and reflection not only helps define the object, but also helps define the object's interaction in a given image space, helping it either fit into the landscape of the image or providing separation from it.

The goal of working with highlights and shadows is to begin to take control of the complexities of shaping an image. The possibilities are essentially endless because of the infinite ways that light and shadow can affect and reflect on a scene. The basics of creating light, shadow, and reflection covered here only scratch the surface of what is possible with Photoshop in working with these elements. However, these basic concepts are essential for creating realistic effects such as reflections on a pond or shadows to fit a landscape.

Applying the same highlight and shadowing in an image in different ways creates very different effects. For example, a simple application of highlight and shadows is used with the Bevel effect in creating the appearance that a button is shaped or contoured. By default, the *up* effect is created by highlighting the upper left of the button while creating a shadow in the lower right, while the *down* effect is created by highlighting the lower right and applying a shadow to the upper left. In fact, by creating the up effect and rotating the image 180°, the appearance will change to the down effect (see Figure 30.1). The effect is a result of human perception: Lighting is most natural and familiar to our perception when it comes from the top. This affects our perception of image objects. Managing these image elements properly will help you control how you want them to appear.

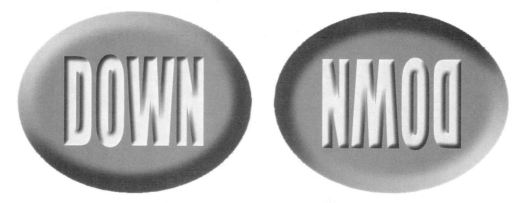

Figure 30.1
At left, a bevel is applied to the button to make it appear raised and the letters to appear inset. Then, the effects are rotated 180° (right). The end result is the left button appears to be raised while the right appears to be indented.

In the same way, the application of highlights, shadows, reflections, and textures can shape objects and give hints to the viewer as to the shape, texture, and material makeup of the object as well as telling about the quality and direction of the lighting. Knowing how to control these applications is imperative to creating realistic effects.

ADDING HIGHLIGHTS AND SHADOW FOR SHAPING

PART
VIII
CH
30

Adding highlights can be done in a number of ways, from manual application to masking, use of layer blending, applying the Lighting Effects filter, and so on. The effects can vary, too, from applying a sharp glint (often known as a specular highlight) to applying more gentle lightening of tone. *Highlights* are areas of the surface of objects in an image that reflect the light that falls on the object. All that really happens is that the object brightens and loses tone in the highlight area. This sounds bad, but the effect is that of light striking the surface of the object. The intensity of the highlighting corresponds to the shape and reflectivity of the object as well as the type and intensity of the lighting striking it.

The following steps show how to apply manual highlighting to a button. This can be accomplished with other simple means (such as using Bevel and Emboss in a Layer Style), but knowing manual techniques can help you control application.

1. Open a new image or an image you would like to use to make a button.
2. Create the button shape as a selection, path, or channel. This can be done with a number of tools including the Marquee tool, the Pen tool, and the shape tools (Custom, Rectangle, and so on). Keep in mind that you will want to make a selection from this for the next step.

→ For more information on working with selections, **see** "How Selections Work," **p. 94**.

→ For more information on working with Paths, **see** "Paths: Bézier Tools for Creating Vector Effects," **p. 175**.

→ For more information on working with masking Channels, **see** "Channels As Selections and Masks," **p. 81**.

3. Load the selection if it is not loaded already.
4. If you have used an image, isolate the button area from the rest of the image by copying and pasting the selected area; if you have opened a new image, create a new layer and fill the area with a color (something in a medium tone would be best for this). The results should appear something like what you see in Figure 30.2.

→ For more information on how to isolate the image area, **see** "Isolating an Image Area," **p. 137**.

5. Use the selection to create an alpha channel if you haven't already. You might want to duplicate this channel before proceeding if this is what you used to create the selection in Step 4.
6. Deselect (Cmd-D) [Ctrl+D].
7. Apply the Emboss filter to the channel created in Step 5. See Figure 30.3 for the results.

Figure 30.2
After Step 4, the area you want to use as a button will be isolated in its own layer. This allows you to apply effects without affecting other areas of the image.

Figure 30.3
Emboss was applied to the channel saved in Step 5 at 135°, a height of 30 pixels, and an amount of 500%. This result will be used to work with and emphasize highlight and shadow.

Note

To increase the depth of the highlight and shadow in the result, increase the height and/or the amount of the Emboss settings. To decrease the depth of the result, decrease the height and/or the amount. To change the angle of the light, change the angle on the Emboss dialog box; the light will come from the same angle represented by the angle on the dialog box.

8. Apply a Gaussian Blur to the mask. A blur Radius of 16 was used for this image, but that will vary depending on the dpi of your image. As the dpi goes up, so should the pixel radius for the applied effect. To soften the bevel effect on the object, increase the amount of the blur.

 If you find your application of blurs or the Embossing filter ends up looking clipped off, see "Giving Space to Blur" in the Troubleshooting section at the end of this chapter.

9. Duplicate the embossed and blurred channel.

10. Apply the Level settings pictured in Figure 30.4 to the original embossed channel (Step 8).

11. Apply the Level settings pictured in Figure 30.5 to the duplicated embossed channel (Step 9).

12. Load the mask created in Step 10.

13. Create a layer, and set it to Group with Previous.

Figure 30.4
Push the right slider on the input levels to 128, and then invert the positions of the output sliders so the white is on the black end and the black is on the white. The settings should be as shown here and will create an effective mask for the highlights in the upper left of the image.

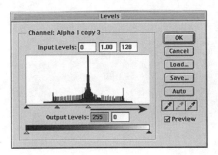

Figure 30.5
Push the left slider on the input levels to 128. This is the only adjustment required. The results should create an effective shadow mask in the lower right of the image.

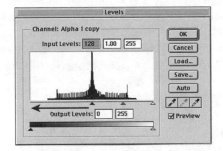

Note

Using Group with Previous will make the shape you isolated in Step 4 act as a clipping group, splicing out any channel information that does not fall over its solid parts.

14. Make the selection a layer mask by choosing Layer, Add Layer Mask, Reveal Selection.

15. Click the layer thumbnail to activate the layer and fill the layer with white to apply the highlight (Edit, Fill with White selected as the Content).

16. Load the mask created in Step 11.

17. Create a layer, and set it to Group with Previous.

18. Make the selection a layer mask by choosing Layer, Add Layer Mask, Reveal Selection.

19. Fill the layer with black to apply shadow.

At this point, you should have a simple button, with the highlight on the upper left of the image. This enhances the shape of the button by providing highlight and shadow to the image area as if there were a light to the upper left of the image. Figure 30.6 shows the results.

Figure 30.6
The highlighting and shadowing create a contour for the button making it appear raised from the back-ground.

Additional highlights and shadows can be added to the image to further enhance the shape and perception of the object. For example, it would be possible to add shadowing at the edge of the button to increase separation from the background and the appearance of depth. The highlight and shadow masks seen in Figure 30.7 were used in clipping groups to create additional effects on the button. The highlight was used as a mask to control a Hue/Saturation adjustment layer in which the Lighten slider was increased to 100%. The shadow was used as a layer mask and the layer was filled with black, but the layer's blending mode was switched to Color Burn. This deepened the blue at the upper edge rather than just putting in a flat black shadow. The final set of layers looks like Figure 30.8.

Figure 30.7
A shaped highlight can also help create and/or alter the reflec-tivity of the surface.

More adjustments are obviously possible, but the result here is that the button looks some-what glossy, has height, and retains good separation from the background—even if it is the same color. These same simple techniques of applying highlights and shadow can be used in more complex ways to shape images and image elements—both elements made from scratch and those in existing images.

Figure 30.8
Most of the layers here are used as a clipping group to help shape the button.

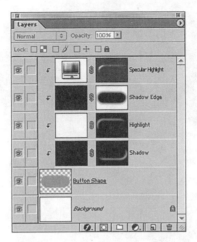

CREATING A DROP SHADOW

One of the easiest effects to create with a selected portion of an image is a *drop shadow*. This is a simple type of shadow often used on Web pages to make an object appear to float above the background or give dimension to buttons or graphic bullets. Photoshop's layer styles can easily do a simple drop shadow for you. However, knowing how to create a drop shadow without using layer styles can help you understand the process and can give you command over shadowing that is not possible using layer styles alone. For example, the layer styles functions cannot bend a shadow to fit the image's landscape or distort effects. Understanding how to make a basic drop shadow rather than how to use only the layer styles functions enables you to create more advanced effects.

MANUALLY CREATE A SIMPLE DROP SHADOW

To create a simple drop shadow, start the same way you would as if using layer styles. All you need to do is make a selection of the image and then use the selection to define the shadow. This is similar to the process used to create the shadow for the button in the earlier example. The shadow is somewhat different here as it is created behind the object as its own layer and can be moved, scaled, or distorted as desired to change the apparent projection.

Use these steps to create a drop shadow.

1. Open the image you want to create the drop shadow in. If there is a separate foreground image element (the object that will be casting the shadow), open that up as well. See Figure 30.9 for the image elements that will be used for this example.

Figure 30.9
The sketchy brick wall pattern was generated using the Mosaic filter and then it was blotched out with a cloud mask to soften the effect, and then the result was embossed slightly and colored. The fire hydrant was pulled out of the stock image using a mask created with the Airbrush. The intent of the wall was to be a fire engine red background for some fire hydrant bullet points.

Tip

Be sure the two images you use fit together before going any further. That is, be sure they are the same dpi, the same color mode and that the foreground element will end up the right size for your purposes in the final image and when placed over the background. The foreground element should probably be smaller than the background; otherwise, the foreground element will not completely fit into the frame of the background document.

2. Make a selection of the image area you want to use to define the drop shadow.

3. Save the selection. For the example, the selection was made around the fire hydrant, and then saved to the brick background image using the Destination selector in the Save Selection dialog box.

4. Use the selection to isolate the image area you have selected over the background. For the example, the hydrant was copied and pasted to the background. If the object being isolated was already in the same image, it would be copied and pasted to place it into its own layer.

5. Create a new layer for the drop shadow between the background and the isolated portion of the image. Call this the Shadow Layer.

6. Duplicate the alpha channel created by saving the selection from Step 2.

7. Working with the duplicate channel, apply a Gaussian blur to soften the edges. The amount of the blur depends on the effect you want. Although this is simplified, if you want the drop shadow to appear as if the item is close to the background surface, use less blur. More blur will create a larger, softer shadow.

8. Load the duplicate channel that you just blurred as a selection (Select, Load Selection, or (Cmd-Click) [Ctrl+Click] the desired channel). Don't worry at this point about the alignment of the selection and the object. You will have the chance to move it later.

9. Be sure the shadow layer is active and fill the selection with black. The shadow might appear darker and more intense than you expect. Leave it for now—we'll fix that in a moment.

10. Deselect (Cmd-D) [Ctrl+D] the selection and then, using the Move tool, move the shadow layer and foreground element into position to produce the effect you want.

11. Be sure the shadow layer is active and select the blending mode and opacity for the shadow in the Layers palette. See Figure 30.10 for a comparison of the result with and without a shadow.

> **Note**
>
> Mode will often work best set at Multiply. Opacity can vary depending on how intense you want the shadow to be. It should probably be set to 10%–50% Opacity—and usually toward the upper end of that scale. This setting might vary widely, however, depending on the intensity of the blur used to create the mask that was filled, the need for separation in the image (if you need to eliminate more noise from the image, the shadow will probably need to be more intense), and personal taste.

Figure 30.10
As the lighting for the fire hydrant and wall seems to be coming from above, the shadow is placed below and a bit to the left. This appears more natural than if the shadow were placed in other positions (right, left, or above) as the shadow complements the lighting already apparent in the image elements.

12. When the shadow is set to your satisfaction, save the image.

The placement of the shadow suggests the placement of the lighting: The light makes the shadow fall on the opposite side of the object. For example, a shadow that appears to be below the foreground image suggests lighting from the top. It is also important when putting together image elements to consider the lighting on the elements themselves. The light should appear to be striking from approximately the same angle.

You can use this type of simple drop shadow for a number of purposes, but one of the most common is to create floating buttons or bullet points for a Web page. Figure 30.11 shows what the sample image might be used for.

Figure 30.11
These hydrants serve both as bullet points and buttons on this firefighter's Web page.

Tip

I have heard people grumble about the incessant use of shadows that drop to the right and down, and although going to the right every time is unimaginative, casting a shadow downward is usually the natural choice when portraying an upright object. The fact is that most lighting will strike any object from the top unless the setting is somewhat unusual. Light from the top most often when creating natural effects in a scene.

The shadow can be burned right into the background or filled and painted behind the foreground object on the same layer, rather than created in its own layer. However, either of these methods can be more trouble than just creating an additional layer for the shadow. Having the shadow alone allows for more flexibility in placement and handling.

Although the steps suggest that more softness in the shadow creates greater distance between the foreground and background, the softness of the shadows can also be affected by the quality and direction of light. Lighting on objects can be focused or diffused. Diffused lighting is the type of lighting you will usually have—to a greater or lesser extent. However, you can create an effect such as focused spotlights. A focused spotlight casts a sharper shadow, regardless of how far the foreground is from the background. The angle of the lighting will also prove more apparent in perspective shifts of the shadow. These possibilities are further explored in Figure 30.12. In the case of the fire hydrant, using focused spotlights makes the lighting seem more consistent with the image, as it evens up the lighting on both sides of the hydrant. With sharp shadows, it is easier to show light angles and shadow overlaps.

Very dark shadows often appear obtrusive and unnatural, especially when more than one light source is apparent. Dark shadows suggest a lack of ambient light. Although it is advised that you most often use Multiply as the blending mode for the shadow layer, Normal, Overlay, Hard Light, Soft Light, and Luminosity modes can often be used with success. If the effect you want is not happening with the Multiply mode, try effecting a change by altering the mode and opacity combinations. Whereas mode will have different effects based on content, opacity will always darken with higher percentages.

Figure 30.12
The drop shadows in this figure were slightly altered in perspective and purposely misaligned to produce a stage-lighting effect— where the angles of lights will not be exactly the same.

> **Tip**
>
> If you are shadowing several items in an image, keep shadows falling in the same direction in the same image unless you have a good reason to change their directions. The global angle in the Layer Style dialog box can help you keep all your lighting and shadows consistent within an image. In some cases, that is a good argument for using layer styles to control drop shadows rather than manual placement.

USE LAYER STYLES TO CREATE A DROP SHADOW

The Drop Shadow option in the Layer Style dialog box can easily render a simple drop shadow similar to the one created here from scratch. There is no reason why you should not take advantage of that feature when creating simple drop shadows. In fact, after creating the drop shadow with layer styles, the drop shadow can be rendered in its own layer and manipulated to create more complex effects. To create a drop shadow with layer styles, simply isolate an image element on its own layer, and then double-click the layer in the Layers palette. The Layer Style dialog box for that layer will open. Click the box for Drop Shadow, and manipulate the controls to get the result you want. When you have created the shadow, simply close the Layer Style dialog box by clicking OK. You can then render the Shadow effect and create it on its own layer by choosing Layer Style, Create Layer from the Layer menu.

Although layer styles provide a quick result, knowing the manual procedure will help you customize application of shadows as needed.

CREATE A SHADOW FOR LANDSCAPES

One step beyond creating a simple drop shadow is creating a shadow for an object in a landscape. Often this is necessary when adding an object to an existing image, although you can use the techniques simply to create effects.

CREATING AND POSITIONING THE LANDSCAPE SHADOW

Much like the series of steps used to create a simple shadow, the landscape shadow is created on a separate layer and then fit to the image, considering lighting on the object and the other objects in the scene. The idea is to create the shadow and then distort it with Skew and Scale to fit the shadow to the elements in the landscape. This can get fairly complicated. The example here will show a simple application in fitting a shadow to a landscape.

Use the following steps to create a shadow that fits to a landscape.

1. Open the foreground image and background you want to use to create the landscape shadow. Be sure to choose images with compatible lighting conditions. See Figure 30.13 for the image used in this example.

Figure 30.13
In the example, only the foreground image will be used on a plain white background to better demonstrate the shadow effects. The statue was shot with a digital camera on an overcast day and then selected out of a dense, leafy background. Harsh sun might have further limited the shadow direction and possibilities.

Shooting Stock Images for Your Use

For the most utility, it is often best to shoot stock images in overcast or diffused light. Although it isn't always possible, this can give you more leeway as to how the image can be used. Directional lighting and direct sunlight can show harshly on the subject and essentially predetermine how the object can be placed in the context of other elements.

---

2. Combine the images and create a simple drop shadow either manually, as described in the step-by-step in the previous section, or by using the Layer Styles. In either case, leave the shadow fairly sharp (apply only a little Gaussian Blur or Spread and Size). In the case of creating the shadow with layer styles, render the layer (Layer, Layer Style, Create Layer) so the shadow is on its own layer before continuing.

3. Taking into account the lighting on the foreground element and the apparent shadows or lighting conditions and landscape of the background, Skew (Edit, Transform, Skew), Scale (Edit, Transform, Scale), and/or Distort (Edit, Transform, Distort) the shadow to a desired angle. Base the skew of the shadow on shadows already apparent in the scene.

In other words, make the shadows parallel to other shadows if they are apparent. If there are no shadows (as in the sample image), use the shadow to define the lay of the landscape. See Figure 30.14.

Figure 30.14
The center handle on the Transform bounding box was used to distort the shadow. This shadow represents a simple flat landscape, but more complex variations are possible.

4. When the shadow appears skewed and scaled appropriately, accept the changes by double-clicking within the boundaries of the transformation box (essentially the same thing as the current selection area), or by pressing the Enter key.

5. Realign the shadow with the object so the shadow appears natural. In the case of the example, the shadow is placed to align with the left edge of the bottom of the pedestal.

6. Touch up any areas of the shadow that stick out from the object. In the example, some of the base is jutting out on the side where the light source is (see Figure 30.15).

Figure 30.15
Thee shadow areas indicated by the arrows obviously have to be removed. Use the Eraser or Airbrush to remove these areas. Do not worry about portions of the shadow mask that fall under the foreground object; the object will mask those parts of the shadow after it is cast. Consider, also, adjusting for elements in the shadow path, such as objects that the shadow might fall on and changes in the terrain.

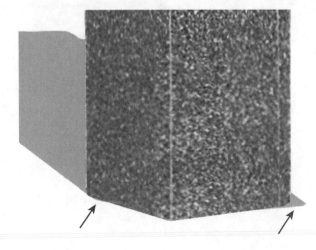

Creating Realistic Shadows

One other concern, at this point, is to try to make the shadow as close to a realistic depiction as possible. The shadow would actually appear like a picture taken of the object from the area of the shadow pointing the camera toward the light source. In the case of the example in Figure 30.15, the light would be coming from above and right. As the perspective of the image was taken from a much different angle, the shadow is not entirely accurate. To create an accurate shadow, two images would have to be shot: one from the current perspective for the image, and one from the shadow as described previously to accurately depict the shadow. In many cases, you will be able to get away with shooting one image as the viewer won't study the shadow for accuracy. However, if you know you will be doing a drop shadow such as this, shoot the extra image if you can so you can create the most realistic shadows.

7. Adjust the intensity of the shadow using the layer opacity. Again, generally the 10%–50% range will work, but this is not an absolute.

At this point, the shadow is essentially done. There are a number of other adjustments you might consider, such as adding additional effects to the shadow to create more realistic effects. For example, the shadow might lighten a bit as it gets longer, depending on the amount of ambient light and other light sources (or reflectors) that are nearby. These other sources might cause secondary shadows as well. Figure 30.16 shows a variation of the shadow created with several simple adjustments.

Figure 30.16
The shadow in this case was blurred using a gradient mask so that the intensity of the blur increased as the shadow moved away from the statue. In addition, the base of the statue was darkened using a copy of the same shadow in a clipping group above the original shadow. The shadow copy was blurred heavily and adjusted using curves.

This is basically the same technique used when making the drop shadow from scratch in the previous section. The only real differences are the more stringent shaping with consideration of perspective and the concentration of additional effects. This type of shadow cannot be cast with Photoshop's Layer Style controls.

CUSTOMIZING THE SHADOW TO THE LANDSCAPE

Shadows can be made to fit into any terrain or image using care in shaping them. This might require custom fitting on occasion, or other manual alterations. Alterations can be accomplished with transformation effects and painting, with your favorite freehand tools.

For example, if a cinderblock wall were to be present near the statue in the sample image, the shadow might cast on the wall. Shadows need to be cast according to the plane they strike. If you just transform the shadow as shown earlier with no alteration for the wall, it just wouldn't look right. In this case, using Photoshop, the shadow can be cast in two parts. The angle and placement of the shadow on the ground can remain the same, but the top—where it contacts the wall—needs to be removed and replaced. The part of the shadow on the wall would be like casting a drop shadow, placed and oriented so it blended with the ground shadow at the base of the wall. Figures 30.17 through 30.20 show the series of steps you could use to create a shadow for the new landscape.

PART
VIII

CH
30

Figure 30.17
In this example, the original statue is placed in a new environment. The different background has different needs when it comes to casting a shadow. The original shadow as created simply doesn't fit the landscape.

The same technique described in the original example can be used to make the portion of the shadow that falls up to the point of the base of the wall, but at that point, the plane that the shadow falls on changes (see Figures 30.18 and 30.19).

Figure 30.18
A second shadow is created, in the same way the original was, to align with that plane. The two shadows are aligned at the base of the wall.

Figure 30.19
A selection is made using the base of the wall as a guide. This will be used to crop the two shadows so that the information for each shadow is restricted to the plane it falls on.

Figure 30.20
When the shadows are cropped to their respective planes, the shadow fits the landscape.

This is just one of the many variations that might be necessary to produce the desired effects so that the shadow conforms to a landscape. All shadow changes work with the same principle and are based on good observation of the elements in the image area. Sometimes it will be best to create the landscape shadow from multiple copies of the original shadow, and sometimes you might want to manually draw the shadow rather than attempt to contour the existing shadow to the landscape. However, the basic techniques shown here should cover most situations that you will have to deal with. Shadows, as mentioned before, do not have to be absolutely accurate to produce their effect. Sometimes simply increasing the amount of blur will solve problems with fitting to a bumpy landscape or diverting attention from the absolute accuracy of the drop shadow.

PART
VIII

CH
30

CREATING REALISTIC REFLECTIONS

Reflections can manifest in a variety of ways and circumstances. One of the basic concepts to master in considering reflection is that the reflection is dependent on the view of the observer.

Creating a simple reflection is actually easier than working with complex shadows. However, creating reflections can become quite a bit more involved when planning to reflect over uneven surfaces, such as waves, or when doing partial and complex surface reflections (such as on warped surfaces). Some of these very complex renderings are probably best left to 3D programs if they involve several levels of reflectivity and unusual angles. However, Photoshop can handle the more straightforward reflections quite easily. All that is required for the basic reflection is vertical duplication and a flip of perspective. Adjusting the intensity of the reflection can be done a few different ways, but again, keeping the reflection in its own layer gives you the most control of the final result.

Use the following steps to create a reflection:

1. Open the image or images you want to use in making the reflection. See Figure 30.21 for the image used in this example.

Figure 30.21
The statue was inserted into a city skyline and given a rather dramatic background of clouds. The goal will be to make the whole city, sky, and statue appear as if they exist at the edge of a lake. Working with a distant, flat shoreline will make this reflection easy.

2. Select all and copy the image. If the image is made up of separate layers, use Copy Merged (Shift–Cmd–C) [Shift+Ctrl+C].

3. Double the vertical size of the image by using the Canvas Size command (see Figure 30.22).

Figure 30.22
To expand the canvas downward below the existing image area, anchor the image using the top-center square of the Anchor grid to make sure the new canvas area will be added below the image. With the Anchor set, double the height of the canvas and enter that into the Height field.

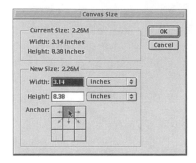

4. Paste the copied image, which will appear in its own layer.

5. Flip the pasted image vertically (Edit, Transform, Flip Vertical). As long as you have done nothing after pasting the image area, the layer you pasted will still be active.

6. Move the flipped layer so it aligns exactly with the original, bottom to bottom (see Figure 30.23).

Figure 30.23
Both images should align bottom to bottom perfectly as one is a duplicate of the other. A curved shoreline would make this effect quite a bit more difficult to produce—although not impossible. The reflection would have to be distorted to fit, most likely using the Shear filter.

7. (Option) Alter the reflection to achieve effects consistent with the surface you want to reflect onto. You can accomplish any number of effects using filters, applying textures, changing the opacity of the reflection layer, or overlaying the reflection with textures or images with opacities at less than 100%. See Figure 30.24 for the options chosen for the example.

Figure 30.24
In this image, the aim was to make the reflection look as if it were over a large and calm lake. The reflection was blurred slightly, using Gaussian Blur, and then a motion blur was applied at 90° (Filter, Blur, Motion Blur). Finally, an area of water was selected from another image and pasted over the reflection. This served the purpose of dulling the reflection somewhat, by cutting a little blue from the water into the reflection colors and adding the slight wavy quality. This could be enhanced more, perhaps using other Wave or Ripple applications, and/or application of a Displacement map.

Note

A gentle blur and careful smudging along the seam between the images (using the Blur and Smudge tools) helped complete the illusion of continuity between the original and the reflection.

8. Crop the image if necessary. At the very least, you will want to remove any excess canvas.

9. Save the result.

It might be a good idea to crop the reflection slightly to de-emphasize the effect of the duplication. Figure 30.25 shows the final result of the application of changes noted in Step 6 with the addition of a crop.

Figure 30.25
The completed scene is a reasonably convincing reflection, even if the scene itself is somewhat surreal. See the color results of this project on ColorPlate 14 in the color section of this book.

Keep in mind when creating reflections that reflective surfaces provide reflection with respect to the viewer's perspective. A relatively flat reflective foreground essentially renders the background exactly as it is—depending on the reflectance of the surface and surface qualities. A mirrored surface, for example, reproduces the reflection pretty much exactly as the original, whereas a dull, streaked polish on a tabletop produces a dulled and blurred effect. Used in conjunction with shadow and appropriate attention to lighting, reflection can help render more realistic results in images that seem to look a little flat, or reflection can just create interesting effects.

Reflections can be cast to numerous image areas, such as the finish of a car, a bay window, a mirror, and so on. Be sure when adding image elements that you account for the reflection of the element in the rest of the image as appropriate. Much like failing to cast a shadow might make an image element seem unrealistic, failing to provide the appropriate reflections can do the same.

Casting reflections across the horizontal plane is very similar to casting them vertically (as was done in the example). For example, if the statue were placed near a parked car or a department store window, you would copy the statue, paste it into the image, flip it horizontally, and distort it as appropriate to fit the contour of the object it was reflecting to—relative to the reflections of other elements in the scene.

Reflections that occur behind image elements are more difficult, as they will have to represent the opposite side of the element. For example, this would be a concern if you moved a person into a scene with a mirror hanging on the wall behind him. The reflection and object would have to convey the back and front of the person instead of just an inverted reflection as in the example. Without a tremendous amount of fudging or using another picture of the same person from the other perspective, this would prove difficult or impossible. The best way to handle the situation accurately would be to use two images of the person: one of the face, and one of the back of the head for use in the mirror.

To create accurate reflections, you might need to reconsider the perspective of the original. For example, the reflection in the lake for our example is not exactly correct. A real reflection of this sort would depict the statue from a lower angle—in fact, it would show the statue image from the reflected angle. This could have been compensated for by shooting an additional image of the statue from the reflectance angle. To examine this effect, place a small object against a bathroom mirror, and then move your head and note the changes in the reflection. Although reflections made without consideration of perspective might be somewhat inaccurate, they can still be effective, much like with drop shadows.

You can use reflection in a number of different ways and intensities. Even simple use of reflection can add a lot to an image. For example, placing an object on a table with basic shadows creates a realistic effect, but enhancing the image with a slight fading reflection gives some texture to the surface it is on (see Figure 30.26).

Figure 30.26
The original image of this camera was taken from a noisy, over-crowded background. Shadows were added to give the appearance and direction of the lighting, and a reflection was added below it to make the surface the camera is sitting on appear reflective. The background is a gradient fill.

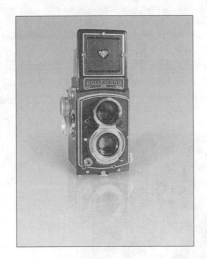

With intense patience, entire scenes can be fabricated.

ENHANCING TEXTURE

The appearance of any object is influenced by its texture. If it lacks richness of texture, it appears flat; if it has texture, it appears to have depth. Enhancing texture and depth can make an object look fuller, and the changes don't have to be extreme.

An easy method of emphasizing dimension is to select the image element and create tonal shifts (for example, using Curves and Levels) to affect image changes. However, this might change the integrity of other parts of the image or element that are fine and these methods might not take complete advantage of the available image information. Alternative techniques borrow from the ideas of applying textures and shadow to help emphasize dimension and texture. For example, it is possible to add edge or backlighting. This can be done by tracing the image element with filters. Other object texture can be emphasized using layer techniques as well, which will finesse image information rather than flat-out change it. Any of these object enhancements can give an image more depth.

ADDING DIMENSION TO IMAGES WITH TEXTURE

This is highly subjective in application to individual images, but the following techniques can be used to alter and/or enhance object texture in a variety of instances. The image selected for this example has lost some texture in translation to print and appears flat. Working with the image can give it more dimension and make it look fuller—restoring it closer to the original state. The changes can be subtle, but the goal is to enhance what is already in the image as existing texture, not to create it anew.

Caution

Techniques used in this example might not be beneficial to all images. The purpose of the steps is more for demonstration of the possibilities than to give a hard, fast solution to every image. Be selective in your choices and image changes.

The three main goals for this image (see Figure 30.27) are to define the image edges (which are currently lost in shadow) and to develop the natural texture of the image. Dimension will be added by selectively working with image edges, highlights, and shadows.

Figure 30.27
This image is of a clay model that had lots of surface texture. Much of the texture was diminished (not lost completely) in the translation to print. A series of steps can be taken to reclaim and improve the image.

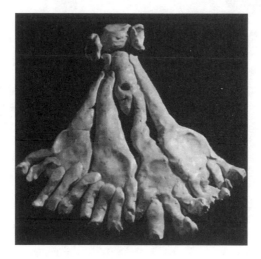

Use these steps to accomplish the goals for this image as previously described.

1. Open the image that contains the element you want to work on. It might be advantageous to select the element you want to work on and isolate it in its own layer.

2. Duplicate the original layer and apply the Glowing Edges filter (see Figure 30.28). The Edge Width, Edge Brightness, and Smoothness need to be varied, depending on the size of the image you are working on. Here settings of 2, 6, and 6 accomplished the desired effect, which was just to thinly outline the object.

Note

Isolation is not done in the case of this image as it is on a pure black background. Instead, Blend If will be used to allow information in other layers to mix in with what is already there.

Figure 30.28
Using the Glowing Edges filter defines the edges of the object where the contrast is high, effectively tracing it. This result can be used both as a mask and/or an element to improve the existing image information. The goal here is to use it as an element to emphasize the object's edges.

3. Move the layer created in Step 2 below the original layer.
4. Double-click the layer in the Layers palette. Adjust the Blend If sliders so the layer created in Step 2 shows a noticeable highlight around the edges of the image. See Figure 30.29.

Figure 30.29
The black slider for Blend If in this Layer was split and set to 6 and 100. This blends tonality between approximately 98% and 61% black with the layers below. The goal was to blend the glow into the darker areas of the existing image to give it the appearance of being backlit without having it infringe too much on the rest of the tonality. This could have been measured but it was faster to just try it out.

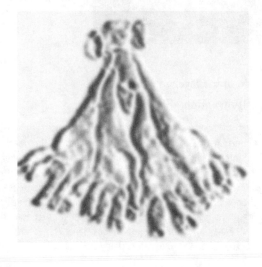

→ For more information on measuring application of and working with the Blend If tool, **see** "Colorizing a Grayscale Image," **p. 514**.

Note

A number of additional things can be done at this point to improve the effect, such as off-setting the Glowing Edges layer, and smoothing out the effects using blur and/or additional layer blending.

5. Duplicate the original layer and move it above the other layers.

6. Emboss (Filter, Stylize, Emboss) using the following settings: 180, 10, and 100. This creates a horizontal embossing effect.

7. Use Levels to isolate the shadow areas by sliding the black input slider to 128.

8. Blur the result using Gaussian Blur. A radius of 3 was used for this image. The result of this example is seen in Figure 30.30.

Figure 30.30
The point of Steps 7, 8, 9, 10, and 11 is to isolate and enhance the contour and shadows already in the image. Blurring softens these elements so they can be used to seamlessly enhance the textures that already exist in the image. See ColorPlate 4 in the color section of this book.

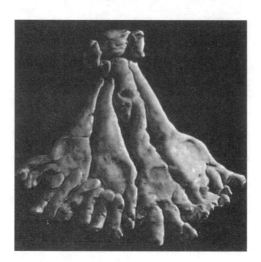

9. Switch the blending mode of the layer to Multiply.

10. Adjust the opacity to position and modify the shadows.

Note

An interesting interplay occurs between these two layers. As the opacity of the upper layer is increased, the interplay in the darkest portion of the shadows (between 98% and 100%) is thrown out of the visual portion of the layer because of the Blend If settings in the lower layer. This keeps changes from adding too much information in areas where there is already dark shadow. The result is that as the opacity increases, the shadows appear to move, and more of the layer two layers below is revealed (increasing the enhancement of the object edges). Further darkening of the shadow layer (for example, using a Curves adjustment layer to darken the tones) would, in turn, enhance this effect.

At this point, you might want to go back and make some adjustments to the layers and effects to be sure everything is blending smoothly and that the enhancement is optimized. Specifically, the Blend If settings of the original layer and the opacity of the upper layer will be important to the effect as created here.

As the highlights in this image were already apparent, and really are enhanced by the increased contrast of the added shadow information, the manipulation is stopped here. However, the highlights could be manipulated in a similar fashion by simply creating a lighten layer using almost the same series of steps as in Steps 6 to 11. The only real difference is that the emphasis would be to enhance the lighter tones. Level settings would change so that the white input slider is moved to 128 after the Emboss, and Blend If could be added to the highlights in the layer below to lessen the possibility that too much detail would be overrun.

Another method of executing similar changes would be to alter the tones using masked layers. An interesting way to proceed is to use one of the image color channels as a mask, or create a mask using calculations. In this particular image, because of the black background, this technique would be most effective with highlights.

These same techniques can be used to enhance and/or correct highlight and shadow color. For example, a color fill layer or adjustment layer could be used to enhance the color of the edge lighting or shadows from the example. Adjustments and effects can be targeted in this way, based on the tonality.

Be aware that these methods will necessarily cause some distortion of the image. Because of this distortion, the techniques are more effective with images that are not too sharp in the first place; used with sharp images, it can cause unwanted blurring and can affect the image integrity. Images scanned from printed matter might be premiere specimens for this type of alteration. Using settings that are not too extreme (a matter of trial and error, depending on the size and tonality of the image you are working on), you can use this set of techniques on portraits for example, to increase aging by a few years, by deepening wrinkles, and so on.

Working with the existing tonality of the image improves the texture and dimension. Adding some emphasis of the image edges helps separate the image from the background. Controlling shadow, highlight, and edges creates better shape and appearance of the image. Making selective changes, based on the image's own tonality, helps to keep the image integrity and shape.

TROUBLESHOOTING

GIVING SPACE TO BLUR

When I apply the Emboss effect to my image as per the instructions, I get a result that seems too clipped off or flattened on one edge. How do I stop that flattening from happening?

Gaussian Blur is far-reaching in the number of pixels it affects. Sometimes it goes on for quite a distance, essentially undetectable depending on your settings, monitor, and so on. Regretfully, although it is undetectable to the eye, it can affect calculations of other filters applied over those areas. The flattening you see at the edge of the embossing effect is probably because the blur you applied earlier ran off the document, and then the element you blurred was moved. When the Emboss filter is run, it applies to everything just like it is supposed to, and ends up emphasizing where the application of the blur met the document boundary. That emphasis in information is where the flat edge forms. See Figure 30.31.

Original Blur   Embossed Result

Figure 30.31
Thankfully, it is fairly easy to solve this type of problem. You might have to step back a few steps to do it, however.

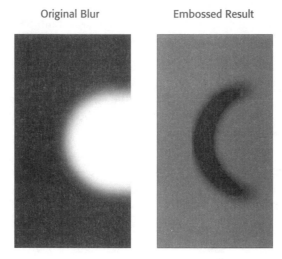

First thing to do is look in the History palette for the application of Gaussian Blur that is probably the culprit. When you find the application, click the step just before the Gaussian Blur in the History palette to return the image to that state.

Note It is possible that you will not find the application. In that case, you might have to return to the original image state and start over.

After you have reverted to the earlier state, increase the size of the document in the direction(s) where you noticed the flattening using Canvas Size (Image, Canvas Size). Increasing the size of the document might require that you fill in or doctor information on layers or channels where it simply runs out. The area of most concern is the area where the filtering was applied. In this case, you will probably want to check the channel where you applied the filters to be sure that you have a continuous tone at the edge of the image after increasing the canvas size. The canvas on channels defaults to black, so if you increase the size of the image, the added dimension on the channels will fill in the added areas with black (see Figure 30.32).

WRONG   RIGHT

Figure 30.32
If the document is expanded, the existing channels might fill in with an undesirable color (left). You will need to correct this before continuing or you will run into even more trouble later.

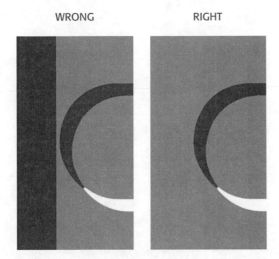

For the most part, you won't have to worry about layers or channels you will not be working with after resizing the canvas. If you intend to crop the image back down after applying the desired effects, you will crop these areas back out of the image anyway. As increasing the canvas size can potentially get very involved, a second solution would be to copy the channel you are applying the effects to into its own document, increase the size of that document, apply the effects, and then copy and paste that altered element back into the original document. Be careful with alignments when returning the element to the original image if using this second method.

PHOTOSHOP AT WORK: EXERCISING HIGHLIGHTS, SHADOWS, AND REFLECTIONS

The best thing to do with the information in this chapter is to explore application of highlight, shadow, and reflection. Depending on your level of experience, any one of the step-by-steps in this chapter could prove useful. Pick one or two of the step-by-steps from the chapter and go to work to re-create the results. Page 30 in the PDF workbook (get the workbook at www.ps6.com if you have not already) includes the original images used in each of these examples, including the fire hydrant, the statue, and the clay model. Simply open the page in Photoshop, crop to the image, and get to work. You will have to supply your own image or background for the reflection exercise, or you can substitute one of the other images.

One other thing you can try with these exercises is changing the image you use for each exercise. For example, the hydrant and statue both have surface textures that could be enhanced, or the clay model could be used to create the reflection. Changing the element for the exercises might give you some additional insight into the techniques involved in producing the results and how these techniques need to be altered to be effective in their application.

CHAPTER 31

CREATING SEAMLESS TEXTURES AND TILING BACKGROUNDS

In this chapter

TEXTURES, PATTERNS, BRUSHES, AND FRAMES AS IMAGE ELEMENTS

Some of the building blocks for creating unique effects in Photoshop revolve around the application of predefined image elements: patterns, textures, brushes, and frames. A *pattern* is simply a rectangular image element that can be used to fill in areas of an image, selection, border, and the like, by tiling end to end in rows. Patterns cover or fill the area they are applied to as an additional visible image element. A *texture* is very similar to a pattern in that they are rectangular elements and can repeat to fill an area. However, the tonality of a texture is used as a map for creating highlights and shadows, which give the appearance of surface texture in the areas where they are applied. Textures modify the area they are applied to rather than cover it. *Brushes* are used with painting tools and can also be defined like patterns or textures from rectangular image areas. Brushes can repeat their patterns, but they do so according to the settings for the application of the brush. *Frames* are elements usually used to surround the image without repetition, much like picture frames. Using Photoshop you can create and store any of these image elements as files to be reused, or you can incorporate them from existing libraries.

Using Photoshop you can prepare effective tiling image elements in both pixel-based and vector formats. Vector formats allow you the advantage of infinite scalability so that the elements created in this fashion can be defined to the exact size of your image, whatever it might be. Applications of these elements include uses in filtering (lighting effects, textures, and displacement mapping), image area fills (pattern fills, layer styles), and painting (stroking paths and selections, using the History Brush or Pattern Stamp). Knowing how to create, save, and use these elements gives you more control over image enhancements and creative development of images. The new Preset Manager feature gives you better ability to manage brushes, patterns, and texture sets, as well as other elements that work with these elements (layer styles, shapes, and contours).

CREATING SEAMLESS PATTERN AND TEXTURE ELEMENTS

Often the key to creating an effective pattern or texture is in making the element tile without seams. Tiling is simply taking the element and placing it in rows and columns end to end repeatedly—like tiles in a floor, but so that the edges touch from one tile to another. This is done as many times as necessary to fill the desired area. A seamless tiling element will tile in such a way that the viewer can't tell where one tile ends and the next begins. Making patterns and textures seamless is usually more useful, as the elements can be applied to large image areas without looking blocky. Unless a blocky look is a desired effect (such as with the Blocks option in the Glass filter), a result with apparent seams will simply look wrong or look like the Photoshop artist made a mistake in application of patterns.

For example, seamless tiling is useful in creating Web backgrounds, which are essentially patterned fills created to tile in a Web browser. If a starry sky background is created without attention to making it seamless, when it tiles, stars that appear at the edge might be clipped and appear unnatural. The purpose of the seamless tiling background is to make a continuous, natural image blend so that the small image can fill a large area.

USING FILTERS TO CREATE A NONTILING PATTERN

To better understand the potential of pattern application, it is best to look at an example. Creating a background pattern from scratch is not very difficult. For example, create a new document that is 2-inch×2-inch in RGB with 288ppi. Reset the foreground and background swatches to black and white by pressing D on the keyboard; then run the following series of filters and adjustments:

1. Clouds filter (Filter, Render, Clouds)
2. Unsharp Mask (Filter, Sharpen, Unsharp Mask: 500,250,0)
3. Difference Clouds (Filter, Render, Difference Clouds)
4. Auto Levels (Image, Adjust, Auto Levels)
5. Hue/Saturation (Image, Adjust, Hue/Saturation: Click colorize, 200,31,45)
6. Unsharp Mask (Filter, Sharpen, Unsharp Mask: 160,46,0)
7. Difference Clouds (Filter, Render, Difference Clouds)
8. Auto Levels (Image, Adjust, Auto Levels)
9. Unsharp Mask (Filter, Sharpen, Unsharp Mask: 160,46,0)

You should end up with an electric, fiery effect with black, blue, and white surroundings. The pattern is what we are concerned with, more so than the color (see Figure 31.1). Your results running the same filters differ depending on how the clouds generate. An action that creates a pattern using the preceding steps is included on the Web site for this book (www.ps6.com) to make creating this on your own easy.

Figure 31.1
This is an example of a random pattern you can create using Photoshop filters. The problem with such patterns is they will not automatically tile when applied to an image area.

PART
VIII
CH
31

This 2-inch×2-inch image (or any pattern generated in a similar way) can be used as a texture or pattern on images that are smaller, or on images with lower resolution, without creating a tiled pattern or using scaling to make it fit. However, if you want to use this pattern to fill an image area having a larger size (greater pixel dimension), the texture has to repeat to fill the image area. Figure 31.2 shows what it would look like to tile the image from Figure 31.1 into a document twice its size (in pixels).

Figure 31.2
The random pattern created for Figure 31.1 does not tile well when given the opportunity. Note the apparent seams where the edges of the pattern meet. A seamless pattern would create a seamless result.

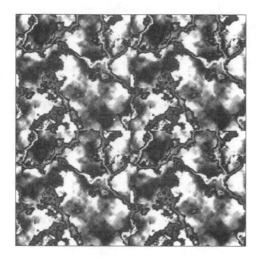

ADJUSTING A NONTILING PATTERN TO MAKE IT TILE

If more care is taken in creating the pattern or texture so that the edges blend when the pattern is tiled, the tiling will not be so readily apparent. Figure 31.3 shows the same image created as Figure 31.1, only a step was added where the edges were blended to be sure the tiling would produce a seamless result. Figure 31.4 shows what happens when the improved image is tiled into a document twice its original size. Although some patterning is inherent in repeating the same image areas, the blocky edges are not overt, and the effect is far more pleasing.

Almost anything can be made to tile seamlessly with some care. The trick is to use Photoshop's Offset filter (Filter, Other, Offset) to simplify correcting the seams. Instead of having to guess where the problems will occur on the seam, you can simply offset the pattern you have created and create a better blend at the seam. The Offset will shift the image so the seams come into view. Figure 31.5 shows Figure 31.1 after an offset of 50 pixels horizontally and vertically. This pushes what were the edges of the image into view. When you can see the seams, a combination of the Clone Stamp applications, and cut-and-paste patches, blend the seam to repair it. You might need to offset one more time to be sure the pattern edge is completely repaired.

→ For more information on techniques for using the Clone Stamp in repairs, **see** "Rubber Stamp Tool Option for Dust Corrections," **p. 585**.

Figure 31.3
This is the same pattern as in Figure 31.1 with some minor adjustments. The goal of the adjustments was not so much to change the appearance of the pattern but to create seamless tiling. Compare the two…it is difficult to notice most of the changes.

Figure 31.4
When the improved pattern is tiled, the result is that the pattern generally looks very similar but tiles seamlessly. The difference can be likened to a good and bad wallpapering job.

Figure 31.5
When offsetting, use the Wrap Pixels option for the Offset. This will take pixels that scroll off the right of the image during the offset and place them on the left of the image.

Some patterns such as the one created previously will not pattern seamlessly because information is randomly generated and fairly dramatic. Other, softer effects can blend as tiles without any work at all. This same offset and blend technique can be used to create seamless textures.

The true power of creating and using patterns and textures comes into play when you can use them effectively in images. Although, you may recognize a pattern and re-create it in Photoshop as an element that can be used in various images. Patterns themselves can be made of other patterns in combination, which in turn form the final element. You can see both patterns and textures at work in the cinderblock wall example that follows.

→ For the example, **see** "Applying Texture and Creating a Pattern," **p. 673**.

CREATING AND SAVING PATTERNS AND TEXTURES

Building a library of your own patterns and textures is important both for knowing how individual patterns and textures work best, and for saving some time when you need a pattern or texture in a pinch. To do this, you'll have to know how to create and save them, as well as how to apply them.

CREATING AND SAVING A TEXTURE

Textures that come with Photoshop are 7-inch×7-inch at 72ppi in grayscale (504×504 pixels). That is a good a size to work with, although your textures can be larger or smaller. Making them too large or small may reduce utility or usability. A texture that is too small might end up being microscopic when applied to your image; if it is too large, the texture you are trying to simulate might not be recognizable in the image because it tiles too large to be apparent. These can often be resized and resaved if necessary without really ruining the effects—unless, of course, you try to resize and resave the same one over and over. Keep originals and resave with a new name as necessary. Textures are used like channels, so should be conceived as grayscale, although you can make them from converted color images.

Use the following steps to create and save a texture:

1. Open a new image at 512×512 pixels in grayscale.

2. Create the texture. You can do this by using multiple applications of filters, freehand drawings, and parts of pictures—any number of combinations is possible.

3. Using the Offset filter as described in the last section, offset the result and patch the seams to make the texture seamless. You can skip this step if it is not important that the texture be seamless.

4. Convert the image to grayscale if it isn't already.

→ For more information on converting to grayscale, **see** "Converting an Image from Color to Grayscale," **p. 487**.

5. Flatten the image.

6. Remove paths and alpha channels.

7. Save the image in the Textures folder in Photoshop using Photoshop native format (PSD) with a unique name.

Note

Textures do not have to be saved into the Textures folder in the Photoshop Presets folder, but putting them there will make them easy to locate when you want to use them. Filters that use textures will not automatically look there, but at least you will know where to find them.

CREATING AND SAVING A PATTERN

Patterns can be saved as both pixel-based art and scalable PostScript vector art that can be rastered to any desired size. Patterns can also be any size, but making them too large or too small again reduces the utility or usability. For example, a pattern to be used in creating a background for a Web page might be any dimension, but if you make it seamlessly tile at the smallest possible size, the background can be smaller and this will help download time. Pixel patterns that come with Photoshop range from about 1 to 2.5 inches square at 72dpi (72×72 pixels to 180×180 pixels). You will have to scale your patterns depending on what you want to accomplish with them.

Use the following steps to create and save a pattern:

1. Open an image that contains an element that you would like to make into a pattern. As an alternative you can create the element.

2. Select the area you want to make into the pattern.

3. Choose <u>D</u>efine Pattern from the <u>E</u>dit menu. The pattern will be saved in the current Pattern set.

Tip

To create a seamless pattern, copy the selection to a new document and then offset the image and patch the seams as necessary before Step 3.

 If you are having trouble with a particular pattern or texture that still has seams or appears to repeat too obviously when you apply it, see "Removing the Pattern from the Pattern" in the Troubleshooting section at the end of this chapter.

APPLYING TEXTURE AND CREATING A PATTERN

The following example shows how to create a recognizable cinderblock pattern using manual and filtered techniques. First, the basic texture for the blocks is established using filters to make a cinderblock surface texture. Then, the texture is saved and applied to a new document using the Texturizer filter. Next, the basic mortar pattern is sketched in by placing paths that will be stroked to build the result. When the small segment of the wall is done, the result is offset to check the seams, and then the final image can be saved as a pattern to tile into other image areas.

Use the following steps to create a cinderblock wall:

1. Create a new document to make a texture. Size it to 7×7 inches at 72dpi in grayscale.

PART
VIII
CH
31

2. Be sure the foreground and background colors are set to the default colors by pressing D on the keyboard.

3. Run the Pointillize filter (Filter, Pixelate, Pointillize) with a setting of Cell Size = 8.

4. Run the Craquelure filter with the following settings: Crack Spacing = 12, Crack Depth = 9, Crack Brightness = 7.

5. Offset the result by 72 pixels horizontally and vertically (Filter, Other, Offset).

Tip

When setting the number of pixels to offset, use a number that will make the offset apparent and easy to find. For example, if you work on an image that is 5-inch×5-inch at 300ppi, you might offset by 300 pixels (1 inch) in both directions. This places the seam along the inch marker on the ruler and leaves plenty of room on each side of the seam to make corrections.

6. Repair the seams that come into view after the offset so that they blend smoothly.

Note

I find it easiest to use the Clone Stamp tool for this type of correction—in this case, a brush with a 9-pixel diameter, hardness of 80, and spacing anywhere between 1 and 80, depending on your preference.

7. Save the texture you have created in the Adobe `Photoshop 6.0\Presets\Textures` folder. Save it in native Photoshop format (PSD). See Figure 31.6 for the result of Steps 1 to 7.

Figure 31.6
The final result of Steps 1 to 7 is a rough-looking texture. You might still want to alter this later to get a better result, but the texture can also be modified in the image after it is applied. This might not work in all applications (where there will be other image elements to worry about) but here it will be fine.

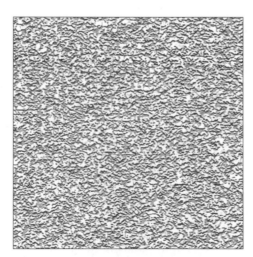

8. Open a new document. For this example, I used a 9×6-inch document at 72dpi.

9. Apply the texture created in Steps 1 to 7 using the Texturizer Filter (Filter, Texture, Texturizer). Use a setting of 50% for the Scaling and 4 for the Relief. Lighting direction can be from the top. You may want to experiment with any one of these settings.

10. Correct the texture to appear as you want it to. In this case, I applied a slight Motion Blur (0°, 10 pixels) and then opened the levels and adjusted the white Output slider to 232 (removing the white from the cement).

Note

You could do Steps 9 and 10 in quite a different way and wind up with nearly the same result. For example, you might color the background in the image a 10% gray, and open and change the texture by applying the Motion Blur to it before it is applied.

11. Make a mortar pattern with the Pen tool, being careful to align the endpoints exactly, top to bottom and left to right. The pen lines can go outside the edge of the document (see Figure 31.7).

Figure 31.7
When using the pen tool for this example, it might be best to hold down the Shift key when drawing the lines. This will lock the alignment in perfectly horizontal and perfectly vertical positions, depending on the direction in which you are drawing the lines.

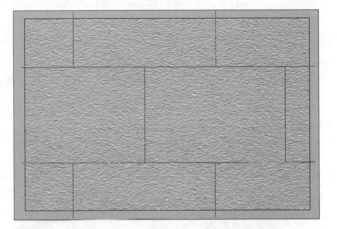

12. Create a new channel.

13. Select the Airbrush tool and a brush that is 13 pixels with a hardness of 95% and a spacing of 1. Change the foreground color to white.

Note

You might not have these settings in your presets so to do this you will either have to create a new brush or adjust an existing one.

→ For more information on creating a custom brush, **see** "Defining a Brush," **p. 692**.

14. Stroke the path created in Step 11 with the Airbrush (choose Stroke Path from the pop-up menu on the Paths palette). See Figure 31.8.

15. Duplicate the channel. You might need to come back to this channel for adjustments.

16. Apply the Diffuse filter (Filter, Stylize, Diffuse) using Lighten Only.

17. Load the channel you have duplicated and altered in Step 15 and 16 as a selection.

Figure 31.8
Stroking the path with a hard brush creates a basic pattern for the mortar in the channel. This will be used to create other channels, as well as to mask other tool applications and possibly to make adjustments.

18. Feather the selection by 2 pixels using the Feather function (Shift-Cmd-D) [Shift+Ctrl+D], and then apply a Gaussian blur with a Radius of 3.

19. Invert the selected area of the channel (Cmd-I) [Ctrl+I]. See the results of this step in Figure 31.9.

Figure 31.9
The result of Steps 16 to 19 is a mask that will be used to define the edges of the mortar and adjust highlights and shadows.

20. Deselect (Cmd-D) [Ctrl+D], and apply the Emboss Filter (Filter, Stylize, Emboss) to the result of Step 19, and then duplicate the channel.

21. Use the channel you duplicated and its duplicate to create highlight and shadow masks using the Levels command (Cmd-L) [Ctrl+L] (see Figures 31.10 to 31.12).

→ For more information on working with highlights and shadows, **see** "Using Highlights and Shadows," **p. 640**.

22. Apply the highlight and shadow masks created in the previous step to the image's Background layer. Load the highlight mask, open the Levels, and move the Output highlight slider to 128, then load the shadow mask, open the Levels, and do the same to the Output shadow slider.

Figure 31.10
Emboss will create an edge of highlights and shadows around the previous mask that can be selected from the result using Levels.

Figure 31.11
The Levels controls are set to create an effective shadow mask from the embossed channel by moving the black Input slider to 128.

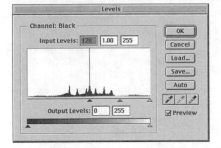

Figure 31.12
Next, the Levels controls are set to create an effective highlight mask from the embossed selection. Note that the Output level sliders are reversed, which saves using an additional tool.

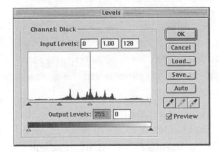

> **Note**
>
> Using these settings, both the highlight and shadow mask areas will darken. You might prefer other adjustments. Those given here are for the sake of simplifying the example. Here you can do some fancier stuff to create shape for the bricks and mortar according to the techniques in Chapter 30, "Working with Shadow and Light."

23. Load the channel created in Step 15 as a selection.

24. Select the Smudge tool and be sure the brush is set to the same brush used in Step 15.

25. Click the work path in the Paths palette, and then choose Stroke Path from the Paths palette pop-up menu. Be sure the Smudge tool is selected and click OK.

26. Choose the Add Noise filter from the Filters menu (Filter, Noise, Add Noise), and apply 5% to 6% noise using the monochrome setting. This should give the mortar some of its original grit.

27. Adjust the middle slider in the Levels dialog box to lighten the mortar and separate it from the brick. I simply moved the middle input slider to 2.

28. Invert the selection and adjust the cinderblocks using Levels. I set the Output sliders to 70 and 180. This limits the tonal range for the surface somewhat while darkening the result (see Figure 31.13).

Figure 31.13
You could still adjust this to be more particular about the shaping. The channels that you saved earlier can help you make adjustments to either the bricks, the mortar, or the highlights and shadows.

29. Offset the figure to check the seams and repair as necessary. If there are any joints out of whack, consider copying and pasting vertical or horizontal areas of the mortar rather than trying to repair. These can be fit into place using the Rotate command from the Transform submenu.

30. After the repairs have been made, save the pattern. You can do this by choosing Define Pattern from the Edit menu. The pattern is ready to be used. See Figure 31.14 for the final result and Figure 31.15 for an example of the pattern applied.

LISTING 31.1   HTML CODE FOR A TILING BACKGROUND

```
<HTML>
<HEAD><TITLE></TITLE></HEAD>
<BODY background="cinder.gif"></BODY>
</HTML>
```

Consider saving the image itself for possible later alterations and changes. For example, you might easily turn this into a red brick pattern by using the selection to colorize the brick, or reform the brick by resizing the path and reapplying the steps to create the mortar.

Figure 31.14
After offsetting and adjusting, the pattern is complete.

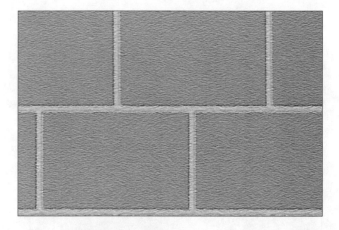

Figure 31.15
After the pattern is complete, the result can be applied. Here the cinderblock pattern is saved as a GIF and loaded into a Web browser using some simple HTML.

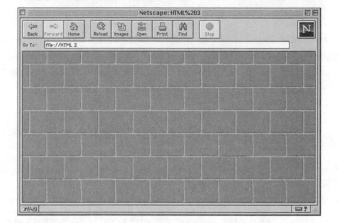

USING ACTIONS TO CREATE TEXTURES AND PATTERNS

It's sometimes possible and desirable to create actions that make particular textures or pattern elements. These actions will be able to generate elements according to the size and sometimes the shape of your image. Essentially, this will scale patterns that you make exactly to the size of the image you are using them with, or can confine changes to a selected area. As long as the pattern does not have to repeat, selective application might be your best option for creating patterns that are difficult to blend at the seams. For example, you can use the action used in making Figure 31.16 with any size document to custom create an effect for any size image. "Cells @ 72ppi" is an action I created to roughly imitate cells with a set of filter applications. It is available on the www.ps6.com Web site. Try it out by opening a document of any size at 72ppi and play the action. When you finish, offset the image to see how difficult it would be to correct the seams to make this a repeating pattern or texture. The feathered edge gives hints as to how you might alter the action to create a corn kernel effect or alligator scales.

Figure 31.16
This pattern is created using an action that will fit the pattern to the image or selected area that you want to apply it to. This pattern creates a very difficult challenge if you attempt to create it as a tiling pattern. Actually, the end result will not improve if you make it a tiling pattern.

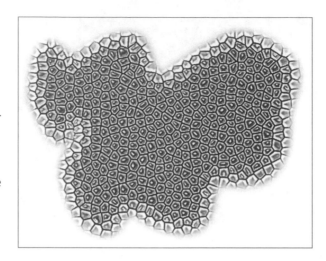

Actions can also replay useful portions of step sets that you use to create effects. For example, recording Steps 12 to 28 will save you a lot of work if you want to use the brick effect frequently and want to change the way it looks, or if you want to try it with different settings or patterns without manually working through the whole thing.

 Sometimes just recording what you do as you go along is the best way to save time.

→ For more information on using actions to record your steps as you work, **see** "Creating Effective Actions," **p. 263**.

CREATING AND SAVING POSTSCRIPT PATTERNS

PostScript patterns provided with Photoshop are in Illustrator format. If you don't have Illustrator, this can make it difficult for you to alter those patterns or create new ones. However, you can create scalable patterns that you can reuse in Photoshop much like the Illustrator patterns provided by Adobe. A template file included on the www.ps6.com Web site for this book and demonstrated in this section of the chapter helps you start creating and exploring new patterns to add to your Photoshop library.

CREATING A SCALABLE POSTSCRIPT PATTERN

You can make scalable patterns in Photoshop that can be used almost like the Illustrator PostScript patterns supplied with the program. The only difference is that there are a few steps added in the application of Photoshop-generated vector patterns—but, depending on how you look at this, it can actually make them more versatile. The paths have to be stroked, or selections created and filled as appropriate after the pattern has been sized to your needs. When the pattern files are saved very small, without fills or strokes, they take up almost no space. Creating the art for the files is done much like creating the path for the mortar seen earlier in Figure 31.8. After the pattern is created, it is stored so it can be sized and stroked or filled on any image.

You can make tiled vector patterns with relative ease—depending, of course, on what you are trying to achieve. To make a tiling pattern, you need to make the result seamless, but you cannot check the success and fix any problems in the vector pattern just by using the Offset filter (as in the previous example). The reason for this is that the Offset filter does not work with path (vector) tools: Although it will wrap your result after you render your pattern, paths will not wrap in the image area. Another way to create these patterns is to duplicate the pattern areas to mirror results and ensure an exact pattern match on all sides of the pattern area. Therefore, when you render the pattern, all lines that leave the pattern on one side will have a corresponding element to match to when the element is tiled.

When making this type of pattern, what you do at the right side of the image will affect what you need to do at the left side. Likewise, what you do at the top affects the result at the bottom and what you do at the lower-right corner affects the upper-left corner. The relationship can get a little complex and, depending on how you draw the curves, can be very difficult to follow. To see just where to draw and where not to draw, I like to use a map to simplify the process. Figure 31.17 is a map that helps show how image areas duplicate. Gray numbers and letters mark areas that correspond to the black lettered and numbered areas inside the image area frame. The orientation of the duplicated parts is the same as the original.

PART

VIII

CH

31

Figure 31.17
This map can help you create effective patterns using the Pen tool. You can use it to develop the patterns directly or copy paths to it to help check or correct them.

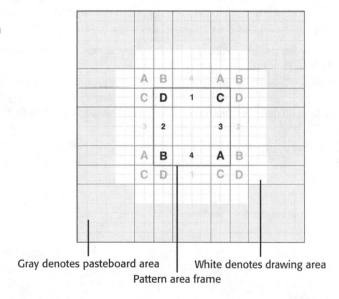

Gray denotes pasteboard area   White denotes drawing area
                    Pattern area frame

The document in the pattern map is actually nine times the size of the final pattern. This gives you room to work, create, change, and experiment with your pattern. The final pattern will be the area in the pattern area frame; you will work in and around that area to construct the pattern. To check all the possible overlaps, tile the pattern parts you create around the parameter according to the map. Checking all the shaded areas would be redundant if you are just checking to see that the pattern works, which is why those areas are shaded. The file (`patterngen.psd`) on the book's Web site (`www.ps6.com`) defines these as red zones to suggest that you do not need to add information in those areas.

The unshaded area shows the absolute critical area where pattern elements affect the final outcome. A regular pattern—more or less a geometric pattern rather than something less structured—will use a slightly smaller critical area. (These are defined in separate layers in the pattern map.) The final step in creating the pattern will be to snip the pattern out of the pattern frame and remove extraneous layers, paths, and channels. If you created the pattern accurately, you can save and use it at any size, and it will tile without seams when you use basic path stroking. You can work larger, if necessary, by scaling the pattern map (using Image, Image Size, and Nearest Neighbor option for the resampling method). The only instance in which you really need to scale the map is by preference; as the resulting paths will be infinitely scalable, you can create it at this size and size it to whatever you need later. This map is large enough so that you can see individual pixels at 1,600% (maximum) magnification.

CREATING A TILING PATTERN WITH IRREGULAR STROKES

It is possible to create a seemingly irregular pattern as paths that will tile seamlessly (or will be very easy to make seamless) after they are stroked. The following steps show how to create an irregular pattern. Steps for creating a pattern with more structure follow this, as do steps for storing and using the PostScript patterns you create.

→ For more information on creating a pattern that has a more regular feel, **see** "Creating a Tiling Pattern with Regular Strokes," **p. 687**.

→ For more information on storing PostScript patterns, **see** "Saving a Photoshop PostScript Pattern," **p. 690**.

→ For more information on using the PostScript pattern, **see** "Using a Photoshop PostScript Pattern," **p. 690**.

1. Open the pattern map you downloaded from the `www.ps6.com` Web site to use as a template. In the layers, be sure the clear Background, Pattern Frame, and Red Zone (Irregular Pattern) are visible. For more control and snap-to points, change your preferences for the Guides & Grid (File, Preferences, Guides & Grid) to add gridlines. This can be set according to how fine you want to measure. Figure 31.18 shows what the pattern map should look like.

Tip

You might want to plan the pattern or sketch the pattern first—either using another layer in the document or on paper (which you could scan and put in as a background to draw over).

2. Turn the Snap on in the View menu if it is not already (Snap should be checked in the list). Also, be sure Guides and Grid are both checked in the Snap To submenu.

Figure 31.18
This shows the pattern map with Guides and Grids turned on. The Guides and Grids are set to 1 inch with 8 subdivisions.

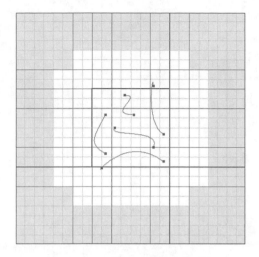

Tip

Snap can be toggled off and on by pressing (Cmd-;) [Ctrl+;]. Another option is to toggle them on and off while using (Control) [Right mouse button].

3. Using the Pen tool, begin to draw your pattern within the pattern area frame. Be sure the Pen tool options are set to Create New Work Path rather than Create New Shape Layer. You can go outside the boundaries of the frame when drawing, but don't go outside the drawing area.

Tip

When using the Pen tool, toggle to the Direct Selection tool temporarily by holding down the (Cmd) [Ctrl] key on the keyboard. If you are drawing a series of lines with the Pen tool instead of one continuous one, a single mouse click off the line you are drawing (with the Direct Selection tool selected) will make the line inactive. With the line inactive, the next point you click will start a new path line.

4. With either the Pen tool or the Direct Selection tool (Press A on the keyboard), select the pattern you have created thus far. To select it, click and drag a selection marquee around the entire pattern (see Figure 31.19).

5. Move the path you have drawn to the upper-left quadrant of the pattern map (see Figure 31.20).

6. Add another path to the path, from the upper-left corner of the Pattern Area Frame to the lower left. The new subpath should snap to the corners of the frame exactly. Although this will be eliminated later, it will help you with alignment.

7. Select all the subpaths in the path.

8. Duplicate the path while dragging to the right quadrant. To duplicate, hold down (Option-Shift) [Alt+Shift] while clicking and dragging any path.

Figure 31.19
Select all the paths you have created for the pattern. If you fail to select all of them, the points you do not select will stay where they are in the steps that follow and this won't work.

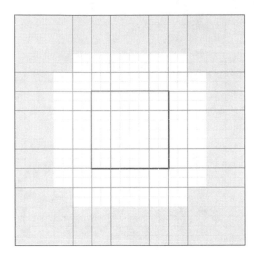

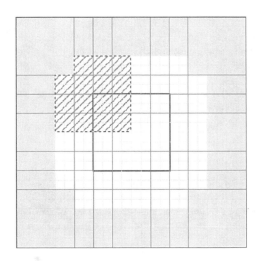
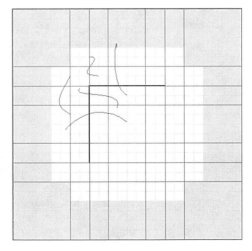

Figure 31.20
The upper-left quadrant is defined by the shaded area. The quadrant and the Pattern Area Frame are the same size and positioning should be relative. Using the snap-to guides simplifies the placement. Turn on the Upper Left Layer if you are having trouble with the alignment. The alignment does not have to be exact in order for the rest of the process to work, but it helps.

9. Align the vertical subpath that defined the left of the Pattern Area Frame to the frame edge at the right. See Figure 31.21 for the result.

10. Using the Direct Selection tool, you can press (Shift-A) [Shift+A] to toggle between it and the Path Component Selection tool. Select the bottom point on the vertical subpath created for alignment in Step 6, and drag the point to the upper-left corner of the Pattern Area Frame. This should make the vertical line horizontal.

Figure 31.21
It should appear at this point that you have duplicated the original set of strokes exactly and aligned them in the upper-right quadrant of the pattern map.

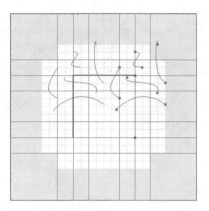

11. Select the entire set of subpaths and duplicate again. This time, drag the result to the bottom of the Pattern Area Frame and align the subpaths there. Check the horizontal line to be sure it aligns to the Pattern Area Frame corners. Move all the strokes you duplicated if it needs adjustment, not just the horizontal line (see Figure 31.22).

PART
VIII
CH
31

Note

During moves, always be sure all the strokes and points in the group you are moving are highlighted.

Figure 31.22
The subpaths in the top half of the pattern map are duplicated and dragged to the bottom of the pattern map. This will mostly complete the creation of the path you will be using for the pattern.

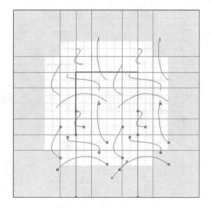

12. Delete the horizontal placement subpath altered in Step 10.

13. Look at the pattern and make adjustments or additions. If adding a subpath, be sure to duplicate the additions in each quadrant. (You might want to use a horizontal or vertical alignment stroke to help with the placement.) If adding to the center area only (inside the center guides), duplication is not necessary (see Figure 31.23). If moving any point or line not in the center, be sure to select the counterparts in each quadrant so the pattern will retain integrity. See Figures 31.24 and 31.25 for examples. Continue arranging, moving, and adding until you are happy with the pattern.

Tip

If this is your first time using the pattern map, I suggest that you make no alterations at this point to keep it simple. You can try some adjustments when you see how the whole process works.

Figure 31.23
Small additions to the center of the pattern will generally never have the chance to alter the larger result. Don't bother duplicating these to the other quadrants. If you try to duplicate these, you will find that the duplications fall into the red zone.

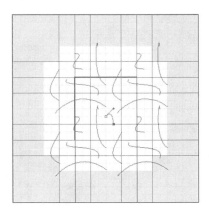

Figure 31.24
If moving any points or lines, select all the counterparts in each quadrant using the Direct Selection tool before making the moves.

Figure 31.25
You can change the position of selected points at the same time in all quadrants using the single handle.

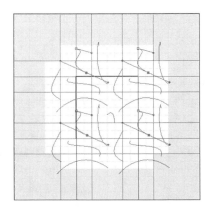

14. When the pattern is set, change the canvas size to 1×1 inch or 300×300 pixels (Image, Canvas Size). This crops the image to the framed pattern area. When you select OK, Photoshop warns you that clipping will occur. This is okay because the vectors remain exactly as they are, even if they fall outside the area of the canvas. The only thing clipping removes is pixel information. Figure 31.26 shows the result. Do not remove any path points, even those that fall completely outside the image area.

Figure 31.26
After the image is cropped, the result will look something like this. When you apply the pattern path to the image (by using Stroke Path, for example), the paths that fall outside the image area can influence the results, depending on settings you use for the tools that you apply.

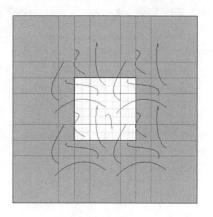

15. Throw away the layers for the frames and red zones.
16. Save the pattern.

When you are done, you have created a path that can be used to create patterns and textures at any size. The path is infinitely scalable and can be stroked with brushes to produce a tilable pattern. This makes it even more versatile than PostScript patterns supplied with Photoshop as you have more control over how they are handled. See "Using a Photoshop PostScript Pattern" for more on how to apply the pattern you have created.

CREATING A TILING PATTERN WITH REGULAR STROKES

A more consistent or regularly patterned set of paths can be created with a similar procedure. However, you will put the pieces together in a slightly different way.

Use the following steps to create a regular pattern:

1. Open the pattern map to use as a template. In the Layers palette, be sure the clear Background, Pattern Frame, and Red Zone (Regular Pattern) layers are visible. For more control and snap-to points, set the grid to 1 inch and 8 subdivisions.

Note

If you have an idea for a pattern, you might want to sketch it in a background layer or on paper to help you plan how to create it.

2. Divide the pattern area mentally into even columns and rows or show the 3×3 grid. I like to use three columns by three or six rows as that configuration usually produces good results, even with complex curves. One and two columns might prove very difficult to work with. Using multiples of three makes the columns overlap evenly on each side.

> **Note**
>
> In the example, the pattern is developed using three columns and six rows.

3. Use the grid to draw a portion of the pattern—staying within the cell size you are working with. Cell size is defined by the number of columns and rows (see Figure 31.27). You can set up guides to help you define the working area.

Figure 31.27
This simple curve will be repeated in the rows and then copied into other columns to create the final effect.

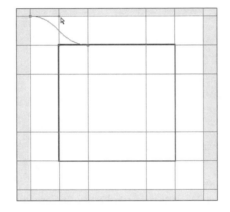

4. Duplicate the path you have created in the first cell to the second cell. To duplicate the path line, select the points with the Direct Selection tool by dragging a selection marquee around the path. When the points are selected, click and drag on the line while holding down (Shift–Option) [Shift+Alt]. Check the guide intersections to be sure the element is placed exactly.

5. Repeat the previous step until the column is filled (see Figure 31.28).

6. When you have completed the left column of the pattern, select all the subpaths using the Direct Selection tool or by pressing A.

7. Copy the path lines by holding down (Shift–Option) [Shift+Alt] while clicking and dragging any line. Align the duplicate exactly in the right column using guides (see Figure 31.29).

8. Highlight and duplicate either the right or left column subpaths and place these in the center column. Again be sure the duplicate is perfectly aligned to the guides. This will complete the basic pattern (see Figure 31.30).

Figure 31.28
The pattern is completed in the column by duplicating the simple pattern in the first cell.

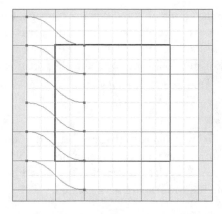

Figure 31.29
The guides will help you align the pattern exactly on the other side of the pattern map. If you have any difficulties, consider using a vertical placement line as used with the example for an irregular pattern.

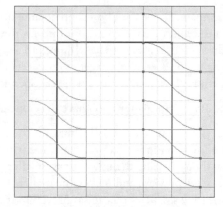

Figure 31.30
The completed pattern should look something like this. All parts should seem to be even and aligned.

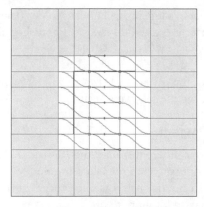

Note

For variation, you could, at this point, flip the center column strokes, or even duplicate and reverse them. The results will work well depending on the original strokes you have created.

9. Shrink the canvas size to 1-inch×1-inch or 300×300 pixels (Image, Canvas Size). Ignore the clipping warning and do not remove any points from the paths. This will size the document down to the Framed Pattern Area, which is all the canvas you need to apply the pattern. (See the next set of steps on using the Photoshop PostScript patterns.)

10. Throw away the layers for the frames and the red zones.

11. Save the pattern.

When you are done, you have again created a path that can be used to create other patterns and textures at any size. This result will have a more regular, predictable patterning. It is saved and applied the same way as an irregular pattern. See "Using a Photoshop PostScript Pattern" for more on how to apply the pattern you have created.

SAVING A PHOTOSHOP POSTSCRIPT PATTERN

Because only important vector information is in the Photoshop document after completing the steps using the pattern map, and vectors are independent of pixels, the document can be changed to a minimum size to help keep the storage space required to a minimum. At this point, nothing in the image will change or become damaged, as it is vector information. It can be resized to any dimension with no loss of integrity when you open the file for use.

Use the following steps to save the PostScript pattern you have developed:

1. Shrink the document to 10ppi (Image, Image Size). Technically, the image can be shrunk even more, but 10ppi allows you to have a preview of the pattern at 1,600% magnification in Photoshop without resizing the image first. Smaller images require that you resize before you can see a preview, and making it smaller than 10ppi does not really make the file size significantly smaller. You can save several variations of the path in one document.

2. Save the pattern with a recognizable name in the Patterns folder (`Photoshop 6.0\Presets\Patterns`). Save the patterns created this way as Photoshop files; do not export paths to Illustrator.

This simple saving procedure will put the patterns where you will know how to find them. To use the pattern you have created, see the following section.

USING A PHOTOSHOP POSTSCRIPT PATTERN

Using Photoshop PostScript patterns is different from using Illustrator PostScript patterns. When opening an Illustrator PostScript pattern, Photoshop prompts you to select a size for rasterizing. When using Photoshop PostScript patterns, the process of rendering is manual. However, because it is manual you have a lot more to do.

Use the following steps to apply a PostScript pattern created using the pattern map:

1. Open the Photoshop PostScript pattern you want to use.

2. Size the image appropriate to the scale you want to use in creating the pattern (Image, Image Size). For example, match the resolution of the image in which you will be using the pattern and increase or decrease the dimensions as appropriate.

3. Use the paths to define the pattern. You can stroke the paths using the Stroke Paths function on the paths palette and you can create selections with the paths to apply other tools, filters, and functions. Also, several effects can be created by stroking with different tools and tool options, using multiple layers, multiple patterns, and/or changing the orientation of the path (90° or 180°). Scaling distorts the pattern if it is scaled separately from the template (see Figure 31.31).

Figure 31.31
Stroking the path using Dissolve or Behind blending modes for the tools you apply can create some interesting effects. In this way, Photoshop patterns are more versatile than Illustrator PostScript patterns that already have color and areas assigned.

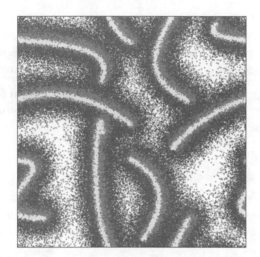

4. When the pattern is created, flatten it if necessary and Select All (Cmd-A) [Ctrl+A]. Set the area to the Defined Pattern (Edit, Define Pattern). The pattern can now be used for fills in other documents (see Figure 31.32).

Figure 31.32
This 4×4 image was filled with the pattern shown as the result in Figure 31.31.

Patterns created in this fashion can also be used for patterns and textures, but they can also be used to create masks, bump maps, and so on. The techniques described enable you to add to the Photoshop library without using Illustrator and to provide a utility and versatility that Illustrator PostScript patterns don't offer (such as altering pattern colors). Because Photoshop vectors allow variation, one pattern is capable of producing an infinite number of effects. Learning how to create and save vector patterns in Photoshop can make basic pattern and texture creation more useful and offers the utility of creating patterns from scratch.

DEFINING A BRUSH

Brushes can produce a variety of effects, and custom brushes can make some unique applications of Photoshop tools. Simply learning to make and save brushes can give you yet another tool to add to the creative arsenal. Stroking vector paths with unique brushes created by using techniques from this section can add even more originality to the effects you create.

A brush can be defined as grayscale from any selected source, as long as it is fewer than 1,000×1,000 pixels. Color sources can define a brush; however, the end result will be grayscale and might be somewhat tonally unpredictable.

Use the following steps to create a brush:

1. Open an image containing an area that you want to use as a brush.
2. Define the brush area by selection. Selections do not have to be rectangles and can be feathered, although you will be filling a rectangular area for the brush.
3. Choose Edit, Define Brush. The brush will be defined in a new square in the Brushes drop-down.

Creative use of brushes will come in handy in creating unique effects with PostScript patterns and stroking. You can use brushes creatively in many ways. Even with simple brush use, it is possible to create effects by stroking paths that are otherwise very difficult in Photoshop. Knowing how to create your own brushes expands the potential of what is possible.

For example, varying brush shapes and spacing can produce unusual and interesting effects. The image of the lunar eclipse in Figure 31.33 was created in two passes using the moon as a brush and then overlaying a black application of a similar-size brush in a second pass. Spacing of 140% was used for the moon and 120% for the black brush. The result required a little cleanup in that the black application fell over the previous moon because of the spacing difference.

Figure 31.33
The result required a little cleanup as the application of the black brush repeated over more than one moon in most instances. However, the cleanup took a few seconds whereas aligning this and creating it manually would have been a bit trickier using other ways to create the effect.

CREATING IMAGE FRAMES

Image frames can help define an image and image areas. Patterns, textures, and brushes (along with filters and other Photoshop tools) can help create reusable frames in several forms. Frames are image borders. Some companion programs and plug-ins (for example, Extensis PhotoFrame) offer libraries of these frames that you can apply to images, sometimes using the third party's interface. What plug-ins and companions do is use a preset mask to alter your image. Masks are relatively simple to make and apply using Photoshop alone, so you can create, save, and apply frames depending only on Photoshop. Knowing how to do this will help you create a library of frames to use with Photoshop, or add to libraries to use with companion programs and plug-ins, if you prefer that method of application.

You can create frames using actions so that they are the size of your image, or you can store them as grayscale or bitmaps to use as masks. Creating frames is different from the procedure for creating patterns or textures, as there is generally no reason to make it repeat. However you choose to create the frame, the goal is the same: to improve the look of your image with the framing. Good planning—either by recording your actions, creating the frame as a scalable vector image, or providing sufficient ppi in the frame—can help you make frames that can be used repeatedly with images of varying shapes and sizes.

Some framing is not too complicated, but frames can be quite subtle or more garish. An example of simple framing would be simply burning in the edge of an image; this is sometimes done in photography to create an almost imperceptible darkening at the image edge, supposedly to help trap the viewer's eye in the image. Another simple method of framing is to expand the canvas size; the color in the background swatch becomes the image border color when the canvas size is increased. Complex framing or compounding frame applications can require several layers, multiple masks, filters, and additional effects—depending on what you want to achieve.

Another effective method of creating a frame is scanning a border or object. This is useful for creating frames that are difficult to imitate or generate using Photoshop, such as tape edges or natural brush strokes. The results can sometimes be achieved more quickly using real objects rather than trying to photorealistically re-create them (see Figure 31.34 for an example). The following steps examine the process for creating frames with actions and vectors and as pixel-based images.

Figure 31.34
This scan of a tape border was done in a few moments by actually applying tape to a black card. The frame can be used in several ways, including selecting the inside of the area created by the torn edges or using the masking tape image itself as a border.

Use the following steps to create a frame and apply it to an image:

1. Open a new document at the size you want to create your frame mask. If you are creating the frame for a specific image and plan to use it as a mask, use the same ppi and dimensions as the image.

Note

It might be quicker and easier to create a new channel in the image itself than to create a new document. However, this exercise assumes you are creating the frame as a standalone document.

Tip

If you are creating the frame at exactly the same size as the image you are going to frame, be aware that the frame will cause some cropping. Be sure the image is not already cropped so tightly that the frame will obscure important image information.

2. Create the frame. You are limited here only by your understanding of the application of Photoshop's tools and filters, the size of the image, and the 256 levels of gray if you are using channels. Essentially, you can create frames for storage in one of three ways: actions, vectors, and pixel-based images. (Discussion and examples for each option follow this exercise.)

3. Save the frame. Use an appropriate name that will help you identify it. Create a Frames directory in the Photoshop\Presets directory, and save the frames there.

It is probably easiest to save any frame type in the Photoshop `Presets` folder, inside another folder called Frames. Make subfolders for each within the Frames folder and title those Actions, Vectors, and Pixel Based to keep them separate. Save actions in their own set in the Actions palette, save vectors as 1-inch×1-inch 10ppi images that can be scaled as needed (see the previous section on creating Photoshop PostScript patterns for more information), and save pixel-based images as flattened grayscale images. With grayscale frames, including the pixel dimensions in the filename might prove handy.

The Presets Folder

Photoshop's Presets folder contains all sorts of stuff that can come in handy when preparing images. It includes actions, brushes, gradients, patterns, duotone presets, color palettes, and more. Essentially, the Presets folder is a storage area for items that can help you customize Photoshop's tools and serves as a library where you can find these items. Many of these are managed from the Preset Manager, but not all. Although you will not have a Frames folder initially, creating one here makes sense, as you will be able to easily find all the creative elements you develop in one place.

Creative application of framing can accomplish a lot in defining how a viewer looks at an image. Framing can be used to highlight words and portions of important images, or framing can exclude extraneous or unwanted image parts. Storing reusable frames in your library can save you from re-creating an effect whenever you need it, and can prove to be very useful in saving time.

FRAMING WITH VECTORS

Use vectors to create patterns that you can stroke to create framing. These paths can be stored in tiny images so that they will hardly take up any space and can be recalled and resized to any image. Used in combination with actions, the paths themselves can be re-created, or actions can be used to apply a series of effects and stroking to achieve the effect. The path in Figure 31.35 was made using grids in a document; then the path was saved separately so it could be applied to other images. Figure 31.36 shows the path applied with various strokes.

Figure 31.35
These vectors were created using the Pen tool, a grid, and duplication/flipping and transforming paths. The results could be saved as a shape and accessed with the Custom Shape tool.

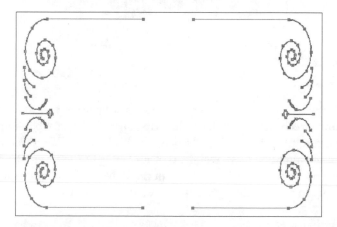

Figure 31.36
While the path is active, stroking the lines with various brushes, colors, and smudging creates an effect for the frame.

FRAMING WITH MASKS

Pixel-based or grayscale frames can either be created in Photoshop or can be the result of scanning something that you would like to use as a frame. Figure 31.37 shows a Photoshop-generated frame, created with a combination of filter applications on a rough Lasso selection saved as a channel. Figure 31.38 shows the frame from Figure 31.37 applied to the same image from Figure 31.36.

Figure 31.37
This pixel-based mask was created with the application of the Wave filter to a selection that was made with the Lasso.

FRAMING WITH ACTIONS

Figure 31.39 shows an example of a frame created just by using an action. Actions can be created by simply recording your steps while creating a frame, troubleshooting the results, and saving the resulting action. The advantage to this is being able to re-create the effects per image so they might be more unique, perhaps better fit the image they are intended for, and allow adjustment to the steps. Actions can create both vector- and pixel-based frames with some limitations on flexibility due to recording limitations.

Figure 31.38
The mask was applied to a separate layer that allowed the area to be filled with a pattern, texture, type, another image, and so on. In this case, Photoshop's Drop Shadow and Inner Glow layer styles are used to create separation between the image and the frame.

Figure 31.39
An action for creating this frame is available on the Web site (www.ps6.com; the action titled "Frame"). To run the action, load it, select the area you want to frame with the Marquee tool, and save the selection; then run the action on the channel to create the frame. Settings for the filters need to be varied to achieve similar results in images with significantly different size.

To use actions, simply play back the action and let Photoshop do the work in re-creating the frame. You might want the action to work on a whole image or just on a selected portion. This is something you will have to keep in mind when creating the action, as you might need to make adjustments accordingly. Creating actions to work with a selection rather than a full frame is probably more versatile in most cases. Be aware that settings for some tools and certain steps for the action might have to be altered to make the result fit the image. Insert stops at these points so you can make the necessary adjustments and take appropriate notes.

Recording Actions
To record actions for creating frames, create a new action by selecting New Action from the Actions palette pop-up menu and then start recording. Start Recording can be selected from the Actions palette pop-up or by clicking the Record button at the bottom of the Actions palette.

➡ For more information on creating actions, **see** "Creating Effective Actions," **p. 263**.

TROUBLESHOOTING

REMOVING THE PATTERN FROM THE PATTERN

I have created a seamless tiling pattern, and although I fixed the seam, the pattern still seems to repeat. What can I do to make it less repetitious?

A number of things can happen in creating a pattern that will make it seem too repetitious. Some are hard to prevent. Because you are working with a square portion of an image, you cannot completely eliminate the possibility of repetition—after all, repetition is the entire point of having a pattern!

Be sure you are not expecting more than can really be done with a pattern. The best and most functional patterns are simple ones. Even the fiery burst pattern I show in the initial example is probably not the type of pattern you will want to be using very often—it is simply an example where I knew the random generation would produce a result that did not tile well without alteration. More often, you will be using patterns that are as simple as the texture created for the cinderblock wall. More complex patterns are certainly possible, but these will almost always have obviously repeating elements. The fiery burst pattern is a good example of that. However, a problem you will probably run into often when creating a pattern from an image element is in the tone of the image. It is very easy to select an area of an image that you want to define as a pattern and find out when you offset that the tone has a very slight grade from one side or one corner to the other. This will make an obvious tonal pattern even if you have smoothed the seams (see Figure 31.40).

Figure 31.40
This image area was filled with a pattern that is seamless, but had a slight tonal grade from the upper-left to the lower-right corner. Although this can perhaps be a useful pattern, it can be a very frustrating thing to attempt to fix if you want a pattern that doesn't look like a pattern.

© PhotoSphere Images, Ltd., photosphere.com

In some cases it might just be best to start over, but there are other things you can do to help reduce the appearance of patterning. First, use simple patterns. Second, use patterns that have desired repeating elements; a pattern of bricks, a carpet pattern, wallpaper, plaids, and so on. Elements that repeat naturally will give you an expected result, while a pattern made from an image of the left half of a pill bottle will usually look odd no matter what you do to smooth the seams. Third, use dramatic scales when creating patterns. By this I mean use the smallest denomination of pixels that will produce the desired result. For the record, the smallest pattern will be 1 pixel. If you want to fill a background with a certain color, or even if you want to store that color, it might be feasible to do it as a pattern. Even a 2×2 pattern can be used to create a fill with particular qualities and pixel order that you want to repeat (see Figure 31.41).

Figure 31.41
If a 2×2 pixel pattern were defined as the image on the left (with just 2 white and 2 black pixels in this array), the pattern could be used to fill areas to create a miniature checker-board that would appear to be gray. This might have more use as a tiny tiling background for a Web page than it does as a true pattern, but it is still viable as a pattern.

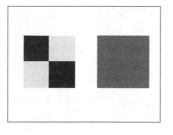

By the same token, a very large pattern might be so big that you would probably never use the whole thing in an application, yet the seamlessness allows you to apply it in any fashion over a large area without having to worry about patterning becoming apparent—even if you do happen to run all the way to the seam. For example, the fiery pattern might be created at 6,000×6,000 pixels (arbitrary measure), which would be large enough to apply it to an image as a border at probably any size without being able to notice a pattern. You might not want to keep this pattern stored in your active pattern set, however, as it may affect bootup time for Photoshop.

Generally, it is good to keep patterns as simple as possible. A good rule of thumb is, the simpler the pattern, the smaller you store it.

PHOTOSHOP AT WORK: CREATING YOUR OWN PUZZLE PATTERN

A common request on email (via listserver) and newsgroup discussions pertaining to Photoshop is for a puzzle pattern, or an action to create a puzzle look. The most frustrating thing about those posts is the poster spends far more time looking for the prepared solution than they would if they just sat down with Photoshop and created the solution themselves.

A great way to create a puzzle pattern is to create a path in the shape of a puzzle using the Pen tool. After the basic shape is created, you can resize the result for application on different-size images. You can use the Pattern Map to help you create a very simple repeating map, work on a freehand version, or use an existing puzzle as a template by scanning it and then using the scan as a background to copy. All you really have to do is draw a vertical line with some bumps in it, and then duplicate and arrange it several times.

Here we will do it quick and dirty, freehand.

1. Open a square image at about 6×6 inches or 480×480 pixels.

2. About 1/4 of the way into the image from the left, draw a vertical line with the Pen tool to define the first puzzle row. Start outside the image and make a vertical line. Go about 1/2 to 3/4 of an inch into the image, then plant an anchor, and draw a bump to the right. Close the bump, draw another vertical for 1 to 1 1/4 inches and draw a bump left. Make another right and another left bump going about an inch every time, and then draw a final path segment off the document (see Figure 31.42).

Figure 31.42
This basic stroke will be the basis for the rest of the pattern.

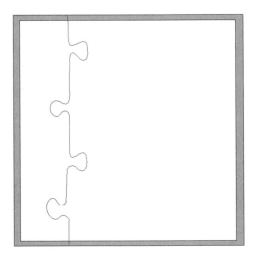

3. Duplicate the path by pressing (Shift–Option) [Shift+Alt] and click-drag on the line. Move it to about 3/4 of the way across the image.

4. Duplicate the path one more time and place it in the center, and then flip the line (either horizontally or vertically will work, but rotating will not).

5. Select the three paths you have created using the Direct Selection tool.

6. Duplicate by click-dragging while holding down the (Shift–Option) [Shift+Alt] keys.

7. Rotate 90° (clockwise or counter, your choice) and position to create puzzle rows (see Figure 31.43).

Figure 31.43
The puzzle pattern is really complete at this point. It can be applied to images in a number of ways from simple stroking to more complex effects.

To apply the pattern, all you need to do is create a shadow and highlight mask as done in Chapter 30, using the Emboss filter. If you do this in a channel, you can create the masks you need to apply the highlights and shadows to etch the puzzle pattern into an image.

1. Create a new channel.

2. Stroke the path in the channel with a small, soft white brush (3px, 0% hard, 1% spacing).

3. Apply the Emboss filter at 135°, 3 pixels, and 100%. You can vary this if you feel comfortable. You might apply a slight blur as well. See Figure 31.44 for the result.

Figure 31.44
This renders a fairly realistic puzzle shape, and it should only have taken a few minutes to do. Save the pattern as a path so you can use it again if you need to.

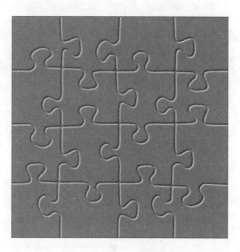

Try to apply the masks and strokes to images using the pattern. When you find a combination that works best for you, record it as an action. After that you can apply the pattern with a keystroke.

COMBINING IMAGES: COLLAGE AND COMPOSITES

In this chapter

COLLAGE, COMPOSITE, AND MORPHING DEFINED

Collage, composite and morphed images are all made up of two or more source images. The materials are combined to achieve different ends, but essentially the process in each is fairly similar: Distinct images are placed together in a single document and are made to work together.

At times, extracting one of these terms from the other is difficult. In fact, some images might include elements of each. It is also very difficult to set a numbered procedure for completing any of these types of images as the result is content specific and really depends on what you are trying to achieve.

- *Collage* suggests images are grouped together in an array that doesn't necessarily have to do with matching content and can be, more or less, random. These can be over-lapped, cut-ups, cropped images, and so on. Collages are technically easier to do than morphing or composite images; in fact, Photoshop layers are a great tool to order and stack collage elements.

- *Composite* images are generally somewhere between collage and morphing. They have a somewhat higher level of refinement in placement and composition than collage, yet will probably not require as much manipulation as morphing objects. Instead of being a composition made up of distinguishable images as a collage, composites mesh the images, probably most often to appear as a unit.

- *Morphing* is creating a hybrid image from two original source images so that the final image is a cross between the two in shape and structure. Usually the morph concentrates on melding the subjects of two different images. For example, when morphing a cat with a tiger, the end result will not look quite like either but will mix the traits of both.

Creating composite images of any sort is where the Photoshop user needs to pull out all the stops and make the most of the program. When creating these images, you will work with multiple source images to create a final image. This can require manipulation of those images individually so they work well together. Simple composites might use only two source images and might take a few simple steps to put together; complex images, however, might require working with multiple documents, with literally hundreds of layers and channels in tow.

Creating effective composites usually depends on paying attention to detail. For example, in an image that has several sources, you might need to orchestrate lighting, shadows, distances, and image interaction in ways simple images do not require. As complex as this might be, the basics for such manipulation and detailing are covered in many of the other chapters. This chapter essentially shows how the practices of individual chapters can be put together into a cohesive whole.

MORPHING IMAGE SHAPES

Making two images into a hybrid is a bit different and perhaps more involved than simply putting two images together in a basic composite. It can require a lot of pixel pushing and adjustment. The goal of morphing is to make a new object out of two different objects, often leaving the flavor and suggestion of both the originals.

Every situation in which you create a morph or hybrid of two images is different. However, you use a similar procedure in creating the final image. The following steps outline that procedure.

1. Select two objects that you think would work well in creating a morph. Generally these objects should have some similarity in shape, design, and purpose.
2. Create digital representations of the objects and isolate the image elements you want to morph.
3. Place the image elements together in a new document that is 20% larger than either of the two source documents.
4. Make rough general adjustments in sizing and shape so the scope of the images is similar.
5. Fine-tune the fit of identifying image elements by enhancing their placement and effect in the image.
6. Fix, replace, or add image detail that might be damaged or needs to be changed to fit the new shape.
7. Add light and shadow effects to the elements to create a realistic sense of lighting and space.
8. Crop the image.
9. Save the image in flattened and full-layered versions.

Along the way are innumerable variables, and the process can become quite a bit more complex than might appear here. However, this does cover the bases.

Tip

Although it is possible to choose quite dissimilar objects to morph, objects that are closer in original form will be easiest to work with. In other words, although I am sure a donut can somehow be morphed with a cathedral, it would be far easier, and probably more effective to make the morphing work with a donut and a car tire.

The goal of the example is to create an intermediate stage between the light meter and computer mouse shown in Figure 32.1. These have somewhat similar shapes and a meaningful result when one considers Photoshop and digital photography.

PART

VIII

CH

32

Figure 32.1
Both of these objects were scanned to create the images. The mouse is easy to select out of the dark background using the Magic Wand and a little touchup. The light meter was somewhat trickier, but was easy enough to outline using the Pen tools.

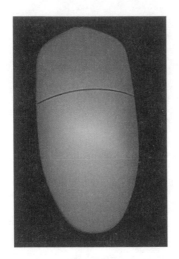

In creating a successful morph, the effect depends on the viewer being able to recognize the separate elements of the different objects with relative clarity. In this example, the elements of the mouse that must be apparent are the general shape and button. The light meter's analog meter and dial are the prominent features, and these help anchor the identity of the light meter.

Note

Doing too good a job of handling and meshing the elements might create an object that looks so real that the effect of the morphing might be lost. There is a balance to strike between effect and desired result.

Of course, some trade-offs occur in image integrity as the distortion of the objects progress. Some of this has to be considered a necessary evil in proceeding to the result.

→ You will find color versions of the visual examples in this chapter in the color section of this book; **see** ColorPlate 15.

The following steps, loosely based on the basic outline for creating a morph, were used to morph the mouse and light meter. This detailed example will help you see how to adapt the steps to what you are trying to accomplish in a real-world scenario.

1. Scans were made of the mouse and light meter using a consumer-grade flatbed scanner.

2. Appropriate selections were made to separate the objects from their respective backgrounds. As these scans were created with separation in mind, the selection was rather simple. Your selections for other morphing projects might not prove to be so easy.

3. A document 20% larger than the light meter was created.

4. The selections created in Step 2 were used to copy the objects to the new document. With the selection active, the element was just copied and pasted to the new document from the original.

5. A change in layer opacity was used to compare the images in size, contour, and place-ment of elements (see Figure 32.2). From the comparison, the mouse needs to be sized up. For best results, it might be wisest to size down the larger item, but there is a lot of manipulation that needs to occur; having the extra pixels seems better at this point than starting to limit them already.

Figure 32.2
The comparison revealed similarities that were not consid-ered during visual inspection. For exam-ple, the curve of the mouse button con-forms somewhat to the arch of the dial and bottom of the meter window. This will be used in a later step to shape that portion of the image.

Light meter

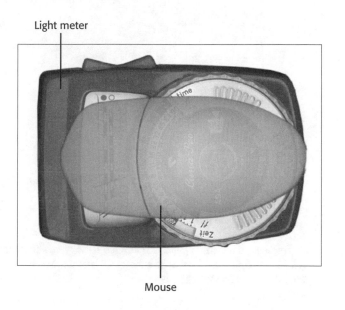

Mouse

6. Overall adjustments were made to the mouse to create a better fit between the objects. Figure 32.3 shows a comparison between the original mouse size, the larger compro-mise size, and the light meter. The mouse was scaled using the Scale transformation (Edit, Transform, Scale).

7. Selections were made for the key elements on the light meter (the dial and meter). As these are geometric shapes, each was selected using the Pen tool. The paths were saved so they could be called later as selections when needed.

8. The selection from Step 7 was used to isolate the dial portion of the meter. The por-tion of the path created to select the dial was selected using the Path Component Selection tool and Make Selection was chosen from the Paths palette menu. After the selection was in place, the light meter layer was activated in the Layers palette, and a new layer was made containing the selected material by pressing (Cmd-J) [Ctrl+J] (the Layer, New, Via Copy command). The layer was then moved to the top of the Layer palette. A drop shadow was applied as a Layer Style.

9. The dial was sized to 90% using the numeric options for the Free Transform command to get it to fit the width of the mouse. To activate the Transform functions, simply select the function you want from the Edit, Free Transform menu. The results appear in Figure 32.4.

Figure 32.3
The mouse was widened and lengthened to fill a larger area and size up to the size of the light meter. Going too much wider might have compromised the mouse shape.

Original Mouse   Enlarged Mouse

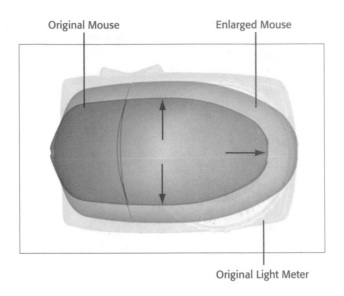

Original Light Meter

Scaling the dial could have been accomplished using the Transform bounding box and handles. To keep the dial's original shape when scaling using the handles, hold the (Shift–Option) [Shift+Alt] keys while making your transformations. This constrains the proportions and scale on center.

Figure 32.4
With the mouse scaled up and the dial scaled down, the two objects fit together better.

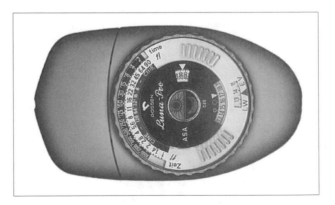

In Photoshop 6 the controls for numeric transformations are no longer in the Numeric Transform dialog box, they are on the Options bar when the Transform command has been invoked.

10. The meter window was selected out of the light meter and placed in its own layer using the portion of the path created for it in Step 7. The process was similar to Steps 8 and 9 for the dial.

11. The meter window was contoured roughly to the front button edge of the mouse using the Shear filter (Filter, Distort, Shear). Figure 32.5 shows the Shear curve used to create the effect pictured in Figure 32.6.

Figure 32.5
As the front edge of the original meter is pretty flat, the curve was altered to look like the front edge of the mouse. The mouse and meter were centered vertically; otherwise, this Shear effect would have been much more difficult to figure out intuitively, and would have required far more trial and error.

Changed arch to match front end of mouse

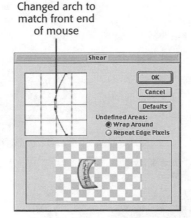

Figure 32.6
The result shapes the whole meter, and doesn't have good ramifications for the back end of the meter, which is distorted at this point and overlays the button edge. This will be touched up in the following steps.

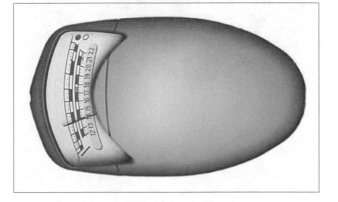

12. Shaping the back of the meter to the button was done in several steps. First, the top white portion of the meter was duplicated and added to the bottom using selection and copy/paste. This area was large enough to fill the area between the bottom of the window and the button line. The copied portion was blended into the rest of the meter by simply running a soft–edged Eraser (0% hardness) on the overlapping portion of the pasted area to reveal more of the meter face below. The bottom of the meter over the button edge was left rough, as it would be redefined in the next step. When the blend was complete, the two-meter face layers were merged using Layer, Merge Down (Cmd-E) [Ctrl+E].

13. The Pen tool was used to trace the curve of the button. This path element was then used to redefine the back edge of the meter face. After making sure the path was in place and active (highlighted in the Paths palette), and the target layer for the meter window was selected, a brush was set up to stroke the path. The Eraser tool was set to Airbrush and a 90% hard brush was selected. Then, the Eraser was used to stroke the path. This erased the bottom of the meter window to match the contour of the button line.

14. A new layer was created. The same path from Step 13 was stroked again using a small Paintbrush with 80% hardness using black. The layer Mode was changed to Multiply; then the opacity was changed to achieve the desired darkness for the button crease. Figure 32.7 shows the result of Steps 12 to 14.

Figure 32.7
The contour of the back of the meter was made to fit using a simple path and stroking. Then, the button line was emphasized so that it both conformed exactly to the path drawn to shape the meter window and darkened so it wouldn't get lost. At this point, the morphing had taken basic shape. There was still more to do.

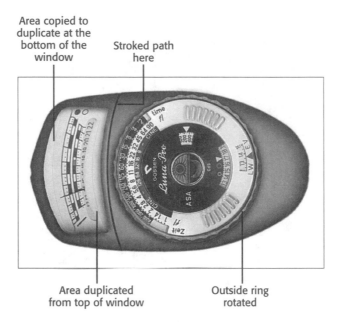

Area copied to duplicate at the bottom of the window

Stroked path here

Area duplicated from top of window

Outside ring rotated

15. After completing the general changes, specific details were improved/added. There needed to be alterations to the meter dial, the number bar, the numbers for the bar, and the meter needle. Figure 32.8 shows the results of all adjustments made for Step 15.

- The dial was in the wrong perspective by 180° considering the light in the composite, and the meter numbers had to be replaced along with the number bar and the meter needle. As the dial was on its own layer, it would have been easy to rotate it 180°, but this would have changed the orientation of the dial to the meter. Instead, the center of the meter was selected with a slight feathering and then copied and pasted to its own layer. When the dial was rotated underneath, the center part of the meter retained its orientation. A slight adjustment using the Move tool was all that was necessary to realign the center of the dial and the ring.

- To replace the number bar, a path was created to approximate the curve, and then it was stroked using the Airbrush. Layer Styles were added to create a very slight embossed inner edge and drop shadow.

- Numbers were added to the bar using a typeface similar to the original, which was kerned and scaled to fit. The arch in the type was created using the Shear filter with a curve similar to that used to reshape the meter window in Step 12.

- The meter needle was replaced by matching the size of the needle width with an appropriate brush, then sampling the needle color and redrawing the needle in its own layer. When the needle was in place, the old needle was removed along with its drop shadow. Layer Styles were used again to replace the drop shadow and to bevel the needle.

Number details put back

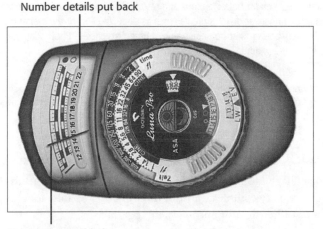

Figure 32.8
A number of minor adjustments were made in Step 15 to bring back detail that had been lost or make it fit to the new form of the object. These changes follow Step 6 in the overall procedure.

Pointer detail added

16. Add shadowing and effects as appropriate to the lighting of the final image. It is best to save these for last because adjustments that you want to make that do not use the Global Light command might be difficult to weed out and correct. If you use the Global Light command for all Layer Styles, the styles can be collectively adjusted using the Global Light dialog box (Layer, Layer Style, Global Light), or they can be changed in the Layer Style dialog box that appears when you select any effect from the Layer Style submenu.

Caution

If you change the angle of a Layer Style with the Use Global Light box checked, it changes the angle for all other Layer Styles currently using the Global Light. To use a Layer Style at a different angle, be sure the Use Global Light box is not checked.

17. Save both the original file with all the layers intact and a flattened version. A variation to this is to save the flattened version and the layers all in one file. To do this, <u>S</u>elect, <u>A</u>ll, then <u>E</u>dit, Copy <u>M</u>erged (Shift–Cmd–C) [Shift+Ctrl+C], and then paste. This creates a new layer from all the elements currently visible.

Starting with the major changes and working toward the smaller changes, as outlined in the basic steps, ensures that you get the best big-picture results. Saving shadows and Layer Styles for later steps helps ensure uniformity. Although some image choices will be obvious when you morph two objects, other choices will be more creative. You might need to try more than one avenue in your alterations to achieve the most satisfactory end. In other words, you have more than one way to morph two objects; if the first attempt does not produce the expected results, use what you learned from the attempt to create a better image.

Morphing Software

Although morphing software is available to help you define intermediate stages between images, manual control with Photoshop gives you far better options and results. As morphing software more or less redefines an image by mathematics, nonlinear developments (such as the extraction of the dial and meter window) are not possible. Although the process might be painstaking at times, practice in Photoshop yields the best results and the best morphed images, without the added expense of another program.

 If you are trying to move an element from one image to another and the Opacity or Blending mode cause you to get different results than you expect, see "Merging Layers with Varied Opacities" in the Troubleshooting section at the end of this chapter.

CREATING A COMPOSITE IMAGE

A composite or collage image is simply a combination of images within one frame. Although these images can be very complex, most of the work is probably done in preparation for the individual images rather than in putting them together.

Again, there are no hard or fast rules for creating composites, but there are trends and tendencies. It is likely that you will create the composite using layers and that selection will play an important role in helping to isolate image areas. Layer opacity can help negotiate the look you want, and layer compositing controls (the Blend If sliders in the Layer Properties dialog box) can play an important role in making the images work together by smoothing the combination of elements. The most challenging concerns are making the images work together as far as lighting and composition are concerned, and making the layered images blend without appearing unnatural.

Although the number of steps for creating a composite is relatively short considering the probable complexity, making a successful composite is a complete exercise of one's Photoshop skills. Planning is an extremely challenging and important step because it defines the work you need to do in compiling the images and how you will put them together.

Use the following steps to create a composite image.

1. Plan your composite. Unless the image you create will be a collage, you should know approximately how you want the image elements to work together and what you want to include. Even for a collage, you need to at least know what images you want to put together. Although things might change when you start looking at the image elements side by side, plan as much of the image as you can.

2. Open the images you want to use in the composite. Start with the background first. This helps you decide the size of the document and gives you a base from which to build.

3. Prepare the separate images as necessary to make them effective parts of the composite. This might require selection, masking, distortion, sizing, alteration, deletion, or other manipulation of image elements. Do only the obvious big-picture alterations. For example, if a picture contains an element that you do not believe will be in the composite, eliminate it at this point. If two elements will be used as a single morphed object, create the element at this point. Do not attempt to shape objects to fit with each other in the composite at this point. That is easier to do in later steps when the images have been compiled to a single document as multiple layers.

4. Add the image elements one at a time to the background in their own layers to create a rough composite.

Caution

It is probably a good idea to save at several points during the development—a good time is after completing each layer addition or alteration in successive steps. If you fail to save and your computer crashes, you will lose all the work you have done.

5. Alter the individual layers so the image elements are positioned to work better together as a whole. The goal is to get images sized and placed appropriately to fit with other image elements as planned in Step 1. You might want to work with manipulation tools (such as the Distort or Scale transformations) to fit objects into place. Click the eye icon next to each layer in the Layers palette to hide and show image elements, so you can better determine proper placement.

6. Blend layers as appropriate. The goal here is to mask, feather, and blend elements so they are seamless and composed.

7. Add shadows and Layer Styles to create depth and separation. These effects should be used in overall consideration of the lighting in the image and as a tool to define the relation of the image elements (in other words, to add depth or help define elements).

8. Create a flattened version of the image and save a flattened version and the version with all layers intact.

An example will hopefully help drive home the procedure. In this case, the plan was to create an image from five elements to link together the concept of digital imaging and photography. The parts shown in Figure 32.9 were collected to accomplish this goal.

PART

VIII

CH

32

Figure 32.9
Each of these elements has a defined purpose in the image plan. These elements were not collected at random in hopes that they would fit together well and create something on their own.

Lens   Vortex Swirl   Light meter   Mouse   Mouse cord

The following steps were completed and roughly conform to the suggested general steps shown earlier.

1. The images chosen for the composite (refer to Figure 32.9) were created or opened. The base image was a scan made with an extra incandescent spot pointing at the lens as it was scanned and an aluminum foil reflector. Although this added some interesting highlights in red, the image still seemed a little monochromatic. The highlights in white seemed to need some color, so a color selection was made using Color Range. When the selection was made, it was feathered and filled with blue. An adjustment layer using Hue/Saturation helped redefine the blue to the green used in the final composite. This would be used as the base to gather the other images.

2. The other composite parts were added to the background in the following order: the vortex swirl, the cord, and finally, the morphed mouse/light meter (which had already been put together). Essentially, this places the elements in their order from the foreground to the background of the image.

3. The swirl was positioned over the lens element, then scaled/distorted to fit the reflective area of the lens. A second swirl was added to the lens and was shaped to fit the cone to lightly accentuate this effect (see Figure 32.10).

Figure 32.10
The image at left shows the first swirl placement. The swirl is then lessened in intensity by reducing the layer's opacity. This allows it to blend with the actual reflection in the lens.

4. The goal of using the swirl in the final image was to blend the cord into the lens as if it were coming out of a swirling vortex. Both applications were intended as suggestions, or quite muted effects. The layer containing the swirl on the lens element was switched to Hard Light blending mode and an opacity of 35%. The Blend If function (Layer, Layer Styles, Blending Options) was used to further mute the effect and blend the swirl with the existing color and tonality of the underlying element. The larger swirl was blended and used on a separate layer at an opacity of 4%, which keeps it barely visible.

5. The mouse and cord were placed so the mouse overlapped the cord end. They are not in the same layer to simplify their placement: after rough placement, the cord will need to be reshaped to fit where it leaves the mouse/light meter. Keeping them in separate layers actually saves some steps as the cord can be distorted separately from the mouse. Shaping the cord was taken care of using the Distort transform function (Edit, Transform, Distort) with a little rotation.

6. To fade the end of the cord into the swirl on the lens element, the Gradient tool was used with the Angle Gradient option to create a mask. With the mask loaded, the eraser was run along the cord end with the cord layer highlighted. The area was then deselected and touched up manually to blend with the swirls and the cord better, using a soft brush with the eraser.

7. To create the illusion that the mouse was floating out of the lens, a drop shadow was placed under the cord and mouse using the Drop Shadow function in the Layer Style dialog box.

Note

Although the mouse shadow fell satisfactorily, the cord shadow overran the lens swirl and fell inappropriately on the inner flange of the lens. If the intent was to make the cord appear to zigzag into the lens cone, only the first arch of the cord would cast a shadow in keeping with the apparent angle of the light. The drop shadow effect would have to be altered to create a more realistic shadow. To correct this, the drop shadow was rendered into a layer by highlighting the layer and choosing Create Layers from the Layer Style submenu (Layer, Layer Style, Create Layers). The shadow areas that went into the cone and under the mouse were erased; then the shape of the shadow was altered somewhat using the Distort transformation function to lengthen it into the mouth of the lens.

8. A bevel was added to the outside of the mouse to give it the appearance of being lit from below and behind, and to add some separation from the background. A little bit of green in the highlight color suggests a green spotlight that matches the green highlights below the lens.

9. A flattened version of the composite and layered version were both saved in the same image. See the result and a variation in Figure 32.11.

Figure 32.11
The result is completed using both the morphed mouse and a version of the original mouse. In some instances, the morphed mouse might prove almost too busy.

The most important element in the result is probably the drop shadow. Without that detail, the result would appear quite a bit flatter—would lack depth and realistic lighting.

Composites such as this can be made from any sources, as long as you can envision the result. Collecting the images to create the final composite will always take longer than actually putting the composite together, especially if you paid attention to the result you are aiming for from the outset and collected compatible elements.

TROUBLESHOOTING

MERGING LAYERS WITH VARIED OPACITIES

I have tried to copy and paste an image element from one image to another and I can see through the result. What can I do to get what I want as a solid rather than a see-through?

If the opacity and blending modes of your layers vary (and often they will when creating complex morphing effects), you might find that cutting and pasting from one image to the next doesn't get the results you thought you would. This might be because you are not copying all the image information from the original, or because opacities and blending modes are not as effective in the target image. The biggest problem will be if the bottom layer in what you want to copy is only semiopaque. There are several solutions to this, depending on the situation. Either you need to collect the information more effectively, or you create a backing to get the solution you need.

The easiest thing to do is probably to make a selection of the element and (Shift–Cmd–V) [Shift+Ctrl+V] to copy a merged version of the area. This will copy at 100% opacity unless the bottom layer of your image is semiopaque (less than 100% opaque). In the latter case, you can do several things:

- Flatten the image and then use the selection to copy and paste the area into the target image.

- Put a mat behind the morphed object to keep it opaque when it is transferred to the target image.

- Change the opacity in the layer causing the opacity to copy at 100%. If this solves the problem with no repercussions, it is probably the easiest and best solution.

The first procedure is pretty simple: Choose Flatten Image from the Layer menu, load the selection you made and saved for the area you want to copy; then copy the area and paste into the target image. This might not always get the results you need.

Creating the mat is only slightly more complicated. First, duplicate the image. You can do this using New Document from the History palette menu or Duplicate from the Image menu (Image, Duplicate). Use the Magic Wand to select the area outside the image area you are trying to retain. You might need to smooth the selection (Select, Modify, Smooth) or use Expand (Select, Modify, Expand) to make the selection fit tightly to the area of the image you are trying to make solid. It is best if the selection is slightly tight rather than too loose.

When the area is selected, create a new layer above the Background (if any) or as the bottom layer in the stack. Fill the selection with white. You can use other colors, but doing so might affect the result unexpectedly. Choose Layer, Merge Visible (Shift–Cmd–E) [Shift+Ctrl+E] with the Background layer hidden. The image area will flatten to the 100% opaque white layer and will now paste opaquely over other backgrounds.

PHOTOSHOP AT WORK: CREATE A MORPH AND COMPOSITE

Page 32 of the PDF workbook (found at www.ps6.com) includes all the images used in this chapter for the morphing and composite examples. The images show the composite I came up with as well as having the elements in separate layers. You can use these images to practice the compositing as outlined in this chapter. Try to imitate the results I got, or alter the goal and planning of the images. The point is to practice composite images and be ready to put that practice to work when it comes to creating your own work from scratch.

PART **IX**

CREATING SPECIAL EFFECTS

CHAPTER 33

Type Effects

In this chapter

CREATING EFFECTS WITH TYPE

The number of effects you can create with type is essentially infinite. Effects or filters and application of plug-ins can be combined in any combination to produce a different effect. However, getting the effect you want rather than just any old effect is not a matter of applying filters at random till you come up with the solution you want. Although many effects are simple, some can become very complex—if you want them to come out looking right. Guiding and tweaking effects that you want to create can become a challenge.

A lot of what you can do with type effects depends on the fonts you have. Most effects require larger, bolder type faces, and often a sans serif type works better than a serif type—if you want the type to remain legible. The wispy tips of serif faces can overcomplicate some effects and can make unexpected things happen—often to the detriment of the effect you want to create.

➔ For more information on typefaces, **see** "Type Control, Placement, and Settings," **p. 221**.

It is easy to overcomplicate the creation of effects so that applying the effect to different images is more complex than it needs to be. For example, you may record your actions while experimenting, discover something interesting, and then save every step you took to get there. However, often you will find that there are intermediate steps that really don't affect the result. It is best to simplify the creation of the effects as much as possible if you are going to get consistent results. Adding extra filter or plug-in applications that don't really need to be used to create the effect not only waste time in application but can cause unexpected complications. For example, when applying an effect you created to an image that has a much lower resolution than the one you developed the effect for might cause the results to be very different. Simplifying the effect might help simplify troubleshooting it.

 If you experience difficulty applying any effect directly to the type, see "The Trouble with Applying Effects to Text" in the Troubleshooting section at the end of this chapter.

WORKING WITH TEXT AS A MASK

The simplest of text effects are accomplished by using text as a mask. Although it is simple, you can accomplish a number of different effects, and it is a great way to make text stand out. Effects can be made using selection of the text area with the mask function of the Type tool; however, it might be best and easiest to control the results using layer masking. With the text in its own layer, the area behind the text can be filled (so the text masks out the background) or the text itself can be covered by a filled layer grouped with it. Filling the text with images or patterns makes it more unusual than a flat color fill or gradient, and if done with style can enhance the image as well as the message.

➔ For more information on working with layers, **see** "Creating Images in Layers," **p. 53**.

TEXT MASKS WITH THE TYPE TOOL

The mask function of the Type tool makes filling text easy. All you have to do is type in the text and fill it with the pattern, image, or color you desire. To access the mask function, click the Type tool and then click the Mask button in the Options bar (see Figure 33.1).

Figure 33.1
These two buttons on the Options bar toggle the Type tool between creating text and creating a text-shaped selection, or type mask.

After the selection area is created, the area can be filled with an image, pattern, and so on. If filled on a separate layer, this selection might prove slightly easier to manipulate and position. If filled with an image using Paste Into (Edit, Paste Into), the image itself will be movable and you will have some flexibility with placing, sizing, and distorting it as necessary (the image will get pasted into the layer with the selection as a layer mask).

Note

The same selection can be created without the Type tool's mask option but will require more steps and more tools. For example, you could simply create the type with the standard type tool in black, and then select the black area of the text using the Magic Wand (if in its own layer, with Contiguous and Use All Layers unchecked). This will create a very similar result (depending on the aliasing for the text and settings for the Magic Wand).

TEXT MASKS WITH THE MULTIPLE LAYER TECHNIQUE

The multilayer masking method is a bit more versatile, and might make it easier to combine a broader range of effects and combinations.

Use the following steps to create the multiple layer type of text mask where the text is filled with a chosen image, pattern, or color:

1. Open an image or new document in which you want to place filled type.
2. Do one of the following:
   - Open or create a pattern to use as the fill
   - Open or create an image to use as the fill
   - Select a color or gradient to use as the fill

Note

If you are using a pattern or part of an image as a tiling fill, select the area (for a predefined pattern this would be Select, All) and set as the defined pattern (choose Edit, Define Pattern). If you are using an image for the fill, select the image (or portion of the image) and copy to fill the buffer with the area that you will paste. If you are using a color or gradient, be sure the gradient is set up in the Gradient tool settings. If using a color, be sure the color is selected in the foreground swatch.

PART
IX

CH
33

3. Select the Type tool.

This can really be any of the type tools, but for the sake of the example we will be using the standard Type tool.

4. Select preferences for the text in the Options bar and the Character and Paragraph palettes.

5. Click the tool where you want the text to begin.

6. Enter the text.

7. Create a new layer (Layer, New, Layer) (Shift–Cmd–N) [Shift+Ctrl+N]. When creating the layer, click the Group with Previous Layer check box. When you click OK, the layer should appear above the text layer (see Figure 33.2).

Figure 33.2
Check the Group with Previous Layer check box to have the layer you create use only the solid parts of the type layer to apply additional effects.

8. Fill the layer created in Step 7 with the image, pattern, color, or gradient that you selected in Step 2. See Figure 33.3 for an example of the result.

9. Apply any additional desired effects and save the image.

The image can be saved in Photoshop native format or flattened for other purposes—although, saving as both might be the best for most cases, so you can easily go back and make changes. In this series of steps, you don't need to render type mask type, unless any additional effects that you apply in Step 9 require it. Leaving the type editable in the Photoshop file format will make it easy to apply the same effects to different words—for example, with use in creating a series of buttons for a Web page.

You can fill the type with anything that you can fill into the new layer, and then you can change the layers independently. In fact, you might find it useful to add additional grouped layers to further refine the effects.

Figure 33.3
After filling the layer above the type with your selected image, the image or pattern will appear only where the text is in the layer below. This is known as a clipping group.

This simple technique can lead to a huge number of variations when combined with other effects and filters. You can fill the text itself, as in the example, or fill the area outside the text (leaving a mask to see through to the background), or both. Figure 33.4 shows what the effect looks like in reverse, where the area around the text is filled, rather than the text itself. To fill outside of the text, simply activate the background layer and fill that with the image, pattern, and so on.

Figure 33.5 takes type fills one step further by filling both foreground and background. A drop shadow was created using a Layer Style to give the image a cutout effect. An inner bevel was added using the Layer Style function to improve separation.

Other alterations might include physical distortion of the lines of the text edges. In Figure 33.6, a Wave filter was applied to the image from Figure 33.2. The image ends up having a sort of quilt cut feel. This can be further embellished to create more enhanced effects. The next several sections explore some popular effects used with text and how to achieve them by isolation and combining text, effects, and filters.

PART
IX
CH
33

Figure 33.4
Really, this is the same as simply placing type over a background, but it is still using type as a mask, and might be considered the starting point for a number of different text effects.

Figure 33.5
Using both foreground and background fills will allow yet more interesting combinations and control. By controlling foreground and background in their own layers, you can easily separate effects.

Figure 33.6
The layered effects in clipping groups allow you to work with image areas independently. Here the shape of the clipping group itself is changed by distorting the text.

CREATING FLAMING TEXT

Building on the ideas of type masking and manipulation, this section explores the popular effect of creating text that looks as though it is on fire. Although you can use plug-ins and other text-effect creation tools, some of the best and most original effects are created by knowing how to do the manipulation yourself in order to create great effects from scratch. This seemingly involved effect can be created easily by following simple steps.

Note

Understanding how to create and control flames manually can lead to better application of the effect than you can create with a plug-in or action.

You can use a number of variations to create flame effects—some more or less realistic, and with more and less utility in creating legible text. The one shown here is perhaps fairly complex, but the best results are not always achieved through Actions. Some of this can be automated, but knowing how to work the techniques manually enables you to alter it to suit your needs far better than stops in an action.

The goal is to make the flame appear realistic. A simple way to create the gradient blending of the flame is by using tritone or quadtone effects. By applying distortion to the text, via the Motion Blur and Wave filters, the basic form for the flame can be created and then adjusted for your purpose. With manual control you will be able to vary flame height, variation, turbulence and color, as well as any number of other factors in creating your flame effect.

→ For more information on using Photoshop's Duotone mode, **see** "Creating a Duotone," **p. 528**.

Use the following steps to create a flaming text effect:

1. Create a document in Grayscale mode, and switch to Duotone mode (Image, Mode, Duotone).

2. Create a tritone using black, yellow, and a red of your choice. For this example, I used process black, process yellow, and PANTONE 171. The curves used are shown in Figure 33.7.

Figure 33.7
Although these curves might seem rather drastic, the result of the tritone is that they blend together fairly well.

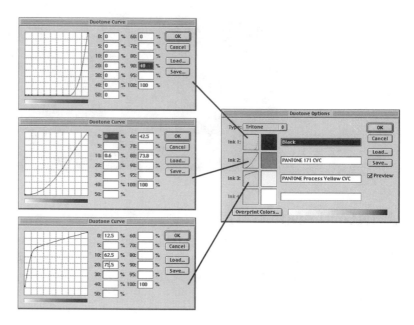

Tip

To shade the flame toward orange or red, strengthen the red curve and/or drop the strength of the yellow. You might also want to increase the brightness or intensity of the white, which can be done by weakening the yellow or removing it completely in the lightest tones.

Note

The tritone for the fire will be available on the book's Web site at http://www.ps6.com.

3. Choose the Type tool and type in the text you want to cast in flames. This effect will work fine with any kind of typeface, but it is suggested that you use a heavy, sans serif face (such as Arial or Helvetica Bold).

4. Save a selection of the text. To make the selection, (Cmd-click) [Ctrl+click] on the layer containing the type. When the selection is visible, save the selection.

5. Duplicate the text layer.

6. Render the type in the duplicated layer (Layer, Rasterize, Type).

7. Apply a motion blur at 90°. Choose a distance based on how high you want to make the flames and the size and dpi of the image you are creating. The greater the distance, the higher the flame. Figure 33.8 shows the effects of applying the Motion Blur filter.

Figure 33.8
The blur is shown here in conjunction with the original text. The vertical blur will give height to the flames, and the duotone will automatically color the flame according to the curve settings in the Duotone Options dialog box because the blur creates a grayscale gradient.

8. Move the blur vertically so that almost none of the blurred text shows below the baseline of the original text. Figure 33.9 shows the result of the alignment.

9. Apply a wave distortion (Filter, Distort, Wave) to the blurred layer. This adds rippling to the flames. Figure 33.10 shows the settings used in the Wave dialog box to apply to the sample figure (the original figure was 300ppi).

Figure 33.9
Moving the blurred layer up leaves less to clean up below the text while heightening the flame.

Figure 33.10
The Wave filter applies a natural wave effect to the flame.

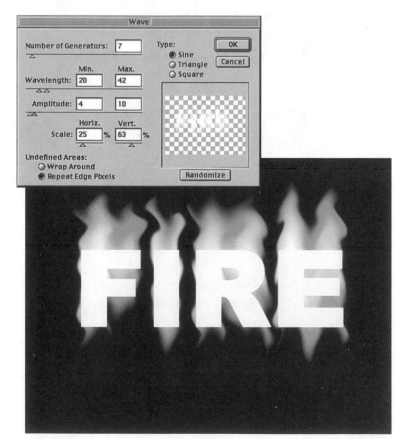

Tip

You might need to tweak the settings and click the Randomize button several times to get the best effect. You can also apply the filter several times and combine with other filters as necessary. For example, a slight blur was applied here after the first application of the Wave filter.

Note

The wave effect can be accomplished in other ways, but the Wave filter seems most consistent and easiest to control. You might experiment with other filters or filter combinations.

Wave Applications

The Wave filter has several settings that will need to be adjusted for the best effect. Number of Generators is the number of waves that will be used to generate the result. This number can be one (simple) to 999 (very complex). The greater the number, the more radical and complex the effect. The Wave length allows you to select the minimum and maximum width of the waves, and amplitude the minimum and maximum height. Again the range is one to 999. Horizontal and Vertical scaling allows you to limit the horizontal and vertical effect between zero and 100%. Wrap Around wraps edge pixels to the opposite side of the image, whereas Repeat Edge Pixels fills in information using the value for the pixels at the edge of the image.

The Type indicates the shape of the wave. Sine will be smooth based on sine waves; Triangle will be a similar generation, but quite a bit more angular than the sine type with more distinct peaks and valleys. The Square type is a hard geometric generation with no apparent blending between edges of the peaks and valleys of the waves. The Randomize feature regenerates the random factors for the wave when you click the button. If you are not sure you like what you see in the preview, try pressing the Randomize button a few times before altering the settings for the amplitude, generators, and wavelength. When you like what you see in the preview, click the OK button.

10. Create a mask to cut off the portion of the flame that doesn't go where you want it to. Essentially, you want to remove the flames that come down below the letters.

Note

Step 10 can be done in a number of ways. The steps I used were

1. Duplicate the original alpha channel (Ctrl-click) [Right+click] of the type selection saved in Step 4.
2. Invert the copied alpha.
3. Using the Gradient tool (set to Linear type) in the Darken mode, blend from the bottom of the letters to the top (from white to black).
4. To soften the edges, apply a slight Gaussian blur to the mask when the blend is complete. Figure 33.11 shows the mask.

Figure 33.11
This is a quick and effective mask for eliminating flames that extend below the letters. The gradient allows some of the spread of the flames to appear as they rise.

11. Load the selection created in the alpha channel in Step 10. (Cmd-click) [Ctrl+click] on the channel you want to load.

12. Press the Delete button. This removes the flame area from below the letters. You might want to duplicate the flame layer before deleting so that you can easily try other variations.

13. Make two copies of the rendered text layer.

14. Bring one of the rendered type layers to the top of the layer pile in the Layers palette and color it if desired. As the image is currently a duotone, only mixtures of white, yellow, orange, and black are possible—and these can be selected by using grays or tones, not the colors themselves. If you want to make other color choices, wait until you change the image to another color mode after it is complete (Step 15).

15. Place the second copy below the foreground layer and apply a slight Gaussian Blur (Filter, Blur, Gaussian Blur). This puts a fiery glow around the edges of the type. To make the glow blend better if it is too harsh, lower the opacity of the layer. Figure 33.12 shows the result.

16. Save the image in Photoshop native format so it can be altered if necessary.

With the steps completed to this point, you might want to convert the effect to another color mode. You might have to flatten the image for all effects to translate properly.

→ For more information on converting the duotone to another color mode, **see** "Printing Duotones," in the Troubleshooting section, **p. 550** and "Converting from Duotone to Grayscale or Color Plates," **p. 512**.

Figure 33.12
A slight glow around the letters will make it appear as if they are engulfed even if the original blur left some edges bare of flame.

In this example, you might try changing the duotone settings and colors. For example, you might want to try to work in some blue as a fourth color so the flames seem extra hot. Another possibility is changing the quality of the flame by using other filters or freehand painting. It is also possible to layer more than one variation of the flame generation to add complexity. Additional effects can be applied to the text as well. For example, in Figure 33.13 the type selection is loaded from Step 4 and the area is filled using the Clouds filter (Filter, Render, Clouds). After the fill, a border is created to define the edges of the type by adding a bevel using a Layer Style.

Many other effects will be possible when changing to a broader color mode. You can use the mask/selection created for Step 4 to help with a number of different applications and effects. For example, in Figure 33.14, the letters were turned into something resembling a charred material, and then the letters were covered with a copy of the flame using the Blend If sliders in the Layer Style dialog box so that the flame didn't just cover the text.

Figure 33.13
The Clouds filter will create a quick flame feel for the lettering while still in the Duotone mode.

Figure 33.14
The letters themselves are made to look as if they are burning in the flames that engulf them by application of a series of filters meant to distort the surface texture.

The effect of charring was created by a string of events. First, the type was copied to its own layer. Then, a series of filters was applied: the Difference Clouds filter to give the text some texture, the Crystallize filter to play up the differences in that texture, the Glass filter to make the effect more extreme still, and then the result was embossed. Applying a slight blur softened the harsh edges, and color was removed using Desaturate (Image, Adjust, Desaturate). Finally, an inner bevel (Layer, Effects, Bevel and Emboss) was applied to round the corners, and Levels was used to darken the letters to cinder.

You can create flames with more complex elements simply by selecting them as you did with the text and applying the same steps. This will, however, only get you the flame. Applying the flame to the image may take some creative manipulation of the elements in a similar way to applying spot color, including placing the flame in its own layer, using Blend If, and selectively clearing or blocking other layer information.

→ For more information on clearing and blocking layer information, **see** "Photoshop at Work: Replacing Object Color with a Spot Color," **p. 550** and "Selecting and Using Spot Color," **p. 540**.

CREATING CHROME TEXT

Chroming introduces specular highlights and distortion in a way that can be used to mimic a variety of hard surface reflections, such as stainless steel, glass, and ice effects. Highlights can be fashioned with a variety of tools, but usually calculations and filters perform the tricks. This technique uses multiple applications of embossing and curves to create highlights and shadow. Multiple and custom embossing creates layered highlights that mimic the specular reflectivity of chrome.

> **Note**
>
> Although there are actions included on the book's Web site (http://www.ps6.com) to aid in this effect (Emboss for Steps 3 through 11, and Chrome for Steps 12 through 16), I recommend that you go through the steps manually before using the actions so that you have a better sense of how the entire process works.

PART

IX

CH

33

1. Open a blank, gray (RGB: 128,128,128) image that fills most or all the width of the screen. The image for the example is 640×260 pixels.

2. Use the Type tool to add the type that you would like to chrome. It should be black type in its own layer.

> **Tip**
>
> Instead of working with the sizing of the type to get it to fit the screen, use any point size, and then use the Transform command (Edit, Transform, Scale) to size the type to the image. The type will remain editable even after scaling.

3. Save a selection of the original text. To do this, (Cmd-click) [Ctrl+click] on the layer containing the type to select the type, and then choose Save Selection from the Select menu.

4. Duplicate the Type layer two times.

5. Change the color of the top layer to 50% gray. To do this, click that layer, then switch to the Type tool, and click the color swatch on the Options bar. Change the color to 50% gray (in Lab color that would be 50,0,0—probably the easiest way to enter this).

Note

Many additional options for changing color of the type will exist if the layer has been rendered, and any other method can be used to change the color of the type.

6. Change the color of the type in the middle type layer to white. To do this, click that layer and then change the color swatch on the Options bar to white.

7. Offset (Filter, Other, Offset) the white layer up and left by 5 pixels (–5,–5).

Note

This can vary in direction and distance if you want to create variations on this effect.

8. Change the color of the type in the bottom layer to black.

9. Offset the bottom layer down and right by 5 pixels (-5,-5). The offset should be in the opposite direction of the movement in Step 4.

Note

The distance can vary in the offsets between Steps 4 and 8, but movements that are equal seem to work best.

10. Flatten the image. Figure 33.15 shows the result to this point.

Figure 33.15
This is a process of manual embossing, which works in the same way as the emboss filter. Being able to do this step manually rather than just using the filter opens up a number of additional possibilities.

11. Apply the Gaussian Blur filter. In this example, a blur radius of 8.5 was used.

Note

More blur adds to the depth of the result and makes the effect less crisp. This is more of a preference rather than a good or bad thing.

12. (Cmd-click) [Ctrl+click] on the type selection saved in Step 2 to load it.

13. Apply the curve pictured in Figure 33.16. This should achieve effects similar to those pictured. The results will vary depending on the typeface you have chosen.

Note

You can experiment with the curves to change the effect. For example, you might want to use more or less frequent waves and alter the amplitudes. More frequent waves and greater amplitude emphasize and exaggerate the effect.

Figure 33.16
In applying the curves, the goal is to keep the midtones light (chrome is a light silver color), so the center of the curve should be high for RGB (as pictured) or low for Grayscale (invert the curve).

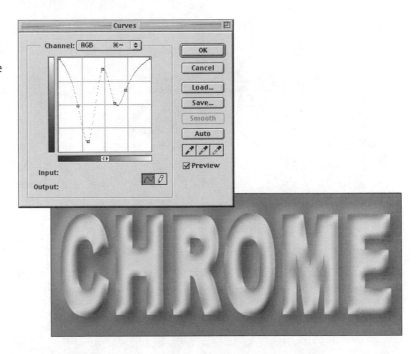

14. Apply the Emboss filter. The settings for this example were 135°, 7, and 245%. The result appears in Figure 33.17.

Figure 33.17
The goal of using the Emboss filter at this point is to accentuate the effect created by the manual embossing (Steps 3 to 11).

15. To increase the effect, apply Gaussian Blur, at about one third the radius applied in Step 11.

> **Note**
>
> The purpose of this step and the blur is to soften the chrome effect somewhat in the final result. You can choose to skip this step and go on to Step 16. If you think the chrome is too harsh after applying Step 16, you can return to the previous state (Cmd-Option-Z) [Ctrl+Alt+Z] and then apply Step 15 to compare. Comparison is aided by taking a Snapshot of the image after Step 16, before the undo.

16. Apply the curve as pictured in Figure 33.18. This should achieve effects similar to those pictured in the result.

Figure 33.18
The goal of this curve is to maintain and emphasize the light appearance of the chrome while adding some specular and reflective qualities.

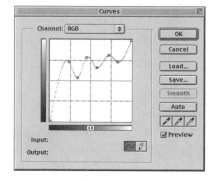

17. Cut and paste. This places the chrome type on its own layer. You can now copy the type to another image, replace the background, or apply additional effects.

Multiple application of the Emboss and Gaussian Blur filters and curves helps to create, accentuate, and isolate highlights. Defining highlights using the contour of the type helps the highlights and shading conform to the proper shape. The wavy curves take advantage of the blurred tonal areas by redefining them as a series of highlights and shadows to mimic the specular effect of shiny metal.

→ For more information on curve variations, **see** "Editing Selections," **p. 112**.

This technique has a number of applications you can create either by varying the parameters of some of the filter applications described in the steps or changing the steps entirely. The goal in any case is to create highlights and tonal variation by applying a series of filters meant to emphasize the existing shape of the type. The chrome curves are just examples of what you might do to create these highlights. Calculations might be used to create similar effects in the channels by combining masking effects. Using the Displace filter might help create offset and depth effects. The technique you use is more of a preference in the way you like to work than an absolute hard fast method.

An easy variation on this is to add color to the type during Steps 3 to 11 where you are creating the manual emboss. This is part of the advantage of making the initial emboss manually, as you cannot colorize the type using the Emboss filter. Any of the type layers colored anything other than a grayscale will infuse the image with tinged highlights, adding some color to the mix.

Figure 33.19 shows the chrome effect used with an image. To unify the image, layers of color grouped with the type were added over the chrome type and filled with color borrowed from the image. Using Blend If sliders in the Layer Style dialog box, these colors were targeted to grayscale areas of the type, enhancing highlight and shadows with the colors from the image.

Figure 33.19
The chrome letters from Figure 33.18 placed over an image result in a unique use for this type of text effect.

Application of other filters might produce yet more effects, such as brushed steel (for example, using noise with crosshatch, other brushstroke filters, Wind, or Motion Blur).

Tip

Don't rush effects. To create good effects, it is often necessary to use a series of filters rather than use one filter as the ultimate and immediate solution. If a quick fix works in some situations, that's fine, but don't be satisfied with mediocre effects.

Hand retouching can make these generated-image effects even better. One choice involves the corners of the letters in the chrome effect, as they might be a bit too square and harsh depending on the end use. They might look far more natural for your purposes when rounded.

CREATING ICE TEXT

Accentuation of the type highlights, texture, and background might turn the chrome effect on type described previously into a successful ice or glass effect. For example, varying degrees of any of the following filters, following the chrome effect in the last section, can produce different ice or glass-type effects when used to intensify the reflective highlights: Glass, Ink Outlines, Glowing Edges, and Bas Relief (as an overlay layer). These added effects can be employed by duplicating the chrome layer and applying the different effects, and then incorporating them with the Blend If sliders, opacity, and layer blending modes in the Layer Styles dialog box.

For this example, we will use combinations of the Glowing Edges (to create streaked highlights) and Glass (to develop texture and distortion) filters to create an ice effect. These will be applied to duplicates of the chrome layer created in the last section. The highlights generated can then be applied to type, which borrows from the image itself, so the ice element appears to take on the reflective quality of its surroundings.

Use the following steps to create an iced text effect:

1. Open an image to place some iced text over.

2. Create the text using the Text Tool. Note the point size you used for later settings.

3. Make a selection of the text and save the selection. (Cmd-click) [Ctrl+click] the type layer, and then choose Select, Save Selection.

4. Deselect (Cmd-D) [Ctrl+D] the text.

5. Emboss the text by choosing Filter, Stylize, Emboss. When you choose the filter, a warning will appear about rasterizing the type. Choose OK. The filter application will be affected by the resolution of the image and type size and imprint, so you will have to adjust the Height and Amount of the emboss to the image. Make the height about 1/10 to 1/20 the point size, and vary the strength of the effect with the Amount.

6. Create a layer under the embossed type and fill with gray. Choosing Layer, New Fill Layer, Solid Color will create the layer and allow you to choose a color for the fill. Then choose Layer, Rasterize, Fill Content. Drag the layer into place below the type layer on the Layers palette if necessary.

7. Merge the type and gray layer. Press (Option+]) [Alt+]] to select the layer above the fill layer and press (Cmd-E) [Ctrl+E] to merge the layers. Choose to Apply the mask when the dialog box appears.

8. Blur the merged layer. Choose Filter, Gaussian Blur. The radius of the blur will have to be adjusted to the size of the image. You want to blur the type, but not obliterate it. Note the radius setting for a later step.

9. Apply the first Chrome curve. See the settings for the curve in Figure 33.16.

10. Emboss the result. Use the same settings as in Step 5.

11. Apply a slight blur. Use the Gaussian Blur filter again but with about 1/4 the radius as used in Step 8.

12. Apply the second Chrome curve. See Figure 33.18 for the curve settings.

13. Apply the Glowing Edges filter. Choose Filter, Stylize, Glowing Edges. Again the settings will have to be adjusted to the size of the type and image. Variations in this step will have dramatic impact on the result, so some experimentation is required.

> **Note**
>
> Step 13 should create some highlights that can be used to gloss the ice blocks that make up the text.

14. Duplicate the result of Step 13. Click the layer in the Layers palette and drag the layer to the New Layer button.

15. Duplicate the channel created in Step 3. Click the channel in the Channels palette and drag to the New Channel button.

16. Blur the channel resulting from the duplication in Step 15.

17. Use Curves to redefine the edge of the blur in the mask. See Figure 33.20 for an example of the curve that might be used.

Figure 33.20
The edge of the blurred selection is probably best redefined using a steep curve. Viewing the alpha channel at the same time as the original type layer will allow you to see how the curve is refining the mask.

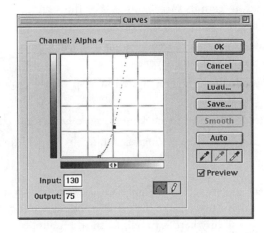

18. Choose Select, Load Selection and load the channel created in Steps 16 and 17.

19. Activate the Background layer by clicking on it.

20. Copy and paste to create a duplicate of the type area of the image in its own layer.

21. Duplicate the layer created in Step 20.

22. Group the layers created in Steps 13, 14, and 21 with the layer created in Step 20. To do this, click and drag the cursor over the layer link boxes in the Layers palette to link the layers, and press (Cmd-G) [Ctrl+G] to group them.

23. Shut off the layer view for the layers created in Steps 13 and 14 (see Figure 33.21).

Figure 33.21
To recount, there should be a grouping stacked on the type layer created from the background using the selection in Step 20. At this point, there should be a total of four layers sitting above the background in the clipping group.

24. Apply the Glass filter (Filter, Distort, Glass) to the duplicate of the type layer (created in Step 21). The purpose of this application is to roughen up the general area of the type using a glass texture.

25. Apply a Levels change to the layer. This can really be any application that will give the type some slight separation from its surroundings. For this example, the middle slider was moved slightly to the left to lighten the text.

26. Activate the layer created in Step 13 by clicking on it in the Layers palette. This will automatically turn on the view for the layer.

27. Change the Blending mode of the layer activated in Step 26 to Lighten (press (Shift–Option–L) [Shift+Alt+L]).

28. Activate the layer created in Step 14 by clicking it in the Layers palette.

29. Apply the Glass filter using the same settings as applied in Step 25 (press (Cmd-F) [Ctrl+F]).

At this point, the basic effect is complete (see Figure 33.22), but there is still a lot more that can be done to make it realistic or just change the effect to blend better with the surroundings. For example, another possibility here is to build a third highlight by duplicating the layer created in Step 13, and applying Steps 11 to 13 another time with different settings to create another specular dimension (see Figure 33.23).

Certainly, these are not the only ways to develop or create these effects. Building on known effects is a great way to make unique, complex solutions and save the effort of rethinking an entire effect from scratch. After you have reasonable results, your personal preferences can help lead the way to making other choices in creating the images you desire. This is why it is good to retain surprise effects recording actions, even if they are mistakes at the time.

→ For more information on ways to save your mistakes, **see** "Creating and Editing Actions," **p. 269**.

Figure 33.22
The basic effect is shown here next to the Layers palette for the image. Layers are related simply without additional changes in Blend functions and Layer Adjustments.

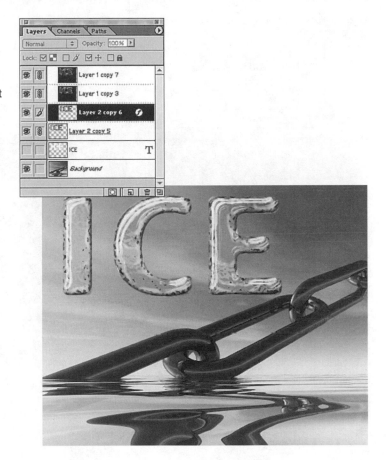

Figure 33.23
A somewhat more complex version of the same solution uses extra layers and a multitude of effects, blends, opacities, and so on. The settings for this image can be explored by downloading the PDF workbook for this book from http://www.ps6.com, page 33.

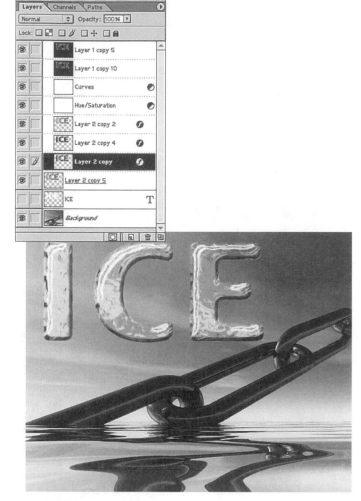

CREATING A TELEVISION TEXT EFFECT

An often-requested technique in newsgroups and listservers is making images appear to be projected on a TV or video display. Certainly, there are a huge number of potential variations for creating, working with, and finishing a TV-type effect. These range from working with different source materials, to using plug-ins, to working with a broad range of techniques. For example, a purist might project the image they want to have appear on a video display on a video display and photograph that to use.

Regretfully, the response is often to look outside Photoshop for some magic plug-in to solve the problem. The main part of the problem is creating the horizontal lines for the screen effect and to use as a mask in adjusting the image. There is no reason to buy a plug-in or look outside of Photoshop to accomplish this.

A simple application of the Patchwork filter can start you with a quick line grid from which you can build the rest of the effect. The grid can be made in seconds, and you can scale the screen lines to your needs. When created, the grid can be used as a mask to darken the lines for the video effect or over the image as a screen in the layers. First, make the grid, apply the grid to the letters (Steps 1 through 12), and then make the rest of the TV tube (Steps 13 through 18).

Somewhat more involved than simply creating an effect is the effort to fit type into an environment (Steps 13 to 18), as was attempted with the ice effect in the last section. No plug-in will create the text environment, as it is not a simple effect. In this case, the goal is to make the text look as though it is projected on a video screen, which means mimicking the projected qualities of the display. These qualities include shape, relative contrast, blurring, and the like. All these qualities have to be created for the image.

Use the following steps to create a TV-type effect:

1. Open a new document to the size you want—approximately the size of your final image. Leave 10% to 15% elbowroom vertically and horizontally, and make the background white.

2. Create a new layer (Layer, New).

3. Invoke the Patchwork filter (Filter, Texture, Patchwork). This will open the Patchwork dialog box (see Figure 33.24).

Figure 33.24
Settings of 7 (Square Size) and 14 (Relief) were used in the example. Use odd numbers for the Square Size to get thin lines; use even numbers to get slightly thicker lines. Odd numbers are recommended, as the width and strength of the line can be adjusted later (Step 6) and the thin lines might be a benefit.

4. Set the Square Size and Relief for the filter. The results of the settings will appear in the preview.

Note

As the background is white at this point, there will be no variation in the Patchwork relief. If you attempt to do this over a background of some sort, you might have difficulties as the filter randomizes the relief based on tonality.

5. To eliminate the vertical lines, apply the Motion Blur filter at high intensity and 0° angle. See Figure 33.25 for the result.

Figure 33.25
The distance has to be only a few pixels to make the effect work, but to ensure there is no problem with consistency, use a high distance setting. Simply push the slider all the way to the right (999)—unnecessary, but effective.

6. (Option) Adjust the vertical blur of the lines using the Gaussian Blur filter to blur the lines and Curves to redefine the falloff. Figure 33.26 shows the curve used in defining the lines in Figure 33.25. This choice leaves a hard falloff from black but still provides a slight darkening in the transition area.

Figure 33.26
The result in Step 3 can be used as is, but the video effect can be adjusted at this point to define the thickness of the lines and how you want them to appear to blend with the image. To adjust the lines, use Gaussian Blur, and then redefine the shape of the lines using Curves.

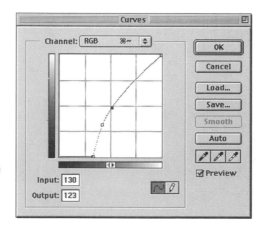

7. Copy the layer to a channel so it can be used as a mask. With the layer active, Select All (Cmd-A) [Ctrl+A] and Copy (Cmd-C) [Ctrl+C]. Create a New Channel (Choose New Channel from the Channels palette menu) and Paste (Cmd-V) [Ctrl+V].

8. Change the Blending mode of the layer with the horizontal lines to Darken or Multiply, or adjust the Blend If sliders in the Layer Style dialog box, so you can see through the white portion of the layer (you might want to blend the grays as well). Blend If will give you slightly more control over the result.

9. Choose the Type tool and insert the type you want to show on the video screen. Select any color for the text except white or black. White will not show up on the white background, and black will defeat some of the purpose and effect of the black video lines. A midtone will work best for most purposes.

10. Center the type if it is not already centered. This can be done by linking the horizontal lines layer and the type layer then selecting horizontal centering for linked layers (Layer, Align Linked, Horizontal Center). The image should look something like Figure 33.27.

Figure 33.27
The horizontal black lines provide a video tube type of video effect. The basic effect is complete at this point, but there are a number of revisions that can be made to improve the results.

PART

IX

CH

33

11. As a variation on this effect, you can apply Motion Blur to the text at 0° to mimic some of the video blur that tends to occur on video displays.

12. Shape the TV tube. There are a number of ways to accomplish this. A simple one is to draw a selection that encompasses the area you want to keep, and fill the outside area. This can be adjusted with a Gaussian blur and curves (again to define the falloff) and can be used in combination to define the effect (see Figure 33.28).

Figure 33.28
The result is actually made up of two tube edges. The first edge is the hard edge (called Tube Edge in the Layers palette), and the second is a blurred edge that helps shape the curvature of the tube (Blurred tube edge).

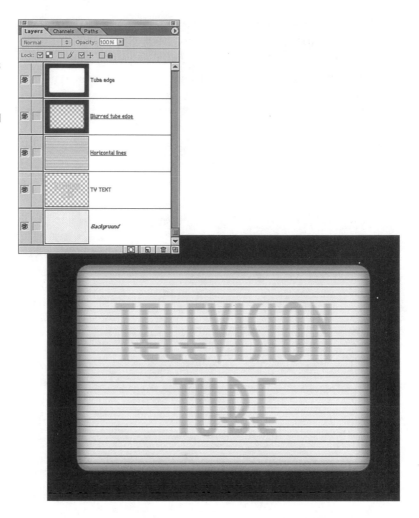

Tip

If trying to imitate the look of a real TV tube and you want the TV to look older, make the shape of the tube with a greater curve. Some very old TV tubes were actually round.

13. (Option) Flatten the image and apply the Spherize filter to make the tube bulge and shape more like a TV tube. For this example, the Spherize filter (Filter, Distort, Spherize) was set to +25°. See the result in Figure 33.29.

Figure 33.29
Use the preview on the Spherize filter to determine whether the canvas size needs to be increased before accepting the changes. If the whole area of the tube isn't affected in the preview, the canvas size needs to be increased. Set the background color to the color of the area around the tube before increasing the size.

After the video lines are defined, they can be used in a variety of ways to create TV-type effects. For example, the text can be used alone as video lines by masking (with the selection saved in Step 7). Simply copy the type layer, load the mask, and press Delete. This cuts the video lines out of the text, for the result as pictured in Figure 33.30.

Figure 33.30
The background was replaced with black so this type would show up better.

The effect completed in this section can obviously be used for more than just text. The line effect and screen edge can be extracted and applied to other images, it can be converted to an image frame, and so on. Figure 33.31 takes the example one step further, by introducing a background image and making the lines tighter. A drop shadow is added to the type, and a motion blur of a few pixels was added to the image. The rounding of the tube was increased to make it seem more like an old, raw TV image.

Figure 33.31
Blurs in the TV effects serve to soften the image and imitate the lack of sharpness on most displays. Coupled with other effects and a drop in contrast, the results here and in the color section do a reasonable imitation of a real display.

TROUBLESHOOTING

THE TROUBLE WITH APPLYING EFFECTS TO TEXT

I am trying to apply effects to some text I placed in an image and I am not able to. Many filters and functions are not available. Why won't Photoshop let me work with text?

Adobe has provided dramatic improvements in Photoshop's ability to handle type, and currently with this ability there are some limitations. One of the greatest improvements is the ability to keep type in the original vector form. This makes it resolution independent, and greatly improves the printed result of type placed in Photoshop.

The downside to this is that unless the type is the type that needs to be rasterized before, many effects (filters, adjustments, and freehand tools) can be applied directly to the type. However, you may not want to rasterize the type to retain editability and sharpness.

A workaround is possible for many effects—which means to simply to create a clipping group with the type at the bottom. In this way, you can apply adjustments (via New Adjustment Layer, using Group with Previous Layer) and apply freehand coloring. However, this still leaves out application of the multitude of filters.

Your only course when applying filters is to rasterize the type. If you have to make a change in the text after it is rasterized (say you discover a spelling error), you'll have to redo the effects you created. To avoid having to redo what you've already done, you'll want to do two things:

1. Duplicate the text layer before rendering the type.

2. Record your actions for the steps you take after rendering to adjust the type.

Duplicating the Type layer will help you start from exactly the point where you rasterized without reverting in the history. Recording your actions from that point will help automate reapplying the effects to the type that you changed so that it is easy to repeat the results.

This is one case in which recording your actions really helps save time, as rebuilding an effect and remembering what you did will be difficult and time-consuming—and just recording the action is such an easy precaution. The action you record may well be one that you can just discard when you are done with the image, as it may be good only in that one situation. Start recording as soon as the layer is duplicated.

PHOTOSHOP AT WORK: UNDER/OVER TEXT WARP

A relatively simple way to apply text effects and keep the text editable is to use the Text Warp feature. Although simple in application, this feature can be used to create relatively complex effects while maintaining text editability.

In this exercise, the object is to create a 3D-text effect by wrapping two lines of text around one another. The trick here is to use layer masking to block out the text in the places you don't want it to appear rather than rasterizing it.

Use the following steps to create the effect:

1. Create a new image (640×300 pixels at 72dpi).

2. Choose the Type tool.

3. Click the Type tool on the image and create the following line of text: The type going over from the bottom. I used a blue color and 30-point type in the example.

Note

The point size of your type may be very different, depending on the typeface that you choose. Make the type fill most of the width of the image.

4. Click the Commit Any Edits check mark on the Options bar.

5. Click the Type tool on the image again to create a second type layer, and type in the following: The type going under from above. I made this type orange and 30-point as well.

6. Click the Create Warped Text button on the Options bar. This will open the Warp Text dialog box.

7. Change the settings for the dialog box as follows: Select Arc, choose the Horizontal option button, change Bend to –50, Horizontal to +40, and Vertical to +10.

8. Activate the blue-type layer by clicking it in the Layers palette.

9. Click the Create Warped Text button on the Options bar.

10. Change the settings in the dialog box as follows: Select Arc, choose the Horizontal option button, change Bend to +50, Horizontal to –40, and Vertical to –10.

11. Position the type layers so that they overlap (see Figure 33.32).

Figure 33.32
The orange type should lie over the blue type and the arcs should intersect at two points as shown.

12. Duplicate the orange-type layer and the blue-type layer.

13. Stack the layers in the following order (from bottom to top): Background (1), blue (2), orange (3), orange (4), blue (5).

14. Group Layer 2 and 3.

15. Group Layer 4 and 5.

16. Make a selection of the left half of the image using the rectangular Marquee tool.

17. Click Layer 3 and make a layer mask from the selection to reveal the selection (Layer, Add Layer Mask, Reveal Selection).

18. Click Layer 5 and make a layer mask from the selection to hide the selected area (Layer, Add Layer Mask, Hide Selection).

19. Double-click Layer 3, and add a drop shadow when the Layer Styles dialog box appears. Use the following settings: Blend Mode: Multiply; Opacity: 50%; Angle: 120; Distance: 26; Spread: 7; Size: 9. Close the dialog box by clicking OK.

20. Copy the Layer Style (Layer, Layer Style, Copy Layer Style).

21. Click Layer 5 in the Layers palette to activate it.

22. Paste the Layer Style to the layer to create a drop shadow. See the results in Figure 33.33.

Figure 33.33
The arc of the text lines should appear to wrap around one another as shown here. Note the setup of the layers in the Layers palette to be sure you have this set up correctly.

The masking and layering confine the effects of the drop shadows and determine what layer information is revealed. The drop shadows create separation of the text lines to make one line of text appear to be first in front of and then behind the other line.

This effect can get even more complex if you add effects to the text layer itself. It becomes increasingly difficult to control the masking and layering. If you've had success with the basic example, add a bevel to the type layers in Steps 3 and 5 and attempt to get the results pictured in Figure 33.34. The bevel creates the need for some additional layering.

Figure 33.34
The Layers palette should give you a clue as to what you need to do here to solve the problem created by beveling the text.

USING FILTERS AND PLUG-INS

In this chapter

A General Approach to Using Filters

In Photoshop nothing is more impossible than trying to explain the proper use of a filter. Filter applications vary, depending on settings and on the images they are applied to. The Filter menu is broad and expandable. Considering these possibilities, a meaningful discussion of the use of each specific filter is out of the scope and page count of even a book this large. The fact is, you could examine a single filter and its application to various images for days, and other than the calculations used in applying the effect, you would probably not come up with much that could be considered definitive.

The reason it is so difficult to explain the proper use of filters is that most filter tools are meant for creative purposes. The exception to this are the filters discussed in the context of repairing images in Chapter 29. There isn't one proper way to apply any filter—even those I point to as most useful—because there is always one or another creative use that falls outside the path of usual practice.

→ For more information on the most useful filters, **see** "Applying Filters to Improve Images," **p. 617**.

My perspective on filters is that they can be fun, and that they are here for when you have time to play and discover what they can do. If you get lucky, you can come away from a session of playing with filters having developed a unique effect that might be applicable to an image in the future. However, luck can be tempered by direction and approach. There are ways you should and should not use filters.

This chapter will give you a good sense of when to use filters (if at all) and which filters give you the most mileage. The chapter also provides a step-by-step example in the Photoshop at Work section at the end of the chapter that shows you a way to use multiple filters in combination to create an otherwise very complicated effect.

When Should You Not Use Filters?

In newsgroups, discussion lists, and forums, someone is always looking for the magic filter or plug-in that will make everything right in an image. Regretfully, there will probably never be a point when the "Read My Mind and Do It for Me" plug-in comes into vogue. The fact about filters is that they perform a distinct mathematical function, yet that function can affect different images and image types in inherently different ways. They will not do anything magically, just like the Magic Wand will not magically select what you think it should. Although some filters—such as the noise filter—have fairly specific uses, most require experimentation to get any viable results, and all can be used creatively.

You should not use a single application of filters in hopes of righting all that is wrong in an image or to create the ultimate effect. If you can apply a single filter, there is a good chance everyone who owns Photoshop can do the same. Although the results might be interesting—and there are probably exceptions to this filter rule—your application of a single filter will be the same as anyone else's—the same old effect. Although singular effects might accomplish a correction goal, combinations of filters, or at least filters in combination with masking, will often improve results.

Unless you are intentionally doing experimentation with a filter and its effects, you should probably not apply it on a completely random hit-or-miss basis where you keep applying filters till you get an effect you like. You could spend quite a bit of time on the hit-or-miss approach, allowing the applications to swallow days and weeks of applying the effects, hoping, and then ultimately clicking Undo.

Tip

> When experimenting with filters, record your actions. There is no telling when you'll hit on a cool combination by accident and produce a great effect that you'll want to duplicate—even if it ends up being wrong for the image you are working on. By recording the action, you'll be able to figure out what you did and save the steps to help you reproduce that effect when you do need it. If you do something you want to remember, stop and take a few notes, including the size and dpi of the image, and anything you need to remember about producing the effect. You're better off taking notes when it is fresh in your mind.

EFFECTIVE USE OF FILTERS

A better approach to using filters is to have a goal in the filter application, and then set out with filters that you know will approximately achieve the effect. Generally, filters will be used in groups to accomplish effects—or effects—that you want to use. For example, the type effects described in Chapter 33, "Type Effects," are not created from a single application of a single filter (or plug-in). Usually, these effects are the result of hours of experimentation and refinement of multiple filter applications. Often the refined result will end up being successful in application to the individual image you are applying the effect to—at least in attaining the desired results. The idea is that many filters will require adjustment with other filters to attain a finished effect. The finished effect often requires adjustment and experimentation.

➔ For the examples of filter application referred to previously, **see** "Type Effects," **p. 721**.

Knowing what filters can do individually is important to directed experimentation (where you have a specific goal). If you have no idea what a filter does—or how it will react—you will be somewhat in the dark when it comes to applying it. You don't want to start experimenting with a new filter when you are close to achieving an effect.

EXPERIMENTING WITH FILTERS TO LEARN THEIR USES

An alternative method to learning filters is to separate your filter sessions into purely experimental sessions and those in which you are trying to achieve an effect with known filters. By known filters, I mean those you are confident using. In the purely experimental sessions, take a filter—just one—and learn what it does by application and experimentation. Open an image, and apply the filter. Be sure the Preview box is checked, change the settings, and see what effect the filter has with the varied settings. Close that image, open another image, and apply the filter again. Apply the filter with and without selection to confine it to a specific area, and with and without feathering on the selection. Preferably, the images used for experimentation should be very different.

As you develop an understanding and a style with each of the filters, you take away another creative tool which helps you create effects in Photoshop. Although the result is calculable (mathematically), the result is not always clear-cut or intuitive—especially in the case of more radical filters—until you gain experience with what the filter can do. A simple grid comparison in a book will not do the possible variations justice, especially considering that it is often a combination of filters and not a single filter that produces desirable results. Learning filters is an ongoing process, like learning any of the other Photoshop or ImageReady tools, but perhaps somewhat more challenging. The filters can be more complex in that different filter settings may produce radically different image results. Experience with using each filter will make use more intuitive and friendly—although you will probably still often be surprised.

USING FILTERS FOR SPECIFIC EFFECTS

After you have some filters under your knowledge belt, and you have some idea where they can lead, then it is time for more directed experimentation. Decide on the effect you want to create and set out to manufacture that from known properties in the filters you understand and have learned through experimentation.

My method for directed experimenting with filters is the following:

1. Decide on an effect that you want to attempt.
2. Open Photoshop. (It is best if all other applications are closed.)
3. Raise the number of History states to 50.
4. Open an image.
5. Create a new action and begin recording.
6. Apply filters, masking, tools, and so on until you achieve the desired effect.
7. Take snapshots to record unexpected and desired results.
8. Take screenshots to store a freeze-frame of the History and Actions palettes after each series of 50 moves or so. (An option here is to increase the number of states stored in the History palette.)
9. Pause the recording during application of tools that you can summarize by description (such as, make a selection of the main subject). This keeps the recording focused on the effect.

Raising the number of History states allows more flexibility in exploring. Recording the action as you work records what you did as closely as possible to the actual chain of events. Snapshots provide reference to image states you might want to return to. Screenshots are a reference to a history of moves that might otherwise disappear, and the point in the Action where the desired state occurred.

When you achieve the effect you desire, stop the recording and edit the steps down in the Action. If you don't achieve the goal, but find another interesting avenue by accident, you might explore the re-creation of that instead. The goal should be to create a reproducible effect. Sometimes you will find a more interesting direction along the way. Following the procedures outlined will help you in retracing steps back so the effect can be re-created.

→ For more information on editing actions, **see** "Creating and Editing Actions," **p. 269**.

Playing with images and developing successful filter effects can be fun and rewarding. Approaching filters with a direction and realistic expectations rather than a random hope for results will end up helping you develop a stronger ability in applying filters to images successfully.

APPLYING FILTERS TO IMAGES

Filters can be applied over the whole image or over a selection, or can be applied using the History Brush. Some depend on other settings in Photoshop (such as foreground and background swatch colors), and most react directly to available image information. The latter is the reason filters might have different effects in different images and image types.

→ For more information on applying effects with the History Brush, **see** "Working with the History Brush," **p. 254**.

There are many filters that come with Photoshop. These are grouped into 14 categories in submenus to attempt to clarify something about their results and/or application. Table 34.1 lists these categories and a brief description of each grouping.

→ For more information on individual filters or filter groups, choose Help Contents from the Help menu in Photoshop, or press (Cmd-?) [Ctrl+?]. This will open Photoshop Help in a Web browser. Select Search from the navigation bar when the initial screen appears, and type the name of the filter or submenu in the Search field, and then press Return.

TABLE 34.1   FILTERS AND THEIR USES

Filter Submenu	General Effects Type	Use
Artistic	Mimics effects created by using different media and media effects.	Special Effects
Blur	Softens an image area by radiating the effect of individual pixels.	Image Correction
Brush Strokes	Mimic painting effects likened to brush strokes.	Special Effects

PART

IX

CH

34

TABLE 34.1 CONTINUED		
Filter Submenu	**General Effects Type**	**Use**
Distort	Creates distortion in an image based on geometric patterns and mathematical shifts.	Special Effects
Noise	Generates or removes *noise* (or image interference) based on existing pixel values.	Image Correction
Pixelate	Defines differences in pixel's areas by accentuating groupings.	Special Effects
Render	Creates rendered and calculated effects with high complexity.	Special Effects
Sharpen	Controls enhancement of contrast in adjoining pixels. Can create the appearance of improved sharpness.	Image Correction
Sketch	Creates sketch-like media effects similar to Brush Strokes or Artistic filters but for hand-drawn media.	Special Effects
Stylize	Renders effects bascd on edge contrast combined with geometric and mathematical displacements.	Special Effects
Texture	Creates effects of applied texture. Somewhat similar to Pixelate effects in creating pixel groupings from existing color and tonal values.	Special Effects

TABLE 34.1   CONTINUED

Filter Submenu	General Effects Type	Use
Video	Filters to adjust video images.	Video-Specific Applications
Other	Filters that seem to fall outside the preceding categories.	Varies

Note

Although plug-ins are not an official category or subfolder on the filter menu, the bottom of the filters list is an area in which some third-party plug-ins will appear when installed. Their application varies widely, from applying digital watermarking (which essentially doesn't affect visible image information) to opening complex interfaces, which can dramatically alter your images.

This text will not attempt to describe each of the individual filters as experimentation is essential to understanding what filters do. Descriptions of individual filters can be found in Adobe Photoshop Help, which is a browser-based help system, accessed from the help menu in Photoshop.

To apply a filter, simply open an image in Photoshop, select the filter you want to apply from the Filter menu, choose the settings you want in the dialog box when it appears (if any), and click OK. There may be more to a successful filter application in the case of some of the more complicated filters (such as the Displacement filter), which require additional setup prior to making application.

USING FILTER PLUG-INS

To use plug-ins, you generally have to put only the plug-in in the Adobe Photoshop 6.0\Plug-Ins folder, restart Photoshop, and then locate the plug-in from the Photoshop menus. I say menus because there is more than one that a plug-in might appear on: the File, Import submenu, the File, Export submenu, or at the bottom of the Filters menu, and some plug-in installers create their own menus. The location of the latter type will be fairly obvious the next time you open Photoshop because new menu items will appear on the menu bar. The other plug-ins will fall into the Import/Export area if they have anything to do with managing import and export types. For example, scanning plug-ins will be found in the Import submenu on the File menu, as will digital camera plug-ins. Most other plug-ins—even those that create menus—appear at the bottom of the Filter menu.

Some plug-ins require installation using the proprietary installer, which either creates the plug-in which you will have to move to the Plug-Ins folder or which installs the plug-in in the appropriate directory for you. Installation might require a serial number.

PART

IX

CH

34

Plug-ins are available as freeware, shareware, and as dedicated program additions sometimes costing several hundred dollars. Function is usually metered in the price, but not always.

Purchased Plug-Ins

One thing to note about the plug-ins you buy is that most or all of the effects these create can be done in Photoshop with the current tools. It might be better to learn the tools in Photoshop than to purchase more tools: These will have additional manuals, additional controls, and additional complexities—yet more things to learn! You might be doing yourself no favors. Another interesting slant on plug-ins is that miraculously the best ideas from these get absorbed into new versions of Photoshop. I am all for support of plug-ins as they are the breeding ground for new features in Photoshop. If there is some function you definitely must have to help speed your work, see whether there is a plug-in to help. However, frivolous spending in hopes of a miracle cure via a plug-in will find you looking for a cure for new ills, such as a depleted pocketbook, and a way to find time to read all the manuals and learn the new tools.

To uninstall plug-ins, generally you will just have to remove them from the Plug-Ins folder.

→ For more information on currently available plug-ins, **see** the Web site: www.ps6.com.

CREATING AND USING BUMP MAPS

Several of the more useful, complex, and creative special effects filters use displacement (or bump) maps in their application. These can achieve some pretty miraculous results, depending on how the maps are developed and applied. Essentially, the filters read areas of light and dark in the maps and adjust the position of pixels in the image according to those light and dark areas. In the bump maps, dark areas cause negative displacement (down and right), medium gray holds placement, and light areas cause positive displacement (left and up). Displacement increases as areas of the map become lighter and darker from middle gray.

Seeing a bump map in action explains a lot more than just hearing a description of it. A great example of what they can do is creating not only the distortion but shadowing. This can be effective in creating ripples in fabric, such as for a waving flag.

Use the following to create a waving flag using a bump map.

1. Open a new document at 300×500 pixels.
2. Select 2 or 3 colors and create a flag. Here I used yellow, blue, and red and imitated a Colombian flag. See Figure 34.1.

Note

This might be a good spot for application of the Custom Shape tool to create stars or draw a quick logo.

Figure 34.1
You don't have to copy this flag. Create whatever type of flag you want. If this is your first time through the exercise, keep it simple so you can more clearly see and understand the effects.

3. Select All.

4. Cut and paste to a new layer (Shift–Cmd–J) [Shift+Ctrl+J].

5. Expand the Canvas size to 440×640 pixels using Image, Canvas Size.

 6. Hide the Background layer by clicking the eye icon next to its name in the Layers palette.

7. Select the Gradient tool from the Toolbox.

8. Click the Gradient Selector on the Options bar (not the arrow to open the gradient selector menu) to open the Gradient Editor.

9. Use the Gradient Editor to create a wavy gradient. See Figure 34.2 for an example.

Figure 34.2
The sliders on the Gradient Editor can be created by clicking below the gradient bar, and then clicking on the slider to alter the color. Click and drag to move. You are trying to generate a series of blended light and dark tones, which will control the vertical displacement of the flag. The lighter and darker the tones and the more frequent the fluctuation between light and dark, the more radical the displacement will be.

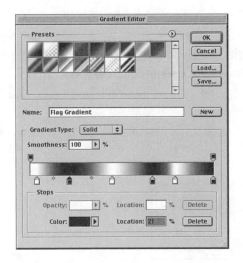

10. Save the gradient and click OK.

11. Create a new channel.

12. Apply the gradient you have created at about a 3.5° angle from left to right. In other words, click at the left edge of the image about halfway up and drag to the right to a point slightly higher. This angle can vary if you want; the idea is to give a little shift to the gradient wave. See Figure 34.3 for the result.

Figure 34.3
The application of the Gradient tool should create a slightly kiltered gradient fill for the channel.

13. Duplicate the channel to a new document by selecting Duplicate Channel from the Channels palette menu. Be sure the Destination Document you select is "new." This will create the channel in a new document as a multichannel image.

14. Change the new document to Grayscale mode (Image, Mode, Grayscale).

15. Save the image in Photoshop native format. This will be used as your bump map.

16. Close the bump map. This should return you to the flag.

17. Select the Displace filter from the Filters menu (Filter, Distort, Displace). This will open the Displace dialog box.

18. Enter 0% for the Horizontal Scale and about 12% for the Vertical Scale (see Figure 34.4).

Figure 34.4
These settings can be more extreme, and you can play with them to see what happens to the application of the map. Again, if this is the first time through, or if you want to duplicate the results as shown, keep to the settings given.

19. Click OK to close the Displace dialog box and the Open dialog box will appear. This is where you will choose a bump map to apply.

20. Locate and select the bump map you saved in Step 15. When you click Open, the bump map will be applied to displace the image pixels. See Figure 34.5 for the result.

Figure 34.5
The map is applied to successfully displace the original pixels. Next, we will apply shadowing to complete the effect.

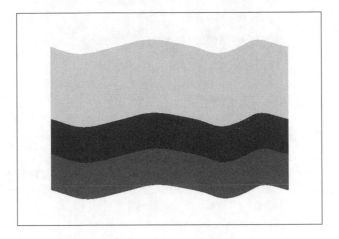

21. Open the Texturizer filter (Filter, Texture, Texturizer).

22. Press the minus button until you get a full view of the flag in the preview (see Figure 34.6).

Figure 34.6
Although it might not seem important to preview here, when you experiment with this filter and the results, previewing will be very important in getting the results you want.

PART
IX

CH

34

23. Select the bump map as the Texture by selecting Load Texture from the Texture pop-up menu.

24. Change the Relief slider to 45 and the Light Direction to Top Right (or Top Left).

25. Click OK to apply the bump map as a texture (see Figure 34.7).

Figure 34.7
The basic wave is complete here. Further applications of bump maps can alter the result further and perhaps improve results. For example, a straight white-to-black gradient (left to right), used as the bump map, would make the flag appear to dip.

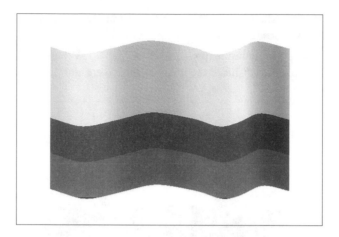

There can still be more to do to this depending on the application, resolution, and so on. For example, you can transform the result to make it better fit a sizing, area, or purpose in an image (see Figure 34.8).

Figure 34.8
The result here was attained by applying a very slight bevel and then using the Distort transform function to alter the shape of the flag even more. The pole was added by applying a bevel (using Layer Style) to a simple filled shape.

Tip

A similar shading effect can be created on the flag by using the Lighting Effects filter. To do this, you would load the gradient channel as the Texture Channel in the Lighting Effects dialog box after choosing Lighting Effects from the Render submenu. The Lighting Effects filter is a little trickier to use; you'll have to play around with the settings to get the result you want. A hint if you go in this direction: Use the Directional Light Type and aim it either horizontally left to right, or right to left.

TROUBLESHOOTING

I CAN'T SEEM TO FIND A PLUG-IN I INSTALLED

I have installed a plug-in but can't seem to find it in the filters menu. Where is my filter?

Be sure that you have followed the manufacturer's instructions when installing your plug-in filter products. Some of these products will require that the plug-in should be installed in different ways, and these might not be limited to simply copying a plug-in to the Plug-Ins directory (`Adobe Photoshop 6.0\Plug-Ins`). Be sure also that you have exited and restarted Photoshop if you have completed the installation while the application is running (not recommended).

If neither of the previous suggestions proves fruitful, try installing the plug-in again after removing/deleting the current copy from the `Plug-Ins` directory. If that fails, see Appendix C, "Your System and Photoshop," for more troubleshooting information.

PHOTOSHOP AT WORK: CREATING A SNAKE WITH FILTERS

A fun experiment with filters is to create a snake with the application of filters. This will create not only the shaping of the snake, but scales and contour as well. This can give you an idea of the type of thing that can be generated using Photoshop. The results of the experiment will end up more or less real, depending on choices you make in the filter applications and adjustments.

If you noticed in the flag example, the nature of gradients creates some interference and distortion in bump mappings. You can actually take advantage of this in the snake experiment.

1. Open an image that is 480 pixels wide × 640 pixels high.
2. Place guides evenly at even quarters, 160-pixel intervals vertically (160 pixels, 320 pixels, and 480 pixels from the top). These will serve as guidelines later, when using the Shear filter.
3. Place two additional guides at 120 pixels and 520 pixels, and then horizontal guides at 240 pixels, 190 pixels, and 290 pixels. These will serve as guides to start your snake shape. After placing all guides, the image should look something like Figure 34.9.
4. Open the Gradient Editor by selecting the Gradient tool and clicking the currently selected gradient.
5. Create a new gradient by clicking the New button, and then create settings as pictured in Figure 34.10. Close the Gradient Editor by clicking OK.

Figure 34.9
This is just a template for the steps that are to come. These guides will act as borders for your selections.

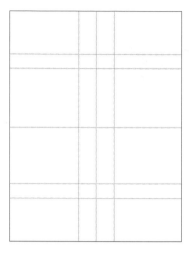

Figure 34.10
The end sliders are pure white placed at 1% and 99%, and the center slider is 99% black, and placed at 50%. The two mid-points are at 50%. Using 1 and 99 will make the result easy to select from the background white using the Magic Wand and 0% tolerance.

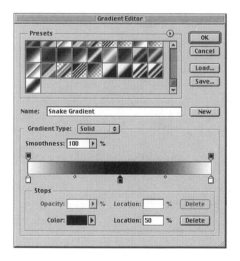

6. Make a selection of the perimeter of the box formed by all the guides you drew in Steps 2 and 3.

7. Fill the selection right to left using the Gradient tool. Use Snap To Guides to fill exactly from left to right. See Figure 34.11.

8. Open the Curves dialog box (Cmd-M) [Ctrl+M] to adjust the tonality for the gradient as shown in Figure 34.12.

Figure 34.11
After filling with the gradient, you will have created a bar. This will be used as the basis for the shape of the snake.

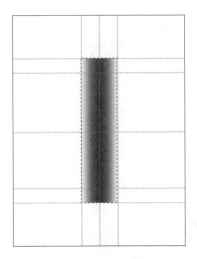

Figure 34.12
You could have worked with the Gradient more to achieve a similar effect, but I think it is harder to achieve. Set the Curve anchors to (0,0), (10,40), (20,60), (40,72), (128,90), (191,128), and (255,255). This creates a sort of center groove of dark and shapes the rest of the bar.

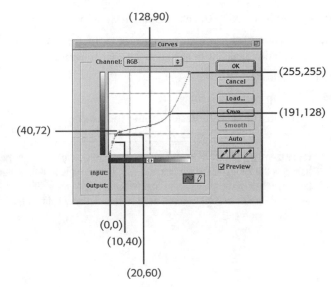

9. Make a selection of the bottom half of the image using the Rectangular Marquee tool.

10. Apply the Pinch filter at 50 (Filter, Distort, Pinch). This will change the contour of the tail end of the snake and add some very slight texture.

11. Choose Edit, Transform, Perspective and adjust the perspective by clicking a bottom corner handle and dragging it into the center (see Figure 34.13).

Figure 34.13
With the application of the Pinch Filter and the Perspective transform, the gradient bar comes to a point at the tail. You won't be able to see them here in print, but zoom in on your attempt if following along and you'll see some texture starting to develop.

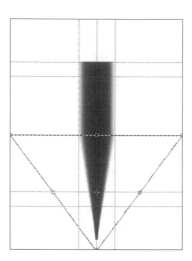

12. Apply the changes by clicking the check box on the Options bar.

13. Select the top portion of the gradient bar between the top line and the horizontal centerline. Use the guides again to help you make that selection.

14. Apply the Pinch filter at –40.

15. Select the entire top half of the image.

16. Apply the Pinch filter at 40. The result should look something like Figure 34.14.

> **Note**
>
> Every time I do this set of Pinch filter applications, I have to realign the top and bottom halves of the image—although I am not exactly sure why. To do this leave the selection of the upper half of the image active and switch to the Move tool, and then use the arrows to slide a few pixels to align. You will need to zoom in very tight on the selection line to see the exact alignment.

Figure 34.14
You can see the body beginning to take shape. When there is a head in place, the more complicated filter application starts.

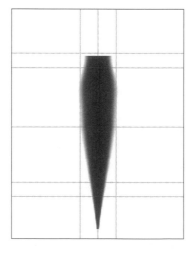

17. Create a new layer.

18. Choose the Elliptical Marquee tool, and with (Shift–Option) [Shift+Alt] held down, start a selection at the top center crosshairs. Pull the selection out till it snaps to the guides.

19. Fill the selection with black. See Figure 34.15 for an example of what you should have at this point.

Figure 34.15
If you don't fill the selection with black, there will be nothing on the layer and you might get an error when selecting the Transform command in the next step.

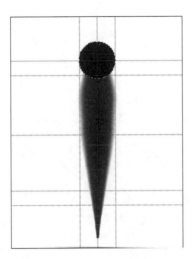

20. Choose Edit, Free Transform and enter these values on the Options bar: Y: 110, W: 80, H: 110. This will move up the ellipse you just created and make it an oval.

Note   You could just transform the selection in the previous Step using Select, Transform Selection, but you will have to fill this eventually anyway.

21. Apply the transformation.

22. Select the inverse (Shift–Cmd–I) [Shift+Ctrl+I] of the current area and fill with white.

23. Double-click the layer you are working on in the Layers palette and change the white This Layer Blend If slider position to 252. The layer below will reappear. This should look like Figure 34.16.

24. Change the blending mode to Darken.

25. Apply a Gaussian blur of about 15 pixels. Be sure the selection is still on the head area. This will feather the head area at the edges.

26. Test the gray value of the center spine on the snake and adjust the dark portion of the head to within a few levels of that using a curve (choose Image, Adjust, Curves). See Figure 34.17 for the adjustment I used.

Figure 34.16
This looks just the same as it did a few steps back in Step 20, but now the surrounding area is filled with white. Without filling that area, the blur in the next step would have blurred to transparent, and there would have been a lot more to do to control the shaping of the head.

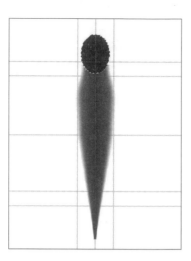

Figure 34.17
As you are following along with these steps, your adjustments should be very similar to mine. I am leaving the head somewhat darker to let it stand off some from the final result. You can make this match better for a better blend. Note the anchor on the curve at 127,127. This keeps the blended area from lightening.

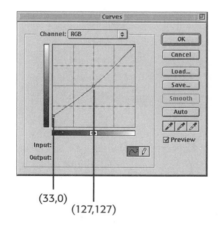

(33,0)

(127,127)

27. Merge the two layers by pressing (Cmd-E) [Ctrl+E] with the upper layer active. See Figure 34.18 for the results.

28. Choose Filter, Distort, Shear and manipulate the curves to look something like Figure 34.19. Then, apply the shear by clicking OK.

29. Create a selection around the snake using the Magic Wand and a Tolerance setting of 10. Click the Magic Wand on the white area outside the snake.

30. Invert the selection and then smooth the selection (Select, Modify, Smooth) by 3 pixels and contract it (Select, Modify, Contract) by 1 pixel. This will tighten the selection around the snake.

31. Save the resulting selection.

Figure 34.18
This is the completed snake shape. This will now be altered with selection and filters only.

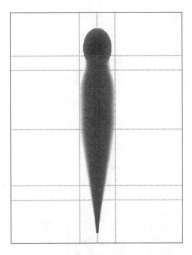

Figure 34.19
For best results here, you are going to want to try to anchor the head at the base using the 25% guideline. The rest of the shape should be controlled using the preview to create something interesting. If you get too wild, the snake will stretch out too thin.

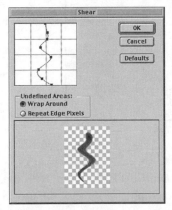

Note

At this point, I like to place the snake in its own layer. This is not necessary as you can do what you need to with the selection just created, but this makes it easier to control the background and results. If you do separate it, put a white background behind it in another layer to help you see what you are doing.

32. Open the Lighting Effects dialog box (Filter, Render, Lighting Effects).

33. Choose a Spotlight Light Type and change the settings to something similar to those pictured in Figure 34.20.

34. Click OK to commit to the changes.

35. Open the Lighting Effects dialog box again.

36. Select an Omni Light Type and change the settings and light placement to something similar to that pictured in Figure 34.21.

Figure 34.20
The potential exists for a lot of variation here. I chose these settings to create highlight effects and to color the snake, which was dull in black and white. To enhance the color, I set the Light Type color to blue and the Properties color to a lime green.

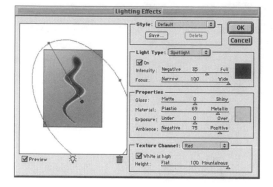

Figure 34.21
This application of light will only help bring out some of the texture that is developing. You might want to do more with lighting applications, but that can be done with other filters as well.

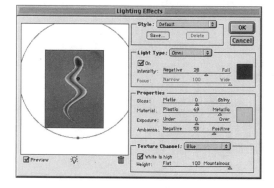

37. Apply the Lighting Effects by clicking OK.

38. Apply the Plastic Wrap filter (Filter, Artistic, Plastic Wrap) with settings of 9, 7, and 7 (Strength, Detail, and Smoothness) to emphasize some of the texture even more. See Figure 34.22 for the results to this point.

Figure 34.22
The Plastic Wrap filter will give a little sheen and contouring to the snakeskin at this point. Many other filters and techniques could be used to work with texture as well.

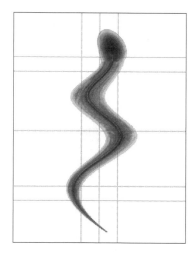

39. As a final step to shaping, a bevel and shadowing was applied through the Layer Style dialog box with the settings shown in Figure 34.23. The final result appears in Figure 34.24.

Figure 34.23
Beveling with these settings makes the snake appear more 3D rather than flat. Notice the bevel is all set to darken using multiply rather than the default settings that highlight one side and darken the other. This is an attempt to give shading and contour to the snake's sides.

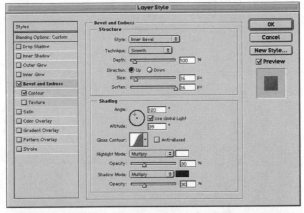

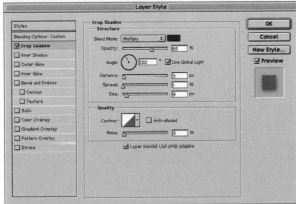

Figure 34.24
Although there is more that you can do to this, such as add eyes, a drop shadow, a background, and so on, I'll leave that up to you. The result of this exercise also appears in the color section of this book, where I added the eyes, drop shadow, and a background color.

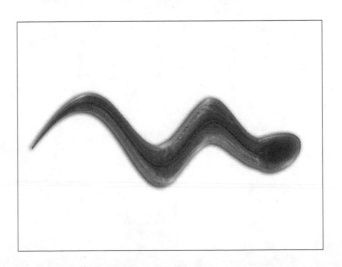

There are many areas where you can alter this example and experiment with the results. The best places are right at the beginning in making the gradient (Steps 2–9); shaping the width of the gradient bar (Steps 5–6); adding texture immediately after the basic shape is done (Step 27); creating the initial wriggle (Step 28); applying lighting effects; and enhancing the result at any point after that. There is a lot of room for creativity in applying filters and effects, and the more you learn about them, the more often you will successfully apply them to achieve results.

PART X

CREATING AND USING WEB GRAPHICS

CHAPTER 35

WORKING WITH WEB FILES

In this chapter

FILE TYPE CHOICES

File type choices for Web images are limited to those that are compatible with and currently supported by Web browsers. Although you can transfer any file type through the Internet, if the file type is not compatible with the browser, the image will not show up in the browser as part of a Web page. The browser will not display the graphic—at least not within the context of the Web page—because it is not built to handle the file type. Creating images that are compatible with browsers and that can be used broadly in Web pages is the primary focus of the next several chapters.

Because of this limitation, saving files for the Web really involves choosing either GIF or JPEG file format. The choice of which format to use is determined by the image contents of the file being saved. Use the following guidelines to determine which type of image you should use when saving.

Generally, you will choose GIF file format for saving, if the image meets any of the following criteria:

■ The image must have transparent properties.

■ The image is a simple RGB image containing 256 colors or less.

■ The image is currently in Grayscale or Indexed Color mode.

■ The image is intended to be an animation.

Choose JPEG if the image meets none of the criteria for the preceding GIF.

Note

The PNG format is not supported by all browsers. Although it is generally considered a Web format and has limited support via browser plug-ins, it is not yet an image type of choice. This might change in the not-so-distant future.

JPEG is the easier of the two to Web images to implement, because the file type can retain RGB color; GIF conversions might require finessing the color a bit. Although there is an advantage to JPEG in retaining image color, the result is somewhat distorted by compression. CompuServe GIF format offers limited color as the means for compression by limiting bit depth. Generally, use the JPEG format with full-color graphics and CompuServe GIF for limited color, like type over a flat color background without a drop shadow.

High compression in a JPEG file creates small full-color image files but does more damage to an image than low compression. JPEG compression runs on a scale of 0 to 12; 0 is the most compressed with greatest loss of image quality, and 12 is the least compressed while retaining the maximum amount of original image information. Regretfully, as the quality of the image goes up, so does the size of the resulting file. JPEGs with higher compression (less than 8 in quality) will probably show visible signs of image damage because of compression.

→ For more information on JPEG files, **see** "JPEG," **p. 329**.

CompuServe GIF (Graphic Interchange Format), often used for Web graphics, is an image compression format designed to speed transfer of images (specifically for the Web). Compression is lossless, but conversion to Indexed Color is not because there is only a maximum of 256 colors.

The GIF format offers more significant compression for limited-color images without apparent distortion. For example, a 6-inch×1-inch, two-color image with maximum JPEG compression (0 quality) will be about twice the size of the same image saved as a CompuServe GIF (3-bit, adaptive), and the GIF would look better. Good Web design will generally keep colors simple, and this fits well with the GIF scheme.

→ For more information on CompuServe GIF file types, **see** "GIF File Format," **p. 328**.

Either of these image types can be used in rollovers, tables, backgrounds, or any standard image placement on a Web page. Often, you will want to use them in combination on a single page, and it might be advantageous to combine them in image tables and even in various states of a rollover in certain circumstances. In the simplest sense, you might want to use GIF shims (or spacers) in a table to take advantage of transparency, whereas the table area itself is made up of JPEG slices to make the most of a color image you are using as a button. In a more complicated scenario, you might want to animate part of a rollover button in the Over state, in a button that is a JPEG in the Normal state. You would have to use a GIF to support the animation—and probably some careful slicing.

→ For more information on rollovers and image states, **see** "Constructing Rollover Buttons," **p. 796**.

→ For more information on juggling image types in an export, **see** "Working with the Optimize Palette," **p. 803**.

Be aware of the advantages each file type offers, and don't just dismiss the use of one over the other in all cases. There will be times when using each format is both sensible and desirable.

KEEPING FILE SIZES SMALL

You should strive to create the smallest possible files when creating images for the Web while still maintaining image quality. Smaller files load more quickly into a browser, and allow faster browsing of your Web pages. This gets the visitor to the content quicker rather than having them sit around waiting for it to load. Regretfully, there is a trade-off in consideration of quality when shrinking file size.

The smaller Web graphics are, the faster they load into a Web browser. This is a simple function of mathematics. Size does not necessarily mean physical dimension. The trick is to make your files as small as possible by choosing to save them in the proper format and keeping the pixel dimensions small enough to fit into browser windows. The trade-off is potential distortion in the images. Weigh the possibilities and potential for compression against the image integrity. This can help you make an informed decision to keep the file sizes small while doing the least damage to your image.

PART

X

CH

35

Why MAC FTP Uploads Change Size

Macintosh users might find that files uploaded to FTP sites change size from what they appear to be when stored on their Macintosh computers. This is because resource forks in the file are removed when it is stored on a Unix/PC Web server. These resource forks tell the Macintosh computer what a file is and control icon previews—which are then also dumped in the upload. As Windows relies on three-letter extensions rather than resource forks (that is, .gif, .jpg, and so on), the resource-fork file inflation is not apparent, unless files were saved from Photoshop with preview images. Files never get larger as they upload. Utilities are available to remove resource forks (BoxTop Software, www.boxtopsoft.com).

The size of your image file is a matter of numbers. The more information an image file has to carry, the larger the file will have to be. By reducing the pixel dimension to the minimum size (reducing the physical dimension), the image will be at its minimum effective size. By reducing the size further using compression (in the case of JPEG images), or reducing the number of colors (in the case of GIF images), images will be as small as possible and will transfer quicker.

Tip

You can check to see that an image you have saved is browser compatible by loading it directly into your browser. Simply open your browser, choose Open (this may be other variations such as Open File or Open Page, depending on which browser you are using), and select the file. If the browser will display the image by itself, and not in a page you have created, it is a problem with the HTML, not the image.

If you resize the image and take advantage of compression in the file type you choose when saving and still feel that the image files you are working on are too large, consider adjusting the cropping. Another consideration might be to redesign so the graphics are smaller. You can change the effective load size of an image by slicing out image areas and substituting a shim or spacer to hold the image space. These spacers take up very little room in a download, and used properly you can save a significant amount of size in a download without affecting the appearance of the image.

→ For more information on working with shims or spacers and tables, **see** "Understanding the Use of Tables to Place Images," **p. 836**.

Yet another option is to use a thumbnail of an image as a button to open a higher-resolution version of the same image. It is far better to shrink the size of the images to get file size down than to put the image information in jeopardy for the sake of compression by using too much JPEG compression or too few colors. Web images that look distorted and altered due to optimizing file size will not impress Web-site visitors.

 If you are having trouble getting consistent results when trying to optimize file size, see "Maximizing Minimum File Size" in the Troubleshooting section at the end of this chapter.

Web Image Resolution

In general, the resolution of all images saved for onscreen viewing should be set to 72dpi. This is true for Web images as well as those that are to be used in video applications. The reason for this is that 72dpi generally matches the resolution of your monitor. This resolution will give you a good representation of size for the graphic because it will actually appear when viewed at 100% on any screen. This will ensure that what you see will be close to what you get on a typical monitor.

> **Note**
>
> Monitors with higher resolution than 72dpi make the image appear smaller when displayed.

Essentially, what happens to your images on screens with higher definition is that they get smaller rather than blurrier, by conforming to the resolution of the screen. However, designing for higher resolutions (essentially, screens with more pixels) might make sites and images too broad to fit on more common screen sizes. It is still best to design for pages and images to go with them at approximately 640×480 pixels at maximum. Although monitor dimensions are often set higher than this (800×600, and so on), this leaves some room for placement of the browser window. As everyone might not run their browser maximized, adding allowance for the browser window is a good idea. Designing for the most common screen sizes and resolutions ensures that the greatest number of people can potentially visit sites and that the content will be the right resolution to display properly on the broadest number of systems and screens.

> **Tip**
>
> Always crop images as tightly as possible to keep file sizes small. If you need extra space around the image on the Web page, you can use a transparent 1×1 pixel GIF as a spacer, or control the image placement using a table in the HTML. Photoshop's new Trim feature helps you crop Web images tightly without losing any important image information.

Saving for the Web

With the Save For Web command, Photoshop gives you the option to compare up to four versions of the image, each potentially using a different optimization method—compression and dithering—to result in various file sizes. This enables you to make a visual comparison of the results before saving, so you can select the smallest image that still maintains the image quality you need. If your image contains slices, you can control each slice's settings and file format independently. In addition, you can output HTML, which will help you control precisely how the sliced image is pieced back together within the browser. Only the Save For Web function has the preview options and HTML export features. Although you can use Save or Save As to create your Web images, you will have to do it without previews and will end up writing the HTML for tables to control the image slices—which will be an arduous task. It is far better to take full advantage of Photoshop's abilities.

Use the following steps to save your images for the Web using the Save For Web function:

1. Choose File, Save For Web. The Save For Web dialog box is displayed. Choose the 2-Up or 4-Up tab to display multiple versions of the file (see Figure 35.1).

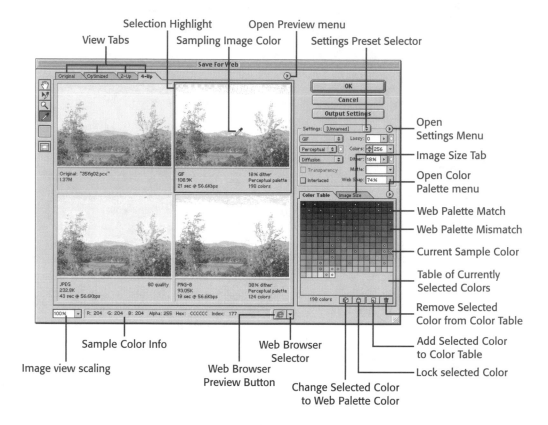

Figure 35.1
You can select different optimization settings for each of the image views. It might be a good idea to leave one of the views set to the original image for comparison purposes. However, you might want to use a single view for an uncluttered look at the result.

2. Select optimization settings for the image, consider options via previews and comparison, and choose Output Settings. See "Optimization Settings and Options When Using Save For Web" later in this chapter for more on these choices.

3. Each time you change any of the settings for optimization, look at the preview to. Ensure that the image quality is still acceptable. The goal is to maintain image quality while reducing the file size (displayed at the bottom of the view) to the lowest possible value. Any increase in lossy compression or reduction in the number of colors reduces image quality as well as image size.

4. When you are done making optimization selections and have decided on a best choice, highlight the choice by clicking the view that you want to retain, and then choose the Optimized tab from the previews.

5. Shut off the view for the slices (if any) by clicking the Toggle Slice Views button, and directly compare the original to the optimization settings you have chosen by clicking the Original and Optimized tabs several times in succession. This will allow you to directly compare the optimized to the original, like toggling layer views would.

6. If the optimized version is acceptable, click the OK button. This will accept the settings and open the Save Optimized As dialog box. If the version is not acceptable, you can adjust the settings for the selected file in the Optimized, 2-Up or 4-Up views, or select another view entirely. If you do not accept the changes, return to Step 3.

7. In the Save Optimized As dialog box, you will be able to choose exactly what you are saving (options for saving HTML, All Slices, or Selected Slices) and again have the opportunity to adjust the Output Settings. Make any necessary adjustments.

8. Choose a location and click OK to save.

At this point, Photoshop will take over. According to the settings you have chosen and the complexity of the file, all the information you have selected to save will be exported, including slices and HTML. Photoshop will automatically name the files according to the naming scheme chosen and will create folders if necessary.

OPTIMIZATION SETTINGS AND OPTIONS WHEN USING SAVE FOR WEB

The Save For Web dialog box offers innumerable option combinations for comparing and optimizing images to be saved for Web use. In the Save For Web dialog box, you can do all the following:

- Create Slices
- Sample/select color table colors
- Choose output settings and defaults for exporting HTML
- Choose output settings and optimization for individual image slices
- Resize images
- Compare views and optimization effects
- Check download rates
- Check a browser preview

This is a very powerful tool for making the most of your Web images by making the least out of their size. The dialog box is segmented into several different areas, which include previews, optimization settings, a color table, image sizing, and several subscreens and menus, including Output Settings and Optimize File Size screens; Views, Settings, and Color Palette menus; as well as the browser preview menu.

PART

X

CH

35

PREVIEWS

The Preview section of the dialog box enables you to make comparisons in image optimizations side by side or individually, and in comparison to the original uncompressed version of the file. There are four tabs, including Original, Optimized, 2-Up, and 4-Up. The Original tab always displays the original view of the file before optimizations. The view cannot be edited or altered with changes in the settings. The Optimized tab displays the currently selected version of the optimized file. This view can be edited using the available settings and displays the file information that will be saved. You can also change the optimized version being viewed or selected by choosing another version in the 2-Up or 4-Up preview screens.

The 2-Up and 4-Up preview screens refer to the number of versions of a preview that you will be able to compare. Each view allows you to choose different settings. A thin black highlight line denotes the currently selected view, which will be used for export whenever the changes are accepted. Photoshop will choose defaults for the views, but you can reset each as desired.

OPTIMIZATION SETTINGS

The Settings portion of the Save For Web dialog box enables you to select a preset optimization type from the Settings list or enter your own settings for each view displayed. The options for settings include choosing a file format, color reduction algorithm, dithering, compression options, progressive loading/interlacing, matte color, Web Snap colors (as a percentage), dithering options, and transparency inclusion.

Although most of these options are discussed elsewhere as part of file type options, some of the options are unique to this palette. The Blur option allows you to choose to blur an image slice before applying the compression. This is used to attempt to reduce the artifacts (JPEG compression damage) left behind by the compression. Web Snap defines relative conformity to the 216-Web color table. A greater percentage will shift more of the colors to match the 216-color palette.

→ For more information on optimization settings and choosing a file format, **see** "Working with the Optimize Palette," **p. 803**, "JPEG," **p. 329**, "GIF File Format," **p. 328**, and "PNG," **p. 336**.

OPTIMIZE FILE SIZE

Optimize File Size, an option on the Settings menu, can help you target a file-size result and choose settings for you to accomplish the particular file-size goal. After choosing the Optimize to File Size from the Settings menu in the Save For Web dialog box, the Optimize To File Size dialog box will open. Specify a target size for the file, and from that choice, Photoshop will determine the optimization settings necessary to get the file down to the size you have chosen. See Figure 35.2 for the Optimize To File Size dialog box.

Figure 35.2
You can allow Photoshop to use your currently select-ed file type, or choose Auto Select, and it will make the choice for you. Files can be opti-mized for the current slice, each slice in the image, or the total of the slices in the image.

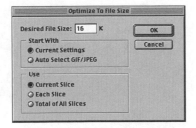

You can load and save optimization settings, Output Settings, and Color Tables by using the Load and Save functions on the associated screen or menu. This will allow you to quickly choose settings you use consistently without the step by step of changing each preference individually.

THE IMAGE SIZE TAB

The Image Size tab offers options for resizing the whole image being saved. The options are much like the Image Size dialog box from the Image menu, but the options are at once more limited and more apropos for Web-image size changes. Dimensions are changed in pixels only, and can be changed by percentage using Bicubic or Nearest Neighbor interpola-tion.

→ For more information on interpolation and resizing, **see** "Resizing an Image," **p. 346**.

OUTPUT SETTINGS DIALOG BOX

The Output Settings dialog box is a center for choosing options for the files created when the image optimization is saved. These options include HTML settings, Background set-tings, and automatic File and Slice naming options. Output Settings can be opened by click-ing the Output Settings button on the Save For Web dialog box, or it can be accessed when saving on the Save Optimize As dialog box.

When the screen opens, it will show the HTML options, but the drop-down selector menu will allow you to change to the other options (see Figure 35.3). With the HTML settings, you can finesse the HTML coding specifics to optimize the code for your use. The back-ground screen allows you to insert a background image or background color to be included in the HTML code. File and Slice naming conventions let you set filenames that will be used both for the HTML files and image files.

PART

X

CH

35

Figure 35.3
You can save your output settings and reuse them for specific Web pages and for compatibility with HTML-authoring applications (such as Adobe GoLive).

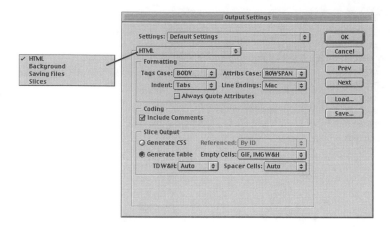

BROWSER MENU

You can view the image in different browsers by clicking the Preview in Browser button. The image is opened in the selected browser, and image statistics are included in the preview. This enables you to see exactly how a specific browser displays an image.

TROUBLESHOOTING

MAXIMIZING MINIMUM FILE SIZE

When I save my images for the Web, sometimes I get great results with file size and sometimes the files seem large, and the download times long. What can I do to keep things small?

Use this checklist to keep your file sizes as small as they can be. Remember that the file size includes the total of all images and the HTML, but not images that you use more than once on the same page.

- Make the file dimensions to the exact pixel size that you want them to appear in your Web page; do not resize with HTML.
- Use 72dpi for the final resolution. You might need to work higher than this to retain detail, especially if using distortion, but the final result should be resized to 72dpi.
- Reduce the number of colors as much as possible in GIF images without distorting the image.
- Use JPEG format for images with more than 256 colors.
- Crop animation tightly to the area of motion. Keep to a minimum number of frames, and use animation sparingly—or eliminate it.
- Keep rollover states to a minimum by using only the states you really need.
- Use repeating image elements (shims and background image fills) to lower the number of image elements used.

- Leave comments out of HTML code.
- Use short filenames.
- Take advantage of optimizing image use by repetition and use of spacers or shims.
- Regenerate code as necessary to reflect changes, and don't leave empty code (that adds nothing to the page, but can't be seen) behind.

Following these guidelines will help keep your pages lithe and effective in design, and they will be better apt to effectively transmit your content.

→ For more information on HTML coding, **see** "Using Photoshop Images on Your Web Site," **p. 827**.

PHOTOSHOP AT WORK: SOME VERY BASIC GUIDELINES FOR WEB DESIGN

Although there is no right and wrong, there is better and worse in Web page design. Better is effective, and worse turns the visitor away. There are enough things to practice in this chapter (sample images appear in the workbook at www.ps6.com), so a review of getting the most from your Web images and design seems in order.

A few simple things can help limit the potential for design problems from several standpoints. Use this list as a checklist to keep within a safety zone for your design. Of course, you can bend and break these guidelines, but they should help steer you in the right direction.

- *Keep the kilobyte total for your entire page below 150KB.* Keep it much lower if possible. If 28.8 modems actually moved data at top speed, this would be a 5-second download or so. However, in the real world that doesn't happen. Lots of people have improved connectivity these days, but designing for the high end leaves much of the market behind. See the checklist that follows.
- *Use a limited number of colors.* Three to five colors will usually do. This helps maintain a look and can keep the design from becoming too busy. It can also help limit colors in graphics to keep them tiny.
- *Sketch out the page before you make it.* Knowing what you want will help you cut corners in creating the elements that go with it. This can keep the pages small in size (KB) and speed the creation process.
- *Use Simple HTML and GIF or JPG images.* Don't depend on browser plug-ins to deliver effects. Standard practice should be to design with the newest standard browsers as a target. There are many cool tools to create amazing Web sites, but the simple fact is that when someone has to download a plug-in to see your page, you risk that they will miss the effect.
- *Create sites offline and test them before and after they are live.* You might get everything working fine offline and then when you set it up you might forget something or a link might be valid only within your directory structure.

- *Create page designs at a browser-friendly size.* A designer once asked me to look at her site and added, "I designed it in 1,280×1,024." At 72dpi, that would need about a 23-inch monitor to display (depending on how the screen resolution was set). Although it is limiting, I sometimes design to 9×6.5 (about 640×480), and do so with the intent that the visitor will not have to scroll.

- *Break up pages at logical points.* This goes along with the previous suggestion in that you don't want to cram so much on a page that it takes forever to scroll through. If you keep sizes small so navigation is quick, adding additional short pages is probably preferable for focusing on information.

- *Make navigation simple and obvious.* There is nothing worse than sitting on a page and not knowing how to get to the next step or where to go—or even if there is more to get to. Good design should play a part in simplifying both the information and access to it.

- *Choose common fonts for the page itself and be aware of potential for reflow.* If design is essential, you might want to consider making most or all your site graphic to control how it appears. Using a +2 sans-serif font (<FONT size="+2" "Arial, Helvetica, sans-serif">) will look very different on a Mac than a PC, depending on the placement and volume of text. To control the look more, you might want to set it in Photoshop.

CREATING PROFESSIONAL WEB EFFECTS

In this chapter

WEB IMAGES AND PHOTOSHOP

With the addition of ImageReady to Photoshop as a suite in version 5.5, Photoshop became the graphics powerhouse it already was, but more specifically empowered for Web graphics. ImageReady is an aid in Photoshop for processing some Web-specific needs, such as creating Java scripts for rollovers and handling animation, much like a high-powered plug-in has. ImageReady has many of the same features as Photoshop, and often it is difficult to tell their functions apart. Because images can be ported from either program to the other while retaining layers, effects, and so on, it almost doesn't matter in which program you are working unless you reach for a specific function that they do not both share. Because Photoshop is the more high-powered of the two programs, generally you will find yourself working in Photoshop to create and finish your images and then porting to ImageReady to complete the final steps of prepping an image for the Web.

The short of it is that you can create Web graphics using any technique described in this book—or any technique you can derive. The only differences between a Web graphic and any other graphic are the file type you save as, the file size, and features of the file type. File types used on Web pages are generally limited to Joint Photographic Experts Group (JPEG), Graphical Interchange Format (GIF), and PNG. The resolution at the final size should be considered at 72dpi, or as actual pixel dimensions (not inches or centimeters).

→ For more information on image size and resolution, **see** "Understanding Resolution," **p. 341**.

Web File Types

I say file type is generally limited not because it really is, but because certain types of images are less supported. You can transport and link to any kind of image from a Web page, but you might not be able to view it in your browser—depending on which plug-ins are available for the browser or how the page is encoded. For example, you could put any image on the Web as a PDF, and the person downloading it most likely would be able to view the PDF. It might even appear in his browser if he has a plug-in, or if it is coded into the page using EMBED and the right browser (EMBED is not a standard HTML code). For the present time—although things are changing—it is safest to use JPEG and GIF images, because they are the most widely supported by browsers.

Although PNG is a fabulous up-and-coming file type for Web application, it is not broadly supported. You can do almost anything with a PNG that you do with GIF or JPEG files, except animation. PNG can have the apparent resolution and color fidelity of a high-quality JPEG while supporting transparency and opacity using a channel mask. It also has lossless compression (with options for lossy). Without the additional compression, it will be larger than GIF or JPEG images. All that said, PNG images might not show up where they are supposed to, so using them is still a little bit of a dice roll.

→ For more information on the PNG and file types, **see** specific file type references in "Selecting a File Format," **p. 319**.

Some of what makes images work is behind-the-scenes programming. For example, rollovers and imagemaps are essentially programs created to make your images "do things." Luckily, ImageReady writes Java for you and even creates complex imagemapping files. All you must know is what to do with the result. Any of the previously listed file types can be used with the programming results.

→ For more information on working with rollovers, **see** "Constructing Rollover Buttons," **p. 796**.

ANIMATION WITH PHOTOSHOP AND IMAGEREADY

Animation is currently supported with only GIF images. *Animation* is the action of making images in a single file appear to move. ImageReady makes putting GIF animations together a snap, as long as you know what it is you are trying to accomplish in the animation and can create the necessary frames. Support for animation is something Photoshop was sadly lacking before. However, things have now become so easy that you can take a Photoshop image in layered frames and turn it into an animation in one simple step.

→ For more information on animation, **see** "Creating a Web GIF Animation," **p. 805**.

CREATING SLICES WITH PHOTOSHOP AND IMAGEREADY

Slices are guides that are placed over an image in a separate slice layer (only one per image). These guides define rectangular areas of the image, which can be saved separately on export. Each of the bounded, rectangular areas is called a slice. When the image is exported (or saved for the Web), Photoshop and ImageReady can cut the image up along the guides and save the slices of the image with different settings and file types. The slices can then be inserted into a Web page using an HTML table. When the page is loaded, the image is reassembled in the browser. This allows you to create links from image hot spots and work with the loading of graphics on your Web pages more creatively.

 Creating slices from an image has never been easier. You can control slices from Photoshop or ImageReady and use ImageReady functions to speed your slicing. The Slice tool is simple to use: Just click and drag and slices will fit to your image, and divide if they already exist. Slices can be reassembled, altered, and refitted, using the Slice Select tool.

Many functions are available for managing slices using the Slice menu in ImageReady, including linking slices, duplicating, deleting, arranging, aligning, and so on. One of the handiest of the automated slice functions is Create Slices from Guides and Create Slices from Selection. For example, you can create slices from guides you drag from the rulers. Just move the guides exactly where you want to slice and choose Create Slices from Guides. You don't even have to run the Slice tool over the image and all the slices will be created for you.

Any sliced image can be exported and ImageReady then writes the HTML for an image table, which will keep the slices tightly together. As long as you don't change the parameters for the table, this can be cut and pasted into both graphic and HTML page design programs with ease.

MAKING A 3D BUTTON

Three-dimensional buttons are common all over the Web for relatively good reason. The appearance of being raised makes the buttons stand off the page and says, "Click Me," to the visitor. This emphasis helps broadcast that there will probably be a link to another page and more information when the button is clicked—no doubt, something will happen. Knowing how to work with shadow and highlights to shape a button is imperative to getting the button to look right and draw attention.

Creating this type of effect is greatly simplified by the use of Layer Styles. The key is to know when to use a complex/custom rather than a "canned" Layer Styles effect. Knowing the difference in application can save you some effort and time. For cases in which simple effects will do—and this is probably most instances—using Layer Styles is the way to go. One of the greatest advantages to using styles over custom manipulations to create an effect is you can copy the styles easily from layer to layer and image to image. This helps you retain some consistency in the look of the page without a whole lot of effort. Keep in mind that your resolution on the Web will be low, so creating the highest-quality effects is sometimes overkill, because you might not be able to present the result.

→ For more information on working with custom highlights and shadows, **see** "Adding Highlights and Shadow for Shaping," **p. 641**.

The key to making 3D images work is the ability to control highlight and shadow. Highlight and shadow add texture to the button, whereas a drop shadow can give it the appearance of being lifted off the page.

Use the following steps to create this very basic Web button effect with Layer Styles:

1. Open a new image about 20% larger than you want the button to be. If desired, you can fill the layer with a color.

2. Create a new layer.

3. Define the shape of the button by selection. (You can easily create more complex geometries in Photoshop than in ImageReady using the Shapes tool or Pen.)

4. Fill the selection with a color for the surface of the button.

5. Double-click the layer in the Layers palette to open the Layer Style dialog box.

6. Click the Bevel and Emboss Style. Adjust the effect as necessary.

7. Click the Drop Shadow Style. Adjust the effect as necessary.

8. Add type to the button, keeping it within the beveled areas of the button. See Figure 36.1 for the result.

Note

In the example, the Bevel and Emboss default was changed so that the Highlight was set to Multiply and the color changed to black so it would act as a shadowing. The Opacity, however, was dropped so that it was significantly lower than the shadow side. The effect is still somewhat like highlighting—although not technically a highlight.

Tip

The other advantage to using Layer Styles is in creating variations and countereffects (for example, emboss down) without complicating the process. This is handy when creating image states for rollover effects.

→ For more information on rollover effects, **see** "Constructing Rollover Buttons," **p. 796**.

Figure 36.1

Effects were applied to the type also, making it appear to be raised and actually elevated slightly from the button by using a slight drop shadow.

Graphic buttons can be created quickly in the same way using images. All you have to do is define the shape of the button, copy and paste the area to a new Layer, and apply the desired effects. This isolates the image area in its own layer. Figure 36.2 shows how this might look using a graphic.

Figure 36.2

Some of the work in shadowing is already done with the natural coloring of the sample image. Note how the lighter top portion makes the bottom appear to be more contoured by shadow. Additional effects were added including a Bevel, a Drop Shadow, an Inner Glow, and manual highlighting to give the button a little gloss. Bevel, Drop Shadow, and Inner Glow all add to the separation from the background.

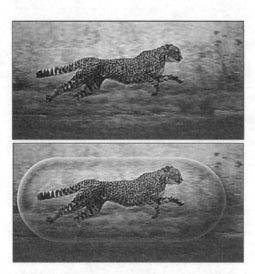

A number of presets are available for button creation in Layer Styles that can create a number of effects for you and also act as a learning tool for how to choose settings to accomplish effects. Take a good look at the settings for the Glass Button Rollovers, for example. These can be loaded from the Styles palette in ImageReady by choosing them from the pop-up menu. Create a layer as in the previous step-by-step (follow Steps 1–4) and then click a Style in the Styles palette. This applies the style to the Layer (really the slice) you have selected. Slices automatically are created for the image based on the button edges. Now you can click the image states and see how the results were put together by double-clicking the button layer to open the Layer Styles.

CONSTRUCTING ROLLOVER BUTTONS

Rollovers are often used as graphical buttons placed on a Web page that appear to be animated depending on action of the mouse on the viewed page. The term rollover comes from the idea that when you roll the mouse pointer over the image it changes. For example, the image can appear to highlight when the mouse pointer passes over a button area. But you can do even more than simple highlighting with rollovers, such as creating complex interactive events, which can be used for simple games or to control display of page information.

Six different potential actions exist for any rollover: Normal, Over, Down, Click, Out, and Up (see Table 36.1). Additional states can be defined as None and have no real bearing on the result.

Note

When creating a rollover, you don't need to use all the states. Also, it is best to use either the Down and Up combination or Click, not all three or other combinations thereof.

TABLE 36.1 ROLLOVER STATES AND ASSOCIATED ACTIONS

State	Appears in Browser When...
Normal	The Web page opens. This is the initial state of the image, but it is also used as an alternate for states that are not defined.
Over	The mouse is hovering over the image area.
Down	The mouse button is clicked and held down. Used in combination with Up as one of two components in an option, replacing Click.
Click	The mouse button is clicked. Used instead of the Down and Up combination.
Out	The mouse exits the image area.
Up	The mouse button is released. Used in combination with Down as one of two components in an option, replacing Click.

Create a quick and easy rollover in ImageReady:

1. Open ImageReady or Photoshop and create the image or button you will be using for the rollover.

Note

See "Creating Images for Rollovers and Animations in Layers" later in this chapter if you aren't sure where to start.

2. Port the image to ImageReady, if you have created it in Photoshop, by clicking the ImageReady button at the bottom of the toolbox; pressing (Shift–Cmd–M) [Shift+Ctrl+M]; or saving the image in Photoshop native format, closing Photoshop, and opening ImageReady and the Photoshop native format you saved.

3. Open the Rollover palette by either clicking the Rollover tab or selecting Show Rollover from the Windows menu. See Figure 36.3.

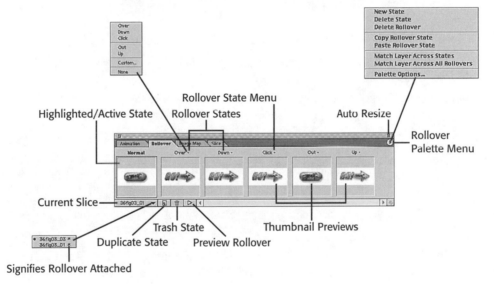

Figure 36.3
The creation of rollover states and selection of options for each are controlled on the Rollover palette through the Palette menu, the State pop-up, and the Slice selector.

4. To create a new rollover state, select New State from the Palette menu.

5. Click the State pop-up menu to select or change the current state. ImageReady creates those states in the order as pictured in Figure 36.3: Normal, Over, Down, Click, Out, Up, and None.

6. Create the number of states you want to use for the image—one new state for each of the states the rollover will contain.

Note

> You don't need to use every state available—in fact, the fewer states you use, the smaller the resulting file will be because there will be fewer images to load and less Java code.

7. Click the Normal state and adjust the image the way you want it to look for this state. For example, you can change the views of existing layers to create the view you want to use during this state, or create new layers and add additional information.

Note

> When managing rollover states, you can change layer opacity with the Opacity slider and Layer views by clicking the view icon for the layers. You can also change the positioning of elements on the layers, and ImageReady will remember those changes between states. ImageReady will not, however, allow you to add and remove layers from the image depending on the state nor will it track specific changes to the layer pixels. To eliminate a layer from a state, shut off the view; don't delete it or create it separately. To change the content of a layer, duplicate it and change it in the new layer, and then shut that view off for states in which it is inappropriate.

8. Select the next state and adjust the view by changing Opacities, Layer views and element placement on the Layers.

9. Repeat Step 8 until all states have been adjusted.

10. Preview the rollover action by clicking the Play button on the bottom of the Rollover palette. After doing this, the image onscreen behaves as the image would in a browser (see Figure 36.4).

Note

> Just treat the image like it was in a browser (put the cursor over it, click it, and move it out) to see the results in the preview. As you move and click, ImageReady shows which state is active by highlighting the state on the Rollover palette. Be sure to have the palette in view. If you are working on a larger image, redraw might not be instantaneous.

11. Edit the action of the rollover. This might require adding or removing states or editing the image layers. See the section "Working with Image States," later in this chapter.

12. Define the action of clicks using the Slice palette. To open the palette, choose Show Slice from the Windows menu or click the Slice tab (see Figure 36.5).

13. Save the document in Photoshop native format for later editing.

14. Export the image and HTML by choosing File, Save Optimized As.

Tip

> You should export a rollover to a separate folder, so you can quickly locate all the pieces. This can come in handy when putting together sites and pages, and is surely better than having to hunt down all the pieces.

Figure 36.4
This series shows the states as they were created in order: Normal, Over, Down, Click, Out, and Up. Normal and Out are the same because you usually will want to return to the original state upon moving out of the image area so everything is as it was. Click and Up are the same by choice; Down, Up, or a derivative state could have been used.

Normal

Over

Down

Click

Out

Up

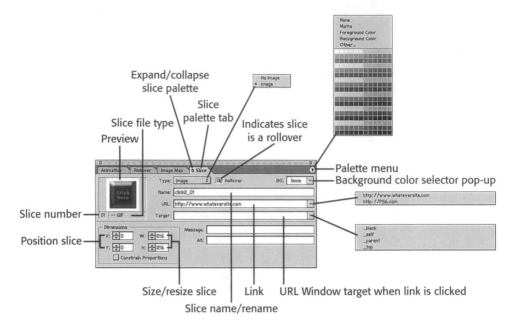

Figure 36.5
To see this expanded view of the Slice palette, click the arrow on the Slice tab. The message appears in the message bar on the browser window, and the Alt text appears before the image does as it is loading or if it fails to load. Target selection creates a new window (_blank), replaces the window contents (_top), or enables you to choose target frames.

15. If you want to place the slices into an existing Web page, move the HTML and images. To do this, open the exported HTML and cut and paste the generated script, slices, and ONLOAD statement to the page in which you want the rollover to appear. Next, copy the image slices to an appropriate reference folder.

→ For more details on how to work with HTML, **see** "Moving the Rollover Code," **p. 800**.

16. Preview the result in a browser. To do this, open the HTML file using the browser's Open File or Open Location command.

The exported HTML can be opened in a browser and viewed immediately without putting the contents into another page. Doing this enables you to preview the rollover and action(s) to ensure everything is working the way you want it to before you either combine the code into an existing page or create more of a page around what you have exported.

 If you have done Step 15 and you can't get the rollover to work correctly or as you expect it to when previewing in a browser, see "My Rollover Doesn't Work!" in the Troubleshooting section at the end of this chapter.

MOVING THE ROLLOVER CODE

ImageReady generates a complete HTML document ready for loading into a browser. You can use that as is, but if you plan to use the rollover in another page, you must move the code. This is simplified by remarks placed in the HTML file that is generated when you export. The markings are clear, and you don't have to know a thing about Java to place the code correctly. You barely have to know a thing about HTML. If you are used to working with pages through a graphic page-designing program and have never worked with HTML directly before, now is the time to click the menu item labeled View Source/HTML.

Moving the code is fairly simple. You must move the script, the ONLOAD statement, and the slices. The following steps show you how to move your rollover code to an existing Web page:

1. Open the page you are moving the code to as text. We'll call this the target page. You can do this by opening the HTML file in a text editor (such as Notepad or Simpletext), a word processor (Word, WordPerfect, and so on), or a page design program in the View Source or View HTML mode (for example, in Dreamweaver, this is Window, HTML, or F10; for other editors, see your software user's manual).

2. Open the HTML that was exported from ImageReady as text in the same program. We'll call this the source page. Figure 36.6 shows a sample of what the HTML will look like.

Figure 36.6
There will be a lot more in your code than you see here, but this is basically all you really have to pay attention to.

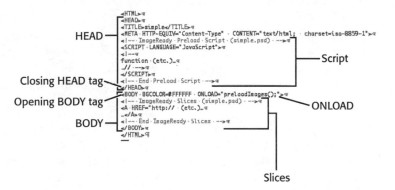

3. Locate the ImageReady Preload Script. This is enclosed by two remarks (remarks are defined by a leading "!--"):<!-- ImageReady Preload Script --> and <!-- End Preload Script -->.

4. Copy all the text from the beginning < in the first remark through the ending > in the end remark.

5. Switch to the target page and paste the text you copied into the HTML right before the closing head tag (the tag looks like </HEAD>; refer to Figure 36.6). Insert the cursor before the opening < and paste.

6. Switch back to the source page.

7. Locate the ONLOAD statement. This is in the opening <BODY> tag and looks like this: ONLOAD="preloadImages();". The body tag in the target looks similar to this: <BODY BGCOLOR=#FFFFFF>. Simply insert the cursor before the closing >, type a space, and paste.

8. Copy the ONLOAD statement only from the O through the closing quotation mark (").

9. Switch to the target page and paste the text you copied into the HTML inside the end of the opening body tag. Place a space before the code you pasted in to separate the ONLOAD parameter from the other parameters in the tag.

10. Switch back to the source page.

11. Locate the slices. This will be enclosed by two remarks: <!-- ImageReady Slices --> and <!-- End ImageReady Slices -->.

12. Copy all the text from the beginning < in the first remark through the ending > in the end remark.

13. Switch to the target page and paste the text you copied into the HTML somewhere between the opening and closing body tags.

14. Save the HTML. Be sure you save it as text only and that your extension is .htm—some word processors can default otherwise.

When you have saved the file, you need to move the images from where you saved them into the folder in which you saved the page. If the images were saved to a folder called Images (this is the default), you can copy the whole folder. If an Images folder already exists where you are copying to, copy the contents of the source Images folder into the target Images folder.

The most difficult step here is Step 13. If you are unfamiliar with where to place the code, you can use a placemarker for the rollover so it is easy to figure out where to put it. All you have to do is paste a dummy image/placeholder into the page where your rollover should go before saving the page. Create the dummy image as a simple white GIF or JPEG at the same size as the rollover image, and call it something you can easily recognize (such as rollover.jpg). When you paste in Step 13, look for the image marker. It will look like this: <IMG SRC="rollover.jpg">. Simply highlight that from the opening < through the closing > and paste. Your rollover will replace the marker. Don't forget to save.

WORKING WITH IMAGE STATES

Rollovers do not have to contain every state. In fact, the rollover can technically have only one state—although that isn't much of a rollover if it does. Usually, you will want to have at least one state in addition to Normal.

 Only one image state of each kind can exist in the rollover, and the fewer states you use, the better. Fewer states require less load time because they generate more code and more images. To edit image states, highlight the state you want to edit and change the Layer views, state type, opacity, or position of elements on the layers. Adding, deleting, or editing layer content can affect other views.

Not every rollover will require a click action. You can use rollovers creatively to change the page contents, and you can even develop simple puzzles and games by hiding and viewing areas of the screen depending on where the visitor's cursor is. These more-complicated rollovers are put together by using different slices to trigger different views.

→ For a demonstration of how you can build a very simple game based on the position of the mouse, **see** "Photoshop at Work: Building a Simple Rollover," **p. 823**.

WORKING WITH THE OPTIMIZE PALETTE

The Optimize palette (a standalone floating palette in ImageReady, and part of the Save For Web dialog box in Photoshop) lets you define file options for individual slices. For each slice you can define file type, compression settings, and so on, as if the slice were an individual image. The palette is context sensitive and changes options depending on what you have chosen as the file type.

 To change the optimization settings for an individual slice, select the slice by clicking on it with the Slice Select tool and change the settings in the Optimize palette. The settings for each slice are stored and exports of slices (all at once, in parts, or individually) will use those settings—unless you change them. Figure 36.7 shows some details of the Optimize palette in ImageReady.

CHOOSING OPTIMIZATION SETTINGS

 Often you will want to save the slices all with the same setting, or you will want to work with slices in groupings. To keep the settings the same across a group of slices, highlight all the slices with the Slice Select tool and link them by choosing Link Slices from the Slices menu. To highlight more than one slice at a time, click and drag a selection box with the Slice Select tool; to add selections individually, hold down the Shift key while clicking the slices you want to include. Targeting optimization settings to particular slices can come in handy, for example, when working with larger sliced images which have both broad areas of flat color and areas with photographic detail. You can save slices as GIFs to keep the flat color uniform (a JPEG would add artifacts), and save the complex color areas as JPEG (where a GIF would tend to fail in reproducing the color well).

To apply the settings you want, several choices are available. You can simply change the settings manually, use a predefined or saved setting from the settings pop-up, or use the Droplet feature. Droplets are miniprograms created with Photoshop or ImageReady which can change settings or be applied like an action. The Droplet takes the current settings and applies them to the slices you drop it on. This feature can also be used to create droplet applications. To create a Droplet from the current settings, simply click the Droplet icon and drag it to the desktop. Images you drag to the icon are then optimized according to the settings.

Figure 36.7
The tab for the Optimize palette in ImageReady expands and contracts choices for each of the file types, and even collapses the menu. The menu has several useful options, such as Create Droplet, Save Settings, and Optimize File Size.

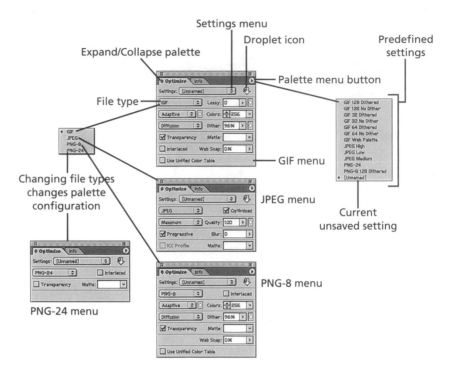

Using Spacers or Shims to Save Bytes

A neat byte saver is taking a 1×1-pixel GIF image and stretching it to fit an area to color it. These are sometimes known as spacers or *shims*. These tiny images can help you create or maintain spacing in a table by filling the space to a specific dimension. You can use them both to take the place of larger, monocolored images, and to create sizing in HTML table columns and rows. You must be somewhat comfortable with code to do this, although some programs enable you to accomplish this by using the graphic page design mode. If there are areas of pure color that you could mark off with slices, you can replace the content with the 1×1 GIF by simply changing the image reference (so long as the Height and Width parameters are used in the code). Shims placed in the topmost row or rightmost column of a table can help you create even spacing in the table (you may have to create an additional row or column, and you will have to set Height and Width parameters). The great part about this is you can use a single 1×1-pixel shim to fill a lot of space on the page. If you are creating a graphic page, every byte counts in lowering the download time, and this can speed up the loading.

You can save settings to make them available in the Settings pop-up menu by choosing Save Settings from the Optimization menu. You can also optimize a current file to a particular size by choosing Optimize File Size. This automatically selects settings for the document and file type to get the file down to the size you select in the Optimize to File Size dialog box.

CREATING A WEB GIF ANIMATION

Animations are an exciting part of Web images. Movement is an advantage unique to the Web medium for most graphic artists not working in video or TV applications. Creating effects involves timing and consideration of space and motion that are somewhat different from still art. Animations can be created using the GIF format and ImageReady, whereas frames can be created in Photoshop. In almost everything else, Photoshop stands alone, but ImageReady is required for animation. Photoshop is well suited to creating individual frames and effects, but it has no feature for compiling and handling frames, as ImageReady does.

Animations work by displaying a series of stepped movements in a progressive order. The steps in movies are counted in frames per second, and GIF animation essentially works in a similar way. The number of frames is used to plan movement and timing. For example, if it takes a cartoon character 3 seconds to walk across the screen at 16 frames per second, 48 separate drawings would have to be created to complete the movement. These drawings would sequentially represent the movement of the character in 16ths of a second.

In creating GIF animations, you essentially need to create a series of sequential movements that accomplish the same thing. You can have control over the timing of the frames, the series of events, and the speed of the movement. The trick is to plan a smooth motion. The trick to planning the motion is to decide how long you want the motion to last, how smooth you want it to be, and what distance or space you want the movement to cover. As with most other Web concerns, you need to work as small as possible while still getting the results you want, and this usually means reducing the number of frames and keeping the animation small. The more frames, the larger the file, and the longer the animation will take to download.

Caution

Use animations with purpose on a Web page, rather than just throwing them up because you can and because it's "neat." Some animations can be distracting instead of useful and might actually encumber and defeat the purpose of your site.

To create an animation, it is best to approach the whole thing tactically. Most likely, a bit of work will be involved, so knowing what your goal is from the outset will help save steps.

Use the following steps to plan your animation and develop parts of the motion. A detailed example follows that can help more with the particulars of how to get still images to appear to move:

1. Decide what you want your animation to look like. This is really a planning step, but it is very important. It might require making sketches or taking notes to define exactly what you want the animation to do.

2. Break down the animation into separate movements, where each change in direction constitutes the end of one action and the beginning of the next.

3. Decide how long you want each of the movements in the animation to last, in seconds.

4. Make a close approximation of the distances you plan to cover using a linear or pixel measure.

5. Decide how many frames you want to use for each movement. This should not be an arbitrary selection, but should be based on the distance of the movement and how smooth you need it to be. Table 36.2 lists some frame rates and suggested use. The frame can vary for each movement—and actually within movements.

Note

Although using a high number of frames per second makes the motion smoother, it also increases the file size. More than 32 frames per second is overkill—especially for the Web. Less than 16fps might make the action a little blocky and rough, depending on the action. However, most Web applications of animation probably fall in the 8fps–12fps category. Slower speeds not only make the animation chunky, but depending on the activity, they can make it hard to follow.

TABLE 36.2   ANIMATION FRAME RATES AND USES

Frames per Second	Frame Speed in Seconds	Use
More than 1		Pause in movement or action
1/sec	1 sec/frame	Stop action effects
2/sec	.5 sec/frame	Stop action effects
4/sec	.25 sec/frame	Very chunky Web animation
8/sec	.125 sec/frame	Chunky Web animation
12/sec	.0833 sec/frame	Minimum smooth Web animation
16/sec	.0625 sec/frame	Quality Web animation; TV cartoon frame rate
24/sec	.04 sec/frame	Top-quality TV/cinema cartoon animation
32/sec	.03 sec/frame	Maximum move export rate; TV/cinema film quality

6. Create the animated parts or repetitive movements that will be part of the larger movements in the frames. Depending on the complexity of the scene you are animating, you might have to build many parts.

For example, if you create an animation of a man going into a barbershop, you animate the man's walk and the spinning barber pole.

Tip

You should animate constants or repetitive action first. That is, if there are separate motions, create those that will appear as constants. Smaller portions of larger moving objects should probably be animated first, and then the elements of the larger object combined.

7. Compile image elements into corresponding steps, and duplicate elements as necessary. Each complete frame's elements should be compiled as a separate layer set.

Using the example from Step 6, you would need to coordinate the steps of the spinning barber pole with the steps of the man as he walks.

Note

Stack the completed frames from the background up in the Layers palette. If a common background exists, leave it as the background and don't bother duplicating it. You can take care of that by showing the right layers when creating the frames for the animation.

8. Make final alterations and fine-tune the image elements. That is, if any image elements in the animation change shape during the course of the basic movement, make those alterations to those image elements at this point.

9. Save the file in Photoshop native format. This will be your backup in case you need to come back and adjust elements in the animation that are not flattened.

This stage takes care of movement that is not repetitive. For example, if you show a ball bouncing, you need to add a little distortion to the ball in frames where the ball impacts the ground. Assuming that the ball's bounce deteriorates—that is, the amplitude decreases as it continues to bounce—each successive impact causes less distortion to the ball, so each instance must be handled differently and the impact on the ball handled separately.

Use the following steps to assemble the animation:

1. Create individual frames from the compiled sets. To do this, flatten the sets. If you are clever, you can build an action that flattens the layer set, moves to the next set, and repeats.

2. Save the image as a PDF again. This is the working version you will port to ImageReady. At this point, you have created all the steps in your animation. You must perform only one more step in ImageReady to complete the animation, as long as the frame speed is the same.

3. Open ImageReady.

4. Open the files saved in Step 2.

5. Choose Make Frames From Layers in the Animation palette menu. This converts the layers to frames.

6. Preview the animation by clicking the Play button on the Animation palette.

7. Make adjustments to the frame views and settings as necessary. This includes adding frames as necessary (using Tween and manual editing), changing timing, and editing frame content directly. For example, if you have a background that goes in all the images, choose Select All Frames from the Palette menu and click the visibility for the Background layer in the Layers palette. This inserts the background as visible in each frame.

Note

Tween is a function that creates intermediate stages between images in a progression. This can help smooth out rough spots in the animation.

→ For more on working with Tween and other editing options, **see** "Editing Animations," **p. 809**.

8. Choose the looping type for the animation (see Figure 36.8). To set a specific number of loops, choose Other from the Loop menu.

Figure 36.8
At the bottom of the Animation palette, you can select Forever (the default), Once, or Other from the Loop menu. This makes the animation loop continually, makes it play through once, or enables you to define the number of plays before it stops.

The loop menu

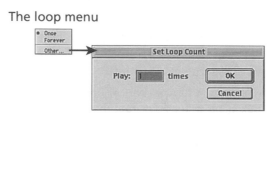

9. Choose the optimization settings you want to use in the export.

10. Save the GIF animation by a name other than the one chosen for the original document in case you need to go back to it.

11. Place the animation on your Web page using appropriate HTML for placing a GIF, just as you would place any other GIF image.

You should be able to see from the complexity of this that it is beneficial to keep animation movements simple unless you are interested in spending a lot of time animating. The other end of this is that the more frames you use and the more time you spend, the less likely the result will be a usable GIF animation. It might end up more suited for video or other applications.

Another option for the Web is to include the animation as a movie instead of a GIF. This is not recommended if you want to place the image directly on the page. What you must do in this case is choose Export Original from the File menu. Then, in the Save Options dialog box, choose Quick Time Movie. You can choose from a number of options for file type and compression (see Figure 36.9). When this file is accessed by a site visitor, it downloads to the visitor's PC and plays in an appropriate movie viewer.

Figure 36.9
A number of Quick Time Movie export options are available. These allow various types of compression and finished quality (and affect the size of the export file accordingly). Photo-JPEG is the default.

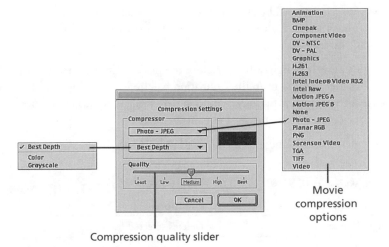

Compression quality slider

Movie compression options

EDITING ANIMATIONS

There are numerous options for working with animation in ImageReady to adjust the results. You can selectively apply changes to the single frames, work with frames as groups, and add and delete frames. For most of this, you will be using the Animation palette and functions found there. See Figure 36.10 for some detail of the Animations palette.

Figure 36.10
There are a number of Animation functions that you will use the Animations palette for that not only control the settings for individual frames, but create frames and content as well.

To edit a frame individually, select the frame by clicking it in the Animation palette. This changes the views on the Layers palette to those appropriate for the frame. You can edit and add layers as desired. If you're adding or deleting layers, be aware that these will be added and deleted to the image and could affect every frame (for example, if you delete or edit a shared background, it is changed in all the frames).

To edit groups of frames, click the first in the series that you want to include and then hold the Shift key and click the last one. This highlights the string. To select nonsequential frames, hold down the (Cmd) [Ctrl] key and click to select or deselect individual frames. Changes you make in layer opacity, views, effects, and timing affect each of the highlighted layers.

Frame speed is selected by clicking the frame speed pop-up below the frames. If you have several frames selected, opening the pop-up from any of the frames and changing the setting affects all the frames.

To add a frame, highlight a frame before the position in which you want the frame inserted and select New Frame from the Animation palette menu. This also can be used to duplicate a frame set and noncontiguous frames. When duplicating noncontiguous frames, the new frames are created after the last frame in the series.

Other palette menu functions are covered in Table 36.3.

TABLE 36.3 ANIMATION PALETTE MENU FUNCTIONS

Menu Item	Function
Delete Frame	Deletes selected frame(s)
Delete Animation	Removes all frames from the animation
Copy Frame	Copies content of frame to the buffer
Paste Frame	Pastes buffer content to frame
Tween	Creates intermediate steps between selected frames
Reverse Frames	Changes the order of selected frames
Optimize Animation	Uses optimization settings to render animation image information
Match Layer Across Frames	Changes active layer (content, opacity, placement) across selected frames
Flatten Frames Into Layers	Creates layers from the content of frames
Add Layer To New Frames	Check option on/off; adds a new visible layer for newly duplicated frames
New Layers Visible In All Frames	Check option on/off; makes newly created layers visible in every frame

AUTOMATING FRAME CREATION USING TWEEN

Tween provides a means for automatically creating intermediate states between two frames that can help speed the creation of an animation and fill in for missing frames and smooth out rough spots in an animation. To use Tween, select the contiguous frames between which you want to create intermediate states, or select the latter of the frames you want to use. Next, choose Tween from the Animation palette menu; the Tween Options dialog box appears (see Figure 36.11).

Figure 36.11
You can choose the target frame for the Tween from the dialog box when it is open, as well as the number of states you want to create in between. Tween works with Opacity, Position, and Effects, giving you control over which elements get included in the Tweening.

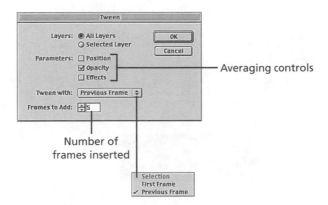

Averaging controls

Number of frames inserted

Figure 36.12 shows a simple example of images that can be used with Tween to blend effects and create a smooth transition rather than an abrupt one. The two images were created for an animation slated to be a logo for the ps6.com Web site for this book. After creating a paint dab animation, the resulting brush strokes were combined by overlaying a gradient so there would be less noise for the type to appear in. This was all well and good, but when it was introduced to the animation, the jump from the paint dabs to the flat gradient seemed too abrupt. Tween was used to smooth out the problem by adding five states between the dabs and the flat gradient that change the color more gently—somewhat similar to the shifting of autumn leaves. See Figure 36.13 for the result.

Figure 36.12
These two states might be interesting in their own right, but abruptly changing from one to the next in an animation didn't work very well. Tween was used instead of the abrupt transition to add intermediate states.

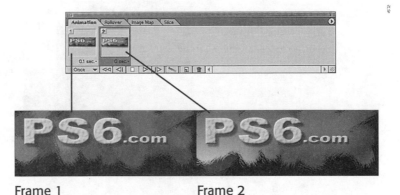

Frame 1   Frame 2

Note

In creating an opacity blend, ImageReady performs an absolute percentage shift in which the percent opacity in the interim states adds up to 100%. For example, if three states were being added to an image that had a single layer for each of the frames involved, and the layers were 100% in their respective frames, the states would have the following opacities: Layer A 25%, Layer B 75%; Layer A 50%, Layer B 50%; Layer A 75%, Layer B 25%. Because this can have undesired effects, enabling some visibility of the layers below, the bottom layer in the example was changed to 100% by selecting the series of frames and choosing Match Layer Across Frames from the Animation palette menu.

Figure 36.13
This shows the inter-
mediate steps created
for the blend, which
gradually shift the
tonality and color by
working with the layer
opacity.

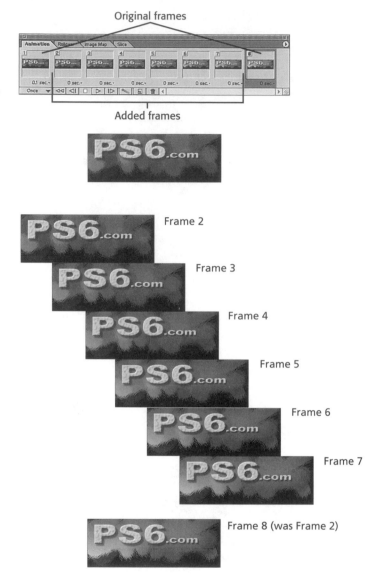

The result can be seen as the opening logo on the www.ps6.com Web site and can be downloaded from there in QuickTime MOV format at a higher resolution.

The option for tweening the position of objects creates intermediate positioning between
layer elements rather than intermediate opacities. Tweening position is done when you want
to create movement directly from and to specific spots in the image. To do this, select or
create frames where the positioning of a layer content is different from the target. For
example, starting with a layer to the left of the image in frame one, duplicate the frame to
create frame 2 and reposition the layer to the right. Applying Tween with the Position check

box checked would create frames in equal, intermediate steps between the positions of the layer in the two frames. This can simulate simple movements without a lot of effort.

ANIMATING ELEMENTS

Animating elements requires attention to detail and an understanding of how motion is handled. For example, objects can accelerate, decelerate, move at constant speeds, turn, and so on, while you handle all the planning and execution of every movement.

ACCELERATION, DECELERATION, AND CONSTANT SPEED

Increasing the distance steadily between a series of elements creates the appearance of acceleration, whereas decreasing steadily causes deceleration. It is recommended that you practice effects of controlling speed and movement in animations. The effects can be calculated using some plain old good sense. Say you want to give a stationary car an acceleration of 6 pixels per frame over 1 second of movement using 12 frames per second. By the 12th frame, that car would have to be moving at 72 pixels per frame (6×12=72). All you need to do is move the car 6 additional pixels with each movement: These movements would be 6, 12, 18, 24, 30, 36, 42, 48, 54, 60, 66, and 72 pixels. Figure 36.14 illustrates accelerating and decelerating movement. By the end of the 12th frame, the car will be moving at 864 pixels per second (72×12, or the number of pixels per frames times the frames per second). To maintain that movement at that point, you would keep the incremental movement at 72 pixels per frame.

Figure 36.14
The figure shows an acceleration toward the right and a deceleration to the left. The tire steadily accelerates or decelerates by adding or subtracting additional pixels for every frame.

You can certainly get more complicated and more accurate than this by applying an acceleration rate according to a bell curve if you have a target. That is, acceleration will gradually become 6 pixels per frame (say .5, 1.5, 3, 4.5, 5.5, and 6 rather than immediately hitting 6). However, we are looking for only a reasonable approximation at this point. The main thing to remember is to make something go more quickly, the distance between where it is and where it was will be less than where it is going to be, and vice versa for deceleration. If you want a constant speed, move in even increments.

COMPILING THE PARTS

As suggested in the steps earlier, you will have simple and complex movements in your animations. In addition, some motions that seem simple are actually complex. For example, tire rotation is a simple form of a complex movement. Not only is the tire rotating, but it is moving forward.

To get the right effects from complex movements, you should attack the parts separately. This is best illustrated by an example. The idea for this example is to build an animated Web page header for a fictitious site called Wreck's End Demolition. A rather simple logo bar is designed, using bright colors, and a toy car selected to use as the "wreck." The goal of the animation is to drive the car across the top of the logo and crash it into the side of the browser—thereby wrecking the end. The motions required are the movement of the car, rotation of the wheels, and action in crumpling the front end of the car on impact (deceleration). A stock photo of a rusty old toy car is selected for use as the car (see Figure 36.15).

Figure 36.15
This car certainly looks like a "wreck," and the idea of it being a toy adds a bit to the less-than-serious nature of the meaning in the name. It was selected and isolated easily from a pure white background.

For the example, the motion is only a second. The plan is to get the whole motion done using 16 frames per second for fairly smooth motion. The car moves at a constant speed, which means the wheel rotation is even. Each frame has a duration of .0625 second, and the total movement is about 400 pixels, or 25 pixels per frame.

The constants are created first: a blue bar for the logo background and, on a separate layer, some type to note the name of the company and the product (see Figure 36.16). The reason for the separate layer is that the type is slightly larger than the bar, and the car would travel behind the type. The movement of the car is created between the background bar and the foreground type by creating new layers in between. The image of the car gets placed in a layer between the type and the background.

The motion of the car is actually pretty simple as it travels along in a straight line horizontally. The movement of the wheel is only slightly more complex because it has to rotate while moving. To make things easy, I would choose to have the wheel rotate 1/8 of a turn per frame: It would make two complete revolutions over the distance traveled. That means eight steps could be created for one complete revolution and then duplicated to make the 16 steps for the tire. This would be quicker and easier than making a separate wheel for all 16 frames (see Figure 36.17).

Figure 36.16
The animation is cre-
ated using this graphic
bar as the base for the
car animation above
it. Later, the area
above the bar is han-
dled separately from
the animation to keep
the file and frames as
small as possible. The
file still is notably
large.

Figure 36.17
This rotation is not
completely accurate
for the ground the car
would cover. To be
accurate, the wheels
would have to spin at
a little under twice
this speed. The idea in
this case is to make
the action apparent
rather than totally
accurate.

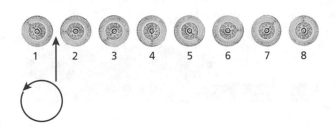

The mechanics of the motion are taken care of by selecting the wheel from the car and
copying it to eight different layers. A selection is made of the wheel in a perfect circle by
holding down the (Shift–Option)[Shift+Alt] keys while dragging a circular marquee from the
wheel hub. After the selection, the wheel is copied once and pasted eight times to make
eight layers. The wheels are then rotated in 1/8-turn increments (45°, 90°, 135°, 180°, 225°,
270°, 315°, and 0°).

Tip

When performing a repetitive action that requires a transformation rather than a straight
copy, such as turning a wheel, do not create subsequent steps from the previous one,
unless the previous is the original. For example, don't copy the original, create a new layer,
turn it 45°, and then copy that layer, paste, and turn it 45° more. Also, always use a new
duplicate of the original for each step and apply rotation and movements accordingly.
Movement and rotation over a series of images can cause unnecessary blurring or distortion because Photoshop needs to reposition the pixels with each rotation, movement,
distortion, alignment, and so on. Eventually, things will get visibly out of whack, blurry,
and bad.

Next, the bottom of the car is aligned so the wheels touch the bar evenly. To do this easily, the ruler can be selected from the toolbox to measure the angle between the bottom of the wheels. The measurement is -179.1° instead of 180° or 0°, so the ruler angle gets changed to the counter of that: 179.1°. When Transform, Rotate is selected from the Edit menu, the car bottom perfectly aligns to the bar. After it's adjusted, the image can be duplicated seven times, so you have the original and seven copies. Because this is a straight copy, you don't need to be concerned about degrading the content. The cars are roughly aligned from right to left from the original up to the last copy. However, a little more attention should be paid to the placement of the bottom and top layer, placing them 175 pixels apart as measured by the back end. Then, the new Align Linked function is used to align the cars at bottom vertically, and Distribute Linked is used to evenly distribute the cars according to the right side. With the links still active, use the Move tool by pressing keyboard arrows to align the car wheels and the bottom of the bar (see Figure 36.18).

Figure 36.18
After the alignment of these cars is complete, duplicating them creates another perfectly aligned set to make all 16 cars. But first, the wheels need to be placed.

To complete the series, the wheels are aligned to the car, again using rough placement and the Align Linked and Distribute tools. Then, the layers are rearranged so the wheels are paired with the appropriate car. Instead of working with layer sets, the tires are simply combined with the car for each of the eight steps in the revolution. Layer sets would have been used if there had been other independent motion in the scene (for example, a bird flying the opposite way at a different speed).

A layer set is created from the eight cars by linking the eight layers and selecting New Set from Linked on the Layers palette pop-up. That set is duplicated using Duplicate Layer Set, and the set is manually aligned using the Move tool. Holding down the Shift key keeps the cars in the same horizontal plane. This results in 16 cars with wheels turning, aligned, and ready to become an animation. The only Photoshop function left to perform is to make the crash.

The car impacts with what is essentially the left side of the browser window. This causes some damage to the car and quick deceleration. The last car from the second set exits the frame and needs to show that impact. Actually, to allow the deceleration, the layer is duplicated and moved only 12 pixels to the left—this shorter movement accounts for some of the deceleration. The car damage is introduced quickly using the wave filter in a selection of the front end, and then scaling. Certainly, there are different ways to accomplish this and other effects. Figure 36.19 shows the progression of the impact on the car.

Figure 36.19
The wave created the zigzagging crunch, and scaling is done to shorten the front end of the car. Some minor touchup with the Stamping and Smudge tools smoothes out the transition at the edge of the selection.

The image is saved at this point and moved to ImageReady. All that has to be done now is open the image, select Make Frames from Layers from the Animation palette menu, and then turn on the type and background for every frame using Match Layer Across Frames. The animation could be exported at this point to a movie or a GIF. See Figure 36.20 for the results.

By creating a series of controlled movements frame by frame, you develop the elements necessary to make objects appear to be animated. Careful attention to image placement, movement, and timing in frames per second can help you decide where image elements need to be placed and how to control them. Although Photoshop can help do the bulk of the work in the compilation and creation of frames, it cannot save a completed animation, and you will have to depend on ImageReady to compile and save the frames as a unit.

Figure 36.20
These are the last eight frames of the movement shown in order. The animation in the example can certainly do more than it does currently, but the effect is interesting and adding more action might make the file even larger.

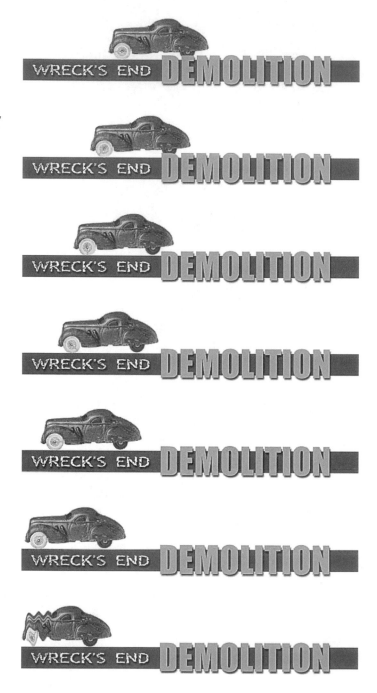

USING IMAGEMAPS

Imagemaps are an alternative means of defining links in an image. The maps are vector shapes used to define hot spots in an image. These hot spots can be clicked when the image—and HTML/code defining the shape—is loaded into a browser to trigger a new URL. A distinct difference between using slices for linking and using Image Maps is that an imagemap can be created in any shape, and can very closely follow the contour of a button, whereas slices have to be rectangular. Imagemaps can be used as slices in combination with rollovers to create more intricate rollovers based on the vector shapes. Imagemaps can be created and manipulated only in ImageReady, although smart development of images in Photoshop can help save some work in creating and managing imagemaps in ImageReady.

There are really two ways to create an imagemap: using the Image Map tool and using the New Layer Based Image Map Area (on the Layers menu). The Image Map Tool lets you draw shapes to create an imagemap manually. The tool comes in four variations: the Rectangle Image Map Tool, the Circle Image Map Tool, the Polygon Image Map Tool, and the Image Map Select Tool (see Figure 36.21). To create an imagemap with the Image Map Tool, simply click and drag for creating with the shapes, or draw a freehand shape with the Polygon tool by clicking point to point (as if setting anchors for a path). In the Image Map palette, you can control the Width, Height, and position (x and y coordinates) of the rectangle; or the Radius and position of the circle.

Figure 36.21
The Polygon Image Map Tool allows you to draw a custom imagemap shape. You can scroll the imagemap tools by pressing (Shift-P) [Shift+P].

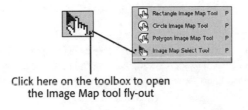

Click here on the toolbox to open the Image Map tool fly-out

The new layer-based imagemap area function uses the contents of a layer to determine the imagemap shape for you. You can choose from three options: Rectangle, Circle, and Polygon. The Rectangle and Circle options draw those shapes for you to encompass the content of the layer, whereas the Polygon draws a custom shape, based on the content and the selected Quality on the Image Map palette. Quality represents how closely the map will follow the layer contents. The shapes are described in the export HTML, using coordinates for the points that describe the shape.

The setting defaults to 80 and can be changed from 1–100, with higher numbers representing greater conformity. The higher the Quality, the more detailed the description of the polygons that you create. Any change to the layer content will prompt ImageReady to redraw the related imagemap. The entire content of the layer accounts for the mapping. For example, if you have buttons that you want to map separately (so that they have distinct function), you have to create them on different layers (see Figure 36.22).

Image preview

Button number

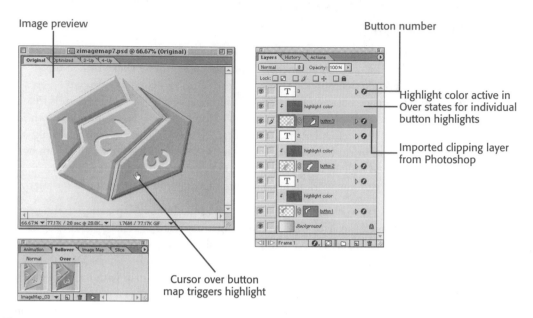

Highlight color active in Over states for individual button highlights

Imported clipping layer from Photoshop

Cursor over button map triggers highlight

Figure 36.22
This set of images shows an image in Web Preview mode, the layer setup for the image, and rollover states for Button 3. Photoshop Layer Clipping Paths were used to create the button shapes, as there is no Pen tool in ImageReady.

> **Caution**
>
> Changing the Quality to 100% for the Image Map Area Polygon settings when using complex shapes can generate a lot of coordinates. Be careful to use lower settings when possible so that you don't increase your page loading time by including imagemaps that describe too much.

 If you are trying to create a map in ImageReady and are experiencing any unusual problems (layers content moving on its own, difficulty controlling the mapping actions, and so on), see "Smoothing ImageReady Performance" in the Troubleshooting section at the end of this chapter.

When created, the imagemaps can be saved as part of the export for use on the Web. There are essentially two ways the code for the imagemap can be saved: Client- or Server-based mappings. The server-based mapping is a bit more complicated to deal with than the client type; it generates two text files (the HTML and a separate file for the map) and the map file must be placed in accordance with server rules in order to function (some servers will not be able to support this option). Processing the map functions, in the case of server-based maps, is handled by the server where the HTML resides. The client-based option is somewhat easier to deal with as the mapping is created right in the HTML and is handled on the machine where the page is downloaded, rather than at the server.

To choose client or server options for the export, you will have to open the Output Settings dialog box (File, Output Settings, HTML; (Cmd–Option-H) [Ctrl+Alt+H]). At the bottom of the dialog box there are imagemap options for the HTML export on the Type pop-up.

You can choose either client- or server-type map handling, or export both types by selecting one of the combination options.

NCSA and CERN are different mapping types. They are not interchangeable. Contact your ISP to find out which method of mapping to use.

If exporting the map as client-side, the map will show up in the exported HTML much like Java scripts are handled for rollovers. If you will be moving the imagemap to another document, you will have to move any Java that was generated along with the ImageReady slices.

→ For more information on moving the code, **see** "Moving the Rollover Code," **p. 800**.

Smart use of imagemaps gives you far more flexibility in design, and greater ability to control the look and feel of your pages.

TROUBLESHOOTING

MY ROLLOVER DOESN'T WORK!

I think I followed the directions and step-by-step to make the rollovers, but they aren't working in my browser when I load the page. What's wrong?

So many things can go wrong here that it is a wonder this ever goes right. This is a pretty simple thing, and most browsers should be able to handle it. However, here is a long list of the things that could skew the workings.

First, and when in real doubt that something is going wrong, reopen the file in ImageReady and export the whole thing (Save Optimized As) to a new directory. Open the HTML file exported to that directory without changing a thing. As long as the HTML works, you are exporting correctly. The problem must be somewhere else.

If you can't even get the exported HTML to work, be sure you have actually seen a rollover work in the browser you are using. If not, you might want to reinstall the browser and get a newer version. Internet Explorer and Netscape are recommended as leaders in the field. They are also free to download. Some rollovers are available on the www.ps6.com Web site for this book, so you can test to see that rollovers work in your current browser.

If you have moved the code, be sure you moved all of it and put it in the proper place. You can't leave off the brackets anywhere, and the code must be placed as specified.

Be sure you are opening the correct HTML file in the browser. If you have saved the original file and the new file with different names, be sure you are loading the file to which you added the Java, and not the original.

Be sure the file was saved to the correct directory. You might have the images in the correct place, but if the file is in the wrong place, it might not know how to find or reference the images.

Be sure you have placed all the images in the appropriate subfolder. If the code tells the browser to look in the Images subfolder and no such subfolder exists, the only error you will get is that the rollovers won't work.

Be sure you have exported all images in a format that is viewable in the browser. For example, if your original settings were for exporting PNG files and you didn't change the preferences for all the slices or all the states, you might be exporting images your browser won't handle.

Review the rollover and be sure you have the events right. For example, if you expect something to happen when you roll over and you have only Normal and Up states in the image, it might very well be that nothing happens in the browser.

Be sure the states are different enough so that you can actually tell a rollover action is happening. Too subtle an action might make it seem that nothing is happening at all.

If still nothing works, make a very simple rollover with a Normal and Over state and see whether you can get that to work using an unchanged export.

If you are at this point and you still can't get it to work, load the files to an FTP site, visit a friend, and try the rollover on her computer. If it works, there is some other problem with your computer that you will have to attend to and that is far outside the scope of this book.

If it doesn't work anywhere, my best bet is that you need to go back and follow the process, step-by-step, one more time.

SMOOTHING IMAGEREADY PERFORMANCE

On occasion, ImageReady will start acting a little strange on me, moving around layer content, exporting HTML that is different than what I set up to export, and generally acting a little buggy. Is there something wrong with the program?

Another thing Photoshop and ImageReady do not share is memory settings. It is easy to forget about assigning these parameters to ImageReady as you will probably have already taken care of them for Photoshop. If you are experiencing odd behavior with ImageReady, you can cure a lot of the ills by assigning more memory to the program. It may also improve performance to change the scratch disk allocation. If there isn't enough memory or room on the scratch disk, unusual behavior such as described may crop up.

→ For more information on increasing the memory allocation to the ImageReady program, **see** "Macintosh Specifics" and "Windows Specifics," **pp. 911-912**.

→ For more information on changing scratch disk allocation, **see** "Scratch Disks," **p. 908**.

Note

Although there is only one possible scratch disk assignment for ImageReady, the suggestions and procedure for assigning scratch disks and handling memory are very similar between ImageReady and Photoshop. Be sure you change the ImageReady settings to change the behavior for ImageReady.

PHOTOSHOP AT WORK: BUILDING A SIMPLE ROLLOVER

Rollovers can do more then just highlight a button or link Web pages. Depending on how you use them they can reveal information and create simple games if you use states creatively. For example, you might use an Over state to jump to another page rather than the Click or Down state if you are comfortable manipulating Java.

The example here will give you just a glimpse of the type of effect you can create, and give you a little practice working with rollovers. You can create an image that is split in half by a slice, and appear to track the position of the mouse for the visitor as they move the mouse on the page.

The following steps walk you through creating this simple effect with slices:

1. Create a 100×100-pixel image in ImageReady.
2. Drag a vertical guide out from the ruler and place it at 50, halfway across the image.
3. Place a dot, centered on the line, as part of the background.
4. Select the Type tool.
5. To the left of the dot, type: **you are left of the dot**.
6. Create a new type layer by choosing the Type tool and clicking on your image.
7. To the right of the dot, type: **you are right of the dot**.
8. Create a slice using the guide by choosing the Slice tool (K) and slicing manually, or choose Create Slices from Guides from the Slice palette menu. This creates two slices for the image.
9. Choose the first slice (untitled-1_01) from the Slice pop-up menu at the bottom of the Rollover palette.
10. Add an Over state and an Out state by selecting New state from the Rollover palette menu. Change the Down state to Out when the new state is created.
11. Set up the states for Slice 1 as follows: For Normal, shut off the type layers; for the Over state, turn on the "you are left of the dot" layer; and for the Out state, be sure the type layers are off. The Rollover palette should look like Figure 36.23.

Figure 36.23
Before you choose the slice in the Rollover palette, the Rollover palette is empty. When the slice is selected at the lower left, a Normal state is created. You must shut off the type layers to get only the dot to appear.

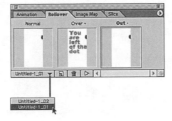

12. Choose the second slice (untitled-1_02) from the Slices pop-up menu on the bottom of the Rollover palette.

13. Add an Over state and an Out state by selecting New state from the Rollover palette menu. You must change the Down state to Out.

14. Set up the states for Slice 2 as follows: For Normal, shut off the type layers; for Over, turn on the "you are right of the dot" layer; and for Out, be sure the type layers are off. The Rollover palette should look like Figure 36.24.

Figure 36.24
Again, choosing Slice 2 creates a Normal state. You must shut off the type again if it is on.

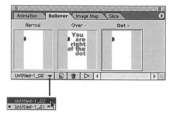

15. Click the Play/Preview button on the bottom of the Rollover palette and roll your mouse over the image.

The states change and appear to know where your mouse is on the page. Of course, this can become far more complicated using more slices and position possibilities. Similar and more complicated tricks (for example, creating concentric slices to control rollover buttons) can be put to work to control the content on your pages. Be aware that heavy use of rollovers requires heavy graphics and causes slower downloads.

PART **XI**

IMAGE PRINTING, OUTPUT, AND USE

CHAPTER 37

USING PHOTOSHOP IMAGES ON YOUR WEB SITE

In this chapter

MERGING PHOTOSHOP AND IMAGEREADY IMAGES WITH THE WEB

Putting up Web pages is simple if you know a little bit of HTML code or have a Web page creation program that does the code for you. Code generators and Web authoring programs (GoLive, Dreamweaver, FrontPage, Cold Fusion, BBEdit, and so on) can help rough in code and simplify the process of authoring. However, it is good to know at least some HTML to get started. With some basic knowledge, you can get up and going without having anything but a word-processing program or text editor.

As you already have ImageReady, some fairly complicated codes can be generated for you to do Java rollovers and complex tables. Java can create some activity on your pages, such as having information pop up on your page depending on when the visitor's mouse rolls, or creating changes in the appearance of buttons to help a visitor know they are active. Tables create an array for your images that help you control where they are placed on the page. Even if you don't know a lot about Web pages or HTML, you can incorporate this complicated code with just a rudimentary understanding of HTML. The purpose here is not to make you a Web page design giant overnight, but to help you understand the controls and options you have for putting your Photoshop and ImageReady images on your Web pages, and to give you the tools necessary to incorporate ImageReady code.

BASIC WEB PAGE HTML

The basic code shell for a Web page is seen in Listing 37.1.

LISTING 37.1   BASIC HTML SHELL

```
<HTML>
<HEAD>
<TITLE></TITLE>
</HEAD>
<BODY>
</BODY>
</HTML>
```

This defines your page without any text or other information, and is simply the basic set of tags used for creating a page. The code is written in *tags*, which are simply markers that denote where an area, type of information, or formatting begins and ends. For example, the <HTML> tag lets the browser know that what follows on the Web page is written in HTML, and defines the absolute beginning (<HTML>) and end (</HTML>) of the code for the page. The closing tag looks the same as the opening tag but with a forward slash. Everything that falls between the beginning and end tag becomes part of that element. Most HTML codes require these beginning and ending tags to define the area in which the tags apply and the content to group under them.

Three additional tags are required, beside the <HTML> tag, to complete coding for a basic Web page: <HEAD>, <TITLE>, and <BODY>. The <HEAD> tag defines header information, or information about what is on the page, as well as scripting and formatting information (if any). The header information includes the <TITLE> tag within it, which contains the page title that appears in the browser title bar. Typing acceptable letters and symbols between the opening and closing <TITLE> tag makes that entry appear in the title bar of the browser window when the page is opened. The <BODY> tag defines the area in which you can place information and images to appear on your page. Typing acceptable letters and symbols between the opening and closing <BODY> tag makes that entry appear in the browser window. These four tags are all that are required to create a basic Web page—and all that are required for you to frame even the most complicated code generated by ImageReady for placing your images.

To put this to the test, if you type the code seen in Listing 37.2 into a text editor or word processor and save the code as a text-only file with the extension .htm, then open that file with a Web browser, it will cause the result pictured in Figure 37.1.

LISTING 37.2 SIMPLE HTML CODING

```
<HTML>
<HEAD>
<TITLE>My First Webpage Title</TITLE>
</HEAD>
<BODY>
This is the body of my first webpage.</BODY>
</HTML>
```

Figure 37.1
This is what the result of the simple code seen in Listing 37.2 will look like in a browser. Additional code can be used to affect color and type size, and place images.

This overview of HTML basics merely sets up your initial page and does nothing that you will be using Photoshop and ImageReady for. Photoshop and ImageReady create images and code that you can insert into your basic Web page in a variety of ways, using different controls. The following section discusses the options you have for using HTML to insert graphics in your Web pages and discusses what you need to know to incorporate images through HTML.

OPTIONS FOR IMAGE INSERTION

There are several ways to use images alone and in combination when inserting them into Web pages. ImageReady can take care of some of the more complicated code writing and methods. However, to know what is going on in the code that ImageReady writes, and how best to use and incorporate it, it is good to understand the basics of the image codes.

BASICS OF PLACING AN IMAGE ON A WEB PAGE

The basic way to insert an image is with an image (<IMG>) tag. This tag references an image that you have saved in a separate file. The tag tells the browser where to look for the file and what type of file it is. It can also control certain parameters about the image such as its size, orientation on the page, text wrapping, and alignment with text, border width, spacing around the image horizontally and vertically, and adding text to display while the image downloads or for nongraphical browsers. Although all these things (and really a few more) are possible in the image tags, the only necessary part of the tag is the identity of the tag and placing the reference to the image. The browser will use default information for the other settings if you don't include it. The basic image tag appears as follows:

```
<IMG SRC="image.gif">
```

This tells the browser that the information that falls between the tags is associated with an image placement and what the source for the image that it should insert is (in this case, the GIF image named "image.gif"). Using the tag in the code from the previous example would resemble the code seen in Listing 37.3 (this code yields the results in Figure 37.2).

> **Note**
>
> "Image.gif" is meant as a generic term for any browser-compatible image (GIF or JPEG). Substitute the entire phrase with the name of the file you want to insert.

LISTING 37.3   USING THE IMAGE TAG

```
<HTML>
<HEAD>
<TITLE>My First Webpage Title</TITLE>
</HEAD>
<BODY>
This is the body of my first webpage.
Here is an image.<img src="image.gif"></BODY>
</HTML>
```

Without other means to control the alignment (for example, tables or the NOBR—no break—tag), alignment can be changed by resizing the browser window. Depending on the goal of your page, this might not be desirable. If you want more control, you have to add more code.

Figure 37.2
The image appears exactly where the tag is placed, aligned to the baseline of the accompanying text.

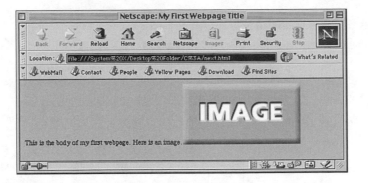

CONTROLLING IMAGES WITH ATTRIBUTES

Other standard controls for the image itself would just be added inside the tag. For example, an ALT statement would display alternative text to the image. To incorporate it, you would simply place the ALT statement following the command within the brackets. It would look like this:

```
<IMG SRC="image.gif" ALT="Placement Only Image">
```

When the page opened and was loading the image, could not find the image, or if it is opened in a nongraphical browser, the text will display in place of the image (see Figure 37.3). Other tag attributes for the image tag would be defined as in Table 37.1.

Figure 37.3
The ALT attribute places text in the space where the image will appear until the image takes its place. Other image tag attributes can help you control the appearance and placement of images on your pages.

TABLE 37.1 ADDITIONAL IMAGE TAG ATTRIBUTES

Attribute Syntax	Description
Width="[number of pixels]"	Width of image in pixels. Can be used to resize the image.
Height="[number of pixels]"	Height of image in pixels. Can be used to resize the image.
Align="[left, right]"	Aligns image to the left or right of the browser window, and text wraps in the open space.

TABLE 37.1   CONTINUED

Attribute Syntax	Description
Valign="[texttop, top, middle, absmiddle, bottom, baseline, absbottom]"	Aligns the text to the noted position in relation to the image. Using this might affect text wraps that would be achieved using Align.
Border="[number of pixels]"	Pixel width of the border around the image. (Border color can be adjusted using BODY settings for text or link color— depending on whether the image is a link or not.)
Hspace="[number of pixels]"	Number of pixels to buffer around the image to the right and left.
Vspace="[number of pixels]"	Number of pixels to buffer around the image on the top and bottom.

Resizing images with the height and width attribute will not do any interpolation in resizing the image. What will happen is the image information will be stretched to fit the area. Generally, it works better when sizing down. However, resizing at all (except in certain circumstances with background areas or in filling sections of a table with solid color) is a questionable practice for images except in some special cases or if trying to achieve an effect. If you need an image to appear bigger on the page, use either a larger version of the image, or do the interpolation in Photoshop where the results will be better. Unless you like the blocky effect that will happen when scaling images up, resizing up in the browser is probably a mistake.

Figure 37.4
This image is resized to twice the height using the Height parameter in the image tag. Note the blocky effect it produces.

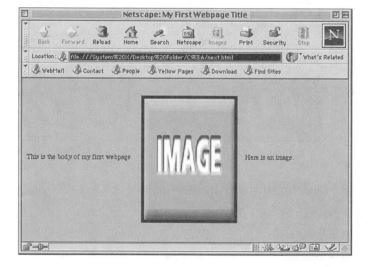

→ For more information on other uses for resizing images, **see** "Understanding the Use of Tables to Place Images," **p. 836**.

When sizing the image down with the Height and Width attributes, the results might look okay, but it isn't the best means of controlling an image in most circumstances, and it isn't really what the tag is for. In sizing the image down using the tag attributes, the image will look smaller in the browser when it loads. However, there will be no associated savings in file size: The file will still take as much memory and time to load as if it were displayed full size. You can save file size by shrinking the image to the display size in Photoshop or ImageReady before saving it for use in the Web page. The only case where it can come in handy to use the Height and Width attributes to resize an image down is when the image appears more than once on the page: at least once at the large size, and then in another place at the smaller size. If you use the same image for both these instances, you will save download time as the image will have to load only once; if you use separately sized images for the two instances, the download time for the page will increase.

Part XI

Ch 37

Importance of Download Time

Using all the tricks you can to keep download time of your pages to a minimum is important. Pages that download more quickly are more attractive to visitors than slow-loading pages because there is less waiting. Be conscious of how you use images on a page, and how you can use them to your advantage in speeding download. In some cases, and with some visitors, every byte is important: If you can, trim a few kilobytes by being careful and making good decisions with your images (and code).

Height and Width attributes are most useful for getting a page with images to load more quickly in general. For example, when loading a page without the Height and Width attributes noted for the images, the text will load for the page and then the page text and sizing will reflow after the image has been located and defined. This can happen a number of times depending on how many images are on the page, where they are situated, and how they load. Noting the Height and Width attributes in the code will lay the page out properly the first time through, with no need to reflow. As a result, the page will load faster (and more smoothly).

Height and Width attributes also can be used to increase the size of images in certain, more advanced uses, such as when an image is used as a spacer or to help the alignment of a table. In these cases, a tiny image (often single color) can be blown up to fill much larger spaces without distorting its appearance.

→ For more information on increasing the size of an image element with Height and Width attributes, **see** "Understanding the Use of Tables to Place Images," **p. 836**.

REFERENCING IMAGES

The reference in the example shown earlier in Figure 37.2 is a simple case where the image will reside in the same directory or folder as the HTML file that is referencing it. For that example, you would upload the HTML file (mypage.html) and the image file (image.gif) into the same FTP directory (the target directory for www.yoursite.com) where they will be referenced. If the image is to be placed in another directory, or even on another server or Web site, that image has to be referenced properly. Depending on where it is located, it might have to be referenced by a full path to the image or possibly by an alternative shorthand.

For example, ImageReady will place images in a subfolder called `Images by default when creating code during an export`, and these images are referenced in the code simply by adding the directory name "Images" to the path in the IMG tag. The browser will look for the `Images` folder before looking for the image. The code for the image tag would look like this: `<IMG SRC="images/image.gif">`. Figure 37.5 shows how the directory structure might look in this case.

Figure 37.5
The HTML pages reside in the base directory in this case, and reference images in the `images` folder. There can be any number of subdirectories in the address for the link to the image, but it is probably best to simplify when you can. The flexibility allows you to organize the images in a variety of logical ways.

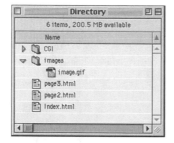

If the image resides in a parallel folder (a folder within the base directory that is not a subfolder), the syntax would look like the following: `<IMG SRC=".../images/image.gif">`. This tells the browser to look at the root directory before looking for the `images` folder. The directory setup would look something like Figure 37.6.

Figure 37.6
HTML pages page2.html and page3.html reside in another directory within the base directory. The ellipses "..." tells the browser to look out to the root directory before attempting to find the `images` folder.

In some cases, such as when the image is on another site, when there are certain types of security, or perhaps even when you are having some sort of difficulty with the link to the image, it might be best to use the full path. This will look like a URL, showing everything the browser would need to locate the image:

```
<IMG SRC="http://www.yourwebsite.com/Images/image.html">
```

The reference method that you use doesn't really matter as long as the image is targeted properly and saved to the right place. For example, if the image is in the same directory as the file that is referencing it, you can reference it with either the shorthand (SRC="image.gif") or the full path (SRC="http://www.yourwebsite.com/image.gif"). The reference will need to be correct, as the browser will not go searching for the image where it isn't told to look.

Caution

Please note that referencing images from other sites without permission can be considered both a copyright violation and stealing. Generally, all images should be referenced from your own libraries, although these might be held in different locations.

 If an image or images fail to appear in your browser tests, see "Finding Images for the Browser" in the Troubleshooting section at the end of this chapter.

USING IMAGES AS BACKGROUNDS

Images can be placed as backgrounds for text and images that appear in the <BODY> portion of the code. These are added in the <BODY> tag itself by including a background attribute directly in the body tag:

```
<BODY background="image.gif">
```

When images are added to the page as a background, they tile to fill the visible area of the browser. This can be very useful as it can allow you to use very small images to fill a very large area. If done correctly, the background will end up seamless and can create a larger pattern—sometimes with very small images, meaning quicker download time.

In Figure 37.7, the sliver image shown above the browser (shown here at 50% so it would fit the viewing page) is used as a background for the page displayed below it.

Figure 37.7
Tiling background images allows very small images to fill large areas, saving file size and download time. The 3KB GIF image used as the background on this page takes an instant to download, and quickly fills the browser window with what appears to be a much larger image.

Image used as a background

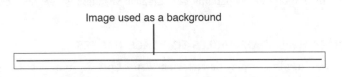

As shown in Figure 37.7, a single row of horizontal pixels can create a vertical pattern. The pixel row needs only to be 1 pixel high, but should be wide enough to fill the maximum viewing size you can expect. Although unlikely, 1,900 pixels is pretty safe for just about any display. However, you might skimp a little if you are counting bytes and want to keep the image as small as possible. Designing with a common pixel width in mind can help you simplify your procedure. Although 1,900 pixels wide will cover almost all situations, 1,280 will be sufficient to cover most configurations and monitor settings—and you can go smaller if you want to skimp on file size.

A vertical pixel row can create a horizontal pattern. Deciding the height of the vertical row to use can be somewhat trickier. There is really no opportunity to scroll right on most Web pages (there is no option to scroll horizontally where there is no content that falls out of the view of the browser window to the right). Because browsers align materials vertically, visitors are used to scrolling down because that is the usual orientation for content. Depending on how the type size is set, how wide the browser is, what defaults the user has chosen for display, and so on, the page might actually be longer or shorter than you expect when the visitor views it in his/her browser. This might affect how you have to size the image for the background and how that image will tile. The height will have to depend entirely on the amount of content you plan for the page. Be sure to leave significant (30%–40%) leeway in creating vertical tiles.

Images as small as 1×1 pixel can be used to tile to color the browser background. To create an image to use as a fill color, all you need to do is open a new 1×1-pixel image and fill it with a selected color, and then save it as a GIF. When the image is referenced as the background image in the BODY tag, the tiny image will tile to fill the entire background of the browser window. Square or rectangular patterns of any size (seamless or not) can be used as well. Be conscious of the size of the pattern and make it as small as possible. Seamless patterns tend to work best for this purpose.

→ For more information on creating patterns, **see** "Creating Seamless Pattern and Texture Elements,"
p. 668.

UNDERSTANDING THE USE OF TABLES TO PLACE IMAGES

Tables are often used to display data, such as lists of prices, item details, and other pieces of information. They have the advantage of being able to break down pages into presized areas, such as neat columns and/or rows, and can be displayed with raised borders to help neatly box and present cells of information. Although tables are certainly useful for defining areas of text and data, they have unique properties that can be used to reassemble sliced images. For the most part, ImageReady or Photoshop will perform the task of formatting the table for you (which can be complex to do if typing the code out longhand). It is, however, helpful to see the code and understand what it does to keep the images where they are supposed to be in case you ever need to make simple adjustments. Figure 37.8 shows a simple, even slicing of columns and rows, and a more complex slicing that might be used to define the areas of a Web page.

Figure 37.8
Tables can be simple rows and columns used for data, or complex configurations of columns and rows useful for defining placement. The simple slicing option might be used for a data table, whereas the more complex slicing can define an entire Web page (note the areas for the header/logo, button navigation, and side-bar information).

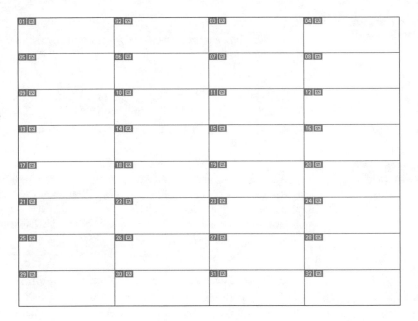

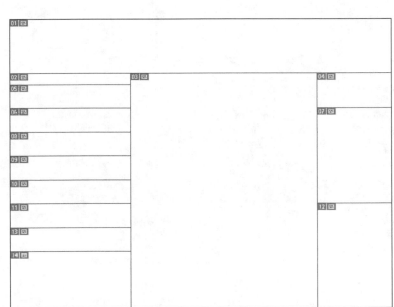

Use the following steps to have ImageReady or Photoshop do the work for you in creating the code for your image table.

1. Create the image. This can be done in either ImageReady or Photoshop.

2. Slice the image as appropriate using the Slice tool.

Note

The Slice tool is now available in either ImageReady or Photoshop, as of version 6.

3. Generate the HTML and slices by choosing <u>F</u>ile, Save Opti<u>m</u>ized As (ImageReady) or <u>F</u>ile, Save for <u>W</u>eb (Photoshop), which will help you automatically save the code and image slices. Be sure to note the folder in which you have saved the files.

Tip

If you want the HTML only, you can also choose to Copy HTML Code, using the ImageReady option for Copy All Slices (<u>E</u>dit, Copy HTML Code, Copy All Slices). Using this command will copy the code to the buffer without having to save it first. The code can be pasted into a text editor directly from the buffer rather than having to open the exported HTML file.

It is possible to choose different defaults for saving the optimized information. Several changes might be in order depending on what you want to accomplish. However, the default setting of Auto for Spacers should be changed to Always in the Output Settings for generating the HTML before creating the tables (see Figure 37.9). Using Always will ensure that the export will generate spacers. These force sizing for the table.

Figure 37.9
ImageReady's preference for spacers can be changed using the Output Settings for HTML (as pictured here) or changing the options in Save Optimized As. Choosing Always as the option for create spacers (rather than the default of Auto) will force the code to create spacers.

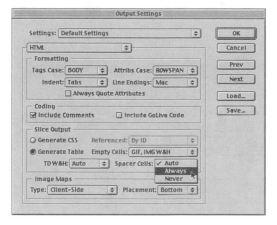

Spacers essentially act as a sort of splint or skeleton to hold the perimeter of the table together in the intended size. They are placed as an additional row and column outside the table, and are filled with a transparent GIF. The GIF image is used to define the space desired for the width of the column or height of the row, depending on where the spacer appears (see Figure 37.10). These are GIF rather than JPEG images as GIF supports transparency, which allows the spacer to perform its function without affecting the underlying image. The spacer is also a 1×1-pixel image, which optimizes its efficiency. This same spacer can be used for a number of different purposes on the page.

Figure 37.10
The spacer row and column define the absolute size of the table and keep the contents of the table aligned. This rather simple 4-panel image will actually have 3 rows and 3 columns when created as a table with spacers. See the code taken from the image using Copy HTML Code in the following example.

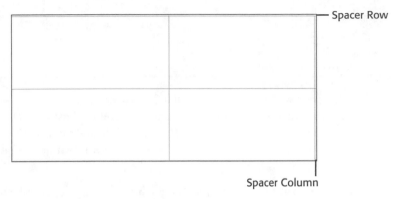

Spacer Row

Spacer Column

As long as none of the content of the cells in the table is larger than the area defined by the spacers, the table will remain the right size and shape. Altering the image size or table size information can alter and/or ruin the effect.

In any case, when the code is exported for the simple four-panel slicing pictured earlier in Figure 37.10, the resulting HTML will look like the code in Listing 37.4. In this case, the code was copied out of ImageReady using the Copy HTML Code command. The Save Optimized command will create the same code, but will create it within a complete coding for the page (including the HTML, HEAD, TITLE, and BODY tags).

LISTING 37.4   IMAGEREADY CODE

```
<!-- ImageReady Slices (Untitled-1) -->
<TABLE BORDER=0 CELLPADDING=0 CELLSPACING=0>
 <TR>
  <TD>
   <IMG SRC="images/spacer.gif" WIDTH=320 HEIGHT=1></TD>
  <TD>
   <IMG SRC="images/spacer.gif" WIDTH=320 HEIGHT=1></TD>
  <TD></TD>
 </TR>
 <TR>
  <TD>
   <IMG SRC="images/imageslice_01.jpg" WIDTH=320 HEIGHT=150></TD>
  <TD>
   <IMG SRC="images/imageslice_02.jpg" WIDTH=320 HEIGHT=150></TD>
  <TD>
   <IMG SRC="images/spacer.gif" WIDTH=1 HEIGHT=150></TD>
 </TR>
 <TR>
  <TD>
   <IMG SRC="images/imageslice_03.jpg" WIDTH=320 HEIGHT=150></TD>
  <TD>
   <IMG SRC="images/imageslice_04.jpg" WIDTH=320 HEIGHT=150></TD>
  <TD>
   <IMG SRC="images/spacer.gif" WIDTH=1 HEIGHT=150></TD>
```

LISTING 37.4 CONTINUED

```
  </TR>
</TABLE>
<!-- End ImageReady Slices -->
```

The TABLE code will contain the beginning (<TABLE>) and ending (</TABLE>) table tags along with defined rows and columns. The rows are defined by <TR></TR> (or Table Row) tags, and columns are defined by <TD></TD> (or Table Data) tags. Images are all defined using Height and Width parameters to be sure of a tight fit within the table. Image Tables require a tight fit to work consistently.

After the image is sliced and exported as the table, separate areas can be used to define links and/or rollovers, or simply to slice up an image to give it the appearance of loading more quickly as it will load in portions. The creation of rollover effects can be done right along with the creation of the image, or separately, depending on how you want to work or what you want to accomplish.

Note

If using any type of linking in the table, be sure you set the border for the image to 0 in the table (this is done by default in the HTML generated by ImageReady). Failing to do this might effectively increase the size of the link image and offset the table. Even if only by 1 or 2 pixels, it might throw the whole table off, depending on how complex the table is.

INSERTING EXPORTED JAVASCRIPT FOR ROLLOVERS

JavaScript for rollovers (and really layer animations) is another method of inserting image information for your pages, albeit somewhat advanced. ImageReady generates the code for the rollover in two portions: the JavaScript, which controls the action, and the table, which controls the placement of the image. These two elements are handled separately in placing the code inside a Web page.

→ For more information on rollover buttons, **see** "Constructing Rollover Buttons," **p. 796**.

After the code is created, it needs to be properly placed in the HTML for the page so that the image will work as expected. ImageReady will generate the full Web page including the script and image tags. You can use this as is, or cut and paste the script and image elements of the code to another page. The areas of code are clearly marked with beginning and ending remark tags. For the script, you will copy everything from "<!-- ImageReady Preload Script ([*filename*]) -->" to "<!-- End Preload Script -->;" For the image area, you will copy everything from "<!-- ImageReady Slices ([*filename*]) -->" to "<!-- End ImageReady Slices -->." In both cases, "[*filename*]" stands for the name of the image as it is currently saved when generating the code. Paste the script into the HEAD of the HTML, and paste the image area information into the body where you want the images to appear (see Listing 37.5).

Tip

Because ImageReady references the filename in the comments in the code for the script, it is helpful to give the file a meaningful name when you are saving it to generate the script. If you don't change the name to something meaningful when saving, remember to change the name accordingly in the markers so that they make sense in defining what they bracket in the file. This will come in handy if you want to move the element again and don't want to figure out the Java and table code.

Tip

You can copy the code with or without the markers; the markers really only serve to tell you where the code begins and ends. An advantage to copying the markers is that if you need to move the script or copy it to another page, you will know where it begins and ends. Copying without will save a few bytes and leave you with slightly less cluttered code. If you are using more than one set of rollovers or multiple tables, you'll have to figure out the code to move the elements if you remove the tags.

LISTING 37.5   JAVASCRIPT CODE

```
<HTML>
<HEAD>
<TITLE>[filename]</TITLE>
<META HTTP-EQUIV="Content-Type" CONTENT="text/html; charset=iso-8859-1">
<!-- ImageReady Preload Script ([filename]) -->
<SCRIPT LANGUAGE="JavaScript">
<!--

function newImage(arg) {
 if (document.images) {
  rslt = new Image();
  rslt.src = arg;
  return rslt;
 }
}

function changeImages() {
 if (document.images && (preloadFlag == true)) {
  for (var i=0; i<changeImages.arguments.length; i+=2) {
   document[changeImages.arguments[i]].src = changeImages.arguments[i+1];
  }
 }
}

var preloadFlag = false;
function preloadImages() {
 if (document.images) {
  [filename]_01_over = newImage("images/[filename]_01-over.jpg");
  [filename]_01_click = newImage("images/[filename]_01-click.jpg");
  preloadFlag = true;
 }
}

// -->
</SCRIPT>
<!-- End Preload Script -->
```

JavaScript —

LISTING 37.5   CONTINUED

```
</HEAD>
<BODY BGCOLOR=#FFFFFF ONLOAD="preloadImages();">
<!-- ImageReady Slices ([filename]) -->
<A HREF="#"
 ONMOUSEOVER="changeImages('[filename]_01', 'images/[filename]_01-over.jpg');
return true;"
 ONMOUSEOUT="changeImages('[filename]_01', 'images/[filename]_01.jpg'); return
true;"
 ONCLICK="changeImages('[filename]_01', 'images/[filename]_01-click.jpg');">
 <IMG NAME="[filename]_01" SRC="images/[filename]_01.jpg" WIDTH=320 HEIGHT=240
BORDER=0></A>
<!-- End ImageReady Slices -->
</BODY>
</HTML>
```

Image Slicing Information

Note

In the code, [*filename*] stands for the current saved name of the image used to generate the code.

The only thing that really needs to be changed or considered about the code as it stands (see the previous example) is that the link for clicking the button has to be placed. The link belongs in the portion of the code that places the image—defined by the statement A HREF ="#". The "#" should simply be changed to the URL of the target. In other words, this should be the place the button was meant to bring the visitor to if it is clicked. This can be shorthand (if appropriate) or the full URL.

When the code is placed in the HTML and the page is saved, you can view the results by opening the saved page in a Web browser.

TROUBLESHOOTING

FINDING IMAGES FOR THE BROWSER

When opening my Web page in the browser, the page opens but the image is missing. Why doesn't the image show?

Usually, images will not show up in the Web page for one of two reasons: The file type for the image is not one that can be opened by the browser (must be a GIF or JPEG), or the images are not properly referenced. If you are using ImageReady to create the image, chances are that the problem lies in the code and references rather than the file type. If this is the case, several different things can be going wrong:

- You might not have the images in the place where you are telling the browser to look for them.

- You might have renamed the image files in the HTML without renaming the images themselves.

■ You might have renamed the images without changing the corresponding reference in the code.

Be sure, simply, that the images referenced in the HTML match in name and placement, or the browser will not find them. If you move the HTML from one directory to another, be sure to move the images, too, if using shorthand references rather than full URLs.

PHOTOSHOP AT WORK: CREATING A WEB PAGE WITH A DOWNLOADABLE IMAGE

Sharing your Photoshop images is one great reason to use the Web. For this exercise to work best, you will need all the following:

■ At least one image you might want to share (perhaps a picture of yourself or family).

■ An active Internet connection.

■ An FTP site to post your work.

Although you can do the exercise without these things, you will encounter some difficulties and you won't get the full effect.

The goal is to put a picture on a Web site so a visitor can download a high-resolution version of it—perhaps even in the format of their choice. The solution will be to show the image in JEPG format for the Web page, but link to another image stored on the site that will download at the click of a button. Of course, the visitor might just download the version of the image that appears on the page, but the point here is that the stored images can be in higher resolution and in other file formats.

Use the following steps to complete the exercise:

1. Locate an image you want to share.
2. Save the image in formats you might like to make available for download.
3. Create the HTML for the Web page with references to the various images.
4. Place the images and associated Web page on the FTP site so they can be accessed via the Web.

Note Be sure each file is saved with the proper extension for the type of image that it is.

5. Send a link for the Web site address in an email to whomever you want to look at the page.

Assuming you have located the image you want to share, you might want to make it available in a variety of formats. For example, you might use Photoshop's native format if there are layers you want to retain, TIFF format for high compatibility across a variety of programs, and a high-resolution JPEG format for those who will not have other viewing capability than the browser. For the sake of this example, save the image as all three of these types. After you have saved the high-resolution versions of the image, save a version for the Web page display. This image can be both smaller than the original and in lower resolution (preferably 72dpi). Making the image small will help save download time for the visitor who is just viewing the page. Be sure all the images are saved either to the directory you will be saving the HTML to, or to a subfolder in that directory (for example, an "Images" directory).

Create the basic HTML for the Web page in a text editor or word-processing program (see the example in "Basic Web Page HTML" at the beginning of the chapter). Title the page something appropriate by adding text between the <TITLE> tags (for this example, I used "The Download Page"). Next, add your image to the body portion of the HTML by inserting the IMG tag. The tag should look something like this:

```
<IMG SRC="mypicturesm.jpg">
```

(where 'sm' stands for small), and should be added between the opening and closing <BODY> tags. For good measure, add the Height and Width attributes for the <IMG> tag. These should be the actual pixel dimensions of the image. If you don't know the pixel dimensions, open the image in Photoshop and look at the Image Size (Image, Image Size). The pixel dimensions will be at the top of the Image Size dialog box.

Note
I will be placing all the files for this example in the same directory for simplicity's sake. You can place them in subfolders, but be sure to make the proper references.

→ For more information on referencing images in HTML code, **see** "Referencing Images," **p. 833**.

The last thing you really have to do to complete the Web page portion is add the links. You can associate the link in a number of ways: You could use simple text links, or you can use image links—perhaps even create rollovers. In the example, I use a combination of text and image links, and make use of the image already placed on the page at full size. The link is the original image resized to 1/6 the size (in this case 48×33 pixels). As the image already has to load for the main image, it adds no significant size to the download (the only addition is the code for the placement of the image).

Adjust other parameters and settings to make the page look as you want it. I worked with this for a few minutes to adjust spacing and alignment, and controlled the layout using a table. Admittedly, I cheated a little on the table, as it was easier to have ImageReady do the code for me. I took the original image, added some size to the canvas, sliced some additional rows, and then copied the HTML from the slices.

Tip

ImageReady can quickly create tables that might take you quite a bit of time to do long-hand. You can use an image you want to cut up to create the table, or a blank image. Cut the area up to approximate what you want the table to look like. If there will be text in some of the boxes (rather than images that fully fill the slice), be sure to change the HTML Output Settings for the <TD> tag's W, H to Always before exporting the code. This will insert Height and Width parameters for each <TD> tag. You might also want to remove all naming parameters in the Saving File Options dialog box (see Figure 37.11). This will allow you to search and replace in a text editor to remove all the image references at one time if you are interested in using the table only.

Figure 37.11
To get to the Saving File Options, choose Save Optimized As (File, Save Optimized As). When the Save dialog box opens, buttons at the bottom right will allow access to the Saving File Options and the HTML Options.

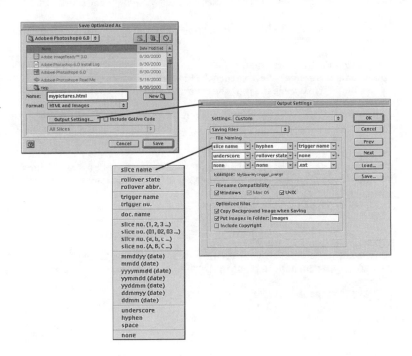

With a few adjustments I ended up with the code you see in Listing 37.6. The results can be seen in Figure 37.12.

LISTING 37.6   EXERCISE HTML CODE

```
<HTML>
<HEAD>
<TITLE> The Download Page</TITLE>
</HEAD>
<BODY BGCOLOR=#FFFFFF>
<TABLE BORDER=0 CELLPADDING=0 CELLSPACING=0>
 <TR>
  <TD>
   <IMG SRC="spacer.gif" WIDTH=288 HEIGHT=1></TD>
```

LISTING 37.6   CONTINUED

```
  <TD></TD>
 </TR>
 <TR>
  <TD>
   <IMG SRC="mypicturesm.jpg" WIDTH=288 HEIGHT=198></TD>
  <TD>
   <IMG SRC="spacer.gif" WIDTH=1 HEIGHT=198></TD>
 </TR>
 <TR>
  <TD width=288>
   To download a copy of this image click on your choice below. </TD>
  <TD>
   <IMG SRC="spacer.gif" WIDTH=1 HEIGHT=49></TD>
 </TR>
 <TR>
  <TD align=right width=288>
   Download a <a href="mypicture.tif">TIFF</a>: <a href="mypicture.tif">
   <IMG SRC="mypicturesm.jpg" height=33 width=48 vspace=8 align=middle></a></TD>
  <TD>
   <IMG SRC="spacer.gif" WIDTH=1></TD>
 </TR>
 <TR>
  <TD align=right width=288>
  Download a <a href="mypicture.psd">PSD</a>: <a href="mypicture.psd">
<IMG SRC="mypicturesm.jpg" height=33 width=48 vspace=8 align=middle></TD>
  <TD>
   <IMG SRC="spacer.gif" WIDTH=1></TD>
 </TR>
 <TR>
  <TD align=right width=288>
   Download a <a href="mypicture.jpg">JPG</a>: <a href="mypicture.jpg">
<IMG SRC="mypicturesm.jpg" height=33 width=48 vspace=8 align=middle></a></TD>
  <TD>
   <IMG SRC="spacer.gif" WIDTH=1></TD>
 </TR>
</TABLE>
</BODY>
</HTML>
```

This same type of Web page setup might be useful in a number of different cases. For example, it might be used to show a product and links to accessories, product literature, or different models in a product line.

There are several things to note in my solution that I chose to add (your solution does not have to be the same). All the additions but the last are elements discussed elsewhere in this chapter.

- I chose to use a table for controlling the placement of elements on the page.
- I used Height and Width attributes in the image or the <TD> tag to control the size of the table elements.
- I used the display image as a type of link button for all the image downloads to conserve download time.

Figure 37.12
The result of the HTML shown earlier is the simple page shown here. Additional code has afforded some control in the presentation. This can be further augmented and improved.

- I used the Align attribute in the <TD> tag to align the text/content for the links to the right.
- I used Vspace around the link images to evenly space the images from one to the next.
- I aligned the link text to the middle of the link image.
- I used separate links for the text and image even though the target was the same. (This keeps the display of the link looking a bit neater. Putting the image and text in the same link will affect the highlighting for the links, covering the space between the words and image.)

Many other parameters can be changed in the HTML and on the page to make the page look different, and a multitude of techniques can be incorporated. For example, text attributes can be changed, styles created, more images can be used, background can be changed, animation added, and so on. Some additional effects are discussed in this book, but more in line with the use of Photoshop and ImageReady images in building a page. A more intensive look at HTML will require a good book on HTML and Web page design.

→ For more information on other Web image effects, **see** "Creating Professional Web Effects," **p. 791**.

CHAPTER 38

USING PHOTOSHOP IMAGES IN LAYOUT APPLICATIONS

In this chapter

INTEGRATING WITH LAYOUT APPLICATIONS

Photoshop images are often imported into applications that have greater control over large quantities of text, multipage documents, and/or stronger vector graphics controls. Page-layout applications such as QuarkXPress, PageMaker, and InDesign all have similar requirements to be aware of when exporting or saving images for use with them. Applications that effectively combine raster and vector data for presentation or design purposes, such as Illustrator or PowerPoint, have additional capabilities and requirements to consider when exporting images. These issues are outlined in the sections that follow.

SAVING IMAGES FOR USE IN QUARKXPRESS, PAGEMAKER, AND INDESIGN

QuarkXPress, PageMaker, and InDesign can embed both raster and vector information, and combine it with its own page and text data. You have several options when saving images from Photoshop for use with these applications. You need to choose the correct image mode for the exported file, the appropriate file format, and whether you want to control transparency in the page-layout applications through the use of Photoshop's clipping paths.

→ For more information about working with clipping paths, **see** "Using Clipping Paths," **p. 855**.

Save the file in an image mode that is supported by the page-layout application into which you are importing. In most cases, this means choosing either RGB or CMYK. Furthermore, if you plan to print the image, you should convert to CMYK mode in almost all cases because Photoshop gives you a high level of control over the conversion process.

For file formats, you should choose DCS 2.0 (Desktop Color Separations), EPS (Encapsulated PostScript), or TIFF (Tagged Image File Format). If you use spot color channels, save a copy of the file as a DCS 2.0. DCS is an EPS variety that supports spot colors. You can also use the DCS 2.0 format if you need support for an alpha channel or a clipping path. If you do not need support for spot colors or alpha channels, save a copy of the file as EPS. EPS is the most widely supported and recognized printing format. Also, use EPS if you need to export a clipping path with the image.

 If your page-layout program shows a low-resolution version of the file when placing an EPS, or shows only a gray box, see "Image Preview of EPS Files" in the Troubleshooting section at the end of this chapter.

If you are having difficulties with either of the EPS formats, because of incompatibilities in either software or operating systems, save a copy of the file as a TIFF. The TIFF format supports one alpha channel, and TIFF is useful when you're importing into a page-layout or illustration program because you can often see the actual image instead of an EPS preview. In addition, by saving a TIFF, you can determine color, transparency, and halftone screen information in some page-layout programs. Use caution when using the TIFF format available from Photoshop 6, however, because some of the newer supported features, such as layers or other compression methods, may not be supported by your page-layout program.

→ For more information on file types, compatibilities, and properties, **see** "File Type Choices," **p. 780**.

WORKING WITH ILLUSTRATOR

Adobe Illustrator can both import and manipulate image data from Photoshop's most common file formats. In particular, Illustrator can import files in Photoshop's native file format. Illustrator's vector editing tools provide a valuable complement to Photoshop's raster editing capabilities. You can exchange raster and vector information between the two applications easily by dragging and dropping, or by importing and placing.

To import Illustrator data into Photoshop, use File, Place. Browse to the Illustrator file you want to import and click OK. You can resize the image by dragging the handles of the bounding box before rasterizing the image (see Figure 38.1).

Figure 38.1
Because you can arbitrarily resize a vector image without altering its quality, you should scale a placed Illustrator or EPS file to the appropriate size before rasterizing the image.

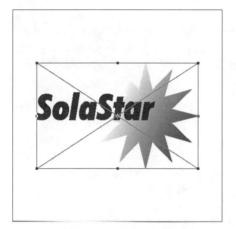

Tip

When importing a vector Illustrator file, it must be rasterized or converted to pixels for use in Photoshop.

You can import Photoshop image information into Illustrator for page-layout purposes, or to use with Illustrator techniques and tools not available in Photoshop. Some examples of features in Illustrator that are not found in Photoshop are the Punk & Bloat filter and creating text along a path. You can save a path you create in Photoshop for use in Illustrator to create text or other effects and then place the Illustrator file with the effects back into Photoshop. You can export any or all Photoshop paths as Adobe Illustrator (AI) files. You can also export a path that shows the document bounds for placement purposes in Illustrator.

→ For more information about exchanging path information between Photoshop and Illustrator, **see** "Using Illustrator to Put Text on a Path in a Photoshop Image," in the Photoshop at Work section at the end of this chapter, **p. 857**.

 Having trouble getting pre–version 6 Photoshop files to display correctly when importing into older versions of Illustrator? See "Image Display Problems in Illustrator" in the Troubleshooting section at the end of this chapter.

Tip

You can also copy and paste path information from Illustrator into Photoshop. When you paste path information from Illustrator, Photoshop asks whether the information should be pasted as pixels or used as a path.

If you are having trouble with blurry or jagged edges when placing an EPS file into Photoshop, see "Bad Edges on EPS Files" in the Troubleshooting section at the end of this chapter.

USING ACROBAT (PS GENERATION)

Adobe Acrobat files have become a popular method of exchanging rich page-layout information because of the widespread adoption of the Acrobat Reader. PDF files are increasingly used in prepress situations as proofs, and as working documents because a service bureau or printer with PostScript Level 3 capabilities can work directly with the PDF file or create a PostScript file to use with older equipment. A highly portable variation of Adobe's PostScript format, PDF files maintain a high level of page-layout information and printer settings.

If you want to create a PDF file just for containing graphics information, for use as a stand-alone PDF, or for combination with other PDF files using Acrobat, use the Save As command and save a copy from Photoshop. If you want to generate a PDF file that contains PostScript printing information, you need to create a PostScript file from Photoshop. For this, you need to have a PostScript printer driver installed through your operating system. You don't need to actually have a PostScript printer, because you are only creating a file.

Tip

Ideally, you should install a PostScript printer driver that matches the output device you eventually plan to use to create the printed image. When installing the printer driver, you can also specify that it should be used to print to a file. You can obtain generic drivers for this purpose from Adobe's Web site (www.adobe.com).

The following steps show how to create a PDF file with PostScript printing information:

1. Choose File, Print Options.
2. In the Print Options dialog box (see Figure 38.2), choose Page Setup.

Figure 38.2
In Photoshop 6, the Print Options dialog box shows a preview of the printed image, including any printing marks.

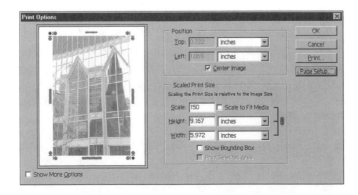

3. In the Page Setup dialog box (see Figure 38.3), select a PostScript printer from the list of available printers. Choose the printing options you want to use and click OK.

Figure 38.3
Some of the settings in the Page Setup dialog box are based on the capabilities of the printer or printer driver you are using.

Note

NEW TO
PHOTOSHOP 6

You can also access the printing options by clicking Show More Options box on in the Print Options dialog box (File, Print Options).

4. To change the color management settings for the PostScript file, choose Show More Options in the Print Options dialog box, and choose Color Management instead of Output from the list (see Figure 38.4).

Figure 38.4
You can control the print color spaces of both the document and the proof in the Print Options dialog box.

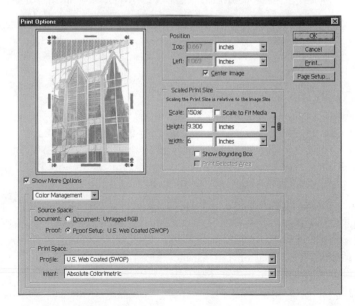

5. Set the Position and Scaled Print Size in the Print Options dialog box.

6. Click Print. In the Print dialog box (see Figure 38.5), make sure that the Print to File box is checked. Set any other print options in the Print dialog box and click OK.

Figure 38.5
By printing to a file using a PostScript driver, you can create a PostScript file. This file can be converted to a PDF.

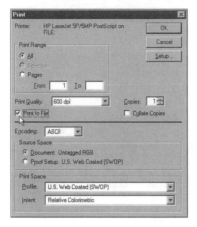

The resulting PostScript file can be used to create a PDF file that contains all the information you specified in the Page Setup, Print Options, and Print dialog boxes. To create a PDF from the PostScript file, you need a tool such as Acrobat Distiller. The PostScript file you create can also be used to print directly to a PostScript printer.

Note

Sending a file to a PostScript printer will require an appropriate driver for creation of the file, as all PostScript drivers are not alike. Drivers are often available free from printer manufacturers. Adobe maintains an extensive collection of links for manufacturers on its Web site.

INTEGRATING WITH MICROSOFT POWERPOINT

PowerPoint is another application into which you may import graphics information. Microsoft PowerPoint is part of the Microsoft Office suite and is used to create onscreen presentations and slideshows. You can import all the common Web formats—GIF, JPEG, and PNG—into PowerPoint. In addition, PowerPoint can import Windows BMP format files, and it also has limited support for EPS and TIFF files.

Generally, the best formats to use with PowerPoint are GIF and JPEG. The same rules that govern the use of these formats on the Web dictate their use with PowerPoint. Use a GIF file for flat-color images, for grayscale, and for images that contain fewer than 256 colors, or if you need to have areas of transparency. Use JPEG for continuous-tone images, or photographs. To import an image into PowerPoint, choose Insert, Picture, From File, and browse to find the file you want to insert.

→ For more information on GIF and JPEG file types, **see** "Effective Use of File Types," **p. 320**.

BLEEDS FOR VARIOUS USES

A *bleed* is the extension of an image beyond the cutline of a page. Bleeds are created when printing to compensate for errors that may be made when pages are cut. Anytime you have parts of an image that should extend to the page edge, whether on a book cover, CD-liner notes, or business cards, you should specify an appropriate bleed. You can create a bleed in Photoshop by specifying a value from 0 to .125 inch (3.18mm or 9.01pts) in the Print Options or Page Setup dialog boxes. This moves the crop marks into the image slightly to show where the edge of the page is expected to fall.

> **Note**
>
> Your image may need to be slightly larger than the actual print size to accommodate the bleed amount.

USING CLIPPING PATHS

When you save a Photoshop EPS file for use in a page-layout or illustration package, by default all the pixels are opaque. A clipping path isolates the areas you want to be opaque. The page-layout program uses transparency for areas outside the clipping path.

1. Create a closed subpath around the object you want to be opaque (see Figure 38.6).

Figure 38.6
The path should define exactly the area of the image you want to print. In essence, the path will be a new document boundary, and is essentially a custom-shaped image box.

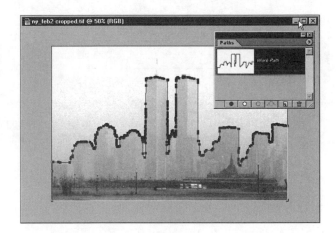

2. Double-click the Work Path to save it. In the Save Path dialog box, enter a name for the path.
3. Choose Clipping Path from the Paths palette menu.
4. In the Clipping Path dialog box, select a path.
5. Enter a value for Flatness. Flatness values range from 0.2 to 100. Smaller values create clipping paths with shorter segments. Larger values create clipping paths with longer

segments. Unless you are receiving printing errors, leave the Flatness value blank to use the printer's default value.

6. Click OK.

7. Save the image as a Photoshop EPS or Photoshop DCS 2.0 file if you are printing on a PostScript printer. Save the image as a TIFF if you are printing on a non-PostScript printer.

When you print the image from a page-layout program, only the pixels bounded by the clipping path print. Note that EPS files with TIFF previews print correctly but do not always display correctly in page-layout programs, depending on how the preview is handled. Most illustration programs, however, display and print the image and clipping path correctly (see Figure 38.7). The true test is outputting to a PostScript printer.

Figure 38.7
The areas defined by the clipping path are opaque and other areas are treated as transparent.

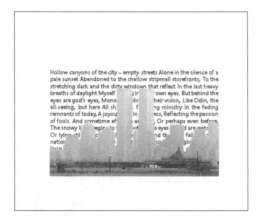

> **Tip**
>
> You can use the Export Transparent Image Wizard to create a clipping path from a selection. Choose Help, Export Transparent Image to start the wizard.

TROUBLESHOOTING

IMAGE PREVIEW OF EPS FILES

Why does my page-layout program show only a gray box or a low-resolution version of the file when I place an EPS?

When you create an EPS file, you can choose what kind of preview to create. You can choose no preview, a 1-bit preview, or an 8-bit preview. If you save the image with no preview, most page-layout applications show only a gray box or test pattern denoting the image bounds. If you save a 1-bit or 8-bit preview, the page-layout application displays only this low-resolution version of the file. In any case, the result is that you may not be seeing exactly what will go to print (either the color or the resolution). A good option for previewing is to create a PDF file and open that in Acrobat Reader. The best option is to test the output on a PostScript printer.

IMAGE DISPLAY PROBLEMS IN ILLUSTRATOR

Why don't my pre–version 6 Photoshop files display correctly when importing into older versions of Illustrator?

Older versions of Illustrator cannot handle layered Photoshop files accurately. If you have any difficulties, try saving a flattened version of the image. To do this, uncheck the Layers check box when saving the image, or flatten before saving. If you need the layers, you can separate and save the layers as separate documents.

BAD EDGES ON EPS FILES

When I place an EPS file into Photoshop, why are the edges blurry and jagged?

Check the Anti-Alias PostScript box in General Preferences in order to anti-alias, or soften, placed Encapsulated PostScript files. Turn off this option to make the edges hard (aliased).

PHOTOSHOP AT WORK: USING ILLUSTRATOR TO PUT TEXT ON A PATH IN A PHOTOSHOP IMAGE

Photoshop is currently at somewhat of a disadvantage when it comes to placing type on a path. Although it will probably not be long before Photoshop will be able to accomplish this, currently it is possible to only mock the effects. Illustrator has always been a stronger type handler than Photoshop. Using Illustrator, you can create type along a path and then import that into Photoshop while retaining the positioning and settings.

Use the following steps to create type along a path in Photoshop by borrowing Illustrator's strength:

1. Create a path in Photoshop (see Figure 38.8).

Figure 38.8
When creating Bézier paths for application of type, keep the segments long and flowing so that the flow of the text will appear smooth. Erratic bumps will probably make the effect just plain look bad.

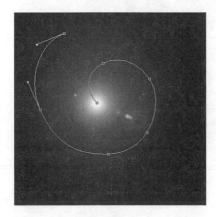

2. Double-click the Work Path to save it. In the Save Path dialog box, enter a name for the path.

3. Choose File, Export, Paths to Illustrator. The Export Paths dialog box is displayed (see Figure 38.9).

Figure 38.9
Choose a path from the Paths list to export for use with Adobe Illustrator.

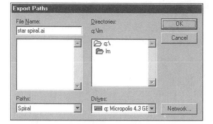

4. Under Paths, select the path you want to export. Select Document Bounds to export a path that indicates the size of the image. Select All Paths to export all the paths in the Photoshop document.

5. Enter a filename and click Save.

To use the path in Illustrator, open the Adobe Illustrator file or use File, Place. Place text on the path or make other modifications using the path, and save the file. Then use File, Place in Photoshop to import the Adobe Illustrator file (see Figure 38.10).

Note

As an alternative, you can just copy and paste the path from Photoshop into Illustrator, then place the type on the path, and copy it back.

Figure 38.10
Exporting and reimporting the document bounds when exporting paths to Illustrator help position the file accurately when you import it back from Illustrator.

CHAPTER 39

IMAGE OUTPUT OPTIONS

In this chapter

HOW DIGITAL OUTPUT WORKS

Digital printing is any output that starts from a digital image or Photoshop file. It is technically the process of defining where ink is placed on paper using numeric representations of your printed data. You may print your final output directly from a digital file, or the digital image may cease to exist when you create film and use analog techniques to define where ink is placed on the page. For the purposes of this chapter, digital printing is any output that starts from a digital image or Photoshop file.

Creating an image in RGB mode is often the first step of the workflow, although your final output is in four or possibly more colors. Your workflow for producing printed images is probably largely unique, depending on the types of images you are printing, your printer, or your service bureau. Your workflow may even change depending on the specifics of the job. There are many printing techniques, and many methods of preparing your digital images for output to paper. Knowing how the image will be printed often requires a relationship with your printer or prepress service bureau, or a bit of trial and error if you are creating output. The preparation of images for print is equal parts science and art.

POSTSCRIPT

Although Adobe has revolutionized several graphics areas with their groundbreaking software, the foundation for everything that Adobe has constructed is PostScript. *PostScript* is a page-description language. Each raster and vector image element is described in PostScript so that it can be output. It is the processors that interpret PostScript data for output on Film Recorders, Laser Printers, and Dye Sublimation Printers, and PostScript's universal adoption that make it particularly powerful. Almost all images that are digitally printed are at some point in their lives in a PostScript format.

There are several different PostScript versions, and you should be careful to make sure that you, your printer, and your service bureau are all working with the same versions, or that you are aware of potential difficulties that might arise because of version and device incompatibilities.

Encapsulated PostScript (EPS) is a highly portable file format that is an offshoot of the PostScript language. EPS files are supported by all page-layout applications and most image-editing applications. EPS files represent image data in PostScript format, but can contain page-description information as well. EPS files can contain screen and halftone information that may not match the settings of your printer, so you may need to make some adjustments during output. Note also that printing EPS files to non-PostScript printers can produce files that do not reflect the true nature of your image.

RIP (RASTER IMAGE PROCESSOR)

A *Raster Image Processor (RIP)* is the software that converts the PostScript, a high-level page description language, into the low-level data that can be sent directly to a printer. You may use only one RIP or multiple RIPs depending on your printers and needs. In the digital print workflow, the RIP processes the device-independent PostScript file, but it can also process a highly device-dependent *PostScript Printer Definition (PPD)* that is embedded into the PostScript file.

LASER OUTPUT

Laser output is produced by laser printers. These use a digital electrophotographic process to create black-and-white output. Because a laser is used to create the output, very high resolutions are possible using this technology, and it is one of the most common, quickest, and affordable printing techniques in use.

PHOTO-QUALITY COLOR

Photo-quality color can be achieved when printing by using one of several printing devices and technologies such as a dye-sublimation printer, continuous-color inkjet printers (such as IRIS), or color electrophotographic printers (such as those made by EFI). These types of prints are often used as proofs, or samples, of what the final output will look like. Printing service bureaus and prepress houses may create these from your original file for you to approve, or you may generate them for your service bureau to use as a guide when creating film or producing the final prints. These processes are not typically used for large print runs because they are relatively expensive and slow compared to four-color, or process printing.

If you want to produce photo-quality color using process printing, you need to take extra care when preparing your file. The correct setup of your color profiles and your output settings is vital. In addition, you need to talk to your service bureau about your expectations and find out about their equipment and limitations.

→ For more information about setting up for printing, **see** "Prepping for Printing: Prepress," **p. 869**.
→ For more information about setting color profiles, **see** "Evaluating Image Color," **p. 409**.

WORKING WITH A SERVICE BUREAU

A *service bureau* is any company that provides either finished output, or more commonly, prepress services, such as film for process printing. Typically, designers develop relationships with a service bureau to ensure that they are going to get the best results possible when printing or setting up their projects. For instance, the service can provide the designer with valuable information about settings in Photoshop that would affect the final output. Before taking a file to a service bureau, you should talk to them and explain the type of job you are printing, the types of software that you are using, and any particulars about the job. Service bureaus can be an invaluable asset to your printing workflow. Service bureaus typically have a variety of high-end printing technologies available, and would have an understanding of the entire printing process.

Over time, service bureaus can anticipate your printing needs and help you set up your files more quickly and economically. Service bureaus also help with the setup and production of your files by providing proofs, or test prints, that enable you to see a reproduction of the final printed piece. Proofs save time and money, avoiding costly setup or unwanted results when printing.

Printing Proofs

A dye-sublimation printer, or thermal dye diffusion printer, creates an image by transferring dye from a ribbon to the paper. The dye is transferred by heating it with a tiny row of heating elements. Continuous inkjet printers (different from the ubiquitous low-end drop-on-demand printers) use a continuous stream of ink to apply an image to paper. These types of high-end prints are commonly used as proofs.

Note

You can create your own digital proofs that can be viewed in Acrobat Reader by creating PDF files using Acrobat Distiller. You should print using the appropriate PostScript driver and create the PDF from the resulting PostScript file, using Acrobat Distiller.

NEGATIVES AND FILM RECORDERS

Film recorder, *filmsetter*, and *imagesetter* are all terms used to describe a process of transferring digital-image information to film so that it can be printed. The higher-end processes mimic analog film: The image is continuous tone, like a negative created by using traditional film. Film for CMYK process printing is generated as negatives on an image setter, and the negatives are used to create plates for printing. The black and white areas on the film, or plate, are used like a mask to describe where the ink will and won't fall on the paper.

Creating negatives or transparencies from your Photoshop images will allow you to have the images printed photographically using traditional processes. Although this may prove expensive, it is often the only way to get optimal quality from your Photoshop efforts.

LARGE-FORMAT PRINTS

As printing technology improves, it has become easier and less expensive to create large-format prints using both low-end and high-end printing technologies. Inkjet methods are the norm as both dye-sublimation and laser techniques require arrays of heating elements and continuous color ribbons or toner. Continuous inkjet technologies, such as IRIS prints, can be generated up to 30×40 inches. Other processes, such as the common drop-on-demand systems, can create prints much larger—typically roll-fed, they are usually 36 inches wide, with maximum lengths reaching up to 50 feet. It is not uncommon for large signage to be produced by connecting these large prints. At the higher (and more expensive) end, large format can also be achieved through a film recorder and the use of more traditional photographic processes.

OTHER TECHNOLOGIES

As printing processes and technologies continue to improve, it has become possible to print some jobs directly from a digital file or multiple files to paper, instead of going through the process of creating film to burn the plates. Such technologies are readily available for black-and-white and color printing, enabling you to create personalized and customized documents. Some processes are used in higher-end DTP (Direct to Plate) printing—which is more like a traditional offset process—and some are strictly digital, like Docutech process, which is a strictly digital print-on-demand technology. The newer digital technologies are meant to reduce costs of creating printed materials, if sometimes at the sacrifice of quality (strictly digital POD processes currently print at only about 600dpi, whereas traditional presses can do 2,540dpi and higher). These can be great alternatives, however, because they can allow shorter print runs and flexibility, whereas traditional processes are more rigid because of processing, setup, and associated costs.

TRADITIONAL OFFSET PRINTING

Offset printing, or lithography, is the most common printing technique in use today. Most often, film is used to burn plates, which determine the areas of the ink. There are four colors of ink in traditional color printing: Cyan, Magenta, Yellow, and Black (CMYK). Depending on the type of lithography used, the images can either be positive or negative on the plates. Water is applied to the plates and is held by the nonimage areas, and then oil-based inks are rolled onto the plate. Water repels the oil-based ink. The layer of repelled ink is then applied to an intermediate cylinder before being applied to the paper. This additional step—offsetting the ink to the intermediate cylinder—gives offset printing its name. One cylinder is used for each color plate. Larger presses may have four cylinders and some up to six (to accommodate spot color and varnishes).

Offset presses can be sheet-fed or web. Sheet-fed presses typically print on only one side of the paper, whereas web-offset presses are designed to print on both sides. Because of this, web-offset presses are used to print the vast majority of magazines and catalogs. Sheet-fed printing tends to be both more expensive and also higher quality than web-offset printing. Sheet-fed printing can often be used with a wider variety of paper types and thickness.

Plates for traditional printing can be created directly from digital files (direct-to-plate) or imagesetters can be used to create lithographic film. Creating film has been the traditional process, and is slowly being encroached on by direct-to-plate. Many prepress service bureaus do not actually produce your final output, but instead, specialize in the creation of the film needed for printing. Using such a service bureau has two benefits. First, it can reduce the setup fees charged by your printer. Second, because you had the film produced, it becomes yours, meaning that you can shop around a bit when looking for printers, particularly when producing the same job in the future.

PANTONE'S SIX-COLOR HEXACHROME PRINTING

Because of the gamut of limitations of CMYK printing, additional techniques have been developed to extend color possibilities on press. One is to use spot colors with the four process colors to create some hues and tints, such as fluorescents or metallics, which are simply impossible to produce using a four-color process. This doesn't solve the problem of the limited CMYK color gamut. *Hexicolor*, based on PANTONE's Hexachrome system, has been developed to expand on the CMYK color space by adding two more inks. By adding a green and orange ink to specially formulated cyan, magenta, yellow, and black inks, the dynamic color range of printed images is increased exponentially. Hexachrome can also reproduce a wider range of PANTONE spot colors, so that the addition of spot-color plates may be unnecessary in some cases where they were necessary before.

Although Photoshop does not produce hexicolor separations directly, plug-ins are available to create the necessary files needed for this type of output. Because of the additional plates and special inks necessary for hexicolor printing, additional expenses are incurred beyond that of CMYK printing. This is currently an option rather than a standard. There are other processes which also add additional color to extend the CMYK gamut (such as by using two or more tones on CMYK inks to create better coverage).

SETTING PRINTING OPTIONS IN PHOTOSHOP

You can set many of Photoshop's printing options directly, although it is a good idea to talk to your service bureau and get their advice about the best settings for their equipment. Knowing what to do with the settings can help you adjust your output and attain the results you want.

LPI VERSUS DPI

Dots per inch (dpi) refers to the addressability of a printing device or a scanner. A higher dpi relates to a higher definition image. *Lines per inch (lpi)* is the number of rows of halftone dots in each linear inch. Higher lpis relate to high-definition images. You should discuss both dpi and lpi with your service bureau. Knowing the final output of your image influences how you set the number of *pixels per inch (ppi)*, or resolution, in Photoshop.

TRAPPING

In offset printing, if the color plates become misaligned, gaps might show between areas of solid color. This can be particularly evident when printing with spot colors or solid areas of Cyan, Magenta, or Yellow that butt up against one another. To remedy this, the colors can be intentionally overlapped along the edges where they meet. If your image is in CMYK mode, you can choose Image, Trap, and enter a value for the trapping. Using the Trap command does not affect spot colors that you may have created on spot color channels. If you need to trap elements on a spot color channel, you can perform a manual overlap. You can trap spot colors and process colors, or perform multiple traps for multiple spot color channels.

1. Choose Select, Load Selection so that you can create a selection from the spot color channel.
2. In the Load Selection dialog box (see Figure 39.1) under Channel, choose the spot channel you want to spread or choke and click OK. You can also hold down (Cmd) [Ctrl] and click the channel to create a selection from it.

Figure 39.1
Choose the channel that you want trap to load as a selection.

3. When the top color is lighter than the bottom color, create a trap that chokes and knocks out the underlying color. To do this choose Select, Modify, Contract (see Figure 39.2). To create a trap that spreads and knocks out the underlying color, choose Select, Modify, Expand.

Figure 39.2
Choose a small value for the trap when expanding or contracting the selection.

4. In the Channels palette, select the underlying spot channel that contains areas you want to knock out. Choose Edit, Clear (see Figure 39.3).

Figure 39.3
By removing the contracted selection from the underlying channel, the color is knocked out and the overlying color is trapped the amount of the selection's contraction.

There is no real need to trap most photographic images, because color will usually blend on its own. Trapping is almost wholly brought about by digital process, where the exact alignment of colors (say, colored type over a solid color background) would otherwise be exactly aligned edge to edge without the trap. Always talk to your service bureau or printer before applying a trap. They can provide you with the appropriate values or, more likely, they may instruct you not to trap because they have specialized software for this purpose.

TRANSFER FUNCTION

A transfer function is used to compensate for color adjustment similar to ICC profiling, but in a way that gives the user manual control. In working with the transfer function, you manually adjust the transfer function curves to modify the ink levels and lighten or darken individual ink applications in targeted tonal ranges. This can be done to fit a single image to various output devices, while not affecting the appearance on screen. When an image will be output from different devices, the quality of the output will hopefully remain fairly constant; the transfer functions allow you to fine-tune the output of an image to the device without redoing or reapplying color correction.

You can alter the transfer function by choosing the Transfer button in either the Print Options or Page Setup dialog box. In the Transfer Function dialog box (see Figure 39.4), you should first choose whether you want to alter all the inks at the same level, or whether you want to change the cyan, magenta, yellow, and black levels separately. Then, you can either drag the curve itself, or enter specific values for each ink percentage. The transfer function is saved with the native Photoshop file and you can also save your EPS and DCS 2.0 files with an appropriate transfer function if necessary. Note that some applications that can use EPS files do not use embedded transfer functions.

Figure 39.4
You can adjust the transfer function's curve directly by clicking and dragging on the curve in the grid.

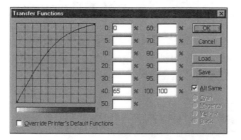

Note

Determining the correct values for the transfer function may require some experimentation or help from your service bureau. After you have a correct transfer function, you can save it to use with other projects that use the same output device. To save the transfer function, choose the Save button in the Transfer dialog box.

KNOCKOUTS

A *knockout* is a printing technique that prints overlapping objects without mixing inks. The ink for the underlying elements does not print (knock out) in the areas where the object overlaps. Knockouts are common when working with areas that overlap with black. Instead of overprinting, or printing one or more colors in the same area, with the black, the non-black, or superfluous colors get removed. It is, however, often desirable to overprint to produce a rich black that is darker than a single coat of black ink can produce.

DOT GAIN

Dot gain is the tendency for halftone dots to spread at their edges. Depending on the amount of the spread, dot gain can cause images to darken. Dot gain is affected by the type of press being used, by the paper, and by the ink. Generally, however, the greatest influence is the paper. Ink spreads differently on newsprint than it does on coated paper. You can compensate for dot gain in Photoshop, or your service bureau can do it before printing. In order to compensate for the dot gain when making the plates, the paper stock that will be used for printing should be taken into account.

→ For more information about setting up for printing, **see** "Prepping for Printing: Prepress," **p. 869**.

PART
XI

CH
39

CHAPTER 40

PREPPING FOR PRINTING: PREPRESS

In this chapter

HOW TO PREPARE A JOB FOR PRINT OR SERVICE BUREAU

The first time you send a job to the printer or service bureau, you might feel a little uncertain about the process. You might not know exactly what to include, or what to expect. Some of the things you should include are not completely obvious. This section is meant to be a primer, not only for preparing and sending out the files properly, but for getting them in order for you and for whoever will be doing the output.

Using the following suggested procedures might go even further than your service requires; however, using procedure assures you that what you send should produce what you expect. It also gives you some safeguards against incurring extra charges or the loss of work and can speed the project to completion.

Proper procedure ensures that you

- Provide necessary information for output
- Provide necessary files for output
- Provide necessary proofs for comparison and matching
- Provide proper, compatible media
- Complete safe archival of your work as file backups

Note

This procedure assumes you have already completed testing for calibration purposes and have run your test file.

CONTACT THE SERVICE

Until you are very familiar with the process and requirements for output, always contact your service before submitting a project—although you might want to make contacting them a regular practice for other reasons. If it is the first time you have contacted them, have them fax or email a copy of their project checklist or their standard submission form; there will undoubtedly be things they forget to tell you if you just ask them about what they need over the phone. The job submission form helps you compile what you need and lets the service know what you have included and need to have done. This form includes information about the materials you are sending for the output, including names of image files, file types, reason for output, screen ruling, and so on. Although you might not really need to contact the service if you know the regimen, you might want to contact them anyway if it has been a while since you last sent anything to them, or even if you just want to consider their turnaround time. Almost any excuse is a good reason to call. The point is a call gives the service the opportunity to update you on any new equipment they might have or changes in their procedure. Output methods change all the time and it is not unlikely that the service will frequently update equipment and/or procedure to keep up with advancements. Calling them will provide them an opportunity to give you an update.

If you are not already sure, clarify with the service that they directly provide the service that you need. Not every service will be able to provide every type of output. This does not necessarily mean you need to switch your service, but that it might be a good idea to have several that you use for different projects, or in unison (both to compare prices, keep prices down, and use the service that is either best or cheapest for what you need). For example, you might find a service that goes out of their way for you to ensure that film comes out right, yet they don't provide a type of proof that you know you can get from the second service. If you push the first service for the same type of proof, they might just job the work out to the second service anyhow. Getting the film from the first and generating the proof at the second will get the results you want and you might save yourself some money.

> **Tip**
>
> Try to get the service to run sample output with specific devices to provide you with a color match to work from so you can match calibrations and see how actual output matches your display. This is very handy for poster plotting or larger, direct digital output, where you will be paying by the foot. It can help you create a more successful image and result. Services may be willing to do a number of things for you on a one-time basis to keep your business. Don't overstep their generosity.

By the time you have hung up the phone, you should be confident that you can give the service what they need so that they can finish the job accurately and quickly. If you need to call them again to clarify anything, do that rather than risk delays, additional delivery charges, or the expense of rerunning a job when it comes out wrong.

Collect Your Files

After you know what the service needs from you, collect all the files necessary for producing the project. This includes the layout file (if any), fonts (if any) and final image files. Collect all the files by copying them to a directory created just for collecting the files (don't just move the files to a new directory). In the directory, create logical subdirectories for the contents. This can simply be a set of directories such as Layout, Fonts, Images or some other clear separation that will help the service locate the files as they need them (the service's instructions might include a description of how they prefer you to do this). You may even choose to include a "Read Me" file in the folder to help describe the contents. This description can be augmented by printouts of complete file lists.

Image Files

The image files you send should include all those used in the layout program and should be in a file type the service can accept (usually TIFF or a type of EPS according to which the service prefers). If you are including DCS separations that are in separate files, be sure to include all five parts of each image. Missing elements will cause failure when the job is run.

Generally, you'll want to include the images as CMYK, unless your service has a preference for making the separations (if this is the case, be sure they are not charging extra for the conversions). A service may have different requirements for different processes. For example,

I use one service that requires CMYK TIFF files for output to film, but RGB files for both their poster plotter and film recorder. Making the effort to provide exactly what they request tends to ensure better results. Be sure you know what file type the service requires for each type of output, and ask if you are uncertain. Checking your files by printing separations (during the proofing) serves as a check to verify that you have included the right file type, and that output will be successful. To test the output, test directly from the files you compile.

When you have gathered all the images, put them in a file/directory called Images.

LAYOUT FILE(S)

If there is only one layout file, you may want to place that in the collection directory by itself in a directory titled Layout, or in a directory titled by the type of file (for example, Quark File, InDesign File, PageMaker, and so on). When you proof the files, you may have to point the layout file to the Images directory so it knows where the high-resolution files are to reference during output. This may require that you archive the originals and remove them from where the layout file can find them, or, even better, try proofing from another computer—if you have one available. After making this change, resave the layout file to keep the reference for the Image files, and back up that new layout to where you have stored the originals.

At any time, if you updated the image files after saving the layout file, you should update the layout file before considering the files complete. This will ensure the changes have not affected the way the images appear (for example, even a minor crop could change the placement of an image and affect how it appears in the image box you have placed it in). If you update, replace the layout file in the Layout folder and reprint any of the proof pages.

FONTS

Be sure to collect all fonts for the output of the job. This includes both the screen and the printer font for every font you used in the layout file. For example, if you use a Dingbat for a bullet, include that in the set of fonts. Most layout programs will assist you with this by providing a listing of fonts used in the layout. However, be sure that you specifically collect fonts used in your Photoshop images that you did not raster. Layout programs may not detect these in the image.

PostScript fonts are created in two parts, a screen and printer font. The screen font is used for the display of the font and the printer font contains the PostScript information for printing the font. On a PC, the screen fonts have an extension of .pfb and the printer fonts have an extension of .pfm. They are generally stored separately by default in the psfonts folder on your hard drive; the .pfb files are stored right in the psfonts folder and the .pfm files are stored in the pfm folder inside the psfonts directory. Non-PostScript (TrueType) fonts are stored in the Fonts directory in the Windows folder. These require only one file for the output, which is used as both screen and printer font. On a Mac, the fonts may be stored in several different ways depending on how they were created and what type they are. By default these are stored in the Fonts folder in the System directory (unless you are using a font management system which allows storage elsewhere). Again the PostScript fonts are made up of a screen and printer font which can be discerned by the icon (see Figure 40.1). These might or might not be collected in a suitcase (also pictured in Figure 40.1). TrueType fonts on the Mac are also only one file used for both screen and print representation. These are stored in the Fonts folder and can be identified by the icon (see Figure 40.1 again). On occasion, TrueType fonts are used for screen representations of PostScript printer fonts. So long as the Printer portion of the font is a PostScript file, the font should be considered a PostScript font.

Note

The preceding descriptions of font placement assume that the reader is not using a font management utility.

Figure 40.1
The Macintosh fonts can be determined from their icons as shown here. Suitcases serve to group a font's files together. Icons may appear somewhat differently from these, but should be similar.

Caution

It is suggested that you use only PostScript fonts for high-resolution output and any output to PostScript printers.

Collect both the screen and printer font for the font set and put them in the Fonts folder, unless this is forbidden by the license agreement with the foundry that created the font (some agreements forbid sending both a screen and printer font when doing output). If you collect only the screen font, you will be able to view the file and not print it. If you collect only the printer font, you will be able to print and not view it. For the sake of output, you can include the printer font only (generally, this will conform to the license agreement with any foundry). To help the service, you might consider keeping PFM and PFB files in different folders.

Caution

Although a service may occasionally suggest that they can substitute their fonts for yours, be sure to include your fonts, and be aware that reflow or other problems with the fonts might be caused by the service being a little lax about using the ones you have supplied. In other words, don't always assume that the problems that arise are your fault; knowing how things work can help you save charges that might not be your fault.

PART
XI

CH
40

SIMPLIFYING FILE COLLECTION USING PDF FILES

You can use PDF files to collect all the images and fonts you need for output into a single file. To generate the PDF, you will need a PDFWriter printer driver, or a printer driver of your choice and Acrobat Distiller. Be sure to select the option to include all fonts as embedded to the file and generate the file in the proper resolution for the output as suggested by your service. PDF files are generally small, transfer easily, and are widely compatible. They can serve as onscreen proofing (what you see is what will print).

Note

For more information about PDF files and Acrobat files, see the Adobe Web site, http://www.adobe.com, or the PDF Zone, www.pdfzone.com.

PROOFING FILES

Proof the files by printing a test from the files you have collected. The proof is best printed from the files you have collected as a test for the collected files. This will help you to be sure that the proofs match exactly to what you are submitting. If using a one-time media, such as a CD, doing the proofs from the collection directory before you copy to a CD is a good way to test to be sure you have what you need before burning the disc. A multiple-session format for the CD will also allow you to change files if necessary.

When proofing, print a complete set of document pages as well as separations for the color pages. To do this, use the Print Separations option in the printer settings. This will vary somewhat, depending on the program you used for the layout, and perhaps the printer driver as well. The goal is to show the plate separations for the color files to be sure the files separate properly. This can serve as a check to be sure that no colors are misassigned and that the files are of the proper type. For example, if you are using CMYK and you print the separations and get a C, M, Y, K, and Blue plate, this probably tells you that you have assigned something an RGB blue or spot color in the layout or image files; if the spot color was not added intentionally, you have the opportunity to adjust it for CMYK. From the plate, you will be able to tell what page element the color was assigned to, and you can adjust it before sending to the service for output. Such correction can save a lot of hourly charges.

SELECT THE MEDIA FOR TRANSPORT

While you are talking to the service, be sure you ask them how they can accept submitted files, including the format (program and file types) and what media they can support. Generally, a service will be pretty flexible with file type: Whatever file type they don't create output from directly, they should be able to convert, or provide options for you to submit the file by another means. For example, if they don't accept files from a lesser-known layout program that you use, they should be able to accept a print file you have generated using a PostScript driver or a file you have converted to PDF.

Tip

One thing you should really require in a service is knowledgeability and willingness to satisfy your needs, even if it is to come at an additional cost. A service that doesn't know what they are doing, how to make things work, or how to satisfy your needs in creating the proper output will not perform well generally. Their lack of knowledge can impede your results.

If you have selected one of the more popular types of archival storage, your service bureau will probably support submission of your project on that media. Personally, I prefer to submit on CD for several reasons. First, the service can't do anything to accidentally overwrite the files as they can't save to the CD. This saves the trouble of having to replace any files (so long as they were readable in the first place). Next, if the disk does manage to become part of the ether (lost, misplaced, disposed, broken, used as a Frisbee), there is negligible cost involved, and you will have a complete backup.

→ For more information on storage, **see** "Peripheral Storage," **p. 901**.

When using the archive media, this can serve as a built-in backup. You should never submit your only copy of anything to a service. As this is the case, you should make two copies of the submission materials. Make one copy for the submission of the materials and an identical copy to retain as an archive in case anything needs a replacement (this is also handy if you need to consult the materials you submitted to answer any questions about the files). After the two copies have been made, the submitted files can be removed from the hard drive. This will leave you with the submission copy and a solid backup, and a little extra disk space. Making the two copies is good practice to use with any important project.

Note

These two copies of the submission should be in addition to making archive copies of the rough materials used for the submission. For example, there may be a number of image files that you saved as PSD files that contain the corrections that you will also want to save from the project. Instead of confusing the collection of files that are necessary for the output, it is probably best to archive the working or in progress files separately.

Another good option for moving files to the service is FTP. Most services will have an area you can upload files to so that there is not even a need to have your own FTP space, or you can attach files to email. FTP is often the better choice as file compression and transport is a little less straightforward when done via email, and more problems tend to occur. A good FTP utility will help you by treating the FTP upload in the same way as moving files around on your hard drive.

Tip

Generally, stick to FTP when using a number of different files, but you might consider email for transfer of PDFs. As a single file, a PDF tends to have fewer issues with email compression and transfer.

EXTRA CHARGES

Services can charge extra for a number of things that you fail to do or that the service performs by your request. For example, if you say, "I need it this afternoon," your service might charge a rush fee. Certainly, if they don't tell you about the fee before they charge it, you can probably negotiate it off the bill. However, if you are aware of the potential charge, ask up front whether a charge will apply, and do what you can to avoid it. In the example of the rush charge, you might avoid that by adjusting your schedule accordingly (either get the job to them sooner or be prepared for delivery the next day—or in 48 hours if they have two-day turnaround).

Really, the service should inform you of any additional charges before performing the work (as an auto-repair shop should). In worst-case scenarios, they might contact you saying that they can't process the job without fixing something on their end. In this case you should consider the cost of having them make the corrections versus your time and expense in doing the same thing. Often it might be worth the few dollars to have the corrections made if they are simple.

Tip

Don't be afraid to negotiate charges with the service if there are extenuating circumstances, or if you get a price from another service that is for equivalent service yet you like another service's product more. Often a service will meet costs to keep your business.

If charges are applied that you don't think are your fault, let the service know. Your proofs (which they should make all effort to match) are your proof of what the output should look like, and if you are able to show a problem between the proofs you provided and their final result (for example, a text reflow), the service won't be able to argue too much with you.

Services might charge for other indirect costs, such as storage. For example, if you run a four-color job and you let them know that there might be a reprint, they might expect a fee for storing your film if it lies dormant for an extended period. Again, you should be made aware of any such charges long before they happen, and you should be given the opportunity to store your own negatives. You will want to take good care of these negatives, because if they are damaged, you are out that cost and will have to run them again if you need them.

Additional items you can expect to be charged for at a service are broad in nature (including pickup, paper, delivery, press time, binding, folding, and any number of minor fixes). Be sure to go over the bill when you get it and question anything that you don't understand.

Finally, make all effort to work with your service. They are providing a needed service and are probably trying their best. Mistakes will happen, probably just due to the sheer volume of work they have to do. Things will go wrong (both on your end and theirs); your efforts to remain amiable and work with the service (rather than being accusatory or stern) tend to get you better, more consistent service with less effort.

WHAT TO EXPECT BACK

All your materials should be returned from the service along with the completed job. You should also get any additional production materials (for example, film), unless you request storage. Materials should be delivered intact, and that is the responsibility of the service: If you get something on delivery that is damaged, it should be replaced—so long as the damage was not subsequent to the delivery. Anything mailed or sent should be packaged in some form of sturdy container, and perhaps wrapped with cellophane, and so on. Damage should never be caused by the packing or packaging. Any missing media should be replaced or deducted as cost. Any discrepancy, problem, or question should be brought to the attention of the service.

PHOTOSHOP AT WORK: THE COMPLETE JOB SUBMISSION STEPS CHECKLIST

The details for submitting your work for printing are really scattered throughout this chapter. Although the bulleted list at the beginning of the chapter is a good overview, the details are not evident. Following a suggested step-by-step procedure for implementing a job and doing the same thing every time will ensure you don't lose steps, work, or spend money that you don't have to.

1. Know what you want to accomplish as a result; decide what the final product should look like.

2. Call services about output options and pricing. Describe the job and ask questions.

3. Decide on a service or services to provide output based on calls.

4. Ask for sample output (if applicable) from your original files to use for color matching and proofing.

5. Make adjustments in Photoshop based on results of the sample if necessary by employing color correction, Transfer Functions, or other changes.

6. Collect the digital files you need for submitting the job by duplicating them to a new folder or directory, including

   - Layout files
   - Fonts files
   - Images files

7. Organize the files you have collected using subdirectories and appropriate naming.

8. Test the output by isolating the output files and printing proofs directly from them.

   - Change the targeting of the layout files, and back up and remove originals from your hard drive. (Moving the output files to a second machine is suggested for proper testing.)
   - Print a complete set of page proofs, showing everything to be output.
   - Print color separations.

9. Check the proofs and correct any problems in the layout or image files.
   - Add missing files.
   - Resave corrected files.
10. Update the proofed pages if changes have been made.
11. Back up/archive collected files by copying submission disk.

With this completed, you have protected your hard work from loss and damage, saved yourself headaches and expense, and added to the potential of getting the best results you possibly can from your image-creation efforts with Photoshop.

PART **XII**

IMAGE PROTECTION AND STORAGE

CHAPTER 41

PROTECTING IMAGES

In this chapter

COPYRIGHTING YOUR WORK

Copyright is protection of artwork, much like patent is protection of intellectual property. It is a formal claim of ownership over use. Copyright is, simply, the right to make copies, or the right to let others make copies with your permission. When you create a new image, you are its creator and own the copyright to the materials. Essentially, you own the copyright to an image when you create it. Copyright applies to tangible creation of materials. These materials can be images, words, music, code, fonts, scripts (Actions), and so on.

There are some gray areas to ownership of copyright in several veins. For example, if you use a source image which you do not have rights to copy in creating an image that is not recognizable as the original, do you then own copyright to that image? Some would argue yes, and some would argue no. Myself, I don't like arguments, and I am not about to say anything that could be legally binding as an opinion. However, it is clearly safest to say that if you did not generate the original image or source, you should seek permission for use from the creator before using it in anything you create. This permission can be granted simply by approaching the copyright owner and requesting the right to copy and use the image. The owner of the copyright can refuse or grant the right, and apply stipulations such as how the materials may or may not be used, and may also require a fee. Respect for copyright is important, and should be embraced by Photoshop users. When in doubt, get permission, or be sure that existing permission allows use.

Some materials can be used freely. For the sake of simplification, these are materials that have expired copyrights or over which the copyright owner has given up copyright and allows free use. That a copyright owner allows free use of materials does not make these materials yours in the sense that you can claim copyright and ownership of the materials. It merely means that you have the right to freely use the materials in other materials you create without paying for the right or clarifying those rights with the owner.

When knowingly using copyrighted materials, and after you have secured permission, there may still be some stipulation or guideline that you will need to follow in order to comply with the terms as assigned by the copyright owner. These may include displaying information about the copyright owner, either in direct relation to the content, or in some reasonable fashion. Most commonly this would include using the © symbol, appropriate date of copyright, and name of the copyright holder. Placing the copyright information appropriately protects you in case someone else uses the materials improperly from a place where you have made them available. For example, if you get permission to use an image on your Web site, and someone takes that image from your site, you will not be liable if that person gets caught and points their finger at you, if you have noted copyright information properly.

Placing the copyright symbol on your materials shows others that you claim copyright and that you expect that copyright to be honored. If the copyright information is removed from an image (such as digital watermarking, copyright tag, or removal of visible copyright information), this can be considered copyright infringement. If copyright is infringed, damages may be due to the copyright holder. You can protect your materials by formally registering them with the government (this requires a fee) or dutifully noting copyright by placement of the copyright symbol, dating, and providing contact information. This generally has to be done only once per work. For example, if you place a copyright notice at the bottom of a Web page, you are claiming copyright to all materials on that page (beside those copyrighted as otherwise noted).

Fair Use

Fair use is the use of an excerpted portion of a copyrighted work. Generally, this applies to written works, not to images. Whereas it is fairly simple to note where ideas and actual verbiage occur in the context of a writing, it is significantly more difficult to do so in the context of an image. Better to simply get permissions for images you will be using than to risk plagiarism and a lawsuit.

WATERMARKING FOR PROTECTION

Traditionally, watermarks are imperceptible. They were originally used as a type of authentication: Documents could be printed on paper with a watermark and when the paper was held up to a light for inspection, a crest, symbol, or other information would appear. Watermarks are still used, for example, on exclusive stationery and in marking some currencies; newer U.S. bills have watermarks of the presidents to the right of the bill. You have to hold them up to the light to see the marking. The purpose of the watermark on the bills is several-fold, but mostly the watermark will not photocopy and reproduce in simpler methods of counterfeiting. It makes the bills much more difficult to copy accurately. Watermarks can be added to images in a similar way so that they can be seen only by a computer.

A watermark on your image provides additional protection for images beyond simple copyright protection. Watermarks can be markings created directly on the images, appearing in some form to visibly mark an image, or they can be electronically embedded markings, which may not appear in casual viewing, or both. Visible watermarks are generally more durable, or often more difficult to remove satisfactorily.

The visible and manual watermarks can be created with a logo (as seen in the action created for Chapter 11); they can be a noise distribution, or a marking on one of the color plates. Applications can range in intensity from a simple knock-out copyright statement that uses the copyright symbol and originator's name in a boldly placed statement to embedding a steganographic message that can be recalled with a simple filter application.

The Digimarc watermarking plug-in, included with Photoshop, can embed a digital watermark that contains a URL address on the Digimarc site where the image creator's information can be found. The filter generates noise to place the digital information in the image, with an intensity based on the settings for Durability as chosen in the Digimarc plug-in dialog box (see Figure 41.1). You will need to register at the Digimarc Web site in order to use the plug-in; the first 99 watermarkings are free. These markings are reasonably durable, but will not withstand heavy changes in the image information (for example, resizing or blurring).

Tip

When registering at the Digimarc site, don't add credit card information unless you intend to pay for something even though the credit card fields have an asterisk by them. Apparently credit card information is necessary, but only if you have a balance to pay. I recommend testing the use of the Digimarc plug-in before just deciding it is the best solution for you and your images.

Figure 41.1
The durability slider is the essential control for the user in controlling the strength of the watermarking. When durability increases, so does the visibility of the noise generated by the plug-in.

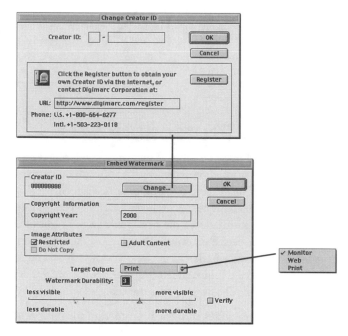

When opening digitally watermarked images, Photoshop displays the copyright symbol in the title bar. When Reading Watermarks that are embedded in the images (Filter, Digimarc, Read Watermark), Photoshop displays saved information in a Watermark Information screen that tells the Creator ID, Copyright Year, Image Attributes, and URL for additional creator information.

Tip

If you are not using the Digimarc plug-in to read or write watermarks, get it out of the Plug-ins folder. On occasion the plug-in will launch when you are opening images to check for watermark information and it can sometimes seem to add an eternity to opening images (although it is really only a few seconds).

No method of watermarking will completely protect an image from someone who wants to use it illegally. The only way to make images completely safe is to keep them hidden. However, noting your copyright in the image can help protect your images from unlawful use, give you rights over use, and may help you gain recognition by exposure.

→ For more information on working with watermarks embedded in images, **see** "Photoshop at Work: Embedding a Watermark with Actions," **p. 280**.

CHAPTER **42**

IMAGE STORAGE

In this chapter

CATALOGING OPTIONS

Although Photoshop has several tools that enable you to create contact sheets and Web photo galleries, there are also a variety of third-party tools available for creating catalogs of your images. These tools often automatically create thumbnails of your images, provide search capabilities, and sometimes even contain some basic image-hediting tools.

There are several popular tools for cataloging images, or media asset management, because most tools support animations and sound files in addition to images. Extensis' Portfolio is available for both Macintosh and Windows operating systems and provides extensive search and thumbnail-creation capabilities. Extensis also provides a server version for image management across an organization and creation of catalogs for the Web. For more information about Portfolio, browse to `http://www.extensis.com/portfolio`.

Platform-specific tools are also available, some as shareware or freeware. Some examples of available tools include QPict and iView for the Macintosh, and ThumbsPlus and Ulead's Photo Explorer for Windows. Whether you choose to go with a high-end media-asset management system, or a personal cataloging tool, make sure that the image formats that you use are supported; that the tool accommodates the number of images that you need to manage; and that the tool provides all the features you consider essential, such as the creation of thumbnails, contact sheets, keyword searches, or Web capabilities.

STORING AND TRANSPORTING IMAGES

Storage and transfer of your images can be accommodated in a variety of ways, from direct electronic transfer through the Internet to permanent storage on CD. Knowing your options and what the advantages and disadvantages are for each can help you choose the right method of transfer and storage for your images, in archiving and in moving them to where they will be used in output.

MEDIA

When you save your image, it is typically stored on your hard disk. It is often necessary to remove the image from your hard disk to create working room for other images. Also, if you have prepared an image for printing, you must determine the best method to provide the image to your service bureau. Because Photoshop images can often be very large, and because media reliability is paramount, several archival technologies are being used by artists and service bureaus worldwide to address both storage and transport of images.

There are three factors in determining viable media options for transporting images. Ideally, the same media can be used for both transport and storage of images, so you should weigh the same factors when choosing your storage option. First, you must discuss the availability of various media options with your service bureau. Most print shops and prepress houses can use a variety of tools, but because investment in each technology is expensive, it is rare to find a service bureau that has access to all the myriad options. If you are concerned only with storage of your images, you should instead consider the availability of media options used by people you collaborate with. Second, you should choose a media format and type that is widely accepted throughout the industry by other service bureaus and collaboration partners. Widely accepted media formats are also viable for longer periods of time. Keeping this in mind, it is often better to invest in newer, but not cutting-edge technology. Wait to see whether a particular media format will be accepted throughout the industry before spending your money. Finally, cost is an issue. This cost may include the storage device itself, appropriate media, and possibly interface cards or installation. For many artists, cost can be the most significant factor in determining a media format.

High-Capacity Disk

One of the most common media types is the high-capacity removable disk drive. For some time, SyQuest dominated this technology with its very successful removable hard drives. Typically available in 44MB, 88MB, and 200MB formats, this standard was widely adopted and is still supported by many service bureaus. Because a SyQuest disk is essentially a single hard-disk platter mounted in a plastic case, using this technology is often as fast as accessing a hard drive. Unfortunately, the media was large and fairly expensive, so competition from newer, lower-cost technology and media all but drove SyQuest out of the market, and the face of removable storage made a drastic shift to lower costs and smaller size.

More recently, a variety of similar technologies have been released that use smaller, cheaper media. Iomega's Zip and Jaz drives have attained widespread acceptance in the market. The ubiquitous Zip disk can hold up to 100MB and runs about $10 U.S., and if bought in volume, this price can be significantly reduced. Iomega has also released a 200MB Zip system that should be sufficient for all but the largest images. Zip drives work best when run from a SCSI controller, but for PC users, printer port and IDE versions are also available and more common. Iomega's Jaz drive must be run with a SCSI controller, and both the device and the media are significantly more expensive—although considerably larger. Jaz disks can hold 1GB of data, and a 2GB version is also available.

> **Tip**
>
> Whenever you provide removable media to your service bureau, be sure that it is included with the printed materials. These disks have a habit of being forgotten and left behind. However, they should not, for the most part, be considered disposable as they can be used repeatedly. Tracking them will save cost.

CD-ROM

One of the best options that has become available as CD technology has improved is CD-R (CD-Recordable) and CD-RW (CD-Rewritable). CD-R drives enable you to burn files onto a CD once. Write speeds of 8× and better are available, and although not as fast as other removable media options, at 8×, 650MB can be copied to a CD in less than 10 minutes. Most significantly, CD-R discs are relatively inexpensive, so the media's return is less important. In addition, CD-R discs are durable and easily distributed because almost all PCs now have CD-ROM drives that can read the information. Slightly more expensive, CD-RW discs can have information rewritten up to 999 times and provide another low-cost alternative for transporting data, although compatibility issues can be a hindrance, as not all readers can access the data on a CD-RW disc.

 If you have purchased a CD-R or CD-RW and are having trouble creating these so that your service can read them, see "The Trouble with CDs" in the Troubleshooting section at the end of this chapter.

FORMAT

Just as important as determining what media your service bureau can accept, you should discuss format capabilities. You should determine whether they have a platform preference or whether they can read both Macintosh- and PC-formatted disks. Generally, they should be able to convert files from one platform to the other.

In addition to disk format, the service bureau may need you to save your files in a specific file format. Be sure to ask them which types of files they can work with, and know their recommendations about the file formats that they prefer. The most common formats that are used are TIFF and EPS, and most service bureaus work with both. Whatever format they specify, be sure to gather more details about the format. For example, if they specify TIFF, find out whether they prefer Macintosh or PC encoded, and whether they will support compression. This can affect your choices not only for providing the files, but in the type of media you will be able to use as well—depending on the digital size of your usual jobs. In addition, if you are providing files in a native page layout format, such as QuarkXPress or PageMaker, be sure to confirm the versions that the service bureau supports. Although most service bureaus are well equipped to handle a vast array of file formats and convert them so that they are usable with their preferred tools, providing files that they prefer gives you greater control over the process and also may decrease some of your setup charges. If a service is not willing or able to adjust to what you can provide, it is time to shop for another service.

  If you are using a Macintosh and working with PC-based companies, be sure to put extensions on your filenames so that the service will have an easier time with the files.

ELECTRONIC TRANSFER OPTIONS: THE INTERNET, FTP, AND EMAIL

As the availability of wide-bandwidth Internet access becomes a reality, this is becoming the preferred method of transferring files between individuals and companies. Transferring files over the Internet is typically independent of the operating system and faster than various overnight delivery services. The simplest method of sending files is by attaching them to an email message. This is useful for smaller files, but can be problematic for larger files usually seen in prepress. Many email applications and service providers limit the size of email messages and email boxes. Many companies, for example, set a 5MB limit on messages. In addition, sending an email forces the reader to download the file when it arrives. The reader must do this even to check other mail. If you do send files as attachments to email between operating systems, you should be aware of the various encryption techniques used in email applications and how to decrypt files that you might receive. For example, it is common for attachments sent from Macintosh files to use BinHex encoding. Although some Windows email applications can decrypt these files automatically, additional tools, such as WinZip may be necessary. Furthermore, Windows users receiving BinHex-encoded files may need to manually add an .hqx extension to make the file readable.

A better alternative is to use an FTP site. Using the Internet's File Transfer Protocol, folder structures can be created and shared with the public. Some service bureaus will create a folder for you to use on their FTP server or create a public folder into which you can upload files. You can upload files and the recipient can download at times when bandwidth is readily available. There are a variety of FTP applications available free on the Internet and most operating systems have at least some primitive FTP capabilities. Some FTP sites require you to have a username and password. Others may provide anonymous login and you can use your email address to access the site. If your service bureau has FTP capabilities, they should be able to provide you with explicit instructions.

Another option, similar to FTP, is the variety of services that have started to become available for file and project collaboration over the Internet. Many of these services are easier to use than FTP sites and can provide additional features such as added security, print work order forms, and version control.

TROUBLESHOOTING

THE TROUBLE WITH CDS

I bought a CD burner thinking it would be great for storage and transfer of images, but it seems no one can read the CDs I burn but me. What is going wrong?

Owning a CD burner is a little more complicated than owning a Zip drive. There are a lot of potential formats for burning CDs, from operating-system–based formats to audio and proprietary. Good software will offer a lot of options for burning—but only some of these options will be broadly compatible.

The first thing to do is to break out the owner's manual and take a look at the options you have for formatting your CD. There can be quite a few options. Although you should understand the use of the options, it should be apparent that not all of them will be necessary and/or desirable for your purposes in image storage and transfer. Usually, you will want to use a format that is versatile and will be able to be read cross-platform. For example, ISO 9660 format is broadly compatible. If you use an operating system compatible format or multiformat/multisession type (CD-ROM XA), you have to be sure the reading party will be able to access the information. The long and the short of it is—don't just stick a CD in and hope for the best. Because you can read a disc with your proprietary software doesn't mean anyone else can. Learn the advantages of the formats by reading your manual and use the appropriate format for the storage you intend to do.

If the problem is intermittent—where it seems other people can sometimes read your discs, and others not—look into the brand of CD you are burning. If you consistently go for sale items, you may not always get consistent results—not so much as there will be bad media for sale as the media is actually different. The color of the plastic and materials used in manufacture may not be suitable for your CD burner, or they may not be suited for reading on the target computer. In short, if you find a CD brand that you have good luck with, it is probably best to stick with that brand even if it may cost a few dollars more when it comes time to restock.

Proprietary CD disc types and burners were on the market for a while when CD burners were first appearing, but some of these did not conform to developing standards (indeed some of them developed their own—ergo, proprietary). If you have one of these drives, they will be good for personal storage, but you can probably not depend on your service bureau supporting them and the results will probably not be compatible with standard CD-ROM readers.

PART **XIII**

APPENDIXES

GENERAL DIGITAL IMAGE INFORMATION

In this appendix

Images are essentially described in one of two ways: as vectors or as pixels. Although there are programs that work with both *vectors* and *pixels*, generally a pixel-based program (Photoshop) will compile images in pixel form, whereas vector-based programs (Illustrator) will compile images based on coordinates and vectors. Neither image type is better, although each type has its advantages. Generally, vector images are illustrative and scalable, whereas pixel-based images are photographic and set size.

Note

> Although vectors are used to describe areas in vector programs such as Illustrator, CorelDRAW, or FreeHand, these descriptions are necessarily displayed on a monitor in pixels as a monitor is a pixel-based display.

PIXELS AND BIT DEPTH

A pixel is the smallest defined unit area of a bitmapped computer image. Pixels are evenly sized squares spread like tiles over the image area. Each pixel is assigned a color within the range of colors possible in the image format and color depth. If you think of pixels as tiny ceramic tiles placed on a wall (without the grout in between), the number of pixels (tiles) in the area of an image remains the same unless the image area (wall) is resized. When resized up (when the wall is made bigger), more pixels are required to fill the area; when the image is resized down (when the wall is made smaller) fewer pixels are required to fill the area. It holds true that resizing the image is not necessarily desirable. As this is the case, certain types of images (notably the image area of a digital camera, or the viewing area of a computer display) are described in an absolute pixel size (for example, 640×480), or total pixels. The amount of information in the images is the same, only the resolution (appearance of the size) might change.

Increasing or decreasing the resolution of a pixel-based image—without changing the canvas size—is like getting closer to or moving farther away from the wall. If you move closer to the wall (lower the resolution), the area of the wall and the size of the tiles appears to get larger from your perspective—although, the same number of tiles actually fills the same area of the wall. If you move farther from the wall (increase the resolution), the same number of tiles will still be there, but they will appear smaller, as will the area of wall from your perspective. The point is that the amount of information in the image stays the same. If you have a 72×72 pixel image at 1 pixel per inch, that image will be 72×72 inches (6×6 feet); that same image at 72 pixels per inch will be 1×1 inch. Both files will be the same size. In the higher resolution, it will be very difficult to see the individual pixels; as resolution goes up, it is harder to see the pixels (when displaying the image at actual size).

Bit depth measures the potential for color variation in a pixel. The measure is referred to as either the number of bits per channel in an image pixel, or the total number of bits per image pixel, although they are very different things. Each bit can be either on or off, so each bit actually has two values. If an image is two bits, there are two bits with two values each that can be paired in any combination (where 1 stands for on and 0 for off: 00, 01, 10, or 11). Each additional bit adds a multiple of two combinations, one additional set of combinations for each potential value. For example, in the set 00, 01, 10, 11, each value could potentially be combined with the 1 or 0 in a third bit if it were added. This would result in the sets (using the off value) 000, 001, 010, 011, and (using the on value) 100, 101, 110, 111—a total of eight combinations. So, to get the total number of combinations per channel, multiply by two for each bit. Eight bits per channel would be $2{\times}2{\times}2{\times}2{\times}2{\times}2{\times}2{\times}2$ (or 2^8) totaling 256 combinations per pixel per channel.

If there is more than one channel, these potential combinations are multiplied together. For example, for three channels (as in RGB), the total possible combinations would be $256{\times}256{\times}256$, or 16,777,216 possible combinations. Sixteen-bit (per channel) images would have 65,536 possibilities per pixel per channel. An RGB image in 16 bit would have about 2.81^{14} potential color combinations per pixel. In other words, increased pixel depth exponentially increases the color possibilities, which is why increased color depth is considered potentially so valuable in color work.

The negative effect of increased bit depth (to 16 bits per channel from 8) is increased image size. In Photoshop this also means losing some functions, as they will not be available for 16-bit images.

VECTORS AND RESOLUTION-INDEPENDENT GRAPHICS

Drawing and modeling programs form shapes made up of vectors which mathematically describe an area. The coordinates of points necessary to describe the shape are stored along with curve information. The area defined is then filled or colored based on other vector patterns or bitmaps. Generally, vector images are created by drawing programs, such as Adobe Illustrator or CorelDRAW, and in 3D modeling. Photoshop's paths use a means of describing areas based on vectors and points, and paths can be used in somewhat of a rudimentary way to create what are resolution-independent images in Photoshop.

→ For more information on paths, **see** "Paths: Bézier Tools for Creating Vector Effects," **p. 175** and "Creating and Saving PostScript Patterns," **p. 680**.

Vector-based images are resolution independent. In other words, because its edges rather than the set pixel content essentially describe the shape, the result is infinitely scalable without a loss of quality. Images created with vectors can print at any size and retain a fine edge on the printing device. The same image would be able to be used in any application where the image was desired.

Images created with vectors are good multiple-purpose images. For example, vector images are good for the creation of logos. Logos generally have few colors, and may be used for a number of purposes, so scalability is important. Because there is no need to describe every pixel in the vector image, except by the vector that encloses the area, vector images are generally smaller than bitmapped images. When used to describe large areas, the information in a vector file remains the same no matter what size, so they can describe images and image areas that are unseemly with pixel images. As usual, knowing the purpose of an image should define your purpose and method of creating it.

Photoshop System Requirements and Enhancements

In this appendix

SYSTEM REQUIREMENTS FOR PHOTOSHOP

Adobe lists minimum requirements for the operation of Photoshop, but keep in mind that these are the bare minimum requirements. Photoshop is a power-hungry program, probably one of the most demanding on the market. You can run the program and view and work with images, but the more serious you are about processing, the more high-end your equipment will have to be to keep up with your processing needs. The more you can do with your configuration and memory parameters to give Photoshop the space it needs, the better off you will be in speeding your processing and working with the program. Considerations include RAM, hard-drive space, and processor, but may include your monitor size, video card, and potential for expansion in other ways as well.

There is often heavy debate about which platform is better for running Photoshop. The simple fact used to be that Photoshop was a Mac tool. The more time goes on, the less the debate matters and the more that centers on how upgradable your equipment is and whether your equipment can handle the demands. There was a time when I was happy to be able to run Photoshop on an old Mac Classic II with 2MB of RAM (minimum RAM suggested was 4MB or 8MB at the time). Adobe now lists the minimum at 64MB, and I feel underpowered with double that. The point is when I was just barely getting Photoshop to open, it served the purpose I needed it for, and I had other (better) workstations to rely on to do serious work. When I open Photoshop now, I may expect a little more from it and my equipment needs to handle that.

Your goal will not always be to have the ultimate Photoshop system. However, understanding the benefits of having more RAM or more speed in your processor (or more processors!) might help you decide whether you need an equipment upgrade to make Photoshop perform the way you expect.

RAM: HOW MUCH IS ENOUGH?

The benefits of having more than the minimum required RAM are manifold. Adobe claims the best way to improve Photoshop performance is to increase the amount of RAM installed on your system. Fewer crashes and freezes, faster processing, smoother operation, and fewer notices from Photoshop about not having enough memory to complete a task are several of the benefits. You can also look forward to an ability to add more states to your History, worry less about purging memory (Edit, Purge), and so on. However, having enough RAM depends on how you work, how much of your RAM you can allocate to Photoshop, and how much RAM you can load into your system.

One thing to be aware of in considering a system upgrade or in buying a new system if you are serious about Photoshop is the maximum amount of RAM the system can handle. You may also want to consider what the cost is to upgrade that RAM. RAM comes in different configurations, and while the prices between types are not always so different, there may be some relative surprises. For example, as of the printing of this book, 64MB and 128MB chips are your best deals on RAM, generally running about the same cost per megabyte.

Other options such as 16MB, 32MB, and 256MB chips are all generally a bit more per megabyte. Pricing depends on demand somewhat, and can often change day to day in the places where you will get the best pricing.

Not all machines can take any size chip. And then you may need SIMMs or DIMMs (although D stands for double, and S for single, you do not need to purchase one double and two singles; the reference is not to how they pair up, but the role they perform). The bottom line is, you need to know what type of memory your machine takes, and how that maximum capacity needs to be filled. As in the preceding Mac example, if you have a 512MB maximum, and that is filled in two RAM slots, you may have to buy two 256MB chips to get to the maximum; if it is in four slots, you need to buy four 128MB chips which may save a few hundred dollars. You have more flexibility with more slots, as long as you are comparing DIMM to DIMM or SIMM to SIMM. If you compare DIMM to SIMM, there have to be twice as many SIMM slots to have the same potential (so long as those slots accept similar configurations). In the example of the machine with two slots, you would have to buy the two 256MB SIMMs at the same time, which would be a costly upgrade; if these were DIMMs you could upgrade one slot at a time, and could do more in increments as your pocketbook allows.

In Doubt About RAM

When in doubt about RAM, call a salesperson and find out exactly what you need. Then call another salesperson and find out exactly what you need again. The two opinions should match. At an Internet pricing service (two are listed in Appendix E), there is information on how to find out exactly what you need. If still in doubt, talk to a professional (www.eritech.com is recommended). Don't ever just buy the cheapest RAM unless you are sure it has the right specifications for your machine. If purchasing through the Internet or via mail, be sure you can return items within 30 days with no restocking fee. Also, if pulling RAM from your machine that you may never use again, consider selling the RAM (either to a company that buys old RAM, or in an exchange). You won't get much for it, but unless you are creating a museum, better not much than nothing.

The RAM available to Photoshop is determined differently on Mac and PC. In Windows, Photoshop will use 60% of available RAM (RAM not being used by anything else when the program is opened), and 50% of total physical RAM on Windows NT. It is possible to change this allocation in the Memory & Image Cache Preferences (File, Preferences, Memory & Image Cache). Performance may not improve with greater allocation if you begin to cut into memory needed for the operation of other programs (such as the operating system). Allocation according to available RAM will be affected by the other programs you have open. Close out of programs that will not be necessary while using Photoshop before you open it for maximum performance. It is suggested that you don't go higher than 60% of the total physical RAM for memory allocation on a typical system.

On the Mac, Photoshop's memory is allocated through settings in the program's Info box. If you have more RAM available, you can increase the amount of RAM allocated to Photoshop. To do this, locate the program icon in the Photoshop folder, click it once to highlight, and then choose File, Get Info. The Info dialog box window for Photoshop will appear, which will show the Minimum and Preferred size of the RAM allocation currently selected for the program. The important thing to do here is increase the minimum so that it is at least at the suggested size (so long as you have that much RAM). Consider the minimum as the least amount of RAM you would like to delegate to Photoshop when using multiple programs; consider the maximum as how much RAM you would like to allocate to Photoshop when it is open by itself.

> **Tip**
>
> Adobe recommends not using RAM performance-enhancing software to go beyond the amount of the physical RAM you have available. Doing so tends to slow performance.

HARD-DISK SPACE

Photoshop requires a great deal of hard-disk space in order to operate efficiently. With the price drop in hard-drive space over the past few years, this is certainly not an area to be skimpy in. If hard-disk space is currently at a premium on your machine, another hard drive (as a replacement or an addition) will probably be your most cost-effective improvement. As of this writing, drives can be found for $100 that are larger than 10GB (or 10,000MB). Although there are other considerations (including drive speed, connection speed, and so on), it is a good idea to make the best use of space available, and get more if you just don't have it.

Photoshop uses hard-disk space as a scratch-disk space to help improve real-time processing. The Photoshop System Requirements suggest keeping 125MB of disk space available for Photoshop, but that seems rather conservative depending on your usage. While this may be okay for most Web site work, it would be insufficient for serious photo retouching. I always have several drives on my machine, and allocate the Scratch Disk settings (Edit, Preferences, Plug-Ins & Scratch Disks) accordingly. Although not all of this space is used for Photoshop, I do have one entire drive that I dedicate just to scratch-disk space. I put nothing else on it and assign that as the first scratch disk on the Scratch Disks Preferences. If you do not have the luxury of a separate drive for a Photoshop scratch disk, you might consider partitioning a current drive. Setting a dedicated space for the scratch disk will keep it clear of other file fragments and debris that can impede performance.

> **Tip**
>
> It is highly recommended that you keep disk space allocated to Photoshop Scratch Disks defragmented, using a utility (Norton's Speed Disk, for example).

Assignment of scratch-disk space should generally be to the fastest drive you have, as that provides the best performance. Internal drives will generally perform better than externals, and removables are probably not the best choice. Photoshop writes to Scratch disks when it runs out of RAM, and can use only a maximum amount of RAM based on the disk space available. That is, if there is 100MB of Scratch Disk available and you have allocated 60% of your 256MB of RAM, only 100MB of the potential 154MB will be used. Dedicating scratch areas to Photoshop using partitions or separate drives removes concern for this potential drop in performance.

PERIPHERAL STORAGE

While peripheral and removable storage devices are not directly related to improving performance, they can help indirectly. Photoshop can generate some very large files quickly, and storing them indefinitely on even a large drive can fill it in a short time. If these drives are used for Scratch Disk space, you may end up choking off your RAM. A good solution to space problems is to use removable storage to archive unnecessary files.

It really doesn't matter what proprietary type of removable storage you choose as long as you are going to be using it for your own storage and nothing else: you can use a Kangaroo drive, a SyQuest 44 that you find at a garage sale, or any obscure thing you can get your hands on. However, it is probably best to consider secondary utility in the drive, such as portability and sharing files. With this in mind, the selections become quite a bit narrower.

If you will be sending files to a service, you will find broad compatibility with Zip drives and recordable CDs (CD-R). Although there are other broadly used options, a CD-ROM is pretty much standard equipment on Mac and PC, and as long as you use proper format, files can be stored on a CD to be read on either platform. The 650MB is also sufficient storage for large files, the disk media is cheap (essentially disposable), and the durability of the media itself is very good. It is clearly the best long-term value. Although Zip drives have become standard on Macintosh (replacing the 1.4MB floppy), their 100MB of space is not sufficient at times for larger projects, and although not incredibly expensive itself, it can cost about 50 times the amount per megabyte of storage. There is only a slight advantage to Zip drives in price of the drive, and, perhaps, the learning curve involved in use (a lot depends on the software you get for processing your CDs). CD-R drives might also have an advantage in that many serve several purposes and can write to more than one media (for example, CD-RW) which may offer added flexibility. The only bad thing about a CD-R is you can write to a space on the disk only once. That dismisses the possibility of updating any files. However, for archiving, this is really preferable, as you can't accidentally overwrite anything.

Note

Although portability via the Internet is becoming an increasingly viable option for file transport, it does not replace the idea of an archival storage system. As the primary concern with peripheral storage is archiving, this cannot be considered a complete solution.

SYSTEM ADDITIONS YOU MIGHT WANT (AND WHY)

There are a number of possible additions to your system that you might want to consider. These are both peripheral to your interaction with Photoshop and directly related to how you work with the interface. They are clearly not necessary, but can certainly help if you plan to get serious about processing images. The purpose of this section is not so much to point you in a direction and say this is what you need, but to suggest some options and have you choose what is to your advantage. The consideration here will cover scanning, navigational tools (tablets, trackballs, and mice), digital cameras, and monitors (large and dual).

SCANNERS

A scanner can be a versatile device in creating or working with images. Although Chapter 18, "Scanning to Create Images," discusses many of the potential uses for a scanner, it does not touch on the idea of the headaches it can save, the money it can save, or the images that you will probably scan that you never would have had you not owned a scanner yourself.

Adding a scanner is not merely a measure of convenience, it is opening up a new creative tool (imagine asking your service bureau to scan a slotted spoon, Q-Tips, or tape border for you as is shown in the example in Chapter 18). Not only can you use it to create image elements, but you can create those image elements as you want them. Although there will be some time involved in mastering scanning—and perhaps the software that comes with the scanner, depending on what you get and how complicated it is—you will not get the type of personalized service you might need. You will also gain better control over your scanning results.

A cheap scanner is probably better than no scanner at all. Some models that would have rivaled the cutting edge of consumer models a few years ago are available for $100 to $200. Some quality flatbed scans can rival drum scans to an extent. However, just having a scanner will give you freedom to explore with images. The quality of the scanner you need is also related to the type of work you will be doing with it. For detailed photo retouching and advertising work, you will need to get a scanner from the upper crust. For working with images to go on a Web page, probably any decent common scanner will do. If you do a lot of serious work with transparencies or negatives, don't think any old transparency adapter is going to take care of your needs—you'll probably have to invest in a high-quality film scanner, or consider other scanning options.

→ For more information on scanning, scanning options, and scanners, **see** "Scanning to Create Images," **p. 361**.

Don't spend too much time learning cheap scanning software. If it is cheap, it may suggest there isn't much thought behind it, that the controls are mediocre, and that the results using the tools they provide will probably be less desirable than just working from the rough scan using Photoshop. However, value is added to scanning equipment by the scanning package—if it is a good package. For example, the LinoColor software adds much value to the cost of any of its line of scanners.

DIGITAL CAMERA: THE PORTABLE SCANNER

A digital camera, like a scanner, can be an invaluable addition to your image-creation battery. Because you can shoot without film and immediately download the results, there is no waiting, and you can shoot things you may otherwise skip over with a conventional camera. These are great for shooting backgrounds, stock images, or scanning 3D objects that you just can't fit on a scanner bed, that won't scan well if you do, or are not at all in a convenient spot for scanning.

Again, these can be a wellspring of image information, which you can use both creatively and in creation of source images. You will need one that can take enough pixels for your purposes (fewer for the Web, more for offset print work, still more for photographic reproduction). As the cost may be prohibitive for a better model, it is probably a good idea to consider this addition after adding a scanner. The reason for this is, although it may seem more versatile than a scanner, you may already have something to shoot pictures with, and a scanner can get those into your computer; in fact, chances are you have a backlog of analog images that can be used in Photoshop. Although there are more potential uses for a digital camera than a standard-type camera, this is clearly the option that can wait.

→ For more information on using digital cameras, **see** "Creating Images with Digital Cameras," **p. 397**.

NAVIGATIONAL INPUT DEVICES: TABLETS, MICE, AND TRACKBALLS

The tools used to navigate your cursor in Photoshop are probably an afterthought for many as it is so easy to use a mouse. However, if you have noted difficulty in making what should be an easy Lasso selection, there may be another option for you. Some Photoshop users swear by their navigational additions, and others swear at them. Like other options, mentioning this subject in a group of Photoshop users becomes an excuse for debate. Like the old PC versus Mac debate, usually the loudest or most persistent wins. The real point here is not to win, but to be aware that there are options and that the options may afford you advantages in the way you work with Photoshop.

HIGH-TECH MICE

All mice are not created the same. Mice that come with systems are usually cheap, performing the basic functions of a mouse with the utmost in near adequacy. Although some actually work, some are flawed in design (or overdesigned), some won't fit your hand (you'll know what I mean if you have small or large hands), some gum up easily, some are gimmicky.

If you are going to use a mouse, get one that can be cleaned easily, has solid tracking, probably a large ball, and multiple buttons (depending on the manufacturer, these can come in handy on a Mac as well as on a PC). Mice fill up with all sorts of gunk, and they need to be cleaned. If you can't get it apart easily (fewer than two screws, and no prying), it is meant to be disposable. If that is the case, throw it away.

I have seen mice that use laser technology on optic grids, and all sorts of mouse shapes. Few are ergonomic for everyone, so it would be smart to go out and try a few on. If you find one that fits, ask a salesperson if you can try it out on a floor model. Don't buy a mouse because you like the way it looks. Several of the brilliant new mouse designs end up being either cumbersome or easy to cause to fail. A low price often means low quality, but there is significant registered doubt that there is a one-to-one correlation. The last mouse I actually bought was $4.95 it still works with no problem and has a lifetime guarantee. It has a one-screw release, a standard-size mouse ball, and I can clean it from the outside without taking it apart. I use it only on my laptop. All that said, I don't use the laptop for serious Photoshop work. My motivation for getting the mouse was so that I wouldn't have to use the awful trackball that came with the laptop. Had I been concerned with using the laptop with Photoshop, I might have considered other options.

TRACKBALLS

Many people I have heard from swear at trackballs rather than by them, but I think this is because, like mice, the introductory models are cheap. If you look at a trackball, pass right by the ones that have a ball that is less than two inches in diameter. The trackball on the laptop previously mentioned was impossible to clean, tiny, and seemingly created for that particular laptop model as an afterthought. The ball was so small that it had to be manipulated with an index finger or thumb. That defeats the purpose of a real trackball.

A real trackball has a large ball so that the user has more control over movement. The large ball also allows the user to get more than one finger on the ball at a time—perhaps the palm—to better control the movement and steady the hand. Again, the device needs to be easy to clean, and any buttons should be situated not so much in a neat array as in places that are convenient to reach. Again, the idea is not to have a pretty device, but one that helps you use Photoshop.

One huge advantage of a trackball over a mouse is that when using a mouse, the mouse has to move but when using a trackball, the ball rolls in a stationary area. What this means, ultimately, is that the area needed for using a mouse is a lot greater than what you need for a trackball. The trackball requires no mouse pad, and is generally more accurate and easy to direct. On a large monitor, you can zip around more easily with a trackball by just flinging the cursor. Try that with a mouse. There is a lot less wrist action required with a trackball as well.

Again, try to get out somewhere and use a trackball before just buying one. I must admit to having just bought mine without trying it when I got the first got one, and at the time I was spending someone else's money. I did some research and found what I thought to be the best thing, and I am still convinced that it is. I ended up getting one for every workstation at that job, and use the same trackball on my main workstation now for Photoshop work.

Note

For a good start on available options, see the Kensington Web site: http://www.kensington.com and Evergreen Systems: www.trackball.com.

Although these may prove more expensive than a mouse, the higher degree of accuracy and control will warrant that expenditure.

GRAPHIC TABLETS

If you have the room for the tablet and like to draw freehand, then a great option for you is the graphics tablet. These are very similar to touchpads and come as a combination of tools (pen and tablet, sometimes with a mouse as well), somewhat more oriented to the hands on graphic artist who has a talent for using a pen. The idea is that you use a familiar pen-shaped tool to control your drawing actions in Photoshop. The tip is pressure sensitive with many of these devices, and there are a number of additional features that make them more of an artistic tool.

As one who is not a wizard with a freehand pen (preferring mechanical drawing, stick figures, image manipulation, and photo-retouching) my abilities don't seem to jibe with the conduct of the tool. That is certainly not to say I do not admire those who can use them. I have tried several and could never seem to justify the expense, or motivate the results as I desired. Although entry-level devices are not outrageous, full-featured models (Wacom now has tablets with LED flat-screen displays that enable you to essentially draw right on the image) are pricey, and that price can help contribute to the accuracy and ease of use.

Tip

For more information on tablets, see the Wacom Web site at `http://www.wacom.com`.

WORKING WITH LARGE AND DUAL MONITORS

A second monitor, be it black-and-white and only 12 inches, might be a very welcome addition for the serious Photoshop user, especially if the monitor you are using is small (less than 17 inches). The second monitor can be used to store palettes and other views while images you work on are on the main screen. What was cramped on a single monitor when both palettes and image needed to be on one screen will become a sprawling landscape with the addition of the second monitor. This allows a better viewing area for the image and the palettes, and is far more convenient than toggling the palettes on and off with the Tab key.

Note

For most machines, using a second monitor requires purchasing a video card. Check your computer's manual or with the manufacturer of the machine.

If one can stand the expense, a large monitor is a great help for the Photoshop user (so long as it is supported by a sufficient graphics card). Larger monitors afford the ability to view an image better, use sharper resolutions, and allow more graphic freedom (as far as freeing up space for palettes and being able to use multiple views to your advantage are concerned, or actually comparing image states side by side). A large monitor coupled with a smaller dual monitor is a heavenly setup. If you are going to spring for the large monitor anyway, my advice would be to tack on $200 or so more for a sidekick to hold the palettes.

YOUR SYSTEM AND PHOTOSHOP

In this appendix

BASIC TROUBLESHOOTING GUIDE

Should you have problems with Photoshop, there are some standard techniques and things to check. Some of these are platform independent. Others are specific to whether you use Photoshop on a Macintosh or a PC.

The following sections will give you a starting place to help you resolve common issues that you might run into when using Photoshop. You might still have to use other sources for help such as Adobe's Help files or Technical Support services; however, the information here will give you a good place to find out what things commonly cause problems and to get quick answers that can help you get back to work fast. Should you need help, Adobe has added both HTML help (Help on the Help menu) and helpful links to the Adobe Web site where you can get technical information, updates, and other help, as long as you are actively connected to the Internet.

VIRTUAL MEMORY

Virtual memory is the use of hard drive space as RAM. The recommended settings for virtual memory vary depending on the operating system. Your virtual memory settings can have a significant impact on Photoshop's performance. You might want to start with the recommended settings, and then experiment with slight variations based on the size of the images that you work on and your particular system.

Tip

Virtual memory settings for your system and using RAM-doubling applications may interfere or conflict with Photoshop's memory management. If you have difficulty, or experience slowdowns when working on larger images, try turning off the virtual memory and disabling and RAM-enhancing utilities. Your performance might actually improve.

SCRATCH DISKS

Scratch disk is an area created on the hard drive in which Photoshop stores information about the image you are working on instead of placing the information in RAM. In this way, scratch disks are very similar to virtual memory management in your operating system. The primary difference between scratch-disk space and virtual memory is that scratch disks are controlled entirely by Photoshop and not by the operating system. Because Photoshop uses the scratch disk as additional RAM, proper understanding and control of the scratch disk is one of the more important keys to gaining optimal performance.

Whenever Photoshop runs out of memory, or cannot fit anything else into physical RAM, it uses the scratch disk as virtual memory. When Photoshop is idle, it copies the entire contents of RAM into the scratch disk. In addition, Photoshop must keep track of more than just the image data. It stores a lot of information, from interface preferences to buffer information, including Undo and History information, information from the pattern buffer, Clipboard data, image thumbnails displayed in palettes, and so on. This can quickly add up to a lot of information and can create demand for a lot of storage.

When you start or install Photoshop, if there is inadequate room on your hard disks for an appropriate scratch disk, Photoshop does not start. In addition, if your scratch disks are full, Photoshop might not perform certain requested actions. Effective use of RAM and optimizing available scratch-disk space depends on how you have set your preferences for the scratch disks. Giving Photoshop more space allows quicker performance. You can help this performance by smart allocation of the scratch drives.

By default, Photoshop creates one primary scratch disk on the startup drive. You can set up to four scratch-disk areas. Photoshop will use this space as needed, limited only by the open or unused space on the disk.

To set the scratch disk, choose Edit, Preferences, Plug-Ins & Scratch Disks. In the Plug-Ins & Scratch Disks Preferences dialog box, choose the hard drives that you want to use as scratch disks (see Figure C.1). If you have multiple drives or partitions, be sure to choose drives that have plenty of unused space on them. If you have more than one physical hard drive, you should choose the fastest hard drives you have (higher RPM and access speed) in order to optimize performance.

APP

C

Note

Do not choose compressed hard drives, removable drives, or mapped network drives for scratch-disk space. It is not recommended and can slow performance.

Figure C.1
Before you start using Photoshop for the first time, you should configure the scratch disks.

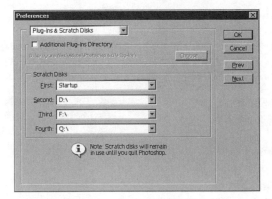

If you get warnings about Photoshop being unable to complete a task because the primary scratch disk is full, you will need to delete files from your hard drive to clear space or change the scratch-disk allocation. It is probably best if you save the current image and spend some time clearing unnecessary files from your drives and archiving what you can. If you try to save and you get an error that there is not enough room to save to the drive, you will have to save to another drive, or clear disk space by removing files.

> **Tip**
>
> If Photoshop does not start and warns you that there is not enough memory to run Photoshop, this is usually an indication that there is insufficient free space on your hard drive. Unless you have changed the settings, this is the hard drive that contains your operating system, and not the hard drive on which Photoshop is installed or one of the scratch disks. It may be necessary to temporarily create open space on the Startup drive to get Photoshop open before you can change memory and scratch-disk allocations. Do this by deleting or moving files. After the program opens properly, you can reallocate the scratch disks.

To avoid this situation, it is best to have one or more drives or partitions dedicated to scratch-disk space for Photoshop. The larger the size of the space you allocate, the better. A longer-term solution is, of course, to increase your available disk space by adding an additional drive. Make sure that the hard drive you use as a scratch disk or as virtual memory is defragmented regularly to keep performance optimized.

> **Tip**
>
> As RAM has come down significantly in price, it is a good idea to get as much RAM as you can afford, or as much as you can get into your system, to reduce the dependence on virtual memory and scratch disks. A significant increase in RAM will speed and improve performance more than an additional hard drive.

PLUG-INS

By default, Photoshop comes with a wide range of plug-ins that provide special effects from the Filters pull-down. They also add valuable functionality to Photoshop, such as the capability to read and save different file formats, and import and export files.

Plug-ins are typically stored in the Plug-Ins folder inside the Photoshop folder. There are subfolders within the Plug-Ins folder to help categorize the filters by purpose and manufacturer. When you start Photoshop, it searches the Plug-Ins folder and all the subfolders for plug-ins. You can choose to search an additional folder if your plug-ins are at another location by selecting Edit, Preferences, Plug-Ins & Scratch Disk and checking the Additional Plug-ins Directory check box. Choosing an additional folder can cause Photoshop to take longer to start up, as it will have to search through more information.

> **Tip**
>
> When choosing a folder for additional plug-ins, be sure it is one dedicated to plug-ins and that it is not a high-level directory (such as the root folder of a hard drive). Photoshop searches all the subfolders in the directory you select for plug-ins; therefore, startup time may increase if you are not careful with placement of plug-ins and selection of directories. It is probably best just to use the `Adobe Photoshop 6\Plug-ins` directory to simplify storage and management of plug-ins.

MACINTOSH SPECIFICS

In the MacOS, you can configure how the operating system allocates RAM to applications. You can configure both the virtual memory and physical RAM allocation when using the MacOS. For Macintosh users, Adobe recommends that you disable Virtual Memory because space that Photoshop could use as scratch-disk space might be used by the operating system instead, which degrades Photoshop's performance. This is good advice for users of older Macintosh systems with smaller hard drives. With the dramatic increase in hard drive sizes and performance recently, however, you can generally leave Virtual Memory turned on while using Photoshop.

To adjust the physical RAM allocation for Photoshop, locate the Photoshop program icon in the Adobe Photoshop 6 directory where you installed the program. Click the icon once to highlight it, then select Get Info from the File menu in the finder, or press Cmd-I. The Adobe Photoshop 6.0 Info screen will open. Select Memory from the Show pop-up menu, and the current memory settings will appear. If your physical RAM allows, change the allocation by increasing the Preferred size, and then the Minimum size (see Figure C.2). The minimum value will always have to be lower than the Preferred.

Figure C.2
Increase the memory allocation by changing the number in the Preferred and Minimum fields. The number represents the number of kilobytes of memory allocated to Photoshop.

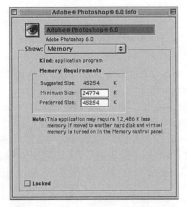 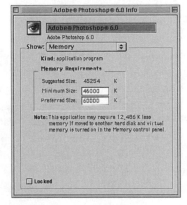

Note

The initial values on the info screen will be default values, which you should not attempt to go below. Photoshop will not start if you do.

The optimal allocation of application memory depends somewhat on how you work, how large your operating system runs, and other factors. For example, if you have 96MB of RAM and your operating system takes 40MB of that, there is really only 56MB left to allocate. If you often use Photoshop in conjunction with other programs, you will have to allocate some of that remaining 56MB to the other program. This could leave very little for you to use in making a change in the current configuration.

Note

If you go to the Info\Memory screen and the memory cannot be edited, Photoshop is currently open. Close the application and return to the info screen and you will be able to edit the memory allocation.

RESETTING PREFERENCES

If you want to reset Photoshop's preferences to the default, you should delete the preferences files. In the Preferences folder in the System folder, there is an Adobe Photoshop 6 Settings folder that contains Photoshop preferences and color settings that can be deleted so that a new set of preferences is created next time you start Photoshop.

Caution

Be aware that resetting your Photoshop preferences will remove preferences for tools, palette placement, and other customizations. Simply manipulating the settings might be preferable to deleting the Preferences.

WINDOWS SPECIFICS

For Windows users, as a general rule, the virtual memory should be set to at least the amount of actual RAM plus another 50%. In Windows 98, the settings for virtual memory can be handled automatically by the operating system, although most users find the automatic settings inadequate for extensive use of memory-intensive applications such as Photoshop. If Windows 98 regularly hangs or freezes, particularly after extended use, try manually increasing the virtual memory settings. In Windows NT, you must set the amount of hard drive space you want to allocate for virtual memory. For any of the Windows operating systems, if you often run other programs at the same time as Photoshop, you might need to dramatically increase the amount of space allocated, depending in large part on the requirements of these other programs. In some cases, allocating 4 to 8 times the size of your physical memory is not unreasonable.

Photoshop's Memory preference is available only on the Windows platform (see Figure C.3). Adobe recommends that you allocate at least 3 to 5 times the size of the average image you work with, plus an additional 5MB or 10MB. The amount of the RAM that Photoshop can use is set in the Photoshop preferences for Windows users.

For Windows users, the default amount of free RAM that Photoshop uses is set to 50%. Photoshop will use up to this amount of RAM or an amount of RAM equal to the remaining scratch-disk space, whichever is smaller. So, even if you have 256MB RAM available, if you have only 16MB of free scratch-disk space, Photoshop will use only 16MB of the available RAM, leaving the rest unused. The amount of RAM specified is actually a percentage of the RAM that is left after the operating system loads. If Photoshop is the only application that you use, or you work on large images, you might want to try setting higher values for the memory usage.

Figure C.3
If you use Photoshop on a PC, you should configure the memory setting to reflect the types of images that you routinely edit.

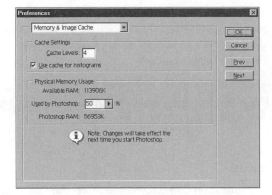

TEMPORARY FILES

Photoshop creates temporary files as it needs to while you work in the application. If Photoshop does not have an opportunity to exit normally (if it or the operating system crashes, or there is a power outage, for example), these temporary files are not deleted. You should check your Temp folders for temporary files created by Photoshop and delete them after any crash or unexpected interruption. Photoshop's temporary files usually have file-names such as ~PSTXXXX.tmp, where XXXX is a four-digit number.

PREFERENCES

In versions of Photoshop prior to 6.0, preferences are stored in a file. If Photoshop does not start correctly and you suspect that the preferences file might be corrupt, or if you want to reset Photoshop's settings to the default, you can delete the preferences file. In Photoshop 6.0, the preferences are stored in the Windows Registry. If you want to reset the preferences to the default, hold down Alt+Ctrl+Shift immediately after launching Photoshop. This will re-create the preferences file.

PHOTOSHOP INSTALLATION OPTIONS

When you get your copy of Photoshop, before you install the software, you should check to make sure that your system has the necessary hardware and software to use the application. In addition, you should become familiar with the installation choices you have both during and after installation of Photoshop. Read the installation instructions and the Undocumented Features file for more information.

PHOTOSHOP SYSTEM REQUIREMENTS AND RECOMMENDATIONS

Macintosh systems must have MacOS System 8.5 or later. Photoshop 6.0 requires an Apple Power Macintosh, 96MB of RAM, and 200MB of open hard-drive space. Memory needs increase to at least 128MB when running Photoshop and ImageReady concurrently. Any increase in available hard-drive space, RAM, and updates to the system software can improve performance.

APP
C

Windows systems must be running either Windows 98 or later, or Windows NT 4.0 (Service Pack 4, 5, 6a required) or later. In either case, an Intel Pentium–class processor is required. You'll need 64MB of RAM and 125MB of available hard-disk space. For Windows and Macintosh systems, a CD–ROM is required.

Tip

One of the single greatest improvements you can make to Photoshop's performance on either platform is the addition of RAM to the system.

INSTALLING ADOBE PHOTOSHOP

Adobe Photoshop 6.0 is distributed on CD. When you insert the CD into your computer running a Windows operating system, the installation program runs if you have your computer set to automatically run CDs. If your computer does not automatically run the setup program, you need to locate the Setup program on the CD and start it, either by double-clicking the icon, or by using Start, Run from your Windows taskbar. For Macintosh users, you need to locate the Installer application and launch it by double-clicking it.

INSTALLING FOR THE FIRST TIME

If you do not already have a version of Photoshop on your computer, the Photoshop setup guides you through several questions about the country of purchase and the license agreement. The installer asks you in which folder you would like to place Photoshop, and which installation option you would like. For Windows users, the options are Typical, Compact, or Custom. For Macintosh users, the options are Easy Install or Custom. Choose the Typical or Easy install methods unless you are replacing specific portions of a previous installation or have some other specific purpose in mind. The installer then asks which file formats you want to be associated with Photoshop, which with ImageReady, and which you want to leave unchanged (see Figure C.4). After you select the installation option, you must enter your registration information: name, business, and serial number. After completion, Photoshop confirms the installation options, and then begins copying the application to your hard drive.

Figure C.4
Choose which image file formats you want to associate with Photoshop. If you need to change these associations later, you need to specify them in the operating system.

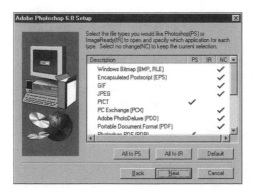

Tip

Keep the serial number for Photoshop in a safe place. You will need it later if you reinstall Photoshop. Write it in your manual cover, on your application box, and consider putting it in your Rolodex, as well.

UPGRADING FROM A PREVIOUS VERSION

If you already own a copy of Photoshop and have purchased an upgrade, the Photoshop installation program verifies that you own a previous version. You can allow the installation program to search your hard drive for the previous installation, you can point it toward a specific directory that contains the previous version, or you can even use the CD or floppy disk from a previous version as verification. After the verification is complete, the upgrade installation continues as the standard installation described previously.

Tip

Look on the CD for free plug-ins and textures, and for plug-ins from previous versions that have been removed from the standard installation.

APP

C

After installation is finished, you are asked to register the program with Adobe. You can do this by filling out and mailing the registration card or by registering online. You can also register with Adobe by choosing Help, Register in Photoshop. By registering with Adobe, you can more easily upgrade to subsequent versions or get replacement media should it become necessary.

HEXADECIMAL COLOR EQUIVALENTS FOR WEB CREATION

In this appendix

HEXADECIMAL EQUIVALENTS

Colors for type and background in Web pages are defined by hexadecimal colors. For example, font color tags and background colors are most often defined by hexadecimals in the form: `<FONT color='#RRGGBB'>`, where Red, Green, and Blue are defined by hexadecimal equivalents. It is currently possible to define some colors with color equivalent names (such as green), but hexadecimal color assignment is prevalent, and you will find it easier to use in creating graphics with Photoshop. Photoshop color palettes allow assignment of color by hexadecimal values.

Hexadecimal is a base-16 system. Each digit can represent a number from 0 to 15, rather than our usual base-10 system where each digit can only represent a number from 0 to 9. The following are allowed as number representations for each digit place: 0, 1, 2, 3, 4, 5, 6, 7, 8, 9, A, B, C, D, E, F, where A–F stand for 10–15. The first digit in the set stands for the number of sets of 16s in the total; the second digit stands for the number of 1s. In other words, if you were counting in hexadecimal from 0, you would progress as follows: 00, 01, 02, 03, 04, 05, 06, 07, 08, 09, 0A, 0B, 0C, 0D, 0E, 0F, 10, 11, 12, and so on. In this way, the first digit keeps track of the number of 16s in the total, just like the tens digit in base ten keeps track of the number of 10s in a total. To convert the number, multiply the value of the first digit in the pair by 16, and add the value of the second. CE, for example, would be 12(16)+14, or 206. In using the hexadecimal system, any number from 0 (000000) to 256 (FFFFFF) can be represented by the digit pairs, and any of 16,777,216 RGB colors can be defined.

Converting RGB values to hexadecimal is a bit more complicated. You would have to take each value for the Red, Green, and Blue, and convert the three-digit number into digit hexadecimal sets. The first digit is the largest whole number (0–15) which will divide evenly into the value, and the second digit is the remainder. Where X=your value for Red, Green, or Blue: $|X/16|$=H1 and X-($|X/16|$)16=H2. The hexadecimal value would be shown as H1 H2. For example, a Red value of 245 would be used in the equation as follows: H1 =$|245/16|$=$|15.3125|$=15, and 15 is equivalent to F; H2 =245-($|245/16|$)16=245-($|15.3125|$)16=245-(15)16=245-240=5, and 5 is equivalent to 5. The values would be placed side by side: F5. You would need to follow the same process in determining the Green and Blue values. As an example, an RGB of 8,106,249 would be represented by a hexadecimal value of 086AF9: Red=8 or 08, Green=106 or 6A, and Blue=249 or F9. These values are strung together to make the hexadecimal representation.

A simple conversion chart for 3-digit RGB values (0 to 255) to 2-digit hexadecimal values (00 to FF) is presented below for your convenience. Table D.1 should simplify conversion to hex values.

TABLE D.1   RGB to Hex Conversion Chart

Number	Hex	Number	Hex
0	00	32	20
1	01	33	21
2	02	34	22
3	03	35	23
4	04	36	24
5	05	37	25
6	06	38	26
7	07	39	27
8	08	40	28
9	09	41	29
10	0A	42	2A
11	0B	43	2B
12	0C	44	2C
13	0D	45	2D
14	0E	46	2E
15	0F	47	2F
16	10	48	30
17	11	49	31
18	12	50	32
19	13	51	33
20	14	52	34
21	15	53	35
22	16	54	36
23	17	55	37
24	18	56	38
25	19	57	39
26	1A	58	3A
27	1B	59	3B
28	1C	60	3C
29	1D	61	3D
30	1E	62	3E
31	1F	63	3F

APP

D

TABLE D.1 CONTINUED

Number	Hex	Number	Hex
64	40	96	60
65	41	97	61
66	42	98	62
67	43	99	63
68	44	100	64
69	45	101	65
70	46	102	66
71	47	103	67
72	48	104	68
73	49	105	69
74	4A	106	6A
75	4B	107	6B
76	4C	108	6C
77	4D	109	6D
78	4E	110	6E
79	4F	111	6F
80	50	112	70
81	51	113	71
82	52	114	72
83	53	115	73
84	54	116	74
85	55	117	75
86	56	118	76
87	57	119	77
88	58	120	78
89	59	121	79
90	5A	122	7A
91	5B	123	7B
92	5C	124	7C
93	5D	125	7D
94	5E	126	7E
95	5F	127	7F

TABLE D.1 CONTINUED

Number	Hex	Number	Hex
128	80	160	A0
129	81	161	A1
130	82	162	A2
131	83	162	A3
132	84	164	A4
133	85	165	A5
134	86	166	A6
135	87	167	A7
136	88	168	A8
137	89	169	A9
138	8A	170	AA
139	8B	171	AB
140	8C	172	AC
141	8D	173	AD
142	8E	174	AE
143	8F	175	AF
144	90	176	B0
145	91	177	B1
146	92	178	B2
147	93	179	B3
148	94	180	B4
149	95	181	B5
150	96	182	B6
151	97	183	B7
152	98	184	B8
153	99	185	B9
154	9A	186	BA
155	9B	187	BB
156	9C	188	BC
157	9D	189	BD
158	9E	190	BE
159	9F	191	BF

APP
D

TABLE D.1 CONTINUED

Number	Hex	Number	Hex
192	C0	224	E0
193	C1	225	E1
194	C2	226	E2
195	C3	227	E3
196	C4	228	E4
197	C5	229	E5
198	C6	230	E6
199	C7	231	E7
200	C8	232	E8
201	C9	233	E9
202	CA	234	EA
203	CB	235	EB
204	CC	236	EC
205	CD	237	ED
206	CE	238	EE
207	CF	239	EF
208	D0	240	F0
209	D1	241	F1
210	D2	242	F2
211	D3	243	F3
212	D4	244	F4
213	D5	245	F5
214	D6	246	F6
215	D7	247	F7
216	D8	248	F8
217	D9	249	F9
218	DA	250	FA
219	DB	251	FB
220	DC	252	FC
221	DD	253	FD
222	DE	254	FE
223	DF	255	FF

THE 216-COLOR, WEB-SAFE PALETTE

Although 16,777,216 colors can be defined, only the set of Web-safe colors should be used for Web-site design. Web-safe colors are colors that tend not to change in display from computer system to computer system. This means that by using Web-safe color, you can better control how your Web site and HTML color picking will match your original intent from system to system. Really, as different systems use different color breakdowns, nothing is completely safe except for black (000000) and white (FFFFFF). For example, Unix uses a different color breakdown than PCs, and that can cause discrepancies in chosen colors. However the 216-color palette offers a best bet for matching colors across systems, as it limits its color use to the most widely acceptable values.

The number 216 is 6 cubed, or 6×6×6. The number of colors represented is actually Red, Green, and Blue in all possible permutations using FF, CC, 99, 66, 33, and 00 as hexadecimal number values. Each color can contain any of the six hexadecimal values in any combination. As long as one of these values is used for each of the RGB colors, the resulting color will be Web safe. For example, 996,600 is Web safe, whereas 969,060 is not.

The 216-color palette is actually trimmed from the 256 colors available. The additional colors are different on different platforms, whereas the 216 colors included in the palette are the same on Mac and Windows. These colors include pure Red, Green, and Blue values of EE, DD, BB, AA, 88, 77, 55, 44, 22, and 11, and grays where Red, Green, and Blue contain equivalent values EE, DD, BB, AA, 88, 77, 55, 44, 22, and 11. To keep it simple, use only the colors designated as follows for the best control. Selecting colors outside those listed here can produce undesired results. To see the colors these values represent, visit the book's Web site at www.ps6.com.

Unix Colors

Unix colors are broken down into 125 variations, with each hexadecimal value assigned as 00, 40, 80, BF or FF (RGB equivalents of 0, 64, 128, 191, and 255). This is a very different color scheme, as shown in Table D.2. However, as these are generally used as servers rather than browsers, a small percentage of visitors to your Web site(s) will be on this platform.

TABLE D.2   WEB-SAFE HEXADECIMAL VALUES

Hexadecimal Value	RGB Equivalent	Hexadecimal Value	RGB Equivalent
FFFFFF	255,255,255	FFCCCC	255,204,204
FFFFCC	255,255,204	FFCC99	255,204,153
FFFF99	255,255,153	FFCC66	255,204,102
FFFF66	255,255,102	FFCC33	255,204,51
FFFF33	255,255,51	FFCC00	255,204,0
FFFF00	255,255,0	FF99FF	255,153,255
FFCCFF	255,204,255	FF99CC	255,153,204

TABLE D.2 CONTINUED

Hexadecimal Value	RGB Equivalent	Hexadecimal Value	RGB Equivalent
FF9999	255,153,153	CCCC33	204,204,51
FF9966	255,153,102	CCCC00	204,204,0
FF9933	255,153,51	CC99FF	204,153,255
FF9900	255,153,0	CC99CC	204,153,204
FF66FF	255,102,255	CC9999	204,153,153
FF66CC	255,102,204	CC9966	204,153,102
FF6699	255,102,153	CC9933	204,153,51
FF6666	255,102,102	CC9900	204,153,0
FF6633	255,102,51	CC66FF	204,102,255
FF6600	255,102,0	CC66CC	204,102,204
FF33FF	255,51,255	CC6699	204,102,153
FF33CC	255,51,204	CC6666	204,102,102
FF3399	255,51,153	CC6633	204,102,51
FF3366	255,51,102	CC6600	204,102,0
FF3333	255,51,51	CC33FF	204,51,255
FF3300	255,51,0	CC33CC	204,51,204
FF00FF	255,0,255	CC3399	204,51,153
FF00CC	255,0,204	CC3366	204,51,102
FF0099	255,0,153	CC3333	204,51,51
FF0066	255,0,102	CC3300	204,51,0
FF0033	255,0,51	CC00FF	204,0,255
FF0000	255,0,0	CC00CC	204,0,204
CCFFFF	204,255,255	CC0099	204,0,153
CCFFCC	204,255,204	CC0066	204,0,102
CCFF99	204,255,153	CC0033	204,0,51
CCFF66	204,255,102	CC0000	204,0,0
CCFF33	204,255,51	99FFFF	153,255,255
CCFF00	204,255,0	99FFCC	153,255,204
CCCCFF	204,204,255	99FF99	153,255,153
CCCCCC	204,204,204	99FF66	153,255,102
CCCC99	204,204,153	99FF33	153,255,51
CCCC66	204,204,102	99FF00	153,255,0

TABLE D.2   CONTINUED

Hexadecimal Value	RGB Equivalent	Hexadecimal Value	RGB Equivalent
99CCFF	153,204,255	66FF99	102,255,153
99CCCC	153,204,204	66FF66	102,255,102
99CC99	153,204,153	66FF33	102,255,51
99CC66	153,204,102	66FF00	102,255,0
99CC33	153,204,51	66CCFF	102,204,255
99CC00	153,204,0	66CCCC	102,204,204
9999FF	153,153,255	66CC99	102,204,153
9999CC	153,153,204	66CC66	102,204,102
999999	153,153,153	66CC33	102,204,51
999966	153,153,102	66CC00	102,204,0
999933	153,153,51	6699FF	102,153,255
999900	153,153,0	6699CC	102,153,204
9966FF	153,102,255	669999	102,153,153
9966CC	153,102,204	669966	102,153,102
996699	153,102,153	669933	102,153,51
996666	153,102,102	669900	102,153,0
996633	153,102,51	6666FF	102,102,255
996600	153,102,0	6666CC	102,102,204
9933FF	153,51,255	666699	102,102,153
9933CC	153,51,204	666666	102,102,102
993399	153,51,153	666633	102,102,51
993366	153,51,102	666600	102,102,0
993333	153,51,51	6633FF	102,51,255
993300	153,51,0	6633CC	102,51,204
9900FF	153,0,255	663399	102,51,153
9900CC	153,0,204	663366	102,51,102
990099	153,0,153	663333	102,51,51
990066	153,0,102	663300	102,51,0
990033	153,0,51	6600FF	102,0,255
990000	153,0,0	6600CC	102,0,204
66FFFF	102,255,255	660099	102,0,153
66FFCC	102,255,204	660066	102,0,102

APP

D

TABLE D.2 CONTINUED

Hexadecimal Value	RGB Equivalent	Hexadecimal Value	RGB Equivalent
660033	102,0,51	3300FF	51,0,255
660000	102,0,0	3300CC	51,0,204
33FFFF	51,255,255	330099	51,0,153
33FFCC	51,255,204	330066	51,0,102
33FF99	51,255,153	330033	51,0,51
33FF66	51,255,102	330000	51,0,0
33FF33	51,255,51	00FFFF	0,255,255
33FF00	51,255,0	00FFCC	0,255,204
33CCFF	51,204,255	00FF99	0,255,153
33CCCC	51,204,204	00FF66	0,255,102
33CC99	51,204,153	00FF33	0,255,51
33CC66	51,204,102	00FF00	0,255,0
33CC33	51,204,51	00CCFF	0,204,255
33CC00	51,204,0	00CCCC	0,204,204
3399FF	51,153,255	00CC99	0,204,153
3399CC	51,153,204	00CC66	0,204,102
339999	51,153,153	00CC33	0,204,51
339966	51,153,102	00CC00	0,204,0
339933	51,153,51	0099FF	0,153,255
339900	51,153,0	0099CC	0,153,204
3366FF	51,102,255	009999	0,153,153
3366CC	51,102,204	009966	0,153,102
336699	51,102,153	009933	0,153,51
336666	51,102,102	009900	0,153,0
336633	51,102,51	0066FF	0,102,255
336600	51,102,0	0066CC	0,102,204
3333FF	51,51,255	006699	0,102,153
3333CC	51,51,204	006666	0,102,102
333399	51,51,153	006633	0,102,51
333366	51,51,102	006600	0,102,0
333333	51,51,51	0033FF	0,51,255
333300	51,51,0	0033CC	0,51,204

TABLE D.2 **CONTINUED**

Hexadecimal Value	RGB Equivalent	Hexadecimal Value	RGB Equivalent
003399	0,51,153	0000CC	0,0,204
003366	0,51,102	000099	0,0,153
003333	0,51,51	000066	0,0,102
003300	0,51,0	000033	0,0,51
0000FF	0,0,255	000000	0,0,0

APP

D

APPENDIX

WEB RESOURCES LIBRARY

In this appendix

OVERVIEW OF WEB RESOURCES

Most of the following Web resources are places where you can download free fonts, graphics, actions, filters, plug-ins, and perhaps unearth some additional Photoshop information or tangential help via newsgroups or forums. I've noted a few handy items for Web development as well, such as where to get free Internet access, free Web space, find low equipment pricing, and get freeware and shareware programs. Some sites listed cover more than just the subject of the sections I have them listed under. The categorization suggests what I believe is the site's strength. Most of the Photoshop specific sites have links to other Photoshop-related sites.

The Web site for this book is `http://www.ps6.com`. You will need to go there to get the workbook, but there are additional items there that may be of help. My plan is to develop the site to augment the book and build according to reader suggestions. I look forward to yours.

The Web site for Adobe is `http://www.adobe.com`. The direct address for Photoshop is `http://www.adobe.com/products/photoshop/main.html`. Here you can find technical support information, forums, and the like.

PHOTOSHOP: FINDING PLUG-INS, FILTERS, BRUSHES, AND ACTIONS

Many of the items on these plug-in lists are the same. This is because most of the well-known plug-ins are on each resource. However, you might find a unique item or two on an individual list, so I thought it best to include several.

Action Xchange

`http://actionxchange.com`

Claims to have more than 1,500 actions available free for downloading. I haven't counted, but there are a lot.

The Action Vault

`http://actions.i-us.com/actions.html`

Not a ton of stuff here, but some useful and educational tidbits can be found. You can learn a bunch about putting actions together by looking at these.

Adobe: Related Third-Party Plugins

`http://www.adobe.com/products/photoshop/plugins.html`

A listing by Adobe of third-party plug-ins they recognize.

Deepspaceweb

`http://www.deepspaceweb.com/plugins.shtml`

Although not everything here is a gem, there is a lot to be learned and quarried here, including plug-ins, actions, and brushes available for download.

The Plugin Head

`http://pluginhead.i-us.com/filplug.htm`

Actions, plug-ins, Filter Factory stuff, brushes, and displacement maps available here.

Ultimate Photoshop

`http://www.ultimate-photoshop.com/filters/`

There is more stuff on this site than just filters. It is just easier to start here.

WebXchange: The Ultimate Collection of Adobe

`http://webxchange.dhs.org`

Fonts, clip art, backgrounds, utilities, actions, and plug-ins to peruse and use.

GRAPHICS AND CLIP ART

The intent here is to collect a listing of a few sites with free graphics. It is easier and probably more helpful that most of the sites listed are directories that contain links to other sites that have free graphics. This gives you a lot more to choose from. I have noted a few good libraries where you can start, but the directories are an invaluable resource. You'll find links to lists of lists—a ton of things to check out.

I can't be sure whether this is a trend or a gimmick in the clip art trade, but several of the directory sites have rated listings. The listings are, however, different with some overlap rather than being identical.

ABCGIANT

`http://ABCGiant.com`

Contains a library of stuff plus links to a number of other free-stuff sites for graphics.

Clipart.com

`http://www.clipart.com/`

A listing of free graphic sites.

Cool Archive

`Coolarchive.com`

Claims to be the ultimate archive. It has fonts, clip art, bullets, sounds, utilities, free services, and more—mostly geared toward Web-site development.

DTP.com

`http://www.DTP.com/`

A listing of free graphic sites.

FreebiesPlanet

`http://www.freebiesplanet.com/graphics.shtml`

A listing of free graphic sites.

GraphicsFreebies.com

`http://www.graphicsfreebies.com`

A listing of free graphic sites.

Designs4Free.com

`http://www.graphics4free.com/main.html`

A large collection of free graphics, mostly for Web sites.

Pambytes Free Web Graphics

`http://Pambytes.com`

This site includes banners, buttons, borders, and the beginnings of a strong font archive.

FONTS

There are all types of wild fonts and standards available on the Internet, and many will not be completely compatible with Photoshop, depending on how they were put together. Programs and conversion utilities are available to help out with problems you might encounter. The following listing includes mostly freebies, but some informational sites as well. All the libraries have previews so you can look at the fonts before downloading.

007Fonts

`http://www.007fonts.com`

A font library of designer faces.

Coolfonts Free Fonts for PC and Mac

`http://www.coolfonts.de`

A listing of listings with a significant library of its own.

FontFace.com

`http://www.fontface.com`

Typefaces for Mac and PC.

The Fonts Zone

`http://www.geocities.com/~fontszone/`

A free font library with descriptions. Some helpful information about fonts, and useful groupings (rather than alphabetical listing).

Free PC Fonts

http://www.freepcfonts.com

A listing of free font sites.

Front Row Fonts

http://frontrow.fontframe.com/

A listing of free font sites.

Graphics.com

http://www.graphics.com/frame.html?section=type

A listing of foundries and typefaces with links to numerous foundries. Helpful if you are looking for a specific font and creator.

Killer Fonts

http://www.killerfonts.com/main.html

Mostly not free, but not expensive, either—a very unusual collection.

Mary Forrest's Free Font Fiesta

http://members.aol.com/mmqchome/fonts/fonts.htm#Links

A listing of listings with descriptions of what those listings list. A seemingly endless supply.

FREE INTERNET (ISP) SERVICE

If you are not on the Web, besides the price of a modem for your computer, there is no longer a reason to wait. There are a number of free Internet providers. Several of the larger and more accessible ones are listed here.

1st Free Internet Access

http://www.1st-free-internet-access.com/

A free Internet provider covering up to 98% of the U.S. and Canada.

Freelane

http://freelane.excite.com/

A free Internet provider available in most of the U.S. and Canada.

Juno

http://www.juno.com/

Probably the most popular and well-known free Internet service provider.

FreeLane

http://www.isps-free.com/

A free Internet provider covering 95% of the U.S. and Canada.

APP

E

Maxis Net

http://www.maxis.net.my/

A free Internet provider.

WEB HOSTING

After you are on the Web, you might want to put up a Web page to show off your Photoshop stuff. Beginners don't need to pay for potentially expensive Web-site hosting. There are free alternatives that give you Web-site space to use, generally in exchange for some type of advertising on your pages.

#1 Free Web Page Listing

http://zap.to/1freewebpage/

Lists a number of services without neat alphabetical listing. However, a valuable resource.

The Free Web-page List

http://freeweblist.freeservers.com

A listing with categorizations by size of space provided.

FreeWebspace.net

http://www.freewebspace.net

A listing of free hosting services—claims to be the largest listing on the Web. Has a great list of service features that you can compare quickly.

HostIndex.com Web Hosting Directory

http://www.hostindex.com/guide1.shtm

Used to list free servers, but now lists paid server comparisons. Lots of information here about services, and a beginner's guide to Web hosting. This link starts with the beginner's guide.

Zarcrom Free Homepages

http://uk.zarcrom.com/freehome.html

List of free servers with minimal descriptions.

SEARCH ENGINE SUBMISSION

For people to find your Photoshop site on the Web, you have to register with search engines. Here you can find information and ways to simplify search engine submission and Web-site promotion. Several are listed as these seem to go in and out of service—or at least the free part does.

Registration Wizard Free Web Promotion Tools

http://www.registrationwizard.com/

Not currently up, but promises to be after a small hiatus. When open, this site allows free submission to many search engines. Maintained by the University of North Carolina at Charlotte.

Easy Submit

http://www.scrubtheweb.com/abs/promo.html

Free submission to about 30 search engines. Navigates your trips to individual search-engine pages and is better than simple automatic submission.

SelfPromotion.com

http://www.selfpromotion.com/

Supposed to act like shareware in that you use the service and if you like it, you pay.

Submit Express

http://www.submitexpress.com/submit.html

Free submission to about 35 search engines. Full service submission is available.

Web Page Design for Designers

http://www.wpdfd.com/wpdhome.htm

http://www.wpdfd.com/resources/Promotion.htm is the promotion page (with reviews of promotion sites and links), but there is a lot of other information to explore here.

PRICING EQUIPMENT AND SOFTWARE

Shopping on the Web can turn up some great pricing for upgrading your system. There are a number of services by similar names, but some seem to accept advertising, which compromises the information you get. I use only the two listed, but if you try variations of the price name (pricewonder.com, pricegrabber.com, pricenetwork.com, pricepulse.com, or price-trac.com), there prove to be significant pricing resources. Comparing between the two below should be astounding enough.

CNET Shopper (was *KillerApp.com*)

http://shopper.cnet.com/

Pricing from a number of vendors and products.

PriceSCAN.com

http://www.pricescan.com

Great pricing from a number of vendors all at once.

FREEWARE AND SHAREWARE

The following is a collection of freeware and shareware sites. These sites offer downloadable software which is either free outright, or free based on your use (if you don't use it, you don't pay; if you use it, you pay on what is essentially an honor system). You can download directly from these sites and archives. These may have utilities to use in conjunction with Photoshop (such as for creating your Web pages, and so on).

Download.com

http://download.cnet.com/

Will start platform specific, but you can jump to various (PC, Mac, Linux, Windows CE, PalmPilot) platforms if desired. A general freeware/shareware listing.

Freeware32.com

http://freeware32.com

A Web-oriented freeware site with a strong graphics orientation. PC only.

Go Network: Downloads

http://www.go.com/Center/Computing/Download

A heavily PC-oriented general freeware/shareware listing.

Rene Guerrero's Comprehensive List of Freeware, Shareware, and Software sites.

http://www.msu.edu/user/heinric6/soft.htm

A listing of sites broken down by platform. Very handy and user friendly.

Shareware.com

http://shareware.cnet.com

More than 250,000 shareware files, which can be searched by keyword and platform.

SoftSeek

http://www.softseek.com/

Software mostly geared toward graphics, the Internet, and Web development.

COPYRIGHT ISSUES

As a reminder to give credit as it is due, this section in Web Resources is about copyright. This is meant to help you be sure you can use what you borrow before you borrow it. If you borrow improperly, it might be considered stealing. These copyright resources contain the information you need to know to tell the difference, and what you have to do to get permissions for use, as necessary.

Ivan Hoffman, B.A., J.D.

http://www.ivanhoffman.com/

This attorney has a site full of information about copyright and use rights. The articles are informative, sensible, and free—with a Web-oriented perspective.

Stanford University: Copyright & Fair Use

http://fairuse.stanford.edu/

Maintained by the Stanford University Library to address issues on usage and copyright.

University of Michigan: Copyright Information

http://www.lib.umich.edu/libhome/copyright/

The UM copyright information site—informative and well maintained.

GENERAL INFORMATION

These sites are more or less handy, general information sites for computers and graphics.

Macworld.com

http://macworld.zdnet.com

A Mac-oriented general information magazine.

PCWorld.com

http://PCWorld.com

A PC-oriented general information magazine.

PDFZone

http://PDFZone.com

Extensive information on Acrobat and PDFs. Includes a lot of digital graphic information.

NEWSGROUPS AND USENET

The following two groups are well-known Photoshop newsgroups. You can access them as a newsgroup, or through Deja.com. I have provided both addresses. These are very useful forums for getting questions answered and learning about how Photoshop is used. Users of all skill levels participate in the discussions.

alt.graphics.photoshop

http://www.deja.com/group/alt.graphics.photoshop

comp.graphics.apps.photoshop

http://www.deja.com/group/comp.graphics.apps.photoshop

APP
E

INDEX

T

Other Related Titles

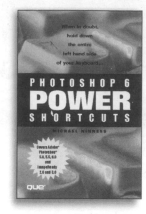

Photoshop 6 Power Shortcuts
Michael Ninness
0-7897-2426-X
$24.99 US/
$37.95 CAN

The Complete Idiot's Guide to Macromedia Flash 5
David Karlins
0-7897-2442-1
$19.99 US/$29.95 CAN

Short Order Macromedia Dreamweaver 3
Steven Moniz
0-7897-2150-3
$19.99 US/$29.95 CAN

Print Publishing: A Hayden Shop Manual
Donnie O'Quinn
0-7897-2102-3
$49.99 US/$74.95 CAN

Short Order InDesign
Patti Sokol
0-7897-2098-1
$19.99 US/
$29.95 CAN

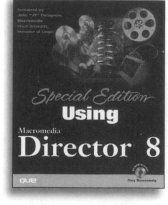

Special Edition Using Macromedia Director 8
Gary Rosenzweig
0-7897-2334-4
$39.99 US/
$59.95 CAN

www.quecorp.com

All prices are subject to change.